Nez Perce Summer, 1877

Nez Perce Summer, 1877

THE U.S. ARMY AND THE NEE-ME-POO CRISIS

BY Jerome A. Greene

FOREWORD BY

Alvin M. Josephy, Jr.

973.8
GREENE
2000

ONTANA
HISTORICAL
SOCIETY
PRESS

Helena

COVER DESIGN BY Kathryn Fehlig
BOOK DESIGN BY Arrow Graphics, Missoula
TYPESET IN Janson and Baker Signet
PRINTED BY Thomson-Shore, Inc., Dexter, Michigan

Royalties earned from this book go to support the programs of Nez Perce National
Historical Park.

00 01 02 03 04 05 06 07 08 09 10 11   10 9 8 7 6 5 4 3 2 1

ISBN 0-917298-68-3

LIBRARY OF CONGRESS CATALOGING-IN-PUBLICATION DATA

Greene, Jerome A.
    Nez Perce summer, 1877 : the U.S. Army and the Nee-Me-Poo crisis / by
Jerome A. Greene.
    p. cm.
Includes bibliographical references and index.
ISBN 0-917298-68-3 (cloth ; alk. paper)
1. Nez Percé Indians—Wars, 1877. 2. Big Hole, Battle of the, 1877 3. Nez Percé
Indians—History—19th century. 4. Nez Percé Indians—Government relations. I. Title.

E83.877.G74   2000
973.8'3—dc21   00-032934
                                                    CIP

In memory of T,
Erwin N. Thompson, 1926–1998, colleague and friend

This book was made possible in part by funding from the Bair Trust and the Montana Historical Society Foundation.

Contents

Illustrations

Maps

Foreword

IT WAS "ONE OF THE MOST extraordinary Indian wars of which there is any record," reported William Tecumseh Sherman, commanding general of the U. S. Army, about the war waged by the government against Nez Perce Indians in 1877. "The Indians throughout," said Sherman, "displayed a courage and skill that elicited universal praise. They abstained from scalping; let captive women go free; did not commit indiscriminate murder of peaceful families, which is usual, and fought with almost scientific skill, using advance and rear guards, skirmish lines, and field fortifications."

Many others, nursing border mentalities like Sherman's about how Indians were expected to behave—but stung by outmaneuvering and humiliating battlefield defeats by the tribal leaders and warriors—agreed with the general. Even in Montana, a principal theater of the war, the frontier newspaper *New North-West* heaped praise on the remarkable Indian adversary. "Their peaceable, leisurely and audacious march through the Bitterroot Valley," the paper wrote, "their quick recovery from surprise on the Big Hole, and tremendous fighting thereafter; their inexplicable conduct in killing without scalping or mutilating . . . their surprise of the vastly superior force of Howard's cavalry and capture of a large portion of his train at Camas Meadows, are incidents that go to make up the inexplicable features of this most wonderful of Indian wars. . . . Their warfare since they entered Montana," the paper proclaimed, "has been almost universally marked so far by the highest characteristics recognized by civilized nations."

The Nez Perces—the *Nee-Me-Poo,* or the real people in their own language—had won the admiration of whites from a time early in the nineteenth century when the two peoples, Indians and whites, had first met each other and the Indians had rescued the Lewis and Clark Expedition from starvation. Thereafter, through three-quarters of the nineteenth century, the Nez Perces, though subjected to numerous sins and injustices by the whites, remained stalwart friends and on occasion even military allies of the Americans in the Northwest. There came a time, however, when some of the affronted Nez Perce bands, including one led by Chief Joseph, could take no more, and the traditional relationship of friendship and alliance exploded into "the most wonderful of Indian wars."

The great fighting retreat of the patriotic Nez Perces, struggling for their lives, lands, and freedom, outwitting and battling off one pursuing force after another, is one of the giant epics of the American West, and the literature about it is immense. But there is no volume like this monumental account of the war by Jerome A. Greene, the distinguished National Park Service historian who has published in the past numerous authoritative works on other Indian wars of the West. Reflecting again a wonderfully massive job of research, Greene provides us now with just about every relevant detail pertaining to the Nez Perce war. In a sense, he has done a good deal of the homework for future historians of that sad and super-dramatic chapter of our western expansion.

—ALVIN M. JOSEPHY, JR.

Introduction and Acknowledgments

NEZ PERCE NATIONAL HISTORICAL PARK, established in 1965, comprises thirty-eight discontiguous sites in four states (Washington, Oregon, Idaho, and Montana) describing the history and culture of the Nez Perce (Nee-Me-Poo) Indians. Several of these properties (including sites authorized by Congress in 1992), along with others within Yellowstone National Park, relate to the warfare between the Nez Perces and the U.S. Army in 1877. Their collective association with the events of 1877 prompted the National Park Service to prepare a study that would bring together site-specific as well as contextual information to aid the planning, management, and interpretation for all major land resources related to the U.S. Army–Nez Perce War.

It is this study, "Historic Resource Study: The U.S. Army and the Nee-Me-Poo Crisis of 1877: Historic Sites Associated with the Nez Perce War," completed in 1996, upon which this book is based. That study was, as is the book that follows, necessarily, a military history, based upon the voluminous body of documentary materials that comprise the history from that perspective, as compared to the relative scarcity of materials that embrace the Nez Perce viewpoint. Nevertheless, Nee-Me-Poo perspective is vital to gaining a comprehensive understanding of the events of 1877, and fortunately, through the efforts of Lucullus V. McWhorter, Walter M. Camp, Edward S. Curtis, and others who actively sought out Indian recollections during the early years of the twentieth century, an important reservoir of first-person participant reminiscences exists that has been incorporated into this study to ensure perspectives from both sides. Similarly, the accounts of participants from other tribes have been included whenever available. Further, because past and recent histories of the Nez Perce struggle have relied heavily upon previously published secondary works, the present study has concentrated more exclusively on archival materials, published government records, and participant accounts, many never before used. With hopes for achieving greater objectivity about the war, the study has refrained from using published secondary renditions beyond those needed to establish background, and those articles and books that focus on specific occurrences considered in the narrative (and required for consideration of interpretations of the events). Two exceptions are Alvin M. Josephy, Jr., *The Nez Perce Indians and the Opening of the Northwest* (1965), and Francis Haines, *The Nez Perces: Tribesmen of the Columbia Plateau* (1955), both recognized standards that were contextually important for this study. Of special value to the fieldwork involved throughout this study was Cheryl Wilfong, *Following the Nez Perce Trail: A Guide to the Nee-Me-Poo National Historic Trail with Eyewitness Accounts* (1990). In addition, as a matter of procedure, all quoted material has been directly footnoted; all other data, unless critically singular in importance, have been consolidated in multiple-citation footnotes.

A note regarding terminology: In recent years there has been a tendency, especially on the part of the federal government, to refer euphemistically to the events of 1877 as a "conflict" instead of as a "war," perhaps in subliminal attempt to soften the reality of what happened to the nontreaty Nez Perces and make it easier to accept. Certainly for the Nez Perces, whose very existence was at stake, their struggle against the army following the outbreak amounted to a defensive war for survival in which they utilized their limited numbers and resources to the maximum. Conversely, as the instrument of the federal government determined to defeat the Nez Perces and thereby protect its citizens, the army employed its own resources in offensively applying the strategies and tactics that characterized its role and very purpose for existence. Moral issues and modern judgments aside, from such perspective the contest was in its purest sense indeed a war and is thus designated as such in the pages that follow.

This study could not have been completed without the help of many people and institutions. Rodd L. Wheaton, Assistant Regional Director, Cultural Resources and Partnerships, Intermountain Regional Office, National Park Service, Denver; and Stephanie Toothman, Pacific West Region, Columbia Cascades Support Office, National Park Service, Seattle, were instrumental in formulating the project, in defining and redefining its scope, and in providing administrative support through its completion. Elizabeth M. Janes, former Chief, Branch of Planning, Eastern Team, Denver Service Center, approved my detail to the (then) Rocky Mountain and Pacific Northwest regional offices for twenty months. I must also thank Franklin D. Walker, then Superintendent, Nez Perce National Historical Park, who provided enthusiastic and total support throughout the research and writing effort. Former National Park Service Chief Historian Edwin C. Bearss promoted my involvement and offered his unique insights and valuable advice throughout the completion of the study. Others in the respective regional offices who extended information and assistance at various times during this work include: Richard J. Cronenberger, Regional Historical Architect; Adrienne B. Anderson, Regional Archeologist; David Ruppert, Cultural Anthropologist; Anne Johnson, Archeologist; Rosemary Sucec, Cultural Resources Specialist; Kathleen McKoy, Regional Historian; and Charles Troje and Christine Maylath, administrative assistants (all in the Rocky Mountain Regional Office, Denver); and Gretchen Luxembourg, Regional Historian; Fred York, Regional Ethnographer; James Thompson, Regional Archeologist; and Wendy Chin, Budget Assistant (all in the then Pacific Northwest Regional Office, Seattle). Douglas D. Scott, Archeologist, Midwest Archeological Center, Lincoln, Nebraska, shared his counsel and expertise regarding Indian wars sites on many occasions.

At Nez Perce National Historical Park, I must thank Susan J. Buchel, former Manager, and Jon G. James, present Superintendent, Big Hole National Battlefield and Bear Paw Battlefield Unit; Mark O'Neill, former Manager, White Bird Battlefield and Upper Clearwater Units; Arthur C. Hathaway, former Manager, Spalding Unit; Otis Halfmoon, Idaho Unit Manager; Teresa Seloske, former Park Ranger, White Bird Battlefield and Upper Clearwater Units; Paul Henderson, former Manager, Oregon/Washington Unit; Robert Chenoweth, Park Curator; Chrisanne Brown, former Librarian; Diana Miles, Park Ranger, Spalding Unit; Linda Paisano, Museum Technician, and Tony Schetszle, former Superintendent, Big Hole National Battlefield—all of whom variously provided resource information and/or administrative support throughout the study. I must also thank Charlie Moses, Chief Joseph Band of Nez Perces of the Colville Indian Reservation, Nespelem, Washington, for reviewing the work. At Yellowstone National Park, Lee H. Whittlesey, Historian, and John Lounsbury, Lake District

Ranger, helped in the collection of documentary materials and reviewed parts of the manuscript. Elsa C. Kortge, Acting Curator, assisted in finding pertinent historic photographs in the park's vast collections. And Aubrey L. Haines, of Tucson, Arizona, furnished information about sites within Yellowstone and loaned me materials from his own extensive files. Still within the National Park Service community, I also received help and materials from Paul L. Hedren, Superintendent, Niobrara/Missouri National Scenic Riverways, O'Neill, Nebraska; Douglas C. McChristian, Historian, Intermountain Region, National Park Service; and Kitty Deernose, Curator, Little Bighorn Battlefield National Monument, Crow Agency, Montana. At the Denver Service Center Library, Jannette S. Wesley and Katherine S. Tudek, Librarians, helped process my many requests for interlibrary loan materials.

Many repositories around the country responded enthusiastically during my research trips or to my mail requests for data. I must thank the entire staff of the Old Military Branch, National Archives, and especially reference archivists Michael T. Meier, Tod Butler, Michael P. Musick, and Michael E. Pilgrim. At the Smithsonian Institution, National Anthropological Archives, Photo Archivist Paula Richardson Fleming gave guidance and assistance. At the U.S. Army Military History Institute, Army War College, Carlisle, Pennsylvania, I must acknowledge the help of Richard J. Sommers, Chief Archivist-Historian; David Keough, Assistant Archivist-Historian; Pamela Cheney, Archives Technician; John Slonaker, Chief Reference Historian; Louise Arnold-Friend, Reference Historian; and Dennis Vetock, Reference Historian. I must thank the staff of the archives and library of the U.S. Military Academy, West Point, New York, particularly Alan C. Aimone, Associate Librarian for Special Collections; Susan Lintelmann, Manuscript Librarian, Special Collections; and Charlyn Richardson and Sheila Biles, Library Technicians, Special Collections.

At the Archives, University of Colorado at Boulder Libraries (Western History Collection), I received most generous help from Cassandra M. Volpe, Archivist; Paulette D. Foss, Assistant Archivist; and David Hays, Assistant Archivist. At the Library and Archives of the Montana Historical Society, Helena, I benefited repeatedly from the knowledge and assistance of former Society Librarian Robert M. Clark. The collections at Washington State University, Pullman, were particularly important to my work, and I thank John F. Guido, Head, Manuscripts, Archives, and Special Collections Division; Lawrence R. Stark, Assistant Archivist; and José Vargas for allowing my examination and use of materials in the McWhorter and other collections. Likewise, Terry Abraham, Director, Special Collections, University of Idaho Library, Moscow, permitted me access to the rich materials in his charge. Also, I must thank Wayne Silka, Manuscripts Curator, The Bancroft Library, University of California, Berkeley; Peter J. Blodgett, Curator, Western Historical Manuscripts, The Huntington Library, San Marino, California; Laura Arksey, Curator, Cheney Cowles Museum, Eastern Washington State Historical Society, Spokane; Dale Johnson, former Archivist, Archives, Maureen and Mike Mansfield Library, University of Montana, Missoula; David F. Halaas, Historian, Colorado Historical Society, Denver; George Kush, Royal Canadian Mounted Police Historian and Curator, Fort Whoop-Up Interpretive Center, Lethbridge, Alberta; Michael Wagner, Braun Research Library, Southwest Museum, Los Angeles; Heather R. Munro, Reference Assistant, Manuscripts Department, The Lilly Library, Indiana University, Bloomington; Vicky Jones, Manuscripts Curator, and John Hawk, Special Collections Librarian, Knight Library, University of Oregon, Eugene; R. Eli Paul, former Research Historian, Nebraska State Historical Society, Lincoln; and Patricia A. Michaelis, Curator, Manuscripts Division, Kansas State Historical Society, Topeka. In addition, various staff members of the following repositories rendered assistance throughout the course of the study: Colorado Historical Society, Denver; Wyoming State Archives and Historical Department, Cheyenne; South Dakota State Historical Society, Pierre; National Library of Medicine, Bethesda, Maryland; Denver Public Library Western History Department; The Frontier Army Museum, Fort Leavenworth, Kansas; Library and Archives Section, Idaho State Historical Society, Boise; Manuscripts Division, Library of Congress, Washington, D.C.; Merrill G. Burlingame Special Collections, Montana State University Library, Bozeman; Archives and Manuscripts Department, Special Collections Division, Harold B. Lee Library, Brigham Young University, Provo, Utah; Manuscripts and University Archives, University of Washington, Seattle; Research Library, Washington State Historical Society, Tacoma; Arvada, Colorado, Public Library; U.S. Geological Survey Library, Lakewood, Colorado; Manuscripts Division, Boise State University Library; Spokane Public Library; and Parmly Billings Library, Billings, Montana.

I must also acknowledge the assistance of many generous individuals who shared with me pertinent materials and also their extensive knowledge of resource areas during the course of my work. Many of them reviewed parts of the manuscript during its draft stage. Lillian Pethtel, of Kamiah, Idaho, gave freely of her time in accompanying me to numerous sites and in providing much valuable data. Eileen and the late Kenneth Bennett, Kilgore, Idaho, lent their expertise regarding the Camas Meadows encounter sites and supplied relevant documentary items, too. For their help in delineating the Nez Perces' possible routes down Clark's Fork, I am indebted to Stuart Conner, Kenneth Feyhl, and Michael Bryant, of Billings, Montana. At the Canyon Creek battlefield, Feyhl and Harold Hagen, also of Billings, and Michael Blohm, of Laurel, Montana, contributed much of their time and specific information about that site. LeRoy ("Andy") Anderson, of Chinook, Montana, shared his insights into the Cow Island, Cow Creek Canyon, and Bear's Paw encounters, while James Magera of Havre, Montana, graciously loaned me important materials from his personal library related to the Bear's Paw battle and accompanied me over the site of that encounter on several occasions. John D. McDermott, of Rapid City, South Dakota, and Don G. Rickey, of Evergreen, Colorado, respectively, gave me access to their vast files of Indian wars documents and contributed their counsel and knowledge of the subject matter. Brian C. Pohanka, of Alexandria, Virginia, readily responded to my request for data from his collection, and Kermit D. Edmonds, of Missoula, Montana, ardently shared his knowledge of Fort Fizzle, Camas Meadows, and other sites. Wayne T. Norman and Jeanne Norman Chiarot generously allowed me to use the 1877 John H. Fouch photograph "Gen. Miles and Command crossing the Yellowstone with Joseph."

Others who contributed valuably in various ways include Paul English, Havre, Montana; Sherry L. Smith, University of Texas at El Paso; Richard Bottomly, U.S. Fish and Wildlife Service, Kooskia, Idaho; Dan Gard, U.S. Forest Service, Missoula, Montana; Alvin M. Josephy, Jr., Joseph, Oregon; Paul A. Hutton, University of New Mexico, Albuquerque; Robert M. Utley, Georgetown, Texas; Mr. and Mrs. Gary N. Dutcher, Stites, Idaho; Colonel Ben F. ("Absaroka Ben") Irvin, Globe, Arizona; Waldo M. Wedel, Boulder, Colorado; Leland H. Reyder, Cottonwood, Idaho; Margot Liberty, Sheridan, Wyoming; Milton Westin, Laurel, Montana; Carmelita Spencer, Grangeville, Idaho; Ruby Rylaarsdam, Grangeville, Idaho; John P. Langellier, Seabee Museum, Port Hueneme, California; John G. Lepley, Museum of the Upper Missouri, Fort Benton, Montana; L. Clifford Soubier, Charles Town, West Virginia; Andrew Masich, Pittsburgh, Pennsylvania; Brad

Dahlquist, Tacoma, Washington; Rom Bushnell, Western Heritage Center, Billings, Montana; James S. Brust, San Pedro, California; Larry Sklenar, Georgetown, South Carolina; the late Erwin N. Thompson, Golden, Colorado; Mary L. Culpin, Denver, Colorado; Virginia Parks, U.S. Fish and Wildlife Service, Portland, Oregon; Michael J. Koury, Fort Collins, Colorado; Janine Caywood, Missoula, Montana; Thomas R. Buecker, Fort Robinson State Museum, Nebraska; Joellen El Bashur, Moorland-Spingarn Research Center, Howard University, Washington, D. C.; Richard W. Sellers, Santa Fe, New Mexico; and Jeffrey Merritt Greene, Arvada, Colorado.

Special thanks also go to Rick Newby, Helena, Montana, and Charles E. Rankin, Martha Kohl, Glenda Bradshaw, Kathryn Fehlig, Molly Holz, and Randi Webb, of the Montana Historical Society Press, and Kitty Herrin, Missoula, Montana, for their assistance in preparing this manuscript for publication.

To all of the above individuals and institutions I extend heartfelt thanks.

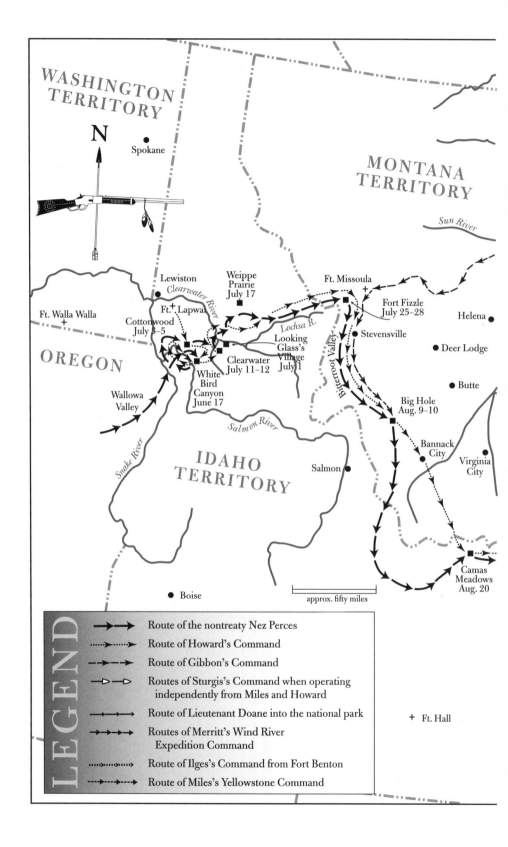

WASHINGTON TERRITORY

N

Spokane

MONTANA TERRITORY

Sun River

Helena

Lewiston

Weippe Prairie July 17

Ft. Missoula

Fort Fizzle July 25–28

Clearwater River

Deer Lodge

Ft. Walla Walla

Ft. Lapwai

Cottonwood July 3–5

Lochsa R.

Stevensville

OREGON

Clearwater July 11–12

Looking Glass's Village July 1

White Bird Canyon June 17

Bitterroot Valley

Butte

Wallowa Valley

Salmon River

Big Hole Aug. 9–10

Bannack City

Virginia City

Snake River

IDAHO TERRITORY

Salmon

Boise

approx. fifty miles

Camas Meadows Aug. 20

LEGEND

→→ Route of the nontreaty Nez Perces

⋯⋯⋯▸ Route of Howard's Command

–▸–▸ Route of Gibbon's Command

–▷–▷ Routes of Sturgis's Command when operating independently from Miles and Howard

→→→ Route of Lieutenant Doane into the national park

▸▸▸▸ Routes of Merritt's Wind River Expedition Command

⋯●⋯●⋯● Route of Ilges's Command from Fort Benton

–▸–▸–▸ Route of Miles's Yellowstone Command

+ Ft. Hall

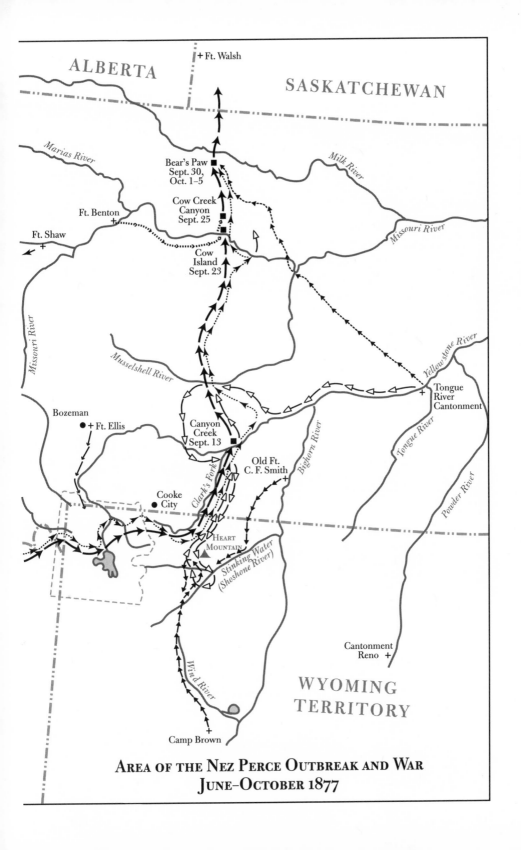

ALBERTA

SASKATCHEWAN

+ Ft. Walsh

Marias River

Milk River

Ft. Benton +

Ft. Shaw +

Missouri River

Bear's Paw
Sept. 30,
Oct. 1–5

Cow Creek
Canyon
Sept. 25

Cow
Island
Sept. 23

Missouri River

Musselshell River

Yellowstone River

Bozeman

● +Ft. Ellis

Canyon
Creek
Sept. 13

Tongue
River
Cantonment

+

Old Ft.
C. F. Smith

Bighorn River

Tongue River

Powder River

Cooke
City ●

Clark's Fork

Heart
Mountain

*Stinking Water
(Shoshone River)*

Cantonment
Reno +

Wind River

WYOMING
TERRITORY

Camp Brown +

AREA OF THE NEZ PERCE OUTBREAK AND WAR
JUNE–OCTOBER 1877

Reasons

IN THE BEGINNING there was the land. The region that today embraces northeastern Oregon, southeastern Washington, and central Idaho was home to the Nee-Me-Poo (Nee-MEE-poo), a term in their own language meaning "The People." The Nee-Me-Poo became known to Euro-Americans as the Nez Perce Indians, a name by which they are commonly recognized today.[1] A broad and topographically diverse area astride the Columbia Plateau, the Nee-Me-Poo homeland—which included their village sites and immediately adjacent and intermittent lands over which they ranged for interband activities and sustenance—stretched westward from Montana's Bitterroot range. It encompassed the rugged Clearwater Mountains, a broken tableland of up to seven thousand feet elevation, as well as an undulating grass plain called Camas Prairie, continuing to include the Blue Mountains and their collateral ranges and valleys in what is today northeastern Oregon.

Several rivers transect the region. The Snake and the Salmon, affluents of the Columbia River from the south and southwest, are ancient, swift-flowing streams whose erosive action created their deep and heavily fissured canyons. Likewise, the Clearwater and its branches radiate from the northeast and southeast to drain the glacially sculpted country west of the Continental Divide. Joining the Snake from the southwest is the Grande Ronde, itself fed by the Wallowa, which traces the valley of that name. Below the Salmon, and between that river and the Snake, lies a steeply rising, tortuously dissected plateau supporting the conifer-shrouded Salmon River Mountains and assorted lakes and streams, while north of the lower Clearwater River the country stretches away into rolling uplands with alternating grass and dense forest cover. Throughout forest and plain, rich soil rests atop volcanic deposits of eons past. A place of moderate seasonal temperatures and precipitation, but with somewhat lengthy winter periods, this broad, variegated tract—historically inhabited by the Nee-Me-Poo and related tribes—covered an area of approximately eleven thousand square miles.[2]

The first documented contact between the Nee-Me-Poo and white men occurred in 1805–6, when the Meriwether Lewis and William Clark army expedition to the Pacific passed through their lands, received assistance from them, and collected initial information about them. Subsequent exploring parties, principally those of the establishing fur companies, provided additional data. Early French-Canadian observers called the Nee-Me-Poo "Nez Perces" (pronounced in French "Nay-pair-SAY," but later anglicized to today's "Nez Purse"), in actuality a term prescribed for numerous groups who pierced their noses with dentalium shells. And although the Nee-Me-Poo apparently never practiced this custom extensively, they nonetheless retained the name. A brave, intelligent, and spiritual people, they had occupied their home territory for millennia, with archeological evidence reaching back for as many as thirteen thousand years. In their traditions, the people believe that they have been here since the time the world was first populated. They lived in several modes of housing, notably rush mat lodges, pine-board structures, and large semi-subterranean bark-covered dwellings, all capable of accommodating several families. Linguistically, the Nee-Me-Poo were of the Penutian language group and spoke a Sahaptian dialect, as did neighboring tribes of the Columbia Plateau. Like the mostly sedentary groups to the west, the Nee-Me-Poo traditionally subsisted on salmon, but they also hunted game in the forests and prairies and consumed local berries, roots, and tubers, especially relishing those of the camas and kouse plants.

Organizationally, the Nez Perces comprised a loose federation of bands, each with a village that habitually occupied a specific locale within the tribal territory. Band members lived their lives with guidance from *Wyakin*, an individually unique nature-force attained through requisite

fasting, praying, and vision-seeking. One's *Wyakin*, the Nez Perces believed, afforded protection, spiritual insight, and guidance in all life
matters, and it furnished strength in deciding such critical issues as war
and peace. Several chiefs, or headmen, governed each band, although
the band only recognized one as the band leader. Chiefs rose in band
hierarchy usually, but not exclusively, through hereditary means, but
war exploits and economic ingratiation proved mighty factors. Once
attained, chieftainship carried numerous responsibilities for the well-
being of the band. Often the chief mediated family disputes and meted
out punishment to headstrong children in the usual absence of parental
discipline. Peer pressure within the band usually governed individual
actions, and laws were few and unnecessary, so that the chief spent more
time dealing with welfare concerns for the entire group. Although war
was no formal prerequisite to chiefdom, some leaders possessed considerable war experience and became noted for their military skills; these
chiefs often commanded the most authority among the people.

While communal within the overall tribe, each band possessed
autonomy that manifested itself in its independent movements and activities. The bands subscribed to a central tribal authority composed of
a council of band leaders that convened whenever tribal necessity demanded. The respective bands maintained distances from one another,
partly, no doubt, because of the topography of the region, but also to
ensure equitable access to game and other food sources. When first
encountered by white men, most Nez Perce villages stood along the
Clearwater and its tributaries, although others bordered the lower Snake
River and the east side of the Salmon. The bands regularly joined for
familial and ceremonial reasons, and sometimes one or more Nee-Me-
Poo groups aligned with neighboring tribes for hunting, fishing, and
other mutually beneficial pursuits.

Although the entire tribe likely numbered well over six thousand
people in 1805, the population estimate stood at less than half that at
mid-century, largely because of rampant disease epidemics introduced
among them. The closest neighbors of the Nee-Me-Poo included the
Cayuses, Yakimas, Walla Wallas, Umatillas, Kalispels, Spokans, and
Coeur d'Alenes on the north and west, tribes of cultural and linguistic
affinity with whom relations were usually friendly; the Shoshones and
related Paiute bands on the south, long considered enemies; and the
friendly Flatheads on the east. One group in particular, the Palouses,

was so closely related to the Nee-Me-Poo that white observers considered it almost a band of that tribe. Intertribal trade was ongoing, and
the Nez Perces periodically journeyed west to barter goods with Pacific Coast peoples and east to trade with the Salish, Kutenais, and
Crows. Historically, the Kutenais, Blackfeet, Gros Ventres (Atsinas),
Assiniboines, and Lakotas often threatened the Nee-Me-Poo on their
occasional trips to the western Montana plains.[3]

The acquisition of horses before the middle of the eighteenth century expedited the journey across the Continental Divide by many Nez
Perces, and seasonal migrations to the plains east of the Bitterroots to
hunt buffalo became annual occurrences.[4] In the exchange of ideas and
products that followed, the plateau Indians soon adopted the portable,
buffalo-skin tipis of the Plains tribes while in transit. Firearms, acquired
after the start of the nineteenth century, facilitated the buffalo hunt
and promoted greater security against enemy tribes while afield. The
pursuit of buffalo—emphasized by some Nez Perce bands more than
others—influenced not only the participants' mode of subsistence, but
their other lifeways and material traits as well. The Nez Perce hunts
took place each autumn through early November, with the tribesmen
passing over the Bitterroots to the plains, particularly areas of west-
central Montana's lush Judith Basin, where the buffalo wintered. Some
of the people returned to Idaho; others occupied semi-permanent villages in the Bitterroot Valley, home of their Flathead allies with whom
they hunted through the winter before returning to their homes late
the following spring. While supplementing their lives thusly, the people
also kindled a sustained and friendly association with the Crow Indians
of the central Montana plains, a small tribe historically surrounded by
enemies. It was principally from the Crows that the Nez Perces acquired Plains-related modifications to their clothing, ornamentation,
songs, and dances. Moreover, the bands who routinely emigrated to
and from the plains gradually contrasted with those Nez Perce bands
who regularly remained at home, contributing to a nascent intratribal
cultural schism that would manifest itself in significant ways before and
during the conflict with the U.S. Army in 1877.[5]

Pervading all aspects of Nez Perce existence was their ancient and
overriding relationship with the land. The earth was the supreme pro-
vider, to be revered—not owned—as the mother of life for all creatures.
Human and earth were inextricably intertwined through birth, life, and

death, in a nonmaterial nurturing that pervaded all aspects of existence. As great benefactor, the earth bestowed life's necessities—among them water, grass, and air—and to the earth, life itself always returned. Central to the Nez Perce concept of land was the notion that the people of the different bands were predestined by a supreme entity to occupy designated areas of the country and were constrained to remain in those homelands. Among the Nez Perces, bands mutually recognized each other's areas as special places set aside to sustain the group economically, socially, and spiritually. Moreover, a band-fostered territorial imperative existed that placed strong emphasis on being born and dying on the same part of the earth. The eternal regeneration of mankind with the land was thus at the root of the Nee-Me-Poo concept of life itself.[6]

Their relationship with the land also accounted for change among the Nez Perces and ultimately provided the vehicle of contention leading to the events of 1877. Following their initial entry onto Nez Perce lands early in the nineteenth century, fur trading companies established long-standing contacts with social implications for the people. Along with sustained association with whites came important modifying influences on Nee-Me-Poo society through routine contact with the traders and through the concomitant effects among the Nez Perces of Christianity, introduced by missionaries in the first half of the century. Ancient Nee-Me-Poo predictions of imminent cultural change—at least partly realized through the loss of game and land resources—proved conducive to their recognition and acceptance of many Christian tenets, including a single creator, the Bible as a source of divine knowledge, ritualized services, and an afterlife.[7] Underlying this acceptance, however, was Nez Perce interest in acquiring the benefits of Euro-American technology.

Although Christianity promoted this objective, its introduction eventually produced cultural schism and factionalism among the Nez Perces. In November 1836, a Presbyterian missionary, Reverend Henry H. Spalding, established a station at the mouth of Lapwai Creek on the south side of the Clearwater. Employing the Nee-Me-Poo language, Spalding introduced agriculture, medical practices, and hymns and prayers that corresponded with the people's traditional forms of worship. In time, chosen Nez Perces became teachers of religious doctrine and worked to spread it among their kinsmen. Missionary activity, initially Protestant (Presbyterians and Congregationalists came in the mid-1830s while Catholics arrived in the region in 1839), concentrated along a relatively heavily populated corridor some sixty miles in length bordering the Clearwater River, home to the Leptepwey, or Lapwai, band of Nez Perces.

For those people, Christianity, along with other influences, changed fundamental aspects of Nez Perce society. Because of the geographic focus of the early proselytizers, not all Nez Perces received equal attention in the acculturation process. The buffalo-hunting proclivities of some bands fostered a cultural exclusiveness that removed them from sustained missionary attention. Compounding this, further inroads by whites flooding into the region via the Oregon Trail during the 1840s escalated competition for land and precipitated violent native reactions against the missionaries among neighboring tribes. Following the Cayuse Indian massacre of the Whitmans at their mission near the Walla Walla River in 1847, and the consequent departure of Spalding from Lapwai, missionary activity ended among the Nez Perces, not to resume in force until the 1870s.[8]

The period immediately following the missionary presence brought continued unrest. Angered by the perceived transgressions of missionaries and intruders into their lands, the Cayuses and Palouses in 1848 resisted troops raised and sent by the provisional government into their Columbia Valley domain in present eastern Washington to punish them for the Whitman murders. Throughout these conflicts, most of the Nez Perces, professing neutrality, remained friendly toward the white Americans. Concurrently, many non-Christian Nez Perces sought spiritual relief from the pressures wrought by the presence of whites through renewed identification with the land. The movement, which affected other Plateau peoples, too, inspired acceptance of the Dreamer religion, a hopeful nativistic theology advocating a return to more traditional tribal beliefs. The Dreamers practiced ritual dances accompanied by rhythmic drumming, and the term, "Drummers," was often applied to them. Strongly adhering to conventional Nez Perce precepts about the land, the Dreamers advocated rejection of white ways and a return to fundamental tribal values.[9]

The rise of the Dreamer religion among the non-Christian Nez Perces reflected a cultural response to a growing crisis brought on by the increasing proximity of white Americans, who were beginning to envelop them. While the people had exuded friendship and forbearance, hospitably accepting whites among them, the growing intrusions threatened that status by introducing a familiar pattern of Indian-white relations wherein the United States government provided for its citizens through territorial confiscation by treaty. Land became the paramount point of contention, philosophically and in actual occupation, as Nez Perce ideas of spiritual bonding with the earth clashed with Euro-American concepts of individual ownership. These convictions, though not always apparent, set the tone for Nez Perce–United States relations from the 1850s into the 1870s.

The treaty period intensified the intratribal estrangement between the Christian and more sedentary Nez Perce bands, mostly situated along the Clearwater River, and the non-Christian bands who continued to occupy remote locations in west-central Idaho and to partake of the seasonal hunting migrations east of the Bitterroots. A principal group of the latter, the Wallowas, inhabited the area west of Snake River and east of the Wallowa Valley of present northeastern Oregon. They perennially camped there and in the nearby Imnaha Valley, beautiful well-watered grassy pockets beneath the Wallowa range. Known for its grazing potential, the area afforded a popular summer rendezvous for other Nez Perce bands and for various Cayuse bands as well. Another prominent non-Christian group, the Lamtamas, inhabited the Salmon River tributaries, including White Bird Canyon, at the western edge of the Clearwater Mountains and southeast of Camas Prairie. The Alpowai band traversed the entire Nez Perce domain, but generally ranged along the upper middle Clearwater and spent much time east of the Bitterroots, often camping along the Yellowstone River. Yet another traditional group was the Pikunans, who occupied the region between the Snake and Salmon rivers. Finally, the closely related Sahaptian-speaking Palouses lived in several villages north of the big bend of the Snake, near its junction with the Columbia.[10]

By the mid-1850s, as the treaty period began, several leaders representing the various Nez Perce bands reflected the growing factionalism in the tribe. One Indian, Hallalhotsoot (Shadow of the Mountain), known appreciatively as Lawyer among whites, had strongly influenced the establishment of a Presbyterian mission at Lapwai near the lower Clearwater. Because of Lawyer's affinity for the Christian religion and his endorsement of missionary activities, church leaders and federal authorities recognized him as nominal head of all the Nez Perces. Other Nez Perce leaders who played significant roles at the outset of the reservation period included the great war leader Apash Wyakaikt, or Looking Glass, a rival of Lawyer for the position of head chief; Tuekakas, known as Old Joseph, of the Wallowa band, who had converted to Christianity in 1839; Timothy, of the Alpowai; and James, or Big Thunder, from Lapwai Valley.[11]

Among these men, Old Joseph played a most significant part in the coming crisis of 1877. When the missionaries had arrived among the Nez Perces, Spalding baptized him a Christian, and the chief moved his people from Wallowa to Lapwai. As a reputable warrior and hunter, Old Joseph had gained enviable status as a leader, and his presence at the mission, where Spalding openly favored him, deprived the local chief, James, of influence and created resentment. After the mission closed in 1847, Joseph returned to Wallowa but continued his Christian ways. He would factor importantly in the imminent developments that created, then modified, the Nez Perce reservation, and he spoke strongly for retaining his people's Wallowa lands: "There is where I live and there is where I want to leave my body." But undeniably, Old Joseph's most important contribution lay in his progeny, as the course of events would prove.[12]

As the intrusion of whites into the Northwest proceeded, the U.S. government took steps to acquire coveted lands and to avoid conflict with the native inhabitants by concentrating them on specially reserved tracts. Through the treaty process, the government extinguished the Indians' right of occupancy to selected areas. In 1855, Washington territorial governor Isaac I. Stevens engineered such agreements with several area tribes, including the Yakimas, Umatillas, Walla Wallas, and Cayuses. The first treaty with the Nez Perces was concluded on June 11, 1855, near Fort Walla Walla, Washington Territory, with Lawyer, Looking Glass, and Old Joseph prominent among the fifty-eight Nez Perces who signed it. The document recognized much of the generally acknowledged geographical perimeter of the ancestral Nez Perce domain, creating a reservation of about five thousand square miles that stretched from the Blue Mountains and upper Grande Ronde River of Oregon Territory, east to embrace the Clearwater Mountains all the way to the Continental Divide, and south from the Palouse River to include the lands between the Snake and Salmon. By the treaty, to which only Old Joseph and Looking Glass among the so-called lower bands acquiesced, the Nez Perces—in return for specified money, goods, and services—ceded to the United States lands on the east running into the Bitterroots, and on the south lands lying far below the junction of the Salmon with the Snake.[13]

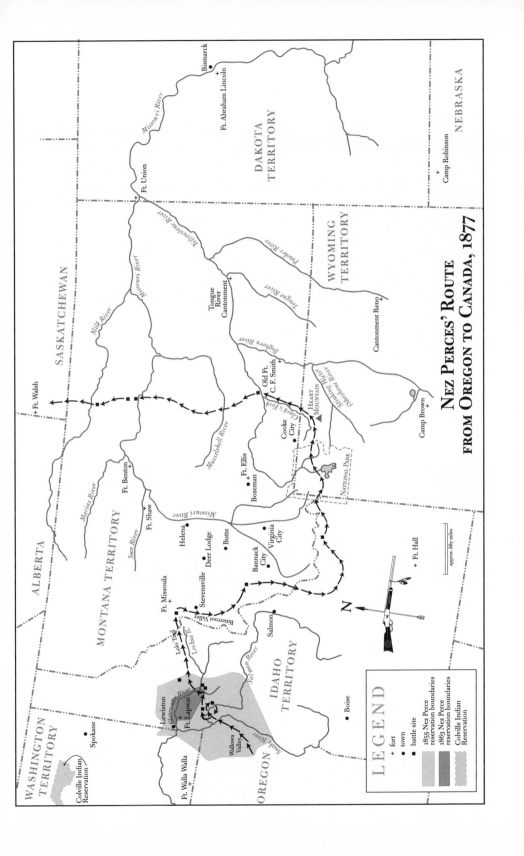

**NEZ PERCES' ROUTE
FROM OREGON TO CANADA, 1877**

WASHINGTON TERRITORY

Colville Indian Reservation

Spokane

ALBERTA

SASKATCHEWAN

+ Ft. Walsh

MONTANA TERRITORY

Marias River

Milk River

Missouri River

Ft. Benton +

Ft. Shaw +

Sun River

Musselshell River

Helena •

Deer Lodge •

Butte •

Virginia City •

Bannack City •

Ft. Missoula +

Stevensville •

Bitterroot Valley

Lolo Trail

Lochsa R.

Lewiston

Clearwater River

Ft. Lapwai +

Ft. Walla Walla +

OREGON

Wallowa Valley

Snake River

Salmon River

Salmon •

IDAHO TERRITORY

Boise •

+ Ft. Hall

approx. fifty miles

N

Ft. Ellis +

Bozeman •

NATIONAL PARK

Cooke City •

HEART MOUNTAIN

Clark's Fork

Old Ft. C. F. Smith +

Bighorn River

Shoshone River

(Stinking Water) River

Camp Brown •

WYOMING TERRITORY

Tongue River Cantonment +

Tongue River

Powder River

Cantonment Reno •

Yellowstone River

Missouri River

Ft. Union +

DAKOTA TERRITORY

Bismarck •

Ft. Abraham Lincoln +

Camp Robinson +

NEBRASKA

LEGEND

+ fort

• town

■ battle site

1855 Nez Perce reservation boundaries

1863 Nez Perce reservation boundaries

Colville Indian Reservation

For many signatory tribes who gradually realized the enormity of their losses by treaty, war seemed the only recourse. Within months of the council, war with the Yakimas erupted, followed by prolonged conflict with the Spokans, Walla Wallas, Cayuses, and Palouses. Thirty-nine Nez Perce tribesmen garbed in U.S. uniforms accompanied federal troops in several of the operations. Significantly, but perhaps not surprisingly, the 1855 treaty immediately caused no major disruption among the Nez Perces because the reservation encompassed much of the traditional band homelands, and notably that of the Wallowas west of the Snake River. But the instrument's inherent failure to recognize a multiple-band tribal composition and its acknowledgment of a head chief concept helped aggravate political divisiveness among the Nez Perces in ensuing years. Besides the alien nature of the transaction, many Nez Perces failed to consider Lawyer a chief. He therefore lacked legitimacy to deal with the whites, and to those bands, his signing the treaty invalidated it.[14]

At a council convened in September 1856, Old Joseph and other of the lower Nez Perce band leaders attempted to clarify their perceptions of the treaty and to explain that their accedence was in no way meant to constitute surrender of their lands. The "Nez Perces are divided in their loyalty," Governor Stevens reported, "one half of them . . . being in favor of, and one half against the treaty."[15] Equally disturbing to Nez Perce adherents of the treaty of 1855 was the failure of Congress to ratify it for nearly four years, a delay that nonetheless witnessed the opening of the Nez Perce cession lands to settlement. Too, even after ratification, the government equivocated over providing the goods promised in the agreement. As Lawyer pointed out nine years later, "we have no church as promised; no school house as promised; no doctor as promised." The government's delinquency was not lost on the Nez Perces who had refused to participate in the pact and who took every opportunity to remind Lawyer's followers of their folly. Compounding all, rich gold discoveries in the Nez Perce country during the summer and autumn of 1860 soon produced an influx of nearly fifteen thousand miners, directly contravening the 1855 treaty. In addition, in 1861 an agreement with the Nez Perces (not confirmed by Congress) permitted opening of a portion of the reservation "to whites in common with the Indians for mining purposes." From staging areas at Walla Walla, Washington Territory, and the newly founded Lewiston, on the Snake opposite the mouth of the Clearwater and itself on the reservation, the miners advanced onto Nez Perce lands without regard for treaty stipulations. In eastern Oregon, too, the Blue Mountains attracted gold seekers. Everywhere their impacts on the Nee-Me-Poo multiplied as boomtowns alternately were founded, flourished, and died along the Salmon and Clearwater and their tributaries. With placer deposits yielding upwards of five million dollars per annum during the early years of the strike, federal officials believed the gold country should remain open.[16]

The invasion by prospectors produced the greatest trauma that the Nez Perces had known in the long span of their relations with whites. Although the people—Christian and non-Christian alike—reaped rewards from the sale of pack horses and cattle to whites entering their lands, they ironically acquired through their transactions a dependency encouraged by ready access to white men's goods, such as firearms, food, and hardware. As roads and trails quickly traced through the country, the miners increasingly subjected the people to all forms of abuse. Whiskey sales and consumption occurred with uncontrolled frequency near the Nez Perce villages, while miners often destroyed or confiscated the tribesmen's property, including buildings and fences. In an attempt to preserve order, the army established Fort Lapwai near the new Indian agency of that name located near Spalding's vacated mission, but the presence of troops had little effect. By late 1862, the Nez Perces, in addition, faced loss of their grazing lands to the covetous intruders, a circumstance that prompted the government to act. In 1863, in an attempt to prevent hostilities, to open the gold country, and ostensibly to protect the Nez Perces from further aggression by whites, commissioners arrived at Fort Lapwai, in the new Territory of Idaho, to negotiate a treaty that would relinquish to the United States a major part of the reservation.[17]

The resulting treaty of 1863 not only removed the extensive land base accorded the Nez Perces eight years earlier, it exacerbated the long-standing political and religious divisions simmering among the tribesmen. Although the largely non-Christian bands attended the deliberations, they steadfastly refused to participate with the bands headed by Lawyer. The treaty, by relinquishing all lands part of Washington Territory and the state of Oregon, drastically reduced the reservation to approximately one-tenth of its 1855 size. The redefined boundaries, dictated largely by the location of gold fields and their supporting communities, created a tract bordering both sides of Lapwai Creek and the middle and south forks of the Clearwater River, but continuing south through the Camas Prairie to some of the northern affluents of the Salmon.[18]

Most important, however, the redesignated area (784,996 acres) co-incidentally encompassed only the lands of the Christianized Nez Perces—about three-fourths of all the tribesmen—whose government-supported leaders readily acceded to the treaty, while excluding those of the isolated Nez Perce bands from the Wallowa and Salmon River regions, whom it nonetheless directed to move onto the new reservation within one year of ratification. By their omission from the newly prescribed boundary, those people lost legal recognition altogether in the Treaty of 1863; in turn, they never recognized the accord. Old Joseph openly renounced his conversion to Christianity. By reaffirming nontraditional forms of government and leadership, the treaty further aggravated fragile intratribal relations, causing the remote lower bands to more completely reject acculturation and to more firmly embrace the Dreamer faith. But the compact engendered anti-white feelings and created certain sympathy among the treaty people, too, and some defections to the nontreaty bands occurred after promised annuities again failed to appear (the treaty was not ratified until 1867). Thereafter, the reservation faction of the Nez Perces, thus endorsed by the government, would benefit not only economically, but militarily, if such support were needed.[19]

Because the Wallowa lands had, in effect, been yielded by the pro-government majority represented by Lawyer's people, the action was repudiated by the lower bands headed by Old Joseph, Looking Glass (son of the chief of the same name, who had died early in 1863), White Bird, Big Thunder, Eagle From the Light, Toohoolhoolzote (Sound), and others, and Nez Perce occupation continued there under tacit consent of the U.S. government. But the Wallowa band and its allies remained off the reservation, and after the death of Old Joseph in 1871, the issue came to crisis with accelerated movement into the Wallowa Valley by white settlers. A commission met with Old Joseph's son, Heinmot Tooyalakekt (Thunder Traveling to Loftier Mountain Heights), known to whites as Young Joseph, and reported favorably that the valley had been permanently reserved for Joseph's people in 1855 and that they had not subscribed to any provisions of the 1863 accord. Furthermore, the commissioners concluded that the pro-treaty Nez Perces had lacked authority to relinquish the Wallowa lands, adding that "if any respect is to be paid to the laws and customs of the Indians, then the treaty of 1863 is not binding upon Joseph and his band, [and] . . . the Wallowa valley is still a part of the Nez Perce reservation." A caveat declared, however, that either the white settlers or the Indians must ultimately leave the area to insure mutual safety.[20]

The secretary of the interior, charged with administering Indian affairs through the Bureau of Indian Affairs, concurred with the commission's report, recommending nonetheless that a designated part of the Wallowa be retained for white settlement. At his behest, President Ulysses S. Grant issued an executive order, June 16, 1873, prescribing that parts of the Wallowa and Imnaha lands "be withheld from entry and settlement as public lands, and . . . be set apart as a reservation for the roaming Nez Perce Indians."[21] The decision to recognize the nontreaties' claim was strangely incongruous, given the government's post–Civil War trend toward restricting the tribes to reservations while opening more lands to white emigrants. Settlers already occupying specific areas of the Wallowa Valley and expected now to leave that place would be indemnified by congressional appropriation. Lapwai Agent John B. Monteith, Presbyterian appointee of the Grant administration under its church-oriented "Peace Policy," notified Chief Joseph of the government's recognition of the nontreaty Nez Perces' claim to the Wallowa.

Yet the presidential order failed either to evict whites already settled on the Wallowa lands or to prevent inroads there by many more. Both treaty and nontreaty Nez Perces continued to use the Wallowa for grazing stock during the winter months; they then generally moved east to cooler elevations each summer. Most whites arrived and established their farms in the summer while the tribesmen were away, then challenged the occupancy of the returning tribesmen.[22] Hoping to prevent clashes, Agent Monteith called on the tribesmen to come on the reservation and protect themselves against the crowding of settlers. Advocating their acculturation, he further urged that the Nez Perces stop going to the buffalo country. "When they go they stay one year, consequently nothing can be done toward civilizing such, and by their example they keep others from settling down." Monteith especially disliked the fact that the nontreaty returnees fraternized yearly with many of his charges along the Clearwater.[23]

Another source of contention that had developed concerned the frequency of Nez Perce murders at the hands of white men. As many as twenty-five tribesmen had been slain in the interval since the onset of the gold rush, and justice had been meted out badly or not at all. A singular case that profoundly affected the course of events three years later was the shooting death of Tipyahlana Siskan (Eagle Robe), a nontreaty Indian, by a settler named Lawrence Ott in the spring of 1874 on the Salmon River. The dispute between the two evolved over land, and although Ott turned himself in, he went unpunished for the crime.[24]

The Ott affair signaled the growing frustration that the Nez Perces felt regarding their relations with the whites vis-à-vis their lands. Finally, Oregon officials demanded all Nez Perce claims to land within the state boundary be extinguished.[25] Bowing to political pressure, on June 10, 1875, President Grant revoked his executive order, thereby restoring the Wallowa tract to the public domain and reopening it for settlement.[26] The fact that Joseph's people occupied the Wallowa but intermittently in their seasonal peregrinations, showing "no inclination to make permanent settlement thereon," was claimed to justify the action, which paved the way for unrestricted intrusions and consequently provoked conflict with the nontreaty Nez Perces.[27] While Joseph counseled restraint, often moving his people to avoid confrontation, conflicts with the homesteaders erupted. A catalytic event was the malicious killing of a Wallowa tribesman by two white men in June 1876, an outrage that, while duly acknowledged, was not promptly mitigated by the authorities.

In July 1876, a delegation authorized by Brigadier General Oliver O. Howard, commanding the Military Department of the Columbia at Portland, met at Fort Lapwai with the various bands of Nez Perces to discuss the complaints of Joseph's people. Howard's assistant adjutant general, Major Henry Clay Wood, chaired the proceeding.[28] Approximately forty Nez Perces attended, among them Reuben, who had succeeded the deceased Lawyer to represent the treaty Nez Perces. Old Joseph's two sons, Joseph and Ollokot (Frog), represented the nontreaty group. Bound by the dead chief's admonition to "never sell the bones of your father and mother," the sons reiterated their claim to the Wallowa, called for the removal of white settlers therefrom, and urged that the murderers of the Nez Perce be punished for their crime. After prolonged consultation, Major Wood promised indictments in the murder case and that Nez Perce witnesses would be called. Wood agreed with Joseph's claims respecting the Treaty of 1863, opining that "insofar as it attempts to deprive them [Joseph's people] of a right to occupancy of any land, its

Commanding Officer and Staff, Department of the Columbia, ca. 1877–78.
Seated, left to right: unidentified, Major Henry Clay Wood, Brigadier General
Oliver O. Howard, Captain Joseph A. Sladen, unidentified. Standing, left to right:
Major Edwin C. Mason, Captain John A. Kress, unidentified.
NEZ PERCE NATIONAL HISTORICAL PARK, SPALDING, IDAHO

provisions are null and void." At the conclusion of the council, General Howard, at Wood's recommendation, called on the Bureau of Indian Affairs to convene a commission to devise means to extinguish Joseph's claim to the Wallowa district and to "effect a just and amicable settlement" for the murder.[29]

The delay in bringing to trial the murderers of Joseph's tribesman, reminiscent of the Ott episode, especially troubled those Nez Perces, and increasingly the tribesmen viewed with gravity the homesteaders' threat to their sovereignty in the Wallowa. On September 3, after nothing substantive had happened following the meeting with Wood, Joseph and his warriors appeared in the Wallowa Valley demanding the surrender of the two perpetrators and threatening to "burn the valley" if the settlers were not gone within a week. Anticipating an outbreak, armed citizens assembled in the valley to fight the warriors. Troops from Fort Walla Walla responded and elicited a promise of restraint from Joseph if the offenders were prosecuted. The incident, details of which were doubtless subordinated by later events, nevertheless loomed large as a manifestation of Nez Perce frustration and represented a contributory cause of the ensuing conflict.[30]

The commission of 1876, headed by David H. Jerome and including among others General Howard, met at the Lapwai Agency in November with the treaty and nontreaty Nez Perces with the purpose, for the latter, "to secure their settlement upon reservations and their early entrance upon a civilized life." At the session of November 13, Young Joseph emerged as principal spokesman for the nontreaty Nez Perces. Tall and eloquent, the thirty-six-year-old leader of the Wallowas presented a forceful yet quietly dignified countenance that inspired his followers and impressed the commissioners. Baptized at birth, the future Nez Perce leader had withdrawn with his father to the Wallowa country following the demise of the missionary movement in the late 1840s. Ever wary of the ways of whites and of the consequent difficulties that their presence posed for his people, Joseph—on assuming his father's mantle—had maintained vigilance while reasserting Old Joseph's commitment to his band. He and his younger brother, Ollokot, had tried to balance the ancestral values and needs of their people with the reality that the times presented.[31] Doubtless his position as chief of the Wallowa band—the most conspicuous nontreaty group affected by the council proceedings—and his leadership skills as perceived by whites, cast Joseph into greater prominence among all the nontreaty Nez Perces, as far as future events were concerned.

Through three days of the Lapwai council, Joseph dominated the scene. "He is in the full vigor of his manhood," reported the commissioners, "six feet tall, straight, well formed, and muscular; his forehead is broad, his perceptive faculties large, his head well formed, his voice musical and sympathetic, and his expression usually calm and sedate, when animated marked and magnetic." "An alertness and dexterity in intellectual fencing was exhibited by him that was quite remarkable."[32] When the commissioners probed the differences between the treaty and nontreaty Nez Perces, Joseph frankly explained: "At the time the [1855] treaty was made we divided. The treaty was the cause of it. From that time we have been separated. We still remain so."[33] On the issue of the Wallowa lands, which the commissioners suggested were only occasionally used by the tribesmen, Joseph imparted his people's philosophy as follows:

Joseph, attired in a Crow war shirt and with colored and otherwise decorated hair,
sat for this formal studio portrait at the Tongue River Cantonment between
October 23 and 29, when he departed for Bismarck.
JOHN H. FOUCH, PHOTOGRAPHER; COURTESY JAMES S. BRUST

That which I have great affection for, I have no reason or wish to
dispose of; if I did, where would I be? The earth and myself are of
one mind. The measure of the land and the measure of our bodies
are the same. . . . If I thought you were sent by the Creator I might
be induced to think you had a right to dispose of me. Do not misun-
derstand me, but understand me fully with reference to my affection for the land. I never said the land was mine to do with it as I

chose. The one who has the right to dispose of it is the one who has
created it. I claim a right to live on my land, and accord you the
privilege to live on yours. . . . I think with reference to the land. I
look upon the land, made as it was, with pleasure. . . . I grew up on
it, and took it as it was given me. As it was created, it was finished
with power. There is nothing should supersede it. There is nothing
which can outstrip it. It is clothed with fruitfulness. In it are riches
given me by my ancestors, and from that time up to the present I
have loved the land, and was thankful it had been given me.[34]

Any government proposals for the Nez Perces' surrender of the Wallowa
lands were thus deemed unacceptable. "We are not to be trampled upon
and our rights taken from us," concluded Joseph. "The right to the
land was ours before the whites came among us."[35]

Rejecting this view, the commission argued that, despite past recognition of the nontreaty Nez Perces' claims that allowed their continued use of the Wallowa Valley, the acquiescence of Joseph's father to
the 1855 treaty, in fact, implied the surrender of such right, rendering
uncertain the Indian claim. Moreover, since the majority of the Nez
Perces (i.e., the Christian bands) had sanctioned the treaty, the minority, under "the law among the whites," must also abide by it. Under this
interpretation, Joseph's people and the other nontreaty Nez Perces were
constrained to remove themselves within the boundaries specified in
1863. In addition, since 1859 the state of Oregon—not the federal government—claimed the Wallowa Valley, and because Oregon law now
prevailed there, the people could be protected only by removing them
inside the Lapwai tract.

On the matter of the killing of the tribesman in the Wallowa, a
matter of great offense to the Nez Perces and for which only minimal
punishment had been meted, Joseph—in a gesture of remarkable forbearance that as well conveyed an intrinsic union between the crime
and the revered Wallowa—stated the following:

With reference to . . . the white man who committed the deed . . . I
have come to the conclusion to let him escape and enjoy health, and
not take his life for the one he took. . . . I do not want anything in
payment for the deed he committed. I pronounce the sentence that
he should live. I spoke to the murderer and told him I thought a
great deal of the land on which he had shed the blood of one of my
people. When I saw all the settlers take the murderer's part, . . . I
told them there was no law in favor of murder. I could see they were

all in favor of the murder, so I told them to leave the country. I told them it was of great importance. You see one of our bodies lying dead... [and] I cannot leave that country and go elsewhere.[36]

The commission recommended that the agent at Lapwai continue to settle the tribesmen on the reservation, but failing that, military force would be used. (A minority report contended that force could not be used until Joseph's people committed "some overt act of hostility.") To promote peace with the white settlers in the meantime, troops would be posted in the Wallowa Valley. Citing "pernicious doctrines" of the Dreamer religion as contributing to the nontreaties' stance, the commissioners urged that its leaders be removed, if necessary, to the Indian Territory (Oklahoma) to curtail their influence.[37]

The report urging the removal of the nontreaty Nez Perce to the reservation set the stage for active military involvement, but at first only to augment the work of the agents of the Bureau of Indian Affairs. In January 1877, Agent Monteith sent emissaries to Joseph reiterating the determination of the government to remove the roaming bands onto the reservation and specifying a deadline of April 1. Joseph replied: "I will not leave it [the Wallowa country] until I am compelled to." In March, the War Department, responding to the Lapwai recommendations delivered through the Interior Department, ordered Major General Irvin McDowell, commanding the Military Division of the Pacific at San Francisco, to implement the removal. Because of its sensitive nature, McDowell directed General Howard to give the removal his personal attention, notifying him "to occupy the Wallowa Valley *in the interest of peace*. You are to comply with the request of the Department of the Interior . . . to the extent only of *protecting and aiding* [its agents] . . . *in the execution of their instructions.*"[38]

Howard responded immediately, directing that—when weather permitted—two companies of the First Cavalry under Captain Stephen G. Whipple be sent from Fort Walla Walla to establish a camp at the west entrance of the Wallowa Valley near the Grande Ronde River. The location was strategic, the companies to be posted "as near the crossing of the Wallowa River as may be practicable, consistent with a comfortable and pleasant camp—a camp to debouch from." An outpost established close by would protect the Wallowa bridge from destruction by the Nez Perces. Howard ordered frame buildings erected for the troops, who would oversee two Gatling guns and secure requisite ammunition at the site.[39] Although placing troops only in the Wallowa country, Howard directed his efforts toward the removal to the Lapwai reserve of the following Nez Perces:

> Joseph's Band, of Wallowa Valley; the Hasotims, on a creek of that name south of the Snake River; the White Bird Indians, located on Salmon River, north of the Snake; and the [Palouse] band of Hush-Hush-Cute [Husis Kute (Bald Head)], scattered along the Snake River to the Palouse country. These, with numerous Indians, malcontents already on or near the Nez Perces reservation, of whom, in a sense, Looking Glass appeared to be the leader, constituted what has been called in reports "The Non-treaty Nez Perces Indians."[40]

On April 20, 1877, several Nez Perces met at Fort Walla Walla with Howard. He explained the requirements of the government for the people to remove to the reservation, although the tribesmen would be permitted to hunt and fish periodically in the Imnaha country. While Joseph did not attend, his brother, Ollokot, tried to convince the general of the people's right to remain at Wallowa. "This is where we were born and raised," he said. "It is our native country. It is impossible for us to leave." To Ollokot's protests, Howard replied only that the people must move.[41]

To hasten that process, Howard agreed to meet with Agent Monteith and representatives of the nontreaty Nez Perces at Fort Lapwai in May and impress upon them "the unalterable purpose of the Government." As a contingency, and doubtless to intimidate the Nez Perces, Howard postured cavalry at Lewiston and near the junction of the Grande Ronde River with the Snake. Elsewhere, more troops assembled to be brought forward if needed. The councils were bitter and turbulent. Alarmed by the message from the Fort Walla Walla meeting, about fifty Nez Perces appeared on May 3 with Joseph and Ollokot, who requested that the proceedings be delayed until White Bird and his people arrived. Howard was adamant that the council begin, and he warned the Nez Perces that, while he was prepared to listen to them, "in any event, they were to obey the orders of the Government of the United States." Agent Monteith read aloud his instructions from Washington, and they were interpreted to the Indians. The Nez Perces, said Monteith, had not responded to his previous invitation to come. Now they must do so. Howard told them that hunting and fishing privileges in the Imnaha Valley were to be granted once the tribesmen settled on the reservation, but he counseled that further delay would cause troops to be sent after them.[42]

On Friday, May 4, the people reconvened with some of White Bird's band in attendance, along with members of other treaty and nontreaty bands. At this session, a confrontation flared between Howard and Toohoolhoolzote, spiritual leader of the Pikunans and a noted orator among his tribe, as the aged warrior tried to explain to Howard the Nez Perce concept of land. Dismissing Toohoolhoolzote as "a large, thick-necked, ugly, obstinate savage of the worst type," the general, with Joseph's concurrence, ordered the meeting adjourned. In his memoirs, Howard recalled, "the Indians at this meeting gave clear evidence that they did not intend to comply with instructions from Washington."[43] On May 7 the council resumed with more of the nontreaty people in attendance. Once again, Toohoolhoolzote held sway, haranguing Howard and Monteith about Nez Perce beliefs respecting their lands. A significant exchange took place, one that explained much of the essence of the nontreaties' position, but which was either misjudged or ignored by Howard, who was determined in his orders. As Howard recounted:

> [Toohoolhoolzote] repeats what he had said at the other council about chieftainship—chieftainship of the earth. . . . I answer, "I don't want to offend your religion, but you must talk about practicable things; twenty times over I hear that the earth is your mother and about chieftainship from the earth. I want to hear it no more, but come to business at once." The old man then began to speak about the land and became more impudent than ever, and said, . . . "You white people get together and measure the earth and then divide it, so I want you to talk directly what you mean." . . . The old man, in a surly way, asked, "What person pretended to divide the land and put me on it?" I answered, with emphasis, "I am that man. I stand here for the President, and there is no spirit, good or bad, that will hinder me. My orders are plain, and will be executed."[44]

After concluding that both Looking Glass and White Bird sub-scribed to these views, Howard reminded the Nez Perces that, for him, the only question that needed answering was, "will the Indians come peaceably on the reservation, or do they want me to put them there by force?" When Toohoolhoolzote persisted in his argument, Howard peremptorily ordered him arrested, led from the assembly, and jailed. (He was released several days later.) The action violated council protocol and infuriated the Nez Perces, but Joseph counseled patience. He later recalled: "I knew if we resisted that all the white men present, including General Howard, would be killed in a moment, and we would be blamed."[45] With the old man removed, the Nez Perces, despite evident misgivings, agreed to inspect the reservation lands. Resignedly, Joseph, Looking Glass, and White Bird the next day rode up the Lapwai Valley with General Howard, observing the tidy farms of many of their treaty kin. At one point, wrote Howard, Joseph allowed that "When I come on the reservation I want a good frame house."[46] But Joseph recalled that "we rode all day upon the reservation, and found no good land unoccupied."[47] On Wednesday and Thursday, Looking Glass and White Bird, again accompanied by Howard, traveled to the Clearwater Valley, where their bands were destined to settle. Looking Glass, recalled the general, "indicated great delight at the peace prospects."[48] Overlooking the valley of the Clearwater on the evening of May 9, the group, wrote Howard, "beheld the best evidence of Indian civilization in the numerous farms on both sides of the river and along the creek, dotted with real houses, and well fenced and planted."[49]

The Fort Lapwai council concluded on May 15. By then, the troops from Lewiston had arrived to effect a show of force. The Nez Perces, reported Howard, agreed to come on the reserve and were assigned tracts as follows: Joseph's band would settle on the upper Middle Clearwater, as would White Bird's band. Husis Kute and the Palouses would also go to the Clearwater, while Hasotin's people would move to the area of the Sweetwater, a tributary of Lapwai Creek. The people were granted thirty days in which to gather their livestock and relocate onto the reservation. Joseph recollected that Howard told them: "If you are not there in that time, I shall consider that you want to fight, and will send my soldiers to drive you on."[50] When White Bird allowed that he could not always control his people who got liquor from the whites, and that he feared those so affected might not come on the reservation, Howard assured him that his soldiers would be ready to assist in bringing them in.[51] The general concluded: "Having now secured the object named, by persuasion, constraint, and such a gradual encircling of the Indians by troops as to render resistance evidently futile, I thought my own instructions fulfilled."[52] Howard returned to

Portland, confident that the Nez Perces would respond by the appointed deadline and that trouble would be averted.

General Howard's expectation that the nontreaty Nez Perces would comply with the Lapwai directive was grounded in his own confidence in his ability to deal with Indians. Forty-six years old in 1877, Howard had enjoyed a diversified, if unspectacular, military career. A Maine native, he had graduated near the top of his 1854 West Point class, and he eventually served at the military academy as professor of mathematics. He saw early duty against the Seminole Indians, but rose rapidly during the Civil War, 1861–65, leading troops at Manassas, Fair Oaks (where, wounded, he lost his right arm), Second Manassas, Antietam, Fredericksburg, Chancellorsville, and Gettysburg. Transferred west in 1863, he took part in operations around Chattanooga and during Sherman's march to Atlanta and the sea the following year. Although his performance leading troops in battle was at best mediocre, Howard emerged from the war a brigadier general with brevets up to and including that of major general.

A complex individual of passionate intellect, Howard was deeply religious and promoted prayer meetings, morality, and temperance among his commands to the extent that he was known by the sobriquet, "the Christian soldier." His professed affinity for the downtrodden, and especially for the recently freed Southern blacks, led to Howard's appointment as commissioner of the Freedmen's Bureau after the war. His administration was controversial and marked by disharmony, but his advocacy of educating the former slaves led to the establishment of Howard University. Howard thereafter took an extreme interest in Indian affairs and Indian rights. His colleague, Brigadier General George Crook, wrote that Howard once told him that "he thought the Creator had placed him on earth to be the Moses to the Negro. Having accomplished that mission, he felt satisfied his next mission was with the Indian."[53] Thus divinely ordained, Howard believed that the Indians should be dealt with through trust and peaceful means, and only lastly through force—a belief that Crook and most other officers on the frontier thought naive. In 1872, his negotiations with the Chiricahua leader, Cochise, produced a tenuous peace in the Southwest, and since 1874, as commander of the Department of the Columbia (which comprised the state of Oregon and the territories of Washington, Idaho, and Alaska), Howard had worked to effect lasting peace among the tribes in that region.[54] When he departed Fort Lapwai in May 1877, it was with the conviction that he had allayed problems with the nontreaty Nez Perces. Yet Howard's diplomatic competence with the Indians was one thing; dealing with them in battle and on a protracted military campaign was quite another, as the events of 1877 soon proved.

Eruption and White Bird Canyon

FOLLOWING THE COUNCIL at Fort Lapwai with General Howard, the Nez
Perces started for their home areas to gather in their livestock and prepare for the move onto the reservation. Joseph and Ollokot crossed the
Snake River at Lewiston and ascended the Grande Ronde River to their
camp near the mouth of Joseph Creek in the Wallowa Valley. White Bird
and Toohoolhoolzote led their bands south to the Salmon River. Looking Glass headed east to his home on the Middle Clearwater above the
subagency of Kamiah and within the reservation boundary. In returning
home, the people traced the geography that became the setting for the
opening stage of the war. Oddly enough, the Wallowa region that so
prominently comprised the crucible of dispute lay beyond the zone
through which they traveled. In its configuration, the area formed a rough,
left-leaning trapezoid with sides about forty miles long that encompassed
some sixteen thousand square miles in west-central Idaho between the
Snake River and the Clearwater Mountains, and that ran from slightly
north of the Middle Clearwater River south to include the mountainous
terrain between the Snake and Salmon rivers. Its northern part comprised the Nez Perce Reservation, as reshaped according to the 1863
treaty, while to the south lay the broad and undulating Camas Prairie,
favorite rendezvous point for all the Nez Perce bands.

Several white communities dotted the scene. From Lewiston, in the extreme upper left corner of the trapezoid, the line of settlement followed east along the Middle Clearwater to the Lapwai Agency and Fort Lapwai, ten miles away, and diagonally southeast some sixty-six miles to the town of Mount Idaho, with approximately a hundred inhabitants, and the adjacent hamlet of Grangeville. The road running between Lewiston and Mount Idaho passed through the low-lying Craig's Mountain range before splitting the Camas Prairie. At a point forty-eight miles from Lewiston and nineteen from Mount Idaho, and near Cottonwood Creek, stood an inn, or halfway house, known as Norton's Ranch or Cottonwood Ranch, where travelers sought rest and sustenance. Several miles south of Mount Idaho, the terrain began a sharp seven-mile descent to the Salmon and its tributary, White Bird Creek, named after the Nez Perce leader whose band inhabited the area. Below White Bird Creek, and along several eastern affluents of the Salmon, stood many scattered homesteads of white farmers and stock raisers. Militarily, the entire area lay within the District of the Clearwater, a part of Howard's administrative domain within the Military Division of the Pacific.[1]

General Howard arrived back at Fort Lapwai on June 14 to be on hand when the nontreaty Nez Perces moved onto the reservation. "The officers, the government employees at the agency, and the friendly Indians," he reported, "all expressed the belief that the 'non-treaties' intended to comply with the promises made to the agent and myself the month previous."[2] Earlier, troops of the First Cavalry from Fort Walla Walla had arrived to support those at Fort Lapwai in anticipation of the Indians' arrival. Visiting the Lapwai Agency on June 4, Sergeant Michael McCarthy of Company H found it lifeless and littered with trash. "The only semblance of animation about the whole agency [was] a few Indian boys catching minnows in a sluggish millrace." Eight days later, it was generally felt that the nontreaties were coming and that the soldiers would have no trouble with them. "A few days and we will return to Walla Walla," penned McCarthy. "Quiet peace reigns. Joseph has put his pride in his pocket and is now I hear crossing his stock and coming in." Unconcernedly, the sergeant recorded that White Bird, "a grand looking Indian whose headdress is decorated with an eagle's wing, is present at our morning drills nearly every day for a week. He is attended by an orderly who rides the regulation distance behind him.

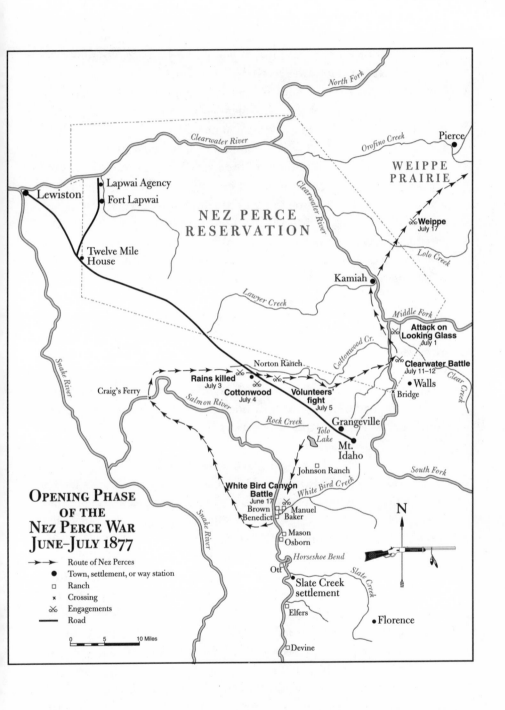

North Fork

Clearwater River

Orofino Creek

Pierce

WEIPPE
PRAIRIE

Lewiston

Lapwai Agency
Fort Lapwai

Clearwater River

NEZ PERCE
RESERVATION

Weippe
July 17

Lolo Creek

Twelve Mile
House

Lawyer Creek

Kamiah

Middle Fork

Snake River

Cottonwood Cr.

Attack on
Looking Glass
July 1

Clearwater Battle
July 11–12

Craig's Ferry

Salmon River

Rains killed
July 3

Norton Ranch

Cottonwood
July 4

Volunteers'
fight
July 5

Walls

Clear Creek

Bridge

Rock Creek

Tolo
Lake

Grangeville

Mt.
Idaho

South Fork

Johnson Ranch

White Bird Canyon
Battle
June 17

White Bird Creek

N

Brown
Benedict

Manuel
Baker

Mason
Osborn

Horseshoe Bend

Slate Creek

Ott

Slate Creek
settlement

Florence

Elfers

Devine

OPENING PHASE
OF THE
NEZ PERCE WAR
JUNE–JULY 1877

→ Route of Nez Perces
● Town, settlement, or way station
□ Ranch
× Crossing
⚔ Engagements
— Road

0   5   10 Miles

We must be of interest to him, so punctual is his attendance." As late as
June 14, McCarthy commented on the tedium at Fort Lapwai, noting
that there "is not a thing to break the monotony except mosquitos."[3]

On that day, Howard received a letter from a Mount Idaho resident stating that the citizens of that community were becoming increasingly suspicious of the tribesmen gathered nearby.[4] The general
instructed Captain David L. Perry, commanding the two companies of
First Cavalry at Fort Lapwai, to prepare a detachment to go the next
day and ascertain the intentions of the Nez Perces known to be camping just off the edge of the reservation. Since returning to their home
areas from the Fort Lapwai council, Joseph, Ollokot, White Bird, and
the other band leaders had readied their people for moving onto the
reserve. Under the watch of Captain Whipple and his cavalrymen, the
Wallowas had spent much of the interval packing their possessions and
corralling hundreds of free-grazing horses and cattle and fording all, as
well as themselves, across the raging and freezing waters of the Snake,
now swollen from the spring runoff. Many animals escaped the roundup
and were later confiscated by white settlers, while others were swept
away and drowned. On May 31, most of the tribesmen crossed at a
point called Dug Bar, near the mouth of the Imnaha and opposite the
mouth of the Salmon, then traveled east for ten miles before fording
the Salmon and moving north through a defile known as Rocky Canyon. They left their cattle below the Salmon, intending to return for
them before the deadline.

Around June 3, the people began converging at the sacred grounds
of Tepahlewam (Split Rocks, or Deep Cuts) on Camas Prairie near a
large pond at the time referred to as "the lake," but today called Tolo
Lake, about six miles west of Grangeville. Those assembling included
the five recognized nontreaty bands, as follows: The Wallowas, with
Joseph, Ollokot, and other leaders, included 55 men; the Lamtamas, or
so-called White Bird band, under their principal chief, White Bird,
included 50 men; the Alpowais of Looking Glass included 40 men (all
were not present at the assembly); the Pikunans of Toohoolhoolzote,
who had travelled over from the Wallowa with Joseph and Ollokot,
included 30 men; and Husis Kute and the Palouses included 16 men,
for a total of 191. Only half of these, say 95, were warriors, the rest
being either too young or old for that designation. There were also
approximately 400 women and children in all the bands, so that the

total nontreaty Nez Perce population at Tolo Lake stood at slightly less than 600.[5]

Tolo Lake, formed at least ten thousand years ago and the sole natural lake on Camas Prairie, had historically afforded a popular early summer rendezvous where the Nee-Me-Poo could observe their Dreamer ceremonies, greet friends and relatives in other bands, race their ponies, exchange gifts, and gather the popular camas bulbs. At Tolo Lake, too, the Nez Perce leaders of the different bands represented their people in the council, and the decisions of the council regarding peace and war became binding on all. Generally, war leadership evolved based on a warrior's record and commensurate ranking status and his ability to attract and maintain a followership. Joseph, a civil leader and descendant of a popular chief, was not regarded as such among the people, and he was, moreover, apparently without extensive military experience. Nonetheless, as co-leader of the large Wallowa band, Joseph stood as an influential force in multi-band councils. Conversely, the other Wallowa co-leader, Ollokot, was highly regarded in military matters, and he provided skilled counsel during the subsequent struggle. Other noted war leaders included White Bird, chief of the Lamtamas, who in his mid-fifties was well past warrior age but possessed considerable knowledge accrued during his many years and was viewed as a senior adviser; Chuslum Moxmox (Yellow Bull), a war leader, also of the Lamtamas; Looking Glass, the Alpowai, fortyish and well respected for his war prowess, and who emerged as perhaps the dominant military leader as the conflict wore on; Toohoolhoolzote, chief of the Pikunans; Koolkool Snehee (Red Owl), an Alpowai headman of Looking Glass's band; Wahchumyus (Rainbow) and Pahkatos Owyeen (Five Wounds), who were not present at Lake Tolo but who shortly joined White Bird's people.[6]

The Lake Tolo councils in 1877 witnessed prolonged and rancorous debate among the leaders of the different bands regarding their imminent movement onto the reservation. Despite the agreements made at Fort Lapwai in May, many tribesmen bridled at giving up their freedom and their lands, and the growing furor over the issue produced much dissension, building resentment and second-guessing over the earlier decision. Against the backdrop of this tense and emotional convocation occurred an incident that further obscured past consensus, intensified the fractiousness and sense of rage among the people, and in

the end provoked irrevocable armed conflict. On June 13, shortly before the deadline for removing onto the reservation, White Bird's band
held a tel-lik-leen ceremony at the Tolo Lake camp in which the warriors paraded on horseback in a circular movement around the village
while individually boasting of their battle prowess and war deeds. According to Nez Perce accounts, an aged warrior named Hahkauts Ilpilp
(Red Grizzly Bear) challenged the presence in the ceremony of several
young participants whose relatives' deaths at the hands of whites had
gone unavenged. One named Wahlitits (Shore Crossing) was the son
of Eagle Robe, who had been shot to death by Lawrence Ott three
years earlier. Thus humiliated and apparently fortified with liquor, Shore
Crossing and two of his cousins, Sarpsisilpilp (Red Moccasin Top) and
Wetyemtmas Wahyakt (Swan Necklace), set out for the Salmon River
settlements on a mission of revenge.[7] On the following evening, Swan
Necklace returned to the lake to announce that the trio had killed four
white men and wounded another who had previously treated the Indians
badly; Lawrence Ott, however, had not been found. Inspired by the war
furor, approximately sixteen more young men rode off to join Shore Crossing in raiding the settlements.

   The news of the killings electrified the assemblage, and now anticipating inevitable confrontation with Howard's soldiers, the bands started
moving away from the lake. The so-called treaty people present in the
camp, afraid of being implicated in the murders, hurried back to the
reservation while the nontreaties traveled to Cottonwood Creek. Seeking to avoid trouble with the soldiers, Looking Glass led his people back
to their tract near the mouth of Clear Creek on the Middle Clearwater,
while Husis Kute camped with his Palouses a short distance away on
the South Fork of the Clearwater. Joseph and Ollokot had been away
from the Nez Perce assembly at Tolo Lake when these incidents happened. They had gone below Salmon River to butcher some cattle and
were sent for immediately after the assembly received news of the murders. Hoping to avert war, the two rejoined their band along the Cottonwood, but by then the tragic course of events precluded further
discussion of restraint among the bands. When the two leaders sought
to bring their camp near that of Looking Glass for security, that chief—
incensed at White Bird over the killings—resisted the approach. They
instead withdrew to the Lamtamas camping ground at the mouth of
White Bird Creek on the Salmon. The killings—and the schisms they

were creating among the Nez Perces themselves—dashed any hope that Joseph and Ollokot might still have retained for a peaceful movement onto the Lapwai reservation.[8]

Despite General Howard and Agent Monteith's outwardly projected confidence that the Nez Perces were about to yield to agency life, there is evidence that the settlers observing the gathering at Tolo Lake thought otherwise. Normally the assembly would have been viewed as a routine affair, for the tribesmen camped there annually. Several accounts suggest that, because of the recent debate at the Fort Lapwai council, the settlers expected a major outbreak, rumored to be scheduled to occur on July 4 at Mount Idaho as they celebrated Independence Day (despite it being more than two weeks beyond the date imposed for the Nez Perces going onto the reservation). Others indicate that a well-to-do Nez Perce cattleman named Black Tail Eagle warned the whites of imminent trouble as he passed through the settlements. On June 13, a Mount Idaho town father named John M. Crooks ventured out to the Nez Perce camp to find out what was happening. By now clearly anticipating trouble from the army, the tribesmen told Crooks that they did not intend to harm the settlers if they did not assist the soldiers.

Ultimately, the attacks came, but possibly in a more incidental manner than the settlers expected. The three warriors who initiated it on June 13, having failed to find Lawrence Ott, traveled to the ranch of Richard Devine, nine miles above Slate Creek, where they shot him to death and took his rifle. Reversing direction and heading north to John Day Creek, the three next day encountered Jurden Henry Elfers, Henry Burn Beckrodge, and Robert Bland, killing them and riding off on their horses. Continuing down the Salmon, they happened on storekeeper Samuel Benedict, out checking his cattle near the mouth of White Bird Creek, and wounded him. Benedict escaped. It was then that the warrior, Swan Necklace, returned to the gathering on Camas Prairie to boast of their exploits and recruit the other young men. Thus reinforced, the warriors attacked John J. Manuel's ranch, two miles above the mouth of White Bird Creek, wounding Manuel and setting his buildings ablaze. Encountering Samuel Benedict again, they shot him as he attempted to flee across White Bird Creek, killing him along with settlers August Bacon and James Baker. On June 15, the warriors continued their raiding, killing or capturing Mrs. Jennet Manuel and her eleven-month-old baby, and killing William Osborne and Harry Mason.

Mrs. Manuel's seven-year-old daughter escaped with wounds. They raped two women, Helen Walsh and Elizabeth Osborn.[9] On the next day, a miner on the Salmon named Frank Chodoze was killed and his cabin burned. The crisis escalated with the killing by volunteers from Mount Idaho of a Nez Perce warrior named Jyeloo southwest of that community, and the Indians' retaliatory slaying later that day of settler Charles Horton. As the reality of the outbreak spread, fear mounted among the residents of Mount Idaho and Grangeville.[10]

In one of the most startling incidents of the outbreak, Benjamin B. Norton, proprietor of Norton's Ranch or the Cottonwood House, twenty miles northwest of Mount Idaho, sought to remove his family and guests to safety late in the evening of June 14. As the settlers' wagons proceeded toward Grangeville, warriors struck in the darkness, killing the horses, then shooting Norton, who died before morning, and wounding F. Joseph Moore, Lew Day, and Norton's wife, Jennie. Moore was an employee of Norton's, while Day had been en route from Mount Idaho to Fort Lapwai with news of the Salmon River killings. Both Moore and Day died later from their injuries. A nine-year-old son, Hill B. Norton, and eighteen-year-old Lynn Bowers, sister of Jennie Norton, fled into the night. In the suddenness of the assault, John Chamberlin and his infant daughter were killed and his other daughter wounded, while Chamberlin's wife was shot with an arrow and raped. Next morning, patrolling citizens found the survivors and ushered them into Mount Idaho before proceeding to the scene of the attack, about five miles west of Grangeville, and rescuing the wounded. The relief party narrowly escaped being attacked by Nez Perces advancing from Tolo Lake.[11]

Beyond the killings, the Nez Perces' raiding left widespread destruction, with many homes, barns, and outbuildings burned and plundered and horses, cattle, and hogs driven off or killed. There were frequent incidents of crops being destroyed. After their rampage along the Salmon, the warriors focused on farms and ranches on Camas Prairie, some near the lake where the bands had assembled. By then, most of the Salmon River settlers had found refuge at Slate Creek, where a stockade was raised, while others sought relief in Mount Idaho and Grangeville. At Mount Idaho, the small hotel was pressed into service as a hospital, and on a hill north of town, residents hurriedly threw up a circular barricade of logs, rocks, and sacks of flour. At Grangeville, an upright stockade was raised around the grange hall. Almost all the people who experienced losses filed claims within months, and most received smaller than requested awards over the next few years.[12]

There is no accounting for what happened in these attacks. Perhaps the events of June 1877 represented the culmination of a cultural crisis that had long simmered among the Nee-Me-Poo. The causes were many: Decades of cultural identity gone awry through repeated land swindles—by both the United States government and individual settlers. Missionary-inspired confusion over what the people should believe of the supernatural and the natural worlds, and over who the people were versus who they should be. The usual litany of broken promises. The repeated cases of physical abuse including the rape of Nez Perce women. The introduction of alcohol. The cupidity of crooked whites. The multitude of other Indian-white contact experiences that promoted grievances without redress. And all these issues led to the intratribal factionalism that had affected so many other tribes in similar ways.

The striking out by Shore Crossing and his followers against individual white men who had at various times wronged the Nez Perces only symbolized the deeper frustration wrought by the myriad issues and the outrage felt by all as they prepared to surrender the vestiges of their homeland. But what followed the first day's killings was a general outburst of the cultural angst that had fomented for years in the nontreaties' psychology, producing a displaced anger and aggression that could not be stemmed. It erupted after the initial Salmon River attacks, helped push the interband leadership away from the conciliation of the past and toward unreserved opposition to what was happening to their people, and reappeared in random explosions over the next three months as the tribesmen tried to elude the army.[13]

The events of June 14 and 15 happened with such swiftness that only on the latter date was the army at Fort Lapwai alerted, although Howard had received intimations of the discontent at Tolo Lake and had heard that the tribesmen might be reassessing their decision. On the fifteenth, Captain Perry sent out a detachment to determine why the Indians had not reported to the agency. The small mounted party had gone but twelve miles when they encountered messengers from Mount Idaho with the first report of the outbreak, whereupon they turned back to the fort with the settlers' plea for help.

Learning of the killings on the Salmon, and of statements by White Bird and Joseph that the people were not coming onto the reservation,

General Howard promptly convened a meeting with Monteith, Inspector Erwin C. Watkins of the Bureau of Indian Affairs, and Captain Perry at Fort Lapwai. Howard directed Perry to ready his two companies to advance to Mount Idaho to relieve the citizens there. Simultaneously, Monteith sent out some friendly Nez Perces, ostensibly to bring in White Bird and Joseph, but more realistically to seek confirmation of the deaths. He then directed the agent at Kamiah to move his family and employees down to the Lapwai Agency. Later that day, news came from Mount Idaho that more whites had been killed. "We want arms and ammunition and help at once. Don't delay a moment," said the message. In answer, Perry's troops, outfitted with three days' rations in their saddlebags and enough for five more carried by pack mules, moved out at eight that evening accompanied by Nez Perce scouts from the agency. Through an aide dispatched to the telegraph at Walla Walla, Howard ordered up the two cavalry companies stationed at Wallowa Valley and the infantry at Fort Walla Walla. Howard then sent a dispatch to Major Wood at Portland requesting the concentration of more troops and supplies at Lewiston. He notified General McDowell of the situation, requested authority to hire more scouts, and closed reassuringly with, "Think we shall make short work of it."[14]

When Captain Perry rode out of Fort Lapwai, his fighting strength consisted of Companies F and H, First Cavalry, 103 men strong. In composition, the two companies more or less typified the enlisted ranks in 1877, many of them foreigners of diverse vocational background, including some recent recruits who were inexperienced in military matters, particularly in such basic cavalry requisites as riding and shooting.[15] Well outfitted for the work ahead, each man wore the issue black campaign hat (or perhaps a civilian-style hat), regulation blue army fatigue uniform, leather gauntlets and boots, and a loaded cartridge belt. Prescribed equipment included a tin canteen, haversack, shelter tent, saddlebags, and a leather carbine sling, and his weapons, consisting of the Model 1873 Springfield .45-caliber single-shot carbine and a holstered Model 1873 Colt .45 revolver.

The officers with the command were all veterans with western service. Connecticut-born Perry, age thirty-six, had been with the First Cavalry since the Civil War and possessed considerable experience of the Northwest Indian frontier. He had most recently participated in California's Modoc War of 1873, where he was wounded, and he owned two brevets for distinguished Indian wars service. Perry personally commanded Company F. His subordinate officer was First Lieutenant Edward R. Theller, attached from the Twenty-first Infantry at Fort Lapwai. Theller was from Vermont and had served with the California volunteers during the Civil War and with Perry during the Modoc campaign. Company H was commanded by Captain Joel G. Trimble, who, like Perry, had seen service with the First Cavalry since the Civil War. Trimble had fought at Gettysburg, Cold Harbor, and Five Forks, and he had been twice wounded in action. His second-in-command was forty-one-year-old First Lieutenant William R. Parnell, an Irish immigrant and veteran of European wars, including the famous charge of the six hundred at Balaclava. He had served with the New York cavalry during the Civil War before joining the regulars and gaining extensive experience under George Crook in Oregon and Idaho during the late 1860s.[16]

The troops traveled all night along the muddy Lewiston–Mount Idaho road, moving part of the way with skirmishers and flankers advanced to counter a surprise attack by the warriors. They reached Cottonwood and Norton's Ranch at about 10:00 A.M. on the sixteenth. After breakfasting there, they proceeded across the rolling Camas Prairie toward Mount Idaho, ascertaining from the smoldering haystacks and ranch buildings they spotted en route that they were entering the zone of conflict. Approaching Grangeville at sundown, they passed by Norton's abandoned wagon and dead horses. At Grangeville, frightened armed citizens presented Perry with details of the outbreak, informing him that a large body of Nez Perces had passed by on the prairie that morning headed in the direction of White Bird Creek on the Salmon. The troops bivouacked in a field, intending to go on to the vicinity of the attacks next day. That plan was scuttled after a delegation of townspeople convinced Perry of the necessity of moving forward and punishing the tribesmen before they crossed the Salmon. At 9:00 P.M., a trumpeter sounded "Boots and Saddles," and the cavalrymen made preparations for a night march. Eleven citizens volunteered to accompany the troops as guides, and all got underway by 10:00 P.M.[17]

For three hours, the soldiers groped south-southwest along the road toward White Bird Canyon, passing en route near Tolo Lake to assure that the Nez Perces had left that area. At about 1:00 A.M., they crested the rise leading into the canyon, the troopers halting to rest and await daylight. About 4:00 A.M., as dawn peeked over the eastern horizon, Perry ordered the march resumed and the cavalrymen started down through a steep and narrow gorge, traversing an old wagon road that led directly into White Bird Canyon. It was Sunday, June 17, and the soldiers moved forward with Company F leading the way in a column of twos, followed by Company H in identical order. Garbed in greatcoats, their carbines and revolvers at the ready, the command traced its way for several miles along a dry creek bed, occasionally skirting around undergrowth and generally paralleling the gradually widening canyon in its descent. Soon the soldiers encountered a woman and two children taking refuge in a ravine. The woman was Mrs. Isabella Benedict, whose husband had been killed by the warriors. Her four-year-old daughter had a broken arm. She told the soldiers that many tribesmen had passed down the canyon during the night.

The men gave the Benedicts food from their haversacks and a blanket, then moved down the grade, soon bearing into a broad valley several hundred yards wide, almost surrealistic in its grandeur and described as "rolling prairie . . . dotted here and there with wave-like swells."[18] The rising hillocks formed a perpendicular ridge dominating the distant front, while a long, rolling ridge paralleled the soldiers' left, beyond which White Bird Creek angled in toward the Salmon, several thousand feet below. One hundred yards in front rode Lieutenant Theller and an advance guard of eight men from Company F, while the citizens and several Nez Perce scouts from Lapwai Agency, riding on either side, served as flankers. In the increasing daylight, Theller's men, now moving up a gentle incline to the ridge in front, could discern an immense pony herd and, beyond that, distant warriors moving toward them. One of the volunteers recalled seeing loose stock running all about. "It was in the breeding season and stallions were fighting, mares squealing, etc., and the noise of all this made many of our horses hard to manage, so that many of the men were badly excited before the fighting began."[19]

The Nez Perce village, containing some thirty lodges with approximately sixty warriors, was hidden from the soldiers' view and strung out along the bottomland of White Bird Creek a short distance from its confluence with the Salmon. Nee-Me-Poo accounts of the battle state that scouts from White Bird's camp had reported the soldiers' advance from Grangeville, and that a party of six warriors, intent on protecting the camp, initially approached them under a flag of truce. But one of the volunteers with the advance—later reported to be Arthur

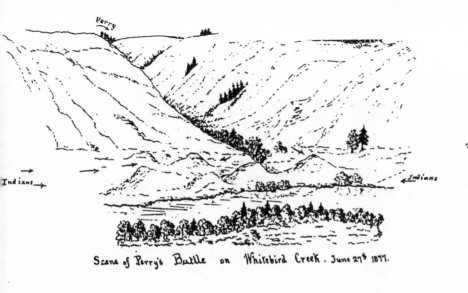

Perry

Troops
→

Indians
→ •

Indians →

Indians →

Indians ←

Scene of Perry's Battle on Whitebird Creek. June 27ᵗʰ 1877.

"Scene of Perry's Battle on Whitebird Creek, June 27th [17] 1877."
INSET DRAWING IN FLETCHER, "DEPARTMENT OF COLUMBIA MAP"

Chapman—opened fire on them, thus precipitating the battle. As many as sixty-five warriors participated in the ensuing combat, many of them armed with repeating rifles, muzzleloading rifles and muskets, and pistols, but also with bows and arrows. Principal Nez Perce leaders present were White Bird, Ollokot, and Lepeet Hessemdooks (Two Moon), the latter leading the opening attack on the citizens at the left of Perry's line, but Toohoolhoolzote and Joseph also took part. Many of the Nez Perce men were worn out from having participated in an all-night spree after consuming whiskey captured in the raiding on Camas Prairie.[20]

When the first shots were fired, Captain Perry hurried Company F forward, moving it left front into line adjoining Lieutenant Theller's right. On Perry's direction, Captain Trimble moved Company H into line on Perry's right. Continuing forward, the troops passed to a point just below, or south of, the perpendicular ridge overlooking the valley and the Nez Perce camp. The terrain to the right of the line rose steadily for two hundred yards, then climbed sharply to a rocky plateau. To the left of the position occupied by Company F lay a large swale through which ran the wagon road the troops had used. Theller's men and several citizen volunteers now commanded the swale. Farther left, a dominating knoll projected, and there the remaining volunteers stationed themselves, prolonging Perry's line and effectually constituting the left

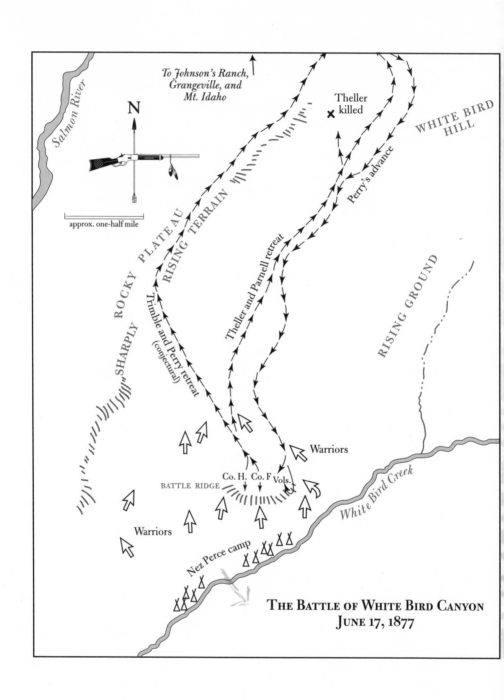

Salmon River

To Johnson's Ranch,
Grangeville, and
Mt. Idaho

N

approx. one-half mile

Theller
✗ killed

WHITE BIRD
HILL

Perry's advance

SHARPLY ROCKY PLATEAU

RISING TERRAIN

Theller and Parnell retreat

RISING GROUND

Trimble and Perry retreat
(conjectural)

Warriors

Co. H. Co. F Vols.
BATTLE RIDGE

Warriors

White Bird Creek

Nez Perce camp

THE BATTLE OF WHITE BIRD CANYON
JUNE 17, 1877

flank. In sum, as the fighting commenced, the whole command with their horses was spread out, precariously exposed along the ridge with no troops in reserve.

Some Nez Perces, moving forward out of the camp at the mouth of White Bird Creek, ascended the sloping canyon bottom to a long, low ridge fronting Perry's command. From behind this ridge, they opened a sporadic fire that knocked some cavalrymen from their saddles and halted Perry's advance.[21] Dismounting, the soldiers sent their horses into the swale on their left and partly behind the volunteers' knoll, then deployed into skirmish formation and returned fire on the warriors. On the left, the volunteers came under sustained fire from warriors hidden behind the bank of White Bird Creek, and within minutes at least one citizen, Herman A. Faxon, had been wounded, causing them all to fall back and leaving the flank vulnerable. Civilian Theodore D. Swarts recalled that "Indians were all around. One Ind[ian] ran out of the brush [near the creek] and called to me 'Stop, stop' (so he could get a shot at me), but I did not stop & he fired two shots, missing me."[22] The warriors now raked the entire length of Perry's line with a blistering enfilade, threatening them from front, left, and rear. Their gunfire took telling effect, and within minutes many of the soldiers unilaterally broke formation to regain their frightened horses, some of which—in their kicking and plunging—were yanking free of their holders and scattering over the field.

Somewhere at the beginning of the growing melee, one of Perry's trumpeters fell dead and the other lost his trumpet, and Perry found it impossible to signal his commands. Further complicating things, many of the Nez Perces' ponies tore over the landscape, kicking up a blinding dust and causing further confusion. More soldiers began falling back in great disorder. "Both companies were by this time mixed in together," wrote Sergeant McCarthy of the withdrawal, "each man occupying any vacant space in the line."[23] As Perry's left collapsed, however, he started the men in his segment to the rear, ultimately gravitating toward the rising plateau on the right. He later wrote, "the men on the left, seeing the citizens in full retreat and the Indians occupying their places and the right falling back in obedience to orders, were seized with a panic that was uncontrollable, and then the whole right of the line, seeing the mad rush for horses on the left, also gave way and the panic became general."[24] "The retreat started from here pell mell," remembered one participant, "soldiers, civilians, and friendly Indians together and all in confusion."[25] Much ammunition was wasted, and more was lost in the saddlebags of the horses stampeded by the warriors.

Thus, the retirement began. "No sooner would one squad halt and face about, than the other, just placed in position, would be gone."[26] To check the warriors, Captain Trimble directed two detachments to the ridge directly behind, or north of, the perpendicular ridge, while his main force pulled back several hundred yards. Other troops took to the right to counter tribesmen in the ravines at the rear of the line. Sergeant McCarthy commanded the right advance squad consisting of six or seven men. Both detachments mounted the ridge, several men serving as sharp-shooters as the others held their horses. McCarthy described the action:

> Looking towards the Indian camp nearly half a mile below on the left front, we could see them swarming out of the brush and occu-pying the round knolls in our front or riding under the cover of them in the direction already pursued by the others by our right flank. We commenced firing but the distance was so great that we could not do much execution and they slipped past our right. . . . Word was passed to us to mount and join the line for a charge, but before we all got back, the order was countermanded and we again advanced to the bluffs, dismounted and opened fire wherever we could see Indians. . . . Looking back towards the line I could see the men firing from their horses' backs, and they appeared half the time enveloped in the smoke of their own guns.[27]

Soon the warriors passed the right and left flanks of the two squads, momentarily exposing the soldiers to an assault from the rear. Orders now came for them to fall back and rejoin the retreating command, and McCarthy's men did so, finally reaching Lieutenant Parnell, who was trying to rally some mounted soldiers to help with the wounded and dismounted. Together, the men made a stand, then Parnell dashed to the rear after telling McCarthy he would bring help. But none came, and the sergeant recalled that the wounded soldiers, "paralyzed with fear or exhausted with fatigue . . . were killed unresistingly before our eyes."[28] When McCarthy at last pulled back and rejoined Parnell, the officer told him, "I could not bring you help, sergeant. You see how everything is going." Parnell and about ten troopers—all that remained alive on the field—withdrew up the narrow defile toward the head of the canyon, all the time firing at the warriors still pressing their front.

While all of this occurred, the citizens started back up the road, apparently for part of the time following Parnell. Volunteer Swarts remembered getting wounded in the retreat:

> I ran onto an Ind[ian] hidden behind a rock directly in my front. I wheeled my horse to the right & he & I fired both at the same instant at a distance apart of about 8 or 10 ft. He shot me in the hip and I shot him through the body. . . . We went back by way of the old "grade," which comes off the mountain a little to the south of the present [1915] stage road.[29]

All the while, Perry, Trimble, and Parnell tried desperately to maintain order in the retreating command. When Perry appealed to Lieutenant Theller to control the men, the lieutenant assembled a body of men and tried to effect an orderly withdrawal. But Theller apparently lost control of himself and at last retreated wildly back up the trail, where he was cut off and killed with seven other men.[30] Trimble, meantime, retired diagonally up the rocky plateau with the several men who had been defending the bluffs on the right. Perry, following, was unable to halt him on reaching the summit. Seeing the command disintegrating about him, Parnell continued his own withdrawal directly over the back road. "I saw it would be suicidal to attempt to reach the bluffs . . . [where Perry had gone], so we slowly retreated up the ravine, holding the Indians in check from knoll to knoll."[31] The climb proved excruciating, the soldiers without horses facing warriors closing on front and flanks. One senior sergeant fought a long-range duel with a warrior before the latter's round finally dropped the soldier.[32] As Parnell's troops passed to the head of the canyon, the troops again encountered Mrs. Benedict and her children. Wrote citizen William Coram: "Having caught a riderless soldier's horse, I now put her on it and two of us took the two children. The little 4 ½ yr-old girl got on behind a civilian & put her hands in his coat pockets & in that way hung on. The little baby about a year old I lashed onto my back with its mother's shawl, like a pappoose, & fetched her to Mount Idaho." While surmounting the divide, Mrs. Benedict's horse stumbled, throwing her to the ground. She fled into the brush, where the Nez Perces found her. Later released unharmed, she walked most of the way into Mount Idaho.[33]

Perry's company continued to retire up the rocky plateau without discipline. En route, Perry became dismounted, adding to his difficulty in controlling his men. Nevertheless, Parnell completed his withdrawal and soon joined Perry's company, now but twenty men strong. Together they faced the Nez Perce marksmen still in pursuit. While surmounting a ravine, Perry's men again stampeded. Two miles to the rear, at Henry C. Johnson's abandoned ranch, Parnell found them sheltered in position behind a rocky knoll. The warriors followed, attacking in front and on the right flank. Perry and Parnell organized their men into a thin skirmish line and began retreating slowly, periodically halting to fire at the Nez Perces. Once, the warriors tried to drive the troops into a deep canyon, but Perry directed volleys of gunfire against them, ruining the attempt. Finally, as they approached Mount Idaho, the Nez Perces pulled back, ending the fight after approximately two and one-half hours. A party of armed citizens reached the troops and accompanied them into the town. It was shortly before 9:00 A.M., and the troops had been gone less than ten hours. "Men and horses were completely exhausted," recalled Parnell. "We had been on the move ever since Friday, and without sleep for two nights."[34]

Moving on to Grangeville, Perry and Parnell found the volunteers, who had retreated rapidly from the canyon and reached the settlement several hours earlier. They also found Captain Trimble and some of the men who had made their way back.[35] Together, the officers took roll call and assessed their losses, which were severe. A tally made several days later noted that, besides Lieutenant Theller, twenty men of Company F and thirteen of Company H had been killed, while but a single man from each company was wounded.[36] (Two of the Mount Idaho volunteers had also been wounded.) Sergeant McCarthy, who had been cut off and left behind during the retreat with Parnell, miraculously escaped detection by the Nez Perces and hiked back into Grangeville two days later.[37] In addition to personnel losses, the troops reported many Springfield carbines and revolvers, with ammunition, lost and abandoned to the tribesmen. Although unknown to the soldiers at the time, Nez Perce casualties at White Bird Canyon amounted to only two or three wounded. None had been killed.[38]

The White Bird Canyon fight almost instantly became the subject of controversy regarding the soldiers' performance and the leadership exhibited by Captain Perry. In the weeks that followed, General Howard sympathized with Perry's management of the battle, but described it as a "rout . . . , a kind of Bull Run on a small scale."[39] Sergeant McCarthy summarized the deficiencies of the combat:

Many of the guns choked with broken shells, the guns being rusty and foul. We were in no fit condition to go to White Bird on the night of the 16th. We had been in the saddle nearly 24 hours and men and horses were tired and in bad shape for a fight. To cap the matter, we were marched into a deep cañon and to a country strange to us, and familiar to the enemy. If there was any plan of attack, I never heard of it. The troops were formed in line and about a third advanced in squads and the remainder very soon afterwards retreated in column up a ridge and out of the canon. The detached advanced squads, each acting independently and extended over considerable ground, were attacked in detail and scattered and scarcely any escaped out of the cañon. . . . Many of these men could have been saved if the retreat of the main column had not been so rapid.[40]

The Mount Idaho volunteers also came under criticism for having largely evacuated their position at the first shooting.[41] The post-battle assessment would continue for years, with most debate centering on Perry's leadership, the problem of numerical inferiority when one-fourth of a cavalry command had to hold horses, and the dearth of training that hurt the soldiers at White Bird Canyon and further demoralized them afterwards. "The explanation . . . is simply that the men had not been drilled, could not manage their horses, and knew little of the use of their arms," wrote one critic.[42] Persistent criticism of Perry's performance, principally at White Bird Canyon, but also at the later engagements at Cottonwood and Clearwater, led to his request for courts of inquiry, which themselves generated controversy but found Perry's conduct acceptable under the circumstances. Despite this cloud, in later years Perry and Parnell received brevet promotions for their service at White Bird Canyon, and Theller won posthumous notice "for brave and soldierly conduct" in the events resulting in his death.[43]

Three days after the debacle in White Bird Canyon, Perry and his command, accompanied by a contingent of citizens, reconnoitered out of Grangeville toward the battlefield, but went only as far as the head of the canyon. No Indians were seen. The troops rested at Henry C. Johnson's ranch, the place where they had stopped on their retreat on the seventeenth, then passed back into Grangeville. That evening, the first medical personnel arrived from Fort Lapwai. General Howard had learned of Perry's debacle on the afternoon of June 17. One of the first reports came from two Company F soldiers, Corporal Charles W. Fuller and Private John White, who had fled at the opening of the battle,

racing their mounts all the way back to Fort Lapwai with the earliest—
though erroneous—news of the defeat.

More accurate reports arrived soon after,[44] and since then, Howard
had busily mobilized reinforcements from throughout his department
and the Department of California. Besides four companies of cavalry
and three of infantry already available at Fort Lapwai and Lewiston,
Howard could expect auxiliaries in the form of six companies of cavalry, five batteries of artillery (intended to function as infantry), and
three companies of infantry, for a total of about 960 men. In addition,
he directed that Major John W. Green's troops at Fort Boise march
north to watch the area of the Weiser Valley and keep tribesmen from
that region from joining the Nez Perces. And with divisional approval,
Howard arranged for troops to be sent from the East Coast.

Some of the department force was on hand and moving out of
Fort Lapwai by June 22, and when Howard departed the next day to
personally lead the campaign, his immediate command consisted of 227
regular soldiers of Companies E and L, First Cavalry; Companies B, D,
E, I, and H, Twenty-first Infantry; and Battery E, Fourth Artillery, outfitted as infantrymen, plus a unit of volunteers from Walla Walla under
Captain Thomas Paige. Other troops were to follow two days later.

Reaching Norton's Ranch at Cottonwood at 1:30 P.M. on the
twenty-third, Howard noted the rampant destruction at the place:
"There is the clothing cut and torn and strewn about—the broken chairs,
the open drawers, the mixing of flour, sugar, salt and rubbish—the evi-
dences of riot run mad."[45] On Sunday, Howard sent instructions to
Captain Trimble at Grangeville to proceed with Company H to Slate
Creek to assist the Salmon River settlers.[46]

On Monday, June 25, Howard and his cavalry visited Grangeville
and Mount Idaho, greeting wounded soldiers hospitalized in the hotel
and meeting citizens and inspecting their makeshift barricades before
moving on to Johnson's Ranch, where the infantry troops had preceded
him. Early the next morning, the command began a reconnaissance
into White Bird Canyon, cautiously entering the defile leading toward
the Salmon with skirmishers advanced. On the battle site, the troopers
stood over their dead comrades in the hills and ravines and dug their
graves, a horrid, detested job that filled them with anguish. Many corpses
had grown disfigured and decomposed over the nine days of exposure
since the combat. "One body of a cavalry soldier gave us some anxious

moments," wrote an officer, "for it was thrust so hard into a small haw-
thorn tree, in the full and life-like position of firing that we did not
approach without guns cocked."[47] Late in the afternoon, in the midst
of a driving thunderstorm, the men found Lieutenant Theller's remains
lying where he and his small force had been entrapped. The body was
wrapped and carefully interred where it lay.[48]

While the burials were taking place, Howard, Perry, and Captain Paige, reconnoitering the Nez Perces, saw the warriors across
the river intently watching the troops. They had crossed at Horseshoe Bend and established their camp on Deer Creek. Underestimat-
ing the tribesmen's ability to negotiate both the rugged topography
and rivers, the general sent word to McDowell that "the longer . . .
Joseph delays with his women, children and abundant stock of horses
and cattle between the Salmon and the Snake, the more certain he is
shut in when Major Green presses up the Weiser and Boise trails."[49]
Believing that the Nez Perces intended to keep his troops from fording,
Howard planned to station a hundred sharpshooters on a ridge across
from the mouth of Canyon Creek, while his other troops engaged the
warriors from the front. To this end, he sent a note to Trimble at Slate
Creek: "Be prepared to follow up a success from us by intercepting
and obstructing trails toward Little Salmon."[50] But on the twenty-
seventh, following a brief and ineffective exchange of fire with the
tribesmen, the command made preparations to cross the raging stream
one and one-half miles above the mouth of White Bird Creek.[51] When
Howard raised the American flag at his headquarters, the Nez Perces
simultaneously raised a red blanket and called for the troops to cross
the river and fight. And as the troops tried to get a rope across the
stream to begin ferrying themselves over, the warriors continued their
baiting, waving blankets and taunting the men to come after them.[52]
That evening, Howard's command bivouacked near the White Bird
crossing. Despite the strain of dealing with Perry's dead, the men
seemed relaxed. As Lieutenant Charles E. S. Wood observed:

> Camp—singing along, telling [stories], and swearing—profanity,
> carelessness. Accepting things—horrible at other times—as a mat-
> ter of course, such as mutilated corpses and death in ghastly forms,
> strewn on every side. Again there is the necessary leaving of last
> messages for sweethearts, mothers, and wives, telling of jokes about
> being killed, about not looking for "my body," &c. Firing expected

tomorrow. The nerve it takes to face the probabilities by writing these last letters and leaving mementoes for loved ones is wonderful,—and one feels demoralized by such acts as these.[53]

On the twenty-eighth, after a delay that he considered unwarranted, still more reinforcements reached Howard, consisting of batteries A, D, G, and M, Fourth Artillery (serving as infantrymen), and Company C, Twenty-first Infantry, boosting the command to almost four hundred men. That afternoon, the general noted, the "Indians charged to the river, a brisk skirmish ensued, after which they left the valley for the heights beyond."[54] The next day, June 29, Howard ordered his train back to Fort Lapwai for supplies; Captain Perry commanded the escort of Company F, First Cavalry, and Paige's Washington volunteers. During the day, two small volunteer units arrived from Lewiston and Dayton, Washington Territory, commanded, respectively, by Captains Edward McConville and George Hunter. McConville's troops were sent forward to Slate Creek to support Captain Trimble's command.[55] That evening, after his men had secured a rope across the Salmon, Howard received word that Looking Glass, heretofore reported to have refrained from openly supporting the people with Joseph and White Bird, was doing precisely that and, moreover, was threatening to join in the conflict. To keep that from happening, Howard sent a force under Captain Stephen G. Whipple to "surprise and capture this chief and all that belonged to him."[56]

Certainly the Nez Perces' defeat of Perry's command must have created a powerful incentive for Looking Glass to explore the option of joining the others. Similarly, the Battle of White Bird Canyon created an inducement for the tribesmen of White Bird, Joseph, and Toohoolhoolzote to continue the fight and perhaps raised false hopes among them as to the eventual outcome. For the army, the battle produced a healthy respect for the fighting abilities of the Nez Perces. It showed that the people could—and would—fight to protect their interests and could deliver a blow swiftly and with stunning accuracy. The troops learned that the warriors were better riders than themselves and expertly adept marksmen capable of inflicting severe casualties in the ranks. Individualistic in their mode of warfare, the Nez Perces used their innate abilities to foil their tormentors and turn them back while operating within the parameters of their group objectives. They employed their ammunition economically and did not foolishly attempt

Looking Glass, leader of the Alpowai band of Nee-Me-Poo, as photographed by William Henry Jackson in 1871. Captain Stephen Whipple's assault on Looking Glass's village on July 1, 1877, effectually drove that chief to support the nontreaty Indians in the widening conflict with the army.

to fire from horseback, as had the soldiers. Their well-trained ponies stood calmly during the tumult while the army mounts panicked and pulled their holders about. If there was any consolation for General Howard in the wake of the White Bird Canyon debacle, it lay in the knowledge that more soldiers were at hand and that the army's resources were renewable whereas the tribesmen's were not. But Howard would learn that irrepressible spirits were sufficient for the course.

3

Looking Glass's Camp and Cottonwood

ON JULY 1, BOATS having arrived from upstream, the troops, horses, pack animals, ammunition, and mountain howitzers of Howard's command negotiated the churning and boiling Salmon to the other side. By then, the Nez Perces had withdrawn into the highland recesses, leaving the army to follow their trail and try to divine their intentions. The region chosen by Howard occupied the lofty terrain lying between the deep gorges of the Salmon and Snake rivers, south of the point where the Salmon angles its flow westward toward the Snake. It is partly dissected plateau, partly steep and rugged canyon breaks, of varying grass and pine forest growth and sharply changing altitude, and partly level grass prairie, in all making river navigation slow and difficult. After fording the river, the soldiers marched for the Snake. In their course of July 2, Captain Trimble and his First cavalrymen and McConville's volunteers joined Howard, having forded at Horseshoe Bend. All pushed toward the summit of Brown's Mountain, where heavy sleet and rain pummeled their bivouac. Several pack animals were lost in surmounting the steep and slippery grades, and the artillerymen, unused to campaigning, complained bitterly as they tried to keep up. The Indian trail, well marked by the passage of their fifteen hundred ponies, was easily followed, but the rugged terrain kept progress to an average of ten or twelve miles per day. Sergeant McCarthy observed that "the command was strung out all the way from base to summit of divide."

Howard believed that the Nez Perces had possibly divided into two groups, with one headed south, and he anticipated that the troops from Boise under Major John Wesley Green might encounter them. (Howard was unduly optimistic about these troops; they had not yet departed Boise.) The other group moved in his own front; his troops had discovered caches of their flour, clothing, and supplies—even abandoned ponies—leading the general to believe that the Nez Perces planned to return to the Wallowa and Imnaha valleys. On the afternoon of July 4, however, while in the process of camping opposite Rocky Canyon, Howard received word that Nez Perce warriors had struck the soldiers posted at Cottonwood on Camas Prairie. Thinking that these tribesmen were but a raiding party from the main group quartered somewhere near the Snake, Howard dispatched McConville's and Hunter's volunteers to ford the river and go in support to Cottonwood.

In fact, the entire body of Nez Perces had gone back across the Salmon, having forded at the then-defunct Craig's Ferry, opposite Billy Creek and some twenty-five miles downstream from White Bird Creek, evidently when they learned that the soldiers had gained the south bank. Realizing that, Howard tried to move back across the raging Salmon on the morning of the sixth, but failed, and he sent word to Whipple that his raft had been swept away by the current. After shooting twenty ponies that the Nez Perces had left behind, Howard's command started on a "Horrible retrograde march" for his earlier fording point miles away and nearly opposite the mouth of White Bird Creek.[1] Sergeant McCarthy recalled the frustration of the moment:

> We were in a bad fix, with no means of crossing the river. We could not cross like the Indians. Our force, except our company, were foot troops. A part of the next day was spent in trying to swim the Cavalry [and their horses] but it was a failure. A raft was tried but it was a failure also. How the whole tribe of Indians with horses, women, papooses, etc., got across was a puzzle. It is yet a puzzle. We didn't seem to have engineering skill enough to devise ways and means to cross and the command marched back two days' march to White Bird Crossing.[2]

Howard's orders to Captain Whipple to arrest Looking Glass proved of dire consequence for the army, as well as for the chief and his people. Until June 29, when he issued instructions for neutralizing those people, however, Howard remained unconvinced that Looking Glass would seriously factor into the conflict, and had written the treaty chief, James Lawyer: "I am glad to hear that Looking Glass remains at home. If the others who gave me promises had kept their word there would have been peace and prosperity—and not war."[3] Howard's change of mind came with reports from Mount Idaho that four volunteers scouting toward the Middle Clearwater had found evidence that Looking Glass's Nez Perces had sacked two homesteads, one between the forks of the Clearwater owned by Idaho County commissioner George Dempster, which they burned, and the other owned by James T. Silverwood. They had also driven off livestock. When the four volunteers tried to approach the Nez Perce camp on Clear Creek, about six miles above Kamiah, the tribesmen motioned them away.

Other reports, some brought to Howard by the Nez Perce scouts, suggested that at least twenty men from Looking Glass's village had already joined the nontreaty bands (however, these people may simply have been visitors to the lakeside convocation who stayed on after Looking Glass had departed) and that the chief and the rest of his people would soon follow. Furthermore, rumors circulated from Mount Idaho that Looking Glass's warriors would attack the settlements within days, and Inspector Watkins characterized the chief as "running a recruiting station for Joseph." Howard's orders to arrest the chief were designed to stop any prospective union and to dissuade further support for White Bird and Joseph.[4]

The directions were explicit and were delivered verbally, as recalled by General Howard:

> Captain Whipple, go with your cavalry and Gatling guns, arrest the Indian chief Looking Glass, and all other Indians who may be encamped with or near him, between the forks of the Clearwater, and imprison them at Mount Idaho, turning them over for safe keeping to the volunteer organization at that place.[5]

At 9:00 P.M., Whipple departed the Salmon with Companies E and L, First Cavalry, his command totaling four officers and sixty-two men. Arriving at Mount Idaho in the early morning of June 30, the captain left two Gatling guns—crank-operated ten-barreled rapid-fire machine guns of .45 calibre, each drawn by three horses—along with a detail of probably four men to operate them.[6] After resting his troops for several hours at Mount Idaho, he pressed forward late in the afternoon toward his objective twenty-five miles away, accompanied by twenty volunteers under Captain Darius B. Randall, so that his effective strength totaled eighty-seven.[7]

The officers of the command represented diversity in their experience. Captain Whipple, who commanded Company L, was the senior, a Vermont native who had led a unit of California volunteers during the Civil War. As a lieutenant colonel, he had seen extensive duty on the California frontier, and he held a brevet for "faithful and meritorious service." Appointed in the Regular Army in 1867, Whipple continued on the frontier in Arizona Territory and joined the First Cavalry in 1870. His first lieutenant was Edwin H. Shelton, from Connecticut, and an 1870 West Point graduate, while his second lieutenant was Sevier M. Rains, an 1876 academy graduate. Captain William H. Winters commanded Company E. He had been appointed from the enlisted ranks, having served with the First Cavalry during the Civil War as a private, corporal, sergeant, and first sergeant before receiving a commission in 1865. Winters had been a captain since June 25, 1876. His first lieutenant was Albert G. Forse, who had figured in the Wallowa incident the previous September. An 1865 West Point graduate appointed to the First Cavalry in June of that year, Forse had spent ten years in the Northwest with the unit. He would be killed in 1898 at Santiago, Cuba, during the Spanish-American War. Second lieutenant of Company E was William H. Miller, an 1872 graduate of the military academy, who had campaigned against the Modocs in 1873, and would one day (1890) be breveted for that service.[8]

Thus officered, the men rode through the night, planning to strike the village at dawn while the people slept, in the customary army tactic of the time used against Indians, and especially against small camps.[9] But the approach was hard, and across rugged, hilly terrain, and through some calculating error, the camp lay ten miles farther than supposed. The troops failed to arrive until 7:00 A.M.[10]—well after daybreak— when the occupants were awake and engaged in their daily routine. The targeted village of eleven lodges stood within the reservation boundary along the right bank of Clear Creek, a short distance from its mouth on the Middle Clearwater and two miles southeast of the present community of Kooskia, which is at the confluence of the middle and south forks of the Clearwater.[11] The site was called Kamnaka, and there the tribesmen had cultivated their land for farming; many were raising dairy

This Nez Perce encampment on the Yellowstone River near the mouth of Shields River, Montana Territory, 1871, as photographed by William Henry Jackson, was similar in appearance to that attacked by Whipple's troops on July 1, 1877. As the conflict dragged on, fewer lodges like these were available for the Nee-Me-Poo, and by the time of the Bear's Paw encounter many of the people were using alternative forms of shelter.

National Anthropological Archives, Smithsonian Institution, Washington, D.C.

cattle.[12] Some of the people, including Looking Glass, had recently returned from the Tepahlewam assembly, professing their disinclination to join in the escalating warfare involving the nontreaty Nez Perces. Looking Glass had turned away nontreaty Nez Perces who had tried to camp near his village.

In 1877, Looking Glass was past forty, six feet tall, and in fine physical condition. His father, Apash Wyakaikt (Flint Necklace), also known among whites as Looking Glass, had signed the 1855 treaty. His son, Allalimya Takanin, reportedly carried a flint arrowhead or a small trade mirror suspended from his throat as his hallmark, and likewise was called by whites the same name. Respected for his bravery and leadership, the younger Looking Glass in 1874 reinforced those qualities when he helped his friends, the Crows, defeat a Sioux war party along the Yellowstone River in Montana.[13] In Idaho, he had rejected war and was secure in his belief that the whites well knew that fact. As it was Sunday, some of the people had gone into Kamiah to attend a Dreamer service. Probably fewer than 20 men of fighting age occupied the camp, which also contained about 120 children, women, and old men.[14]

Nez Perce testimony given years afterward clarified much of the detail surrounding the attack on Looking Glass's village. Whipple tersely reported that "an opportunity was given Looking Glass to surrender, which he at first promised to accept, but afterward defiantly refused, and the result was that several Indians were killed."[15] But a Nez Perce participant, Peopeo Tholekt (Bird Alighting), gave a somewhat different account. Halting at the crest of a hill less than one-quarter mile west of the village, the troops announced their presence. Looking Glass sat in his lodge eating breakfast. Alerted to the soldiers, he sent Peopeo Tholekt to tell them he wanted no trouble, that his people were peaceful and wanted to be left alone. The warrior rode across Clear Creek and met several officers and a volunteer interpreter, all mounted. The troops had dismounted and spread out, leaving their horses on a flat of the hill to their rear. In another version of the event, the interpreter, J. A. Miller, of Mount Idaho, told Whipple that Looking Glass agreed to meet him at a point almost a mile away from the village.

The Nez Perce account refuted the promise of a meeting, however. After the warrior delivered Looking Glass's first message, he was directed to return and bring the chief. But Looking Glass distrusted the officers, and he sent Peopeo Tholekt back with another man carrying a white cloth on a pole. According to Peopeo Tholekt, he told Whipple: "Looking Glass is my chief. I bring you his words. He does not want war! He came here to escape war. Do not cross to our side of the little river. We do not want trouble with you whatever!"[16] But Whipple and two or three others, along with an interpreter, demanded to see the chief and

Peopeo Tholekt (Bird Alighting), photographed in 1900, was with Looking Glass on July 1, 1877, and provided an important account of the army attack on the chief's village.

DELANCEY L. GILL, PHOTOGRAPHER; SMITHSONIAN INSTITUTION COLLECTION, NEZ PERCE NATIONAL HISTORICAL PARK, SPALDING, IDAHO

rode across the creek to his tipi. Just as they approached the lodge, someone on the hillside fired a shot that struck a villager.[17]

At that, the officers wheeled their horses and dashed back across the creek to the command, while a general fusillade tore into the camp, ripping through tipis and creating general panic among the tribesmen. Warriors and their families, Looking Glass among them, raced out of

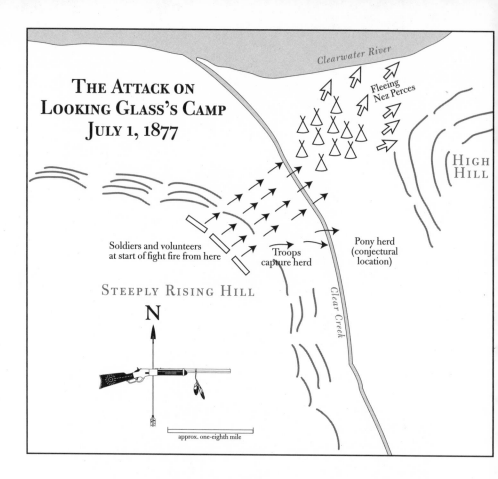

THE ATTACK ON
LOOKING GLASS'S CAMP
JULY 1, 1877

Clearwater River

Fleeing
Nez Perces

HIGH
HILL

Soldiers and volunteers
at start of fight fire from here

Troops
capture herd

Pony herd
(conjectural
location)

STEEPLY RISING HILL

Clear Creek

N

approx. one-eighth mile

the north and east sides of the village and into the bushes and trees as
they sought to hide from the troops. In one instance, the volunteers
wounded a herder who was quickly rescued by two warriors on horseback who pulled him up and rode off.

Presently, the firing subsided and the soldiers moved down the slope
in skirmish formation, wading through the creek and advancing on the
camp. Then the firing opened again. Peopeo Tholekt, struggling to get
away on his horse, heard bullets striking lodge poles about him before he
could join the refugees up the river. Some villagers fled over a hill to the
east to get beyond range of the army carbines. Despite the lateness of the
hour, the attack had come as a surprise, and there occurred little return
fire as the families evacuated. One warrior is reported to have leveled
some shots at Whipple's men. At one point, an Alpowai woman wrapped
in a wolf skin advanced on the soldiers, but she eventually withdrew with
the others. Another woman with a baby strapped to her back plunged her
pony into the icy Clearwater to get away, but fierce currents pulled them

under and all drowned. Several more tribesmen received bullet wounds in their scramble from the camp.[18]

One essential component of the army assault was the capture of the Nez Perces' horses, intended to immobilize them for the present and future. This likely happened as the skirmishers advanced on the camp. Lieutenants Forse and Shelton with twenty mounted men accomplished it quickly, and Forse remembered "driving the Indians out of the rocks above us, then surrounding the herd and driving one or two Indians out of it who were evidently about running them off." He noted that, in the process of completing the task, his detachment was well beyond supporting distance from the balance of the command, located on the opposite bluff. "Passing the old camp I drove the volunteers out of it and destroyed it by burning."[19] Actually, only two of the lodges caught fire, and in ransacking the tipis, one volunteer recalled retrieving two buffalo robes along with a buckskin bag of gunpowder and another containing vermilion. Another commented favorably on the performances of Captain Winters and Lieutenant Rains, and the latter later won a citation for "gallantry and daring" in "advancing alone into the enemy's camp and endeavoring to seize the chief."[20] Yet another volunteer, Peter Minturn, received notice in the press as having been "hungry for Indian meat, and proved himself to be a dead shot" during the attack.[21]

Whipple's assault was devastating for Looking Glass's people. Reports are unclear as to the extent of their casualties, one stating that "four Indians were killed and left on the field" and "many others were wounded," while another cited one killed and three wounded. The most detailed Nez Perce account enumerated three killed (one dying of his wounds) and three wounded in the affair. There were no casualties among the soldiers and volunteers.[22] Whipple and his men returned to Mount Idaho on the evening of July 1, bringing with them about six hundred ponies captured during their attack on Looking Glass.[23] Peopeo Tholekt described the aftermath experienced by the Indians:

> After the soldiers left, we returned to our ruined homes. Several tepees had been burned or otherwise ruined. Much had been carried away and many objects destroyed or badly damaged. Brass buckets [kettles] always carefully kept by the women, lay battered, [and] smashed. . . . Growing gardens trampled and destroyed. Nearly all our horses were taken and every hoof of cattle driven away.[24]

Despite Whipple's seeming success, it did not altogether please General Howard. Because Whipple had arrived late at the village, he had effectually failed in his mission to arrest Looking Glass, capture his people, and escort them as prisoners to Mount Idaho, thereby removing them entirely as factors in the widening conflict. News of the episode perturbed Howard, who wrote the captain:

> Your report of 2 July is just rec'd. I am glad you came upon the Indians, but am sorry you did not succeed in capturing that band, for I counted much on it. I said to you verbally: "Go to the forks of the Clearwater, resting only a couple of hours at Grangeville, and capture them before they can move across the river.["] By the delay till night you allowed them to get the usual warning of your approach, and therefore they escaped. Perhaps I expected too much of [your tired] horses.[25]

In the end, the ill-conceived and poorly executed attack on Looking Glass netted the army nothing but another complication in its goal to contain the outbreak. With the loss of his village and its contents, the chief—previously an advocate of peace—aligned his fortunes with those of White Bird, Joseph, and the others. Moreover, besides adding people to the cause, Looking Glass's presence—as a man respected for his military talent and leadership among all the Nee-Me-Poo, besides one who knew well the buffalo country to the east—brought significant dimensions with which the troops would have to contend.[26]

Back at Mount Idaho by midnight, Whipple met Captain Lawrence S. Babbitt of Howard's staff with orders to proceed to Norton's Ranch at Cottonwood. Early on July 2, with the two Gatling guns in tow, the troops rode down the road to Cottonwood, there to await Perry's arrival from Fort Lapwai with supplies and to intercept the Nez Perces if they passed that way. Since crossing the Salmon, Howard had learned that the tribesmen were attempting to ford near Rocky Canyon, and from his headquarters, he notified Whipple that, if Perry did not arrive, to "leave no stone unturned to ascertain for me where the Indians are heading, and report to me as often as you can. I expect of the cavalry tremendous vigor and activity even if it should kill a few horses."[27] Howard later maintained that "the object of this movement was to meet the enemy and hold him in check should he anywhere attempt to recross the Salmon and turn upon my communications."[28]

"Cottonwood House — two days fight — Whipple and Perry — July 5th"
INSET DRAWING IN FLETCHER, "DEPARTMENT OF COLUMBIA MAP"

In 1877, Norton's, or Cottonwood, Ranch was the only major structural complex at Cottonwood. Situated in a sheltered gulch bordering the south side of Cottonwood Creek, which emptied into the South Fork of the Clearwater River about twenty miles east, the ranch straddled both sides of the Lewiston–Mount Idaho Road, with the house or hotel proper on the south side. In 1862 a man named Allen had built the way-station with logs from a cottonwood grove that lined the bottom. It consisted of a store, saloon, hotel, and stage station. After a year, two individuals, Wheeler and Toothacher, bought the property, and in 1864 John Byrom acquired it. Later, two other men, Joseph Moore and Peter H. Ready (a Mount Idaho volunteer in 1877), owned the ranch before selling it to Benjamin Norton, who operated it at the time of the outbreak.[29] Besides the hotel building proper, the ranch included barns, stables, and horse corrals. When Captain Whipple's Companies E and L, First Cavalry, arrived on July 2, the Norton property, unharmed by the warriors following its abandonment on the night of June 14, began service as a command headquarters, a use that would cause it much injury.[30]

Cottonwood stood on the western edge of the Camas Prairie. West of Norton's Ranch, the road to Lewiston gradually climbed over undulating ground punctuated by ravines and gorges of tributaries feeding south into Cottonwood Creek. The open terrain changed to light forest cover as the road crept up the east slope of Craig's Mountain, a hilly divide stretching roughly northeast-to-southwest, its crest approaching forty-five hundred feet altitude, or a thousand feet higher than at Norton's, about two and one-half miles east. The path of the road leading from

Norton's made the distance longer, but kept generally to high ground before passing through a gentle saddle, followed then by a steep rise toward the crest of the divide.

After deploying his force at the ranch and throwing up defensive entrenchments, Captain Whipple—following Howard's instructions—sent two scouts, William Foster and Charles Blewett, out on the morning of July 3 to range south of Cottonwood looking for signs of the Nez Perces. The scouts traveled west on the Lewiston Road, or "stage road," to the point where it crossed Boardhouse Creek, then veered left on the Salmon River trail toward Lawyer's Canyon.[31] Meantime, the body of Nez Perces, with their livestock, had forded the Salmon and headed for Camas Prairie, intending to cross to a familiar camping ground at the mouth of Cottonwood Creek on the South Fork of the Clearwater. They, too, had sent out scouts from their village, and at a point about ten miles from Cottonwood, near Lawyer's Canyon leading to the Salmon, Foster and Blewett sighted tribesmen and started back to report their discovery. En route, at least one warrior shot at the scouts, who fired back. As Foster and Blewett retreated, Blewett's horse suddenly stumbled, throwing its rider and leaving Foster to press on alone and gain Cottonwood.[32] On Foster's arrival, Captain Babbitt, who had gone to Norton's with Whipple, immediately dispatched the information to Howard via Mount Idaho:

> Cottonwood, 4 P.M. (Tuesday)
> One of our scouts just in reports seeing twelve or more Indians from here toward Salmon river. On returning he was fired upon by a single Indian and he and the other scout returned the shots. In some way one scout was dismounted and took to the brush and the other was obliged to leave him. These Indians were coming from the direction of Salmon river on the trail leading toward Kamai [Kamiah] and crossing the road passing the place about eight miles from here. The whole command starts in a few moments and may bag the outfit unless the whole of Joseph's force is present.
> Babbitt commanding.[33]

As the trumpeter sounded "Boots and Saddles," Whipple ordered ammunition distributed and otherwise readied his cavalrymen for action, planning to move in the direction that the warriors had been sighted. He ordered Lieutenant Rains of Company L, adjutant for the

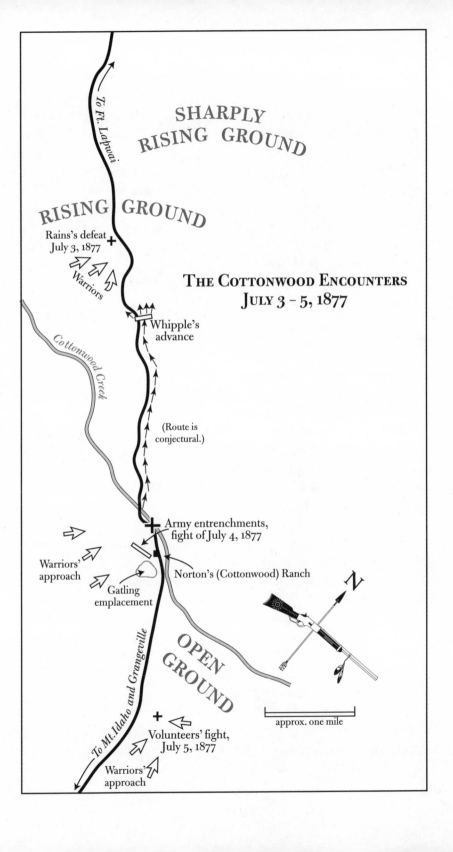

To Ft. Lapwai

SHARPLY
RISING GROUND

RISING GROUND

Rains's defeat
July 3, 1877

Warriors

THE COTTONWOOD ENCOUNTERS
JULY 3 – 5, 1877

Whipple's
advance

Cottonwood Creek

(Route is
conjectural.)

Army entrenchments,
fight of July 4, 1877

Warriors'
approach

Norton's (Cottonwood) Ranch

Gatling
emplacement

N

To Mt. Idaho and Grangeville

OPEN
GROUND

approx. one mile

Volunteers' fight,
July 5, 1877

Warriors'
approach

command, to take ten men and go out as the advance guard, reconnoiter the Nez Perces' position, and try to find and help Blewett. In his report to Howard, Whipple said that "I particularly cautioned Lt. Rains not to precede the command too far, to keep on high ground, and to report at the first sign of the Indians."[34]

Rains immediately called for volunteers, got together five men each from Companies E and L,[35] and with Foster leading the way, started at 6:00 P.M. along the road winding up over the ridges west of Norton's Ranch. Second Lieutenant Sevier McClellan Rains was twenty-five years old, a Georgian (though born in Michigan) from a distinguished family. His father, Gabriel J. Rains, graduated from the U.S. Military Academy in 1827, served in the Seminole campaigns in Florida and in the War with Mexico, and rose to become a brigadier general in the Confederate army. Oddly enough, the elder Rains had served in the Northwest in the 1850s, had commanded the guard of soldiers attending the Walla Walla councils in 1855, and had taken an active part in the multitribal wars that followed.[36] Young Rains, who graduated on the eve of the military disaster at the Little Bighorn in Montana Territory in June 1876, had at the news applied for a commission in the Seventh Cavalry, but accepted one in the First Regiment, his original choice.[37] With his advance guard of ten men, plus Scout Foster, Rains moved rapidly, putting distance between his men and Whipple's main command. Up the winding road and along the ridge that diverged from Cottonwood Creek, Rains led his party. Two miles northwest of Norton's Ranch they descended into a broad saddle, then began moving up the slope of Craig's Mountain. To their left rear, and extending south from the saddle, ran a broad coulee leading down to the creek.

Unseen by the lieutenant and his men, Nez Perce warriors, having observed the advance, moved into the creek bottom and toward the coulee. After the party passed through the saddle and started up the divide, the warriors raced out of the coulee in their rear, effectively cutting off their retreat toward Cottonwood and charging the soldiers. Rains's men hurriedly took cover among some large boulders south of the road, probably expecting Whipple momentarily to appear and counter the Indians. But Whipple did not come forward. Scout Foster galloped his horse away to the north, but warriors pursued and killed him in the open. They surrounded Rains and his band and killed them all, evidently after a stout defense by the soldiers. From the dearth of evidence, it is difficult to conclude what, if any, tactical deployment occurred. When the bodies of the soldiers were found among many expended cartridge cases, most had been shot in the head, leading some to conclude that they had exhausted their ammunition before the warriors rushed their position and wiped them out.[38]

Whipple, meanwhile, galloped his seventy troopers ahead when the shooting started, but halted them on the eastward brim of the saddle one-half mile away. There the men of Companies E and L listened and waited until the firing died away. Again they advanced, this time as skirmishers, until they sighted approximately a hundred warriors in their front who sent scattered shots at them.[39] After two hours spent "menacing each other," Whipple's men turned around, formed a square enclosing the horses, and at dusk fell back to Norton's, where the captain composed a dispatch for General Howard:

> Cottonwood, 10:30 A.M. [P.M.] (Tuesday)
> Joseph with his entire force is in our front. We moved out at 6 A.M. [P.M.] to look after the Indians reported. Rains, with ten men moved on ahead about two miles. We heard firing at the foot of the long hill back of Cottonwood, and mounting a slight elevation saw a large force of Indians occupying a strong position in the timber covering the road. Nothing could be seen of Rains and his party and we fear they have been slaughtered. We moved up close enough to see we were greatly outnumbered by enemies strongly posted. Night was approaching and after a consultation of all the officers it was decided to return to this place and hold it until Perry . . . should arrive. There was no diversity of opinion in this case, and there is no doubt that the entire command would have been sacrificed in an attack. We shall make every effort to communicate with Perry to-night and keep him out of any trap.[40]

The withdrawal from in front of the Nez Perces occasioned much grumbling in the ranks because Whipple had neither attacked the warriors nor sought to learn Rains's lot. A report out of Mount Idaho complained that "Brave Rains and his followers were left to their fate, and Whipple with his command retreated (without firing a shot) to Cottonwood."[41] During the night, Whipple dispatched two men to go through to Perry. They became lost and later returned—apparently having unknowingly passed by Rains's dead command. Later, a friendly Indian brought word of the approach of the pack train from Fort Lapwai. With the loss of Rains's party, the captain had but seventy men available.

Nonetheless, fearing that the Nez Perces would attack Perry, Whipple led his troops out at dawn on July 4, deployed in double skirmish lines. Passing west of Cottonwood, they found the remains of the advance guard, leaving them by the road as they urgently pressed ahead. Once, spotting a lone horse on a hill to the right, Whipple feared it might be a decoy for an ambush and kept the soldiers moving. Eight miles out they joined the train, seventy-five loaded mules guarded by twenty-nine men of Company F, then turned back to Cottonwood.[42] At the site of Rains's defeat, the cavalrymen attempted to bury the dead, but Nez Perce marksmen hidden among the boulders and trees of Craig's Mountain opened fire on them, and the effort was, for the moment, abandoned as the troops withdrew back to the fortified ranch complex at noon.[43]

Because no soldier with Lieutenant Rains survived the encounter with the Nez Perces, the Indians' accounts of the episode alone describe what happened before and after the party advanced beyond the saddle. A warrior named Seeyakoon Ilppilp (Red Spy) had killed Charles Blewett in the encounter where Foster escaped to Cottonwood. Several warriors followed to look for soldiers, finally sighting their bivouac and the surrounding earthworks at Norton's Ranch. When notified of the discovery, a larger group of warriors moved forward led by the prominent military men, Five Wounds and Rainbow. They discovered Rains's advance guard moving on the road and attacked from front and rear. The soldiers whipped their horses to flee, but all fell within minutes. The warrior Two Moon remembered that "the rocks where some of them took shelter did not save them from the bullets sent against them. Their horses, guns, and ammunition we took."[44] Another warrior, Yellow Wolf, interviewed in 1908 and again in 1930, described how a Nez Perce man decoyed Rains and his men forward while the remaining warriors circled and came in from the rear. As the command was wiped out, one soldier, his face bloodied from a wound in the head, survived repeated attempts by the Nez Perces to kill him, but finally succumbed to his multiple injuries. No warriors died in the attack on the Rains group.[45]

Kawownonilpilp's recounting supports these accounts:

> Instead of making a charge down on the tents [at Norton's], the warriors turned and went after this artillery company [sic]. I was the one who had seen these soldiers first. As we chased them, two soldiers got off their horses. These men were killed, and we went right

over them, not knowing who killed them. We kept on after the remaining soldiers, whose way was blocked by the ten men [warriors]
on the hill. . . . We began moving up from behind, and then made a
charge. No soldier was left alive. All in that squad were killed.[46]

Yet another Nee-Me-Poo stated that Looking Glass, having joined
the others following Whipple's attack, led the assault against Rains:

> The Indians cut them off from Cottonwood, as the soldiers instead
> of endeavoring to return to that place veered off in another direc-
> tion, apparently determined to take chances on their horses. Before
> reaching a high ridge four of the soldiers dismounted and fought
> bravely. The four who dismounted were all killed by one Indian, a
> noted warrior named Wat-zam-yas. The other seven were overtaken
> on the ridge. . . . White Bird says the soldiers at Cottonwood could
> have saved this party if they had been brave enough, but they did
> not even start out from their camp.[47]

Yellow Wolf, however, was adamant that Looking Glass did not
join the main body of tribesmen until they reached the mouth of Cottonwood Creek on the Clearwater. Logistically, following Looking
Glass's recent loss via Whipple's attack, Yellow Wolf's assessment seems
appropriate. In 1957, one of the surviving Mount Idaho volunteers
named Elmer Adkinson stated that in about 1935 an aged Nez Perce
named Johnson Boyd claimed that he had killed Lieutenant Rains.[48]

On July 6, three days after the loss of Lieutenant Rains and his
men, a burial party arrived on the scene. The Nez Perces had taken the
guns and saddles and stripped the bodies to their underwear. Rains's
gauntlets were still on his hands, and his West Point ring remained on
his finger.[49] A courier from Howard who arrived at Cottonwood on
July 5 was told that Rains and his men had been found south of the
road, the lieutenant, "as if in life, was reclining against a large rock, a
lesser one in front of him. He seemed to have died in the act of firing his
last charge. His comrades lay dead around him."[50] Assistant Surgeon
William R. Hall initially stated that the body of one soldier, Private
Daniel Ryan, had not been found, but later amended his report to include Ryan. Surgeon Hall was unable to describe the character of the
wounds.[51] Most of the bodies, including that of Scout Foster, who had
been shot in the forehead, were buried near the road in the area of the
fatal encounter. The party lifted the body of Lieutenant Rains into a

roughly fashioned casket and transported it for interment "with military honors" the next day at Norton's Ranch. In June 1878, the remains of Lieutenant Rains and his men were received at Fort Lapwai, where funeral services preceded their burial in the post cemetery. When that post closed in 1884, the remains were reinterred in the cemetery at Fort Walla Walla.[52] The army posthumously cited Rains "for great gallantry in endeavoring to check the advance of the entire hostile force, with but a handful of men, in action against hostile Nez Perce Indians, at Cottonwood Ranch, . . . when he was killed."[53] Foster's grave remained along the road leading west from Cottonwood, known locally as the Cottonwood Butte Road. During the 1880s, a stone monument purchased in Walla Walla was raised at the grave and a wrought iron fence placed around it.[54]

After the pack train moved into Norton's Ranch on July 4, the soldiers, with Perry now in command, worked to strengthen the position Whipple had originally occupied two days earlier. Captain Winters described the military topography of the vicinity as follows:

> This house [Norton's] facing to the north-east is located in a narrow ravine from which the ground rises gradually on every side. To the north-east and north-west the ground is broken by small ravines, which with the points or spurs thus formed, radiate from the larger ravine in which the house, barns &c are situated. To the southwest of the house the ground rises somewhat more abruptly to a high table land or mesa, trending off to the west and south-west, and on the south-east at the distance of about eight hundred yards from the house terminating in a high prominent hill which commanded all the ground in the vicinity and from which could be had a general view of the whole surrounding country, including Craigs Mountain to the north-west and Camas Prairie and the town of Mount Idaho to the south-east.[55]

Perry established major entrenchments, one series consisting of rifle pits arranged in a semicircle on the large hill immediately southeast of the Norton place, the other occupying a rise southwest of the house. According to Corporal Frederick Mayer, the soldiers had "excellent material" for building breastworks. "There was a pile of brown stone good for building a wall. They were all shapes and sizes about 3 and 4 inches thick, fine for a breastwork. We formed a half circle on the hill around the Ranch."[56] One soldier remembered that the day was "hotter than blaze."

Between 1:00 and 2:00 P.M. on July 4, the Nez Perces appeared in force. Several approached from the upper reaches of Cottonwood Creek, disrupting the Rains burial detail and driving those soldiers back to the ranch. Other warriors arrived and soon surrounded the troops. Perry reacted quickly, directing twenty-eight men of Company F into the southernmost rifle pits on the hill to meet the warriors. Ten more men of Companies E and L took up positions in the westward pits, where Lieutenant Forse commanded a Gatling gun.[57] A sergeant at the works on the hill called for a Gatling gun, and it was hurriedly hauled into position. Captain Winters described the action:

> Galloping around with shouts and songs they soon completed the investment of our lines. While mounted they usually kept at long range, but frequently dismounting they approached under cover of ridges and ravines close to our lines, but always advancing cautiously and avoiding exposure to our fire.[58]

The warriors circled, making repeated bold attempts to storm the position on the hill, some closing to within one hundred yards. But the soldiers managed to keep them away. As Mayer recalled, "Sergeant St. Clair had the Gatling gun right in the center of our line [ready] to open fire when he thought it necessary." Finally, "somebody hollered [']open up Jersey, let them have it,['] and Jersey did open up. There were horses and Indians turning all kinds of summersets [sic]."[59] Another account stated that, "One fellow [warrior] came down across the road and had his horse shot from under him, and was himself wounded, and broke down the creek out of sight. The Indians soon gave him another horse, and he made an attempt to get up to the pits."[60] In the assault, the warriors generally maintained sufficient distance among themselves to keep the Gatlings from being effective. Once, the soldiers unleashed four revolutions (twelve shots) with one of the guns directed at a group of five warriors, but only hit some of their ponies. The warriors pulled back, but kept up a steady fire until after 9:00 P.M., when they withdrew.[61] General Howard later described the July 4 activities at Cottonwood: "There were doubtless plenty of flags flying; plenty of firing from carbines and Gatlings, to make the old Craig Mountain ring; add the Indian yellings and shootings and the day we celebrate was here properly honored."[62] In the fighting at Cottonwood on July 4, neither the soldiers nor the Indians suffered casualties.[63]

Nez Perce accounts provide more dimensions to the attack on the entrenchments at Cottonwood. One participant recalled the fortifications: "Five hollows [rifle pits] were dug so deep that the warriors could hardly do anything with guns, only to go up close to them. . . . When we reached the first hollow, the soldiers moved out and ran away. When nearing the second hollow fortification, one of the . . . [warriors] made the remark that we must quit for a little while, right where we were."[64] Another account stated that Joseph took part in the encounter and that the warriors succeeded in capturing two dozen army horses, although army records specify only "5 public horses" as being lost in the action.[65]

During the night of July 4, the soldiers threw up additional rifle pits. On the hill where the major entrenchments stood, they raised a special work where the reserve ammunition could better be protected. Perry's command now numbered 7 officers and 113 men, besides the packers and several citizens who had come in during the night. Companies F and L now occupied the southwest hill, and Company E covered the rest of the ground. Winters placed his men "on all the elevated points and in some of the intervening ravines."[66] The fighting from the trenches at Cottonwood, now designated Camp Rains, resumed at about 9:00 A.M., July 5, as the Nez Perces approached the southwest side of the south hill and opened a sporadic fire on Perry's command. Simultaneously, the men in the pits watched as the entire Nez Perce village, strung out several miles away in a caravan and with some sixteen hundred head of cattle and horses, proceeded diagonally across the prairie, crossed the road to Mount Idaho, and headed toward the Clearwater River.

Late that morning, the soldiers spotted two figures approaching down the road from Mount Idaho to the east. As they drew nearer, a party of twenty warriors moved out of the Nez Perce camp to cut the men off. Perry directed a part of L Company down the hill to saddle their horses preparatory to going to their aid. Two miles from the earthworks, the pair opened a race with six of the warriors to gain Cottonwood while Perry's men sent volleys of gunfire over their heads and succeeded in halting the warriors. The men proved to be members of Company L, couriers from General Howard sent out by Whipple thirty hours earlier. They reported that the Indians had attacked a group of volunteers en route from Mount Idaho to Perry's command. The party of seventeen had left Mount Idaho that morning on receipt of the news of Lieutenant Rains's defeat.[67] Forty-year-old Captain Darius B. Randall commanded the outfit, and as they went along the road to Cottonwood they sighted signal fires atop Cottonwood Butte straddling the Craig's Mountain range. Then they saw the Nez Perce village ten miles in the distance moving down from the area of Craig's Mountain to the prairie. Electing to push on, the volunteers presently found the warriors confronting them, perhaps 150 warriors who had filed off from the caravan and split into an unequal "V" formation, its long arm generally paralleling the road on the east side while its short arm stretched across the road, perhaps a mile south of Shebang Creek, to prevent passage and to intercept Randall's men. Before the envelopment could be perfected, however, Randall sent his men charging through the Indian line toward the creek, where he hoped to make a defense until Perry could send troops to their relief. While the breakthrough succeeded, the men were unable to outrun the warriors and reach the creek. Most gained a slight elevation about one and one-half miles southeast of Cottonwood and about one-quarter mile east of the road near a trail leading to Elk City. Captain Randall and four others were cut off in an adjacent swale. All the men dismounted and began shooting, some gaining cover behind a fence. Almost immediately, Randall, a Civil War veteran and a well-respected local citizen, dropped mortally wounded.[68] Another volunteer, Benjamin Evans, also fell dead and three more men were wounded as the small force labored to establish a perimeter to ward off the attack.

The warriors, meanwhile, soon diverted their position to the east of the volunteers' line and opened a brisk fire, felling several horses tended by holders. They later reported losing only one man in the fight. He was Weesculatat, also known as Mimpow Owyeen (Wounded Mouth), and he was shot three times when his horse, spooked by the volunteers' firing, ran directly among the party at the start of the fight. Although the warriors succeeded in retrieving the badly injured man, he died later, the first Nez Perce casualty identified by name since the war with the army had opened in mid-June. Another of the fighting men was Ollokot, who was unhorsed during the engagement and whose wife brought him another mount. According to Nez Perce sources, the party that attacked the volunteers numbered only twelve or fourteen, a figure unaccountably in stark contrast to that estimated by the volunteers and the army. By that time, however, the Nez Perces were principally concerned about moving their large village across the prairie, and most of them did not

become involved in the fighting near Cottonwood on July 5.[69] Regardless, in their fight with Randall's men, by changing their position to a
point east of the volunteers, the warriors left open a corridor leading to
Cottonwood, and it was in that direction that the volunteers now looked
for help.

From their defenses, Perry's soldiers watched the unfolding combat with growing apprehension, realizing that Randall's men would be
wiped out if relief did not arrive soon. At one point, the volunteers
fired a volley to attract Perry's attention. One of the cavalry officers,
Lieutenant Shelton, prepared to lead some soldiers of Company L forward. Yet Captain Perry hesitated to send help, believing that it was too
late to do any good and fearing that warriors in the rear would overrun
his own position and capture the train of ammunition and supplies meant
for Howard's main command. Perry later stated that he thought the
action "a ruse on the part of the Indians to draw us out." The delay
brought vigorous protests from his men, and Perry's individual leadership abilities were again called into question. When Whipple asked
him about the fighting, Perry replied that "some citizens . . . are surrounded by Indians, and are being all cut to pieces." Any help, he said,
would be "too late."[70] A tense command situation erupted at this juncture, causing tempers to flare over Perry's dilatory manner. A man in
the ranks complained sarcastically to George Shearer and within ear-
shot of the officers, "Shearer, you need not come to the 1st Cavalry for
assistance, as you will not get any."[71] Finally, defying Perry, Shearer
and Paul Guiterman rode off to join Randall's men, Shearer's horse
being shot just as he reached the volunteers. After nearly an hour, and
apparently after Sergeant Bernard Simpson, of Company L, threatened
to lead out a squad on his own,[72] Perry relented, directing Captains
Whipple and Winters and Lieutenant Shelton forward with about sixty
men and a Gatling gun. Winters recalled:

> As quickly as possible the men were drawn in and marched down
> the cañon at a run. Reaching the open ground Captain Whipple,
> with about 15 men, was seen marching obliquely to the left across
> my front, and was soon joined by Lieut. Shelton with his mounted
> party who had just preceeded [sic] me. . . . Deploying my men as
> skirmishers the advance was continued for about a mile when a note
> was received from Captain Perry with instructions not to go too far

as the Indians were coming in on our right. My line, then some four hundred yards in rear of where the citizens were, was moved to the left a short distance and halted, the flanks well thrown back. Captain Whipple with his men, including the mounted party under Lieut. Shelton, moved up to where the citizens were.[73]

Protected in his advance by the line of skirmishers, Whipple approached to within two hundred yards of the scene, then hesitated. Nonetheless, the presence of troops with the gun created the desired impact on the tribesmen. They watched from afar, to the right and left, and beyond firing range, and, reported Winters, "manifested no disposition to close in on the command." The relief proceeded. In all the excitement and activity, the soldiers had fired no shots. Late in the afternoon, the dead and wounded were placed in a lumber wagon brought out from Cottonwood, and Whipple and his men escorted the remaining members of the so-called "Brave Seventeen" back to Norton's house. One of the wounded, D. H. Howser, died that night.[74]

On the evening of July 5, as the Mount Idaho volunteers tended their wounded following their relief by Captains Whipple and Winters and Lieutenant Shelton, the citizen troops of Captains McConville and Hunter arrived at Cottonwood, having been dispatched the previous evening by General Howard below the Salmon upon receiving word of the attack on Rains's men. The next day, Perry's soldiers buried the dead enlisted men from Rains's fight (the lieutenant was buried on July 7). The volunteers set out across Camas Prairie for Mount Idaho, escorting the dead and wounded from the previous day's fighting. Randall and Evans were buried at Mount Idaho on July 8. That day the volunteers from Mount Idaho, Lewiston, and Dayton hastily reorganized into a single battalion under McConville, then pressed north seeking the trail of the Nez Perces. Perry's men left Cottonwood late on July 8 and, near midnight at Grangeville, met the van of Howard's command, most of which had by then recrossed the Salmon opposite White Bird Canyon. As the men labored up the grade from the river, they saw that the heavy rains had washed away the soil, exposing many dead from the battle of June 17. But they could not halt. Early on Monday morning, Howard led his reunited force north out of Grangeville to find the Nez Perces.[75]

Taken together, the actions at Looking Glass's village on July 1, and at Cottonwood, July 3–5, had the effect of further escalating the warfare in the wake of the battle at White Bird Canyon, thus precluding any possibility of a peaceful solution to the outbreak. At Cottonwood, where General Howard had established a station overlooking Camas Prairie to confront the Nez Perces should they flee north, the tribesmen succeeded in executing ample diversionary actions to circumvent that strategy and permit the passage of their combined village toward the Clearwater and an important union with the refugees from Looking Glass's camp, an event that was to plague the army through the balance of the war.

Clearwater

As the tribesmen of Joseph, Ollokot, White Bird, and Toohoolhoolzote bypassed the soldiers at Cottonwood and crossed Camas Prairie to the South Fork of the Clearwater River, warriors from their company raided abandoned farms and ranches, continuing the pattern established at the start of the outbreak. A number of forays occurred on the prairie, but the most damaging were those to homesteads along the Clearwater, where the warriors plundered and burned houses, barns, and outbuildings. On Camas Prairie, ten miles from Mount Idaho, Henry Croasdaile's house was "completely gutted & torn to pieces inside, all the furniture, bedding, blankets, [and] groceries . . . stolen or broken up." James C. Cearley, who had fought with Randall's men near Cottonwood, lost his barn, while John Flynn and John Healey reported that the Nez Perces "burned our House, Barn, shedding, & all our clothing & provisions." The home of D. H. Howser, who had died of wounds following the volunteers' engagement, was burned on July 6, and farmer J. C. Harris reported that the tribesmen had ruined sixteen acres of wheat and timothy at his place. Along the South Fork of the Clearwater River, the Nez Perces burned houses and barns and destroyed fences and crops belonging to George Dempster, D. M. Jones, William Grotts, James T. Silverwood, Thelbert Wall, and Arthur Williams.[1]

After diagonally traversing the country between Cottonwood and Grangeville, the Nez Perces followed the narrowing canyon of

Cottonwood Creek to its mouth, at last setting up their village on the South Fork of the Clearwater River. The large camp occupied both sides of the stream, but mostly straddled the ground on the west side. There the refugees from Looking Glass's destroyed village met them about July 7, bringing their number to approximately 740 men, women, and children. On the eighth, possibly in preparation for moving east across the Bitterroot Mountains, the Nee-Me-Poo forded many of their animals to the north side of the Middle Clearwater. At about the same time, many people in the Clearwater camp rode over to Kamiah and crossed the middle fork to attend a Dreamer service.[2]

It was after the tribesmen had established their village on the banks of the South Fork that the reorganized battalion of volunteers found them. Colonel McConville had left Mount Idaho with seventy-five men on the morning of July 8 after receiving ammunition from Howard's command at the mouth of White Bird Creek.[3] McConville's command crossed to Cottonwood Creek, then followed that stream until dark and unknowingly camped a short distance from the village. During the night, picket guards informed McConville of the proximity of the Nez Perce village less than a mile away, and the colonel dispatched a rider, John McPherson, to notify Howard of the discovery. McConville sent ten of his men to a high hill about one-half mile away, directing them "to hold the hill at all hazards, and to give the alarm in case of the approach of the Indians."[4] Presently, two more volunteers, George Riggins and P. C. Malin, rode off to Mount Idaho to find Howard. Before daylight, two of McConville's men, Lieutenants Luther P. Wilmot and James Cearley, reconnoitered the Nez Perce camp, approaching to within one-half mile of the village. As Wilmot recalled:

> We counted 72 big teepees. We counted over 150 horses tied at different places around the teepees. We was satisfied the whole bands [of] the Indians were in this camp. We watched until the sun come up and begin to shine on the teepees. Soon life began to show. . . . Fires began to start and once in a while men began to move around. Boys began to start out on to the hills on to the opposite side of the river. Finally we went back to our camp and reported.[5]

After a thorough discussion, the men decided to stay put and after dark get word to Howard and to assist the army troops in an attack.[6] But on the afternoon of July 9, the inadvertent discharge of a rifle by one of McConville's men brought instantaneous attention from the Nez Perces and changed the plan.[7] As the warriors responded, McConville and the balance of his command filled kettles and canteens with water and joined the lookouts on the hill in raising rock fortifications. "It was flat on top," recalled Wilmot, "and one of the finest places any one could wish to make a stand."[8]

For the next day, Nez Perce warriors surrounded and isolated McConville on the hill, which became known alternately by the appellations, "Misery Hill," "Mount Misery," or "Fort Misery." Climbing an adjacent ridge, the warriors began the confrontation by verbally challenging the men to fight. Near midnight, they "suddenly burst forth [with] a succession of the most unearthly yells, screeches, and screams of wild birds, among which were distinguishable the notes of the curlew . . . , the bark of the prairie wolf, [and] the scream of the panther."[9] Then, at 1:00 A.M. on July 10, they opened a "strong fire" against the volunteers, keeping it up until dawn.[10] During the night, they stampeded the men's horses, capturing forty-three animals. At 7:00 A.M., the Nez Perces opened a mocking dialogue, then formed themselves in a line ready to attack. But suddenly they pulled back and returned to the South Fork.[11] McConville's men waited on the hill until late in the afternoon when they saw thirty of the warriors move upstream to attack a small party of volunteers coming from Mount Idaho under the battalion's major, George Shearer. McConville directed Wilmot and twenty men forward, and they headed off the warriors, shooting one and killing a pony, after which the tribesmen pulled back, allowing Shearer's party to reach Misery Hill. McConville learned from Shearer that Howard had crossed to the east side of the South Fork. (Howard had attempted to contact McConville, to tell him to "be encouraged and keep all the brave men you can, barricading your position if necessary," but the presence of the Nez Perces had prevented his couriers from reaching McConville's camp.[12]) Late that day, Adjutant Morris of the volunteers drafted the following for delivery at Mount Idaho:

> Fort McConville, July 10
> . . . George Shearer arrived safe to-day. All are well. We see plenty of Indians around us. We are fortified for the present on an elevated place near a log cabin between the buttes of Kamai [sic]. A few shots have been exchanged but the enemy keeps shy. Lew Wilmot made a crack shot this afternoon and knocked one Indian off his

horse. Maj. Shearer and the boys made a narrow escape in getting
to camp without fighting. The Indians occupy both sides of the river.
The part of our stock [stolen from the citizens around Mount Idaho
over the previous weeks] from what we can see is on the east side of
the Clearwater below the east or middle fork. Col. McConville has
in all eighty-one men including the three that leave with this message. Col. McConville is waiting for the co-operation of Gen.
Howard from the other side. The Col. and all of his men are anxious to test the enemy's strength when the proper time arrives.[13]

After Shearer's arrival, McConville sent Wilmot and Benjamin Penny to
find Howard and coordinate with his force. It was agreed that, if Howard
attacked the village the next day, Wilmot was to signal the action with a
bonfire. Wilmot reached Howard that night, and the next day, he rode to
Mount Idaho before starting back to McConville.[14] Meanwhile, on the
morning of July 11, the warriors seemingly distracted and his men low
on provisions, Colonel McConville led them afoot out of their hilltop
fortifications. They halted for the night at Cearley's ravaged property,
and on the twelfth, his men mounted on animals obtained from the citizens of Mount Idaho, McConville reversed direction on word from
Howard that the Nez Perces were withdrawing toward Kamiah. The
movement to contain the Nez Perces south and west of Howard's position occupied the volunteers over the succeeding two days.[15]

Few Nez Perce accounts discussed the skirmishing at Misery Hill.
Yellow Wolf stated that the place was named Possossona (Water Passing),
that the fighting occurred sporadically, and that the warriors departed
after sundown. They returned later, but the volunteers did not prevent
them from capturing the horses, which Yellow Wolf identified as having
been stolen from Looking Glass's camp. "We took them all, except a few
we did not want," he said, describing the shooting in the darkness as "just
like fireworks." According to the Nez Perces, only one warrior received
injury in the fight with McConville's volunteers. He was Paktilek, who
lost his right-hand forefinger as he made off with two ponies.[16]

By his withdrawal from Misery Hill on July 11, McConville lost all
chance of coordinating with General Howard in an attack on the Nez
Perce camp. On the ninth, Howard—informed of the location of the
Nez Perces and now accompanied by Perry's cavalry—started north, in-
tent on following "Whipple's route to Looking Glass's camp via Jackson's
Bridge, with the hope of taking the enemy in reverse."[17] Therefore, he

went on to Thelbert Wall's burned ranch,[18] four miles beyond the bridge and on the east side of the South Fork of the Clearwater, where he went into bivouac. There he awaited the arrival of his exhausted artillery/ infantrymen who had to be transported from the Salmon River in wagons sent down from Grangeville and who reached camp at about 8:00 P.M. At Wall's, most of the men bivouacked on a high hill beyond the burned buildings. Before daylight on the tenth, Howard's restive pickets opened fire on each other, but no one was hurt. The command laid over, still awaiting the artillerymen.[19]

At 7:00 Wednesday morning, July 11, the command, numbering 350 men and guided by local resident James T. Silverwood and a contingent of scouts headed by Arthur ("Ad") Chapman,[20] at last moved out together along the high ground between the forks of the Clearwater, their left flank generally paralleling the South Fork.[21] The cavalry battalion, composed of four companies of the First Cavalry commanded by Captain David Perry, led the way, followed by that of the foot soldiers, five companies of the Twenty-first Infantry under Captain Evan Miles, and the artillery, acting as infantry, comprised of five batteries (companies) of the Fourth Artillery under Captain Marcus P. Miller. Following the artillerymen came two howitzers and their crews, commanded by Second Lieutenant Harrison G. Otis of the Fourth, and the two Gatling guns and their attendants.[22] Besides the civilian guides, several newspaper correspondents also went along, representing such tabloids as the Portland *Oregonian*, San Francisco *Chronicle*, Portland *Standard*, and Idaho *Tri-Weekly Statesman* out of Boise.

Captain Trimble's Company H, First Cavalry, had the honor of leading the advance guard, with six mounted troopers at the very front of the column. The day was clear and breezy, not yet hot. The army kept to the high ridges, marching in column on ground nearly one thousand feet above the bottomlands of the South Fork, and heading in the direction of Looking Glass's former camp at the mouth of Clear Creek on the Middle Clearwater. A few miles out, the troops came upon a small group of horses, mares and colts that Chapman identified as having been stolen from his ranch on the Cottonwood. At this sign of the possible proximity of Indians, skirmishers deployed and the advance resumed. At about 11:45 A.M., as the cavalry passed over a long crest leading toward Clear Creek, Howard's aide, First Lieutenant Robert H. Fletcher (Twenty-first Infantry), and Scout Chapman, while reconnoitering along the bluffs, peered down from the height and first observed the large Nez Perce village at the mouth of Cottonwood Creek. They were quickly joined by another aide, First Lieutenant Melville C. Wilkinson (Third Infantry), along with Captain Trimble, Silverwood, and several others. A newspaper correspondent described the sight:

> A very pretty scene met our view. The ranches looked fresh and fertile, the dingy river—now not worthy the name of "Clearwater"—only served by its ugliness to heighten the effect by contrast with the gardens, dotted here and there along the river bank. The company soon sighted the enemy on a flat, hedged in on the river by a dense underbrush, with a few pine trees interspersed on the flat. About, the hills rose steep, making it equally as good a place for attack as for defense.[23]

Informed of the discovery, General Howard rode to the bluff and saw the village, which stood about one mile southwest of his position. The Indians had already sighted the command, and the officers watched as they herded their livestock upstream and away from the camp. After deciding that they were not reservation Nez Perces, Howard ordered a howitzer brought forward and placed on the bluff overlooking the South Fork. (This bluff is immediately north of what today is called Stites Canyon, down which a modern road leads to the community of Stites.) The gun, overseen by Captain Lawrence S. Babbitt, Howard's ordnance officer and acting aide, and commanded by Lieutenant Otis, quickly opened against the rapidly emptying Indian village. But because the distance was too great, the howitzer shells burst high in the air and did no damage beyond frightening the fleeing people.[24] After ten minutes, Howard directed that both of his howitzers, along with the two Gatling guns, supported by Captain Winters's Company E, First Cavalry, and Captain George H. Burton's Company C, Twenty-first Infantry, be shifted to another promontory on the bluff to the south and across a large ravine (present Stites Canyon) leading to the river bottom. While the distance was but a half mile on a straight line, the defile (termed by Howard "a deep and rocky transverse ravine") necessitated a detour of one and one-half miles around its head to reach the bluff where the pieces were then deployed. At Howard's direction, Captain Miller sent Trimble and his company ahead down the river to reconnoiter.[25]

In the meantime, warriors from the camp crossed the South Fork and began a spirited approach through two large ravines leading to the bluff tops along which Howard's troops marched. (These ravines were opposite of and south from the village; they ran east on either side of the feature today called Dizzy Head.) When shooting by the Indians erupted behind and to the left of the column, Howard—anxious to join the battle after consecutive debacles—first countermarched his men, then deployed them into line to return fire on the warriors. Captain Miller placed his companies "along the crest of a ravine to the right, to connect on the left with the Infantry."[26] Wrote Second Lieutenant Charles E. S. Wood, of the infantry: "It was a test case—all the hostiles under Joseph against all the soldiers under Howard."[27] Back at the north, on orders to move to the main body, Trimble's Company H, First Cavalry, which was as much as one-half mile in front of the column, dismounted and, leading their horses, turned back and encountered Captain George B. Rodney and Company D, Fourth Artillery, who were escorting the pack train.[28] Placing the animals between the two units, Trimble and Rodney passed through the depression at the head of the ravine (present Stites Canyon) to gain the open plateau on which the balance of the column was deploying into a rough semicircle, with the curve facing the bluffs. As Trimble and Rodney extended their men into the line, the pack animals proceeded several hundred yards to the rear and center, where Howard established his headquarters and hospital and where the other cavalry animals had been sent. One officer recalled that the headquarters was built "with the aid of the Pack Saddles piled in a circular manner, though the protection was very slight."[29]

The Nez Perces who confronted Howard's troops had been taken by surprise. Many had been engaged in routine activities in the camp. Some were racing ponies on the flat land along the river bottom north of the village and others were swimming in the South Fork, when the booming of the howitzer and the crash of the shells fragmenting caught their attention. A scout came riding down the hill east of the river and announced that the soldiers were surrounding the camp. Twenty warriors grabbed their weapons and cartridge belts, then fell in behind Toohoolhoolzote, the aged leader who Howard had jailed at Fort Lapwai. Together, they raced upstream about one-half mile to a shallow ford, then crossed and ascended the ravines to attack the troops and keep them from approaching the camp. Tying their horses in the trees, the warriors crept along the brow of the bluff, occupying several points between the spring and the large draw up through which most

"Battle of Clearwater. Howard, July 11–12"
INSET DRAWING IN FLETCHER, "DEPARTMENT OF COLUMBIA MAP"

of them passed. Armed with an old muzzleloading rifle, Toohoolhoolzote crawled up the slope and killed two soldiers, among the first to fall in the battle. Other warriors piled loose stones into crude ramparts, then moved ahead, fired at the troops, and fell back behind the barricades.

Because the troops had miscalculated the location of the village, they had actually passed on toward Clear Creek before discovering their error, and it took them time to reverse direction and march back to the blufftop plateau, where they were when Toohoolhoolzote attacked and caused them to assume their defensive line. While this initiative held the soldiers in place, more warriors—having moved their families from danger—now swept into the large ravine and gained the heights. Many of them followed the military leaders, Rainbow and Ollokot. The total number of fighting men at the top at this time probably did not exceed one hundred.[30]

As the principal Nez Perce firing settled in the large ravine below the blufftops on the south, Howard's men adjusted their own position. Miller with two infantry companies, plus Company A and part of Company E of the artillery, withdrew toward the sound of the gunfire. The roughly skewed, crescent-shaped defensive perimeter of the soldiers fluidly settled into place to meet the warriors. From its southernmost extremity to its northernmost, the command deployed as follows: Companies F and L, First Cavalry; artillery battalion; infantry battalion; Companies E and H, First Cavalry. Before long, about twenty-five warriors appeared on the south end of the perimeter, galloping as if to flank the troops. Instantly divining their plan, Major Edwin C. Mason of the Twenty-first Infantry—Howard's chief of staff who was supervising the placement of troops—took Burton's and Second Lieutenant Edward S. Farrow's Companies C and E, emerged from the line, and with Captain Winters's cavalry on their far right, moved ahead "under a hail of fire" to disrupt the movement. Meanwhile, two civilian packers and their laggardly pack mules loaded with howitzer ammunition hove into sight from the south, hurrying to reach the command. When within three hundred yards of the skirmish line, the warriors dashed in, killed the two men, and moved off with three of the animals and their baggage.[31] Fire from Perry's and Whipple's cavalrymen helped dissuade the attackers, and soon Lieutenant Wilkinson, aided by Rodney's company, arrived to escort the remaining mules into the line.[32]

All this time, the gunfire from the edge of the bluffs—and especially from the Nez Perce position in the forested gulch opposite Howard's left—continued to increase in volume, as the warriors sent a barrage of bullets among the troops. "They gave it to us hot," said one observer. Supplementing the soldiers' rifle and carbine fire was that from the howitzers and Gatlings commanded by Lieutenant Otis, for the moment still stationed at a pivotal site on the bluff and capable of dominating both the village and the principal Nez Perce position in the ravine.[33] Eventually, one howitzer, then the other, was drawn up behind the left of the line and nearly opposite this latter position.[34] Occasionally, the warriors attempted assaults on this front. These charges were made "in regular daredevil style, nothing sneaking about it," remembered Sergeant McCarthy. "They were brave men, and faced a terrific fire of musketry, gatling [sic] guns and howitzers."[35] One attack came from a ravine opposite the right of the line in which a spring was located. (This draw is presently called Anderson Creek Ravine.) Several men of Company B of the infantry resisted this assault, during which Private Edward Wykoff was killed and another man was wounded.

McCarthy recollected details of the warriors' attacks:

> The Indian battle formations were excellent. Commands were mostly given by signals. A chief on some point out of range directed the movement by waving a blanket or circling his pony. They rode to the attack or in pursuit in small squads of 3 or 4. Each squad seemed to be an independent unit. Their horses were gentle and when an Indian wanted to shoot he rolled off the pony to the ground, took

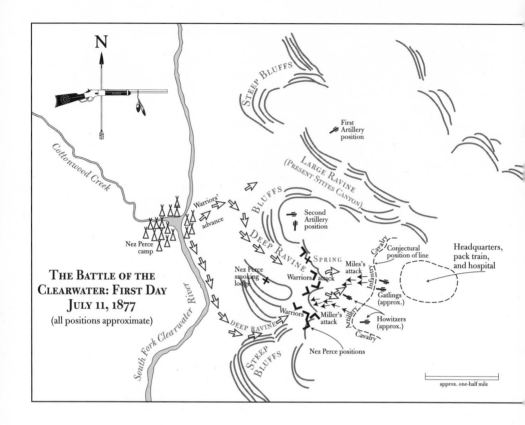

THE BATTLE OF THE CLEARWATER: FIRST DAY JULY 11, 1877 (all positions approximate)

N

Cottonwood Creek

STEEP BLUFFS

First Artillery position

LARGE RAVINE (PRESENT STITES CANYON)

BLUFFS

Warriors' advance

DEEP RAVINE

Second Artillery position

Nez Perce camp

Nez Perce smoking lodge

SPRING

Warriors' attack

Miles's attack

Conjectural position of line

Cavalry

Infantry

Headquarters, pack train, and hospital

Gatlings (approx.)

Warriors

Miller's attack

Artillery

Howitzers (approx.)

Cavalry

South Fork Clearwater River

DEEP RAVINE

STEEP BLUFFS

Nez Perce positions

approx. one-half mile

deliberate aim and crawled on again, the pony remaining quiet and patient during the firing. . . . I saw several of these squads go by. They were singing, one of the bunch giving out the song, the others joining in the chorus. . . . The leader, a medicine man, harangued the warriors during the battle in a voice heard all over the field.[36]

About midafternoon, the warriors opened an attack on the left front of the army line. Captain Evan Miles led Companies B, D, E, and H, of the infantry, and A and part of E, of the artillery, in a spirited drive that cleared some of these tribesmen from the ravine. A Civil War veteran of marked ability, Miles had served with the Twenty-first since 1866.[37] Captain Marcus P. Miller and the balance of the artillerymen supported Miles's movement, in which Captain Eugene A. Bancroft, Company A of the artillery, was shot through the lungs and Lieutenant Charles A. Williams of the infantry through the wrist and thigh.[38] Miller described the action:

[I] saw that a party of Indians had attacked the part of my line occupied by Battery "A," 4th Art'y, [and] that the left half of the battery was slowly retreating. . . . I instantly rallied this battery—gave the order to cheer and charge. [I] directed that [First] Lieut. [James A.] Haughey commanding the Infantry company next on the right to do the same and with what other men I could get hold of near them, all rushed upon the Indians, the Indians turning back and running like whipped dogs. This cheer and charge was taken up all along the lines and a general advance was made. The charge relieved temporarily the attack on the lines about the Howitzers—but shortly the Indians returned to attack these.[39]

A correspondent told of Miles's action:

The soldiers stood their ground manfully and held their own. The artillery company came to their assistance on the double quick. They dropped in the grass for a moment or so, and then, "up guards and at 'em". . . . The Indians ran and a rousing cheer broke from the whole line. The gatling [sic] gun and howitzers had already taken up their positions, and on the stampede opened a splendid and rapid fire on the enemy.[40]

Although the artillery pieces played on the Nez Perce positions, the warriors managed to kill or wound four members of one howitzer battery. Private William S. LeMay, the sole remaining cannoneer, was able—by lying on his back between the wheels—to load and fire the weapon and drive back the warriors.[41] So determined were the warriors that, at one point, they practically enveloped the howitzer and Gatling. First Lieutenant Charles F. Humphrey quickly gathered some men of Company E, Fourth Artillery, and facing a blistering fire from the warriors, retook the pieces, the soldiers having to haul them manually. Captain Miller reported: "That party had to cross grounds seen to be exposed to severe fire from the Indians—but following the example of Lieut. Humphrey the men went bravely on. Two of them were wounded in getting there."[42] But Humphrey's maneuver seemed to determine the warriors in pressing their attack, and they continued their push toward the battery. Many army casualties happened at this point. As one observer reported:

So exposed were the soldiers, and so fast did the killed and wounded fall, that the command "halt" was given before reaching the enemy's line. In this charge was most of the loss sustained by the troops.

There were more men killed and wounded during twenty minutes than were lost during the rest of the fight.[43]

The dead lay where they fell; wagons took the wounded to the hospital, where the surgeons had raised an awning for their comfort. The warrior Yellow Bull claimed that the warriors had planned to capture some of the soldiers alive. One named Pahatush prepared to go out. "Just as he was about to start, a volley was fired by the soldiers, and the smoke was so thick that we could not see. Pahatush was shot in the right hand as he held his gun, and the gun was broken."[44]

Soon afterward, forty-two-year-old Captain Miller led another charge on the bluff to the immediate right of the ravine held by the greatest number of the warriors. According to Miller,

> Gen'l Howard ordered me with Capt [Stephen P.] Jocelyn's Co. B, 21st Infantry, and Winters' troop of Cavalry on foot, to take the ridge. . . . I tried that, but with only partial success and temporary relief to the line—but sufficient time was given to allow the men there to use their entrenching tools and gain some shelter.[45]

Miller's actions here and on the next day were roundly hailed, and he emerged from the battle a genuine hero. Miller's charge on the Nez Perce positions at Clearwater succeeded in significantly advancing the army perimeter in that critical sector. Correspondent Thomas Sutherland wrote:

> The words . . . Miller used were these:—"Men, get up and go for them; if we don't do something they will kill us all." At this every man in that part of the line sprang to his feet, and all made one impetuous, irresistible charge, driving the Indians from their barricades on the edge of the canyon down a steep bluff into the wooded canyon below. . . . Some of the Indians did not leave their posts until the soldiers were within twenty or thirty yards of them, all the time keeping up a continuous fusillade of bullets. Strange to say, only one man was shot during this charge; he was killed outright.[46]

Participating in this action were Companies B, C, H, and I, of the infantry, along with Company E of the cavalry. Simultaneously, on the right of the army position, Lieutenant Wilkinson opened a lively demonstration with the remaining available men, while the howitzers leveled a bombardment on the Nez Perces' position. The firing from the right perhaps contributed to the recall of Miller's men from their farthest advance, for it was soon discovered that his soldiers were being fired upon from behind. Seeing what was happening, Second Lieutenant Harry L. Bailey—dashing out between the lines—shouted, "Cease firing[!] You are firing into your own men[!]" After a few minutes, order was restored and Miller's troops withdrew several paces back.[47] Bailey recounted an incident that occurred as he scolded one of his men for recklessly exposing himself. "'I tell you, Lieutenant, this is a ticklish business.' I told him it would be more ticklish if he did not keep his place. At that moment a rattlesnake reared up at his elbow, and he forgot the bullets for a second!"[48] Howard concluded the maneuver a success: "Miller's charge gained the ridge [along the bluff top] in front and secured the disputed ravine near Winters's left [present Anderson's Draw]. Further spasmodic charges on the left by the enemy were repelled by Perry's and Whipple's cavalry, dismounted, and Captain Arthur Morris's artillery, Company G."[49]

This bold attack by Miller's men succeeded in driving many of the Nez Perces with Toohoolhoolzote away from the brow of the hill. The warrior Yellow Wolf remembered the event. "Indians and soldiers fighting—almost together. We could not count the soldiers. There must have been hundreds. Bullets came thicker and thicker."[50] When the soldiers crested the brow, the warriors dashed away through the trees, many leaving their ponies behind as they moved down the ravine. They evidently returned after Miller's troops pulled back from their farthest advance. Some of the warriors who fought there were later identified as Wahlitits (Shore Crossing), Sarpsisilppilp (Red Moccasin Top), Tipyahlana Kapskaps (Strong Eagle), Pahkatos Owyeen (Five Wounds), and Witslahtahpalakin (Hair Cut Upward). Yellow Wolf later joined a party in the area of the spring, the members of which were engaged in a contest with the cavalrymen on the line. Here, the tribesmen suffered their first battle losses when Wayakat (Going Across) was shot and killed and Yoomtis Kunnin (Grizzly Bear Blanket) received a fatal wound. Another man, Howallits (Mean Man), incurred a slight wound. Here, too, Yellow Wolf was instructed to shoot at officers rather than common soldiers.[51] (The Nez Perces continued to pursue this unique tactic in subsequent engagements with the army.)

During the day, one of Howard's Nez Perce scouts deserted the troops. He was Elaskolatat (Animal Entering a Hole), whose father had been killed in the volunteers' fight at Cottonwood. At an appropriate

moment, the scout dashed his mount across the field and into the Nez
Perce lines, where "he threw off his citizen's clothes and dressed as an
Indian for battle." Later that day, while joining in a horseback charge,
the former scout received a gunshot wound.[52]

Howard established his line to protect his supplies and ammunition. The occasional offensive thrusts were, in fact, part of an overall
defensive scheme adopted to allow the general and his staff to determine how best to counter the tribesmen. Captain Trimble depicted the
position "as in some respects good, as the ground was higher and sufficiently undulating to make temporary earthworks easy of erection.
Furthermore, as the whole line was clear of the timber, any hostile seen
emerging therefrom could easily be stopped."[53] The roughly semicircular line covered all areas of approach, although the heaviest concentration of soldiers was in front, where Howard stationed his infantry
and artillerymen, doubtless because of the greater range and accuracy
of their rifles over those of the cavalry, who rested on the flanks. (The
discrepancy in the arms was not lost on the Nez Perces, who generally
maintained appropriate distances relative to the positions of the cavalry and foot troops.[54]) The line ran about eight hundred yards north
to south, but in its convolutions stretched in overall length for more
than two miles. Once it was established, many of the men had to lie flat
to avoid being hit by Nez Perce bullets; they then worked to erect small
semicircular breastworks from the many rocks that dotted the terrain.
Others threw up rifle pits where the ground was soft enough for digging. Although the Nez Perces' gunfire reached all along the line, the
heaviest return fire continued left of the center and opposite the main
warriors' ravine. Once, recalled Sergeant McCarthy:

> a squad of about a dozen mounted Indians came out of the woods . . .
> and stray shots struck the ground about us from time to time, but
> on the other side of the line, the firing was very heavy. We could not
> see what was going on there, but there was one continual peal of
> musketry and the howitzers and gatlings [sic] were being used freely;
> and the yells of the Indians, shoutings of our men and the braying of
> our pack mules made a terrible din.[55]

During one lull in the afternoon, Lieutenant Shelton and part of
Company E of the cavalry crept out in front to a position from which
they could rake the warriors' defenses. "As soon as this was discovered

by Captain Perry he had the recall sounded, it being in violation of orders to leave the skirmish line in any direction."[56] The battle intermittently raged in this manner until dark. "The Infantry and artillery all behaved splendidly and held all the exposed and dangerous points," wrote McCarthy. "The Indians found them more formidable than they did the cavalry at White Bird Canyon."[57] At about 9:00 P.M., the men heard the Nez Perce leader mentioned by McCarthy "haranguing" the warriors, his voice rising above the tumult and continuing his message for an hour, when the shooting subsided to just an occasional shot. "Now and then," remembered Trimble, "the female voice could be detected in a plaintive wail of mourning, sometimes in low and tremulous unison, then breaking into a piercing cry."[58] Those close to the tribesmen in the large ravine could hear them working on their barricades. "I heard the piling of cobble stones some thirty yards in my front," remembered Lieutenant Bailey.[59] He directed the howitzer at his rear to open on the place indicated. "I was amazed to see the flash of a discharge close behind me, and then came the shell so near over my head that I could have touched it by reaching up, and to my joy the shell exploded right in the place I had indicated."[60] At dusk, one soldier spotted a lone white horse loping toward him. "Suspecting some deviltry, I went out, when the horse came right up to me. He was in perfect terror, shot just above the nose, the ball passing completely through his tongue. He had on an Indian rope, and was completely covered with human blood."[61]

Through the night, the ammunition was replenished all along the line. The troops held their respective positions about five paces apart, and they followed orders to enlarge their breastworks, "two or more to occupy them during the night, the occupants . . . to relieve each other in watching."[62] Without food, the soldiers could only work on their defenses and wait for dawn. The spring in the ravine near the crest of the bluffs—that had been taken by Miles's and Miller's charges—had not been completely secured and continued to draw much attention. It lay about two hundred yards west of the right side of the soldiers' line. During much of the day, Nez Perce sharpshooters, some seemingly firing from treetops,[63] had succeeded in keeping the troops from the water, and the men—their canteens empty—and some three hundred cavalry mounts and pack mules confined in the center suffered from thirst. In at least one instance, an officer drank from a muddy mire through which the mules had walked, and later he became ill. After dark, when water was more easily obtained, Surgeon (Major) George M. Sternberg organized a force of officers, packers, and hospital attendants (including General Howard) to pass back and forth to the spring. To counter wild claims circulating among the men as to the extent of their casualties, Howard—who was out on the line reconnoitering his position between 3:30 and 4:30 A.M.—provided the men with an accurate report and encouraged them with prospects for victory on the morrow. He withdrew Captain Rodney's company from the line, placing the men in the rear as a reserve force. That night, wrote Lieutenant Wilkinson, "the bright stars looked down on our little Army, exhausted but not discouraged. Our torn and bleeding comrades give us cheer by their brave words spoken, and silent suffering."[64]

During the night, about half of the warriors left the ravine and returned to guard their village. Many elderly noncombatants stayed at a "smoking lodge," an enclosure of stones about twelve yards long by eight yards wide about eight hundred yards west of the army position (near present Dizzy Head) and protected by trees and ridges from immediate danger. At the smoking lodge (or smoking pit), the day's events were discussed and counsel offered to the Nez Perce leaders charged with the fighting. Some of those who met at the smoking lodge were Weyato Kakin, Helam Kawot, Two Moon, and the Palouse leader, Husis Kute. Later, some younger men reportedly shirked their duty at the front to find shelter there.[65]

At daybreak, July 12, the gunfire began anew. Most of the warriors' shooting continued from the heavily occupied ravine, and several times braves on horseback dashed, shooting, from the declivity onto the plain to see the situation before them. Once they tried to drive a herd of several hundred ponies through the line to disrupt and stampede the pack animals, but the attempt failed. Within minutes of daylight, Nez Perce marksmen had rousted several cooks who had gone to the spring for water to make coffee, sending them scampering across the plateau to the line, some tossing their kettles aside as they ran. Howard ordered Captain Miller to take the spring, and that officer again moved forward, this time with Captain Perry's dismounted cavalrymen and Lieutenant Otis's gun battery, and with Rodney's company in support. The maneuver shortly drove the warriors away, and by 9:00 A.M., Miller reclaimed the spring and the cooks got their water. Following this exchange, the gunfire died down all along the line. The cavalry horses were watered at the spring,

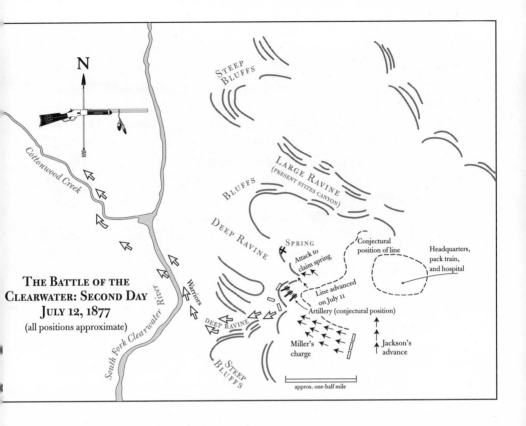

N

Steep Bluffs

Cottonwood Creek

Large Ravine
(Present Stites Canyon)

Bluffs

Deep Ravine

Spring

Conjectural
position of line

Headquarters,
pack train,
and hospital

Attack to
claim spring

Line advanced
on July 11

THE BATTLE OF THE
CLEARWATER: SECOND DAY
JULY 12, 1877
(all positions approximate)

Warriors

Artillery (conjectural position)

Deep Ravine

Miller's
charge

Jackson's
advance

Steep
Bluffs

South Fork Clearwater River

approx. one-half mile

and the men settled in their breastworks received coffee and freshly baked bread—their first meal since the battle started.

But the warriors aggressively persisted in their enterprise, keeping up their intermittent appearances on all sections of the front. One officer, writing a few days later, depicted the warriors' mode of combat:

> They ride up behind little elevations, throw themselves from their ponies, fire, and are off like rockets. Lines of them creep and crawl and twist themselves through the grass until within range, and with pieces as good as ours tell with deadly aim that they are marksmen. They tie grass upon their heads, so that it is hard to tell which bunch of grass does not conceal an Indian with a globe-sighted rifle. They [also] climb trees and shoot from them.[66]

The day passed with each side trying to anticipate the movements of the other. In the afternoon, Howard withdrew Miller's artillery battalion

from the line, closing it with the thinly spread soldiers of the cavalry
and infantry and moving the line ahead so that it more directly faced
the bluff and the ravine sheltering the warriors. The general and his
staff now planned an offensive movement to be executed by Miller's
men, assisted by a howitzer: They would rush out from the line on the
left of the Nez Perces' ravine, then charge into it and strike the warriors from behind. The remaining troops would join in the assault.[67]

But at 2:00 P.M., the plan changed with the discovery far to the
south of the anticipated supply train from Fort Lapwai with Captain
James Jackson's Company B, First Cavalry, in escort. Instead of leading
his charge, Miller extended the left of the line, then moved his companies (A, D, E, and G) out along the ridge for two miles, "clearing the
way with a howitzer," and interposed his force between the Nez Perce
position and the approaching train. Jackson had reached Grangeville
the previous night and had left on the morning of the twelfth to join
Howard.[68] Then, at about 3:00 P.M., as Miller countermarched guarding Jackson's approach, the artillerymen suddenly wheeled and charged
double time across the plateau straight toward the warriors in the ravine. When some warriors moved out and around, attempting to pass
Miller's left, the reserve company under Rodney deployed, outflanking
them. Miller wrote of the assault on the warriors' position:

> On the charge . . . I was delayed slightly by the hesitating move-
> ments of D Battery, at the most important juncture, while close to
> and opposite the Indians' stone shelters. A & G Batteries had out-
> flanked the Indians to their left. Seeing it, both Capt. Morris and
> myself yelled to the men to take the works. There was no officer
> with them. When [First] Lieut. Wm F. Stewart, 4th Art'y, my adju-
> tant, seeing the trouble, sprang forward to where the men were and
> took them over and into the works and advanced in pursuit.[69]

Reported Howard: "For a few minutes there is stubborn resistance at
the enemy's barricades. Then the whole line gives way."[70]

Overall, the onslaught was sudden and swift and caught many of the
warriors behind their defenses. Quickly following Miller in the charge
came the infantrymen and Winter's dismounted cavalry moving as skirmishers. "One bullet went through the top of my hat and removed a
handful of hair," wrote Second Lieutenant Edward S. Farrow.[71] As the
rush proceeded, the companies of Jackson and Trimble advanced with a

Gatling gun and the two howitzers to the brow of the bluff and opened a brisk but ineffective fire on the retreating tribesmen.

McCarthy gave a vivid account of the movement:

> The Indians had all along held possession of the trail leading down to their camp, and had built stone forts capable of holding 10 or 12 men each at the point where the trail commenced. . . . As soon as the Indians at the head of the trail, or cañon, found their position was turned, they abandoned their forts and fled down the trail, and a general stampede up the other side [of the river], which was a gradual slope, was commenced. Our whole line advanced to the edge of the perpendicular bluff, and the artillery in some instances advanced down the less steep path and trail. . . . The cavalry were then ordered to their horses, and boots and saddles sounded, and as soon as mounted we moved forward towards the trail.[72]

The soldiers chased down the ravine after the warriors, who quickly negotiated the high South Fork waters and raced their ponies up Cottonwood Creek and into the hills after their families. Most of the cavalrymen did not join in the pursuit, but dismounted and led their animals carefully down the trail. Sergeant McCarthy took note of the Nez Perces' stone fortifications:

> They were horseshoe shaped, high enough for a man to stand up in, and on the top willows were so placed as to cover a gun barrel and shade the eye. In front of the Indian line of forts and a few yards distant from the rifle pits occupied by the Infantry lay a dead Indian who had advanced beyond his comrades. He was nearly naked and lay as if asleep on his back, one arm down over his head and knee bent. He was a magnificent[ly] shaped man and very large, in fact almost gigantic.[73]

According to the few Nez Perce sources about the Clearwater battle, most of the men had withdrawn before the soldiers began rushing down the ravine. Wottolen (Hair Combed Over Eyes) explained that dissension among the tribesmen had largely ended their resistance to Howard's army. "They quit for a reason," he said. "There was a quarrel among the Nez Perces. Some kept riding back and forth from the fighting to the camp. That was not good. The leaders then decided to leave the fighting, the cowards [i.e., warriors who disagreed with them] following after."[74] "We were not whipped!" asserted Yellow Wolf. "Not until the last of us

leaped away did the soldiers make their charge."[75] Because of the impromptu decision of the warriors and chiefs to leave the action, the women
still in the camp had no opportunity to pack properly for moving. In any
event, Yellow Wolf looked around the ravine and discovered that he and
Wottolen alone remained, and both quickly left, passing down and through
the mostly abandoned village, where Yellow Wolf assisted Joseph's wife
and infant daughter who had not yet fled the camp.[76] Peopeo Tholekt
recollected the movement thusly:

> Everybody was running, some leading, some falling behind! All skip-
> ping for their lives, for the camp! Every warrior, afoot or who had a
> horse strong enough to carry him, hurried from the ridge. They
> followed the families, the moving camp, guarding them from the
> pursuing soldiers. The cannons boomed and the Gatling gun rattled,
> sending out shot after shot after the fleeing families.[77]

Another Nez Perce, Eelahweema (About Sleep), who was fourteen years
old at the time of the fight and who was one of the boys who brought
water up the hill for the warriors, also remembered the withdrawal:

> When the cannon-guns belched, rocks were showered and limbs of
> trees cut down. Smoke from that gun was like grass on fire. . . . I
> jumped out from there and ran! Soldiers must have fired at me, for
> bullets sang by but none touched me. Reaching my horse, a gray
> cayuse, I sprang on him and made for the camp. . . . The foremost
> reaching camp told the women that they better rush to the brush. In
> about fifteen minutes I saw soldiers coming in sight down the bluff
> and hillside. They began firing across the river among our tepees. A
> few horses were hit but no Indians killed. We hurried packing, get-
> ting ready to move, the bullets falling around.[78]

During the running fight from the top of the bluffs, Joseph evidently
preceded the warriors, rushing forward to warn the remaining villagers
of the impending attack.[79]

At the river, Howard's infantrymen halted, unable to ford the deep
stream. On Perry's direction, Trimble and Whipple crossed with their
companies and took up skirmish positions along the bank beyond the
deserted camp. Jackson's company and later the others ferried the foot
soldiers across, and because of the delay in fording, Howard had to call
off the pursuit. "An opportunity was lost on that occasion for effective
cavalry work that was inexcusable," wrote Lieutenant Parnell.[80] Instead,

at about 5:00 P.M., pickets were thrown out and the troops encamped amid the abandoned lodges. On the west side of the village, the soldiers discovered extensive log barricades facing west, suggesting that the tribesmen had anticipated an attack from that quarter, likely from McConville's volunteers only recently gone from the area. Howard's aide, Wilkinson, drafted a missive to McConville, lamenting that the volunteers "did not wait for him" and urging them to "harness the retreating Indians."[81] At least one elderly woman was found, who vigorously fought the sergeant who was detailed to bring her to Howard.[82] Some of the men spent the evening rummaging through possessions discovered in the tipis and in caches made in the soil.[83] They included buffalo robes, blankets, flour, dried meat and salmon, coffee, beadwork, and cooking utensils,—in short, "everything but their arms and horses."[84] Others roamed the bivouac sporting buckskin clothing and moccasins rifled from the camp.[85] Most wrapped themselves in their blankets and slept soundly.

Army casualties in the Battle of the Clearwater (Howard "denominated" it the "Battle of the South Fork of the Clearwater") numbered twelve men killed, two officers and twenty-five enlisted men wounded (two men died later), and one missing (counted among the killed). The breakdown of casualties by branch was: infantry, twenty-two; artillery, ten; and cavalry, eight. Virtually all the infantry and artillery losses took place on the first day of fighting.[86] "Their fire was deadly," wrote Lieutenant Wood of the warriors, "the proportion of wounded to killed being but two to one."[87] Furthermore, officers, noncommissioned officers, and trumpeters made up nearly one-half of the casualties, clear evidence that the Nez Perces comprehended army hierarchical structure and sighted their weapons accordingly to cause as much disruption as possible among the command. (This feature of the Clearwater engagement continued a trend that had been apparent at White Bird Canyon, wherein one-fourth of the total army casualties had been leadership personnel.) The soldier dead were buried in a long, single grave, with military honors, on the plateau on which they fought. Sergeant McCarthy noted the preparations as he prepared to leave the bluff top after the fighting: "As we passed headquarters, the burial party were putting dead bodies in a wagon for burial. The bodies were already black. There was a wagon full, about 15 or 16, principally infantry & artillery, who had borne the heaviest of the final desperate charges of the Indians."[88]

"The Idaho Indian War—Return from the Battle of July 12, 1877."
Probably taken near Kamiah, this stereopticon card view is the only known photo of
troops actively involved in field activities during the Nez Perce campaign.
COURTESY DOUGLAS D. SCOTT

On the thirteenth, Surgeon Sternberg conducted the twenty-seven wounded to Grangeville, twenty-five miles away. He wrote:

> The means of transportation furnished by the Q.M.D., three wagons and thirty pack mules. . . . I immediately constructed 15 litters, each to be drawn by a single mule. They were made of lodge poles [from the village] and canvas lashed with rope yarn. The larger ends of the poles were lashed to the sides of the pack saddles. The other extremities dragged upon the ground. A cross piece was lashed fast about the middle of the poles. . . . The litters answered their purpose admirably and the wounded arrived in as good condition as possible.[89]

On July 19, Sternberg conducted the wounded, transported in eighteen straw-filled wagons, to the post hospital at Fort Lapwai, en route
spending nights or resting at Cottonwood, Mason's ranch, and White's
ranch (where Sternberg performed a leg amputation) and reaching the
fort on the morning of July 21.[90]

Nez Perce losses in the battle, according to Howard's report, stood
at twenty-three warriors killed and "at least twice as many wounded,"
although this figure is clearly exaggerated.[91] Most reliable sources show
that their casualties were surprisingly low, with as few as four killed and
six wounded. The dead were Going Across, Grizzly Bear Blanket,
Heinmot Ilppilp (Red Thunder), and Whittling, while the wounded
included Mean Man, Kipkip Owyeen (Wounded Breast)—who received
his name from his injury—Pahkatos Owyeen (Five Wounds), Old Yellow Wolf, Animal Entering a Hole, and Yellow Wolf. None of these
stopped fighting after being hit, although Wounded Breast's injury was
severe. Other Nez Perce accounts, including that of Joseph, agree that
four of their people were killed.[92]

Despite the minimal Nez Perce losses and despite Howard's greater
casualty count, the Battle of the Clearwater was a clear victory for the
army in a campaign heretofore plagued by questionable strategy and repeated defeats. For one thing, military authorities—and especially General Howard— interpreted the result in the most positive terms as a clear
sign that fortunes were turning in their favor. In what officers believed
had at last been a rout of the tribesmen, the Nez Perces lost prestige not
only among their protreaty brethren, but also with neighboring tribes,
some of whom reportedly had vowed their support in the struggle against
the white men's oppression. For another, the outcome boosted the morale of the officers and enlisted men charged with quelling the outbreak
and restored a belief in their capabilities, a belief that was not altogether
justified. It also restored a sense of confidence in the settlers in their
physical and economic survivability in the Salmon River and Camas Prairie
country of Idaho Territory. Unknown to the settlers at present, it would
free them from the threat of further conflict; the Nez Perces, now faced
with the consequences of their actions, were forced to leave the region to
pursue an existence elsewhere. Some observers believed, however, that
the Clearwater encounter taught the Nez Perces that United States troops
were their superiors, a hollow presumption that was to be repeatedly
disproved on other fields in the weeks ahead. Yet future successes for the

Nez Perces would be due in large measure to individual leadership, for the Clearwater fighting revealed transcendent difficulties in Nez Perce leadership and followership based upon culturally ingrained processes that threatened to paralyze group unity and undermine common objectives.[93]

Despite the obvious barrenness of his victory, General Howard used it as a subterfuge, milking the event to every advantage as if his job depended upon it. In fact, it did. Frustrated by perceived inaction and consecutive reverses that seemed to border on incompetence in command, President Rutherford B. Hayes—on the advice of his cabinet— appeared ready to sack Howard in favor of Hayes's close friend Crook, and the news of a signal defeat of the Nez Perces could not have come at a more critical juncture. Probably at Howard's urging, his adjutant in Portland, Major Henry C. Wood, breached the chain of command in telegraphing the news directly to the president (for which Wood was afterwards sternly rebuked by General McDowell). Wood forwarded an announcement from the field that stated, "Nothing can surpass the vigor of General Howard's movements and action," while Oregon politicians Henry W. Corbett and Joseph N. Dolph, noting that Howard "appears to be master of [the] situation," asked Hayes and Secretary of War George W. McCrary to "suspend judgment" on replacing him.[94] In the end, because of Clearwater—and only because of that encounter of questionable result—the president relented and retained Howard in command. And on the local front, Howard's stock soared, too. Rumors that he had been burned in effigy on the streets of Lewiston proved baseless, and in the wake of Clearwater, local officials endorsed his "judicious guidance & management" of the campaign.[95]

Four days after the engagement, Howard offered his congratulations to his troops. Predicting that the Battle of Clearwater "will surely bring permanent peace to the Northwest," the general expressed gratitude that "not one officer or soldier . . . failed to do his duty, and more gallant conduct he never witnessed in battle."[96] Eventually, performance honors were bestowed all around. Besides Lieutenant Humphrey, who received a Medal of Honor for his action at Clearwater, twenty-eight officers won citations for gallantry and meritorious conduct in the battle, one was cited for "gallant service," and another was recognized "for energy and pluck displayed." Three enlisted men received certificates of merit, entitling them to two dollars extra pay per month, and one was cited for "conspicuously brave conduct."[97]

Kamiah, Weippe, and Fort Fizzle

THE BATTLE OF THE CLEARWATER was indisputably a watershed in the army's campaign against the Nez Perces. By not pressing them in their retreat from their village, General Howard lost both the initiative and an opportunity to finally curb the nontreaty Nez Perces and end the war. He later claimed that he had driven the tribesmen away from the settlements, thus ending the threat along the Salmon River and on the Camas Prairie. But Clearwater proved only a temporary setback to the Nez Perces; despite the loss of their homes and supplies, they were enabled to continue to pursue their apparent objective of reaching the buffalo plains beyond the Bitterroot range. In failing to intelligently predict that course, Howard could not properly capitalize on his victory by blocking and thereby denying to the Indians the strategic umbilical posed by the Lolo trail—the primary route leading from the rugged Idaho fastness to the open plains of Montana. From a military perspective, it was a failure of colossal proportion that was to haunt the army through the next twelve weeks.

On July 13, after much delay in moving the howitzers down from the bluffs east of the river, and after burning and otherwise destroying the Nez Perce village and its contents, as well as the rich caches of supplies, Howard's troops took up their march along the Nez Perces' trail about 9:00 A.M. They skirted a corner of the Camas Prairie, then bore north past McConville's vacant Misery Hill post toward the sub-agency at Kamiah along the north side of the Middle Fork of the Clearwater. Howard had received word that the warriors were threatening the reservation tribesmen. Yet his movement proceeded slowly over the nine-mile course, the cavalry halting periodically to permit the foot soldiers to keep up with them. Finally surmounting the hills overlooking the river opposite the agency about midafternoon, the command saw the tribesmen already across the stream. "From where we were halted," wrote Sergeant McCarthy, "we could see the main body of the Indians. They were in line mounted on a hill about half a mile back, and along the hill were some stoneworks."[1] The troops spotted an immense herd of live-stock on the bluffs behind the agency buildings.[2]

Instantly, Howard directed the gun battery forward, and Lieutenant Wilkinson's detachment descended ready to open the howitzers and Gatlings on the tribesmen, who had by then completed their passage. At the same time, the cavalry was rapidly deployed, Perry and Whipple veering right and toward the river while Howard with Jackson's company skirted the base of the bluffs and headed to the river. Companies F and L rode down the bluffs and advanced on the riverbank in a maneuver that elicited the first gunfire from the Nez Perces. Captain Whipple described the movement:

> Passing down the bluffs, Captain Perry with his company and mine kept a half mile or so to the right until near the river, then changing direction to the left marched down the river to join the main column which had halted. When within about 300 yards of the main column, a brisk fire was opened upon Captain Perry's column from the enemy concealed on the other side of the river, and that officer ordered the gallop and, as soon as out of direct range, the halt. Three men became demoralized at the first volley, dismounted, and came in on foot through a grain field on the left. This was the first and only instance of panic, fright or unsteadiness I saw among the men on the entire campaign.[3]

Another observer commented that "the horses became wild and unmanageable for a time, so that many men dismounted from them and let them go."[4] Yet another noted that the cavalrymen "walked into an ambush. . . [which caused] a great stampede for a short distance."[5] Correspondent Thomas Sutherland watched as Perry's and Whipple's men buckled under "a very brisk fire (say fifty shots in two minutes)."

"The men jumped from their horses and took to the grain fields on their left," eventually reaching the ford where Wilkinson's Gatling guns responded.[6] The performance of the cavalry at Kamiah disgusted Howard, who complained to Perry.[7] Despite the long-distance shooting, the gunfire remained lively. Two soldiers were injured in this exchange, one sustaining a severe head wound.[8] Trumpeter Bernard A. Brooks commented: "One man was shot within ten feet of me . . . and the bullet whistled dangerously near my own head."[9] One account said that army sharpshooters killed two Indians eight hundred yards away, but this was questionable.[10] Meantime, the artillery pounded the woods on the north side of the river without apparent effect and stopped after an hour. Because the reservation people had removed all their boats to the north side to keep them from falling into the hands of the nontreaty people, Howard could not immediately cross his command. Regardless, such a venture at that time would have been risky. The troops withdrew several hundred yards and went into camp, remaining there for the rest of the day. That night and the following day, the soldiers bathed and washed their uniforms—the first time in several weeks that they had clean persons and clothing. During the fourteenth, the pickets occasionally fired their weapons, but the warriors did not respond.[11]

At 6:00 A.M., Sunday, July 15, Howard led a command composed of Companies B, F, H, and L, First Cavalry, and forty volunteers who had arrived the previous day under Colonel McConville, in a march of twenty miles downstream to Dunwell's Ferry. He planned to ford the troops, then overcome the Nez Perces on their side of the river and cut them off while his remaining men under Captain Miller crossed at Kamiah and closed on their rear. But the plan proved short-lived. Four miles out of Kamiah, the column halted when the general was suddenly called back to the camp opposite Kamiah by word that a messenger from Joseph wanted to see him. Perry's Company F returned with Howard, while the remaining units, under Captain Jackson, kept on. Later, Company H was recalled and returned to the camp about midnight.

The parley with Joseph's messenger, a man named Kulkulsuitim, occurred on the south side of the Clearwater, a short distance from the army encampment. Major Mason joined Howard in the discussion. The meeting raised expectations that the Nez Perce leader was about to surrender, reportedly on the unconditional terms proposed by Howard, and the general made extensive preparations to receive the chief. But as the officers talked with the messenger near the river, shots rang out, reportedly from the north bank, and the meeting ended. Nonetheless, Howard remained optimistic, penning the following dispatch to divisional headquarters:

> Joseph has promised to break away from White Bird and give himself up to-morrow. He said he was forced to move to-day. The indications are that they have but little ammunition or food, and sustained large losses of everything in their hurried crossing of the river here at our approach. I see evidence of the band's breaking up, and shall pursue them a little farther with vigor.[12]

Howard also wrote another, less definite, statement that suggests that he was not as sanguine about the outcome:

> Joseph may make a complete surrender to-morrow morning. My troops will meet him at the ferry. He and his people will be treated with justice. Their conduct will be carefully investigated by a court composed of nine (9) officers of my army, to be selected by myself. [Brevet Lieutenant] Colonel M. P. Miller is designated as the officer to receive Joseph and his arms.[13]

But Joseph never appeared, and Howard became convinced that the event was but a ruse designed to further impede the army while allowing the tribesmen time to move their noncombatants and livestock toward the Lolo trail.[14] Instead, seventeen warriors, including a leader named Red Heart, came in with twenty-eight women and children. These people, recently returned from the buffalo country, had met with White Bird, Joseph, and the others at Weippe, about twenty miles north, and had decided against aligning themselves with the nontreaty Nez Perces. They brought with them another leader, Three Feathers, and a few of his people who did not want to continue the fighting. Red Heart's people turned in two guns. They reportedly claimed that other Nez Perces would soon follow their lead and that Joseph had been compelled over his objection to go with White Bird and the others to the buffalo lands. Some of the Indians were considered reservation dwellers. Despite this and the previous noninvolvement of most in the fighting, all were arrested and taken to Fort Lapwai and jailed.[15] These surrenders led some officers to conclude that dissension had set in among the people and that "the war seems virtually ended."[16]

On the sixteenth, when Jackson rejoined, the command took the entire day in fording the Clearwater "after considerable humbugging with our horses, which had to be towed across as usual."[17] By then it was virtually certain that the Nez Perces had started east over the Lolo fork trail, but Howard needed positive information. At 4:30 A.M. Tuesday morning, Major Mason led the cavalry, along with about twenty of McConville's volunteers and a howitzer detachment, to reconnoiter beyond the intersection of the Lolo and Oro Fino trails to Weippe, a popular Nez Perce camas-gathering spot. Six Christian Nez Perce scouts accompanied the command, among them John Levi (Sheared Wolf), Abraham Brooks, and James Reuben, their leader. The march was difficult because fallen timber in the forest barred much of the way. At about noon, after traveling about twenty miles and passing across the open Weippe Prairie, the troops paused briefly for lunch. They next entered the timber on the far side, eventually reaching a summit overlooking Lolo Creek. They continued along the Lolo trail, the volunteers leading the way, and at midafternoon came to open ground. Here McConville directed the scouts ahead, and they moved quickly across the break and into the timber. As they advanced, they were suddenly fired upon, Reuben and Brooks being wounded and John Levi killed. One of the volunteers recalled seeing three of the scouts, "coming toward us, dismounted and without their guns, and motioning with their hands for us to go back. They were hardly in sight before three sharp volleys were heard from the trail ahead and the next moment the rest of them came out of the timber as fast as their ponies could run."[18] Most of the scouts raced past the volunteers, who had no interpreter, leaving them in front and anticipating a major attack. The men who fired at the scouts were warriors from the main body, which was moving several miles away on the Lolo trail. They had learned of the presence of the troops from tribesmen who had remained behind as a rear guard. At the surprise, McConville's men fell back, taking cover behind fallen trees, and waited. But nothing happened. "As the moments glided by," remembered participant Lieutenant Eugene T. Wilson, "the situation became ludicrous and we began to speculate upon the success Colonel Mason would have with a mountain howitzer in timber too thick to drag a cat through."[19] McConville was shortly joined by Captain Winters, who directed him at Mason's order to go forward, and the volunteers and Company E advanced into the underbrush, the cavalrymen arrayed as skirmishers with every fourth man holding the horses in the rear. Presently, they found one severely wounded scout (Brooks) and the body of another (Levi), then took position at the edge of the woods anticipating an attack. After awhile they slowly withdrew, half of each company mounted and the other half dismounted. Emerging from the forest, McConville saw that Mason had dismounted his entire force, "it being utterly impossible for a mounted man to make his way through the timber."[20] Gaining open ground with Lieutenant Forse guarding their withdrawal, all the men mounted, turned about, and marched to Lolo Creek.[21] The volunteers fashioned a travois for the wounded scout, and the dead man was slung across a pony and carried out. Not far from the trail, the volunteers and scouts halted while a grave was dug and the dead scout interred. McConville's men ascended the trail until near midnight when, their horses exhausted from the climb, they bivouacked. Next day they overtook the balance of Mason's command. Determining the trail to be unsuited for further cavalry operations, the major concluded to return to Kamiah.[22]

On the morning of the eighteenth, the troops reached Howard's camp, the wounded scouts borne most of the way by the volunteers. During the day, a detail searched the agency buildings and found "3 hostiles, 2 of whom were wounded," evidently during the Clearwater battle. Most of the soldiers were ferried to the south bank, Company H of the cavalry alone remaining to entrench for the night on the agency side.[23] On July 19, Howard started his troops downstream, intending to stop at Lewiston for supplies, then go north and east through the Spokan and Coeur d'Alene country—a longer but faster route—and intercept the Nez Perces at the east end of the Lolo trail. He left three companies—one each of cavalry, infantry, and artillery—to stand watch opposite the Kamiah subagency in case the tribesmen returned, and he anticipated that the arrivals of Major John Green and Colonel Frank Wheaton would further secure the region. The volunteers would return to the site of the South Fork village and finish destroying caches found there. Their duty was to continue protecting Grangeville and Mount Idaho; Howard directed them to drive several hundred excess captured ponies into Rocky Canyon near the Salmon River and kill them to ruin any possible incentive for the warriors' return to the area.[24]

Yet Howard's march was short-lived. Before he reached Cold Spring en route to Lewiston, he received notices from Watkins and Monteith that the tribesmen had turned back toward Kamiah. Further news came that warriors had burned property on the North Fork of the Clearwater. Finally, the night after Howard left Kamiah, the Nez Pérces struck the subagency, running off as many as four hundred of their kinsmen's ponies and mules and killing some cattle. The soldiers on the south side of the river heard the disturbance, and a few shots were fired in their direction. Eventually "the men were dismissed with orders to lie down without undressing and to be ready at the slightest warning."[25] In the morning, the reservation tribesmen commenced to cross over into the army camp, each party waving a white flag as they approached. They reported that Looking Glass had led the raid on their homes and that head chief James Lawyer had gone into hiding for fear of losing his life during the attack.[26]

Word of the attack on the Kamiah people decided Howard to forsake his original plan and to pursue the Nez Perces in a direct movement across the Bitterroot Mountains on the Lolo trail. Over the next few days, he formulated his plan while awaiting reinforcements. Essentially, he would proceed with three columns. The right column, personally commanded by Howard, would keep on the nontreaties' trail all the way to Missoula. It would consist of a battalion of Fourth Artillery under Captain Miller—Companies A, C, D, E, G, L, and M; a battalion of infantry under Captain Miles—Company H, Eighth Infantry, Company C, Twelfth Infantry (both arrived from Fort Yuma, Arizona Territory), and Companies C, D, E, H, and I, Twenty-first Infantry; and a battalion of First Cavalry under Major George B. Sanford—Companies B, C, I, and K—all cavalry companies not previously extensively involved in the campaign. This command of 47 officers, 540 enlisted men, 74 civilians and Indian scouts, and approximately 70 packers would depart Kamiah on Monday, July 30. The left column—designated to march through the Coeur d'Alene country over the Mullan Road to Missoula, where it would meet Howard—was, at Inspector Watkins's behest, to check potential allies of the Nez Perce fighters among disaffected area tribes while cooperating with Howard's principal force. This column, commanded by Colonel Wheaton, would comprise the ten companies of his Second Infantry, en route from Atlanta, Georgia, since July 13; Companies F and H, First Cavalry; and two companies of mounted volunteers from Washington Territory. Wheaton's command numbered 36 officers and 440 enlisted men. To protect the settlers on the Salmon and the Camas Prairie from further harassment, Howard would posture his reserve column under Major Green, First Cavalry, at Henry Croasdaile's ranch, a centralized location on Cottonwood Creek ten miles from Mount Idaho and sixteen from Kamiah.[27] This command comprised Companies D, E, G, and L, First Cavalry; and Companies B and F, Twelfth Infantry, besides a unit of Warm Springs Indian scouts. The force numbered 22 officers, 245 enlisted men, and 35 Indian scouts. Green would oversee an army subdepot at Kamiah with an artillery detachment and two pieces stationed there, while manning an outpost at Mount Idaho for the local volunteers. Green's command would make frequent patrols of the crossings of the Salmon River and the South Fork of the Clearwater, and the country between the Salmon and the Snake, with instructions to bring in any parties or families associated with the nontreaty Nez Perces.[28]

Colonel Wheaton and the Second Infantry reached the theater of operations on July 29, having traveled by rail to Oakland, California, by steamer to Portland, and by boat up the Columbia River to Lewiston. Howard returned to Kamiah on July 26, ready to spend the next three days crossing his enlarged command over the Clearwater in canvas boats

"Pack train encamped at Cottonwood during 1877 war." These troops perhaps composed part of Howard's reserve that remained at Croasdaile's ranch near Cottonwood while his immediate command moved into Montana.
IDAHO STATE HISTORICAL SOCIETY, BOISE

preparatory to marching east on the Lolo trail. That same day, Companies (Batteries) C and L, Fourth Artillery, arrived from San Francisco to augment Miller's battalion with nearly fifty more men. Two days later, Howard accompanied McConville's men northeast to Weippe Prairie and returned without finding any Nez Perces. Following that scout, the Washington volunteers were discharged. Also on the twenty-eighth, Major Sanford with Companies C, I, and K, First Cavalry—the head of Green's column—arrived at Kamiah from Fort Boise, adding 140 more soldiers to Howard's army, along with 24 Bannock scouts, traditional enemies of the Nez Perces who were decked out in uniforms with bright sashes of stars and stripes. With the additions, Howard's force numbered some 730 officers and men. Also, a mule train of 350 beasts made ready to haul supplies for the army, while the artillery complement of two Gatling guns, two howitzers, and a small Coehorn mortar, all dismantled, would also be transported by mules. While the expedition assembled, Captain Jackson's company of cavalry patrolled as a picket guard a short distance up Lolo trail. On the evening of July 30, Sanford and the last soldiers crossed the Clearwater. Outfitted with twenty days' rations, General Howard's army ascended the Lolo trail on Monday, July 30, beneath a driving rainfall that "renders the mountainous trail slippery and exceedingly difficult." It had been two weeks since the Nez Perces departed for Montana Territory over the same route.[29]

In 1877, the Lolo trail stood as the major east-west linkage between the Bitterroot Valley in Montana Territory and north-central Idaho Territory. From the area of Kamiah, the trail ran approximately one hundred miles northeast, penetrating densely forested lands in traversing Idaho's Clearwater Mountains and Montana's Bitterroot range. A product of Pleistocene glaciation, the region was drained by the Bitterroot River on the east and the Lochsa and Selway rivers flowing west from the mountains to form the Middle Clearwater. The country—composed of myriad landforms of undulating ridges, swampy meadows, and peaks rising to seven thousand feet in elevation—in 1877 afforded a lush beauty complicated by an inaccessible character that made passage an arduous undertaking. Two primary features were the Lolo Pass (now called Packer's Meadows), a spacious, level hollow of about fifty-two hundred feet elevation at the divide between the Bitterroots and the Clearwater Mountains, and, a short distance below on the Montana side, the thermal waters known as Lolo Hot Springs, a traditional place for wayfarers to rest and relax. From there the trail paralleled Lolo Fork, an eastward flowing tributary of the Bitterroot River. The route had been used by Indians for generations preceding the arrival of white men in the region. Lewis and Clark followed portions of it in their passage to and from the Pacific Ocean in 1805 and 1806, and the trail—also known as "Lou Lou" or "Loo Loo"—had assumed its present designation by the 1860s, when early topographers referenced it on their maps. Its passage was never easy, owing to its heavy timber growth and commensurately large proportion of uprooted trees felled by windstorms and heavy snows. Moreover, the trail alternately ascended and descended numerous mountains and saddles rather than following one long ridge, a wearing trek for those constrained to attempt it. In 1866, at the time of the Idaho and Montana gold rushes, a congressionally funded party—headed by Wellington Bird and Sewell Truax—surveyed and started building a wagon road on the Lolo trail, the ax men clearing many trees along the route and grading some of its steeper sections. It was along the line of the Bird-Truax improvements that the Nez Perces and Howard's soldiers traveled in 1877.[30]

While the army remained in the area of Kamiah awaiting supplies and reinforcements, the Nee-Me-Poo took advantage of the delay and, in effect, stole a march on Howard. They started for the Lolo trail on July 15, just as Howard moved to ford the Clearwater and head them off on the north side, a plan that failed. At Weippe, twenty miles from Kamiah, the leaders paused to council—the first of several meetings held over the course of the next several weeks to define what their objectives should be and what means they should adopt to attain them. According to Nee-Me-Poo testimony regarding the Weippe council, the leaders were divided about what to do. Some, including Joseph and Ollokot, wanted to follow the Lolo trail to the Bitterroot Valley, then pass south and return to the Salmon and Snake river country via the Elk City Road or Southern Nez Perce Trail and Nez Perce Pass (southwest of present Darby, Montana). White Bird advocated going into Canada, while others, notably Looking Glass, argued forcefully for gaining the buffalo plains, where they might join with their friends the Crows. In the end, the proponents of going to the plains prevailed; Joseph, White Bird, Toohoolhoolzote, the Palouse leader Hahtalekin (who had joined with sixteen warriors), and Husis Kute all proclaimed unity in the plan. Although each band maintained its element of independence as before, Looking Glass seems to have emerged from the conference as the recognized military leader; because of his seniority and experience, his opinions carried the most weight among all the people.

On the sixteenth, their animals packed and the great herd of ponies moving forward, the Nee-Me-Poo started out on the trail to Montana. They left scouts behind to watch the movements of the soldiers. It was these warriors who alerted the people about Major Mason's advance on the seventeenth, which resulted in the exchange near Weippe Prairie. Looking Glass later led the warriors in the attack on the Kamiah subagency and the running off of many of the reservation people's horses. All this time, the main Nee-Me-Poo column, consisting of the leaders and warriors and their families, including the very old and very young, the wounded and lame, besides some two thousand horses and hundreds of dogs all stretched out for several miles, kept moving farther away from the army and deeper into the recesses of the wooded and mountainous terrain. What might have appeared a logistical ordeal occurred with precision and dispatch, the tribesmen's mobility due to the culturally ingrained responsibility each family unit had in organizing, packing, and completing the daily transport of its property and members in harmony with other band and tribe members, plus their long experience in the rigors of mountain-plateau travel.[31]

When the Nee-Me-Poo reached Lolo Hot Springs, they paused at a traditional camping site nearby.[32] There they received information that some soldiers lay ahead on the trail watching for their arrival. Although the people had succeeded in leaving Howard's troops far behind, they seemingly were unprepared for finding more soldiers in their front. In a significant statement transcribed much later, Looking Glass responded to the information, stating in essence "that he did not want to fight either soldiers or citizens east of the Lolo because they were not the ones who had fought them in Idaho." These people, he believed, had nothing to do with their problems. He directed his warriors to fight only in self defense and not to instigate trouble.[33] In retrospect, the Nez Perces' parochial perspective of the war, and their failure to comprehend the scale and span of the United States government's resistance to their flight, became key ingredients in their ultimate tragedy.

In fact, the Nez Perces' movement was well known, having gone from frightening rumor to confirmed fact, and soldiers stationed near

Missoula anxiously began preparations to receive them. These troops belonged to another administrative division—the Military Division of the Missouri, commanded from its Chicago headquarters by Lieutenant General Philip H. Sheridan. Within this vast military domain, the largest in the country, Montana Territory lay within the Department of Dakota, commanded by Brigadier General Alfred H. Terry from St. Paul, Minnesota. When the Nez Perces crossed the Bitterroots into Montana, they entered the department's District of Western Montana, commanded by Colonel John Gibbon from Fort Shaw. On word from Howard through Terry, it was Gibbon's soldiers who anticipated, and first encountered, the Nez Perces as they came east along the Lolo trail.[34]

The soldiers stationed in western Montana Territory had been there only a few weeks, having been sent into the area to build a post near Missoula City to police intertribal conflict over hunting grounds and to offset rising fears of an Indian war among Bitterroot Valley settlers as the government attempted to remove area tribesmen to a reservation farther north. Lieutenant Colonel Charles C. Gilbert, Seventh U.S. Infantry, selected the site of the new post four miles southwest of the community. On June 25, 1877, Captain Charles C. Rawn established the Post at Missoula (formally named Fort Missoula in November, 1877) with soldiers of Companies A and I, Seventh Infantry, out of Fort Shaw.[35] As building progressed, Captain Rawn, a Civil War veteran with sixteen years in the regiment, visited the different tribes in the region and gained statements of continued friendship from their leaders. In particular, Chief Charlo of the Flatheads, longtime allies of the Nez Perces, pledged neutrality in the escalating conflict, but promised to provide the army with intelligence of Nez Perce movements (and later more openly sided with the troops). As a precautionary measure, Rawn hastily fortified the new post, then sent an officer and four men "to watch the Loo-Loo [sic] trail from a point where it can be seen six or eight miles and report the approach of any large band of Indians from the west side."[36]

The detail under Second Lieutenant Francis Woodbridge was the one that had been reported to Looking Glass at Lolo Hot Springs. Woodbridge ascended the trail for several days. On June 21, Rawn, having heard nothing from them, dispatched First Lieutenant Charles A. Coolidge with one soldier and several civilian volunteers to learn Woodbridge's whereabouts. Coolidge's party encountered them a day later, as Woodbridge returned down the trail. That same day a mixed-blood Salish Indian named Jim Simonds (more commonly known as Delaware Jim), who lived with one of the Nez Perce women, brought word to the detachments of the arrival of the Indians at Grave Creek Meadows and Woodman's Prairie,[37] and the news, immediately forwarded to Rawn, spread quickly through the Bitterroot Valley creating consternation among the settlers.[38] Four days later, Rawn led four officers, thirty enlisted men, and about fifty volunteers six miles up the trail to a point "in what I considered the most defensible and least-easily flanked part of the cañon between the Indians and Bitter Root Valley." "My intentions were," reported Rawn, "to compel the Indians to surrender their arms and ammunition, and to dispute their passage, by force of arms, into Bitter Root Valley."[39] Rawn's command advanced into Lolo in skirmish formation. One soldier recalled that as they entered a narrow part of the canyon Nez Perce pickets fired on them, after which "the main column closed up and we went ahead into the defile." No further shooting occurred.[40]

Also on the twenty-fifth, Delaware Jim communicated with the Nez Perces, relaying the information to Rawn, who notified district headquarters of his status:

> Am intrenching twenty-five regulars and about fifty volunteers in . . . Lou Lou cañon. Have promises of more volunteers but am not certain of these. Please send me along more troops. Will go up and see them to-morrow and inform them that unless they disarm and dismount will give them a fight. White Bird says he will go through peaceably, if he can, but will go through. This news is entirely reliable.[41]

On Thursday evening, July 26, Rawn, accompanied by a group of regulars and volunteers, and carrying a flag of truce "fashioned by tying a white handkerchief to a gun barrel," met with the tribesmen and demanded that they turn in their arms and horses. Both Looking Glass and White Bird attended the council, and Joseph appeared as the proceeding ended, apparently concurring in a decision to meet Rawn again the next day.[42] That same day, Montana Territory Governor Benjamin F. Potts, who had arrived in Missoula with an escort, issued a call for volunteers and then hurried to the front. He wanted no trouble with the Nez Perces.[43]

On the twenty-seventh, Captain Rawn, accompanied by Potts, Captain William Logan of Company A, Seventh Infantry, and three volunteers, along with Chief Charlo, and backed by about a hundred armed men, approached the meeting place. Rawn and Potts met Looking Glass and Joseph between the lines at the edge of Woodman's Prairie and beyond rifle range of the warriors "drawn up in line on a ridge to show themselves."[44] Volunteer John Buckhouse remembered that "they were all well armed, and appeared a decent lot of fellows."[45] Delaware Jim interpreted, and the meeting lasted less than an hour. In return for being allowed to peaceably pass by the troops and through the Bitterroot Valley, the Nez Perces offered to surrender ammunition but not their arms. Rawn refused. A volunteer remembered: "The situation was just a little bit tense and strained as we sat facing each other with guns ready for instant use and each side watching for the first sign of treachery."[46] Finally, Looking Glass told Rawn that he needed to consult his people and that he would inform the captain next morning of the decision. Rawn asked to be informed by midnight, and the council broke without agreement.[47] That evening Governor Potts returned to Missoula, while Rawn filed the following report:

> Had a talk with Joseph and Looking-Glass this afternoon and told them they had to surrender arms and ammunition or fight. They are to consider to-night. I think that for want of ammunition or Charlo[']s threat they are wavering. Charlo has sent them word, that if they come into the Bitter Root he will fight them.[48]

By that time, Rawn's mixed command of 216 men lay prepared for the Nez Perces behind a hasty field fortification that stretched from the bench overlooking the creek and trail from the north. Each unit, regular and volunteer, had labored to raise its own barricade, consisting of log breastworks built of felled timber laid horizontally atop the dirt dug to create a trench in the rear. Corporal Charles N. Loynes described the construction: "A tree would be dropped, then another, called a head log, would be placed upon it, with a small limb in between giving the required space to get the rifles through."[49] A few rifle pits were apparently located farther up from, and to the rear of, the line of trench and log works. Although it appeared strong enough to face an opponent approaching directly from the west, the barricade's position on the floor of the canyon made it susceptible to enfilade fire from the heights on either side.[50] Volunteer Wilson B. Harlan recollected that "it was the belief of most of us, that in case of a fight, especially before our reinforcements arrived, it would have been another Custer massacre."[51] Following the

meeting on the twenty-seventh, many of the approximately 150 volunteers, on learning of the people's intent to pass by their homes peacefully
and unwilling by their presence to risk their hostility, peremptorily abandoned Rawn's entrenchment "in squads of from one to a dozen," leaving
only about thirty to man the work. Helping to offset this loss were Charlo
and twenty Flatheads, who tied white cloths about their heads and arms
to distinguish themselves from the Nez Perces.[52] Thus, on Friday evening,
Rawn's total force at the barricade stood at thirty regular soldiers, about
thirty volunteers, and twenty-one Flathead Indians.[53]

The command passed a restless night in a drizzling rain. As the
hours went by, three unarmed Nez Perces came into the works and
were captured.[54] Early Saturday morning, the soldiers and volunteers
behind the log breastwork braced themselves for an attack. But it never
came. Instead, despite the confidence of Rawn and his men that the
Nez Perces could not get by them, they did exactly that.

Some distance west of the entrenchments, the tribesmen, with all
their families, horses, and baggage, skillfully climbed north up a ravine,
then took to distant slopes and ridges out of view of Rawn's command.
They then went back down to the Lolo Creek drainage three miles east
of the works. In effect, their route was "making an arc of a circle in the
movement."[55] Volunteer Harlan, acting as an advanced picket, watched
the circumvention of Rawn's position from a mountainside:

> About nine o'clock I sent word that the Indians were driving in their
> horses and breaking camp. Another man was sent in when it was
> seen that they had packed up and had started down the valley to-
> ward us. . . . I reported to Captain Rawn that the Indians were be-
> ginning to climb the ridge a fourth of a mile above our camp and
> were evidently going around us. . . . I saw squaws and children with
> camp stuff going up.[56]

While the passage was occurring, a party of thirty or forty volunteers,
led by Lieutenant Coolidge, moved back along the base of the mountain on the north and climbed a short distance to guard against a surprise from the right rear of the barricade. A few random shots were
fired, but no one on either side was injured. "The truth was," wrote one
volunteer, "some of our citizens were pretty badly scared."[57] Late that
afternoon, after the Nez Perces completed the passage, they went across
the bottom and emerged into the Bitterroot Valley south of Lolo Creek.

Rawn led troops after them, later reporting that "I abandoned the breast-works, formed a skirmish line across the cañon with my regulars and such of the volunteers as I could control, and advanced in the direction the Indians had gone."[58] At the mouth of the Lolo, the remaining Bitter-root volunteers left Rawn and moved up the valley, warily approaching the Nez Perces' camp. Looking Glass appeared, professing friendship, promising to pass through the valley peaceably, and offering the men safe conduct through the village, an offer that the volunteers accepted.[59]

Meanwhile, Rawn and his soldiers, along with the volunteers from Missoula and adjacent communities, returned to their stations amid unfolding criticism of the regulars' inaction. Editorialized one territo-rial paper: "The Nez Perces, fresh from the victorious slaughters of Idaho, were permitted to pass an entrenched camp . . . under command of a Regular army officer without a shot being fired."[60] "Everybody went home," recalled a volunteer, "the majority mortified and disgusted at the turn affairs had taken."[61] In the aftermath of what became known as "Fort Fizzle," Captain Rawn came under severe criticism from the volunteers for not attempting to prevent the passage of the Nez Perces. "So far as infantry goes," opined the Helena *Daily Herald*, "they are as useless as boys with pop-guns."[62] Argued one participant:

> How Capt. Rawn can make it appear that it was not safe to oppose the passage out of the Lolo when he had 250 well armed men under his command and more arriving hourly, I fail to see. Before dark on Saturday, 28th of July, there would have been 400 men to the front, and by noon the following day one to two hundred more would have been added.[63]

Correspondent Thomas Sutherland, who was with Howard's force, complained that "the conduct of Captain Rawn and the volunteers . . . is very reprehensible and admits of no defense." Concerning the Nez Perces, he wrote, "there is no earthly excuse for their escape."[64] Yet many of Rawn's volunteers had deserted him before the tribesmen passed by, refusing to do anything to cause the warriors to strike back at the Bitterroot residents. The Nez Perces credited Rawn for withholding his men's fire, thereby preventing their disastrous defeat at the barri-cade.[65] There was also criticism of those volunteers from Missoula, Philipsburg, and Deer Lodge, who turned back at the same time as Rawn, thereby leaving the Bitterroot Valley settlers to meet the threat by themselves.[66] Later, cooler, more reflective assessments voiced approval of Rawn's prudence and judgment.

Of course, while the Fort Fizzle imbroglio was unfolding, General Howard's force was still making preparations to leave Kamiah, over a hundred miles to the west. By the time Howard's various dispositions had been made and the troops were underway, the Nez Perces were well advanced in their journey up the Bitterroot Valley.[67] Howard's march was not easy. After leaving on July 30, the command made sixteen miles to Weippe Prairie and there encamped. "A severe rain . . . kept us company for the entire day, making the marching, which was single file on account of the narrowness of the path, one of the most slippery, sticky, mucky and filthy of the trip."[68] Over the next several days, the soldiers wound their way across "fallen timber and miry bog-holes," ascending along a winding divide "where we find scarcely grass enough to keep our animals alive."[69] Dr. Jenkins A. FitzGerald wrote his wife on August 1: "Last night we had rather an unpleasant time. . . . We went to bed without our tents, and it began to rain about midnight. So I had to get up and make a shelter with a tent fly. . . . Today some beef cattle arrived to serve as food for us all, poor things."[70]

The command was large and unwieldy in its movements across the narrow trail. Far in advance ranged the Indian scouts, followed by a pioneer unit, initially of dismounted cavalrymen but eventually of civilian skilled laborers (later dubbed "skillets" by the soldiers) commanded by Captain William F. Spurgin of the Twenty-first Infantry. The pioneer unit led the way through "the most God-forsaken country troops ever went over." Often the infantry and cavalry alternated in working to clear the road of fallen trees to ease the passage of the column. In one instance, Major Sanford was cited for allowing his men to water his horses "one by one on the trail," a procedure that greatly impeded the soldiers following behind. Insufficient forage for the pack mules additionally slowed progress.[71] At one point, the soldiers came upon an Indian sign, which they interpreted as one of defiance. "It is in the shape of a bow, at least ten feet in length, cut out with a perfect line of beauty, on the bark of a huge black pine tree."[72]

The ponderous advance left some officers doubting whether Howard's force could ever catch and strike the Nez Perces.[73] But conditions improved after the command crested the summit and entered Montana. At Lolo Hot Springs, recalled an officer, "every one, down to

the most stoical mule in the packtrain, felt cheered."[74] Dr. FitzGerald
again reported to his wife:

> Last night we had the most picturesque camp I have ever seen—a
> very remarkable spot where there are 4 hot springs. The steam from
> them this morning rose up as if from a number of steam mills. I
> bathed my feet in one of them last night and found it as hot as I
> could bear comfortably. There was good trout fishing in the Lolo
> nearby, and [Brevet] Colonel Sanford and I got quite a fine string
> and had them for breakfast. . . . The rumor is that Joseph has left
> White Bird and Looking Glass and is somewhere in the mountains
> by himself with his band. . . . Do you know . . . that for nearly every
> morning of this month [of August] we have found ice in our wash
> basins and buckets?[75]

By crossing into Montana Territory, General Howard left the Department of the Columbia, in McDowell's Division of the Pacific, and
entered the Department of Dakota within Sheridan's Division of the
Missouri. He acted on direct orders from Commanding General William T. Sherman, through McDowell, to forsake administrative boundaries in running down the Nez Perces.[76] On August 4, Howard learned
from messengers that the Nez Perces "had been permitted to pass
through the Lo Lo Cañon," and that Colonel Gibbon's force was approaching Missoula from Fort Shaw. This news at least quelled fears
that the tribesmen would somehow double back past Howard to the
Camas Prairie.[77] It inspired Howard to move forward next day with
Sanford's cavalry and the artillery, leaving the infantry and most of the
packs to follow behind, and join Gibbon as quickly as possible. His
detached command consisted of "192 cavalrymen, 13 officers, 20 Indian scouts [plus] 2 Howitzers and a Coehorn, with 15 men, 1 officer."[78]
He also sent couriers over the back trail to report by telegraph to division headquarters that he had learned that the tribesmen were then
camped near the community of Corvallis, in Bitterroot Valley, and likely
intended on moving "toward Big Hole Prairie on [the] Elk City trail."[79]
On August 6, Howard grazed the animals at Summit Prairie (presently
called Packer's Meadows), then pushed on to Lolo Hot Springs, where
a courier from Gibbon notified him that the colonel had left Missoula
and was pressing down the Bitterroot Valley after the Nez Perces. Gibbon requested cavalry, and Howard sent him word that he was hurrying en route with two hundred horsemen:

I shall join you in the shortest possible time. I would not advise you to wait for me before you get to the Indians, then if you can create delay by skirmishing, by parleying, or maneuvering in any way, so that they shall not get away from you, do so by all means if you think best till I can give you the necessary reinforcements. I think however that the Indians are very short of ammunition, and that you can smash them in pieces if you can get an engagement out of them. Your judgment on the spot will be better than mine. I will push forward with all my might.[80]

From the bivouac at the hot springs, Howard also sent an aide to Missoula requesting that supplies and forage be forwarded to the mouth of Lolo Creek on the Bitterroot. On the eighth, the troops reached Rawn's vacated barricade. A citizen pointed out the Nez Perces' route around the work on the heights on the north. "The position was a very strong one," noted Howard, "and it is to be regretted that the Indians could not have been met and driven back upon me. . . . In truth, I should have been in Missoula by the northern route . . . had I not been detained by reports of the return of the hostiles [to Kamiah] after they had started for Montana."[81] Later on the eighth, Howard reached the mouth of Lolo Creek. Because the Nez Perces had turned south after debouching into the Bitterroot Valley and were now targeted by both Howard's force and that of Colonel Gibbon, he sent a directive north to Colonel Wheaton of the left column to shorten his marches "till you hear from me, for you may not be obliged to come through to Montana."[82] Then, reprovisioning his cavalry and artillery detachment with supplies from Missoula, and the Lolo trail now behind him, Howard set out on Gibbon's trail up the Bitterroot Valley.

Bitterroot and the Big Hole

THE NEGOTIATIONS AT Woodman's Prairie, a mile west of Fort Fizzle, and the aftermath of that event made it seem apparent to the Nez Perces that their departure from Idaho and arrival in Montana meant that past conflicts lay behind them—that a new beginning was at hand and that the settlers of the Bitterroot Valley could be assured of their peaceful intentions. Many of them had traveled back and forth through the area for years, and many individuals were well known among the white populace. But their newly felt relief proved fleeting. Their false sense of security was based as much on a misunderstanding of the role and regional responsibility of the United States military as it was a tragic miscalculation that other tribes on the northern plains would receive them with friendship. Both beliefs would be shattered completely in the days and weeks ahead.

On the evening following the passage around Captain Rawn's barricade on the Lolo, the Nee-Me-Poo leaders met to deliberate again over their objectives. According to tribal testimony, the council came about at the urging of Joseph and Toohoolhoolzote. There was obvious friction among the leadership about where to go; this friction carried over from the Weippe session of two weeks previous. Into that mix came reports from three Nez Perces who had been among the Crows scouting for the army against the Lakotas of the eastern Montana plains. The leader of the three, Grizzly Bear Youth, admonished the headmen of the military presence to the east, urging them to travel north of Missoula through the Flathead Reservation and by Flathead Lake to the British Possessions.[1] The advice implicitly countered the leaders' view that conflict with the army lay in the past and that the peoples' longstanding relationship with the Crows would somehow benefit them.

In the council, Looking Glass, White Bird, and the others debated whether to continue toward the buffalo plains or go north into Canada. White Bird and Red Owl favored the latter course, but it appears that the others were not so inclined and that the discussion regarding Canada died quickly. Most of the talk then turned on how best to reach the plains, and while there were various routes to be considered—particularly one that ran more or less directly east up the Big Blackfoot River, through Cadotte Pass, and down Sun River to near Fort Shaw—Looking Glass, as before, argued forcefully for going by way of the Big Hole Basin and ultimately east down the Yellowstone River to the land of the Crows.[2] Looking Glass claimed a superior knowledge of this route over others, and he may have been interested in bypassing the various posts and mining camps. Yet objections to this course arose, with a man identified as Pile of Clouds[3] disputing Looking Glass and complaining that the Crow country was too open for fighting. Pile of Clouds urged the chiefs to go back to the Salmon "where there are mountains and timber, and we can fight." Throughout the discussion about Canada and going to the plains, Joseph had remained silent, possibly because he was interested in neither course. When he did speak, he counseled against further fighting, for Montana was not his country. "Since we have left our country, it matters little where we go." Quite possibly he entertained the notion of Pile of Clouds, which would entail the tribesmen's continuing along the Bitterroot and then returning through Nez Perce Pass to the Salmon River country.[4] Ollokot's position on the matter is unknown, and Toohoolhoolzote, Five Wounds, and Rainbow apparently aligned with Looking Glass.[5] Eventually, after the council closed, Looking Glass's seniority and respected abilities in military matters again prevailed, and the group collectively yielded to his preference. Despite the real potential for fragmentation of the body, White Bird urged unity, saying, "If we go to the Crows, we must all go." And although the Canadian option had clearly emerged during the conference, it was just as clearly not yet the favored alternative.[6]

At this stage, two tribes—the Flatheads and the Crows—figured importantly in the Nee-Me-Poo effort to get to the plains. The Flatheads were old friends of the Nez Perces who shared peaceful passage of the Lolo trail in treks to the west to harvest salmon. They were intermarried with the Nee-Me-Poo. Whether the Flatheads would present an obstacle following their show of support to the army and the Bitterroot volunteers in Lolo canyon needed to be determined. In reality, Charlo's people had no good alternative to the course that he had selected for them. As chief, Charlo had to put on a good show and control his young men lest he reap local white retaliation. With Charlo's friendship now in question, some of the Nez Perces apparently advised against going north of Missoula for fear that the Flatheads might attack them. The reality was that the Flatheads, disarmed and dependent on the whites for protection, were themselves fearful that the Nez Perces would strike them, and were perhaps more interested in obtaining horses than in fighting. At any event, as long as the Nez Perces remained in the Bitterroot Valley, the Flatheads refused to deal with them.[7]

As for the Crows, whose allegiance to the troops was well known in 1877, the uppermost question for the Nez Perces was whether that allegiance to the army would take precedence over decades of intertribal friendship and mutual support. The two tribes had occasionally fought each other, but generally had been allies against hostile neighbors on the plains. Their rapport strengthened after an 1855 treaty designated the area lying between the Yellowstone and Missouri rivers east of the Crazy Mountains as Nez Perce hunting grounds. The Crows also ranged this country, and inevitably the two peoples bonded even more. Intermarriages increased, and the tribes helped each other in their conflicts with the Blackfeet, Teton Sioux, Northern Cheyennes, and Assiniboines.[8] In the wake of the gold strikes in Idaho, the Nez Perces seemed to extend their visits among the Crows. For example, in 1871, one group of thirty-five lodges requested to stay and begin farming with the Crows at their agency at the mouth of Mission Creek on the Yellowstone River. Thus, in the turmoil that forced the Nez Perces to move from their Idaho homes, Looking Glass expected that the Crows would give them a permanent welcome.[9]

Yet there is evidence that conditions on the plains militated against the Crows' unconditional acceptance of the Nee-Me-Poo among them. The fact was that the immense herds of buffalo that attracted the tribes no longer existed, many of the animals having been slaughtered by white hide hunters. Although the Nez Perces continued to hunt the region in 1877, the diminution of the herds meant competition for all the peoples whose basic lifeways were tied to the beasts, a reality that may have cumulatively begun to affect the Crow–Nez Perce relationship by that year. Practical like the Flatheads at this point in their history, the Crows simply believed that alienating the whites constituted too great a risk to their tribal well-being.[10]

But trouble with the Crows only loomed as a possible danger as the Nez Perces set out through the Bitterroot Valley on July 29. From the mouth of Lolo Creek, the valley stretched south along the Bitterroot River for sixty-five miles to a point where the stream forked. The fertile valley was broad and flat and was nine miles across at its widest place. It had early attracted white settlers. The major community was at Stevensville, which had grown up since the 1850s around the stockaded adobe trading post of Fort Owen, long abandoned by 1877.[11] Fifteen miles up the valley was Corvallis, and farther up the Bitterroot lay Skalkaho.[12] Each of these communities took precautionary measures at word of the Nez Perces' outbreak in Idaho. Neglecting their fields and crops, the residents at Stevensville made hasty attempts to upgrade Fort Owen, generally in good shape except for parts of the front and north end, which were crumbling. "We cut green sods and built it up again," recalled Henry Buck, who also noted that the people renamed the structure "Fort Brave." At Corvallis, the people built a fort of green sod, inside of which were living rooms fashioned of tents and wagon covers and partitioned with lumber. It was named "Fort Skidaddle," after its occupants, mostly Missourians who had "skedaddled" rather than face repeated Confederate incursions during the Civil War. Similarly constructed, the post at Skalkaho was called "Fort Run," after the propensity of area citizens to rush inside its gates when it was finished.[13] Armed with obsolete muzzle-loading weapons provided by the territorial government, the Bitterroot volunteers thus set about protecting their homes and families from the Nez Perces.

On July 10, Wilson B. Harlan, of Stevensville, informed the governor of the state of readiness in the valley:

> Since the settlers have been supplied with arms they have confidence they can defend themselves and their homes if given a little notice of invasion. The families with one or two exceptions are at their homes. There was not the panic that was reported. Four or

five families went to Missoula, and 19 or 20 to Fort Owen, while fully 50 staid [sic] at their homes somewhat uneasy but not apprehending immediate trouble.[14]

When Rawn finally called for assistance, the people herded their families into the forts before setting forth to the Lolo. After the Nez Perces had passed Rawn's fortifications, however, and following Looking Glass's profession of friendship for and peaceful intentions toward the Bitterroot residents, the volunteers returned quickly to their homes to await developments.[15] At Stevensville's Fort Owen, 258 citizens had taken refuge, and early word from the Lolo held that the men were being "cut to pieces" by the tribesmen. In time word arrived that, in fact, no fighting had occurred.[16]

From their first camp at J. P. McClain's tract, on Carlton Creek west of the Bitterroot River, the Nez Perces on Sunday, July 29, began a long procession up the valley, "apparently as unconcerned and indifferent to the circumstances as though on an ordinary journey to the buffalo country."[17] They were secure in the knowledge that Rawn would not strike them, that the Bitterroot occupants would let them pass, and that Howard's army was far behind. At 10:00 A.M. on the thirtieth, the van of the Nez Perces arrived on the flat west of the river opposite Stevensville. Witness Henry Buck described the scene:

> I sat on top of the fort where I had a plain view of the caravan and watched their passing. As was always customary with Indians traveling on horseback, they jogged their ponies along on a little dog trot. Being curious enough to gain some idea of their number, [I] took out my watch and timed their passing a given point. It took just one hour and a quarter for all to move by and there were no gaps in the continuous train. There was no unusual confusion or disorder and none came over on our side of the river.[18]

The Nez Perces halted and went into camp three miles southwest of Stevensville on Silverthorne Creek, not far from the home of the Flathead leader, Charlo. Evidently, some of Stevenville's leading citizens loaded their wagons with flour and drove out to the camp and received cash for their goods.[19] Early the next day, the tribesmen crossed the river and visited the Buck Brothers general store,

> [We] were busy arranging the goods on the shelves, when low [sic] and behold a band of squaws from the Nez Perce camp, accompanied

by a few armed warriors, appeared. They soon made known their
wants to us, saying they needed supplies and had money to pay for
them, but if we refused to sell, would take them anyway. Our stock
comprised but a handful of such articles as they wanted. However,
we held a consultation over the matter and decided that "prudence
was the better part of valor," so decided to trade with them. Flour
was their main desire and we had none; but near Fort Owen was
located the flour mill to where they repaired for a supply.[20]

Despite the amicable appearance of the Nez Perces, the citizens all slept in
the fort that night, content that the Indians would soon be on their way.

Instead, the people stayed another day at Stevensville. The relative calm of the preceding day was shattered when Looking Glass and
more than one hundred warriors arrived, all reportedly armed with repeating rifles. "We were lost to know what this day would bring forth,"
wrote Buck. He described their appearance as "formidable," while at
the same time "the finest looking tribe of Indians I have ever seen."[21] A
man passing through the community "found it full of Nez Perces, warriors, buying whatever they could get, provisions, clothing, etc., and of
course wanted whisky [sic] and ammunition, both of which I believe
they got in small quantities."[22] At least one shopkeeper refused their
business and locked his store.[23] They paid for their purchases in gold
coin, silver, gold dust, and paper currency, possibly at exorbitant prices
charged by the merchants, but this day many indeed bought whiskey,
which money-conscious purveyors made readily available to them.
Looking Glass stationed himself on the street to police his people and
keep them in hand. Two individuals, David Spooner and Jerry Fahy,
were reprimanded by the storekeepers for dispensing liquor to the men.
As Buck remembered: "The older people of the Nez Perce tribe were
well disposed and tried in every way to keep the peace and deal squarely
with us; but the younger warriors knew no bounds and were hard to
control, especially when under the influence of liquor." In one instance,
Looking Glass publicly rebuked a warrior involved in a scuffle and sent
him back to the camp. By 3:00 P.M., the Nez Perces, having expended
more than twelve hundred dollars in Stevensville, had all left town and
returned to Silverthorne Creek, and it was here that some of the tribesmen purchased ammunition from whites who approached their village.[24]

While the Nez Perces replenished their supplies in Stevensville,
six lodges of Nez Perces under Wahwookya Wasaaw (Lean Elk), better

known as Poker Joe, who had been summering in the Bitterroot, joined the main body, thereby augmenting the force and providing fresh horses.[25] All the while the tribesmen meandered along the bottom, a scout for Captain Rawn observed them and reported back daily on their progress. Speculating that the people, including a reported 250 warriors, were heading to Big Hole Prairie, Rawn informed Governor Potts that he would lead fifty or sixty regulars in pursuit, but, on instructions from Gibbon, would "temporize" his march so that he and Howard could catch up. "I am pretty well satisfied," Rawn wrote Gibbon, "that they will not hurry out of the Valley until they know that your command and Howard's have arrived. They are watching and know nearly everything that is going on." Rawn then delayed his movement to await Gibbon's arrival at the post at Missoula.[26]

On July 31, Governor Potts issued a second proclamation (his first was on July 26), this time calling for 300 volunteers. In response, several Montana communities announced their readiness to aid in the subjugation of the Nez Perces. The towns and mining camps of Philipsburg, Deer Lodge, Cable, Bear, New Chicago, Yreka, Bear Mouth, Yamhill, and Pioneer could together provide a total of 75 men. Butte raised three companies totaling about 150 men, while Helena and Pony each offered to raise 50 if they received arms from the territory. But the call was premature, and the War Department denied Potts's request to organize volunteers without congressional authority; moreover, Generals Sheridan and Terry believed they could provide sufficient regular troops to handle the crisis. Nor could Potts legally obligate the territory for costs incurred in raising and supporting troops. The organization of local militias was suspended. General Sherman wrote Potts that "if the citizens, in their own interest, will join the regular troops and act with and under them, the commanding officers will loan them arms and ammunition when possible, and may certify to beef or food taken *en route*."[27] The statement seemed to justify the formation of some spontaneously raised groups, such as those from among the Bitterroot Valley residents bent on protecting their homes and families.[28]

By coincidence, while all these events proceeded, General Sherman and a small entourage was in the territory, having come up the Yellowstone to consult with Terry, Crook, and Sheridan concerning the Sioux question, before touring the Yellowstone National Park preparatory to passing through western Montana en route to the west coast.

While at Fort Ellis on August 3, Sherman wrote Secretary of War George W. McCrary. In a statement suggestive of the imperviousness of the army hierarchy to the causes of the conflict, Sherman declared that "these Nez Perces should be made to answer for the murders they committed in Idaho, and also be punished, as a tribe, for going to war without any just cause or provocation." Furthermore, he declared his preference to stay aloof from the conflict. "I do not propose to interfere, but leave Gibbon or Howard to fight out this fight," wrote the general. Although Sherman thereafter maintained a keen interest in the course of the pursuit, he deferred to McDowell and Sheridan to manage the overall strategy for stopping the Nez Perces.[29]

In the meantime, over the next several days the people continued their leisurely pace up the valley. They proceeded past Corvallis, some of the diehard entrepreneurs of Stevensville even following them in wagons hoping to prolong the commerce. Farther up the valley, one group of young men with Toohoolhoolzote ransacked the ranch home of a settler named Myron Lockwood, taking large quantities of flour and coffee and several lesser items. Reportedly, Looking Glass demanded that the men leave seven horses in payment. Elsewhere, the warriors took five cattle, which they later killed to eat. The assemblage paused at the sacred Medicine Tree, offering prayers and gifts in a traditional homage observed by area tribes for generations and practiced still.[30] The slow progress agitated some of the Nez Perce leaders, and White Bird admonished Looking Glass for dragging lodgepoles that further impeded the advance. Moving at about fifteen miles per day, the travelers paralleled the East Fork of the Bitterroot River, surmounted the Continental Divide, and moved their caravan down a tributary of the Big Hole River, intending to rest for several days before beginning the long trek to join the Crows.[31] As Yellow Bull averred, "From the friendly talks we had had with the soldiers in Lolo Pass, we did not suppose there would be any more fighting, especially if we did not disturb the settlers, and we had not molested them."[32]

In fact, as the Nez Perces settled into their camp along the north fork of the Big Hole River (Ruby Creek), new soldiers were gaining on them. Colonel Gibbon had mobilized troops from Camp Baker, Fort Benton, Fort Ellis, Fort Shaw, and a camp at Dauphin Rapids on the Missouri River, finally setting out from Shaw on July 28 with eight officers and seventy-six enlisted men. Traveling 150 miles via Cadotte

*A Lamtama Nee-Me-Poo war leader, Chuslum Moxmox (Yellow Bull), photographed ca.
1878, was a veteran of Gibbon's attack at the Big Hole and most of the other 1877 encounters.*
NATIONAL ANTHROPOLOGICAL ARCHIVES, SMITHSONIAN INSTITUTION, WASHINGTON, D.C.

Pass and down the Big Blackfoot, Gibbon and a mounted detachment,
including a few men from the Second Cavalry, reached the post at
Missoula on August 2, followed the next day by his infantrymen, who
arrived in wagons sent out to meet them.[33] On his arrival, Gibbon immediately requested Governor Potts to send militia to guard the passes
leading into the Big Hole Basin once the Nez Perces had passed through,

hoping thereby to trap the tribesmen while Gibbon advanced to fight them. "Please give instructions . . . to have no negotiations whatever with the Indians, and the men should have no hesitancy in shooting down any armed Indian they meet not known to belong to one of the peaceful tribes."[34]

An experienced and resourceful soldier and author, John Gibbon had logged many years on the frontier. Graduating from West Point in 1847, he served against the Seminole Indians in Florida before becoming an instructor of artillery tactics at the Military Academy (Gibbon authored *The Artillerist's Manual*, published in 1863). He was successively a brigade (the famous "Iron Brigade"), division, and corps commander during the Civil War, leading troops at South Mountain, Antietam, Spotsylvania, and Petersburg, and he received wounds at Fredericksburg and Gettysburg. By 1864, Gibbon was a major general of volunteers. In the postwar reorganization of the army, he was appointed colonel of the Thirty-sixth Infantry. In 1869 he took command of the Seventh Infantry, and he played an important role in the Sioux Campaign of 1876 preceding and following the Little Bighorn battle. His position as commander of the District of Western Montana insured Gibbon's prominent involvement in army efforts to thwart the Nez Perces' movement into Montana.[35]

At 1:00 P.M. on August 4, Gibbon's command, augmented by the addition of Rawn's two companies as well as Company G, which had arrived from Fort Ellis on July 29, started rolling down the Bitterroot Valley in wagons accompanied by a large number of supply wagons and pack animals. His small army consisted of Companies A, D, F, G, I, and K, Seventh Infantry, totaling 15 officers and 146 men (including 8 men of the Second Cavalry), besides a twelve-pounder mountain howitzer. Eight hours later they pulled up at Stevensville, camping south of town on the east side of the river where Gibbon learned of the "pitiful spectacle" of the townspeople's bartering with the Nez Perces. Next day, amid news that as many as 150 citizens were en route from Bannack City to head off the tribesmen, the troops pressed on, picking up 34 volunteers from the Bitterroot Valley despite some argument in the civilian ranks over the propriety of their pursuit of professed peaceful Indians. On the sixth, they encountered the ransacked Lockwood house, then advanced twenty-four miles on the trail, ascending the rugged divide separating them from Ross's Hole to a point short of the summit, where they camped. Gibbon noticed that the Nez Perces, to lighten their load, did not drag their lodgepoles with them on the trail but cut temporary poles for use at each campsite. More important, the trail passed the start of the route to Idaho through Nez Perce Pass, signifying that the people had not intended to return immediately to the Salmon River country.[36] In the afternoon the troops ascended out of the bottom, climbing "a long steep incline" before bivouacking without water. On August 7, joined by two additional officers of the Seventh Infantry, they moved up and forward thirteen miles to reach the foot of the Continental Divide.[37] Gibbon reported: "We had up to this time been passing regularly the Indian camping-grounds, which showed that they were moving at the rate of about twelve or fourteen miles a day, so that if we could continue to double this distance the question of overtaking the enemy was simply one of time."[38] He estimated the fighting strength of the Nez Perces at 250 warriors.

At the suggestion of First Lieutenant James H. Bradley, Gibbon dispatched him and First Lieutenant Joshua W. Jacobs with about 60 mounted soldiers and volunteers to make a night march, catch the Nez Perces before dawn, and stampede their horse herd, thus immobilizing the village while Gibbon and the remaining troops pressed ahead. Starting at 5:00 A.M. on the eighth, Gibbon's force labored greatly in surmounting the divide, being compelled to remove much fallen timber in its path and to double-up the horse teams before wagons could proceed.[39] It took six hours to cover the two miles leading to the summit, before lumbering at a somewhat faster pace for twenty miles into the Big Hole Basin. But a courier from Bradley informed Gibbon that the distance to the village had been underestimated, and that Bradley had not been in position before daybreak to launch his attack. Bradley's command was in hiding awaiting Gibbon. Afraid that the tribesmen would discover Bradley's men, the colonel drove the command ahead. But "as our impatience to get forward increased," he later recorded, "the difficulties of the route seemed to redouble. Again and again we recrossed the creek into the 'glades' on each side, struggling through thick timber and in places swampy flats, in which our wagon-wheels sunk to the hub."[40] Finally, Gibbon left his wagons and 20 men as guards to follow and pushed on with the howitzer, reaching Bradley near sunset and still about five miles from the Nez Perce camp. That evening after the train caught up, the troops downed a meal of hardtack and water and rested. "The genial campfire, stimulating coffee and soothing pipe were forbidden," remembered Gibbon's adjutant, Second Lieutenant Charles A. Woodruff.[41] At 11:00 P.M., the fighting command of 17 officers, 132 men, and 34 scouts and volunteers moved out on foot. In preparation for battle, each soldier carried ninety rounds of ammunition. On Gibbon's order, the mountain howitzer would proceed at dawn, accompanied by a pack mule bearing two boxes (two thousand rounds) of ammunition. All animals, save those of Gibbon, his adjutant, Lieutenant Jacobs, and a guide, were corralled near Placer Creek with a guard detail. The soldiers left their greatcoats and canteens behind.[42]

Gibbon gave the lead to Lieutenant Bradley's command and the thirty-four citizen volunteers under Captain John B. Catlin, all now dismounted and their horses left behind. In 1877, thirty-three-year-old James H. Bradley was considered one of the frontier army's rising stars. The Ohio-born soldier served as an enlisted man with state troops during the Civil War. He was commissioned in 1866 and joined the Seventh Infantry in 1871. An officer of literary talent, his prose and poetry frequently graced the pages of the territorial newspapers. An able historian and masterly chronicler, Bradley had researched treatises on the fur trade in the Northwest, and his riveting account of his discovery of the dead on Custer's battlefield of the preceding year, when he was Gibbon's chief of scouts, constituted a significant record of historical merit (and is recognized as such today). As recently as March, Bradley had through public notices solicited subscriptions for his upcoming book about the Sioux campaign of 1876.[43]

The dispositions made, the advance got underway in single file. Astonished at the Nez Perces' apparent failure to have any scouts or picket guards in the vicinity of their camp, Gibbon feared the possibility that he, and not they, would be surprised. Whispered orders passed among the officers and men. The night was clear and starry as the troops passed along through alternating pine woods and marshlands for three miles. "We tripped over fallen timber, and now and then crossed streams and marshy places where we sunk over shoetops in mud," remembered Gibbon.[44] Occasionally, parts of the column got lost, requiring the balance to wait for them to catch up. Presently, the country leveled into a broad basin. Hugging the foothills overlooking the confluence of Trail and Ruby creeks, the soldiers bore left paralleling the North Fork of the Big Hole, or Wisdom, River and soon came within view of the glow of fires in the distant village and heard dogs baying. After passing around a point of timber extending into the valley, they came upon a herd grazing on the hillside above and across the river from the camp. "As we silently advanced they commenced neighing," wrote Gibbon, "but fortunately did not become alarmed, and by the time we had passed through the herd the outline of the tepees could be made out in the bottom below."[45]

At that point, Gibbon ordered a halt, and the command laid down and quietly anticipated daylight amid "the barking dogs, crying babies, and other noises of the camp."[46] It was 2:00 A.M., and still, but "of the quiet that precedes a tornado," remembered Corporal Loynes. Realizing the importance of capturing the herd behind him, Gibbon nonetheless demurred, fearing he might wake its guards. The soldiers took position along the hillside, below and somewhat north of the grazing animals and perhaps thirty yards above the heavy willow thickets fringing its base and adjoining a deep and thicketed slough, which itself adjoined the river. The stream ran approximately twenty feet across and contained numerous bottom undulations so that both it and the slough were anywhere from knee- to armpit-level deep. About four hundred feet east of the command and across the river lay the village of eighty-nine lodges, arranged in a northeast-to-southwest alignment— "a straggling open V," said Gibbon—with the main concentration of tipis adjoining a westward-extending bend of the stream. The camp occupied an open meadow directly opposite from where the troops waited. Farther east, the ground rolled away into an ascending benchland that typified the basin topography.[47]

At about 4:00 A.M.—just before dawn—Gibbon ordered the advance. Captains James M. J. Sanno and Richard Comba, their men arranged as skirmishers, moved forward opposite the village, while on the extreme left Bradley's soldiers with Catlin's volunteers started off with Captains Rawn and Constant Williams remaining behind in support. One company under Captain William Logan stood somewhat to the right on the hillside, in reserve. "All pushed forward in perfect silence," wrote Gibbon, "while now scarcely a sound issued from the camp."[48] Then the advance quickened, the men of Bradley and Sanno forging through the underbrush into the muddy slough. Comba's men simultaneously moved across a boggy loop in the meandering stream and approached the willows along the west bank across from the camp. "We had orders to fire low into the tepees," remembered seventeen-year-old civilian

△ Indian Village
→→ Gibbon's 1st position
=== Second in timber
Indians fire timber

Big Hole Battle — Gibbons. Aug. 9.

"Big Hole Battle—Gibbons [sic]—Aug. 9"
INSET DRAWING IN FLETCHER, "DEPARTMENT OF COLUMBIA MAP"

participant Horace B. Mulkey, whose father's ranch stood only four miles away.[49] Then, abruptly, a gun shot shattered the calm on the left, quickly succeeded by others. A single tribesman, Hahtalekin, out tending his horses drew the first fire and fell dead. At this, Comba's company drew up short of the river and began leveling volleys into the tipis. Then they waded the stream and charged the village. Sanno's company likewise raced toward the lodges. On the right, Logan brought his Company A in on the run, as did Bradley on the left with his command of assorted infantrymen, volunteers, and dismounted cavalry, and instantly the entire line erupted in gunfire directed at the skin-covered tipis. Corporal Loynes, moving in support with Rawn's Company I, recollected the attack:

> We had previously received orders to give three volleys through the camp, and then charge, . . . and as we gave three volleys into the camp, we rushed to the water's edge, every one seeming to want to get to the opposite side first. So into the water we leaped, not knowing its depth in the dim light of the moon, through it and into the camp of the Indians we followed with a yell that would do credit to the Indians themselves.[50]

By now, the men under Comba and Sanno had waded the stream, mounted the bank, and struck the village at the north edge of the principal concentration while still shooting into the lodges, now rapidly disgorging their occupants as frightened, half-clad Nez Perce families ran for cover in the morning twilight. "Fortunately for us," recalled

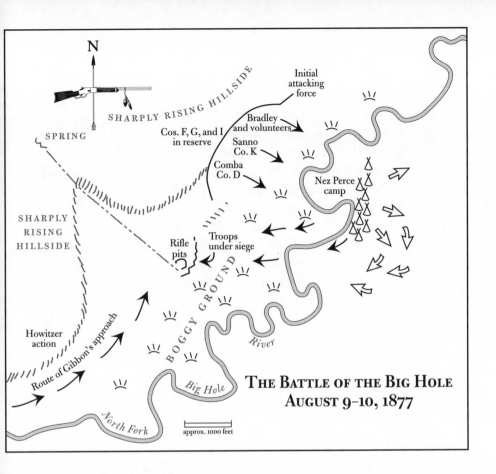

N

SHARPLY RISING HILLSIDE

SPRING

Cos. F, G, and I
in reserve

SHARPLY
RISING
HILLSIDE

Initial
attacking
force

Bradley
and volunteers

Sanno
Co. K

Comba
Co. D

Nez Perce
camp

Troops
under siege

Rifle
pits

BOGGY GROUND

Howitzer
action

Route of Gibbon's approach

River

Big Hole

North Fork

approx. 1000 feet

THE BATTLE OF THE BIG HOLE
AUGUST 9–10, 1877

Woodruff, "[they were] a little dazed and nervous from the shock of surprise."[51]

> Men, white and red, women and boys, all take part in the fight, which is actually hand to hand, a regular melee, rifles and revolvers in full play, men are powder burned, so close are they to death dealing guns, the dingy lodges are lighted up by the constant discharge, the ground is covered with the dead and dying, the morning air laden with smoke and riven by cheers, savage yells, shrieks, curses, groans.[52]

Bradley's charge collapsed, the lieutenant killed instantly while leading his men through the thickets, and his men gradually moved up the stream to merge with Sanno's soldiers, so that the extreme northern end of the village was not enveloped by the command.[53] "The fighting at the stream was desperate," reported a participant, "and dead bodies of Indians and whites fell and floated down together."[54] Many of the people took cover in the brush lining the stream; others hid behind the bank of the sharp bend fronting the village and opened a rigorous discharge against the soldiers of Sanno's and Bradley's units as they completed their crossing and mounted the open ground. While many of the villagers fled east and south to escape the onslaught, Logan's soldiers coursed through the stream and turned and leveled their weapons against the people hiding behind the river bank. "Here the greatest slaughter took place," reported Gibbon. Here, too, the gray-haired Logan, with twenty-seven years service in the army and who but recently had lost a daughter and grandchild, died in the rush, a bullet in his head as he admonished his men against shooting noncombatants.[55] Lieutenant (Adjutant) Woodruff recounted that "[Private Philo O.] Hurlburt of K killed the Indian that shot Bradley. Jacobs killed three, [Lieutenants Edward E.] Hardin & [Frederick M. H.] Kendrick one each. I didn't get a chance to kill any of them."[56] Lieutenant Jacobs, armed with two revolvers, reportedly "fought like a lion."

Meanwhile, Captain Sanno was nearly shot by one of his own men, the bullet just grazing his head. In the charge on the village, the soldiers met Nez Perce boys who tried to protect the families by wielding knives against the troops. Sanno used the butt of his rifle to knock the youths out of the way. In similar fashion, Private Charles Alberts of Company A fought his way out of a tipi filled with women and boys who came at him with knives and hatchets. One soldier, apparently stunned by a spent ball, awoke to find a Nez Perce woman dragging him into a lodge, whereupon "he kicked her from him, secured a rifle, and dispatched her."[57] To expose those hiding in the lodges, the soldiers tore at the covers. Others used lariats to pull them over while their comrades waited to shoot at the occupants. A sergeant remembered seeing a dead woman, her eyes staring vacantly while a living infant lay astride her, painfully flailing its gun-shattered arm. The same man described people jumping into the stream beneath robes or blankets and trying to get away. "As soon as we discovered this trick we only had to notice where the blanket or buffalo hide was slightly raised, and a bullet at that spot would be sufficient for the body to float down the stream."[58] When Gibbon crossed the stream at the upper end of the camp from his position on the hillside, he encountered three women, one with a baby, hidden behind bushes in the water. "As I passed along one of them made me a salutation with her hand, as if to claim my protection. I tried to explain to her that she was safe, and beckoned her to come out, but none of them moved."[59] Twenty minutes after the initial attack, the soldiers held the village and began to destroy it.

Nez Perce accounts of the struggle in the village describe it as one of almost indiscriminate slaughter on the part of the soldiers. The Nee-Me-Poo had camped here in the Big Hole Basin on the evening of August 7 on the recommendation of Looking Glass, despite perceptions of imminent danger on the part of some tribesmen. Apparently, too, some of the people had spotted Bradley's men scouting the camp. There had occurred heated discussions about what to do, but nothing was done to improve their security, a dereliction that proved tragic. The site was a traditional camping place, known as Iskumtselalik Pah (Place of the Buffalo Calf), and the tribesmen set to work cutting and preparing lodgepoles to take with them to the plains.[60] They were also hunting and preparing camas. The night before the attack, the Nee-Me-Poo had held a routine dance until late and were sleeping soundly when Gibbon struck them. Accordingly, many noncombatants were killed during the tumult of the opening volleys directed on the camp and before they could even arise. White Bird lamented the deaths of five children together in one lodge. And Nee-Me-Poo testimony reveals that an officer shot in the head by a woman in the camp was likely Captain Logan, who had just shot her husband. A volley from the troops shortly felled her.

Nee-Me-Poo narratives of the opening attack reveal poignant, personal incidents that underscore the trauma that affected so many families. Yellow Wolf, who was in a lodge at the lowermost end of the camp, remembered that it "was just about daylight when I heard it—a gun—two guns! . . . I was half sleeping. I lay with eyes closed. Maybe I was dreaming?"[61] Closer to the action was Husis Owyeen (Wounded Head), who recollected:

> The bullets came like hail on the tepee and the poles. Quickly I lay flat to the ground. The guns now continued, and after a short while I thought it my time to get up and fight instead of waiting for the bullets to cease. Getting up, I took my gun and ammunition belt, and stepped out the doorway. I ran up the creek. . . . I met a friend of mine who was wounded, shot above the stomach. I crossed into the tepee and sat down with him, then came out a moment later, going across the creek. I climbed the bank, on the lower side, to join in the battle.[62]

A youth, Young White Bird, aged nine or ten, fled with his mother to the stream and raced into the water, both of them wounded. "Five of us were there, and two more came," he remembered. "One little girl was shot through the under part of her upper arm. She held the arm up from the cold water, it hurt so. It was a big bullet hole. I could see through it."[63] Like many others, Yellow Wolf rushed to where the fighting was going on. "These soldiers came on rapidly," he said. "They mixed up part of our village. I now saw tepees on fire. I grew hot with anger. Women, children, and old men who could not fight were in those tepees."[64] The warrior, Kawownonilpilp, described his role in the fighting in the village:

> I saw the . . . warrior who had called the people from the tepees [when the attack began], not far away, crouching low with his rifle. I went to him, dropping close to the ground beside him. In about three minutes, I saw a soldier come around the tepee I had just left. He fired at us, but missed both of us. The warrior, having the gun, shot and killed the soldier instantly. In a few moments a second soldier came from behind the tepee—the same way—firing at us. The warrior killed this soldier also. There were two soldiers going around the tepees—passing on either side—thus circling them. One of them came only a few feet from us and fired quickly. He missed, and the Indian shot, the bullet striking somewhere on his head, knocked the soldier down. He fell, pitching towards us. The soldier's partner, coming around from the other side of the tepee, shot the Indian through the arm. Four other soldiers now came from behind the same tepee. One of them fired and shot my friend, shot him squarely through the breast.[65]

Significantly, as the shooting escalated, the Nez Perces' horse herds that were scattered over the hillside above the camp began collecting "like frightened sheep" and moved off, soon accompanied by mounted warriors, so that the infantrymen and volunteers would never seize the animals. Moreover, it was soon evident that the Nez Perces were not about to give up. Many turned back and took positions behind distant trees and ridges, some in the rear of the command. Their gunfire joined that of warriors still ensconced behind the riverbank against the soldiers engaged in burning the lodges, compelling the officers to first direct a vigorous response and, when that failed, to withdraw the command from before the blistering Nez Perce counterattack that came from every direction. The warriors' marksmanship was deadly. "At almost every crack of a rifle from the distant hills, some member of the command was sure to fall."[66] Clearly outnumbered, the troops could not hold the camp. "There was so much brush and high bluffs," wrote Woodruff, "that we couldn't occupy all the place at once."[67] Furthermore, many of the tipis, some of canvas and the others of skin, were wet from dew and would not ignite.

About two and one-half hours after the battle began, under the rain of Nez Perce bullets, the soldiers abandoned the village. "We lost a lot of valuable time trying to burn the lodges," opined volunteer captain Catlin. "We soon found we had more important work on hand."[68] Rawn's company, deployed as skirmishers, advanced on the Nez Perces in the brush in front and covered the withdrawal, which was confusing and involved some hand-to-hand combat. With what wounded they could retrieve, the men moved back across the stream to the foot of the hill where they had started their assault, then hiked upstream through the willow thickets, driving villagers before them, and began entrenching behind trees and fallen timber on the wooded point they had passed during the night. The point, in fact, constituted an alluvial fan created by a wash emanating from the hill directly west. Some of the men began to run, and it was possibly at this point that Gibbon, who was among them, cried out, "Don't run, men, or I will stay right here alone," at which order was restored. First Lieutenant Charles A. Coolidge was shot through both thighs during the withdrawal (and was later wounded again). Rawn's men, facing the camp, then gradually withdrew to the point themselves. The selected defense site was about one-half mile west of the south end of the village. The warriors followed, taking up position in the timber and bushes above and below, and kept up a withering, unremitting fire on the soldiers, wounding several. It was during this exchange that Gibbon, his horse killed, received a flesh wound in the leg. Adjutant Woodruff was wounded in the heel and both legs. First Lieutenant William L. English was also hit, and his injuries later proved mortal.

It was White Bird and Looking Glass who rallied the warriors into turning about, facing the troops, and driving them back from the village. Incensed at the attack, Looking Glass reportedly called to Shore Crossing, Red Moccasin Top, and Swan Necklace, three of the instigators of the outbreak: "This is battle! These men are not asleep as were those you murdered in Idaho! . . . Now is the time to show your courage and fight[!]"[69] During the movement of the soldiers and citizens from the village, a group of warriors located near the upper end of the camp took deadly aim at the soldiers in retreat, felling many and later recovering their rifles and cartridge belts. As the soldiers withdrew through the willow thickets, the warrior Grizzly Bear Youth got into a hand-to-hand fray with a volunteer who nearly killed him. Another warrior shot and killed the citizen, the bullet breaking Grizzly Bear Youth's arm as it passed through.

As the command took position, the howitzer belched forth two rounds above and southwest of Gibbon's defensive position, having approached and ascended the hillside with its crew to open against the villagers. With the gun came the pack mule bearing the extra ammunition that Gibbon had directed be sent. The warriors presently subdued the gun detachment following a rigorous engagement in which one man (Corporal Robert E. Sale) was killed, two were wounded, and two more fled. The driver, momentarily pinned under a dead horse during the fight for the gun, eventually freed himself; all the surviving soldiers succeeded in making their way back to the wagon train. Nez Perce accounts indicate that one warrior who arrived on the scene after the gun was dismounted lamented its loss, since he had learned how to fire the piece during past army campaigns against the Yakimas and Cayuses. Yellow Wolf and Peopeo Tholekt together identified the Nez Perces involved in this incident as themselves, Old Yellow Wolf, Weyatanatoo Latpat (Sun Tied), Pitpillooheen (Calf of Leg), and Ketalkpoosmin (Stripes Turned Down). And Peopeo Tholekt, who wanted to turn the piece against the soldiers, gave the name of another man—Temettiki—as involved in the capture of the gun. Stated Peopeo Tholekt: "They . . . left me with the cannon. I tried to drag the wagon [carriage] along, but soon got stuck on a rock. I then unscrewed the wheels, taking them off the spindles. I took the gun from its resting, rolled it down a steep bluff, where I buried [hid?] it."[70]

Through the balance of the day the command was pinned down by the intermittent harassing gunfire. The hillsides north and west, as well as the willow thickets and timber to the east, provided ample cover for the warriors who sent scores of rounds into the defenses. Officers positioned the troops to best advantage and counseled the men to use restraint in their firing, for ammunition had begun to run low. Even Gibbon took an active part in the defense, firing at the warriors with his hunting rifle. When a westerly breeze arose, the Nez Perces ignited the brush in an effort to smoke them out. The troops feared that they might suffocate or that warriors would charge on them, occasioning much suspense and eliciting prayers from both officers and men. Lieutenant Woodruff told his wife: "Some of the wounded covered their heads and expected to be killed."[71] But the grass was too green to catch fire and the wind changed and the attempt failed. Later, amid moans and wails of grief emanating from the village, the soldiers heard Nez Perce leaders exhorting the warriors, and late in the afternoon they watched and listened as the tribesmen began dismantling their tipis and packing, and with their horses started south, leaving the warriors to deal with Gibbon's refuged force. Nee-Me-Poo accounts mention that the soldiers and volunteers suffered greatly from their wounds and from their famished and thirsty condition. Peopeo Tholekt and Yellow Wolf remembered hearing their crying from the entrenchments during the day and into the night.

During the night, several men crawled to the river for water, filling numerous canteens and returning despite the fire of Nez Perce sharpshooters who—undeterred by the darkness—succeeded in killing at least one volunteer. The others labored to raise breastworks, some of the soldiers employing their trowel bayonets to effect, while across the stream the Nez Perces found and killed some of the wounded who had been left behind. "It seemed as if daylight would never come," penned Lieutenant Woodruff.

> The nights are cold in the mountains, even in summer; the men have no covering; their clothes have been soaked in crossing and recrossing the river. More than one-third of the command are killed and wounded; they have no medical attendance, and some of the wounded suffer intensely and their groans are very trying.[72]

With ammunition becoming a critical factor, Gibbon sent runners through the dark to find the train. Others departed for Deer Lodge with messages requesting supplies and medical help. Toward dawn, Sergeant Oliver Sutherland of Company B, First Cavalry, managed to gain the defenses, bringing to the beleaguered men welcome news that Howard was on his way. Sutherland had left Howard at the hot springs as his force struggled over the Lolo trail. Some of the volunteers disagreed with Gibbon's management of the situation and set off on their own, somehow eluding the warriors. The Nez Perces kept up their sporadic shooting, but it was clear from their activity that the major fighting was over and they were moving out, leaving but a few warriors to continue harassing the command. By the next morning they were gone.[73]

Gibbon's fears that his train had been captured proved false, and on August 10, although small parties of warriors still hovered in the distance, the colonel sent Captain George L. Browning and twenty-five men to usher it forward while his famished soldiers, their rations having been soaked in their haversacks while crossing the river, carved flesh from Woodruff's dead horse (without salt or fire, however, many "preferred to remain hungry"). Gibbon meantime sent a fan of skirmishers up the slope to determine the fate of the howitzer crew. The Nez Perces had not only disabled the howitzer, but also made off with the gun implements and dispersed the shells after killing the mules. More important, they captured the two thousand-round ammunition supply on its way to Gibbon. Army losses at the Big Hole aggregated twenty-nine (two officers, twenty-one enlisted men, and six citizens) killed and forty (five officers, thirty-one enlisted men, and four citizens) wounded, with two men dying later of their injuries, an exceedingly high casualty rate for an Indian battle and ample testimony of the Nez Perces' resolve and fighting abilities. On the other hand, the Nez Perces themselves apparently endured substantial losses. Gibbon claimed they lost at least eighty-nine killed and with an unknown number of wounded. Later Nee-Me-Poo testimony offered various figures ranging between forty-five and one hundred killed and wounded, although most accounts stress the disproportionate number of women and children among the dead. Young Horace Mulkey said that he counted seventy dead Indians on the field. Nez Perce casualties probably stood at between sixty and ninety killed, with many wounded who expired on the march over the next days or weeks. Regardless, among the dead were prominent Nez Perce fighting men Shore Crossing, Red Moccasin Top, Five Wounds, and Rainbow, and the Palouse leader, Hahtalekin. Practically every Nee-Me-Poo family endured a loss at the Big Hole. The bloodshed had come at the hands of not only Gibbon's troops—which the tribesmen, having left Rawn's soldiers behind without a fight, had not anticipated—but of the Bitterroot settlers, with whom they had an agreement and had but recently transacted business, and that violation of trust contributed to the shock they felt and likely accounted for some of their subsequent actions.[74]

On Saturday, August 11, Gibbon buried his dead. At 10:00 A.M., General Howard with a small escort reached the stricken command.[75] Since detaching himself and Major Sanford's cavalry from the rest of his column on the Lolo trail on the fifth at word from Gibbon, Howard had doggedly pushed on through the Bitterroot, his infantry and artillery complement following in wagons two days behind. At Corvallis on the ninth, he learned that the Nez Perces, followed by Gibbon, had gone through just a few days earlier, and next morning he pressed on hurriedly with his escort of twenty cavalrymen and seventeen Bannock scouts, making fifty-three miles. Nightfall found them just eighteen miles from the battleground where some of the departed volunteers met them with news of the battle and Gibbon's besieged situation. By the time Howard reached the site next morning to exultant cheers of men bathing in the stream, the Nez Perces, aware of his approach, had completely withdrawn. Medical help in the form of Surgeon Charles T. Alexander and Assistant Surgeon FitzGerald, escorted by twenty cavalry, arrived at 6:00 A.M., August 12, and immediately went to work. Major Mason and the remaining cavalry came in that afternoon.[76]

If it had profound meaning, the Battle of the Big Hole served to let the Nez Perces know that their transgressions in Idaho had not been forgotten, despite their relative ease in passing by the troops in Lolo Canyon and their smooth passage up the Bitterroot Valley. It also jolted them physically in the loss of so many of their people and resources, and the repercussions would prove long lasting and probably insurmountable, despite their moral resolve to continue. Big Hole unequivocally played a role in the Nez Perces' subsequent group behavior, too, as the frustration level rose to extended heights needing release. For the army, the bloody confrontation that Sheridan termed "one of the most desperate engagements on record"—which militarily has to be classified as a draw at best—did not achieve its anticipated objective of stopping the tribesmen and ending the conflict, although it did partially atone for the embarrassing loss at White Bird Canyon. (As a military operation, Big Hole represented one of the rare instances—and certainly the most dramatic—in the history of trans-Mississippi Indian warfare that infantry troops—i.e., a dismounted force—acting alone accosted an Indian village in a maneuver usually left to the mobility of cavalry to perform.) For the moment, Big Hole became caught up in the romantic fervor that governed media attention of military events in the late nineteenth century. "That the price of victory was paid in the loss of nearly half of the attacking party, makes the victory itself all the more precious," editorialized the *Army and Navy Journal*, "and we trust that Congress will reward every man that fought at the Big Hole battle for his heroism."[77] And as forthcoming kudos and medals proved, the army was as adept at rationalizing its errors as government policy as a whole was in creating an atmosphere in which they could occur. Nonetheless, six enlisted men received Medals of Honor for their performances at the Big Hole; six more garnered Certificates of Merit. And in 1890 fourteen officers, including Gibbon and the deceased Bradley, Logan, and English, won brevet promotions for their gallant service at the Big Hole.[78]

Camas Meadows

COLONEL JOHN GIBBON's active involvement in the Nez Perce conflict was largely finished after his bloody confrontation with the tribesmen at the Big Hole. All day long on August 12, his wounded men received treatment from Howard's medical officers while the Bannock scouts who accompanied the general's advance showed their disdain for the fallen Nez Perces by digging up and desecrating the bodies buried beneath a collapsed river bank. On the thirteenth, Gibbon departed for Deer Lodge, ninety miles away, the nearest place where the injured of his command, drawn forward in travois, could obtain extended medical care. Before leaving, he assigned fifty men under Captain Browning, First Lieutenant George H. Wright, and Second Lieutenant John T. Van Orsdale to continue the pursuit with Howard in wagons as far as Bannack City, sixty miles away. Gibbon reached Deer Lodge in two days, followed by the balance of his men on August 16.[1]

Howard's cavalry pulled out on the Nez Perces' trail on the thirteenth. Most of his infantry and artillery, following behind, camped near the battlefield on August 14 and continued after Howard the next day, although fifty men comprised of Batteries A and E of the artillery under Lieutenant Humphrey and Company H, Eighth Infantry, under Captain Daniel T. Wells, rolled forward in wagons and reached the general's bivouac on the evening of the thirteenth, twenty-three miles from the battleground.[2] Major Mason, in a letter to his wife, explained what was doubtless Howard's thought on pressing the chase:

> I think a few days will determine whether we will pursue the hos-
> tiles further. If they go east after passing Bannack City or go over
> the old Mormon Road and down past the Salmon River and thus
> sweep around through Pleasant Valley—between Market Lake and
> Henry Lake [west of present Yellowstone National Park]—we will
> send word by telegraph to General McDowell that having chased
> the Indians through the Dept. of the Dakota, into the Dept. of the
> Platte, we will give up the chase—as the Indians are in General
> Crook's Dept.—who is so well able to take care of them.[3]

At his camp of the thirteenth, Howard received word via couriers from Bannack that the Nez Perces had killed some citizens on Horse Prairie Creek and were likely on their way back into Idaho, having passed farther to the west than Howard had supposed they would. The news made Howard think that the tribesmen perhaps intended to head back to the Snake River country in his department, where he might combine with Major Green to close on them. If they, however, contin-ued east, Howard—citing his "extraordinary marches"—questioned the advisability of pursuing "unless General Terry or General Crook will head them off and check their advance. . . . Without this cooperation," he notified McDowell, "the result will be, as it has been, doubtful."[4] Nonetheless, Howard sent word to Captain Miller, with the balance of the command, hoping "that you will be able to overtake us before we become engaged with the enemy."[5]

In fact, after leaving the carnage of the Big Hole, the Nez Perces had traveled slowly over long days to put as much territory as possible between them and Howard's troops. It was a difficult journey, the people saddened by their losses in the fighting as well as the deaths of many wounded along the trail. Their route, evidently in no way modi-fied because of their recent confrontation with the soldiers,[6] took them up the Big Hole River, southwesterly and west of the present commu-nities of Wisdom and Jackson, and within ten or twelve miles of Bannack City. They crossed Bloody Dick Creek and Horse Prairie Creek, camping at the west edge of Horse Prairie, traditionally famil-iar to the Nez Perces, and historically the site where Lewis and Clark acquired horses from the Shoshones in 1805. As the Indian vanguard appeared in their country, many white settlers in their path fled for safety into Bannack City.[7]

On the evening of August 12, in a post–Big Hole rage reminiscent of the initial outbreak and evidently aimed at all manifestations of white culture, some warriors attacked a ranch owned by Messrs. W. L. Montague and Daniel Winters where several families resided, the women and children having been evacuated to Bannack. Killing Montague and Thomas Flynn in the house, the warriors ransacked the place and shot to death two more men, James Farnsworth and James Smith, working in a field. Daniel Winters and two men escaped by hiding and fleeing, and they eventually reached Bannack. Five miles farther the warriors surprised four men, John Wagoner, Andrew Meyers, Alexander Cooper, and a Mr. Howard near a ranch, killing Cooper while the others managed to escape to some willows and hide until the Nez Perces left. Of course, at both places the raiders took horses, too, apparently totaling about forty. They also pilfered and destroyed the ranch of John and Thomas Pierce in the area.[8]

Leaving Horse Prairie on August 13—the same morning that Howard was leaving the Big Hole battlefield, approximately two days' march behind them—the Nez Perces dropped south and crossed the Continental Divide through Bannock Pass, reentering Idaho Territory not far from the Lemhi Indian Reservation and briefly passing along the bottom of the Lemhi, a branch of Salmon River that separated Montana's Bitterroot Range from Idaho's Lemhi Range.[9] Whereas, before the Big Hole encounter with the soldiers, by common consent Looking Glass's regulation had prevailed, that disaster resulted in his subordination as far as the daily marches were concerned. By mutual consent of the band leaders, general direction of the caravan devolved on Poker Joe, who had joined the people near Stevensville in the Bitterroot and who was recognized for his familiarity with the region the tribesmen would traverse in gaining the plains. As the warrior Wottolen said, Poker Joe "would have the people up early in the morning, and travel till about ten o'clock. Then he ordered a stop and cooking was done while the horses filled up on grass. About two o'clock he would travel again. Kept going until about ten o'clock at night."[10] Looking Glass, especially regarded for his military acumen, maintained the people's confidence in that discipline but was likely chagrined at his subordination after Big Hole. Probably, too, Ollokot gained in prestige for his military experience in the wake of Big Hole, while Joseph, known for his diplomacy, continued his oversight of the Wallowas and the nonmilitary aspects of the overall train. While their hierarchical marching system probably remained the same as before, with scouts well out ahead of the column, the primary leaders in front, followed by secondary leaders, common men, women and children with the baggage, and finally the driven horse herd, after Big Hole the marching and camping followed a strict regimen that ensured awareness of all around them.[11]

Settlers in the Lemhi Valley anticipated the Nez Perces' arrival and built two stockades (one at Salmon City and one at Junction) to protect themselves. Nor were the local Indians, Lemhi Shoshones under the leadership of Chief Tendoy, receptive to their age-old adversaries. After pausing several hours near Junction at the mouth of Timber Creek, during which they assured the settlers of their peaceful enterprise, the tribesmen proceeded east a short distance to camp in the mouth of a canyon where they killed some cattle and readied rifle pits in their newfound security-consciousness.[12] Next day, the Nez Perces turned up the Lemhi Valley on the old Mormon Road and passed southeast over to Birch Creek Valley, a monotonous gravelly plain bordering a tributary of the Snake River. On Wednesday, August 15, along Birch Creek, sixty miles from Junction, a group of warriors attacked a horse-and-mule-drawn freight train, killing five men—James Hayden, Albert Green, Daniel Combs, all of Salmon City, and two unidentified men (a man named Albert Lyon escaped through the creek)— and burning three wagons and three trailers loaded with general merchandise, including canned goods, crockery, window glass and sash, and whiskey, en route from the Union Pacific Railroad transfer point at Corrine, Utah Territory, to Salmon City and Leesburg, Idaho Territory. Two Chinese cooks rode with the train. One of them, Charles Go Hing, later testified about the raid as follows:

> We camped for dinner about noon on Birch Creek, had finished dinner and were lying under the wagons when we heard the clatter of horses' feet, looked up and saw a party of armed and mounted Indians advancing towards us at a gallop. The men all started for the wagons to get their guns, but before they could get them the Indians had surrounded us and leveled their guns and commanded us to surrender, which we did. I counted them and there were 56 of them, all well-armed and mounted. . . . The Indians after eating made us hitch up the teams and drive up to their main camp about a

mile away, where they made us go into camp. The men started with some Indians to drive the animals out to feed. I never saw any of them again. The other Indians broke into the wagons and helped themselves to goods. The Indians said they were Nez Perces and belonged to Joseph's band.[13]

As the warriors celebrated, the cooks managed to get away in the night and made their way to Junction. The forty animals from the train were absorbed into the Nez Perces' herd. On the night of August 16, Tendoy and some fifteen of his Lemhi warriors caught up with the Nez Perces and in the darkness ran off seventy-five of their stock, some of which had been taken in the Horse Prairie raid. Next day, a party headed by Colonel George L. Shoup of the local Idaho volunteers (later first governor of the state of Idaho and U.S. senator, 1890–1901) arrived at the scene of the smoldering train and buried the dead.[14]

From Birch Creek, the Nez Perces began moving easterly, skirting the foothills of the Rocky Mountains and crossing Medicine Lodge Creek and Beaver Creek to reach an area twenty-five miles south of Pleasant Valley below the Montana line. Here, on August 16 and 17, they crossed the Corrine Road a few miles north of present Dubois, stopping to gather in their scattered stock and taking over the Hole-in-the-Rock Stage Station, disrupting travel on the road, and destroying the telegraph lines. Word of their presence threw a brief scare into the residents of Virginia City, Montana, sixty miles away. One man in the vicinity of the road reported seeing dust "on the trail direct to the south fork of Snake River, and which leads to the head of Wind River valley" in Wyoming. But the tribesmen, in fact, continued gradually northeast to Henry's Fork of the Snake River, then on toward Henry's Lake, hugging the boundary between the territories just west of the national park.[15]

All the while the Nez Perces were skirting the Rockies, General Howard—convinced that they "were only deviating to blind our pursuit" while resupplying their cavalcade—marched his men east and south, intent on heading them off before they reached the stage road or, at worst, Henry's Lake. On the fourteenth, with his primary infantry complement trailing two days behind in wagons, the general and his available force traveled twenty-five miles amid further word of the attack on the Horse Prairie settlers. Next morning, Howard and his men passed by Bannack City to an ovation of the townspeople, who were relieved at the presence of the troops. "Gen. Howard was the great attraction," wrote Major Mason. "We camped [on Horse Prairie Creek] about 12 miles beyond the town, but the people filled our camp all afternoon, all full of advice as to what should be done, and giving their opinions in an offensive manner."[16] While Howard collected provisions in Bannack, a message from Colonel Shoup alerted him to the presence of the Nez Perces in the Lemhi Valley and decided him on his course to intercept them near the stage road from Corrine. "We have the inside track and are very hopeful of taking them on the hip," wrote Mason.[17] Learning of the attack on the freight train at Birch Creek, Howard on the sixteenth pushed forward, momentarily bolstered by the presence of two volunteer companies from Deer Lodge that peremptorily returned home after a too-brief scouting foray.[18] He dispatched a courier to Miller, telling him to pick up two weeks' supply of provisions at Bannack. "You must not obtain more supplies than the pack train can carry, [f]or we may be obliged to drop the wagons at any point."[19] Miller's battalion, tired and weary from the constant pursuit, had trouble keeping together on the trail, and many rode in the wagons. As driver Henry Buck recalled, "My duty mostly was to pick up and haul foot-sore and worn out soldiers as we traveled along. I usually started out empty, but by camp time—say twelve or one o'clock—I would have all the men that could get into the wagon."[20]

On August 17, after detaching Captain Browning's Seventh infantrymen to go on to Deer Lodge and then on to their home station at Missoula, Howard traveled to Junction Station. That night he sent forty cavalrymen under First Lieutenant George R. Bacon, together with several Bannock scouts under Orlando "Rube" Robbins, to proceed via Red Rock Lake to Raynolds Pass near Henry's Lake, constantly probing the country to their right in an effort to find the Nez Perces. If he encountered them, Bacon was to somehow hinder their approach while sending the information back to Howard.[21] At Junction Station, another contingent of fifty-three Montana volunteers—these from Virginia City and most of them under Captain James E. Callaway—joined along with a mountain howitzer. Some of them, like those from Deer Lodge, took French leave and went home, although Callaway and about forty stayed with the troops. (The howitzer was left at Pleasant Valley, and Callaway's men never reached Howard until he stopped at Camas Meadows.) Scouting ahead of the cavalry, Howard also learned of the sightings of the Nez Perces farther south on the stage road, and he sent several citizen scouts forward to Pleasant Valley, just below the Montana line, to more precisely assess their whereabouts.[22]

On the morning of August 18, Company L, Second Cavalry, under the command of Captain Randolph Norwood, joined Howard's force. Norwood had started from the Tongue River Cantonment on the lower Yellowstone River on July 18 as escort to Commanding General Sherman, who was set to visit the national park, but at Fort Ellis, Sherman had sent Norwood's unit—fifty-nine men—forward to aid Howard in the prosecution of the Nez Perces. Norwood's horses were tired, but offered a striking contrast to the condition of Howard's own depleted animals. Because of Sanford's need to graze and rest his horses, Howard allowed the major to remain in bivouac that morning while he moved on to Pleasant Valley.

Late that evening, the cavalry having rejoined Howard, the command camped at Dry Creek Station, eight miles below Pleasant Valley on the stage road, from which point "the best possible road" led east to Henry's Lake. Here First Lieutenant Henry M. Benson, Seventh Infantry, joined the troops. He had been sent from Deer Lodge by Gibbon to work with the volunteers, but because most of them had returned home, Howard attached Benson to Norwood's cavalry company. That evening scouts brought information that the Nez Perces were encamped at Camas Meadows, eighteen miles east. Howard, after consulting his officers, determined that his weary cavalry mounts could not undergo a night march and went into camp.

On Sunday, the nineteenth, the command started east and shortly encountered the broad trail of the Nez Perces—"fifty to one hundred and fifty feet wide, and the vegetation . . . almost entirely obliterated by the tramping of their several hundred ponies and the dragging of scores of travois poles."[23] Along the way, the soldiers saw fresh graves, apparently those of more Big Hole wounded. A Second Cavalry sergeant reported seeing "numbers of conical piles of pony droppings, evidently built by hand," which the Bannocks said had been fashioned by youths to show their contempt for the troops. Reports from Howard's scouts suggested that the tribesmen were headed for the Wind River plains in Wyoming, and "miles and miles away" the soldiers could see the dust of their caravan.[24]

As the army trailed east they passed along the broad country geologically termed the eastern Snake River Plain. In many ways identical to the land the Nez Perces had passed through in the Lemhi Valley, the eastern plain presented an incongruous mix of desert and intermittent wetland trending northeast practically all the way to the Wyoming line. Bounded on the north by the Centennial Range of the Rockies, the zone traversed by the Nez Perces and the army in 1877 was marked by residue in the form of basalt-lava flow outcroppings left from volcanic upheavals that occurred more than one-half million years earlier. Camas Meadows, a low and lush grassy area punctuating the basalt fields, is named for the plant whose blue flowers blanket the country each spring. Camas Meadows is watered by a network of streams converging varicosely from the northwest, north, and northeast into two major courses, Camas Creek and Spring Creek (the latter an affluent of Camas Creek, which is westernmost of the two). The two creeks begin to roughly parallel each other approximately two and one-half miles south of the present community of Kilgore, Idaho. The main channels of these streams are generally separated by about one-half mile, although minor tributaries of each transect the intervening ground, creating a boggy condition that is present part of the year, but in August is mostly dry. One southwardly flowing intermittent tributary of Spring Creek appears on early maps as "Camas Creek," and was apparently so designated in 1877. Several miles farther south, Spring Creek and what was then Camas Creek converge, with Camas Creek continuing on to join Mud Lake forty miles southwest. Camas Meadows encompasses an area approximately five miles east-to-west at its widest point, and ten miles from north to south. Today it is bordered on its east, north, and west by parts of the Targhee National Forest.[25]

Into this region Howard's fatigued troops marched eighteen miles from the stage road, establishing their bivouac of August 19 along the high ground fringing the bottom of Spring Creek, on the east side of Camas Meadows. Howard described the camp as follows:

> [It was] a very strong natural position on the first elevated ground which overlooks the meadows toward the west and some lava-beds toward the north and east. The cavalry [apparently excepting Norwood's company—see below] was posted in line of battle covering the camp; the infantry in reserve near the creek, and great pains taken by my inspector, Maj. E. C. Mason, Twenty-first Infantry, to cover the camp with pickets in every direction. Before night every animal was brought within, the horses tied to the picket-ropes, the

animals with the few wagons, to their wagons, and the bell-mares of
the pack-trains were hobbled. Captain [James A.] Calloway's [sic]
volunteers came up and encamped about one hundred yards from
me, across a creek. They are between two streams of water whose
banks were fringed by thickets of willows.[26]

In a reminiscence published four years later, Howard provided additional particulars of the site:

> We took for the centre of our night camp one of these [lava] knolls
> which was near to the meadow bottom. From my tent I looked back
> [west] to the parallel streams. Across the first one, the Calloway
> [sic] volunteers encamped. Norwood's Cavalry and the forty infan-
> try occupied the west side [of the then Camas Creek]. The other
> companies of cavalry covered all approaches to my own, the central
> position, which was upon a comparatively high lava pile, that, stud-
> ded with bushes, constituted our castle-like defence.[27]

As depicted in contemporary accounts, including Howard's report,
most of the troops comprising Sanford's cavalry battalion took position
according to their column formation, or "in line of battle," along the
high ground, probably within the roughly defined 150-yard-radius of
high knolls on which Mason and the soldiers raised bulwarks of large

*"Fight at Camas Meadows—Sanford—Aug. 20" represents the scene at Howard's
camp on the morning of August 20, 1877, looking west.*
INSET DRAWING IN FLETCHER, "DEPARTMENT OF COLUMBIA MAP"

pieces of basalt scattered through the area. The infantry, consisting of Humphrey's Fourth artillerymen and Wells's Eighth infantrymen, presumably along with the wagons, occupied the strip of ground immediately west, bordering the east side of Spring Creek. As indicated, Callaway's Montanans set up their camp in the median between Spring Creek and the then Camas Creek, a short distance from where their horses grazed and approximately 100 yards from Howard's bivouac.[28] Immediately west of Callaway, and across the latter stream, Norwood's cavalry guarded the perimeter. The untethered pack mules likewise grazed between the streams; the bell-mares—horses with soft-toned bells strapped to their necks to which the pack animals responded—were hobbled to keep the mules from wandering off in the night. "Gen. Howard placed a line of pickets outside of the herd [of mules], along the northwest and west sides of the meadow."[29] Meanwhile, Sanford's horses, probably also left to graze for a time between the streams, were by nightfall within the infantry line east of Spring Creek and tied to a picket rope, while the wagon teams were tied to their vehicles.[30] The Camas Meadows site, with its lush grazing and trout-laden streams, rewarded both men and animals. "With only a small portion of the men fishing, enough were taken to feed the entire command," remembered Sergeant Harry J. Davis.[31]

As Howard and his men settled in for the night, the command numbered slightly more than 260 men, including the Bannock scouts and the Montana volunteers. Of this force, it would be the cavalry that would play the most important part in the forthcoming action with the Nez Perces. The commander, thirty-five-year-old Major George B. Sanford (1842–1908), had served with the First and Second Dragoons in the West during the opening months of the Civil War, and had later campaigned with Grant and Sheridan in the eastern theater. Most of his subsequent service had been in the trans-Mississippi West. Captain James Jackson, who had joined Howard near the end of the Clearwater battle, had risen from the enlisted ranks during the Civil War, as had First Lieutenant John Q. Adams, veteran most recently of the Modoc conflict in California. Both Captain Camillus C. Carr and First Lieutenant Charles C. Cresson had also advanced from the ranks, but Carr had spent his entire military service in the First Cavalry. Lieutenant Benson, a veteran of the California volunteers, joined the regulars in 1866 and transferred to the Seventh Infantry three years later.[32]

But it was Captain Randolph Norwood's Company L, Second Cavalry, that would see the most action at Camas Meadows. Norwood (1834–1901) was from Maryland and served in that state's volunteer cavalry during the Civil War in the Shenandoah Valley and at Petersburg, Virginia. He joined the Second Cavalry in 1866. After serving in the West for several years, Norwood went on recruiting duty and after that managed an extended sick leave, first to his home in Baltimore and then, during the summer of 1875, to Europe. In 1876, a citizen wrote the Secretary of War that Norwood "has been loafing around our streets for over 2 years," and an army retirement board found "no disqualification for active service" and urged that Norwood rejoin his command. The captain arrived back in Montana in time to participate in the closing operations of the Great Sioux War, including the fight with Lame Deer's Sioux at Muddy Creek in May, 1877.[33]

During the hours before nightfall, August 19, a few tribesmen appeared in the distance, but such sightings were routine and thus given little consideration. In camp, some of the men crawled under the wagons to sleep, while others pitched shelter tents. Feeling secure for the first time in several weeks, many troops undressed before going to bed. The night was occasionally rainy, and clouds partly obscured the moon.[34] Apparently some Nez Perce warriors had stolen among the pack animals, either cutting the hobbles or the bell-straps on the bell-mares, and at around 3:30 A.M.,[35] after the moon had set and in the predawn darkness of August 20, a column of horsemen (according to Howard's report) approached the picket line from the north, above the area of the Montanans' camp and from the general direction that Lieutenant Bacon was expected on his return from Henry's Lake. When the pickets' challenge went unanswered, the soldiers fired at the column—"three or four shots fired in rapid succession," said one man—and suddenly an attack by Nez Perce warriors opened on the command, with the immediate fire directed against the citizens' camp. It sounded, said one participant, "like the discharge of several Gatling guns."[36] Captain Norwood reported that "the camp was startled and hurriedly aroused by a volley or heavy discharge of fire arms and loud yelling and whooping from [the] hostile Indians."[37] The warriors rushed into the area between the streams, startling and stampeding most of the volunteers' horses, as well as all the neighboring pack mules, and attempting to drive off the cavalry mounts. Recounted a volunteer:

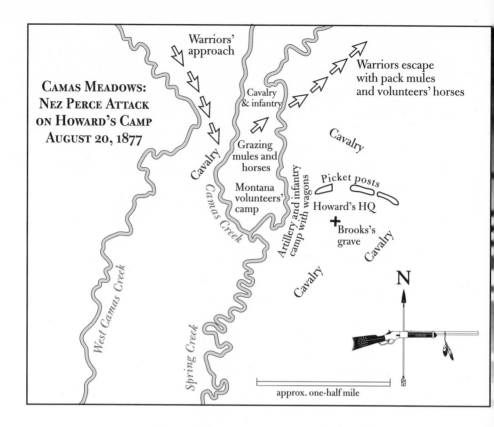

CAMAS MEADOWS:
NEZ PERCE ATTACK
ON HOWARD'S CAMP
AUGUST 20, 1877

Warriors'
approach

Warriors escape
with pack mules
and volunteers' horses

Cavalry
& infantry

Cavalry

Grazing
mules and
horses

Montana
volunteers'
camp

Artillery and infantry
camp with wagons

Picket posts

Howard's HQ

Brooks's
grave

Cavalry

Cavalry

Cavalry

Cavalry

Camas Creek

West Camas Creek

Spring Creek

N

approx. one-half mile

Fortunately for the citizens, the camp was pitched on low ground, and the Indians overshot them, and although the bullets flew like hail around them, no damage was done by the fire beyond the killing of a horse and slight abrasions inflicted upon two of the party by spent balls. The Indians gathered up stock from all parts of both camps, and posted a line of about twenty-five men in front of the citizens' camp, within fifty yards of the wagons, and kept up their terrific fire at that distance, while the remainder of the raiders . . . were driving the animals across the creek and into the open country beyond.[38]

In the initial tumult, some volunteers took to the icy creeks for protection, while others scrambled to reach the regulars across Spring Creek. A reminiscent account stated that two of the citizens "made a bee line for Gen. Howard's tent, crying at the top of their voices every time they hit the ground: 'White men [!] Don't shoot [!]'"[39] Amid the gunfire and confusion, the soldiers raced from the shelter tents on hands and knees, quickly dressed, and rushed to meet the warriors.[40] "Every-one was out in a minute," recalled an enlisted man, "and all we could

see was a magnified imitation of a swarm of fireflies flitting in the al-
ders, as the rifles spoke; while the trampling of hundreds of hoofs added
to the din."[41] Most of the soldiers dashed for the willow thickets bordering Spring Creek, "and in less than two minutes from the com-
mencement of the firing, not half a dozen men were left upon the
camp-ground."[42] Because of the darkness, and because the citizens' camp
lay directly across the stream from the regulars, the soldiers withheld
their fire, although their presence along the line of Spring Creek prevented the warriors from driving off the cavalry horses and the wagon
mules. Yet they made off with 150 pack mules and most of the volunteers' horses in the strike. "Sweeping around our camp," penned correspondent Sutherland, "could be distinguished a herd of stampeded
horses and mules, galloping at their highest possible speed, with a considerable band of Indians behind them goading them on with loud cries,
and discharge of rifles."[43] "Except [for] the noise we were making ourselves, nothing could be heard but receding hoofbeats and faint yells."[44]
Then they were gone, apparently heading northeast from the camp,
leaving the command bewildered and in suspense in the half hour of
darkness left before dawn. Despite all the shooting, only the two citizens and one soldier were slightly wounded.[45]

Nee-Me-Poo accounts of the raid on Howard's camp at Kamisnim
Takin (Camas Meadows) all agree that Looking Glass played the primary role in orchestrating and overseeing the event. Some informants
suggested that the notion for the attack stemmed from a vision experienced by Grizzly Bear Youth or Black Hair, or perhaps both men.[46]
Scouts had anticipated Howard's selection of the bivouac (where the
people had camped the previous night) and had reported such to the
Nez Perce leadership. Looking Glass arranged for a group of warriors
to join him in the attempt to capture the animals.[47] Some Nez Perce
recollections indicate that the party numbered 28 warriors, while others
place the figure at 120 or even 225.[48] In the darkness of morning on
August 20, however, the raiders were unaware of the presence of the
volunteers' camp and targeted their efforts on what they thought was
the horse herd—in reality the pack mules congregated north of the
citizens' bivouac. "We know American horses are afraid of Indians,"
Looking Glass reportedly said. "Make all the noise you possibly can, as
by so doing we may be able to stampede the whole herd at once." And
that was exactly what was done, although the warriors were surprised

to discover later that they had captured mules instead of horses. (Whereas the obvious objective of the Nee-Me-Poo men was to get horses and complicate Howard's pursuit, the presence of the hated Bannocks among the troops probably provided yet another incentive.[49]) The Nez Perce Yellow Wolf was one who went among the animals and cut some loose. He and others discounted the notion that the warriors approached in column formation as reported by Howard. They said that they advanced on the soldier camp in two or three parties, and that an individual named Otskai (Going Out) prematurely fired his weapon to start the action.[50] While some of the Nee-Me-Poo desired to uncharacteristically attack the camp on foot, Wottolen stated that the idea was to go among the soldiers, find General Howard, and kill him and his officers, but that plan lost out because the warriors wanted to attack the camp on horseback and, perhaps more importantly, Looking Glass would not allow it. Besides Looking Glass, other leaders and principal warriors present included Ollokot, Toohoolhoolzote, Teeweeyownah (Over the Point), Two Moon, and Espowyes (Light in the Mountain). Despite some Nez Perce accounts that maintain that Joseph was present at Camas Meadows, others—and at least one explicitly—deny his participation.[51]

Informed of the loss of the animals, Howard directed Major Sanford's cavalry to pursue as soon as daylight came and try to retrieve the mules and horses taken in the raid. Two of Sanford's companies rode out shortly, consisting of Companies B (Captain Jackson and Lieutenants Adams and George S. Hoyle) and I (Captain Carr and Lieutenant Cresson), First Cavalry. They were joined by Company L, Second Cavalry (Captain Norwood and Lieutenant Benson), whose horses had pulled up a picket pin in the melee and had milled "'round and 'round and twisted themselves into a grotesque puzzle."[52] Companies C and K of the cavalry battalion remained with Howard and the infantry and volunteers in the Camas Meadows camp and prepared for another possible attack.

At the time that Sanford's cavalry left the bivouac at Camas Meadows, the warriors and the captured animals could be seen four or five miles in the distance, doubtless from the cloud of dust that they raised. According to the account of Sergeant Davis, who was with Norwood, "one company of the 1st Cav. was to make a detour to the right and the other to the left, and our company was to follow the trail."[53] In their pursuit, the cavalrymen managed to close on the warriors, and about three miles

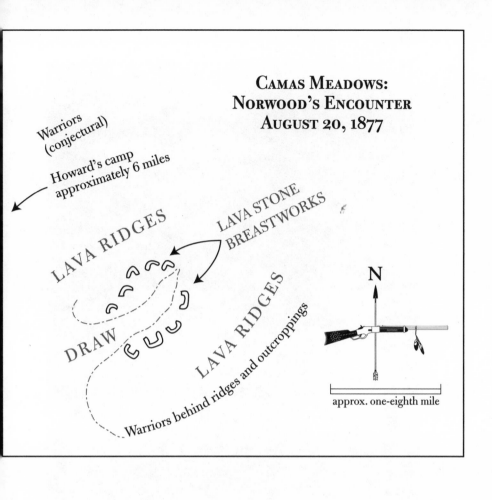

CAMAS MEADOWS:
NORWOOD'S ENCOUNTER
AUGUST 20, 1877

Warriors
(conjectural)

Howard's camp
approximately 6 miles

LAVA RIDGES

LAVA STONE
BREASTWORKS

DRAW

LAVA RIDGES

Warriors behind ridges and outcroppings

N

approx. one-eighth mile

from the bivouac, Norwood's company succeeded in retaking about seventy-five mules and horses, but in the tumult most of the animals again broke away toward the warriors and only twenty-five were reclaimed.[54] Eight miles from the camp, the warriors halted beyond a timbered lava ridge, "the first roll of the foothills," remembered Davis, and when Captain Carr's company appeared ahead of the other units, the warriors opened fire on them from behind rocks, causing them to dismount. Carr and Norwood formed in line to meet the seeming ambush, and Captain Jackson assumed the right next to Norwood, with all number fours going to the rear with the horses. Sergeant Davis said that Norwood's men, crawling up to the brow of the ridge, could see the line of warriors about one thousand yards in the distance. As the shooting became general, the Nez Perces directed a heavy fire against the left of the soldiers' line and began

*Trumpeter Bernard A. Brooks, Company H, First Cavalry, wearing his dress uniform,
ca. 1876. Brooks was killed during the skirmish at Camas Meadows, August 20, 1877.*
COURTESY EILEEN BENNETT

to turn it at that location, causing Sanford to direct his men to fall back after an hour in that position, possibly after Sanford communicated with Howard.[55] Almost simultaneously, the pressure from the warriors increased on the right. Jackson found himself embroiled in a desperate contest with warriors starting to outflank his right. Amid the skirmishing, Jackson's trumpeter, Private Bernard A. Brooks, fell dead, a bullet through his heart, and Jackson, aided by one or two of his men, dismounted from his horse and dashed out and recovered the body.[56]

Soon both Carr and Jackson withdrew their companies, and after twenty minutes Norwood's thirty-five men, too, started in the direction of the horse holders. When Sanford sent his adjutant, Lieutenant Cresson, directing Norwood to retreat, the captain told him that "we had better hold the position." Regardless, Norwood soon found that he could not safely withdraw, so he took up a temporary position on ground slightly higher than the surrounding terrain, planning to take appropriate measures to cover his rear before pulling back.[57] Up to this point, few casualties had occurred on either side, largely because, as Davis explained, "the range was long for our Springfields and longer for their Winchesters."[58] Lieutenant Benson, however, was hit, a bullet penetrating his buttocks. Norwood later declared that had he retired after "the 1st Cavalry . . . company uncovered my [left] flank, . . . my company would have been annihilated."[59]

In his official report, Norwood described his movement as follows:

> I fortunately dismounted my men under cover of a small ridge of lava and deployed them for action. It was a position of great peril or danger; my flanks were exposed by the hurried withdrawal of Captain Carr's company. He having received an order to withdraw, and so did I, but I declined to obey it. If I had obeyed, my company would have been slaughtered.[60]

The exposed location quickly decided Norwood to move farther back in the general direction of Howard's camp to a stand of aspen where the horse holders had gone. At first, the troopers could not see the horses, and they momentarily panicked until a trumpeter blowing "recall" alerted them to their presence. Sergeant Davis explained that

> the race to that thicket was something never to be forgotten, for a cavalryman is not trained for a five hundred yard sprint; luck was with us, however, and no man was hit in that mad race for safety. I

had a horse's nose-bag slung over my shoulder containing extra cartridges, and a bullet cut the strap and let it fall to the ground. A hero
would have stopped, gone back and recovered that bag, but not I.[61]

Norwood reported that the troops withdrew "to the left and rear about
1200 yards."[62] The captain continued:

> I got my men in position very rapid[ly] and informed them to for-
> tify, as I proposed to hold it, which I did . . . [for] four hours. After
> the two companies of the 1st Cavalry under [Brevet] Col. Sanford
> withdrew, the . . . whole fighting force of Indians concentrated on
> my position.[63]

The area occupied by Norwood's command—called the "frying pan"
in some accounts—was located seven miles diagonally northeast from
Howard's camp and approximated ten acres on a slightly elevated series
of lava ridges overlooking the surrounding desert and bisected by a gully
or wash extending north-to-south. Sergeant Davis described it as "a sort
of basin . . . with a rim high enough to protect our horses, and filled with
young cottonwoods in full leaf."[64] Probably the trees that grew in the
gully were aspen, and the company horses were sheltered there while the
soldiers fortified the ridges. There they hastily raised breastworks of loose
pieces of basalt and built them facing in all directions to ward off the Nez
Perce attackers. At least twenty-five such fortifications of varying size,
generally sufficient to contain from one to two (sometimes three) men
each, were thrown up along an irregular perimeter adjoining both sides
of the gulch. Some of the breastworks took advantage of natural declivi-
ties in the terrain, with openings shored up with rocks to protect their
occupants. Some were crescent-, oval-, and horseshoe-shaped and open
at the rear for entrance and exit, while a few were completely enclosed.
Some structures measured about four by five feet; others ran ten feet in
length. While most of the Nez Perce marksmen seemingly remained
behind rock-strewn ridges several hundred yards away, some warriors
were able to approach behind a lava crest perhaps fifty yards south of
the defense site.

It was this ability of the Nez Perces to draw near the soldiers that
likely produced the greatest number of casualties. Besides Lieutenant
Benson, who had been wounded before Norwood pulled his men back,
these included Private Harry Trevor, hit in the right breast, and Samuel

Glass, who received a bullet in the bladder; both subsequently died of their wounds. Another bullet struck Corporal Harry Garland in the hip, driving two cartridges from his belt into his body. Three other soldiers and a civilian received wounds in the fighting before the warriors withdrew. Davis reported that Sergeant Hugh McCafferty climbed a tree and, hidden by the foliage, kept the troops informed of the warriors' movements. According to a contemporary report, the Bannock, Buffalo Horn, "stood by Norwood all the time, and by all accounts, kept up his old reputation of being the bravest of scouts."[65]

In their accounts of Camas Meadows, the Nez Perces did not emphasize the fighting with Sanford's battalion and Norwood's company as much as they did the previous stampeding of the command's animals, although one narrative mentioned the presence of the Bannock scouts with these soldiers. The Nez Perces later told prospector John Shively in the national park that six or seven warriors had been killed in the fight with Norwood.[66] Peopeo Tholekt provided one of the more complete renditions of the Nee-Me-Poo movements, as follows:

> Scouts on swift horses to the rear brought word the soldiers were in pursuit. Mounted, they came swiftly, and while some of the warriors went on with the mules, the rest of us lined up behind a low hill awaiting the enemies. Soon some of them appeared on top of the ridge, and seeing us, dropped back from sight. Not long until shots came from that ridge. . . . Soon those soldiers with horses skipped for the cottonwoods some distance away. Then we turned to those soldiers [Norwood's] on the ridge who were doing long-distance firing at the Indians still holding the line. We must have hit one or two of them slightly, for they became scared when they saw our [their?] horses gone. A bugle sounded down among the timber, and those soldiers skipped for their lives for that shelter. . . .[67] After this driving [of] the soldiers, Indians creeping to hiding about that woods saw several soldiers wounded or killed. Some of us, a very few, got in among rock holes on a bluff and fired from there. No Indians killed. A bullet hurt Wottolen's side only slightly. A bullet clipped me here [in the head]. . . . When I returned to life [consciousness] I was at the bottom of the bluff, and some rock bruises on me. . . . Not feeling to do more fighting, I recovered my gun and went to where I had left my horse. The fighting did not last long.[68]

Meanwhile, following the first attack on the bivouac, Howard had reorganized his remaining force and had improved the defenses on the lava knoll near his headquarters, bolstering the points with basalt rock.[69] On learning of Sanford's situation, Howard made preparations to advance. First, he sent the following verbal message via an orderly to Captain Miller, still on the trail with the balance of Howard's troops.

> Tell [Brevet] Col. Miller that the Indians stampeded some of our packmules [sic] this morning and [Brevet] Col. Sanford immediately started in pursuit with 3 cos. Cav. He now reports the enemy in strong force and that they are getting around his left flank. Tell the Col. to hurry up as soon as possible.[70]

Apprised of Norwood's situation a short time later, Howard sent another orderly out with instructions to "Find Capt. Norwood and tell him if he can do so safely to retire, but without hurry, and then you are to return to me and let me know his situation."[71] Howard then moved out of the bivouac with Captain Wells's Eighth infantrymen and Captain Henry Wagner's Company C, First Cavalry, together with a howitzer under Lieutenant Otis. Reaching Major Sanford's two companies that had drawn back, Howard inquired, "But where is Norwood?" "That is what I am trying to find out," replied Sanford. Howard placed the infantry on the right of Sanford's command and together they pushed forward, eventually gaining Norwood's position.[72] Wrote the captain: "I suppose if not for General Howard's approach [the Nez Perces] would have made desperate efforts to annihilate the company."[73] The small independent body of volunteers, having found most of their horses, also rode forward to relieve Norwood, but they had not advanced far before encountering the command coming back with its wounded and with Brooks's body strapped over a horse.[74] By 9:30 A.M., it would appear, the major part of the Camas Meadows fighting was over.[75] Following Norwood's return to the camp, "much bitterness was expressed concerning the action of the other companies" doubtless by the captain himself. He evidently believed that "had he been vigorously supported a decisive victory would have been obtained," and "had not the troops been so well sheltered by the rocks among which they were entrenched, the company must have been annihilated."[76] Whether or not the fact that Norwood's recently joined Second Cavalry company was not a part of the dominant First Cavalry battalion with Howard in any way affected its performance in relation to the other companies is not known, although that possibility must certainly exist. In any event, wrote an unidentified participant in the fighting at Camas Meadows, "it must be admitted that Joseph worsted us."[77]

Back at the camp by 3:00 P.M., Howard's men prepared meals and further strengthened their defenses. "Every precaution taken in camp to prevent stampede," wrote Lieutenant Wood.[78] A single grave was prepared by Jackson's men on the ground east of Spring Creek and below the lava-stone fortifications raised by the men. There Trumpeter Brooks's body was placed. General Howard made remarks and Major Mason read the Episcopal service as Brooks's comrades said good-bye. Then the farewell volleys of the Springfields echoed across Camas Meadows. As Howard defined the moment, "the remains of young Brooks were left, to rest there in loneliness till the resurrection."[79] At seven that evening, just as the funeral concluded, Captain Miller and the remaining 230 infantry of Howard's army arrived and went into camp after an "extraordinary march" of forty-six miles, during which the men alternated riding in the wagons and walking. Plans got underway for continuing the pursuit the next morning, one of Howard's major objectives now being to realign his wagons, horses, and available mules to compensate for those run off by the Nez Perces.[80]

For his daring recovery of Trumpeter Brooks's body, the army awarded the Medal of Honor to Captain James Jackson, but not until 1896 and with supporting verification provided by Howard and then-Colonel Mason. In 1878, however, four enlisted men received the Medal of Honor for their performances at Camas Meadows: Corporal Harry Garland (also for his service at Muddy Creek, Montana, earlier that year), "wounded in the hip, the bone being shattered so that he was unable to stand, but continuing to direct the men with excellent judgement"; Farrier William H. Jones (also for service at Muddy Creek), "wounded in the knee . . . but continued at his post"; First Sergeant Henry Wilkens (also for service at Muddy Creek), "receiving . . . a very painful wound in the head, but continuing with the company displaying excellent judgement and courage"; and Private Wilfred Clark (also for his service at Big Hole), who "though wounded in shoulder and chin, continued at his post." In addition, Captains Carr, Norwood, and Wells, and Lieutenants Benson, Adams, Cresson, and Guy Howard (the general's son), would in 1890 win brevets for service at Camas Meadows.[81]

On Tuesday, August 21, General Howard started his wounded on the back trail to Virginia City escorted by all but eight or ten of the Montana volunteers. One of the casualties, Blacksmith Samuel Glass, shot through the bladder during Norwood's action, died August 22 on the way at Pleasant Valley and was buried there.[82] Howard's command, at last together, again pushed on after the Nez Perces and made eighteen miles on the twenty-first before stopping at Shot-Gun Creek. Wagoner Henry Buck ably recorded the marching formation used by the army throughout the post–Civil War Indian wars period:

> The wagon train and the pack animals were placed in the center; ahead of us was a company of cavalry to lead the way, while another company of cavalry brought up the rear. The infantry marched on either side of the wagons about one hundred feet distant, while on the outside of these the balance of the cavalry took their places in the grand parade across the prairie following Joseph's trail.[83]

That day and night more Bannock scouts joined from Fort Hall, Idaho, 120 miles southwest, in the charge of civilian scout "Captain" Stanton G. Fisher and escorted by Captain Augustus H. Bainbridge, Fourteenth Infantry, and ten soldiers of that regiment. Bainbridge, who started back to Fort Hall with his escort on the twenty-third, informed the general that the additional scouts, which brought their total complement to fifty, had been sent on the advice of General George Crook, in whose department Howard was now operating.[84] The presence of the Bannocks added a note of excitement to the command. One observer, calling them a "gorgeous set of warriors," portrayed them in this manner:

> Some carried long poles, on which were single eagle feathers tied loosely with sinew which whirled about in the breeze like toy windmills, which, with other poles having dangling scalps, meant war. They were in full paint—some all red, others red, green and yellow. Many had dyed their horses' manes and tails and decorated them with bunches of different colored feathers and jingling sleigh bells. They all wore dresses of buckskin, beautifully ornamented with bead work, and their brightest blankets.[85]

Howard was immediately desirous of having the Bannocks try to retrieve the livestock taken by the Nez Perces at Camas Meadows.[86]

Over the two following days, the army moved northeast along the Henry's (or North) Fork of the Snake River and began to enter the deep woods around Targhee Pass, two miles east of Henry's Lake and on the fringe of the national park. In their camp of the twenty-second, the troops feared another nighttime assault by the Nez Perces and largely

went without rest. Still hoping to corner the Indians near the pass before they entered the park, at 2:00 A.M. the soldiers were on the road
again. But the Nez Perces had already departed, continuing east, and
the news demoralized the command. Lieutenant Bacon had been in the
area with his cavalry, but acting on his orders, Bacon had reconnoitered Raynolds Pass fifteen miles away from Targhee Pass. Having seen
no Indians, the lieutenant had returned to Howard's trail on the stage
road on the assumption that the tribesmen were going in another direction, which, in fact, they were.[87] Now with exhausted men and animals,
Howard's army could not go on without supplies and rest, compelling
him to temporarily stop the chase at Henry's Lake for four days while
he personally set out with two teams for Virginia City, seventy-five miles
away, to obtain clothing, shoes, blankets, and pack horses, and to telegraph Generals Sherman and McDowell.[88] To watch for the Nez Perces'
approach into the buffalo grounds, however, Howard sent Captain
Norwood's company, with an artillery complement under Captains
Edward Field and Harry C. Cushing, to the Crow Agency, east of Fort
Ellis on the Yellowstone River. The Bannock scouts, meanwhile, would
keep tabs on the Nez Perces, report on their movements, and capture
their livestock if opportunity permitted.[89]

At Henry's Lake, General Howard offered a realistic albeit defensive appraisal of his command's performance that was undoubtedly intended to dilute lingering criticism of his effort:

> From Kamiah to Henry Lake, at which point the cavalry and infan-
> try arrived together, the command was marching continuously with-
> out a day's halt 26 days, making an average of 19.3 miles a day;
> baggage carried generally by pack-trains, the Indian trail from
> Kamiah to the Bitter Root Valley being impassable for wagons. The
> command suffered often for want of shoes, overcoats, and under-
> clothing during the latter part of the march, owing to the rapidity of
> the march and the difficulty of procuring the supplies in Montana.[90]

In a letter home, Major Mason lamented the conditions. "I am anxious
on the men's accounts to have the campaign close. But I don't expect it
will, for the craving over newspaper applause overrides other considerations."[91] Another officer wrote home that "the whole command is weary
and tired of marching. . . . The only visible strategy is troops, troops,
and more troops."[92] If truth be known, Howard wanted desperately to

curtail his operations and go home, and so did his men. As one of them put it: "The feeling of the command is . . . that he should turn back and leave the further pursuit to . . . Terry and Crook. . . . To be ordered to the Yellowstone country or not to be—that is the question."93

The question was resolved in Virginia City beginning August 24, in a heated exchange of telegrams among Howard, McDowell, and Sherman, who was at Fort Shaw, Montana. Replying to Howard's earlier question about continuing, McDowell told him pointedly that his instructions were to go on, and Howard responded, telling his chief that "My duty shall be done fully and to the letter without complaint."94 But to Sherman he remonstrated that "My command is so much worn by overfatigue and jaded animals that I cannot push it much farther." If other troops could head off the tribesmen in their front, Howard could "in a few days work my way back to Fort Boise slowly, and distribute my troops before snow falls in the mountains."95 Sherman interpreted the message to be that Howard wanted to quit, and he replied that he "should pursue the Nez Perces to the death, lead where they may. . . . If you are tired, give the command to some young energetic officer. . . . When the Indians are caught, your men can march to the Pacific Railroad and reach their posts by rail and steamboat. They are not needed back in California and Oregon now, but are needed just where they are."96 The implicit reprimand gave Howard new resolve, and on August 27, back at Henry's Lake, he shot off a message to the commanding general: "You misunderstood me. I never flag. It was the command, including the most energetic young officers, that were worn out and weary by a most extraordinary march. You need not fear for the campaign. Neither you nor General McDowell can doubt my pluck and energy. . . . We move in the morning and will continue to the end."97

The National Park

THE LAYOVER OF General Howard's command on the shores of Henry's Lake coincided with a broadening of the army's pursuit of the nontreaty Nez Perces. After Henry's Lake, matters became increasingly complex for both the troops and the tribesmen. As Howard pursued, a military cordon slowly began to encircle the tribesmen on north, south, and east. This envelopment was composed of commands from the departments of Dakota and the Platte, overseen, respectively, by Brigadier Generals Alfred H. Terry and George Crook. On August 13, on Sherman's authority, Lieutenant General Sheridan directed Terry to cooperate with Howard, "even to temporarily placing such troops as you may have to spare under his command." At Camp Brown, Wyoming, Crook was alerted to the approaching Nez Perces and his men prepared for field duty. When Howard expressed concern that the Indians might be intending to join Sitting Bull's Sioux somewhere below the Canadian line, Sheridan responded that "such junction is preposterous." Yet to forestall efforts by the Nez Perces to gain a foothold in the Yellowstone country, Terry directed that troops be sent to watch the area of the Musselshell River and Judith Basin above the Yellowstone.[1]

In fact, such efforts were already underway. At the Tongue River Cantonment (soon to be known as Fort Keogh) on the Yellowstone, Colonel Nelson A. Miles, as early as August 3, had sent First Lieutenant

Gustavus C. Doane with Company E, Seventh Cavalry, and about sixty Crow scouts to the Musselshell River to watch for signs of the Nez Perces. According to a directive to Doane, the lieutenant was to "use every effort to either capture or destroy the Nez Perces band of hostile Indians that have recently been engaging the troops in Idaho, and who will doubtless, if defeated, endeavor to retreat and take refuge in the Judith Basin or vicinity."[2] Of major concern at this juncture was maintaining the allegiance of the Crows, and Doane was expected to use whatever diplomacy he could muster to that end.[3] On the twelfth, underscoring Miles's determination to stop the Nez Perces, he sent Colonel Samuel D. Sturgis with six companies of the Seventh Cavalry up the Yellowstone to observe the country about the Judith Basin, some 250 miles northwest of the Tongue River post.[4] Another directive to Doane asserted:

> Your objective is now the band of Nez Perces, and you will please use every effort to assist [Brevet] Gen. Sturgis in capturing or destroying them. If the Crows will take part in it they can easily surround the Nez Perces, and compel them to lay down their arms; the warriors, or at least all of the principal men should be marched to this place, and their arms destroyed. Provided the Crows assist in the work, the ponies and ammunition may be given to them and the remainder of the [Nez Perce] band left with the Crow tribe for the present. You can withhold any ammunition or rations [from the Crows] until this is accomplished, and then the Crow Camp can return to their agency where they will find an abundance.[5]

Seven days later, Sturgis deployed his force on the Musselshell, but shortly removed to the mouth of the Stillwater River on the Yellowstone "with a view of taking up a central position where we might guard the various passes by which the Indians might attempt to debouch from the mountains."[6] Sturgis also received notice from Howard stating that, based on information from his scouts, the tribesmen "will probably cross Stinking [Water] River one hundred miles south east of Crow Agency."[7] Much against Sturgis's wishes, Lieutenant Doane, acting on orders received from Colonel Gibbon, moved his scouting force to Fort Ellis and, on August 29, set out for the upper Yellowstone leading into the national park.[8]

All the while that Howard's troops and animals had been resting at Henry's Lake, his Bannock scouts trailed the Nez Perces east through

Targhee Pass, across the valley of the South Fork of the Madison, and into the national park. There, along the main Madison River on August 25, they came upon two men, William H. Harmon and Charles Mann, whose party had been captured the previous day by Nez Perce warriors. This information, plus news of the general course of the Nez Perces relayed to Howard on his return from Virginia City, confirmed in his mind that they were headed for the Crow Agency near the Yellowstone River and ultimately for the buffalo grounds above that stream. "I believed that the route of the enemy, conforming to the features of the country, would be through [the] National Park to Musselshell Valley, by way of Clarke's [sic] Fork, or possibly leading further south by way of some point between Crow agency and the Stinkingwater [present north fork of the Shoshone River], crossing to the valley of the Musselshell."[9] It was in looking to the possibility of heading off the tribesmen that Howard had sent Captains Harry C. Cushing and Norwood to Fort Ellis. Those troops had instructions to keep Howard posted and to communicate with Colonel Sturgis's patrolling command.[10]

As Howard pondered the Nez Perces' objective points, unknown to him General Sherman, following up on his previous communication with Howard, and possibly in response to continually mounting criticism of his brigadier, had set in motion plans to gently remove him from command. On August 29, from Helena, Sherman wired Sheridan:

> I find Genl [Lieutenant Colonel Charles C.] Gilbert here & will send him up the Yellowstone to the park to overtake Howard with all news & to advise him to have his command follow the Nez Perces till killed or captured, when the men can return to their posts on the Pacific, meantime advising Howard to give his command to Gilbert & in person to overtake me & go with me to his department. It is not an order but only advice.[11]

Two days later, Colonel Gilbert departed Fort Ellis with Company L, Second Cavalry, now under command of Second Lieutenant Charles B. Schofield, to find Howard and take over the general's column in accordance with Sherman's wishes.[12]

The missive Gilbert carried to Howard outlined the troop dispositions underway in Sheridan's division and noted that his column, as the "pursuing force," had "not much chance of a fight." In it, Sherman continued:

Really I see not much reason for your commanding a Detachment, after having driven the hostile Indians out of your Department across Montana, and into Genl. Sheridan's command. I find . . . Lt. Col. C.C. Gilbert here [at Helena], who has served long in this Territory, and is familiar with the Indians, and the country in which they have taken refuge. I don't want to order you back to Oregon, but I do say that you can with perfect propriety return to your command, leaving the troops to continue till the Nez-Perces have been destroyed or captured, and I authorize you to transfer to him, Lt. Col. Gilbert, your command in the field and to overtake me en-route or in your Department.[13]

The effort by Sherman to remove Howard reflected not only the commanding general's deep-seated frustration toward the overall progress of the campaign, but also his extreme anger at the Nez Perces themselves. His harsh views toward the Nez Perces were evident in a telegram to Sheridan sent from Deer Lodge on August 31:

If the Nez-Perces be captured or surrender it should be without terms. Their horses, arms and property should be taken away. Many of their leaders [should be] executed preferably by sentence of a civil court for their murders in Idaho and Montana and what are left should be treated like the Modocs, sent to some other country; there should be extreme severity, else other tribes alike situated may imitate their example. These are my conclusions, but after capture or surrender you had better consult the Washington authorities. All here think they will fight hard, skillfully, to the death.[14]

Oblivious to all this, Howard, on Tuesday morning, August 28, pulled out of camp at Henry's Lake. There the Montana volunteers departed, as did most of the wagons hired in Missoula. The command marched through Targhee Pass to the Madison River, on the very course the tribesmen had taken six days before. As the troops coursed up the Madison, they encountered "a most wretched figure, worn and ragged." He was Henry Meyers, another escapee from among the same group of tourists accosted by the Nez Perces four days before at Lower Geyser Basin. Later, yet another man, Albert Oldham, appeared, having been shot in the face by the warriors and in a "famished condition."[15] Howard camped that night on the Madison River, leading into the park.

The national park, informally called "Wonderland" because of its variety of natural features ranging from vast and nearly impenetrable

forests intertwined with lakes and streams to unique geologic formations and abundant thermal phenomena, had been established by Congress in 1872 "for the benefit and enjoyment of the people." The park
then encompassed nearly 3,313 square miles, principally in northwestern Wyoming Territory (the west and north boundaries were in Idaho
and Montana territories, respectively), running approximately sixty-two
miles north-to-south by fifty-four miles east-to-west. Besides the Madison and its contributory streams, the Gibbon and the Firehole—encountered by the Nez Perces as well as by Howard's command as they
proceeded into the park—two major rivers draining the area were the
Yellowstone, flowing northward through the park to form high-alti-
tude Yellowstone Lake, and the East Fork of the Yellowstone (later
named the Lamar River), which converged with the primary stream in
the north-central part of the park as it angled northwest and beyond
the boundary. Numerous affluents joined these streams everywhere as
they coursed across the mountainous park topography. In 1877, there
were no major roads and few trails leading through the Yellowstone
wilderness, although wagons traveling up the Madison and Firehole
rivers could reach the area of the Lower Geyser Basin. Across the
Yellowstone River, above its confluence with the East Fork (Lamar), a
wooden bridge had been erected by Collins J. ("Yellowstone Jack")
Baronett, enabling travel between Mammoth Hot Springs, where a log
cabin hotel stood for the benefit of tourists, and the route east to the
mining region around Cooke City.[16] All of the activity related to the
Nez Perces and Howard's army in that year took place in the northern
half of the national park.

Oddly enough, as the course of events unfolded, the pinnacle of
army leadership had left the national park just days before the Nez
Perces entered it. Commanding General William T. Sherman, on a
tour of western posts during the summer of 1877, had left Fort Ellis on
August 4 with an entourage of two officers besides himself, his son, a
packer-guide, three drivers, and only four soldiers, a total of twelve
persons. "I do not suppose I run much risk," he wrote Secretary of War
McCrary, "for we are all armed, and the hostile Indians rarely resort to
the park, a poor region for game, and to their superstitious minds associated with hell by reason of its geysers and hot springs."[17]

From August 6 to 17, Sherman's group ranged through the north
and west parts of the park, visiting Mammoth Hot Springs, Mount

Washburn, the Lower Falls of the Yellowstone and the geyser basins, and Old Faithful, impressed by its beauty and geologic features. At Mud Volcano, the general's people peered inside the boiling, churning enigma, deciding it was not of volcanic origin but of "muddy water, and . . . thick mud, puffing up just like a vast pot of 'mush.'"[18] On August 16, they were overtaken by a courier bearing news of Gibbon's battle at the Big Hole, and the next day, en route back to Fort Ellis, Sherman's party received dispatches, telegrams, and newspapers describing the event. Back at the post on August 19, the commanding general wrote McCrary that "we saw no signs of Indians, and felt at no moment more sense of danger than we do here."[19]

Sherman had no knowledge of his proximity to the Nez Perce cavalcade that entered the park only six days after the general's party had vacated it. On Tuesday, August 21, the tribesmen camped at Henry's Lake, their livestock fairly blanketing a three-square-mile tract as it grazed. On the following day, the people filed into Madison Basin along the road from Virginia City to the Lower Geyser Basin, their presence creating a brief scare along the Madison Valley as panicky residents fled toward Virginia City. That night a party from the Nez Perce camp raided a small band of miners twenty miles away along the West Fork of the Madison and got away with most of their horses.[20] The arrival of the Nez Perces in the national park on August 23 opened to them a myriad of possibilities regarding their course throughout it and egress from it. One of the army's principal authorities on the park was Colonel John Gibbon, who had explored the region on a visit in 1872, subsequently lecturing and authoring articles describing its wonders for the public.[21] On Sherman's direction, he offered Howard his views of the route the tribesmen might take:

> The Nez Perces having entered the Geyser Basin have two ways open to them. They may turn up the Fire Hole Basin and reach Wind River by the trail to the south, passing west of Yellowstone Lake, or entering the lower Geyser Basin move eastward to the Yellowstone River either near the falls or near where it emerges from the Lake. Here they may cross the River by fording and turning south follow Capt. [William A.] Jones trail east of the Yellowstone Lake to Wind River, or they may continue down the River to the bridge at the forks, go up the East fork and so over into Clarks fork or one of several passes leading towards the Yellowstone or Bighorn. East of the Yellowstone River and Lake, elk and deer are plentiful and both

are filled with quantities of large trout. Your best and surest plan is
to cling to the trail to the last, as you may rest assured other troops
will sooner or later get in front of these Indians hampered as they
are with their wounded and large herds. By sending for it you can
get any quantity of beef on the hoof down the Madison in the Gallatin
Valley, and on the Yellowstone below the mouth of Gardners River.[22]

Gibbon proved correct in predicting at least part of the Nez Perces'
route. It is apparent that the people themselves, for a major portion of
their trek through the park, remained uncertain of their course. Few
Nee-Me-Poo accounts addressed the matter of their route, and whatever clues to the mystery of where they went have been derived from
non–Nez Perce sources, principally from the account of Howard's leading scout, Fisher, who with the Bannocks trailed them for much of the
way, and that of John Shively, a prospector who was captured and held
by the Nez Perces during their passage (and then escaped). It is the
latter stage of the people's course through the park that is open to question and has been the focus of considerable debate.[23]

As stated, the Nez Perces entered the national park via the Madison River Valley on August 22, the day that Howard camped along the
Henry's (or North) Fork of the Snake River en route to Henry's Lake.
On Thursday, August 23, Howard's scout, Fisher, led his Bannocks
through Targhee Pass into the Madison River Valley. Atop the Continental Divide, Fisher espied the Nez Perce camp along the Madison
River; a short time later his scouts encountered their trail. Reaching
the South Fork of the Madison at sundown, Fisher halted his scouts,
sending forth a few who returned shortly to report that the Nez Perce
camp lay but a few miles away, and that it could be taken easily by the
Bannocks. After some deliberation, Fisher acceded in the plan, fearing
that the cavalry could not arrive in time to surprise the camp. Yet after
all proper dispositions were made, including the Bannocks readying
themselves for an assault, several of the scouts returned to report the
camp deserted, and the offensive plan collapsed entirely.[24]

Besides the Nez Perces, the Bannocks, as well as other tribes of the
Great Basin and Plateau, had since the 1830s journeyed through what
became the national park to the Montana plains to hunt buffalo. The
standard route, known by the 1870s as the Bannock Trail, started at
Camas Meadows and, moving east, crossed Targhee Pass and the basin
of the Madison River. It then penetrated the Gallatin Mountains to the

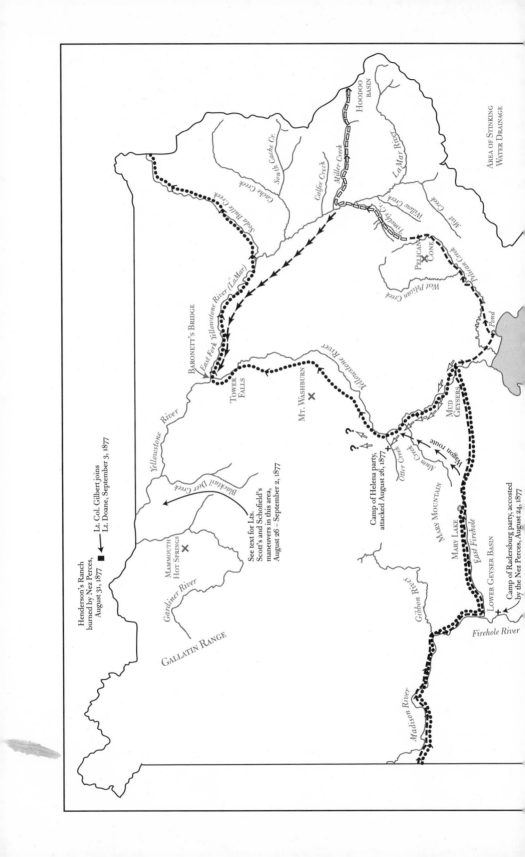

AREA OF STINKING
WATER DRAINAGE

HOODOO
BASIN

South Cache Cr.

Cache Creek

Soda Butte Creek

Cauffee Creek

Miller Creek

La Mar River

Willow Creek

Mist Creek

Cloudy Cr.

PELICAN
CONE ×

West Pelican Creek

Pelican Creek

Pond

BARONETT'S BRIDGE

East Fork Yellowstone River (LaMar)

TOWER
FALLS

Yellowstone River

MT. WASHBURN ×

Yellowstone River

MUD
GEYSERS

Otter Creek

Alum Creek

Wagon route

Camp of Helena party,
attacked August 26, 1877

Yellowstone River

Henderson's Ranch
burned by Nez Perces,
August 31, 1877 ■

Lt. Col. Gilbert joins
Lt. Doane, September 3, 1877

See text for Lts.
Scott's and Schofield's
maneuvers in this area,
August 26 – September 2, 1877

Blacktail Deer Creek

MAMMOUTH
HOT SPRINGS ×

Gardiner River

GALLATIN RANGE

MARY MOUNTAIN

MARY LAKE

East Firehole

LOWER GEYSER BASIN

Camp of Radersburg party, accosted
by the Nez Perces, August 24, 1877

Gibbon River

Firehole River

Madison River

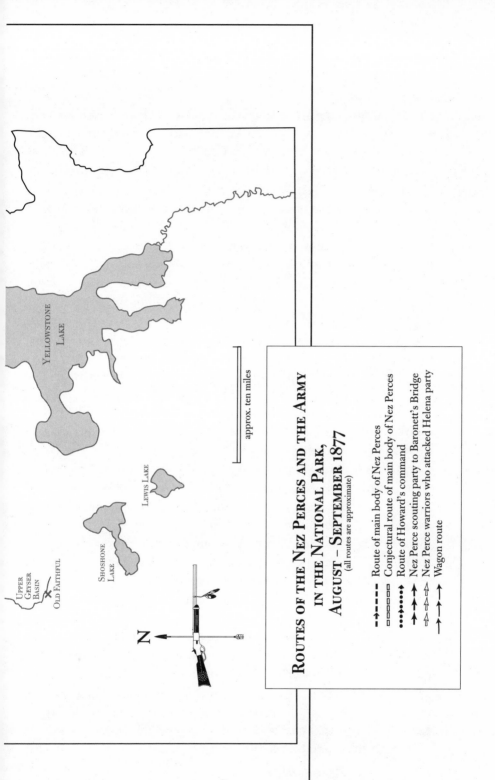

UPPER
GEYSER
BASIN
✗
OLD FAITHFUL

SHOSHONE
LAKE

LEWIS LAKE

YELLOWSTONE
LAKE

N

approx. ten miles

**ROUTES OF THE NEZ PERCES AND THE ARMY
IN THE NATIONAL PARK,
AUGUST – SEPTEMBER 1877**
(all routes are approximate)

- ∙—∙—∙→ Route of main body of Nez Perces
- ◻◻◻◻◻◻ Conjectural route of main body of Nez Perces
- ∙∙∙∙∙►► Route of Howard's command
- ⇒⇒⇒⇒ Nez Perce scouting party to Baronett's Bridge
- ⇨⇨⇨⇨ Nez Perce warriors who attacked Helena party
- →→→ Wagon route

vicinity of Echo Peak and passed down Indian Creek to the Gardner River. The trail then led through Snow Pass, reaching Mammoth Hot Springs before continuing up Lava Creek and across Blacktail Deer Creek Plateau to the Yellowstone and the East Fork of the Yellowstone. It then proceeded up the East Fork Valley, branching to enter the Absaroka Range and emerge in the valley of Clark's Fork, from which place its users might travel to the Yellowstone Valley or Wyoming Basin.[25] In 1877, however, the Nez Perces chose not to follow the Bannock Trail, instead opting to pursue a hunting trail with which they were largely unfamiliar. The reason for this decision is not altogether clear; perhaps it was meant to confuse the army, or possibly the tribesmen were wary of troops operating in the northern reaches of the park.

The Nez Perces did not tarry long at the site on the Madison River subsequently located by Fisher and his scouts. In one of his accounts, Yellow Wolf indicated that late in the day "the Indians were getting ready to move camp." It was soon after that that Yellow Wolf and Otskai, roaming several miles away from that camp, happened on fifty-two-year-old John Shively, a prospector who was crossing the park from the Black Hills gold country in Dakota Territory. As Shively ate supper late that day in the Lower Geyser Basin, the Indians approached him. (Shively maintained that four warriors approached him while at least twenty more surrounded him at a distance.) Taken to the Nez Perce camp, Shively attended a council of the leaders in which "they asked me if I would show them the best trail leading out of the park to Wind River, where they were going." Fearing for his life, the miner replied affirmatively. Later, Shively learned that the Nez Perces had taken that route rather than the customary Bannock Trail "to get away from Howard." The warriors then detained Shively for several days, until the night of September 2, when he managed to escape.[26]

Although Fisher noted in his journal that the Nez Perces' presumed camp (that he found abandoned) was on the Madison, "a few miles above us," and "on the opposite side from where we were," in fact, as indicated by Yellow Wolf and as discovered by Fisher, the tribesmen had broken that camp and gone on late in the afternoon, and that Yellow Wolf had gone in advance "about six miles" before encountering Shively. Actually, Yellow Wolf and the tribesmen had to have traveled much farther to camp along the Firehole River in the area of Lower Geyser Basin, where Shively was and where he said the Nez Perces camped. If Fisher spotted the abandoned camp of the Nez Perces only a few miles from his position on the South Fork of the Madison, it seems that the tribesmen traveled up the Madison all the way to the Firehole and then covered the distance to Lower Geyser Basin, a total distance of around ten miles, all before darkness fell.[27]

Determining the subsequent course of the Nez Perces through the west and central areas of the park becomes easier after August 24, for on that day they encountered the tourists from Radersburg, Montana. Yellow Wolf claimed to have seen lights from their campfire on the night of the twenty-third, but decided to wait until morning to investigate because of boggy ground over which they must proceed. (A wise decision, considering the many hot springs in the area.) Early the next day, the Nez Perces surprised the group of seven men and two women as they prepared breakfast, and, as discussed below, over the succeeding two days the fate of its various members hung in the balance. Some of the party escaped relatively quickly, and some were found by Howard's troops and scouts as they fled for safety.

That day, August 24, the Nez Perces passed from the Firehole River up the East Fork of the Firehole (later designated Nez Perce Creek), ascending Mary Mountain and skirting Mary Lake (about one-half mile long, north to south, and one-quarter mile wide) and Hot Sulphur Springs (today Highland Hot Springs) on the Central Plateau. They camped along the edge of a basin about three-quarters mile in circumference, inside which their immense horse herd grazed.[28] On Saturday, the twenty-fifth, they continued down the slope and through Hayden Valley and along Elk Antler Creek to the Yellowstone River, fording the stream above the Mud Volcano, about five miles north of Yellowstone Lake (the crossing is known today as Nez Perce Ford), and camping on the east side of the river. Here the Nez Perces released the remaining tourists, providing them with food, horses, assistance in recrossing the river, and directions toward Mammoth Hot Springs far to the northwest.

Earlier that day, as they passed through Hayden Valley, the warriors had captured a recently discharged soldier, James C. Irwin, from Fort Ellis and still in uniform. His sojourn with the Nez Perces lasted six days until September 1, when he managed to escape. Across the Yellowstone River, they continued south, crossed Pelican Creek, and camped near a pool on the north shore of the lake later named Indian Pond. There the people, aware of Howard's location at Henry's Lake far in the rear, evidently passed two days without concern of the soldiers, leaving on the morning of August 28 to ascend winding Pelican Creek east and north. By then, Fisher's Bannocks (numerically reduced to forty after the departure of fifteen deserters) were in close pursuit, having crossed from Lower Geyser Basin on the twenty-sixth and reached Mud Volcano on the twenty-seventh, where they killed and scalped an elderly Nez Perce woman who had stayed behind so as to not hinder the progress of her people. Fording the Yellowstone the next day, Fisher approached the camp site in the timber near Yellowstone Lake, but was too late to find the Indians.[29]

Scout Fisher's journal of his reconnoitering of the main Nez Perce caravan on the days after August 28, together with the account of John Shively, who remained with the caravan following his capture, provide the only known contemporary evidence that enable the approximate tracking of those people until the time they left the national park. The following estimate of the course of the tribesmen—who could have traveled through the park in more than one group—is based on these sources, on period cartographic information, and on previous judgments of that course. Regarding the cartographic data, it is important to note changes in Yellowstone Park nomenclature since the time of the Nez Perces' passage. Specifically, Pelican Creek, as referenced on the Hayden Survey Map of 1878, is today called Raven Creek. In 1877 and 1878, the stream known as Pelican Creek trended generally north and east from Yellowstone Lake and passed to the east of "Pelican Hill" (now Pelican Cone). The only major affluents of Pelican Creek shown on the 1878 map were "Lake Creek" (present Astringent Creek) and "West Pelican Creek" (today's main Pelican Creek), both joining the major stream from the north. Smaller, unnamed tributaries also lead into the primary stream from the southeast. Furthermore, by 1878 a trail paralleled Pelican Creek for much of its length and beyond its headwaters, passing near or across the heads of several tributaries (particularly Timothy Creek) of the East Fork of the Yellowstone (Lamar River).[30] Shively's recollections, given but a few days after his escape from the Nez Perces, are not altogether clear on details of where the people were at different points. Based on his detailed interview account published in the Deer Lodge New-Northwest, his role as guide was briefly usurped by a Shoshone chief (probably Little Bear). On August 28, according to this account, the tribesmen followed the Shoshone, apparently continuing up Pelican Creek, but then bearing left toward the Yellowstone River and going "around a mountain" before correcting their course and emerging on the East Fork. In reaching the East Fork, the Nez Perces might have descended Timothy Creek. In any event, on the thirtieth, according to Shively, they moved down the East Fork "four or five miles towards Baronette's Bridge" at the junction of the East Fork with the Yellowstone, but on the thirty-first, going on, they decided to send scouts some twenty miles to the bridge, which ultimately was burned at the direction of the Shoshone leader. According to Shively, the Nez Perces "did not like the idea of coming down that stream." Possibly because of potential confrontations with troops or miners, they turned back "to seek an outlet toward the Big Horn." Still on the thirty-first, the Nez Perce council reconvened, and Shively, now reinstated, told them he could guide them to Clark's Fork River and scouts were sent to explore that area.[31]

Fisher's journal, while otherwise spotty and unclear on many points, precisely mentioned Pelican Creek—no forks or subordinate affluents— as the stream he ascended during his scout after the Nez Perces. On August 28, he followed their trail up Pelican Creek for "about ten miles," then climbed a mountainside from which he "could plainly see the smoke in the enemy's camp."[32] From this point, Fisher turned back, not to actively resume his reconnaissance until September 1, when he and a group of scouts started up Pelican Creek on the trail again. At sundown that day, they suddenly encountered the discharged soldier, Irwin, who said he had left the Nez Perce camp that morning "about thirty miles from here." According to Fisher's dispatch to Howard, the encounter with Irwin happened three miles up Pelican Creek:

> We have just met an escaped prisoner from Joseph's band, his name is James C. Irwin, lately discharged from Co. G, 2d Cavalry, Ft. Ellis. He says he left the hostile camp about 8 o'clock this morning. The enemy have been lost or bewildered several days. They are now some-where between Soda Butte and Clark's Fork silver mines. This man Irwin will come to your camp [and] explain the situation. It will be very important to keep this man with you. I shall proceed slowly and carefully, in fact from Irwin's statement it will not be necessary to follow the trail, but take the cut off he took on his escape.[33]

Next day, as Fisher resumed his probe, Irwin started for Howard's command. On arrival September 2, he told the general that the tribes-men were no more than forty miles away, "having been lost for several days in the pine forests." Irwin further said that there were 216 warriors, "besides boys and squaws, who use guns at times of battle." Poker Joe (Lean Elk) had assumed a major leadership role and was apparently so familiar with Virginia City and Bozeman that "he sent word by Irwin to a man named Kennedy to look after a house and lot of his at the latter place." Evidently misconstruing Joseph's designated role with the noncombatants of the train, Irwin reported that he had been "supplanted" as chief and spent his time "packing mules and building fires." The leaders had sent four emissaries to the Crows to try to gain their support; meantime, the people were well supplied with dried meat, sugar, and ammunition, but lacked flour, salt, and coffee. Finally, Irwin told of Shively's captivity among the Nez Perces working as a guide.[34]

Meanwhile, Fisher continued up Pelican Creek on September 2, but did not start until late afternoon, after having taken some observations from a mountainside and then gotten delayed in "swamps and fallen timber" which retarded his party's advance. "We made about six miles over a very bad trail through fallen timber," he noted in his journal. Yet the scout recorded that he and his Bannocks crested the Pelican Creek divide to reach the waters of the East Fork of the Yellowstone River.[35] Based on the cartographic data cited above, the "waters" could logically have been the upper reaches of Timothy Creek, the headwaters of which extended sufficiently westward to bisect the trail shown on the Hayden map, and the course of which leads naturally northeast to the East Fork. On Monday, September 3, the scouts followed the trail "through the roughest cañon I ever undertook to pass through," wrote Fisher.

> About every foot of it was obstructed with dead and fallen timber and huge blocks of granite which had fallen from its sides. We found plenty of dead and crippled horses that had been left by the enemy. They evidently had a hard time getting through this place for the trees and logs were smeared with blood from their horses.[36]

While other creek bottoms might more directly align with Fisher's description, that of Timothy Creek also conforms well, according to observations by park authorities who have studied and hiked over the terrain.[37]

On the fourth, Fisher and a white scout named A. K. Gird ascended to "the divide" and by noon had approached within a mile of the Nez Perce village, which was in process of breaking camp—"gathering their horses together and pulling their lodges down preparatory to leaving."[38]

The "divide" was perhaps the high ridge on the south side of Miller Creek, separating that stream from the East Fork (Lamar) River, and reached by climbing the canyon wall directly east of the East Fork, from which point the upper Miller Creek drainage could be observed below and to the east. According to Fisher, the Nez Perces then traveled "nearly east" up the canyon. The Bannocks told Fisher that the area was called the "trap" and that "there is no way of getting out of it except at each end and that it is about fifteen miles long."[39] In fact, the area of upper Miller Creek—with its exit-impeding features as noted by modern hikers—configures well with reference to a "trap."[40] That afternoon, Fisher and his colleagues heard gunfire in the canyon below. They tried to descend to the bottom, but found the canyon edge to be perpendicular and impossible to negotiate. Later, they learned that some of Fisher's Bannocks had accidentally run into a rearguard of some forty Nez Perces and had a brisk exchange in which "at least a hundred shots were fired." They reported having killed one Nez Perce.[41] It is hypothesized that, from the "trap" of upper Miller Creek, the people continued east to a grassy summit near the headwaters of Miller, Papoose, and Hoodoo creeks known as Hoodoo Basin. John Shively reported that the tribesmen camped on "a beautiful, grassy ridge" east of Yellowstone Lake that conceivably could be the same area. (It was from this place that Shively, after pointing the Nez Perces in the direction of the Crow country, made his escape on the night of September 2.[42]) Park superintendent Philetus W. Norris noted in 1880 that he had found the remains of numerous Indian lodges, some of which were still standing "near the summit of an open, grassy pass between Hoodoo and Miller Creeks."[43] And while the lodge poles might have been left there by other tribes, the location aligns well with the presumed route of the Nez Perces as they headed toward Crandall Creek on Clark's Fork River.

On September 6, Fisher's party traveled from their camp on the East Fork twelve miles "down the stream over an exceedingly rough trail." He wrote: "The enemy's trail followed down the same creek that we came down today to a point where it formed a junction with another stream and then turned in a south of east direction, making up this last mentioned creek. Following their trail upward, we came upon some cattle they had killed."[44] This imprecise entry[45] suggests that Fisher's reconnaissance on September 4 failed to detect the departure/return of a Nez Perce scouting party down the East Fork to Baronett's bridge and that the bands likely were traveling in more than one group. Fisher's comments indicate that a major group of Nez Perces apparently turned right up Calfee Creek or Cache Creek, probably the latter, then turned southeast up South Cache Creek, or traveled along the divide between Calfee and Cache creeks, either to rendezvous with the other groups on the grassy slopes near Papoose Creek or to pass east down Timber Creek to Crandall Creek.[46] Fisher's scouts followed the trail an unspecified distance and discovered the butchered cattle identified as having been slaughtered by the Nez Perces seemingly because of their practice of taking small quantities of meat (particularly internal organs) and leaving the carcasses mostly untouched.[47] Then the scouts eventually moved three miles to Soda Butte Creek, and after going two more miles they made camp. "There is just an even dozen of us now," wrote Fisher of his dwindling scouting force as more of the Bannocks departed.[48] On the seventh, Fisher caught up with Howard's command, which had preceded him up Soda Butte Creek and out of the national park.

In reporting on his lengthy encounter with the Nez Perces, John Shively supplemented the important intelligence of their status given by Irwin. He said that the camp of 125 lodges numbered 250 warriors, but that the total population was between 600 and 800. There were two thousand horses, with each lodge's occupants responsible for its own animals. "Every lodge drives its own horses in front of it when traveling, . . . [and] the line is thus strung out so that they are three hours getting into camp." A few Crows had reportedly joined the body, as well as seventy-five Shoshones under Little Bear. (All of these people seemingly had left the group before the Nez Perces emerged from the park into Yellowstone Valley.) Regarding leadership, Shively said that "no particular chief seemed to be in command," and that "all matters were decided in a council of several chiefs." He had not knowingly seen White Bird, but Looking Glass was considered the "fighting man"; he noted that "Joseph would come in if it was not for the influences of the others." He described Joseph as "about thirty-five years of age, six feet high, and always in a pleasant mood, greeting him each time with a nod and smile. . . . Joseph wears one eagle feather." Shively further reported that the Nez Perces told him they had lost forty-three warriors in their battles to date.[49]

The Nez Perces' prolonged contact with Shively and Irwin represented two of three encounters directly with the main body of the

tribesmen as they passed through the park, the other, as indicated, being their involvement with the Radersburg party of tourists, beginning
on August 24 in the Lower Geyser Basin. Whereas those with Shively
and Irwin were purposefully and peacefully sustained by the warriors,
the contact with the Radersburg group was brief—and violent. Their
experience was also significant because their interrelationship with the
Nez Perces gave knowledge about the tribesmen's early movements in
the park. The Radersburg party—so-called because its members were
from that community between Helena and Three Forks, Montana Territory—consisted of nine people: George F. Cowan, his wife Emma,
her brother Frank D. Carpenter, and sister Ida Carpenter, besides
Charles Mann and a young teamster, Henry ("Harry") Meyers—all from
Radersburg—plus three friends of Frank Carpenter's from Helena,
Andrew J. Arnold, William Dingee, and Albert Oldham. Leaving
Radersburg on August 5, the party had entered the park on the fourteenth via Henry's Lake, Targhee Pass, and the Madison River and had
followed a road leading to Lower Geyser Basin, finally establishing their
permanent camp on the left bank of Tangled Creek and about one-half
mile west of Fountain Geyser.[50] From that point they had toured the
Upper Geyser Basin, and some of the group had gone over to see the
Lower Falls and Yellowstone Lake. By August 23, the party had reas-
sembled at the permanent camp, ready to start for home the next day.
Camped nearby was William H. Harmon, a Colorado prospector who
was to experience the subsequent events with the Radersburg party.
They had settled in for the night, not knowing of the capture of John
Shively a mile north of their camp. That night Nez Perce scouts, in-
cluding Yellow Wolf, sighted the Cowans' campfire. At about 5:00 A.M.
Friday morning, as Dingee and Arnold prepared breakfast, three tribesmen approached, dismounted, first identifying themselves as Shoshones
("Snakes") and then confessing that they were Nez Perces belonging to
Looking Glass's band. They asked about soldiers in the vicinity, saying
that they were friends of white men but would fight the soldiers. As the
conversation continued, more warriors appeared in the distance, some
strolling the adjoining area to watch the geysers. Initially, the Radersburg
party, confronted with the warriors, tried to leave and began packing
their baggage wagon. But the Nez Perce warriors requested food, which
Arnold began to dispense to them until George Cowan intervened,
stopped the disbursement, and probably angered the tribesmen.

Hoping to avoid a serious confrontation, the tourists, joined by Harmon, harnessed their teams and saddled their four riding horses, then started down the Firehole with their two wagons (a double-seated carriage, or spring wagon, and a half spring baggage wagon) toward where the vast Nez Perce assemblage was moving up the East Fork of the Fire Hole (present Nez Perce Creek). Frank Carpenter described the procession:

> As far as we could see, up and down the river, they were moving abreast in an unbroken line ten or fifteen feet deep, driving ponies and constantly riding out and in the line. We could see about three miles of Indians, with one thousand or fifteen hundred ponies, and looking off to the left we could see more Indians looking at the geysers in Fire Hole Basin.[51]

Close to the mouth of the stream as many as seventy-five warriors on horseback blocked their way and directed them to follow the Indians.[52] "Every Indian carried splendid guns, with belts full of cartridges," remembered Mrs. Cowan.[53] At this point, Frank Carpenter demanded to see Looking Glass and was led away from the other members of the party for that purpose.[54] Two miles up the creek they came on so much felled timber that the wagon could not go on, whereon they took some provisions and blankets and headed after the Nez Perce camp accompanied by the warriors. Other men then tore into the wagon and its contents, destroying the vehicle by knocking out the wheel spokes to use in making quirt handles. The team horses were saddled for Mrs. Cowan and Ida to ride. Six miles farther east, near the foot of Mary Mountain, the entire body halted to eat, and there the tourists were reunited with Carpenter. There, Poker Joe—who the Cowan party initially thought was Joseph[55]—told them that they would be released if they traded their horses, arms, and bedding for some of the Nez Perces' jaded mounts. Captive Charles Mann remembered that, after taking most of their guns, the Nez Perces "robbed us of what we had left," then began moving their procession again.[56] Poker Joe told the captives to go on their way, cautioning them, however, to get off the trail and into the woods and to beware some younger troublemakers among the people. "He seemed to act in good faith with us," recalled Mann. But as they started back, "they discovered that they were closely followed by forty or fifty of the worst looking warriors in the band."[57] After laboring among the fallen trees, however, most of the tourist party returned to the trail and shortly found themselves surrounded by the warriors, who started them east to the Nez Perce camp on the pretext that the chiefs wanted to see them again. Mann suggested that the warriors had become incensed when two men of the party, Arnold and Dingee, had bolted into the underbrush at their approach.[58] One or two miles farther east, at a point just past the earlier meal stop and at the base of Mary Mountain, the warriors paused the remaining members of the group and took the balance of their effects. George Cowan and his wife later described to a reporter what happened next:

> These warriors . . . took the party along with them about one mile where heavy, thick timber was reached. While ascending a small, sharp knoll in this timber, Mr. Cowan and his wife being in advance of the other members of the party, . . . two Indians came dashing down the trail from the front, and, stopping their horses within about fifteen or twenty steps of Mr. Cowan, one of them raised his rifle and fired, the ball passing directly through Mr. Cowan's right thigh. Another Indian who had been riding close to Mr. C. then leveled his gun on Mr. Cowan's head, but to avoid this shot he slipped from his horse, and being unable to use the wounded leg, fell to the ground. Mrs. Cowan was the first person to reach her husband after his fall and was bending over him, when two Indians who had jumped from their horses came running up, one of whom asked Mr. Cowan, who had raised up on his elbow, if he was shot through *here* pointing to his own breast, and upon being told no, that he was wounded through the leg, he immediately drew a large revolver and presented it at Mr. Cowan's head. Mrs. C, observing the movement threw her arms around her husband's head and her body in front of his face, shielding him from this shot. The Indian then caught Mrs. C. by the right hand and attempted to drag her away from her husband, but she still clung to his neck with her left hand. This movement gave the second Indian a full view of Mr. Cowan's head, when, with a quick movement he drew a revolver from beneath his blanket and fired a shot therefrom which took effect in the upper part of Mr. Cowan's forehead, rendering him perfectly insensible and oblivious to everything else that then transpired.[59]

Years later, Emma Cowan recalled looking up just before the warriors shot her husband in the head: "The holes in those gun barrels looked as big as saucers."[60] As the firing broke out, Charles Mann felt a bullet slice through his hat "without touching my hair." Albert Oldham, meanwhile, had been hit in the face, the bullet tearing through his cheeks "without [major] injury to his teeth or tongue," but knocking him down. Instantly, he had turned on his attacker, pointing an empty rifle at him, and the Nez Perce bolted while Oldham dove into the brush, where he roamed for an agonizing thirty-six hours sustaining himself on crickets until rescued by Howard's column. Charles Mann likewise took to the bushes, lying there for four hours before finding his way back to the Lower Basin camp and then heading down the Firehole where the army scouts found him the next day.

Mrs. Cowan and Ida Carpenter went unharmed in the melee. Frank Carpenter had also run into the brush, but when a warrior trained his gun on him, he made the sign of the cross and the warrior did not fire but took him captive.[61] Henry Meyers and William Harmon both fled into a marsh and hid among the reeds. Harmon was picked up the next day by Fisher and his scouts on the Madison six miles below its junction with the Gibbon and Firehole rivers soon after Mann was found. Harmon, "exhausted from hunger and fatigue," the next morning went down to join the command; Mann kept on with the scouts for four days searching for others of the party. Meanwhile, Arnold and Dingee, who had initially fled from the warriors, managed to get away through the woods after abandoning their mounts and eventually reached the Gibbon River. Henry Meyers found Howard's command at Henry's Lake and told of the presumed deaths of Cowan and Oldham at the hands of the Nez Perces. Dingee and Meyers soon departed for their homes via Virginia City, while Arnold stayed with the command.[62] In fact, George Cowan, having been shot, had afterwards been nearly brained by a warrior who struck the prostrate man on the head with a large rock. Left for dead, he came to within hours of his wounding, tried to stand upright, but was shot again— this time in the hip— by a warrior lingering nearby. Cowan did not move, and after several Nez Perce men passed by driving horses without observing him, he waited awhile and then pulled himself along the ground by his elbows through the stream and along it for a distance of one-half mile. He alternately crawled and rested and, over the next four days, traversed about twelve miles. Near the place where the wagons had been abandoned, Cowan found his bird dog, who stayed with him through his subsequent journey. At one point in his travail, Cowan saw Fisher's Bannocks, but fearing they were Nez Perces, he remained hidden. Finally gaining the camp site at Lower Geyser Basin, he found a dozen matches, and with potential meat and fire at hand, and strengthened with

George and Emma Cowan in 1901, visiting the site in Yellowstone National Park where George Cowan was left for dead after being shot.
YELLOWSTONE NATIONAL PARK ARCHIVES, MAMMOTH, WYO.

some weak coffee he managed to brew in an old fruit can, Cowan rested overnight, then started back to the mouth of the East Fork of the Firehole, confident of being rescued. Howard's scouts with "Captain" Rube Robbins encountered Cowan on August 29 and were able to inform him that his wife and sister-in-law had been released safely. The next day, Howard's surgeon treated his wounds. Cowan, Oldham, and Arnold continued with the troops, but later departed for Bozeman via Mammoth Hot Springs and Bottler's Ranch.[63]

Probably because of the timely intervention of Poker Joe, the Nez Perces did no further injury to the remainder of the Cowan party, but kept the two grief-stricken women and Frank Carpenter with them until the next day.[64] In her narrative of the event, Mrs. Cowan recounted the passage of the Nez Perce procession up Mary Mountain on August 24 in a paragraph that probably described the character of the people's trek through the park:

> Over this mountain range, almost impassable because of the dense timber, several hundred head of loose horses, pack horses, camp accoutrements, and the five or six hundred Indians were trying to force a passage. A narrow trail had sufficed for tourists. It was a feat few white people could have accomplished without axe or implements of some sort to cut the way. It required constant watching to prevent the loose horses from straying away. As it was, many were lost and recovered by the Bannack Indians [scouts] later. The pack animals also caused trouble, often getting wedged in between trees. An old squaw would pound them on the head until they backed out. And such yelling! Their lungs seemed in excellent condition.[65]

At the camp that night on the east side of Mary Lake, Emma Cowan noticed that the tribesmen lacked tipis and instead protected themselves from the cold and rain with pieces of canvas stretched between poles or over bushes in the form of rude wickiups.[66] Frank Carpenter remembered that the camp was "on the outer edge of a circular basin about three-fourths of a mile in circumference" with its perimeter dotted with campfires and in which many of the horses were corralled.[67] Carpenter also stated that he met Joseph that evening and that the Wallowa leader had expressed displeasure with the actions of his kinsmen in opening fire on the Radersburg people.[68] On August 25, following a council of leaders, the Nez Perces released Mrs. Cowan and the Carpenters from their camp on the east side of the Yellowstone

above the Mud Volcano. "We did not want to kill those women," remembered Yellow Wolf. "Ten of our women had been killed at the Big
Hole, and many others wounded. But the Indians did not think of that
at all."[69] Given horses and clothing, and escorted by Poker Joe to the
west bank of the river, the three kept to the timber as they went along,
fearful of encountering more scouting parties. In their course, they
crossed Sulphur Mountain in the evening and night of August 25. On
the twenty-sixth, they forded Alum Creek, surmounted Mount
Washburn, and passed through the camping grounds near Tower Fall
before stumbling onto a detachment of Second cavalrymen from Fort
Ellis commanded by Second Lieutenant Charles B. Schofield near
present Tower Junction. The troops escorted the trio to Mammoth Hot
Springs, and from there on August 27 they started down the road to
Fort Ellis and Bozeman, with Emma Cowan eventually to be reunited
with her husband following his own ordeal.[70] In his wire to Gibbon
from Mammoth, Schofield reported intelligence, perhaps gleaned from
Mrs. Cowan and the Carpenters, that the Nez Perces were en route to
Wind River and Camp Brown for supplies; however, the lieutenant offered his own belief that they were headed for the lower Yellowstone by
way of Clark's Fork. [71]

The Radersburg party was not alone in their experience with the
Nez Perces. A few miles from where the bloody eruption involving
Cowan and Oldham occurred on the Mary Mountain trail, another group
was about to fare even worse in their meeting with a group of warriors
from the caravan. The so-called Helena party of ten men included Andrew
Weikert, Richard Dietrich, Frederic J. Pfister, Charles Kenck, John
(Jack) Stewart, Leander Duncan, Leslie N. Wilkie, Benjamin Stone,
and two youths, Joseph Roberts and August Foller, aged twenty and seventeen, respectively. Several of the party under Weikert had left Helena
on August 13, reaching Mammoth Hot Springs on the twentieth, where
they met the other members. Together, they started sightseeing two days
later, visiting Tower Fall and traveling to Falls of the Yellowstone, near
which they camped on the evening of August 23, at about the time
prospector John Shively was being approached by the Nez Perces near
Lower Geyser Basin. The next day was spent further touring the falls,
and on Saturday, the twenty-fifth, the party crossed Alum Creek and
passed up Sulphur Mountain enjoying the scenery as they headed toward the Mud Geyser. Late in the morning, from the heights about

This stereopticon view of the Radersburg refugees and others at Bottler's Ranch, en route out of the national park on August 30, 1877, was taken only five days after the Nez Perces released the Carpenters and Mrs. Cowan. Left to right, front row: Ida Carpenter, Emma Cowan, and Frank J. Carpenter. Back row: Packer Boney Ernest, "Texas Jack" Omuhundro, and Captain Bailey and Mr. Birmingham, both of the British Army.
CALFEE AND CATLIN, PHOTOGRAPHERS; MONTANA HISTORICAL SOCIETY, HELENA

Sulphur Mountain, they observed the Nez Perce assemblage several miles to the south as it passed through Hayden Valley toward the Yellowstone, at first mistaking the throng for a herd of elk or a large group of tourists. "We could see something alive coming, but did not know what it was," stated Ben Stone. A mile or so farther, "on reaching the top of a small hill, [we] saw a large camp across the Yellowstone. Duncan exclaimed: Indians! Indians! My God, it's Indians!"[72] On discerning their identity, the Helena party hurriedly consulted and decided to remove their camp back from the falls and await the departure of the tribesmen. Stated Andrew Weikert: "We went into camp between the forks of the first creek [Otter Creek] above the upper falls, about a mile and a half above the falls, and felt quite secure."[73] Nevertheless, some of the party spent a restless night.[74]

On the twenty-sixth, two of the group, Weikert and Wilkie, rode out to see if the tribesmen had moved as the rest of the party lolled about camp. Evidently informed of the presence of the Helena tourists by the discharged soldier, James Irwin, whom they had picked up on the twenty-fifth, at least one scouting party of Nez Perces had mounted an effort to seek them out, doubtless to obtain whatever provisions they possessed.[75] Yellow Wolf's narrative, the only known Nez Perce source that touched on the subject, suggested that the party was led by either Kosooyeen or Lakochets Kunnin (Rattle Blanket).[76] In the afternoon, without warning, several warriors dashed into the camp firing their weapons. The attack was swift and caught everyone off guard, but they scattered nonetheless, running into the brush with the warriors in hot pursuit. As Ben Stone recalled, "Duncan sprang up like a deer and we were not long in following suit."[77] Frederic Pfister and Richard Dietrich ran off in the direction of the Yellowstone, but Dietrich failed to jump Otter Creek and landed in it, where he remained for several hours while the Nez Perces plundered the camp. Leander Duncan also ran into the woods and hid until dark and then started for Mammoth Hot Springs. John Stewart and Charles Kenck ran off nearly together, but the warriors wounded Stewart in the leg and hip and chased Kenck until they caught up with him, then shot him twice. Stewart heard Kenck cry out, then go silent. Shortly, one warrior returned and demanded money from the wounded Stewart, who turned over $263 and his silver watch. Unable to find Kenck or any others of the party, Stewart managed his way back to the camp after the warriors had gone, retrieved an overcoat, soaked his hip wound in the stream, and set out on what he expected to be an arduous hike to Mammoth Hot Springs. Soon, however, he chanced upon his own horse, but was unable to balance himself with no saddle. At Cascade Creek he washed his wounds and then moved on; after a mile or so, he encountered Ben Stone. At the initial shooting, Stone had run and somersaulted down the hill and landed in the stream, remaining hidden there for three hours while the warriors completed their raid. "I asked him if he was wounded," related Stewart, "and he said he was not. I told him I was, but whether badly or not I could not tell. I then asked him if he would stay with me and help me through to the Springs, and he said he would."[78] Together, they ate lunch and started down the trail.

Weikert and Wilkie, meanwhile, on returning from their lookout on Sulphur Mountain, ran directly into the warriors near the Yellowstone at the mouth of Alum Creek. The warriors were dismounted, and Wilkie had no trouble turning his mount and getting away. But as Weikert spurred his horse to follow, the Nez Perces fired at him, clipping his shoulder blade. Another bullet ripped into his gun stock. His horse stumbled and threw him, but Weikert was able to remount and escape with Wilkie. Both then raced up Alum Creek and circled through the timber back to the camp in an attempt to warn their colleagues, but on their arrival they realized that they had been too late. The warriors had taken their blankets, tents, and saddles and made off with fourteen horses. They had smashed several shotguns and burned whatever they did not want.[79] Provisioned with a ham found in the camp, Weikert and Wilkie started for Mammoth and soon overtook Stewart and Stone. With Stewart mounted on Wilkie's saddle horse and the lame Stone on Weikert's, the four men ascended and descended Mount Washburn and continued down the Yellowstone, gaining the hot springs shortly before 6:00 A.M. next morning, August 27. At McCartney's hotel they found their colleague, Frederic Pfister, who had reached Lieutenant Schofield's command near Tower Junction the preceding evening, within hours of the arrival there of Emma Cowan and Frank and Ida Carpenter. Pfister had gone back to Mammoth with Schofield's detachment, and on the morning of the twenty-seventh he started with the troops to Fort Ellis. An ambulance was summoned to transport the wounded Stewart to Bozeman, and he started down on Thursday morning, August 30.

Another of the Helena party arrived at Mammoth on the morning of August 27. Leander Duncan had also escaped the Nez Perce attack; he reported that Richard Dietrich was on the back trail two miles away, exhausted, and Weikert—his wound cleansed and dressed—rode out with an extra mount and brought him in. Dietrich refused to go down in the ambulance with Stewart, protesting that he could not leave until Joseph Roberts and August Foller were found. On Wednesday, the twenty-ninth, Weikert and hotel proprietor James C. McCartney started back to the Otter Creek camp to bury Kenck and to try to learn something of the whereabouts of the two young men. Next day they found and buried Kenck's body, but a search of the area through the thirtieth failed to disclose what had happened to Roberts and Foller, and on the thirty-first Weikert and McCartney headed back to Mammoth Hot Springs. (Weikert would later learn that Roberts and Foller had somehow escaped the attack and survived several days and nights until they reached the Madison Valley, where they ran into some freight wagons en route to Howard's troops and acquired food. Then they set out on their own for Virginia City, reaching that place without incident on August 31 where they erroneously reported the death of Ben Stone.) On the way, and within twenty miles of the springs, Weikert and McCartney engaged in a spirited encounter with eighteen Nez Perces who succeeded in dismounting them and driving them into the underbrush along the base of Mount Everts.[80] "The Indians never let up shooting, but kept picking up the dust all around me," recounted Weikert. "I think they must have fired fifty shots at me, but only cut a piece out of my boot leg and killed my horse."[81] Wilkie's horse spooked and ran off. Yet somehow eluding their pursuers, the men forded the Gardner River and walked the rest of the way into Mammoth.[82]

Exhausted from their ordeal, Weikert and McCartney arrived at Mammoth Hot Springs to find that the warriors had struck there.[83] On the thirtieth, Jake Stoner, an ambulance crewman who had remained behind at the springs, while hunting spotted a party of Indians near Lava Creek. Quickly returning to McCartney's place, Stoner warned Richard Dietrich and Ben Stone of the appearance of the Indians, and both men fled into the brush to hide. The warriors approached the cabin-hotel and searched around it. Ben Stone, who had retreated up a gulch to a wooded point of rocks behind the hotel, narrowly avoided the Nez Perces as they searched the area. But the Indians presently moved north beyond the park boundary toward Henderson's ranch, a complex established by James Henderson in 1871 and in 1877 managed by his son, Sterling, who provided mail service and provisions for area miners. (The ranch stood about six miles below Mammoth Hot Springs and two and one-half miles northwest of the present town of Gardiner and along the wagon road to Bozeman.) On the morning of August 31, when the Nez Perce scouting party of eighteen appeared at the ranch, five men were present—two at the house and three fishing in the Yellowstone some three hundred yards away to the east. Those at the house, John Werks and Sterling

Henderson—observing the warriors' advance a mile distant—hurriedly gathered up arms and ammunition belts and raced to join those at the river: Joseph Brown, George Reese, and William Davis. Meantime, the Nez Perces split into two groups, a party of eight continuing the approach while the remainder stood their horses and watched from afar. The ranchmen assumed a strong defensive position among some boulders one hundred yards from the house and, as the eight warriors began emptying horses from the corral, let loose a volley of shots against them.

The firing spooked the Nez Perces' own animals, leaving the tribesmen dismounted and seeking cover behind the house and barn, from which they returned the fire. After two hours of sporadic shooting in which neither side gained an advantage, Henderson and the others withdrew to the river and crossed in a boat to the other side. The mounted warriors then came forward and sent a few bullets over the stream after them while the party at the ranch set fire to the log house, retrieved their own horses, and escorted the captured stock back toward Mammoth Hot Springs. No one was hit in the exchange, but as the warriors completed their withdrawal from Henderson's ranch, Lieutenant Gustavus C. Doane—en route with Company E, Seventh Cavalry, forty-two Crow Indian scouts, and a few wagons—coincidentally came on the scene, having seen a plume of smoke as he passed Cinnabar Mountain. The Doane party had left Fort Ellis on August 27, under orders "to push up the Yellowstone to the [Baronett's] bridge at the mouth of East Fork, cross that, and feel for the Indians up the right bank of the Yellowstone."[84] As Doane's column passed along the Yellowstone, numerous anxious citizens had attached themselves to the command. Racing after the Nez Perces, a detachment from Doane's command managed to take back nineteen of the stolen horses.[85] The warriors went back into the park. By then, Richard Dietrich, who was a music teacher in Helena, thinking it safe after the previous day's alarm, had returned to McCartney's place for food. As he stood in the doorway of the cabin, a Nez Perce warrior named Chuslum Hahlap Kanoot (Naked-footed Bull), still enraged over the loss of family members at the Big Hole, took aim at Dietrich and killed him.[86] A short time later, a detachment of ten men from Doane's command under Second Lieutenant Hugh L. Scott, guided by a local man, Collins J. ("Jack") Baronett, arrived to find Dietrich's still-warm body, which they removed to the floor of the cabin. "He had plunged forward on his face," remembered Scott, "and had been shot again, the bullet going the length of his body."[87] The warriors had started back up the Yellowstone River to rejoin the main camp. Trailing past the base of the Liberty Cap geyser cone, Scott's men pursued the warriors to Lava Creek and then, at Baronett's insistence, returned to join Doane at Henderson's ranch, where they bivouacked.[88] Following their skirmish with these same Nez Perces, Weikert and McCartney arrived to find Dietrich dead on the floor. With Ben Stone also missing and presumed dead, the two continued down the road to Henderson's. In fact, Stone had escaped the warriors' rush on the cabin on the thirtieth; his harrowing ordeal to elude the Nez Perces involved his hiding in the branches of a tree and an encounter with a bear before he, too, reached Henderson's ranch that night for a reunion with Jake Stoner, who had previously arrived there, and with Weikert and McCartney, who came in an hour after Stone. The next day, Weikert with some soldiers and citizens from Henderson's went back up the river to McCartney's hotel to bury Dietrich in "an old bath tub," for they had no lumber for a casket. Six weeks later, Weikert returned to Mammoth Hot Springs and exhumed both Kenck and Dietrich for reburial in Helena.[89]

On Saturday, September 1, Doane directed Scott to take twenty men and scout down to Baronett's bridge, which crossed the Yellowstone just above its confluence with the East Fork, to determine if the Nez Perces had forded there and to fire the grass on his return to frustrate their passage along the valley.[90] Scott moved out approximating a pony trail that led from Blacktail Deer Creek to the bridge. He refused his Crow scouts' advice to stay on the trail for fear of an ambush by the Nez Perces. He described his procedure of advancing:

> We did not go over a ridge until we were assured all was safe beyond. With great difficulty in getting the horses down and up, we crossed the deep, narrow box cañon of Blacktail Deer Creek where there was no trail. The edge of the cañon was held by ten men to hold back any Indians who, though unseen by us, were doubtless watching us all the time, to keep them from coming up on the edge and killing us all like rats. The other ten went down with me, and we climbed out on the other side. Then we held the cañon edge for the others. I felt very uneasy at putting the cañon between me and the command, but had to carry out my orders.[91]

Reaching Baronett's bridge without sign of the Nez Perces, Scott's men set the grass on fire, but rain shortly extinguished it. Then the troops turned back. On the way, they came upon two scouts sent from Colonel Sturgis's command east of the park who were to try to find Howard. John J. Groff and J. S. Leonard had been fired on by warriors as they traveled Blacktail Deer Creek Trail. The warriors had wounded a fifteen-year-old Warm Springs Indian boy who had accompanied them, and Groff had been shot through the neck. The boy disappeared into the woods and was not seen again.[92] The two men went ahead to Henderson's, where Groff received treatment for his wound and rode in a wagon down to Fort Ellis. (Later, on his way back to Sturgis with dispatches from Fort Ellis, Leonard was over-taken and killed by the Nez Perces on Clark's Fork.) That night, Doane assumed a defensive position in some dry irrigation ditches and established a number of sentry posts around the bivouac.

Doane, a conscientious veteran officer revered by Scott as "a thor-ough plainsman," decided to proceed up Gardner River on the morrow on the advice of the Crows. He would leave the citizens with sufficient supplies at Henderson's. But Doane's movement was preempted by the appearance of a courier from Lieutenant Colonel Gilbert with instruc-tions for him to await his arrival.[93] Gilbert's message, written at Fort Ellis on August 31, read as follows:

> General Sherman and [Brevet Major] General Gibbon had a con-ference in my presence day before yesterday, the issue of which amounts to this, that I am to overtake you, assume Command of you and your party, and then communicate with General Howard whose presence General Sherman much needs in the Department of the Columbia, and should Howard go at once I am to take the Command of his column. I expect to camp about 10 miles out from this Post this afternoon of Sept. 2d, that is to say the third day out.[94]

Doane took it upon himself to notify General Howard, then passing through the park, with the following message:

> The enclosed letter received by me last evening will need no expla-nation. I am here with one Co 7th Cavalry, about 30 citizens, and 42 Crow scouts. Camped at a burning ranch, fired by the Nez-Perces yesterday. Will await Col. Gilbert here but to-day am sending you this to anticipate him. Please return a courier with the bearer of this (who may be able to find you to-night). I will look for an answer tomorrow night. Gen. Sturgis on Aug. 29th was at Crow Agency. His command of 450 men, and Crow scouts besides, should be on Clarks Fork about Heart Mt. but I fear he is *not* there.[95]

Bearing Sherman's message to Howard regarding the transfer of his command, Gilbert and Company L, Second Cavalry, under Lieutenant Schofield, reached Doane's force on September 3 and refused to allow the lieutenant to proceed on his mission. Doane, with years of Indian experience, firmly believed that the Nez Perces intended to move down an age-old trail that paralleled the Yellowstone to where Livingston, Montana, stands today and then cross to the Musselshell and through Judith Gap to the hunting grounds. So anguished was Doane by Gilbert's directive that, according to Scott, he wept. Taking command, Gilbert marched the combined force back down the Yellowstone and away from the Nez Perces to Miner's Creek; he then followed an old trail to and up the West Gallatin River to the Madison long after Howard had left Henry's Lake. Hardly a "young energetic officer," as specified by Sherman, Gilbert (1822–1903), at fifty-five, was eight years older than Howard. A West Point graduate (1846), Gilbert served in the Mexican and Civil wars and had been wounded at Wilson's Creek in 1861. Appointed acting major general and brigadier general of volunteers in 1862, his star fell quickly after perceived command deficiencies at the Battle of Perryville, Kentucky, and he ended the war a major at a desk job. In 1877, according to Scott, Gilbert mismanaged Doane's cavalry so badly that the horses were starving. "We piled up twenty-five saddles on the West Gallatin and left them there, unable to transport them, and we sent twenty-five horses down the Madison by easy stages to Fort Ellis to recuperate."[96] Several dismounted cavalrymen escorted the animals to Ellis. "We went down the Yellowstone a badly broken up command," said Scott. Gilbert never found Howard, never delivered Sherman's missive, and never took over Howard's command. The troops traveled slowly through the park on his trail, at one point camping at a spot formerly occupied by the Nez Perces, where Scout Jirah Allen found several baby moccasins. "I could not repress a wish that the fleeing, hunted creatures would get through all right."[97] Gilbert's men passed up and over Mount Washburn, then on down the Yellowstone to its junction with the East Fork. Here Doane and his fatigued men and animals departed for Fort Ellis via Mammoth Hot Springs. Gilbert, with about twenty men, continued on Howard's trail over to Clark's Fork before abandoning his mission "on account of the worn-out condition of the animals" and returning through the Crow Agency to Fort Ellis. Had Gilbert foregone his convoluted pursuit of

Howard and marched instead to Baronett's bridge, he would have intercepted the general on his way down the Yellowstone on September 5.[98]

On August 29, Howard's army pushed slowly up the Madison and camped in the canyon within the park boundary. The general sent a dispatch to McDowell, explaining that the Nez Perces might diverge southeast to avoid the troops from Fort Ellis.[99] He sent a courier to Fort Ellis requesting that Sturgis be informed "that the Indians will [probably] go by Clarke's [sic] Fork, or make a wider detour, if bothered by troops, in order to reach the Yellowstone. . . . I [now] do not think they will go to Wind River country unless forced in that direction." He directed that Captain Cushing move out and join Sturgis, if possible, and sent word to General Crook to watch for signs of the tribesmen moving southeast.[100] Howard also took the opportunity to prepare a field order lauding his men for their sacrifices and attempting to put a bright face on a campaign of, at best, mixed success, with hollow assurances that their "disciplined spirit" would be rewarded "in the conscientious performance of duty."[101] "The chief incident of the day," penned Major Mason, "was finding by the roadside the poor fellow who was shot through the face by the Indians and afterwards escaped—he was almost dead from hunger and cold."[102] Albert Oldham was "all covered with blood and withal . . . a sad looking spectacle."[103] Advancing farther into the park on the thirtieth, Howard found many impediments to his advance. "The country in which I was now operating was a river-gorge, or cañon, walled in by precipices and choked by marsh and undergrowth, the river so winding that in one day it had to be crossed five times."[104] That day they crossed the mouth of Gibbon River and started up the Firehole, camping on "a fine level piece of land partly covered with pines and partly meadow," about one mile above the mouth of the East Fork of the Firehole.[105] Later that day, the wounded George Cowan, who had been found the previous day by Howard's white scouts, was brought in for treatment by the surgeons. As the column settled in camp, many of its members took the opportunity to visit the geysers, marveling at the "puffing steam, squirting boiling water, lakes of clear blue hot water, holes full of boiling mud, chalk vats that made bubbles as large as your hat, bountiful formations of soda and magnesia, [and] needles of pure sulphur." On Friday, the column with its eleven wagons pushed up the East Fork of the Firehole on the trail, encountering one of the Radersburg party's wagons off to the right and slowly clearing a path for the army supply wagons as they went.[106] At the base of Mary Mountain, the troops stopped for the night.[107] Next morning, September 1, Captain Spurgin of the Twenty-first Infantry brought his engineering talent to the fore, ably directing his civilian "skillets" in preparing the route up and over Mary Mountain.[108] As Henry Buck explained:

> A route was laid out, not continuing on the old Indian trail, but following up ridges and gullies, also along some very steep side hills to pass from one ridge to another, where it would be necessary to use guy ropes fastened to the top of the wagon box, and men walk[ing] along side of the wagon, holding fast, thus preventing its capsizing. The last stretch of about one-half mile of heavy grade followed a sort of canyon or washout that was wide enough for the passage of our wagons. The bottom was filled with huge rocks, many of which it was necessary to roll aside before we could proceed. Our camp was on a nice little prairie at the foot of Mary Mountain, thence it was a dense forest to the summit, an estimated distance of three miles. There had been a fire that had swept through the pines, and trees lay criss-cross over each other on the way; much chopping had to be done and also some pick and shovel work. It took until the middle of the afternoon of the second [September 2], before we could make a start with the train.[109]

Thus, from the Firehole River, Howard's route paralleled the north side of the East Fork of the Firehole, gravitating northeast as it ascended Mary Mountain and skirted the west side of Mary's Lake. About one mile north of the lake, the road turned east, then south, cutting along the east side of Highland Hot Springs and continuing southeast for two miles before leveling east for ten miles across the south edge of Hayden Valley to the Mud Volcano and the Yellowstone River.[110]

On the morning of September 1, Howard moved his troops ahead of the workmen to Mary Lake, where they went into camp. During the day, more of the Bannocks began deserting the command and tried to make off with about forty horses belonging to the laborers. Eight of the scouts were arrested, and Howard made their release contingent on the return of the stolen animals, which by the next day had been accomplished. The remaining Bannocks (not counting those with Fisher) were released and then left the command. "The brave Bannock Indians have all deserted us," noted a correspondent, "and when we come to weigh their usefulness against their perfidy the latter largely predominates."[111] On the second, with the road completed, the wagons began their ascent of Mary Mountain. "My wagon was in the lead," recalled Henry Buck. "We hooked eight horses to it and made the start. Other teams were doubled up in like manner and our train was on the move." By noon on the third, all the wagons had reached Mary Lake; they then proceeded across Sulphur Mountain down to Alum Creek and toward the Falls of the Yellowstone.[112] Crossing a gentle plateau, they shortly approached a wooded ridge extending toward the river. Henry Buck remembered the details of the descent at what became known as "Spurgin's Beaver Slide":

> We . . . came to the conclusion that the only way to get down was to take a jump of some five hundred feet. Someone suggested to prepare a slide and go down hill like a beaver. The pines were not thick and the ground was smooth, although about as steep as the roof of an ordinary house. We picked a place that looked most suitable for our descent and commenced clearing a roadway. . . . We had with us a very large rope—one hundred feet long—for emergency cases and were now all ready to "go". . . . One end of the rope was fastened to the hind axle of my wagon, then two turns were made around a substantial tree, with several men holding onto the end of the rope so that the wagon could not get away, they payed it out as fast as the descent was made. Nothing daunting, I climbed up into my spring seat and gathered up the lines—not even taking off my leaders. I made the start downward and nearly stood up straight on the foot rest of the wagon, it was so steep. Slowly and carefully we went the length of the rope, when a halt was called and, with the aid of a short rope made fast to the hind axle and securely tied to another tree, we then loosened the long rope and came down and made another two turns around a nearby tree and was then ready for a second drive; thence a third and so on until the bottom was reached in safety. The rope was then carried up the hill and another teamster took courage to try his luck and his wagon, too, was landed at the bottom of the hill. This routine was continued until all the wagons in our train were safely landed on the little flat together.[113]

The wagons then proceeded to the Yellowstone River, to a point about two miles above the upper falls, where they stopped for the night. Passing through cold and rainy weather, on Tuesday, September 4, the wagons stalled at Cascade Creek. "From here we could see our soldiers camp on the high plateau across the canyon, about on the same ground where the Canyon Hotel now stands [in 1922]," remembered Buck.[114]

Again, the "skillets" stepped forward and cleared a roadway through the trees and erected a pole bridge across the stream. "The rope-act was here repeated to get our wagons down and teams again doubled up for the long climb to camp on the flat where the command lay waiting for us."[115]

Howard's troops, meanwhile, had camped at the ford, about six miles below Yellowstone Lake and near Mud Volcano, on the first, where they found "plenty of wormy fish." Next day, the command awaited the arrival of wagons from Fort Ellis bearing rations and badly needed clothing; many had been wearing the same outfits over the past several weeks. That afternoon, Captain Robert Pollock ordered Company D of the Twenty-first to strip and bathe in a medium-temperature hot spring. "Red flannels got a washing as did some choicer hides which had not seen water since leaving Wallula."[116] And on the evening of the second, the discharged soldier James Irwin had appeared, having escaped the tribesmen and encountered Fisher and his scouts up Pelican Creek. As previously indicated, he provided Howard with important news of the composition, organization, condition, and general location of the Nez Perces. Reported Howard: "The fact that they had a white man detained as prisoner and compelled to act as guide was encouraging as showing their ignorance of the country."[117] The general's Bannock scouts supplemented Irwin's information that the Nez Perces were headed in the direction of Clark's Fork, and Howard sent this word back by courier to Fort Ellis, attempting to coordinate with Captain Cushing's and Colonel Sturgis's columns. Howard also took Irwin's advice to follow down the Yellowstone River by a more accessible route than that of the Nez Perces. Therefore, on the afternoon of the third, the provisions having arrived, the troops marched down the left bank of the river and camped "on a little flat just above and nearly abreast of the lower falls."[118] On Tuesday, the general, distressed over Irwin's news that the Nez Perces had sent envoys to the Crows, dispatched a notice urging "that steps be taken to capture this delegation and prevent the Crows from forming an alliance with them."[119]

Because of the difficulty and delay in moving the wagons forward, Howard decided to cut loose from them, directing Spurgin to take them out of the park to Fort Ellis. Spurgin then continued down the Yellowstone, through Dunraven Pass and into Carnelian Creek valley, then slowly moved toward Tower Creek and down that stream to its junction with the Yellowstone. On the way, his men sighted Indians on a distant mountain, and Spurgin broke out the ammunition and, assuming a defensive position, braced for an attack. But they proved to be some of Doane's Crow scouts, and the excitement waned. The wagoners and civilians then detoured around Tower Fall, journeyed down the Yellowstone to strike Gardner River about one and one-half miles above its mouth, and erected a bridge to cross it. Then they went on down the Yellowstone and out of the park.[120]

Forging ahead with his supplies now carried by the pack animals, Howard's force on September 5 reached the confluence of the Yellowstone with the East Fork to find that Baronett's bridge had just been burned. (The act was probably accomplished by a Nez Perce party that included the "Snake chief"—probably the Shoshone, Little Bear—who, Shively told an interviewer, had burned the bridge. This party had traveled down the East Fork about August 31 from the body or bodies moving in the vicinity of Cache or Calfee creeks.[121]) Howard quickly made repairs utilizing logs found in an abandoned house and crossed his army, continuing up the East Fork of the Yellowstone after having learned from miners about the Nez Perces' attack on Henderson's ranch and Mammoth Hot Springs. (A group of Howard's scouts under "Captain" Robbins also rode to Mammoth and Henderson's to survey the destruction there.) He also heard that Colonel Gilbert had undertaken a "stern chase" in the wrong direction to find Howard. On the sixth, the soldiers started up Soda Butte Canyon, and on the seventh, couriers from Sturgis appeared, bringing Howard his first concrete knowledge of that officer's position near Clark's Fork, east of the park. The general sent three couriers to Sturgis (none of whom reached him) and dispatched orders to Cushing at Fort Ellis to hurry supplies forward to Clark's Fork. "Indians are between me and Sturgis," he told Cushing, "and I hope we shall entrap them this time. By marching toward Clarke's [sic] Fork you will be ready to re-enforce either Colonel Sturgis or myself."[122] Continuing northeast up Soda Butte Canyon (which Howard renamed "Jocelyn Canyon" for that Twenty-first Infantry officer), the troops arrived at the New Galena Smelting Works, there veering off east-southeast to intersect Clark's Fork, which they traversed on September 8, descending to the mouth of Crandall Creek where reports had indicated the Nez Perces were headed. Meanwhile, his scouts followed the tribesmen's trail from the mouth of Soda Butte Canyon that probably led up Cache Creek and its tributaries to Hoodoo Basin. Observed one member of that party:

The Indians camped here and it looks as though they had got brushed, or rather, lost; for the trail is new and they have had a most difficult matter to get out, but out they have got of course, and over a trail that beats anything we have yet found. . . . A great curiosity consists of a washed-out basin, where the constant action of the elements has left pinnacles, towers and battlements of titanic structure. . . . [The Indians] now number, nearly 200 lodges; their strength has been largely increased as is evident by the more numerous lodge fires we found at their camping places.[123]

As the Indians passed through and exited the park, the troops of several commands had begun converging on them, hoping to close their way to the north and east and to compel their surrender. In fact, the time spent by the Nez Perces in getting out of the national park actually facilitated that troop deployment. But the experience of the soldiers and the Nez Perces in the national park was also important from several other standpoints. For one, it compounded the difficulty the tribesmen faced in their efforts to reach the buffalo country and their anticipated union with the Crows, and it may consequently have affected decisions about their final destination. Furthermore, the delay of the people in getting through the park made it additionally unlikely that the Crows—ever more firmly fixed in their service capacity to the army command—would provide the relief and support they sought. While in the park, the Nez Perces' dramatic encounters with the tourist parties pointed up not only the fragmentation of control authority that existed among them, but revealed the mix of searing hatred toward whites still evident among some warriors in the wake of the Big Hole, with that of the compassion evinced by elements of their leadership. But as it affected the Nez Perces, the trek through the park wilderness also further tried the endurance of Howard's weary men. For their commander, while the objective of the Nez Perces' defeat and surrender was not realized, a residual benefit came in the nature of the knowledge gained from scouts and informants about their strength, composition, and condition that could contribute to produce their final subjugation. Having finally pushed through the park, and thus encouraged by the notices that the tribesmen were at hand, a reinvigorated General Howard remained confident that, between his own force and Sturgis's strategically poised command, the long and trying odyssey of the nontreaty Nez Perces was at its end.[124]

Canyon Creek

ON AUGUST 26, General Sherman wired Sheridan in Chicago: "I don't think Howard's troops will catch Joseph, but they will follow trusting to your troops heading them off when they come out on the east of the mountains."[1] Among the commands assigned by Sheridan to head off the Nez Perces as they emerged from the national park was that of Brigadier General George Crook, commander of the Department of the Platte. Both the Indians and General Howard's soldiers were presently operating in his administrative jurisdiction. Uncertain as to the exact direction the tribesmen were traveling, but nonetheless responding to the reports of scouts and other observers that they perhaps intended to reach the buffalo country via Wind River, Crook—on orders from Sheridan—prepared to confront them accordingly in the area south and east of the park. Crook planned an offensive from Camp Brown, Wyoming, to include six companies of the Fifth Cavalry and one of the Third, most of them permanently stationed at Fort D. A. Russell near Cheyenne.[2] These troops would cooperate with a battalion of five companies of the Fifth under Major Verling K. Hart. This battalion was already afield from Cantonment Reno on Powder River and was searching the area of north-central Wyoming for vestiges of the Lakota-Cheyenne alliance left from the Great Sioux War. At Sheridan's direction, a contingent of Oglala Sioux scouts started from Red Cloud Agency, Nebraska, for Hart's command, which on September 6 got underway for the Bighorn River and the site of Fort C. F. Smith, abandoned since 1868. Originally, Crook was to personally lead the expedition, but problems arising at Camp Robinson, Nebraska, and environs after the death of the Lakota leader, Crazy Horse, took precedence, and Colonel Wesley Merritt, regimental commander of the Fifth Cavalry, assumed the command.[3]

Sheridan's design called for Major Hart and his four companies (7 officers and 239 enlisted men) to converge on the Stinking Water River (present Shoshone River) if the Nez Perces came down that stream.[4] If they exited the park and traveled down Wind River, Hart and/or Merritt would proceed there to stop them. On September 10, Crook reported to Sheridan that his scouts had found no sign of the Nez Perces on the Stinking Water, but that the Nez Perces had told the Bannocks with Howard that they were en route to join the Crows. "The fact of their loitering around the mountains in the Yellow Stone country would indicate that they were holding communication with other Indians so as to determine what their future movements should be," said Crook.[5]

Despite Crook's belief that the Nez Perces would not come south, Merritt moved out of Camp Brown (north of present Lander, Wyoming) with his seven companies (approximately five hundred officers, men, scouts, and teamsters) on September 9, hoping to cooperate with Hart and keeping fifty of the eighty-four Shoshone scouts under Chief Washakie posted well in front to intercept any news of the Nez Perces' approach.[6] With wagons instead of pack mules to carry its rations, the column on September 12 had difficulty surmounting the summit of the Owl Creek Mountains in a rainstorm and only slowly proceeded north-west toward the Stinking Water. Two days later, Merritt cut loose from his wagons, and on the fifteenth, the troops passed through a snow squall en route to crossing the Greybull River and trailing up Meteetse Creek to reach the Stinking Water on September 17, where a recent cavalry trail was discovered. Camping between the forks of that stream (above present Cody, Wyoming), Merritt sent out scouts who identified the trail as having probably been made by Sturgis's command operating from the vicinity of Heart Mountain, just twelve miles away. Later, the scouts established contact with Hart's battalion, which had ridden west from Fort Smith and then south through Pryor Gap in the Pryor range to reach the Stinking Water. The scouts led them back to join Merritt at the forks of that stream. The combined force then marched for Clark's Fork, but arrived far too late to join Sturgis and Howard, now well across the Yellowstone, and found only a few abandoned cavalry mounts. The aptly named Wind River Expedition concluded with the return of the eleven companies to Camp Brown on September 28, having been too late and too far removed to help find and subjugate the Nez Perces.[7]

Thus, for the moment, as the Nez Perces passed through and out of the national park, it remained for Colonel Samuel Sturgis to assume the principal role of confronting them. Sturgis's involvement in the campaign would constitute an important change in the direction and conduct of the army's pursuit of the tribesmen, for with the introduction of the aggressive Colonel Nelson A. Miles and his Yellowstone Command onto the scene (of which Sturgis's Seventh Cavalry was a major component), it now became a matter only of time and opportunity for the war with the Nez Perces to conclude. Anticipating the Indians' goal of gaining the buffalo grounds north of the Yellowstone, and perhaps uniting with the Sioux under Sitting Bull near the British line, Miles, on August 12, as mentioned, had sent Sturgis and part of the Seventh Cavalry west from their camp opposite the Tongue River Cantonment (on the Yellowstone River at the mouth of the Tongue) to strategically poise themselves in the Judith Gap, a stretch of prairie land lying north of the Yellowstone and between the Little Belt and Big Snowy mountain ranges through which the Nez Perces might logically attempt to pass. Miles's orders to Sturgis were as follows:

> With six companies of your regiment and the Artillery Detachment [a bronze twelve-pounder Napoleon gun] with your command you will proceed by rapid marches, via the valley of the Yellowstone and Musselshell Rivers to the vicinity of Judith Gap, sending forward rapidly to Fort Ellis, M.T., to obtain all possible information regarding the movements of the hostile band of Nez Perces. . . . It is the object of your movement to intercept or pursue, and capture or destroy them. . . . The Crows and Nez Perces have hitherto had friendly relations, but it is deemed probable that the former will act with your force against the Nez Perces, as they are hostile to the Government. You will please use your discretion as to the extent to which you can rely upon them (the Crows) for the object you have in view, being careful to avoid exciting hostility on the part of the Crows. . . . Your command will be provided with thirty six-mule

> teams, two ambulances and the pack train now at your camp. . . . In
> addition, . . . you will have driven with your command Beef Cattle
> for 25 days supply.[8]

Miles next day followed up with the comment: "I think it desirable that as much force as possible be brought to bear against the Nez Perces, with a view to striking a decisive blow and bringing them into complete subjection to the Government."[9]

Fifty-five-year-old Samuel D. Sturgis (1822–1889) graduated from West Point in 1846. He had gone immediately as a lieutenant of dragoons into the war with Mexico, where he was captured before the Battle of Buena Vista and not released until its conclusion. Until the Civil War, he served primarily in the West, where he garnered experience in numerous campaigns against Apaches, Kiowas, and Comanches. During the war, Sturgis fought in many engagements in the eastern and western theaters, rising to the rank of brigadier general of volunteers after his performance at Wilson's Creek, Missouri. He fought at Antietam and Fredericksburg in 1862. But his reputation as a commander faded after his rout by the Confederate cavalry leader Nathan Bedford Forrest at the Battle of Brice's Cross Roads, Mississippi, and after an investigation, Sturgis spent the rest of the war "awaiting orders." Appointed to command the new Seventh Cavalry in 1869, Sturgis endured Custer as a subordinate (unless assigned detached service elsewhere) until after the Battle of the Little Bighorn in 1876, which saw half his regiment annihilated and his beloved son, Second Lieutenant James G. Sturgis, a recent graduate of the military academy, among the killed. Following that tragedy, Sturgis assumed personal command of the regiment, leading it west from Fort Abraham Lincoln, Dakota, the following spring to participate in Miles's closing operations against the Sioux and Northern Cheyennes, thus availing his troops to counter the Nez Perces.[10]

Sturgis's command consisted of Companies F (Captain James M. Bell, Second Lieutenant Herbert J. Slocum), G (First Lieutenant George D. Wallace, Second Lieutenant William J. Nicholson), H (Second Lieutenant Ezra B. Fuller, Second Lieutenant Albert J. Russell), I (Captain Henry J. Nowlan, Second Lieutenant Edwin P. Brewer), L (First Lieutenant John W. Wilkinson), and M (Captain Thomas H. French, Second Lieutenant John G. Gresham) and numbered about 360 officers and men. The troops were divided into two battalions of three companies each, with F, I, and L commanded by Major Lewis Merrill, and G, H, and M under Captain Frederick W. Benteen.[11] Sturgis's adjutant was First Lieutenant Ernest A. Garlington. The march along the north side of the Yellowstone to the landmark of Pompey's Pillar was hampered by a dearth of rations occasioned when a supply steamer sank above the cantonment; the shortage was relieved only by sending a detachment to obtain provisions at the Bighorn Post (later Fort Custer) then under construction at the confluence of the Bighorn and Little Bighorn rivers.[12] (Although supplies arrived on the twentieth, the loss of proper rations haunted the troops for the duration of Sturgis's campaign.) Also, alarming rumors reached Sturgis from Miles that Sitting Bull with his Lakotas had recrossed from Canada into the United States, headed toward the mouth of the Musselshell on the Missouri River. Therefore, wrote Miles, "it is important that the hostile Nez Perces should be captured or neutralized to prevent their joining the band of hostile Sioux." And later he urged Sturgis: "Keep your force between the Nez Perces and Sitting Bull, if possible, and [I] should be very glad if the former could be struck first."[13] Sturgis reached the Musselshell on August 19, having marched cross-country from Pompey's Pillar. "At this time," wrote engineer officer First Lieutenant Luther R. Hare, "the valley was covered with immense herds of buffalo."[14] On the twenty-first, the troops continued upstream toward Judith Gap, where Lieutenant Doane was already maneuvering with his Crow scouts. A courier from Second Lieutenant Ezra B. Fuller, who with five men had previously ridden up the Yellowstone from the cantonment to Fort Ellis, brought word that the Nez Perces were still in the vicinity of Camas Meadows and, moreover, were likely en route to Wind River.[15] This news decided Sturgis to turn back toward the Yellowstone, to near the mouth of the Stillwater, and, as he notified Governor Potts, to keep watch for the Nez Perces' possible emergence into or along the Yellowstone Valley or to be ready to move his command toward the Stinking Water or Wind River. As Doane departed for Fort Ellis in accordance with instructions from Gibbon (and much against Sturgis's preference), Sturgis had hired John J. Groff and J. S. Leonard, with the Warms Springs boy, to scout the Clark's Fork and Stinking Water region and "to penetrate the park until they could bring me definite information in regard to the hostile Indians."[16] (It was these two men that Lieutenant Scott encountered in the park on September 1.) On the twenty-fifth, Sturgis forded the Yellowstone and then moved up the Stillwater to the Crow Agency, where he hired six Crows and a French guide named Rogue. These he sent forward into the Clark's Fork and Stinking Water region after receiving a telegram from Howard citing the latter stream as the likely objective of the Nez Perces.

Miles also directed Sturgis to proceed farther south "to near Stinking Water." "You may yet capture or destroy the Nez Perces," he wrote on August 26. He advised that Sturgis might initiate their surrender by "sending a small party of Crows, or any white man that knows them . . . demanding their surrender on the same terms as other Indians who have surrendered to this command, assuring them that they will receive fair and just treatment from the Government."[17] Next day, Miles changed his mind, writing Sturgis, "I would prefer that you strike the Nez Perces a severe blow if possible before sending any word to them to surrender."[18] Meanwhile, angered by the meddling of Gibbon in directing Doane up the Yellowstone ("cruel interference with my orders and plans"), Sturgis waited at the agency for his scouts to return until August 31; then, hearing nothing and fearful that the Nez Perces were passing east through the park, he moved his force toward Clark's Fork.[19] His plan, as he notified Colonel Miles, was as follows:

> In case I should learn that the hostiles had moved up the East Fork of the Yellowstone [Lamar River], then I would move up the cañon of Clark's Fork, going on if necessary until we should encounter them in the Soda Butte Pass; otherwise I would establish my camp near Heart Mountain, and from that central point observe the outlets both on the Stinking Water and Clark's Fork, all depending on the information I might receive in the mean time.[20]

But Sturgis's difficulties were just beginning. Reaching the mouth of Clark's Fork Canyon on September 5, he continued to a tributary two miles away and went into bivouac, where his hungry men used grasshoppers to hook many fine trout.[21] The colonel had discovered, in fact, that no trail led through the canyon, and he therefore determined to march next day northwest up a stream that would lead, ultimately, to Soda Butte Pass. Word from his Crow scouts and the Frenchman, Rogue, however, that the country to his right was impenetrable, and that, moreover, the Nez Perces could not descend via that route, turned his attention toward the Stinking Water. On the sixth, Sturgis sent his wagons with twenty-five men back to the Crow Agency for provisions expected to arrive from Fort Ellis. His Crows also departed for the agency, and the colonel dispatched Rogue and a prospector named Seibert with a notice to miners in the Clark's Fork area regarding the proximity of the Nez Perces ("As they are hostile and murdering all the unarmed people who come in their way, I send this to put you on your guard.").[22] These men on the eighth met Howard's command and alerted that officer to Sturgis's location, but somehow failed to return and alert Sturgis to Howard's presence. On September 7, Sturgis marched his men again for Clark's Fork Canyon, fully intending to start for Heart Mountain, a lofty pinnacle shooting up from the plains some fourteen miles southeast from his position. Next morning, scouting parties struck out in divergent directions for the Stinking Water and the upper reaches of Clark's Fork, led, respectively, by Lieutenants Hare and Fuller. At 3:00 that afternoon, Hare returned to report having found Rogue and Seibert sixteen miles away, one dead and the other badly wounded, apparently having been attacked by Nez Perce warriors coming from the Stinking Water. The injured man was subsequently treated and sent in company with several prospectors back to the agency.[23] Fuller, too, brought word that from a mountaintop he had sighted the tribesmen moving toward that same stream before they disappeared beyond some mountains. "The guide who accompanied him," Sturgis later reported, ". . . assured me that from the point where the Indians had disappeared behind the mountain range, it was altogether impossible for them to cross over to Clark's Fork, and that they must necessarily debouch on the Stinking Water."[24]

Sturgis's next decision was inadvertently horrendous as it affected army plans to close on the Nez Perces as they emerged from the park. Apparently against the advice of some of his senior officers, he resolved to drive his force cross-country to the presumed outlet of their route and head the people before they gained the Stinking Water, then follow up on that route until he met them or turned them back onto Howard's army, "wherever it might be." Perturbed that Doane's command was unavailable to help monitor both potential routes of the tribesmen, on the evening of September 8, after sending the balance of his train and the Napoleon gun back to the agency, Sturgis set out with pack animals for the Stinking Water, moving up Pat O'Hara Creek, a tributary of Clark's Fork, and camping after fifteen miles, probably on Skull Creek, near the base of Heart Mountain.[25] Next day, his command negotiated the rough terrain west and south of Heart Mountain and forded the Stinking Water about noon east of its canyon. "The sulphur fumes are distinctly noticeable a mile from the stream," wrote Lieutenant Hare, "all coming from the sulphur-beds in the cañon."[26]

On the morning of the tenth, in a "tedious march" owing to the "continuing rarity of the atmosphere," his men recrossed the Stinking Water (both forks)[27] and turned up a tributary (probably Rattlesnake Creek) leading northwest from the North Fork of the Stinking Water. They crossed the divide to Dead Indian Creek, an affluent of Clark's Fork, where they found the trail of the Nez Perces and camped at high altitude, probably in the vicinity of Dead Indian Pass. The tribesmen's path suggested that they had turned back and descended into Clark's Fork, effectively circumventing Sturgis's troops while leading, and thus evading, those of Howard yet on the back trail coming from the park. Sturgis, wrote Hare, had been misinformed by "the ignorance of the guides and their confusion." On Tuesday, September 11, Sturgis roughly paralleled Clark's Fork Canyon to reach the river below the mouth of the canyon directly on the Nez Perces' trail. Late in the day, the troops came on an abandoned government horse bearing a First Cavalry brand, evidence that Howard's army probably lay somewhere ahead on the trail.[28]

General Howard's command, after discovering signs of the Indians at the mouth of Crandall Creek on Clark's Fork on September 8, had, in fact, continued down the stream, where Sturgis's couriers to the miners found them. Howard quickly responded with a message telling Sturgis of the Nez Perces' presumed course (possibly even toward the Stinking Water) and urging cooperation. "If you can check them in front, I will be able to close on them and strike them from the rear."[29] (As previously stated, however, the couriers did not reach Sturgis.) In the rain and cold of Sunday evening, the ninth, one of Fisher's men killed a wounded Nez Perce discovered near the scout's camp. Another man scalped the dead tribesman, hiding the trophy from Howard's view when he approached to alert them of Sturgis's presence "within twenty miles" and that a fight seemed imminent the next day. Instead, on the tenth, Fisher's scouts found the Indians' trail bearing southeast through the foothills toward the Stinking Water and then detected their apparent stratagem in turning Sturgis in that direction. As Fisher explained:

The enemy followed the trail towards the Stinkingwater about two miles, and then attempted to elude pursuit by concealing their trail. To do this, the hostiles "milled," drove their ponies around in every direction, when, instead of going out of the basin in the direction they had been traveling and across an open plain, they turned short off to the north, passing along the steep side of the mountain through the timber for several miles. When we reached the point where the enemy had endeavored to *cache* their trail, we scattered out in every direction looking for it. At first the scouts were at a loss to know which way they had gone but after spending some time in the search I was so fortunate as to stumble onto the trail. I then went back to apprise the command of this new change of direction.[30]

Fisher and his men later trailed the Nez Perces through what Fisher described as "a very narrow and rocky canyon" leading down to Clark's Fork. While the Nez Perces' course to Clark's Fork is not known with certainty, several scenarios based upon longtime study of the terrain are possible. One possible route would have the Nez Perces milling their horses in a grassy swale a mile or two south of Dead Indian Pass, then moving first north and then northeastwardly down Bald Ridge, parts of which would have afforded some concealment from Sturgis's scouts. By this route, they could have reached the upper end of Newmeyer Creek and followed its slope eastward, then northward to reach Clark's Fork two miles below the mouth of Clark's Fork Canyon. Another course would have them mount Bald Ridge and move two miles southeast toward the Stinking Water before milling their animals in a swale, then move east-northeast via the head and main course of Paint Creek to reach Clark's Fork. Finally, a somewhat longer and less direct route would have the Nez Perces move south up Dead Indian Creek, surmount a divide leading to the upper drainages of Trail and Pat O'Hara creeks, mill their horses in a swale along the latter stream, and then follow it in swinging east and north, circling around the east flank of Pat O'Hara Mountain and through Oxyoke Canyon before heading north to Clark's Fork. These routes (not all of which have been completely evaluated) either contain, or are likely to contain, at least some topographical elements that might conform to Fisher's "narrow and rocky canyon" reference. Whichever route the tribesmen chose, however, it is certain from the military documents and reminiscences that Howard's command trailed them over the same course and that Sturgis's command eventually did likewise in its return to Clark's Fork.[31]

Howard followed with his men, disappointed that he was still at least one day behind the Nez Perces and that Sturgis had not stopped them. His command continued down the right bank of Clark's Fork and bivouacked about two miles below the canyon. During the day, the scouts found and buried the bodies of three prospectors killed by the warriors as they passed. "They will kill everybody who falls into their hands now," wrote Major Mason, "in order to prevent the news of their movements from being known to those in front."[32] On the eleventh, joined by a few Crows arrived from the agency, they found a wounded German who reported that his two partners had been killed by the Nez Perces on Crandall Creek.[33] "If we ever get these fellows," allowed Mason, "they must swing—unfortunately, catching comes before hanging."[34] Again, Howard tried to communicate with Sturgis, telling that officer that the Nez Perces were now in his (Howard's) front and admonishing him that they must be stopped before reaching the Yellowstone. "Let me know just where you are and what you are doing," he wrote.[35] That evening, when Howard's soldiers camped along Clark's Fork, Sturgis's men, having that day followed the trail from Sunlight Basin, saw their fires and camped only four miles behind them. At Sturgis's approach to the spot he had vacated the evening of the eighth, Howard, with Major Mason, rode back to assume overall command. The two conferred, and, reported Sturgis, "we entered into mutual explanations, and had the poor satisfaction of exchanging regrets over the untoward course which events had taken."[36] A witness commented on the meeting: "[Sturgis was] so bitterly chagrined at the escape of the Indians from one of the best laid traps of nature and man, that he exclaimed:— 'Poor as I am I would give $1,000 if I had not left this place.'"[37] On consultation, the two agreed that Sturgis should press on after the Nez Perces by forced marches, accompanied by Lieutenant Otis's two mule-mounted howitzers, Major Sanford and fifty cavalrymen under Captain Charles Bendire, and Lieutenant Fletcher's twenty-five scouts. Hopefully, this force could overhaul the tribesmen and strike "a telling blow" before they crossed the Yellowstone. Howard would follow with the balance of the command "as rapidly as possible."[38] They further agreed to send a dispatch to Colonel Miles at the Tongue River Cantonment, explaining how the Nez Perces had managed to get past them, their (Howard's and Sturgis's) intended movements, and the anticipated route of the caravan after crossing the Yellowstone River. In the missive, drafted September twelfth, Howard asked Miles "to make every effort in your power to prevent the escape of this hostile band [should Sturgis fail to halt them], and at least hold them in check until I can overtake them."[39]

At 5:00 A.M., Wednesday, September 12, Sturgis and his augmented force, "almost breakfastless" despite meager provisions that had arrived from Fort Ellis, proceeded down the river toward the Yellowstone through a mist that grew into a torrential rain. They were also impeded by the necessity of fording Clark's Fork numerous times. "We had nothing to eat," recalled one trooper, "so we merely drew our belts one hole tighter, took a drink of water, threw the saddles on our horses . . . and hit the trail."[40] Sturgis drove his force mostly at a trot, and by 1:00 P.M., at the first halt, they had covered thirty miles. At 4:00 P.M., the men passed an abandoned Nez Perce camping site, but Sturgis kept on for seven more hours before calling a halt for the night about eight miles above Clark's Fork's confluence with the Yellowstone. Trooper Theodore W. Goldin described the scene:

> Some one discovered a fallen tree, and every one fell to bringing in arms full of brush, among which was some that was dry enough to kindle into flame. In a few moments that old tree was blazing merrily, and the outfit, officers and enlisted men alike, in wet, steaming overcoats, edged in as close to that roaring fire as they dared, seeking to thaw out the stiffness of their day's ride which we were told exceeded sixty miles.[41]

Most of the soldiers then succumbed to their weariness and "sank into a damp, restless, unrefreshing sleep." On directions of the officers, the packers set the mules to graze to stop their braying, fearful that the noise would warn any Indians nearby of the troops' presence.[42]

The Nez Perces, were, in fact, close at hand, having forded the Yellowstone on September 12 and moved downstream about six miles to camp. According to their own sources, a young man named Ilatakut (Bad Boy) had guided them in the circumvention of Sturgis and the evasion of Howard in the mountains and foothills. The large body of tribesmen, with all their horses and belongings, had beaten both officers to the Yellowstone, crossing below the mouth of Clark's Fork.[43] They at last recognized the futility of attempting a union with the Crows, whose tribal interest dictated their continued allegiance with the government, although it is likely that much sympathy of the Crows rested with their old friends in their plight. By now, the once-remote Canadian option loomed invitingly as the Nez Perce leaders cogitated over what to do and where to go, as it had increasingly since their sojourn in the national park.

On fording the Yellowstone, the tribesmen continued downstream to the grassy flats bordering Canyon Creek above its mouth, then turned up the creek bottom perhaps three miles where they encamped for the night, unaware that Sturgis was significantly gaining on them. Below Canyon Creek, the Yellowstone Valley narrows to less than one mile in width. The presence of the community of Coulson at that spot perhaps influenced the Nez Perce leaders to avoid an encounter with the settlers there by moving instead up Canyon Creek.[44] The lush Clark's Fork bottom of the Yellowstone Valley had only recently attracted settlers, and many had moved into the area in June.

Early the next morning, Thursday, September 13, a party of warriors started down the Yellowstone Valley to forage for supplies and encountered several newly established homes. Near the mouth of Canyon Creek, they alarmed settlers Elliott Rouse and H. H. Stone, who fled downstream to a neighboring ranch. The warriors stopped at the stage station built in the summer of 1877 on the east side of Canyon Creek and about one-half mile from the Yellowstone, and as the driver and passengers in an arriving coach—one a vaudeville entertainer named Fanny Clark bound for the mining camps—scurried into the brush, they fired the buildings and haystacks, scattered the mail, and tried to destroy a mowing machine. (While in hiding, Edwin Forrest, who ran the station, killed Miss Clark's little dog, which persisted in barking and drawing the Nez Perces' gunfire. He tried to slit the throat of his own somewhat larger dog, but the animal broke free of his grasp. "Nursing the cut kept the dog too busy to bark any more," wrote Scout John W. Redington.[45]) Reportedly, some warriors then mounted the coach and drove it over the prairie for amusement. Farther downstream, they found Bela B. Brockway's ranch and burned his hay house and corral. Again, most of the settlers found refuge in the bushes. But at the tract of thirty-year-old homesteader Joseph M. V. Cochran on the rich bottom five miles below Canyon Creek, two wolfers, Clinton Dills and Milton Summer, occupied a tent on the property when the Nez Perces arrived and killed both of them. Cochran himself was with some loggers upstream toward Canyon Creek when the warriors appeared.[46] Armed with a rifle, he approached and talked with them, and they eventually turned and rode off with his horses, but without harming Cochran. When he returned home, he found the bodies and that the Nez Perces had taken much property from his ranch, including clothing, utensils, tools, and ammunition. Some warriors ranged farther down the Yellowstone to the settlement of Coulson, near present Billings, where they burned a shack and exchanged shots with residents secured in hastily prepared rifle pits. They kept on to near the present town of Huntley before turning back to rejoin the main assemblage, then in process of moving up Canyon Creek.[47]

While all of this was occurring, Sturgis's command had descended Clark's Fork and crossed the stream to a plateau lying between it and the Yellowstone. Turning north, the soldiers located a ford (near where the present bridge crosses into Laurel) and, at about 10:00 A.M., began swimming their horses across the Yellowstone. Sanford's and Bendire's cavalrymen, along with Lieutenant Otis and the artillery, had dropped far behind because of their fatigued animals. Sturgis, in fact, seemed ready to halt his weary men, possibly intending to give up the chase altogether after gaining the north bank. While his scouts continued on the Nez Perces' trail, he penned a note to Miles, enclosing Howard's dispatch that had arrived, and sent it in duplicate via couriers down the Yellowstone to Tongue River.

The country entered upon by the Nez Perces and Sturgis on the north (west) side of the Yellowstone River was strikingly different from that they had known over previous days in the vicinity of the national park. The Yellowstone's left bank retreated in rolling fashion to form a lofty, broken scape of yellow clay ridges and plateaus, succeeded beyond by more, a tableland interspersed with broad valleys and sandstone buttes carved and weathered by millions of years of erosional action. Canyon Creek, on which the Nez Perces had camped the night of September 12, was dry in September except for infrequent alkali pools and represented more of a deep-walled slash through the grassy terrain. From the highlands bench overlooking Yellowstone Valley, the bed snaked its way south and east twelve miles down to the canyon mouth. Inside the canyon proper, a north fork fed into Canyon Creek. From the mouth, dominated by towering yellow, red, and gray-hued walls up to four hundred feet high, Canyon Creek ran southeast, entering the northeasterly flowing Yellowstone some six miles downstream from the place that Sturgis's troops forded. On either side, the bottom spread through a broad, mostly treeless, valley, or cove, through which rare tributaries fingered their way to the creek.

As the balance of Sturgis's troops waited on the left bank of the Yellowstone for the pack mules and rear guard to come over, a Crow scout rode up to announce that the Nez Perces lay just below and were headed toward the troops.[48] This news startled Sturgis. Peering downstream, Scout Fisher and his men could see a plume of smoke rising from buildings and haystacks ignited by the warriors miles away on the Yellowstone bottom.[49] Soon one of Sturgis's white scouts appeared with news that the main village was "going in a northwesterly direction" up Canyon Creek six miles away. The trumpeters sounded "To Horse," and the command set out at a trot. Two miles downstream, the troops received word from the scouts that the Nez Perces were headed toward the canyon of Canyon Creek, approximately ten miles north of the river.[50] At this, Sturgis veered his men north, away from the Yellowstone and toward the bluffs rising sharply four miles north to try and head off the tribesmen somewhere along Canyon Creek. Major Lewis Merrill's battalion of Companies F, I, and L (Bell, Nowlan, and Wilkinson)—150 men strong—led the advance as the troops rode ahead with Company L in the lead. Wilkinson deployed his unit in line and advanced behind the scouts, while Companies F and I followed in columns of fours at his flanks. Captain Benteen's battalion—minus Company H, which served as rearguard for the command, but with Sturgis in attendance—followed in reserve.[51]

As Merrill's battalion advanced, in Wilkinson's front a long ridge rose up to three hundred feet above the surrounding ground and ran roughly southwest to northeast toward Canyon Creek. Its top constituted a broad plateau of up to one mile in width, and from this point, probably before noon, warrior marksmen first fired on Wilkinson's soldiers as they attempted to skirt the ridge and head off the main body of Nez Perces. The shooting brought the troops to a halt; they then began moving forward in mounted skirmish formation and started up the slopes of the ridge, firing their Springfields as they went, while Merrill's other companies under Captains Bell and Nowlan, strung out behind because of their worn-out animals, closed in and similarly disposed themselves. Gaining rising ground, the command could see the Nez Perce column bearing up the north side of Canyon Creek, the tribesmen and

their camp dunnage moving along and the pony herd stretched out for
a mile, all bound diagonally northwest, apparently headed for the mouth
of the canyon that could not yet be discerned by the soldiers. As the
troops trotted up the ridge (which Merrill at first mistakenly believed
was the south side of the canyon), the warriors retreated, now bracing
themselves behind the northwest edge of the plateau to deliver a rapid
fire but ultimately withdrawing in the direction of the continually moving caravan. The army scouts, meanwhile, found themselves in front of
the troops who were ascending the plateau and momentarily got caught
in a crossfire—"a hot place," said Fisher. On top, the soldiers dismounted
with Company F on the right and quickly stepped across the broad
tract, finally settling at its northwest edge and continuing their desul-
tory shooting at the warriors, who returned a brisk fire from the ravines and washes punctuating the broken ground that stretched to the
canyon two miles distant. Fisher complained that the cavalrymen, "instead of charging which should have been done, dismounted about five
hundred yards from the enemy's lines, deploying to the right and left,
and opened a very rapid fire."[52] On the other hand, Merrill explained
that "the men were almost entirely recruits, but dismounted and formed
under fire, and moved rapidly to the front, driving the Indians with
perfect steadiness and unexpected coolness and absence of confusion."[53]
With the plateau cleared and in Sturgis's control, the troops finally
beheld the panorama before them. Wrote Merrill:

> The farther edge of the plateau being taken, it was then discovered
> that this was not the flank of the cañon, which could now be seen,
> with a broad valley some three miles wide intervening, amply inter-
> sected by ravines and gulches, in which the Indians were taking shel-
> ter to dispute further progress toward the cañon mouth.[54]

In fact, the "flank of the cañon," southwest of its entrance and forming
its south side, was an imposing sparsely wooded four-hundred-foot yel-
low-walled butte (today called Calamity Jane Horse Cache Butte) that
ran back nearly one mile from the mouth, while the opposite wall consisted of abruptly rising palisaded rimrock towering four hundred feet
above the creek bottom. The half-mile-wide mouth, or gorge, lying
between thus assumed both tactical and strategic importance, for
through it the people needed to pass if they hoped to get away from the
soldiers and protect their families and stock; they also needed the route

in order to gain the open plains leading north. By blocking the canyon, Sturgis's soldiers could prevent the Nez Perces' entrance and likely end the conflict.

After nearly thirty minutes of largely ineffective firing from the brim of the plateau, Merrill's dismounted skirmishers pressed down its slopes and proceeded through the sage-and-greasewood-covered flat, pushing the warriors back toward Canyon Creek and the Nez Perce column, still in motion toward the canyon's mouth. A cold, fiercely blowing wind seems to have affected the shooting ability on both sides, and the soldiers, at least, had trouble gauging the distance and accordingly adjusting their sights because their bullets, when striking the damp ground near the warriors, kicked up but little dust. Fisher observed that the warriors stationed themselves between the soldiers and their own horse herd. They "fought entirely on horse-back, firing mostly from their animals and at long range, doing but little harm."[55]

On gaining the plateau behind Merrill, Sturgis immediately comprehended the situation before him. His primary objective became the Nez Perce pony herd driven by the noncombatant women and children; he knew that to corral those animals would effectively stymie the people's advance. With the ground to his front torn up with ravines and ditches, Sturgis sent Captain Benteen, who with his battalion (reduced to Companies G and M) had assumed position on Merrill's left on the plateau, to ride to the west, skirting around the ravines and reaching

"Fight at Cañon Creek, Sturgis. Sep. 13th." Lieutenant Fletcher's drawing affords a compressed (and thus distorted) view of the action, showing the positions of troops engaged on the ridges in the foreground and the Indians' withdrawal into the mouth of the canyon.
INSET DRAWING IN FLETCHER, "DEPARTMENT OF COLUMBIA MAP"

negotiable ground near the base of the hills on the left, two miles away in a direct line, but about double that distance by traveling behind the plateau occupied by Merrill and then turning northeast toward Horse Cache Butte.[56] Benteen had earlier dispatched a platoon of Company M under Lieutenant Gresham to the western foothills, and he followed with the rest of his men. (Benteen's route on turning north probably approximated the course of the present Buffalo Trail Road north of Laurel.) On reaching the level plain beneath the west hills, Benteen was to charge his horsemen diagonally northeast, across the front of Merrill's troopers and across Canyon Creek, cutting off at least part of the horse herd before it entered the mouth of the canyon.

Simultaneous with the passage of Benteen's battalion across his front, Merrill was to mount his men, advance rapidly to flank the rear of Benteen's command, and guard it against Nez Perce sharpshooters who were increasingly posting themselves atop the buttes and ridges surrounding the mouth of the canyon. Benteen followed his intended route without disruption until he reached a point beneath Horse Cache Butte, from the top of which warriors delivered a blistering volley that dropped several men from their saddles as the troops rode past. Otherwise, Benteen's movement, reported Sturgis, "was executed with great promptness and vigor, gallantly driving the enemy before him all the way to and beyond the creek."[57] The captain succeeded in driving out warriors sheltered in a dry bed who fled up the creek to find cover behind rocks near the canyon mouth.

But at that point things went awry for the troops, for Merrill was unable to bring his men ahead as planned to guard Benteen's movement toward the horses. Sturgis later explained that Merrill's men had become exhausted from their having skirmished on foot across nearly three miles of rough terrain, a factor compounded by the failure of the holders to bring the led horses forward for the men to mount. "Either by reason of the difficulty of leading them over such broken ground when tied together in fours, or through some misunderstanding of their orders on the part of those having charge of them, [the horses] had become too far separated from the troops to be available in time."[58] Further complicating matters, a contingent of mounted warriors suddenly appeared near the led horses in the right rear, posing a threat to the ammunition-bearing pack animals and causing Merrill to halt his skirmishers while the warriors' purpose was divined. They proved to be Crows doubtless drawn

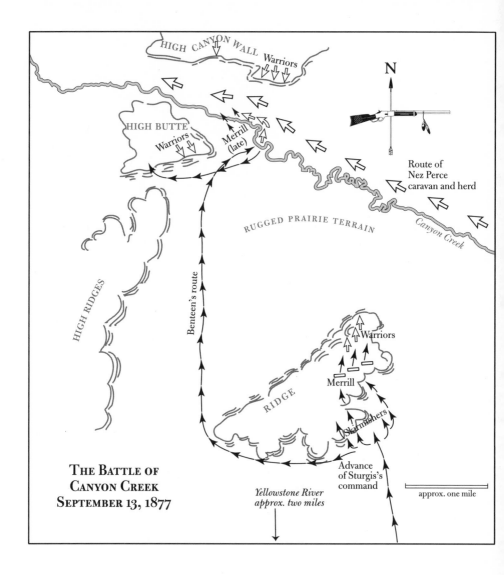

N

HIGH CANYON WALL   Warriors

HIGH BUTTE
Warriors
Merrill (late)

Route of
Nez Perce
caravan and herd

Canyon Creek

RUGGED PRAIRIE TERRAIN

HIGH RIDGES

Benteen's route

Warriors

Merrill

RIDGE

Skirmishers

Advance
of Sturgis's
command

**THE BATTLE OF
CANYON CREEK
SEPTEMBER 13, 1877**

Yellowstone River
approx. two miles

approx. one mile

by the possibility of obtaining Nez Perce mounts. As a consequence of these developments, and with the resulting lack of protection, Benteen scuttled the balance of his maneuver, thus halting his command—and apparently withdrawing it back across the creek—while most of the remaining Nez Perce horses reached the canyon.[59] Yet Sturgis exaggeratedly reported that the tribesmen lost as many as four hundred of their horses that could not gain the canyon mouth before being cut off. Whatever the number, they were undoubtedly captured by the Crows.[60]

PLAN of the Battle Ground.

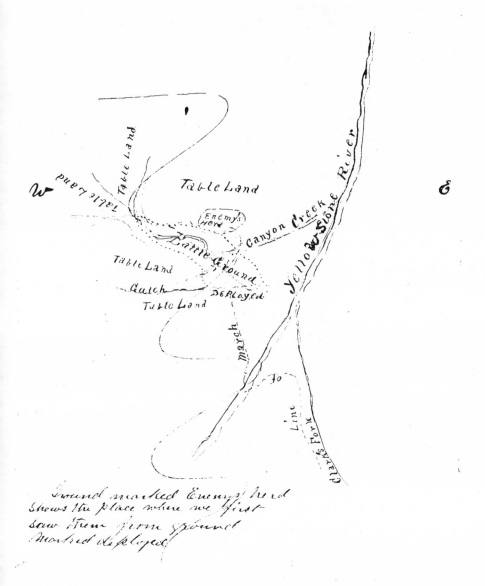

Scout Fisher's "Plan of the Battle Ground" of Canyon Creek, September 13, 1877
MONTANA HISTORICAL SOCIETY, HELENA

Merrill's men pushed on afoot and reached the mouth of the canyon after the Nez Perces, who left a rearguard of warriors to stiffly contest any further advance by the soldiers. "Here the hardest fighting was done," observed Fisher, "the hostiles having the advantage of being concealed behind the rocks and timber while we were on the open grassy bottom."[61] As long as Nez Perce sharpshooters poised atop the high bluffs and ridges surrounding the canyon entrance effectually controlled access into it, the soldiers lost all hope of gaining a tactical advantage, and Sturgis therefore turned his attention to clearing the heights. Nowlan's Company I was pulled back and placed in reserve on the right, the rest of Merrill's line extending to fill the vacated ground. At Merrill's order, ten soldiers from Company I in charge of Sergeant William Costello dashed their horses west across the valley to scale Horse Cache Butte, from which point they might enfilade the Nez Perces' position. "Orders were given the whole line to advance at the charge as soon as the first shots from Sergeant Costello's party showed that he had gained the bluff."[62] Soon after, Sturgis directed Benteen to lead his troops across the valley and gain a lodgement on the same butte, but beyond Costello. At about 4:00 P.M., that officer started with Companies G and M, joined by the just-arrived Captain Bendire's Company K of the First Cavalry and Otis's battery of one howitzer (the other had fallen into the Yellowstone while crossing), both delayed because of their severely weakened horses. Fisher said that he tried to direct Otis to a place where his gun would be most effective, but to no avail, and "I left him in disgust."[63] The artillery never saw action at Canyon Creek.[64]

According to descriptions given by Private Goldin, Benteen circled Horse Cache Butte to the south side, there passing through a narrow saddle-like aperture where the warriors again fired down on his men from the top of the butte. The soldiers spurred their horses up the steep slope as far as they could, then dismounted and continued their climb, urged onward by Benteen and Captain French, until they emerged on the plateau, deployed as skirmishers, and swept across to the north edge.[65] But by the time Benteen's men gained the height, most of the Nez Perces had withdrawn. Wrote Goldin:

> When they reached the top not an Indian was in sight. Not another shot was fired at us. We moved rapidly across the plateau on top of the bluffs [Horse Cache Butte] and dismounting crept cautiously to the edge and peered down into the draw below us. At first we saw

only a few fleeing Indians, well out of range, then some one discovered a party of fifteen or twenty in a deep draw, evidently holding some sort of a council. Although they were fully four hundred yards away, we gave them a volley and when the smoke lifted we could see a bare half dozen of them streaking it for safety down the draw, while the others lay there, dead or wounded.[66]

Meanwhile, as Benteen negotiated Horse Cache Butte, Costello's detachment had preceded his men to the top. As shots from Costello's troopers rang out, Merrill's line surged forward and into the canyon causing the warriors to fall back one to two miles into its upper recesses. But this action did not end quickly, as depicted by Fisher:

The Indians were driven very slowly from point to point up the gulch. . . . A squad of cavalry came up the gulch to a point nearly opposite us [scouts], but they did not stop long as the Indians opened a red-hot fire on them and they speedily retreated down the gulch again. We still tried to hold our ground, but the enemy got so numerous among the rocks above us that we could not raise our heads above the bank to shoot without receiving a volley in return. . . . It soon became apparent that we could not do any good by remaining where we were and that we would have to get out.[67]

The cavalrymen had themselves turned about and left the canyon, Captain Bell mounting his company in column of fours—"a foolhardy thing to do under fire," recalled Private Edwin F. Pickard. Merrill's men moved to the north side of Canyon Creek, where Company H, which had served as rearguard during the day's activities, joined them. This unit, commanded by Lieutenant Fuller and supported by Wilkinson's Company L, moved some eighteen hundred yards to the rimrock along the east side of the valley, there to scale the bluffs and "secure a lodgement." Farther to the right, Nowlan's I Company attempted the same. Captain Bell, meanwhile, led Company F back up the canyon to guard against any surprises by the Nez Perces against Fuller and Nowlan. Although the warriors tried to counter this movement, the attempt by the soldiers to surmount the perpendicular upper escarpment failed because of physical impossibility—"unscalable for even a goat," wrote Benteen. Wilkinson's covering gunfire proved ineffective because the warriors were well hidden behind overhanging rocks, and Fuller, at Sturgis's direction, presently withdrew to protect the hospital. Nowlan and Wilkinson in turn rode to the relief of Bell, who had become engaged with warriors in the upper part of the canyon. The major fighting, which had started at about 11:30 A.M., was over by 4:30 or 5:00 P.M. By nightfall, the Nez Perces had departed, leaving the troops to return to the mouth of the canyon, where Sturgis had set up his field hospital and where, it was learned, the Crows had advantaged themselves of the day's distractions, appropriating many items of personal equipment as well as some horses and pack animals. "The Crows took no part in the fight," protested Fisher, "but staid in the rear and stole every thing they could get their hands on."[68]

Within hours of the close of the encounter, Sturgis dashed off a note to be telegraphed to his superiors: "We have just had a hard fight with the Nez Perces lasting nearly all day. We killed and wounded a good many & captured several hundred head of stock. Reports not yet in and cannot give our loss but it is [a] considerable number killed & a good many wounded."[69] In fact, Sturgis's casualties in the Canyon Creek fighting totaled three enlisted men killed and an officer (Captain Thomas H. French) and eight men wounded, one of whom died later while being transported down the Yellowstone. Wilkinson's Company L, which was in the forefront in opening the action, sustained the heaviest losses, with two men killed and two wounded. The dead on the field were Private Edgar Archer (who actually survived until the fourteenth) and Private Nathan T. Brown, Company L, and Private Frank T. Goslin, of Company M.[70] (Brown served as acting sergeant major with Benteen's battalion.) That evening the soldiers buried Brown and Goslin in a trench. A witness said that the men "were literally shot to pieces, but no time was taken or effort expended in fixing or cleaning them up in any manner, but they were put into the trench with spurs, belts or other wearing apparel upon them." An officer conducted a service and a shot was fired over the graves.[71]

During the fighting at Canyon Creek, several episodes of a personal nature occurred regarding the soldiers. In one, a mixed-blood Bannock with Fisher went into the fray sporting "a bright scarlet Indian war-dress, topped out with an eagle-feathered war-bonnet." Although the scout, Charley Rainey, warned the soldiers not to shoot at him, apparently not all got the word. As Rainey and another scout, Baptiste Ouvrier, huddled among the sage cleaning their weapons after the fighting was well under way, a company of passing troopers spied them and, thinking them Nez Perces, leveled a volley their way, "cut-

Contemporary media views of the Canyon Creek engagement as they appeared in
HARPER'S WEEKLY, *October 27, 1877*

ting the feathers out of Charley's bonnet, shooting several holes through their clothing and tearing up the brush and dirt on all sides of them."[72] In another instance, Private James W. Butler of Company F was left behind in Merrill's initial advance because his mount was too fatigued to continue. Butler "followed rapidly on foot until he captured a pony, which he mounted bareback and galloped forward to the skirmish line, where he behaved gallantly during the fight."[73] The various scouts, both of Sturgis's and Howard's commands (evidently not constrained by the military discipline of the proceedings), ranged about—"bushwhacked around," said Redington—during the fighting and got involved in several small-scale skirmishes with the warriors. Redington was incredulous over one of these, in which a dozen or so scouts atop a knoll drew the warriors' attention:

> A shower of hostile bullets went slap-bang right among and through them, zipping and pinging and spitting up little dabs of dust under their horses' feet, and before and behind them. Logically, every one of those scouts was scheduled to get shot. And yet neither man nor horse was hit. Why? Don't know! . . . Must have been thirteen guardian angels watching over each scout and diverting bullets by inches and half-inches.[74]

Later, while joining his colleagues in a flank attack on a Nez Perce position, Redington received a wound in the knee. "One of my fellow Boy Scouts took his mouthful of tobacco and slapped it onto the wound, making it stay put with a strip of his shirt. It smarted some, but caused hurry-up healing, and the few days' stiffness did not hinder horse-riding."[75] Redington further remembered the aftermath of the battle, when "we had to cut steaks from the horses and mules shot during the day. The meat was tough and stringy, for the poor animals had been ridden and packed for months, with only what grass they could pick up at night. But it was all the food we had."[76]

Trooper Jacob Horner recollected the lack of food and water during the day-long fight, and the suffering of the wounded soldiers afterwards, many of whom, over objections of medical personnel, drank stagnant alkali water collected from buffalo wallows to relieve their thirst. Horner also recalled Colonel Sturgis's tendency to spit tobacco "in every direction. The other officers moved away to avoid him."[77] On one occasion, Horner acted as a messenger for Sturgis:

Sturgis noticed that the troops, who were dismounted and firing on their bellies, were removed too far from their horses. He turned to me and ordered me to deliver a verbal message to Major Lewis Merrill to bring the horses closer. . . . I mounted and headed for the puffs of smoke. When I got into the center of action I suddenly had a strange feeling. I saw that I was the only mounted trooper in sight. What I had to do, had to be done quickly. The bullets were whining over the field. I spurred on to where I thought I might find the major. Suddenly I recognized him in the grass. The sun sparkled on his glasses. I knew it was him. I yelled the order and he acknowledged it with a grunt. I lost no time in wheeling my horse around and heading for headquarters. I escaped being hit.[78]

Horner recalled watching Sturgis when a man was brought to the headquarters area with a severely wounded heel. He saw the colonel wince at the sight of the injured youth, possibly reminded of the loss of his son with Custer the previous year. Horner watched as a buddy was brought in with a badly wounded arm requiring removal. "He asked me if I wanted to watch the amputation. I told him I would rather not."[79]

Most of the personal accounts agree that Benteen displayed great coolness and bravery in the Canyon Creek combat. One stated that after his surrender Joseph asked to see the officer who rode the buckskin horse at Canyon Creek and whom the warriors had tried repeatedly but unsuccessfully to shoot. He was described as having a "trout rod in his hand and a pipe in his mouth." It was Benteen. And although the accounts of Goldin and others are quick to condemn Sturgis's management of the engagement (some stated that he was afraid because of what had happened to the regiment at the Little Bighorn), most such judgments are without foundation. Even though Sturgis failed to finally deter the tribesmen at Canyon Creek, Private Horner remembered the colonel as genial, energetic, and cool in battle, and said that he was highly regarded by his soldiers.[80] From all indications, too, some Seventh Cavalry soldiers showed certain compassion for the Nez Perces in their struggle, perhaps because they had but recently joined in the campaign against them as opposed to Howard's men who had been in the field since June. The men of the Seventh had been reading of their plight in the newspapers for most of the summer, and Goldin not only confessed that "our sympathies were with the Indians," but noted admiringly that "the resourcefulness of those Indians was the cause of much talk among our men." He added that "we felt they had received more than the traditional Double Cross. We fought them, of course, but our hearts were not in it as in the case of the Siouz [sic], Cheyennes and Apaches."[81] Similarly, Trooper William C. Slaper of Company M recalled thinking that "the Nez Perces were a good people and very much abused by our pin-head Government officials."[82] Even those who had been on the trail now for months grudgingly admitted respect for their cause. Wrote Dr. FitzGerald of Howard's command, who had accompanied Sturgis to Canyon Creek: "Poor Nez Perces! . . . I am actually beginning to admire their bravery and endurance in the face of so many well-equipped enemies."[83]

Most of the Nez Perce accounts of the fighting at Canyon Creek, which they called Tepahlewam Wakuspah (Place Similar to the Split Rocks at Tolo Lake),[84] suggest that the immediate appearance of the troops was unforeseen, and that perhaps the warriors were so engrossed in their foraging activities down the Yellowstone on the morning of the thirteenth that they failed to keep scouts posted on the back trail. It is likely that had the Nez Perces not already been packed and on the move, Sturgis's attack would have had devastating results for them. Yellow Wolf indicated that only as the village packed up did he receive knowledge of the troops' advance. "I saw soldiers near, and across the valley from us. The traveling camp had nearly been surprised. Soldiers afoot—hundreds of them. I whipped my horse to his best, getting away from that danger."[85] As the families and horses began entering the mouth of the canyon, Yellow Wolf briefly joined the warrior, Teeto Hoonnod, who singlehandedly kept part of the troops at bay. This prominent man warned Yellow Wolf to get away, as he was drawing fire, and Yellow Wolf proceeded to withdraw and join the warriors guarding the families as they filed into the canyon. He saw what apparently was Benteen's movement to cut off the horses, interpreting it as a drive to capture the noncombatants. "They tried to get the women and children. But some of the warriors, not many, were too quick. Firing from a bluff, they killed and crippled a few of them, turning them back."[86] Referring to the climbing of Horse Cache Butte by some of Sturgis's troops late in the fighting, Yellow Wolf noted that these soldiers killed two horses and wounded a man named Silooyelam "in the left ankle." Two other Nee-Me-Poo casualties at Canyon Creek were Eeahlokoon, hit in the right leg, and Animal Entering a Hole, wounded in the left hip and thigh by a single bullet. Although Sturgis claimed that sixteen Indians were killed at Canyon Creek, the sole fatality acknowledged by the Nez Perces in the engagement was Tookleiks (Fish Trap), an elderly man who was trying to retrieve one of his horses when he was shot by the Crows.[87] The warrior Teeto Hoonnod stayed in position at the mouth of the canyon, performing a rearguard function until the tribal assemblage had gotten safely inside its walls.[88] After the battle, as the troops withdrew and went into camp near the mouth of the canyon, the Nez Perces bore left up the main branch of Canyon Creek. Yellow Wolf and others raised a barricade in the upper reaches to impede further pursuit.[89] "It was after dark when we reached camp. Staking our horses, we had supper, then lay down to sleep."[90]

Other than that of Yellow Wolf, few Nee-Me-Poo accounts described the combat at Canyon Creek, noting only that a confrontation occurred. Several, however, observed its significance for the people, primarily in that although the women and children and most of the livestock managed to escape, "we lost a large part of our herd of horses. This loss was a serious blow to us." The misfortune of losing the ponies at Canyon Creek (most of them appropriated by the Crows), with further such losses the next day, ultimately meant that the remaining animals had to compensate, and probably slowed the rate of march after that to an extent that it facilitated the army's effort to stop the Nez Perces. As Yellow Bull stated, "At Canyon Creek fight we lost many horses, and this crippled our transportation, making it hard work for us to get along."[91] Just as important, the loss of the animals—possibly coupled with the onset of a perceived deficiency in the amount of their available ammunition—seems to have contributed to growing dissension and outright quarreling among the people,[92] doubtless aggravated by the knowledge of the Crows' betrayal in direct opposition to what Looking Glass had predicted.[93] These factors, added to the real likelihood that the people were becoming physically exhausted from their three-months-long ordeal, constituted but part of the significance of Canyon Creek. Of greater magnitude, based on the perspective of later-unfolding events, was the critical loss of a full day's travel by the Nez Perces as the engagement with Sturgis occupied and thus delayed their progress. Although Sturgis failed to win a solid victory and stop the Indians and end the war, his action so thwarted them materially, physically, and psychologically that its significance, although perhaps not recognized at the time, became compelling in view of what happened to the tribesmen over the ensuing three weeks, and how, in turn, it affected their final defeat by the army.

The wounded of Sturgis's command suffered desperately from thirst on the days following the fighting. The colonel and his men departed on the trail on September 14, leaving them to the attention of appropriate medical personnel until the arrival of Howard's column and requisite transportation. First Lieutenant Charles A. Varnum, regimental quartermaster officer, then escorted the wounded forty miles down the north bank of the Yellowstone to Pompey's Pillar, where on the eighteenth a wide-bottomed mackinaw was engaged to carry them on to the Tongue River Cantonment. On the march from Canyon Creek, Varnum's procession encountered the famous Martha Jane ("Calamity Jane") Cannary, who reportedly had lived in a dugout near Horse Cache Butte on the battlefield and who had experienced a brief run-in with the Nez Perces near the Yellowstone. She now agreed to accompany the injured downriver as a nurse. Later on the eighteenth, at Terry's Landing, opposite the mouth of the Bighorn River, the boat halted while the body of Private James Lawler of Company G, who had died that day, was removed for burial. The remaining seven wounded reached Tongue River four days later where they were hospitalized.[94]

Virtually every officer who appeared on the field at Canyon Creek on September 13, 1877, received belated recognition for "gallant service in action" in the engagement when in 1890 Congress permitted the retroactive award of brevets by the War Department. By then, many of them were retired or deceased. Assistant Surgeons Jenkins A. FitzGerald (died in 1879) and Valery Havard were cited "for repeated exposure to the fire of the enemy in their humane efforts to extricate and take care of the wounded." Thirty enlisted participants likewise received citations for their efforts at Canyon Creek.[95]

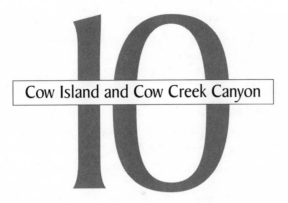

Cow Island and Cow Creek Canyon

THE NEZ PERCES' successful deliverance up Canyon Creek Canyon after the fight with Colonel Sturgis enabled them to reach the high plains that rolled gently away to the Musselshell River, twenty-five miles north. They probably camped the night of September 13 in the area of present-day Molt, Montana, and Big Lake Basin before traversing the open ground and multiple tributaries to reach the area of modern Lavina, where they turned west to about where Ryegate is today. There they forded the Musselshell and continued toward the Big Snowy Mountains. The trek was not easy, given their depleted condition and loss of horses coming out of the Canyon Creek encounter, and the pursuit by Sturgis—and especially by the Crow scouts—made it even worse. Some Nez Perces later claimed that after Canyon Creek Joseph began to exude more authority than heretofore; that his assertiveness increased measurably as the tribesmen left Sturgis farther behind and they became more confident that they would reach Canada safely; and that, as the intratribal unity that had been born of the common threat and danger began to fray, disputes and disharmony broke out with greater frequency.[1]

Sturgis started on the trail with pack mules at dawn on the fourteenth, and early into the day's march, a large party of 150 Crows caught up with the command.[2] They were "gaudily arrayed in war costume, but more eager for Nez Perce ponies than for Nez Perce blood," wrote the colonel.[3] Because their own horses were so fresh, Sturgis sent them ahead, hopeful that they might catch the tribesmen and somehow hold them until the troops arrived. The scouts raced forward, but were unable to stop the Nez Perces. They did harass them sufficiently to cause them to abandon about four hundred more ponies (some that were recovered proved to be mules taken from Howard's command at Camas Meadows), and, joined by some Bannocks, they kept up a running skirmish with the Indians' rear guard that resulted in their killing five Nez Perces.[4] Also, on the fifteenth, the Crows and Bannocks tried unsuccessfully to cut off and capture the families, but were prevented by the Nez Perce guards. "My heart was just like fire," recalled Yellow Wolf.

> I do not understand how the Crows could think to help the soldiers. They were fighting against their best friends! Some Nez Perces in our band had helped them whip the Sioux who came against them only a few snows before [in 1874]. This is why Chief Looking Glass had advised going to the Crows, to the buffalo country. He thought Crows would help us.[5]

The moving encounter with the Crows, coming on the heels of the Canyon Creek engagement in which those scouts had appeared, must have confirmed to the Nez Perce hierarchy the propriety of finally adapting their course toward the British Possessions.[6] Theodore Goldin witnessed the distant affair and years later recollected what he saw:

> The Crows had come up with a considerable body of the enemy and were hotly engaging them near the edge of a belt of timber, but the fighting seemed to be at fairly long range. As we watched the fight, still spurring forward with the hope that we might soon have a part in it, we were surprised to see the Nez Perces ride out of the timber in almost perfect line of battle formation; there were possibly a couple of hundred of them and for some distance they moved forward in what appeared to be perfect alignment, then the two flanks opened out into a perfect skirmish line with the seeming purpose of flanking the Crows. This style of fighting was too much for our allies; they couldn't understand it, and as practically all of them were young warriors, they fired a few hasty shots and then broke and fell back in great confusion. In fact by far the larger part of them kept on falling back until they reached the reservation miles away.[7]

Following far behind, Sturgis's officers also caught glimpses through their field glasses of the Nez Perce procession moving far ahead of their rear guard. During the march, the troops came across the bodies of two dead Indians on the trail, evidently having died of wounds received the previous day.

After making about thirty-five miles, by nightfall Sturgis's soldiers were so fatigued that men and horses were strewn over the back trail for ten miles, with at least one-third afoot. "Captain Bendire's detachment," reported Sturgis, ". . . did not arrive in camp until late at night, with every officer and man on foot."[8] That evening a courier brought orders for Howard's troops to return to the Yellowstone, and next day Major Sanford with Bendire's company (along with Fisher and his scouts, whose one-month enlistment time had expired) started back while Sturgis with the Seventh Cavalry pushed ahead to the Musselshell, which they reached on Saturday, September 15. By then, the condition of the horses and the men had become so critical that Sturgis decided he could go no farther. The men had been on half rations for the past few days and now were reduced to eating pony meat. Ninety-three of the Seventh's horses had been lost, either killed in the fighting, wounded and abandoned, or played out and abandoned on the trail, leaving an equal number of the men dismounted. Compounding this, a painful hoof disease appeared among the remaining cavalry mounts, making them too sick to carry their riders, most of whom had themselves become too weak even to walk.[9] "Under these circumstances," declared Sturgis, "I felt compelled to suspend further pursuit, in order that both men and animals might rest, and the troops provide themselves with game until our supplies [en route by wagon from Fort Ellis] should overtake us."[10] He sent a letter to Howard notifying him that the Nez Perces were heading toward the Judith Basin and that he was reluctantly abandoning "a hopeless pursuit before my horses are completely destroyed."[11] The fact that the Nez Perces faced similar afflictions with the loss of even more of their horses, and that he believed that they, too, would commensurately slow their progress after the troops stopped pushing them, made Sturgis's decision all the more palatable. On the nineteenth, the colonel's adjutant read aloud an order acknowledging his men for their hard service—"a bombastic card of thanks," recalled one Seventh cavalryman.[12] Sturgis remained in camp on the Musselshell and one of its tributaries until September 22, during which period his men continued to subsist on pony, mule, and buffalo meat, along with locally available buffalo berries, "which we broke off in great clusters as we rode under the trees that bore them," remembered Redington. "Those berries are certainly the best puckerers on earth. They put on a pucker that never comes off."[13]

While Sturgis rested his troops on the Musselshell, General Howard with his own force moved to catch up. On learning by courier of Sturgis's encounter on Canyon Creek, Howard left his command near Rocky Creek in charge of Major Mason and rode thirty-five miles through the night with fifty mounted men, reaching the battlefield on the morning of the fourteenth after Sturgis had departed in his pursuit of the tribesmen. He notified Sturgis that he expected supplies from Fort Ellis and that he had brought forward five hundred pounds of freshly slaughtered beef for Sturgis's men. Howard then sent to the Bighorn Post (Fort Custer) for supplies for his own troops, and after the balance of his command got in (including the troops sent back by Sturgis), he started with the Canyon Creek wounded down the Yellowstone to Pompey's Pillar on September 17. From there, two days later, the column started north over the prairie, reached the Musselshell on the twentieth, and marching west joined Sturgis the next day.[14]

With the certainty that Colonel Miles would march diagonally northwest from the Tongue River Cantonment based on the information contained in Howard's September twelfth dispatch, Howard and Sturgis continued purposefully to slow their pace, thereby causing the Nez Perces to correspondingly decrease their own rate of advance, ultimately to the benefit of Miles's movement. (Although most evidence for this purposeful delay by Howard and Sturgis appeared in writings and documents filed *after* the fact of most of the Nez Perces' containment and surrender at Bear's Paw, there is indeed pre-Bear's Paw documentation to support it. However, all contemporary evidence suggests that their troops and animals were likely too severely fatigued to continue the march even had they been disposed otherwise, and that the intended delay was more of a happy coincidence.[15]) With Sturgis's soldiers now constituting a part of Howard's command, and the supplies from Fort Ellis having arrived, the weary troops crossed the Musselshell on the twenty-second and plodded their way west, up Careless Creek toward Judith Gap, amid rumors that their campaigning was at an end. "The latest scheme for our return," wrote Captain Stephen P. Jocelyn, ". . . is to march from here north to the Missouri River at the mouth of the Musselshell. There or at Fort Peck (east down the river) we take steamer to Omaha."[16] Grazing for the animals was difficult because the buffalo herds the troops had seen there in August had eaten almost all the grass. On the twenty-fourth, the men moved eight miles to Elk Creek, and next day skirted the Big Snowy Mountains and entered the Judith Basin. There the scouts came on a recently vacated camp of River Crows with several dead inhabitants lying around; according to Redington, it was the village of Dumb Bull, upon which the Nez Perces had taken vengeance on September 21 by attacking, wrecking their property, taking their dried meat, and running off their ponies.[17] Reaching Beaver Creek on September 26, Howard next day sent Major Sanford's four First Cavalry companies homeward, believing that Sturgis's Seventh companies would suffice for the duration of operations.[18]

Also on the twenty-seventh, a courier brought word that the Nez Perces had crossed the Missouri at Cow Island. Deeming it no longer necessary to follow directly on the trail, Howard now determined to get to the Missouri River and find a steamer to transport him upstream. Over the succeeding four days, Howard's column followed the road to the trading settlement of Carroll City, located on the south side of the Missouri about twenty miles above the mouth of the Musselshell. There he learned of Miles's movement from the Tongue, and on October 1, the general and one hundred foot soldiers boarded the steamer *Benton* and started for Cow Island, forty miles west, resolved to there pick up the Nez Perces' trail; the rest of his command would remain with Sturgis at Carroll pending Howard's further communication with Miles. "The plan is to turn over the closing of the campaign to Miles and then start for home," wrote Major Mason.[19]

Cow Island, situated in the Missouri River about 120 miles downstream from the river port of Fort Benton, served as the head of navigation during low-water each autumn. Cow Island, in fact, in 1877 comprised two large islands (both extensively covered with cottonwoods) and several smaller ones, located in a major bend on the south side of the stream. The width of the river to include the islands was approximately twenty-two hundred feet, although the navigable channel spanned only about five hundred feet. Across from the island proper, on the north bank of the river and west of the mouth of Cow Creek, stood Cow Island Landing, where steamboat cargoes were unloaded to await delivery upstream by freight wagons to Fort Benton for military and commercial use. A road paralleled Cow Creek to ascend the pine-dotted bluffs leading from the canyon to the open benchlands north of the Missouri. South of the river, the bluffs rose sharply in similar fashion, but without access to the river.

During the summer of 1877, a civil engineer unit upstream from Cow Island was working to remove obstructions and stabilize the river channel at Dauphin Rapids, near the mouth of the Judith River. Company B, Seventh Infantry, from Fort Benton, served as guard to the engineers. On August 18, a detail of men started for Cow Island to guard commissary supplies. No permanent buildings stood at the landing, only tents surrounded by a drainage ditch, approximately two and one-half feet deep, with its excavated dirt thrown outward forming an embankment that could double as an entrenchment in an emergency. The tents and ditch stood about four hundred feet upstream from the landing area above the mouth of Cow Creek.[20] By the afternoon of September 23, when several hundred Nez Perces appeared on the south bank,[21] the garrison at the landing numbered twelve men in the charge of Sergeant William Molchert, who had been sent down from the project just a day earlier to obtain additional rations from the army stores located there, plus four civilian disbursing clerks who represented the freighting interests in the region. One of them was Michael Foley, chief clerk for the agent of the *Josephine* line of steamboats, Colonel George Clendenin, Jr., a breveted former Union army officer.[22] Fifty tons of government and commercial freight lay under tarpaulins at the landing awaiting shipment by wagon to remote corners of the territory, including Deer Lodge, Missoula, Helena, and Fort Shaw.

The Nez Perces had approached the Missouri River (which they called Seloselo Wejanwais—colored paint—or Attish Pah—place of the Cave of Red Paint) after having passed through the Judith Basin, where they had encountered Dumb Bull's Crow encampment. From that point, they had veered slightly northeast, stopping at Reed's Fort, a trading post on Big Spring Creek (just west of modern Lewistown), and traveled west of the Judith Mountains, passing close to where the modern community of Winifred stands today.[23] Most likely they crossed familiar terrain visited often in times past in their pursuit of the buffalo herds. At Cow Island, at about 2:00 P.M., some of the people moved upstream to ford the river; others crossed below and directly opposite from the landing while Sergeant Molchert and his party watched, withdrawing into their defenses in preparation to receive them.[24] The passage was orderly and controlled, with twenty warriors riding in advance to meet any attack, followed by the pack animals and families who were in turn guarded by the remaining warriors on the south bank. Once across, the procession moved two miles away and went into camp. Then two of the Nez Perces approached the landing to ask for food. Clerk Michael Foley, who claimed a knowledge of Indians, advanced and spoke with them, but returned to tell Molchert that the tribesmen wanted to talk with the person in charge of the soldiers. Molchert went forward unarmed and was surprised to learn that the tribesmen "spoke English as well as any one could" and readily expressed their friendship. Molchert refused to allow them to approach closer than one hundred yards from the defenses. When the Nez Perces requested provisions from the freight deposit, the sergeant turned and walked away, whereupon the tribesmen called him back to beg for food. Molchert returned to his defenses, got a sack with some hardtack and placed a side of bacon with it, then walked back and handed it over. Then he shook hands with the Nez Perce leader, whom he later declared was Joseph.[25] The Indians withdrew. Years later, Molchert described what happened next:

> Things went along for a while quietly till we saw an Indian coming between our breastworks and the foot hills stripped naked, when we know this means fight. Having previously distributed the ammunition and giving each man his place, we were standing around and taking our supper as I jokingly remarked to the men that this might be their last sow belly and hard tack, when without any warning they commenced to fire from the hills, the balls going in every direction between us but luckily nobody was hurt. This was sun down and from that time on till day break we were fighting for our lives. Of course the freight we could not save as it was piled right up against the bluff. The agent had a hospital tent there for his quarters with 500 sacks of bacon piled against it, which they set on fire that lit the country up for miles. . . . They charged us three times during the night through high willows, impossible to see any one.[26]

Two civilians, E. W. Buckwalter and George Trautman, were wounded in the opening volley on the party in the entrenchments.[27] The warriors apparently approached the supply dump via a coulee located on its opposite side, so that their movements went largely undetected by the soldiers and citizens. There they took whatever food, tinware, and other supplies they desired. "We had privilege to do this," reasoned Peopeo Tholekt. "It was in the war." The igniting of the sacks of bacon—the work of "bad boys," said Yellow Wolf—produced an enormous blaze that enabled the defending party to witness the proceedings and most likely kept the Nez Perces from approaching the earthworks too closely. "I believe the fire was what saved us," said Foley. That night he composed a message for Agent Clendenin, although it was not likely delivered until the next day after the warriors had departed. The message read:

> Rifle Pit at Cow Island,
> September 23, 1877, 10 A.M. [P.M.?]
> Col: Chief Joseph is here, and says he will surrender for two hundred bags of sugar. I told him to surrender without the sugar. He took the sugar and will not surrender. What shall I do?[28]

In the morning the firing died down, evidently at the instigation of the Nez Perce leadership, and by 10:00 A.M. the people had departed Cow Creek and the river canyon, passing up a ridge to the benchland and heading in the direction of the pass between the Bear's Paw and Little Rocky mountains. The tons of supplies continued to burn well into the afternoon, when Agent Clendenin arrived from downstream. "Calicoes, stationery and other drygoods, were strewn over the surrounding hills and through the gulches for miles."[29] No fatalities had occurred on either side in the skirmish at Cow Island; besides the two injured civilians, one warrior—Wounded Head—had been grazed in the head by a piece of wood splintered by a bullet.[30]

While the events at Cow Island progressed on September 23, troops from Fort Benton—alerted to the presence of the Nez Perces in the region—were moving close at hand. On September 21, on receipt of news that the advancing Nez Perces were threatening the defenseless trading post of Fort Clagett, on the south side of the Missouri below the mouth of the Judith River, Major Guido Ilges, post commander at Fort Benton, started a force downstream to its relief. The garrison of Fort Benton, reduced to a single depleted company of the Seventh Infantry, required Ilges to enlist volunteers from among the adjacent citizen population, each man to furnish his own horse, gun, and ammunition. Second Lieutenant Edward E. Hardin, with thirteen men of Company F plus two citizen volunteers and a mountain howitzer, boarded mackinaw boats and set out down the Missouri, reaching Fort Clagett in the forenoon of the twenty-second. Accompanied by thirty-eight citizens and a single enlisted man, Private Thomas Bundy of Company F, all mounted, Ilges started overland for the well-fortified post, which he reached late in the afternoon of the twenty-second.

After determining from his scouts that the tribesmen had gone toward Cow Island, Ilges at dawn on the twenty-fourth directed his force sixty-five miles downstream "to protect people and property (both private and public) against the hostile Nez-Perces." The command reached the south bank opposite the Cow Island landing past sundown, long after the warriors had lifted their siege of Molchert's party and departed, although the destroyed freight was still burning. En route down the river from Clagett, Lieutenant Hardin picked up Sergeant Molchert and his men, who were trekking to Dauphin Rapids, and brought them back to Cow Island.[31] The next morning, Tuesday, September 25, Ilges used the mackinaws to ferry his men and horses across the Missouri. At 9:30 A.M., he started with his mounted civilian force on the Nez Perces' trail up Cow Creek amid reports that a wagon freight train bound for Benton, and a light wagon containing military personnel and civilians, including four women, lay ahead on the road. Ilges hoped to rescue any members of either group who might somehow have escaped from the tribesmen. "Any one who has ever traveled through Cow Creek Canyon, with its 31 crossings, its narrow bottom, its high and precipitous sides, shutting off the traveler from the outside world, will know what a task was before the volunteers should the Indians still be in the canyon and disposed to dispute its passage," averred the publisher of the Fort Benton *Record* after interviewing a member of Ilges's expedition.[32]

A Prussian soldier immigrant possessing extensive Civil War and frontier service,[33] Major Ilges led his command only ten miles north of the Missouri before his scouts sighted the Nez Perces, whose warriors had surrounded the wagon train and its eight men in Cow Creek Canyon. The train, which included a herd of cattle, belonged to Messrs. O. G. Cooper and Frank Farmer and had left Cow Island on September 22, camping on the benchland above the Missouri. On the twenty-third the train moved on, but muddy roads and the numerous crossings of Cow Creek made progress slow, and it was but a matter of time before the Nez Perces caught up with it after they had left Cow Island. Some warriors approached the wagons unthreateningly, and the entire Nez Perce assemblage camped the night of the twenty-fourth within one and one-half miles of the train. In the morning, as Farmer and Cooper went up the creek to look after the cattle, some of the warriors shot and killed a teamster named Barker, and at the sound of the firing the two men ran into the hills, where they found most of the other teamsters.

The warriors had shot Barker seemingly at the approach of Ilges's men, and the seven other teamsters managed to flee into the willows as the combat began, all unaware for the moment that the shooting involved the volunteers from Fort Benton. The warriors simultaneously set the train afire and started down the canyon to meet the command. A thousand yards from Ilges and his force, they split into small groups, disappearing from view as they sought advantageous positions on the high ground in Ilges's front and among the hills on his right, from which they opened a long-range fire on the men. The major distributed his force as appropriately as the topography of his position in the canyon would allow, placing his wagon and horses in the creek bed, and commenced to return the fire. His position generally lay exposed to Nez Perce marksmen shooting from the surrounding heights, and as the fight opened, Ilges dispatched Private Bundy, the only other soldier present, to go back to the landing and bring forward Lieutenant Hardin and his men and the mountain howitzer. Bundy, traveling by foot, succeeded in reaching the river, and Hardin started immediately. The exchange between Ilges and the Nez Perces, which started at noon, lasted for about two hours, during which one of the citizens was killed. Another, Judge John J. Tattan, was saved when a bullet struck his belt buckle, merely bruising his abdomen. Finally, the warriors stopped shooting and withdrew up Cow Creek Canyon. Fearful that the Indians, by their disappearance, might be attempting to flank his command by the left, and recognizing his decided disadvantage in numbers compared to the warriors, Ilges himself began a slow and cautious withdrawal down the canyon floor. Three miles from the Missouri, he and his men joined the advancing troops under Hardin and returned to the Cow Island entrenchment at 6:00 P.M.

Ilges's casualties amounted to the one volunteer (Edmund Bradley) killed, along with one privately owned horse. He claimed that two Nez Perces were wounded. The major reported that "the citizens . . . behaved well during the fight, with a few exceptions, but they are not a very desirable material to handle under disadvantageous circumstances."[34] He recommended that Private Bundy receive "such recognition as the proper authorities can give to a brave and good soldier."[35] On the twenty-sixth, the troops and civilians returned to the site of their engagement to bury Bradley and Barker and to search for the other teamsters who had fled at the outset of the fight. That night the steamer *Benton* arrived, discharging fifty tons of freight, while the *Silver City* approached Cow Island landing with one hundred tons more. On the twenty-seventh, Ilges sent two of his volunteers as couriers cross country to Colonel Miles, operating near the Little Rocky Mountains, to tell him of his work and to provide concrete information of the location of the Nez Perces. "They are traveling slow and cautiously, resting and delaying daily," he wrote.[36] As insurance against future attacks, the *Benton* transported logs from the island to the landing to be erected into a blockhouse.[37] Lieutenant Hardin remained at Cow Island with twenty-five men and the howitzer while Ilges and the volunteers started up the Cow Creek road on their return to Fort Benton, encountering the burned-out train, its thirty-five tons of goods destroyed or removed by the Nez Perces. Over the next two days, Ilges's party found evidence of further depredations by the Nez Perces, including the body of a man killed between Birch and Eagle creeks. After long marches, Ilges and his volunteers pulled into Fort Benton on the afternoon of September 29, tired but satisfied in the success of their mission.[38] From a military perspective, of course, the Cow Island affair and its aftermath, including Ilges's fight with the Nez Perces, constituted another delaying obstacle in their movement north.

When the Nez Perces left Cow Island headed north, they were less than eighty miles from the United States–Canada boundary. Convinced that they had outdistanced Colonel Sturgis and General Howard and that the army was at least two days behind them, the tribesmen began a leisurely movement dictated as much by the condition of the families and their animals as by rifts appearing among the leadership. The grueling three-months-long journey toward oft-changing and uncertain objectives had taken a severe toll; the people had lost many friends and relatives in the various combats since leaving Idaho, and the pressure and worries connected with obtaining food and supplies while staying ahead of the soldiers amid mounting cold weather had sapped their strength and energy, if not their spirit. The freighter O. G. Cooper made a careful observation of the Nez Perces when they camped near his train on September 24 preceding its destruction the following day. Cooper's remarks represent an important appraisal of the Nez Perces late in their journey and but a few days before they encamped along Snake Creek north of the Bear's Paw Mountains:

While the Indians were around the wagons I tried to count them, but of course could not do so accurately. As near as I could make out, however, there were between seven and eight hundred men, women and children, perhaps more, and I should judge about four hundred warriors. I noticed that all the young sprightly bucks had but a few cartridges in their belts, while the old fellows, and the middle-aged, seemed better supplied; but I think they were all short of ammunition, as they were very anxious to buy from us. They had but a few lodges with them, and they cut green poles when they went into camp. They were armed with all sorts of guns, and many had cavalry carbines. . . . Their animals were very poor, and many had sore backs and feet, but they had some fine horses with them, and I think one—a fine sorrel covered with a blanket—was a race horse. I saw at least a dozen different branded horses. A brown and white pinto and a bay were branded "PI;" several had a heart on right shoulder and an "M" on left; a large bay was branded "circle a," and some mules with harness marks were branded "W.G." There were also a number of Gov. mules and horses. About twenty of their horses, crippled and dead, were left along Cow Creek.[39]

Cooper's estimate of the camp population was close to that given earlier by former captive John Shively in the national park, although his apparent inclusion of young males inflated his estimate of the number of warriors present.

Nee-Me-Poo sources indicate that the internal dissension that had marked their journey from the Yellowstone River continued after they moved north from the Missouri. One dispute among the leadership again involved Poker Joe, who had taken charge of the procession following the Big Hole battle, and Looking Glass, who now asserted his right as a chief to resume that function. On September 25, at the first camp following the skirmish with Ilges, the argument between the two flared anew when Looking Glass complained of the constant hurrying forward mandated under Poker Joe's leadership. With Canada looming ahead, the troops far behind, and with the weakened animals and the weariness of the elderly and the young so pervasive throughout the column, Looking Glass now challenged the need to keep up the pace. With approval of the interband leadership, the change was carried out. The Nee-Me-Poo emerged from the Cow Creek drainage by a natural ridge leading up to the prairie benchland. Then, moving slowly over the next few days to reserve their strength, they skirted the east and northeast edges of the Bear's Paw Mountains until they reached the bottom of Snake Creek, just forty miles south of the British line. There, on Saturday, September 29, amid heavy fog and increasingly frigid autumn temperatures, the tired and weakened people set up their camp at Tsanim Alikos Pah (Place of the Manure Fire), fully aware of their proximity to Canada and freedom from the soldiers.[40]

Yellowstone Command

THE TONGUE RIVER Cantonment was but a year old in September 1877, when troops from the post began to play an integral part in the widening Nez Perce War. Constructed on the left bank of the Tongue River at that stream's confluence with the Yellowstone, the cantonment—little more than a ramshackle collection of mud-chinked cottonwood log huts with earthen roofs—already boasted a record of accomplishment in the army's prolonged campaign against the Sioux and Northern Cheyennes in the wake of the Little Bighorn battle. By September, operations out of the cantonment against those tribes had significantly subsided following Colonel Miles's aggressive campaigning through the autumn and winter of 1876 and the spring and early summer of 1877. Miles's campaign had resulted in the surrender of many of the people at the cantonment and at the agencies in Dakota Territory and Nebraska. Sitting Bull, the Hunkpapa visionary at the heart of the Sioux-Cheyenne coalition, had gone into Canada in the spring of 1877 and posed but a lingering, if not altogether remote, objective for Miles and his Yellowstone Command. In the interest of maintaining accord with Great Britain, however, General Sherman temporarily precluded further operations by Miles north of the Missouri River.[1] Meanwhile, signs of the permanent military occupation of the Yellowstone hinterland came with the start of work that spring on a substantial new post slightly upstream, to be christened

Fort Keogh, after one of Custer's dead officers, next to the hovels constituting the cantonment. Construction of a sister fort, Bighorn Post (later called Fort Custer), was underway at the junction of the Little Bighorn and Bighorn rivers about one hundred miles southwest of the cantonment. Anchored squarely at the epicenter of the area recently occupied by the Sioux and Cheyennes, the twin stations were to insure that those tribes never again achieved hegemony in the region.[2]

In his conduct of operations from the Tongue River Cantonment with troops of the Fifth and Twenty-second infantry regiments, supplemented with a battalion of the Second Cavalry from Fort Ellis, Miles had molded his command into an efficient fighting force reflecting his own aggressive leadership. Like many of his contemporary career officers, Nelson A. Miles (1839–1925) lacked the professional credentials of a West Point education, rising instead through the echelons of rank afforded by service in the Civil War. Born in Massachusetts, Miles worked in a crockery shop before the war erupted. An interest in military precepts prompted him to raise a company of volunteers in 1861, and he joined the Massachusetts volunteer infantry as a first lieutenant, quickly distinguishing himself to his superiors for his bravery and judgment in battle. By the conclusion of the Civil War, Miles was a senior officer, a veteran of many hard-fought contests, including Fair Oaks, Antietam, Fredericksville, Chancellorsville (for which service he received a Medal of Honor in 1892), and Petersburg. Wounded four times in combat, he received many brevets, and in May, 1864, he won promotion to brigadier general of volunteers. Miles commanded the First Division, II Corps, Army of the Potomac, during the fighting leading to Appomattox, for which duty, at age twenty-six, he was appointed major general of volunteers in 1865.

After the war, Miles served as custodian for the deposed Confederate leader Jefferson Davis, drawing much negative and unwarranted notice from Southerners for his treatment of the ex-president. Reverting to his regular army rank of colonel upon the reduction of the postwar army in 1868, he married the niece of General William T. Sherman, opening a relationship that the ambitious Miles exploited for personal gain in subsequent years. When the army was reorganized in 1869, Miles received appointment to the Fifth Infantry, and it was with this unit that he first gained notice for his success as an Indian campaigner. His work in 1874–75 in the Red River War on the southern plains marked him in his superiors' eyes as a dedicated, resourceful leader, and in 1876, in the wake of the Little Bighorn, the army leadership turned to Miles to subdue the Sioux and Northern Cheyennes.

Miles's adept prosecution of these tribesmen through the balance of 1876 and into the spring and early summer of 1877 virtually ended the Great Sioux War. The colonel hoped that the reward for his work would be his upgrade to brigadier general and achievement of an independent command. In pursuit of the former objective, and in what must have seemed awkward to both men in light of later events, Miles in February 1877 solicited the favor of none other than General Howard:

> Since the war it has fallen to my lot to successfully engage larger bodies of Indians than any other officer, and to have gained a more extensive knowledge of this remote frontier than any living man. I feel that I have earned it [promotion] and should prize your endorsement very highly. If you please you can communicate with Genl. Sherman on the subject.[3]

Although a brigadier's star was not immediately forthcoming, in the creation of the District of the Yellowstone in September 1877 with himself as commander, Miles attained his goal of an independent command.[4]

As indicated, Miles anticipated a role for his soldiers in the Nez Perce conflict and signaled his involvement as early as August 3 and 12, even before receiving instructions from department and division headquarters, when he sent Lieutenant Doane and then Colonel Sturgis west from Tongue River to the Judith Basin to seek out, intercept, and destroy the Nez Perces after they emerged from the national park. Early in September, he had dispatched Second Lieutenant Hobart K. Bailey, Fifth Infantry, with a small detachment to Carroll City, on the Missouri, to guard ammunition at that place. Miles's motivation for this activity lay in his anxiety that the Nez Perces were passing through country only recently occupied by Sitting Bull's Sioux, and that in Canada (or near the line), the two tribes might collaborate in new warfare on the frontier settlements.[5] Thus, for Miles the Nez Perce threat was important as it could potentially affect his longstanding fixation on Sitting Bull. As he wrote Sturgis: "If they [Nez Perces] could be destroyed it would have an excellent effect on all the Indian tribes, and relieve all the troops in northern Montana."[6] That the self-exiled Hunkpapa leader was still considered a potent concern to United States officials was manifested in the creation of the so-called Sitting Bull Commission, headed by General Terry, which was in late September slated to cross the border north of Fort Benton, meet with the chief, and induce him to surrender. On September 14, in accordance with directions from department headquarters, Company K of the Seventh Cavalry, under Captain Owen Hale, crossed the Yellowstone en route up the Missouri to serve as escort to Terry's party. Two days later, Miles received orders to send the battalion of three companies of the Second Cavalry under Captain George L. Tyler instead of Hale's unit, and these troops ferried the Yellowstone and headed out accordingly.[7]

Miles's personal involvement in the army campaign against the Nez Perces began on the evening of September 17, when a courier reached the cantonment at 6:00 P.M., bearing the Howard/Sturgis dispatch of the twelfth from Clark's Fork, more than 150 miles west of the post.[8] In his letter, Howard described the movements preceding the fight at Canyon Creek and appealed for Miles's help:

> COLONEL: While Colonel Sturgis was scouting toward Stinking Water, the Indians and my force in close pursuit, passed his right, and they, after a short detour, turned to Clark's Fork, and by forced marches avoided Sturgis completely.
>
> I have sent Sturgis with Major Sanford, First Cavalry, and Lieutenant Otis, Fourth Artillery, with howitzer battery in fastest pursuit, and am myself following as rapidly as possible with the remainder of my own immediate command. The Indians are reported going down Clark's Fork and straight toward the Musselshell. They will in all probability cross the Yellowstone near the mouth of Clark's Fork, and make all haste to join a band of hostile Sioux. They will use every exertion to reach the Musselshell country and form this junction, and as they make exceedingly long marches it will require unusual activity to intercept or overtake them.

But it was Howard's final remark—in effect, a plaintive cry for help—that impelled Miles to action: "I earnestly request you to make every effort in your power to prevent the escape of this hostile band, and at least to hold them in check until I can overtake them."[9]

Miles immediately fired off a dispatch to General Terry, enclosing a copy of the Howard-Sturgis missive. "I will leave nine (9) companies of infantry and one (1) of cavalry at this point and on the Yellowstone. With the remainder I will strike across by head of Big Dry, Musselshell,

Crooked Creek, and Carroll, with the hope of intercepting the Nez Perces in their movement north." He requested that "an abundance of rations and grain" along with quantities of clothing be sent up the Missouri by steamer from Fort Buford for his own men and for the destitute commands of Howard and Sturgis.[10] Miles also sent a cautionary note to Howard: "I fear your information reaches me too late for me to intercept them, but I will do the best I can." He asked that "the movement of my command be kept as secret as possible, so that it may not become known to the Crows or other friends of the enemy."[11] As the couriers departed, Miles made preparations through the night of the seventeenth for assuming the chase. He directed that supplies, thirty-six wagons, two ambulances, artillery (one breech-loading 1.67-inch caliber Hotchkiss gun, one bronze twelve-pounder Napoleon cannon) plus its requisite ammunition, small arms ammunition (two hundred rounds per man, with fifty rounds on the person and the balance carried in the wagons), mule teams, pack mules, horses, baggage, and troops be ferried to the north bank of the Yellowstone preparatory to leaving in the morning.[12] "All was commotion from the time the order was rec'd and no sleep for anyone," noted Captain Simon Snyder.[13] By sunrise, all was in readiness for departure. General Sherman's young niece, Elizabeth, visiting at the garrison since July, stood under an American flag at Miles's quarters waving two small flags as the troops departed.[14] "My command," remembered Miles, "slowly wound its way up the trail from the Yellowstone to the high mesa on the north side of that river. Then commenced a most laborious and tedious forced march."[15]

When Miles dispatched Sturgis into the field in August, that officer had taken the strongest companies of the Seventh Cavalry with him, leaving the most underofficered and understrengthed units of the regiment at the cantonment. Therefore, Miles's command on leaving the Yellowstone on September 18 consisted of Companies A (Captain Myles Moylan), approximately 30 men; and D (Captain Edward S. Godfrey, First Lieutenant Edwin P. Eckerson), approximately 40 men, Seventh Cavalry. En route, Miles would overtake and absorb Company K of the Seventh (Captain Owen Hale, Second Lieutenant Jonathan W. Biddle), with approximately 44 men, plus Captain George Tyler's battalion of Second Cavalry, consisting of Companies F (Tyler), about 54 men; G (Second Lieutenant Edward J. McClernand), about 50 men; and H (Second Lieutenant Lovell H. Jerome), about 60 men. Departing the cantonment with Miles were units of his own Fifth Infantry regiment riding captured Sioux ponies and consisting of Companies B (Captain Andrew S. Bennett, Second Lieutenant Thomas M. Woodruff), about 26 men; F (Captain Simon Snyder, commanding mounted battalion), about 28 men; G (First Lieutenant Henry Romeyn), about 23 men; and I (First Lieutenant Mason Carter), about 28 men; plus a complement on foot consisting of Company K (Captain David H. Brotherton, Second Lieutenant George P. Borden), about 29 men, with 21 men attached from Company D, to act as escort to the wagon train and to serve the artillery pieces (the latter in the charge of Sergeant John McHugh). First Lieutenant George W. Baird (on temporary duty at Fort Peck) served as Miles's command adjutant, First Lieutenant Frank D. Baldwin his aide-de-camp, Second Lieutenant Oscar F. Long his acting engineer officer, and Second Lieutenant Marion P. Maus his commander of several white and 30 Indian scouts. Surgeon (Major) Henry R. Tilton and Assistant Surgeon (First Lieutenant) Edwin F. Gardner accompanied as medical officers. There were 20 packers, a detachment of around 12 men to service the artillery, plus teamsters. Altogether, Miles's troop complement after incorporation of the units of the Seventh and Second cavalry regiments totaled approximately 520 officers, men, scouts, and civilian employees.[16] It was the largest command Miles had fielded since arriving on the northern plains in August 1876.

Miles's commissioned officer corps mostly reflected experience and commitment in past frontier service. While all played significant roles in the days and weeks ahead, several deserve special mention. Captain Owen Hale (1843–1877), commander of the Seventh Cavalry battalion and of Company K, had served with the New York volunteer cavalry during the Civil War. He was commissioned first lieutenant in the Seventh Cavalry in 1866 and captain in 1869. His twenty-two-year-old second lieutenant, Jonathan W. Biddle (1855–1877) from Pennsylvania, had been appointed scarcely a year earlier, August 31, 1876. Captain Myles Moylan (1838–1909), a Civil War veteran, had risen from the enlisted ranks and had been with the Seventh Cavalry since its formation in 1866. He had reached the grade of captain in 1872 and had commanded Company A at the Little Bighorn. Captain Edward S. Godfrey (1843–1932), who commanded Company D, had been with the regiment since his graduation from West Point ten years previous and had served in most of its campaigns and engagements with Indians, including the Washita,

Indian Territory, in 1868; the Yellowstone and Black Hills expeditions of 1873 and 1874, respectively; and the Sioux Campaign and its resultant Little Bighorn battle in 1876. Godfrey's lieutenant, Edwin P. Eckerson (1850–1885), appointed from civilian status in 1872 and dismissed from the Fifth Cavalry in 1875, had rejoined the army into the Seventh Cavalry in May 1876, but was on detached service at the time of the Little Bighorn.

Among the other units, Captain George L. Tyler (1839–1881) had served with state troops during the Civil War, with the regulars since 1866, and had been with the Second Cavalry since 1870. Both of his subalterns, Edward J. McClernand (1849–1926) and Lovell H. Jerome (1849–1935), graduated from the military academy in 1870 and had been with the Second since then. Of the Fifth Infantry officers, Simon Snyder (1839–1912), who commanded the mounted battalion, had served with the regiment since 1861 and as a captain since 1863. Captain Andrew S. Bennett (1834–1878), a Wisconsin infantry officer during the Civil War, joined the Fifth regulars in 1871 (he would be killed in action with Bannock Indians within a year), while his second lieutenant, Thomas M. Woodruff (1848–1899), had been with the regiment since his 1871 graduation from West Point. Mason Carter (1834–1909), commanding Company B, a Georgia native who fought on the Union side in the Civil War, had been a first lieutenant with the Fifth since 1864. First Lieutenant Henry Romeyn (1833–1913), a breveted Civil War veteran, had joined the regiment in 1869 in that grade. Of Miles's staff, Adjutant George W. Baird (1839–1906) had ended the Civil War as a commander of black troops and joined the Fifth Infantry in 1869, while Second Lieutenant Marion P. Maus (1850–1930), an 1874 academy graduate, was attached to Miles's command from the First Infantry. Second Lieutenant Oscar F. Long (1852–1928), an 1872 West Point graduate, had served with the Fifth Infantry since June 1876. Major and Surgeon Tilton (1836–1906) had served in the army since the start of the Civil War, while Assistant Surgeon Gardner had joined the regular army only in August 1876.[17]

Many of Miles's officers and men, while new to the Nez Perce war, represented seasoned campaigners recently involved in arduous campaigns against the Teton Sioux and Northern Cheyennes. Following the disaster at the Little Bighorn that had decimated the Seventh Cavalry, Miles had led his Fifth infantrymen on lengthy and successful campaigns in the

Yellowstone-Missouri wilderness, meeting the warriors in several pitched encounters that had contributed to the collapse of the Indian coalition early in 1877. His troops, augmented by a battalion of Second cavalrymen from Fort Ellis and part of the reconstituted Seventh regiment from Fort Lincoln, had spent the spring and early summer in running down small groups of tribesmen as they fled from or to the agencies or sought to reach Sitting Bull's people in Canada. Weathered and worn from their weeks afield, Miles's force was nonetheless tried, vigorous, and overtly optimistic in the fashion of its commander as the men set out after the people now commonly referred to as "Joseph's Nez Perces."

On Tuesday, September 18, the departing command passed through the camp of captive Sioux and Northern Cheyennes, who had surrendered to Miles the preceding March, as the troops made their way nearly eighteen miles northwest up Sunday Creek, an affluent of the Yellowstone, before halting at 5:00 P.M. The march was not easy because the train had difficulty negotiating the prevalent quicksands of the alkaline stream. Cognizant of Sherman's stricture against crossing north of the Missouri, Miles expected to confront the Nez Perces before they reached the river; his immediate objective, therefore, was to gain the mouth of the Musselshell River on the Missouri in the shortest time possible and work accordingly from that point. He sent a directive to Captain Tyler, out ahead with his battalion of Second Cavalry en route to General Terry, to unite with Hale's company of Seventh Cavalry and together to keep watch for the Nez Perces and exercise vigilance to prevent surprise. Miles proposed meeting Tyler's command at the Musselshell.[18]

On Wednesday the command continued tracing the stagnant pools that comprised Sunday Creek, the landscape turning into badlands as they passed seventeen more miles and stopped early in the afternoon on a branch of the stream to await the wagons, which arrived two hours later. That night they subsisted on buffalo, deer, and antelope, but had poor-quality water and built their fires from buffalo chips, the only fuel available. The twentieth saw them off at 5:15 A.M., proceeding northwest through the "dreary waste" of the divide between the Yellowstone and Missouri rivers, a parched, treeless scape deprived of all water but for rain-caused pools. Atop the divide, they "obtained a most perfect view of the varied and extensive scenery of the surrounding country," before camping on a tributary of the Big Dry, having traveled thirty-one miles.[19] That evening, thirty Northern Cheyenne warriors joined the command from the camp near the cantonment to serve as scouts for Colonel Miles. Miles increasingly used his civilian and Indian guides as he neared the zone where he might logically expect word of the Nez Perces, and felt constantly to his left front with what he called "a cloud of scouts and videttes" during his movement to the Missouri.[20]

On September 21, the troops arrived at the southern branch of the Big Dry River—"the first running-water stream since leaving the Yellowstone," wrote Lieutenant Long. Along the cactus-and-sage-strewn prairie this cloudy day at noon, they reached the four Second and Seventh cavalry companies, halted since receiving Miles's directive not to proceed to Fort Benton. The command bivouacked along a stream with alkaline water and plentiful game but without timber, again awaiting the wagons and escort. On the following day, Saturday, great herds of buffalo came in sight, but Miles had issued an order to prevent the firing of weapons. "No shooting was allowed," wrote Private William F. Zimmer, "for fear of stampeding them and putting the Indians on their guard, if there is any near."[21] "The lumbering fellows act as if they had received a copy of the order," observed Dr. Tilton. "They cross our trail, running between the advance guard and the next battalion."[22] The travel was difficult, the road winding among arroyos and through barren hills as the soldiers transected various tributaries en route to Squaw Creek, finally camping long after dark amid towering cottonwood groves, having covered thirty-six miles.

On Sunday, the twenty-third, the troops moved five miles, camping on Squaw Creek within sight of the high bluffs of the Missouri. Anxious that he might be delayed in crossing the river, Miles sent Lieutenant Biddle of the Seventh Cavalry with five enlisted men ahead to stop a passing steamboat to ferry the Second Cavalry battalion to the north side. Later, a courier from Biddle announced that a vessel, *Fontenelle*, en route from Fort Benton to St. Louis, awaited Miles's use. Moreover, the boat's captain had no knowledge of the Nez Perces having crossed above, so Miles believed he was still ahead of them. Dispatches also arrived from Tongue River with news of Sturgis's encounter with the tribesmen at Canyon Creek, terming the action "a running fight from the Yellowstone to the Musselshell." Howard told Miles of his intention to slow his own march to allow the colonel sufficient time to advance his force.[23] After marching about twenty-two miles, the command reached the mouth of Squaw Creek on the Missouri at 7:00 P.M., about six miles below the mouth of the Musselshell. As the soldiers went into camp, Scout George Johnson ill-advisedly tried to cross the river and drowned.[24] Despite this loss, the mood remained high. Wrote Lieutenant Long: "Since leaving the Yellowstone we had marched 146 miles, and the miserable water from the alkalescent to the strongly alkaline had begun to tell on men and animals, but the refreshing draughts of the pure Missouri River water served to reinvigorate to restore the spirit and animation, and to relieve the fatigue."[25] And Lieutenant Biddle wrote home: "I think Joseph has had so many hard knocks . . . that he will surrender if he finds this command ahead of him."[26]

At the Missouri, Miles made plans to start Tyler's battalion to Fort Benton for Terry's commission to Sitting Bull, telling him, however, "should you en route find any indications of the Nez Perces having crossed the Missouri, you will use your force to intercept, or pursue them."[27] At the mouth of Squaw Creek, Miles therefore crossed only Tyler's men and their train of twelve wagons on the *Fontenelle*, and used the steamer to begin transferring his own supplies and the artillery to the left bank of the Musselshell on the Missouri, leaving the rest of his wagons at Squaw Creek with Captain Brotherton's company. Still laboring in the conviction that the Nez Perces would most likely be encountered south of the river, he wrote Terry: "I will move up on the south side of the Missouri to Carroll, and possibly Judith Basin, to intercept and, if possible, prevent any of the Nez Perces from going North."[28] Thus intending to go on west below the Missouri, Miles outfitted his troops with fifteen days' rations and began a complicated and complex movement to get them and their horses and pack animals across the Musselshell.[29] Lieutenant Long described the situation on September 24 in excruciating detail:

> We are up early this morning and actively engaged all day in ferrying the train and [Second] cavalry across the river. In the angle formed by the Missouri and Musselshell rivers, to the south of the former and east of the latter, is an upheaval of nature terrible to contemplate for military purposes—the high sterile bluffs separated by deep gorges, ravines, and gulches, worn by waters coursing through the loose soil until cañons are formed; and through this kind of a country we must . . . find a pathway for our pack animals. Starting at 7 P.M. in the darkness, after considerable trouble we find a buffalo trail and follow its crooked windings, balancing ourselves on the precipitous side of a bluff, at whose base, hundreds of feet below,

flows the Musselshell, or ascend the steep slopes of the high banks only to find a steeper declivity awaiting us. However, we soon reached a gravelly ford of this river, about 100 yards in width and 18 inches deep, some 3 miles from its mouth. Crossing to its left bank, we passed down its valley cut by arroyos and with a heavy growth of sage-bushes; crossed Crooked Creek, and at 11 P.M. reached the Missouri again on the west side of the Musselshell, near its mouth. No odometer could be used, and the estimated distance of our night's march is 8 miles.[30]

During the night of the twenty-fourth, the steamer *Benton* passed up the Missouri, dropping off Miles's adjutant, Lieutenant Baird, with the provisions he had arranged for at Fort Peck, eighty miles down the river. Two of Miles's scouts, Luther S. "Yellowstone" Kelly and George Abbott, also joined from Bailey's detachment at Carroll.[31] Meanwhile, the *Fontenelle* completed transferring Miles's supplies and, by early the morning of September 25, had departed downstream. Then, as the troops gathered near the Missouri, a small boat arrived from above bearing a note penned that morning by Lieutenant Bailey at Carroll:

> A mackinac has just arrived from above with a letter from Col. Clendenin which I enclose. By it you will see the situation up to 11 P.M. yesterday. I sent you at midnight yesterday a large sized mackinac in which you can cross everything. It is large enough to carry an empty wagon I think. . . . I think I can defend this place without much trouble. There is a building large enough to get everyone into and so situated to command the place from three sides. . . . The despatch was brought to me by a Corpl of the 7 Infy and a citizen both passing on the *Silver City*.[32]

Clendenin's letter, of course, told of the Nez Perces' sacking of the stores at Cow Island after they crossed the Missouri at that point on the twenty-third, as well as their likely course to the border: "I think the Nez Perces are keeping up Cow [Creek] & will pass through the [Little] Rockies & Bears Paw & so north to the line."[33]

The news brought an abrupt change in Miles's strategy. He abandoned his plan to continue along the south bank and decided to cross over and prolong his trajectory northwest, now intent on intercepting or pursuing the Nez Perces somewhere in the area of the Little Rocky or Bear's Paw ranges. "I decided to place my force as speedily as possible in the gap between the northern ends of the Little Rocky and Bear

Paw Mountains, between which ranges the Indians had started north-ward," he reported.[34] Immediately, he directed Sergeant McHugh to fire three rounds from the Hotchkiss gun as a signal to the *Fontenelle*, by then several miles below the command. Lieutenant Baldwin, aboard the steamer sick with pneumonia that precluded his further involvement in the campaign, heard the distant firing and the shots bursting in the air and ordered the vessel turned about.[35] The rest of the day and night was spent in transferring Miles's entire command, including pack train and wagons, to the north bank in preparation for renewing the pursuit. Kelly and the civilian scouts rode far ahead, seeking a tall butte from which to scan the horizon. Shortly after dark, the Second Cavalry battalion started for Fort Benton, still intent on joining Terry's commission.[36] On Wednesday, a cold and windy day, Miles wrote his wife: "We start right north for the Little Rocky and Bear Paw Mountains with the hope of heading them off or getting on their trail. I intend to move as rapidly as possible."[37] After a difficult labor getting the wagon train up from the river bottom, Miles and his troops marched away from the Missouri, covering fifteen miles before bivouacking among the low hills of a gradually ascending plateau. "To the northwest the blue outline of the Little Rocky Mountains is seen," noted Lieutenant Long.[38]

On September 27, Miles and his troops reached Fourchette Creek, gradually ascending that stream and its Dry Fork toward the northeast end of the Little Rockies. The view was spectacular. "To the east and west of us," wrote Long, "as far as the eye can see, stretches a vast expanse of undulating prairie land, with waving grasses that furnish food for the numerous herds of buffalo and antelope that graze on every side."[39] After traveling less than ten miles, the troops overhauled Tyler's battalion. Miles "put a stop to our movement," wrote Private Zimmer, and the companies formally merged with his field command. They all stopped to await arrival of the train, and the horses and mules were allowed to browse. "While our stock is grazing, a few buffalo quietly join the herd, to seek the refining influence of government mules," noted an officer. "For fear that they may stampede [our] flock, orders are given to shoot them."[40] Surgeon Tilton celebrated the "swift running mountain streams of palatable water, which were a Godsend to us."[41]

Late that afternoon, leaving his wagons and the Napoleon gun with forty soldiers under Captain Brotherton and Lieutenant Borden, Miles pulled away with his mounted force, rationed for eight days, plus the Hotchkiss gun and pack train, passing through the gently rolling lands of upper Dry Fork Creek, probably but a few miles west of present Shed and Beam lakes. Tilton noticed an abundance of ducks; "some are lighting and dashing the spray. . . . Others are . . . taking wing. They need have no fear; we are not hunting ducks today."[42] With the scouts well out in front, toward evening the men entered the low foothills of the Little Rockies, camping long after dark without wood and near some holes containing rainwater "thick with mud." The distance traveled this day was little more than twenty-four miles.[43]

By traveling east of the Little Rockies, Miles hoped to screen his presence from the Nez Perces while his scouts ranged far and wide among the high points of that range seeking the people.[44] "Every precaution was taken to conceal the command as far as possible, and the march was made with all the celerity and secrecy practicable," he recalled.[45] Friday, September 28, was windy and cold, and the troops arose at 3:00 A.M. to build fires of buffalo chips for cooking breakfast. They continued on the prairie, approaching the eastern flanks of the "rough-looking" Little Rockies and spotting a "herd" of twenty bears about two miles from their column. From the narrow valley of an affluent of Beaver Creek "choked by the growth of cactus and sage-brushes," the soldiers began climbing the rolling ground near the foot of the mountains. Long described them thus:

[They rise] to the height of nearly 1,000 feet, impress all with a lavish display of grand and imposing scenery. The whitish precipitous rocky face of the range, checkered by the sunlight and shadow, is relieved by the warm gray lichens which cover it in spots, and the sparkle of tiny streams of water that trickle down its surface. The hardy pine crowns its summit and flourishes in the grand solitudes and silent wilderness of the comparatively unknown region.[46]

The command traced around the northern slopes and through a pass—perhaps following the upper North Fork of Beaver Creek—to reach Little Peoples Creek and its tributaries. That evening, after having gone twenty-eight miles, the soldiers camped along a stream with plenty of wood and grass nearby.[47] Probably sometime on the twenty-eighth or twenty-ninth, the two couriers, Charles Bucknam and William Gantes, sent by Major Ilges, reached Miles with direct information about the course of the Nez Perces after they left Cow Island.[48]

On Saturday, the twenty-ninth, after carefully extinguishing all fires before dawn, the command resumed its march northwest. Game abounded, with large herds of deer, antelope, and buffalo on every side as the men navigated the drainage of Little Peoples Creek and approached the southwest side of Three Buttes, a dominating landmark that afforded a sweeping view in all directions. Lieutenant Long was among those who climbed the highest peak. "The Bear's Paw Mountains are plainly seen stretching toward the southwest and the Little Rockies, a little east of north, to the northeast [sic—southeast], and many miles distant, the dim outline of Wood Mountains in the British possessions are seen on the horizon."[49] In the afternoon, the weather turned colder and intermittent rain turned to snow as the column drew nearer to the Bear's Paws. "Fortunately for us the clouds drifted very low and thus shielded us from observation," recalled Captain Godfrey.[50]

Sensing his closing proximity to the Nez Perces, Miles sent his scouts to range in all directions over the countryside and "to be circumspect" in finding some sign of the people's impending arrival or recent passage. "Yellowstone" Kelly described the meticulous search for the elusive tribesmen on the twenty-ninth:

> Beyond People's Creek to the left extended a broken plain to the foot of the Bear Paw Mountains, hazy and dim in the distance. From the Bear Paw to the Missouri every ridge was scrutinized for signs of travelers, for it was apparent that no great company of people with a multitude of live stock could conceal from view their movement on that open plain, nor would they try, expecting pursuit only from the rear. We looked long and earnestly, but no object appeared to move, not even buffaloes where one might expect plenty.[51]

Several inches of snow had accumulated by the time the troops, after twenty-six miles, encamped among the foothills along a fork of Peoples Creek, probably within fifteen miles of the Nez Perce village on Snake Creek. Again without wood (although a few men went into the mountains in search of it), the troops built fires fueled with buffalo chips. Their tents having remained with the wagons, they prepared for an uncomfortable night. That afternoon, a courier rode in from General Howard with dispatches telling of that officer's position near Carroll and of his decision to terminate his campaign, send his own cavalry home, and keep Sturgis's battalion, along with his own infantry, on the Missouri River.

Still driven by the potential of a Lakota presence as much as a desire to stop the Nez Perces, Miles responded that he hoped "to prevent their forming a junction with Sitting Bull" and urged Howard to keep on the trail. But the reality was otherwise. Howard's message "made it clear," recalled Miles, "that whatever encounters we might now have with the Nez Perces, we were entirely beyond support."[52]

In fact, on the twenty-ninth, a major clash with those tribesmen grew increasingly imminent. Lieutenant Maus with some soldiers and civilian scouts, operating a considerable distance southwest of Miles's force as it crossed the prairie from the Little Rockies, came upon fifteen or twenty Nez Perce warriors leading some ponies and opened a running engagement with them. Maus thought that two of the warriors had been wounded in the exchange of fire, and his men captured fourteen ponies. Late in the day, they and some of the Cheyennes returned to Miles to report the Nez Perces' trail directly in his left front. Miles sent Maus and two soldiers back out with Kelly, Corporal John Haddo of Company B, Fifth Infantry, and Milan Tripp and William F. Schmalsle, both civilian scouts, to renew their survey of the country; they searched until dark, finally camping in a fine, cold mist.[53] But a few miles away, in the closing hours of September 29, Miles and his men camped in the shadow of the Bear's Paw Mountains, awaiting anxiously for whatever the morrow might bring.

In entering the country lying between the Little Rocky and Bear's Paw mountains, the Nez Perces and Miles's troops penetrated lands more or less permanently inhabited by three mobile tribes not always friendly to each other, the River Crows, the Assiniboines, and the Gros Ventres (Atsinas). The country was well known for its rich game resources, particularly buffalo and antelope, that gave sustenance to these native peoples. Other regional tribes, such as the Flatheads, Lakotas, Blackfeet, Plains Crees, and Yanktonais Sioux, motivated by trade and subsistence needs, frequently hunted there and their presence variously inspired armed collisions with each other as well as with the traditional occupants. Like some other Columbia Plateau tribes, the Nez Perces found the area accommodating and usually passed through during their seasonal trans–Rocky Mountain buffalo-hunting excursions. Historically, the Nez Perces factored into this mix, carrying on an intense rivalry with the Blackfeet, in particular, that included open warfare. Their relationships with other transient and settled tribes in the area alternated between friendship and hostility, depending on the economics of game availability, their relative affinity for the U.S. government, and their proximity to each other.[54]

The Bear's Paw Mountains provided the Nee-Me-Poo with ample game as well as outlying buttes and ridges high enough to discover approaching enemies while affording a visual shield to their presence. The Bear's Paws rise sharply from the surrounding plain and stretch approximately twenty miles north-to-south and about forty east-to-west. Appearing from afar as a cluster of partly interconnected conical volcanic peaks, the Bear's Paws, in fact, constitute an elevated, dissected tract of ridges rather than a true mountain range. Their grass-covered slopes exhibit occasional breaks of contrasting dark volcanic rock, while aspen and cottonwoods dot their valleys. Their highest peak, Baldy Mountain (formerly called Bearpole Peak), ascends to 6,916 feet in the western sector; most of the other peaks stand well under 6,000 feet in elevation, and those composing the easternmost are considerably lower. The highest prominences on the northeastern edge of the Bear's Paws are McCann Butte (formerly Eagle Butte), rising about 900 feet above the plain, and Miles Butte (formerly Gray Butte), about 1,500 feet, two miles directly south. From the high western core of the cluster, streams radiate in all directions but trend toward the Missouri River, to the south, and to Milk River, about twenty miles north. Snake Creek heads in the northern part of the mountains, not far from Peoples Creek, the major artery transecting them, and courses through the foothills and rolling prairie northeast to Milk River.[55]

It was at Snake Creek that the Nee-Me-Poo, after skirting the eastern and northeastern sides of the Bear's Paws, established their camp on September 29. In the early afternoon, the convoy of families and animals paused to dry hides and meat of some buffalo killed at the site by advance scouts as they came north from the Missouri River. Only the evening before had their scouts reported seeing people moving at a great distance from the tribesmen, but they could not confirm they were soldiers. As Yellow Bull remembered:

> We discussed it and there arose a dispute. Not knowing anything about the presence of Miles' troops, one side said it could not be Howard, for we knew the worn-out condition of his men and horses; therefore it must be other Indians moving camp. The other side said they did not like to take the risk and insisted that scouts be sent back to find out, but they were not sent.[56]

Yellow Bull also recalled that almost everyone wanted to continue, realizing that Canada still lay some distance away, but following a fractious interlude, Looking Glass—who wanted to stop—again influenced the council of leaders. He prevailed, and the halt was made. Perhaps more important, some of the horses were experiencing a painful sickness in their hooves (possibly the same affliction affecting the army mounts) and the Nee-Me-Poo leaders wanted to let them feed on the plentiful grass.[57]

By that season, summer's verdure had given way to dry, drab desolation, an appearance heightened by the frequently leaden autumn skies. Probably influenced partly by defensive considerations, the Nez Perces selected a site on the grassy bottom generally bordered on the north, south, and east by an intersected network of gentle and brush-filled swales, coulees, and wavelike ridges that might afford limited protection in the case of an assault by a determined foe. Chiefly, however, the site offered comfortable refuge from the seemingly ceaseless cold winds and breezes that swept the open prairie, while simultaneously providing a water source, shrub fuel and buffalo chips for cooking, and a place for concealment. At the south, in particular, a high, abruptly sloping bluff with an adjoining cut bank rose forty feet from the bottom near the creek to meet the surrounding treeless plain, undulating southeastwardly in ascending to the mountains six miles away. Near the west base of this bluff, the channel of Snake Creek angled sharply northwest for several hundred yards before turning south toward the mountains. West of the village, the bottom stretched back from the mostly dry and willow-fringed channel, gently rising through the adjacent hills to an open plateau ideal for grazing ponies. Along the right (east) side of the creek on a slightly intermediate and roughly crescent-shaped flat "covering about six acres of ground," remembered one officer, the Nee-Me-Poo set up their camps, each band or interband group occupying a specific site within a linear space measuring approximately one-quarter mile south to north and two hundred yards east to west. Full-fledged lodges of hide or canvas were scarce among the people as most had been abandoned at the Clearwater and the Big Hole and they had had little time to cut new poles. Presumably, many found shelter under pieces of canvas brought along, purchased, or captured on the way from Idaho. Southernmost lay the camp of Joseph's Wallowas, along with Husis Kute's Palouses, roughly two hundred yards from the high south bluff and containing at least fourteen families. To the northeast and across a swale stood the shelters of Looking Glass's Alpowais, at least nine in number, while adjoining these on the north were eleven more dwellings, principally Lamtamas under White Bird. Finally, fifty yards farther northwest stood the Pikunan camp of Toohoolhoolzote, which included as many as fifteen family dwellings and wickiups. This band unit occupied a generally triangular-shaped tract, each side about eighty yards long, which rose between the forks of a rivulet entering Snake Creek from a coulee directly east.[58] Just above the southern extremity of the camp, the course of Snake Creek angled southwest, and a tributary entered through a coulee from the east and southeast.

Early on the morning of September 30, even before the Nee-Me-Poo started their daily routine preparatory to continuing their trek north into Canada, the troops under Miles were in motion. Already Miles's scouts had dispersed. Lieutenant Maus, Kelly, and the several civilian guides had camped in the foothills, apparently off to the southwest, while the main body of Cheyenne and Lakota scouts searched northwest for the village.[59] Scout Louis Shambo, riding with ten of them, notified the colonel when he reached the trail discovered the previous day. Three or four miles farther, Shambo's party saw a dozen or so people in the distance running buffalo. "I soon noticed that they were Nez Perces as they had striped blankets and the other tribes had solid colors," he recalled. "I sent another Indian back to say that we had found the Nez Perces and that the command had better hurry up." Shambo and the Cheyenne scouts then followed the Indians at a safe distance as they returned to their village. From afar, because the camp was situated in the depression, they saw only the pony herd on the tract north of the stream.[60] Shambo's description of this event correlates well with that given by the Cheyenne, Young Two Moon. He claimed that two of his fellows, Starving Elk and Hump, using field glasses had spotted smoke rising far off in front and rode ahead to reconnoiter. An officer kept the two in sight; if they found the camp they were to signal back to him by separating, then riding back and crossing each other's path. When this occurred, news of the discovery was sent back to Miles. Meanwhile, the other scouts advanced to meet Starving Elk and Hump, wishing to view the Nez Perce village. Young Two Moon peered over a hill and could see the pony herd, but that was all. The scouts then started back to join Miles's command.[61]

The troops were up and about at 2:00 A.M., the cooks preparing breakfast over frozen and hard-to-light buffalo chips. "The moon and stars shine in a clear sky, the air is chilly," wrote Tilton. "We march as early as we can see to move."[62] At about 4:40 A.M., the column slowly wended southwestwardly from the bivouac site toward and into the foothills, looking to intersect the trail reported by Maus the previous day. Morning evolved bright and cloudless, the mist hanging on the mountains slowly evaporating in the sun. The order of march placed the troops of the Fifth Infantry mounted battalion in front, followed by the battalions of the Second and Seventh regiments, respectively, by the foot soldiers of the Fifth Infantry, and lastly by the pack train.[63] En route, the troops forded several iced-over tributaries and headed ever more directly south with word that some Indians had been sighted in that direction. At 5:30 A.M., Lieutenant Long, at Miles's behest, rode ahead to verify the existence of the trail found by the scouts and pronounced by them to be two days old. At 6:30, the column halted briefly to rest their horses on what Long reported was Peoples Creek, but perhaps more logically was Suction Creek, described as "10 feet in width, with clear running water and gravelly bed." Proceeding on, the troops encountered the trail of the Nez Perces leading from the mountains. Godfrey stated that this occurred at 8:20 A.M.[64] Almost simultaneously, the Cheyenne, Brave Wolf, appeared with the news that smoke from the village had been sighted about six miles ahead. At this, Miles prepared his mounted force for battle. He sent an officer rearward to hurry the lagging ammunition packs, then placed all extra dunnage with the remaining mules, the Fifth Infantry foot soldiers to follow in reserve with the train. Most of the men wore caped greatcoats. Each cavalryman carried a pistol and Springfield carbine, each mounted infantryman a "long Tom" Springfield rifle; each man took one hundred rounds of ammunition. Miles's own appearance was described in considerable detail by two civilian guides:

> He looked the leader that he was—rough, tough and ready. Weighing nearly two hundred pounds, he sat on his charger like a centaur, his brown mustache and side whiskers, slightly mixed with gray, adorned features that are heavy but pleasing, and were overshadowed by a broad-brimmed, slouched drab hat. A wide blue ribbon encircled its crown, with blue streamers behind. He wore a red blanket frontier shirt and a black necktie, its ends floating over his shoulders; outside

the shirt, a buckskin coat, short at the hips and carelessly buttoned; the light blue trousers of a private soldier, with black stripes down the seams, and coarse boots completed his attire.[65]

As the preparations continued, a messenger started back over the trail to find the wagon train with orders that the Napoleon gun and its ammunition be brought up quickly. In suddenly reversing direction to the north, Miles's column reformed with the Seventh Cavalry battalion in front, followed by the Second Cavalry and the mounted Fifth Infantry soldiers. At approximately this time, off to the left on a slope of the Bear's Paws, a few Nez Perce scouts suddenly appeared. Some of Miles's Cheyennes went after them, and a bit of long-range intertribal maneuvering occurred that the officers and men watched with interest from the distance.[66] Perhaps it was at this juncture that several officers of the Seventh Cavalry, anticipating the coming action, conversed among themselves, as recalled by Captain Godfrey:

> Capts Hale, Moylan and self were together, when after a silence [Hale] said with a rather cynical smile: "My God! Have I got to be killed this beautiful morning?" Then his smile pursed, his countenance became serious and his eyes to the ground. Not a word was spoken for several minutes; then the Adjutant, Lt. Baird, rode up with orders to mount.[67]

As the troops started northwest, they passed "through a gap near the northern end of the range" (perhaps the area south of McCann or Miles buttes, which would have brought them to Peoples Creek about seven and one-half miles southeast of the village) and ascended a rise between Peoples and Snake creeks (west of the presently designated Sand Rocks?) from which Miles could see the Nez Perces' herd on the bench west of the village, but not the village itself.[68] At one point in the advance, the mounted troops encountered a ravine so deep and potentially hazardous that they were compelled to cross it in single file. The Seventh completed the crossing and formed on the adjoining plain, but the other units experienced difficulty.

Even before the companies of the Second and Fifth cleared the ravine and separated from the pack animals, the battalion of the Seventh Cavalry had crested a rise ahead and moved beyond view. By now, Shambo and the remaining scouts had returned with definite knowledge of location of the camp, the Cheyennes and Lakotas announcing that the fight had already started, referencing either their sighting of the camp or their encounter with Nez Perce scouts on the mountain slopes. They underwent "an almost instant transformation . . . [with] hats, coats, leggins, shirts, blankets, saddles and bridles . . . quickly thrown into one great heap in a ravine," said Miles, as they stripped themselves for the coming battle, applying paint to their bodies, donning breechclouts, moccasins, feather headdresses, and other adornments, and mounting special war ponies brought along for the occasion.[69] Thus readied according to their custom, the scouts dashed off to take the lead on either side of the troops in front.[70]

Armed with knowledge of a village of imprecise size somewhere ahead on the trail, and at least aware of the likelihood that the Nez Perces had been alerted to his presence and probably were beginning to get away, Miles planned to execute the traditional army tactical strike that became classic throughout the post–Civil War Indian campaigns—one that would physically shock and demoralize all the camp occupants—men, women, and children, both young and old—before they could respond effectively to counter the blow. Considered conscientiously immoral by modern standards, especially in its targeting of noncombatant populations, the tactic—while never formalized in the military precepts of the day—theoretically took root in the "total war" concept engendered by Union commanders during the Civil War, although it had been used previous to that struggle against Indian villages. Time-tested on numerous fields of the northern and southern plains during the postwar period, the reality-based tactic, most effectively implemented at daybreak, was embraced by field commanders hard-pressed for results against the highly mobile and particularly elusive tribesmen of the plains. Miles had used the tactic the preceding May in assaulting the village of the Minneconjou Lakota, Lame Deer, and it had resulted in the capture of the Indians' pony herd, the destruction of their camp, the killing and scattering of the people, and the psychological and emotional devastation and ultimate surrender of most of the refugees. A major difference, however, lay in the fact that the attack on Lame Deer had occurred at dawn, when most of the village occupants were asleep, while the Nez Perces who camped along Snake Creek were not only fully awake and into their daily activities, but—based on rapidly unfolding events regarding their scouts—they would anticipate, and gear up defensively to meet, such an attack.[71]

Soon after daybreak, the Nez Perces prepared to start north again, still confident that the great distance from Howard's army assured their security. In the village were approximately 700 people, of whom perhaps 250 were warriors, the rest women, children, and the elderly.[72] Some of the men rode off to hunt, while some women left the camp to skin, butcher, and pack the meat from buffaloes killed the preceding day. Other tribesmen, including Joseph and his twelve-year-old daughter, Kapkap Ponmi (Noise of Running Water), were out catching horses from among the herd located west of Snake Creek, while still others packed selected animals for continuing the movement into Canada, now but forty miles distant. Children played with sticks and mud balls. Some people were still eating breakfast when two scouts who had been visiting an Assiniboine camp raced in from the north, yelling that soldiers must be approaching and that the troops had stampeded some buffalo the two had seen during their return to the camp.[73] According to Yellow Wolf, Looking Glass downplayed the warning, saying that the people had plenty of time to move. (Looking Glass also discounted a dream the warrior, Wottolen, had had about an imminent attack.) "About one hour later," Yellow Wolf recounted, "a scout was seen coming from the same direction. He was running his horse to its best. On the highest bluff he circled about, and waved the blanket signal: 'Enemies right on us! Soon the attack!'"[74] At this immediate alarm, the warriors sprang to action, arming themselves, with some racing out to secure the horses. Women and children, some leading previously packed animals, started north out of the village. More warriors tore through the camp, running along the flat and through gullies toward the high cutbank and bluff overlooking the creek bottom on the southern perimeter, the direction of the greatest threat. "Soon, from the south came a noise," recalled Yellow Wolf, "—a rumble like stampeding buffaloes."[75]

Gallery of U.S. Military Participants

*Brigadier General Oliver
Otis Howard, Commander,
Department of the Columbia*
MOORLAND-SPINGARN RESEARCH
CENTER, HOWARD UNIVERSITY,
WASHINGTON, D. C.

*Colonel John Gibbon,
Seventh Infantry*
WESTERN HISTORY DEPARTMENT,
DENVER PUBLIC LIBRARY

*Colonel Nelson A. Miles,
Fifth Infantry*
STANLEY MORROW, PHOTOGRAPHER;
COURTESY BRIAN C. POHANKA

*Colonel Samuel D. Sturgis,
Seventh Cavalry, ca. 1864*
WESTERN HISTORY DEPARTMENT,
DENVER PUBLIC LIBRARY

*Lieutenant Colonel Charles
C. Gilbert, Seventh Infantry*
SPECIAL COLLECTIONS,
U.S. MILITARY ACADEMY LIBRARY,
WEST POINT, N.Y.

*Surgeon (Major)
Henry R. Tilton*
NATIONAL LIBRARY OF MEDICINE,
BETHESDA, MD.

Major Henry Clay Wood,
Assistant Adjutant General,
Department of the Columbia
OFFICERS . . . WHO SERVED IN
THE CIVIL WAR

Captain Lawrence S. Babbitt,
Ordnance Department,
Department of the Columbia
COMPANIONS OF THE MILITARY ORDER

Captain Frederick W.
Benteen, Company H,
Seventh Cavalry
LITTLE BIGHORN BATTLEFIELD
NATIONAL MONUMENT,
CROW AGENCY, MONT.

Captain Edward S. Godfrey,
Company D, Seventh Cavalry
LITTLE BIGHORN BATTLEFIELD
NATIONAL MONUMENT,
CROW AGENCY, MONT.

Captain Owen Hale,
Company K, Seventh Cavalry
LITTLE BIGHORN BATTLEFIELD
NATIONAL MONUMENT,
CROW AGENCY, MONT.

Captain Stephen P. Jocelyn,
Company B, Twenty-first
Infantry
OFFICERS . . . WHO SERVED IN
THE CIVIL WAR

Captain Evan Miles,
Twenty-first Infantry
OFFICERS . . . WHO SERVED IN
THE CIVIL WAR

Captain Myles Moylan,
Company A, Seventh Cavalry
LITTLE BIGHORN BATTLEFIELD
NATIONAL MONUMENT,
CROW AGENCY, MONT.

Captain David Perry,
First Cavalry
NEZ PERCE NATIONAL HISTORICAL
PARK, SPALDING, IDAHO

*Captain
Darius Bullock Randall,
Idaho volunteer*

*Captain Simon Snyder,
Company F, Fifth Infantry*

*First Lieutenant and
Adjutant George W. Baird,
Fifth Infantry*

*First Lieutenant
Henry M. Benson,
Seventh Infantry*

*First Lieutenant
Mason Carter,
Company I, Fifth Infantry*

*First Lieutenant
William R. Parnell, Company
H, First Cavalry*

*First Lieutenant
Henry Romeyn,
Company G, Fifth Infantry*

*Second Lieutenant
Jonathan Williams Biddle,
Company K, Seventh Cavalry*

*Second Lieutenant
Lovell H. Jerome,
Company H, Second Cavalry*

*Second Lieutenant
Oscar F. Long, Fifth Infantry*

THE HUNTINGTON LIBRARY,
SAN MARINO, CALIF.

*Second Lieutenant Sevier
McClellan Rains, Company L,
First Cavalry, in 1876*

SPECIAL COLLECTIONS,
U.S. MILITARY ACADEMY LIBRARY,
WEST POINT, N.Y.

*Second Lieutenant
Charles Erskine Scott Wood,
Twenty-first Infantry*

SPECIAL COLLECTIONS,
U.S. MILITARY ACADEMY
LIBRARY, WEST POINT, N.Y.

*Second Lieutenant Charles A.
Woodruff, Seventh Infantry*

OFFICERS . . . WHO SERVED IN
THE CIVIL WAR

*Corporal Roman D. Lee,
Company H, First Cavalry,
first army fatality in
the Nez Perce War*

LIBRARY OF CONGRESS,
WASHINGTON, D.C.

*Stanton G. Fisher, civilian
scout for General Howard*

BRADY, NORTHWESTERN FIGHTS
AND FIGHTERS

*Hump, Minneconjou Lakota
scout for Miles's command,
photographed in the 1890s*

R. L. KELLY, PHOTOGRAPHER;
SOUTH DAKOTA STATE HISTORICAL
SOCIETY, PIERRE

*Luther S. "Yellowstone" Kelly,
scout for Miles's command*

WESTERN HISTORY DEPARTMENT,
DENVER PUBLIC LIBRARY

*Young Two Moon,
Northern Cheyenne scout
for Miles's command*

NATIONAL ANTHROPOLOGICAL
ARCHIVES, SMITHSONIAN
INSTITUTION, WASHINGTON, D.C.

12

Bear's Paw: Attack and Defense

WORD OF THE PRESENCE of the village ahead, coupled with reports that the Nez Perces might already be fleeing to the north, impelled Miles to hurry his troops forward. It was shortly after 9:00 A.M.[1] Operating on knowledge gained from his scouts that the village lay between four and six miles ahead over generally open terrain, the colonel started his cavalry forward at a trot, the Indian scouts well out in front. The battalion of the Second Cavalry caught up with the Seventh, and on direction each unit formed into columns of fours. Lieutenant McClernand remembered that "the 7th was directed to move to the right of the Second and on a line with it, taking sufficient interval to form left front into line."[2] Miles ordered Tyler to follow the lead of the scouts and charge directly through the Nez Perces' camp, while the companies of the Seventh would come in closely behind in support. The mounted Fifth infantrymen would follow in reserve, followed by the Hotchkiss gun and pack train.

The distance to the village proved to be several miles greater than reported, and perhaps with the belief that the Nez Perces might be getting away, Miles ordered the horsemen to spur into a gallop.[3] Eventually, the command, still moving northwesterly, crested the low divide from which the Nez Perce horse herd could be seen on the flat west of Snake Creek; some witnesses reported seeing parts of the village, yet two miles away, as the troops started the gentle descent toward the bottom. Here the column momentarily slowed, the battalions reforming left front into line preparatory to opening the assault.[4] The final configuration kept the Seventh on the right, the Second on the left, and the Fifth somewhat behind and between the former battalions.[5] The Cheyenne scouts hurried their own advance far in front, and as they closed on the camp, they swerved gradually left, sweeping broadly toward the pony herd grazing on the bench west of the camp. Tyler's battalion, following some distance behind—probably believing that the ponies and Nez Perces moving among them represented the main part of the encampment, most of which still lay hidden in the creek bottom—responded in kind, veering left after the scouts.

Miles was riding close to the Seventh troopers as they resumed a trot down the slope leading toward the south end of the village. As Tyler's men diverged, Miles saw what was happening and quickly ordered the battalion of the Seventh Cavalry to lead the charge into the camp, Captain Hale transmitting the directive to his company commanders and reforming the companies back into columns of fours.[6] Miles reportedly yelled, "Charge them! Damn them!," drawing a chorus of approving shouts in response as the horses broke into a gallop, Hale leading the way.[7] "He was splendidly mounted on a spirited gray horse," wrote Miles, "and wore a jaunty hat and a light cavalry short coat. . . . [He had] a smile on his handsome face."[8] The descending plain lying before the charging column was flat and broad, and gradually the soldiers reached a point where their view in all directions became obscured by the rising ground ahead. Whatever glimpse they had previously had of the village was now lost as they plunged ahead, now moving up a moderate slope toward the crest of what appeared to be a gentle hill leading down to the village, but what, in fact, was a much more precipitous drop into the creek bottom. Approaching over the broad flat now bordered on its right by a gradually narrowing coulee, the Seventh troopers, revolvers drawn, charged ahead with Company K, under battalion commander Hale, on the right, Moylan's Company A on the left, and Godfrey's D in the center.[9] As their horses thundered toward the top of the hill rising south of the bottom, the field suddenly narrowed as the coulee extending on the right increasingly crowded the command. Hale's men, pressed by Godfrey's company on their left, deviated right, riding into and through two swales, while Moylan and Godfrey stayed on course.

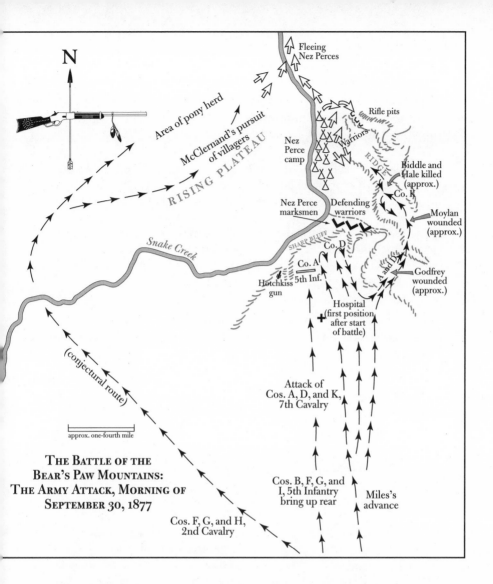

N

Fleeing
Nez Perces

Area of pony herd

McClernand's pursuit
of villagers

RISING PLATEAU

Rifle pits

Nez
Perce
camp

Warriors

RIDGE

Biddle and
Hale killed
(approx.)

Co. K

Moylan
wounded
(approx.)

Nez Perce
marksmen

Defending
warriors

Snake Creek

SHARP BLUFF

Co. D

A and D

Godfrey
wounded
(approx.)

Co. A
5th Inf.

Hotchkiss
gun

Hospital
(first position
after start
of battle)

(conjectural route)

approx. one-fourth mile

**THE BATTLE OF THE
BEAR'S PAW MOUNTAINS:
THE ARMY ATTACK, MORNING OF
SEPTEMBER 30, 1877**

Attack of
Cos. A, D, and K,
7th Cavalry

Cos. B, F, G, and
I, 5th Infantry
bring up rear

Miles's
advance

Cos. F, G, and H,
2nd Cavalry

What followed happened quickly. Passing through the swales, Hale's company ascended a flat ridge leading from the southeast down toward the Nez Perce camp. Warriors hidden in the coulees and washes suddenly opened a devastating fire on them that abruptly stopped their advance. Almost simultaneously, Companies A and D, galloping full stride, converged as they arrived on the top of the bluff, their horses grinding to a halt within twenty yards of its edge.[10] "We could then see the village," remembered Private Fremont Kipp. "All of it lay within 400 yards of us, to our right, at the mouth of a coulee."[11] Before the troops could react, a group of warriors suddenly sprang up from beneath the crest of the bluff and delivered a point-blank volley into them. Some riders fell or were shot from their saddles, the momentum of the charge carrying their mounts to stumble over the bluff. Private John McAlpine of Company D recalled:

> Those Indians stopped our charge cold. The bullets flew fast and thick. My horse went down . . . , and when I pulled myself free a slug took my hat off. There was a man . . . riding beside me. His horse was shot and as he got to his feet a bullet caught him square in the forehead. . . . I reached over and took his hat. It was a fur one, and I wiped the blood and brains off it and put it on.[12]

Hopeless of carrying a mounted assault beyond the precipice, Captain Moylan commanded the troops to fall back. "The movement was executed by 'Fours left about,'" he recalled. "In the execution . . . some confusion occurred for the very good reason that the men were under a heavy fire from the Indians, and that the large majority of them had never been under fire before, being mostly all recruits."[13]

Intent on withdrawing and reforming the battalion components, Moylan started his own men to the rear. Before Godfrey could follow suit, however, a Nez Perce marksman let loose, his shot striking and killing the captain's horse, throwing the officer to the ground. Godfrey later described the incident:

> I saw an Indian taking aim at me. I was not more than 50 to 75 yards from him. [He was] to my left. I was riding on an iron gray horse and my men were mounted on black horses. This of course made me a conspicuous mark and I was quite a bit nearer to the Indian, looking [to see] if it were possible to get down in columns of fours. His rifle cracked and down went my horse, dead. The momentum (we were galloping) threw me forward; I lit on my head and shoulder, leaving my shoulder strap and hat on the ground, but I turned a complete somersault and lit on my feet. I had my revolver in my hand, and as soon as I had recovered somewhat from the daze of the stun, I tho[ugh]t I'd try to defend myself, but when I tried to raise my pistol found my right arm was disabled, paralyzed at the shoulder. While advancing to the charge my trumpeter, [Private Thomas] Herwood, who was a boy recruit, gasped to me, "Ca-Ca-Captain, there'll be a good many of our saddles emptied today, won't there?" I replied, "Well, perhaps yes; but you keep right along with me and you'll be all right." Soon after this I had occasion to speak to him again and I found he had recovered himself.[14]

The actions of Trumpeter Herwood and Sergeant Charles H. Welch probably saved Godfrey's life. As the captain lay prostrate near his dead horse, his company moving to the rear, Herwood rode his own animal between the Nez Perces and the officer, drawing the warriors' attention to himself while Welch delivered a covering fire until Godfrey could regain his feet. During this heroic endeavor, Herwood received a gunshot wound in his side.[15] With Godfrey thus incapacitated, Lieutenant Eckerson took charge. Eckerson turned the head of the column back to the rear, and the partly stunned Godfrey ran after them. Seeing this, Moylan rode up, halted the reversal, and on orders from Colonel Miles, directed Companies A and D to dismount and face front, adjoining the right of the mounted Fifth infantrymen who had arrived on the field. Together, the Fifth and the two units of the Seventh now occupied a line perhaps two hundred yards back from the edge of the bluff.[16] Miles next commanded the two cavalry companies to connect with Hale's K, then under intense fire from the warriors. Thus far, casualties among the two units remained light, with only three soldiers killed and four wounded, mainly, Moylan believed, because of the presence of a large depression in the terrain some distance from the edge of the bluff and between the Nez Perce warriors and the troops. This "protected them somewhat, the Indians overshooting them."[17]

Company K, meanwhile, was sustaining severe losses more than three hundred yards away on the right. There, Hale's men had advanced in formation along a flat ridge descending toward the southeast side of the Nez Perce position, only to find themselves isolated and exposed to sharpshooters in gullies adjoining the bluff on the south who now turned on them with telling effect. Hale ordered his men to dismount and to move forward in skirmish formation, their shooting forcing the Nez Perces from their position below the bluff embankment from which they had fired on Companies A and D. In the exchange, Lieutenant Biddle was one of the first casualties, killed by Nez Perce fire, according to one witness, while in the act of kneeling to shoot. From this point, the battle intensified, the warriors quickly circling through the swales and gulches to flank the soldiers and drive off and capture their animals, and when the troops approached the edge of the coulee, the fighting became hand-to-hand.

But as the dismounted troopers of A and D drew nearer in support, moving at double time, their horses advancing with the holders, the warriors gradually withdrew, assuming a protective stance behind ridges and in gullies between the soldiers and their village, where many noncombatant family members now lay hidden. Hale took advantage of the pause to pull back and reassemble his company, leaving several dead and wounded on the ground in his front. Private Peter Allen was among those hit:

> While we were on our retreat I was wounded, one bullet crushing my left arm from elbow to wrist, another passed through my belt and clothing grazing the skin on my right side, and a third bullet passing through my hat plowing a ferrow [sic] through my hair across the top of my head, which rendered me unconscious for a short time. After I realized my condition and the position I was in, being about midway between the two lines of battle under cross firing, I gave the comrade just in front of me a signal to cease firing while I crawled over in rear of our line of battle, my over-coat having nine bullet holes in it. Capt. Owen Hale . . . directed me to go to the Hospital.[18]

Some injured soldiers struggled back to the line, while others, unable to move, lay helplessly near the edge of the coulee until caught and killed in the ensuing crossfire. Godfrey recalled that "they were in the line of fire from both sides, and these bodies had many shot wounds that were made after death."[19]

Yet the break in the shooting was brief, for when their maneuver exposed the flank of Companies A and D, the warriors opened again, this time raking and inflicting heavy losses among the men of those units. Moylan and Godfrey, who was again mounted, led their troops through a veritable rain of bullets toward where Hale and his men were engaged about one hundred yards from the Indians. Adjutant Baird, en route with an order for Hale respecting the holding of his position, took a bullet in the left arm that shattered the bone, while another tore off part of his left ear. Entering the large ravine immediately to the right of the plateau on which A and D had charged forward, the dismounted men found themselves easy targets for the Nez Perces.[20] Godfrey remembered that the overcoats encumbered his soldiers, but they could not take the time to remove them as they hurried ahead. As Godfrey stepped up the bank of a ravine, a bullet struck him in the side; within minutes, he slid from his mount, grabbed the pommel of the saddle, and used it as support as he made his way to the rear seeking medical aid.[21] Shortly thereafter, as Company A arrived on the scene,

Captain Moylan dismounted to get instructions from Hale and took a bullet in his upper right thigh that "sent him springing around." Moylan headed to the rear seeking treatment for his wound. And Captain Hale, who had been encouraging his men, had just completed reloading his revolver behind the skirmish line when a bullet tore through his neck, breaking it and killing him instantly, leaving Lieutenant Eckerson as the only commissioned officer still engaged of the three Seventh Cavalry companies. When the soldiers reported their ammunition running low, Eckerson mounted, raced to the rear, and brought forward a new supply, despite his horse being wounded in the effort.

Lieutenant Oscar Long, who in continuance of the wounded Baird's mission had arrived with instructions for Hale to attempt to connect with Companies A and D, temporarily took charge of the dwindling members of Company K and ultimately effected the union.[22] As in the past, the Nez Perces had successfully targeted commissioned and non-commissioned officers. "Any insignia of rank was almost a death warrant," noted a correspondent.[23] Already, the three first sergeants of the battalion (George McDermott, Company A; Michael Martin, Company D; and Otto Wilde, Company K), along with several more sergeants and corporals, lay dead or dying on the field. Eventually, the horse holders let their animals go and assumed positions on the line. "Our horses went back without leaders," remembered Private Allen. "Every man stayed and fought. . . . After the battle that morning our horses were found grazing back in the rear."[24] Dr. Tilton, who with his assistant surgeon managed to move over the field attending the stricken troops amid the galling fusillades, depicted the scene: "Riderless horses are galloping over the hills; others are stretched lifeless upon the field; men are being struck on every side, and some so full of life a few moments before have no need of the surgeon's aid."[25]

Captain Snyder's mounted infantrymen, meanwhile, had completed their deployment by the time Companies A and D of the cavalry began their pedestrian movement to join Company K. Leading their Indian ponies by lariats, the foot troops pressed forward over the ground that A and D had charged in on during the initial assault and took position on the bluff overlooking Snake Creek. From this vantage, the Fifth soldiers, lying prone, began firing volleys against the warriors still sheltered in surrounding draws who were harassing the Seventh troopers to their right front across the coulees. At one point, Company G of the Fifth began to

deploy in skirmish order "by the right flank" to gain a more advantageous position on the line. Lieutenant Romeyn described what happened:

> The Bugler was ordered to sound the deployment. "I can't blow, sir;
> I'm shot!" said the brave fellow, and a glance toward him showed him
> on the ground, with a broken spine. Another man lay still when the
> movement began, his head toward the enemy. A Sergeant in his rear,
> creeping crab-wise toward his new position, was directed to have him
> move along. "He can't do it, sir; he's dead," was the reply.[26]

The arrival and placement of the Hotchkiss gun on the brow of
the ridge immediately west of the south bluff was intended to bombard
the Nez Perce positions, but the muzzle of the piece could not immediately be lowered sufficiently to be effective and the precise shooting by
the warriors in its front soon forced its temporary abandonment.
Throughout the opening phase of the action, Miles rode back and forth
in the rear observing and directing operations, sending staff officers
ahead with orders to the commanders of the Seventh Cavalry and Fifth
Infantry. Tilton described him as riding "here, there, and everywhere.
When the first horse is blown a fresh one is mounted, and off again."[27]
Lieutenant Long reminded Miles years later that "the fire of the Indians
was often concentrated on you, so much so, in fact, that Colonel [then
Captain] Snyder, Captain [then Lieutenant] Carter and others begged of
you to dismount for their sake as well as your own, for on your safety
that of the whole command depended."[28] Miles nonetheless ranged over
the field, occasionally calling to the tribesmen to surrender and stop
the fighting.[29] At one point he approached the position of the beleaguered Seventh Cavalry engaged at the far right. "I was shocked to see
the lifeless body of that accomplished officer and thorough gentleman,
Hale, lying upon the crest of a little knoll, with his white charger beside
him. A little further on was the body of the young and spirited Biddle."[30]
A crisis in leadership of the Seventh Cavalry troops now facing him,
Miles directed Lieutenant Romeyn of the Fifth to move forward through
the gullies on the right with his own Company G and take command of
the crippled battalion of the Seventh.[31] At the same time, the effective
shooting of Snyder's infantrymen poised on the bluff sent the Nez Perces
to find cover, thereby relieving the cavalrymen sufficiently to allow them
to begin a semblance of withdrawal from the catastrophic field.[32]

Nez Perce recollections of the opening assault by Miles's force present an indelible account of the terror it aroused among the people and their reaction to it. But for the quick response of the warriors to warnings by their scouts of the imminent strike, the camp would have been defenseless. Like many others preparing to move, the young man, Black Eagle, had started toward the herd when the commotion arose in camp. "Turning, I saw everybody in confusion; those scattered rushing back to camp and getting their guns. . . . I knew well what that meant, and I ran for the horses." Black Eagle recalled, "I had soldier shoes on which were too large and heavy for the swift going. I stopped and took them off, leaving them there on the ground."[33] When Joseph heard the tumult, he was still with the horses. He told his young daughter to catch one and flee with the others starting north from the camp. Then he raced back, the bullets from soldiers tearing through his clothing and wounding his horse. "As I reached the door of my lodge, my wife handed me my rifle, saying: 'Here's your gun. Fight!'"[34] The warrior, Shot in Head, remembered the shouting: "'Soldiers, soldiers, soldiers! Soldiers have come!' Then the crack of guns filled the air. Everybody was outside, running here, there, everywhere." Shot in Head with several others, in their enthusiastic fighting, later got outside the soldiers' lines and had difficulty returning to protect the camp.[35]

In the initial confusion following the alarm, Yellow Wolf, like the others, ran to the herd intent on saving the horses. From the high ground of the plateau above the village, he looked across to the plain beyond camp and saw "hundreds of soldiers charging in two wide, circling wings. They were surrounding our camp."[36] Yellow Wolf joined about twenty other warriors in the dash for the top of the bluff south of the village. When the Seventh troopers charged forward, it was this group that fired into them and stopped the assault. "We were only a little way from the soldiers," said Yellow Wolf. "We had a fight. We stood strong in the battle. We met those soldiers bullet for bullet. We held those soldiers from advancing. We drove them back."[37] During the first part of the battle, few of the warriors were hit; one who died was Joseph's brother, Ollokot, the respected military leader shot in the head by a soldier's bullet.[38]

While all of this action had been occurring, Captain Tyler's battalion at the outset of the attack had diverted left to sweep around and isolate the herd of about five hundred animals (horses, ponies, and mules) grazing on the high plain three hundred yards west of Snake Creek and the Nez Perce village. But fording the creek and negotiating some adjoining broken terrain retarded Tyler's movement until after the Seventh had become engaged. Meanwhile, the Cheyenne and Lakota scouts, being far out in front of the troops, initiated contact with the Nez Perces as they approached the herd.[39] Following a discussion over the propriety of their attacking before Tyler's men appeared, Young Two Moon led the assault, which consisted of the scouts' approaching the camp apparently from the southwest and firing on it from some distance away.[40] According to Young Two Moon, "the Nez Perces all rode out and looked. Then they began to shoot and the scouts began to charge back and forth in front of the camp." The Nez Perces mounted two feints toward the scouts, but fell back after the Cheyennes shot one person from a horse.[41] All the scouts then advanced for a charge across Snake Creek and into the camp, but only three—Young Two Moon, Starving Elk, and Little Sioux—actually carried forward, mounting two sallies at the camp, evidently with little or no shooting. During the second rush, as many as seventy Nez Perces, probably responding to the cavalry assault south and east of their camp, began evacuating to the northeast with a body of horses.[42]

Presently, Tyler's force came onto the scene, their horses moving at a gallop over the open ground west of Snake Creek as they attempted to cut the herd off from access to the village occupants. The animals reacted sluggishly, perhaps because of the sickness afflicting many of them,[43] and one officer remembered kicking at them to get them to run. Tyler's maneuver succeeded in corralling most of the 500 animals and driving them away from the camp, although perhaps 250 others had been taken by the mounted tribesmen moving northeast in their attempt to flee the village. (Still other horses were present in the village when the troops attacked.) When Tyler's men sighted these people, they were approximately one-half mile from the camp. Acting on orders from Miles sent via the wounded Baird to stop the tribesmen and capture their horses, Tyler sent Lieutenant McClernand's Company G ahead. These troops opened a long-range running encounter, forcing the Indians—who McClernand identified as "mostly men and boys" but who in reality included women and small children, too—over the course of about five miles to relinquish many of their ponies which were then confiscated by the soldiers.[44]

According to a Cheyenne account, the Nez Perce men were out in front, trying to keep the horses from being run off, while the women followed. The troops and scouts tried to get between the two parties,

> but the women would not stop and the Nez Perces crowded the
> scouts so closely that they had to get out on the other side of the
> Nez Perces. The soldiers did not reach the Nez Perces men. The
> Nez Perces were very brave and crowded on the soldiers, who after
> a little while mounted and rode off.[45]

McClernand recalled: "As the men had to be detached from time to
time to guard the ponies the Indians were forced to abandon, the enemy finally became stronger than what remained of the troop, and began to work around on our flanks and rear."[46] This factor, as well as the
sounds of distant shooting from the direction of the village, prompted
McClernand to start back immediately. He described the withdrawal in
considerable detail:

> For the purpose of covering our retreat as well as possible, a long
> and deep ravine leading down to the creek near to the Indian camp
> was selected, and into this were driven the two hundred and fifty
> ponies captured since leaving Tyler. The troops then moved into
> the ravine and dismounted. At this time the Indians closed in from
> all sides except immediately in the rear, where they had not yet time
> to get. When the troop was dismounted, there were not more than
> thirty men with it, and these divided into two platoons alternately
> took position in the lateral ravines that put into the main one. The
> first platoon would hold the enemy in check until the second had
> taken position several hundred yards to the rear, when the first pla-
> toon would fall back, and so on. By this means a disaster, which
> seemed imminent at the commencement of the retreat, and of which
> some of the men had begun to speak, was averted.[47]

Nez Perces who took part in the encounter with the cavalry north
of the village recalled their tumultuous attempt to escape. A young boy,
About Sleep, had left the village just as the shooting started and got caught
up with the herd and the Cheyenne scouts. About Sleep fled with the
group heading north, his brother mounted behind him.

> Our warriors are passing shots with the cavalrymen. They are close
> together, mixing up. Soldiers continue sending shots at us, but they
> cannot stop us. My little brother, holding right to me, has one braid
> of hair shot off close in his ear. Two soldiers pursue us but are driven
> back before they catch us.[48]

Another youth recalled trying to get from the herd to the camp when he encountered the same group. "About this time I looked and the high bank back of the camp was black with soldiers." His immediate party succeeded in eluding the pursuers and continued north. "We camped that night . . . on the same creek on which the battle was fought. That afternoon we killed two buffalo and roasted the meat that night and had plenty to eat. All of us were mounted. The next night we camped on Milk River and from there we went on into Canada."[49]

McClernand's maneuvering to capture the stock occupied two or three hours, during which his soldiers crossed to the east of Snake Creek.[50] By the time they returned to the vicinity of the battlefield, the firing had died down. He posted Company G "to hold in check the Indians who had been following us." Most of these people managed to get back into the village and assist in its defense, although some who had left the village earlier evidently stayed away. From his unit's position in the hills northeast of the camp, McClernand went afoot to find Tyler and the balance of the command, encountering some dead and wounded of the Seventh Cavalry on the way. "One wounded sergeant begged me piteously for a drink of water, which I did not have to give. He could not move, or give me any information about our position."[51] Eventually, McClernand returned to his company and removed to a nearby position designated by Colonel Miles.[52]

After the main part of the herd had been captured, Lieutenant Jerome brought his Company H up on the left bank of the creek opposite the village at the time the Fifth Infantrymen were firing into the Nez Perces' positions to relieve the Seventh Cavalry troopers pinned down east of the camp. Jerome's men opened a fusillade for several minutes that kept the warriors occupied and further helped Hale's soldiers.[53] (It may have been at this time that Jerome heard a voice call out from the Nez Perces' position: "Who, in the name of God are you? We don't want to fight."[54]) The action appears to have been preparatory for a general assault ordered by Miles on the Nez Perces' positions in the ravines adjacent east of their camp. There, in deep recesses, both natural and created by digging, the families kept out of sight, the warriors posted in neighboring coulees delivering enough firepower to keep the troops from advancing closer. By early afternoon, the warriors still trained a rigorous discharge against the disparate parts of the command that covered them on the east, south, and west. By then, too,

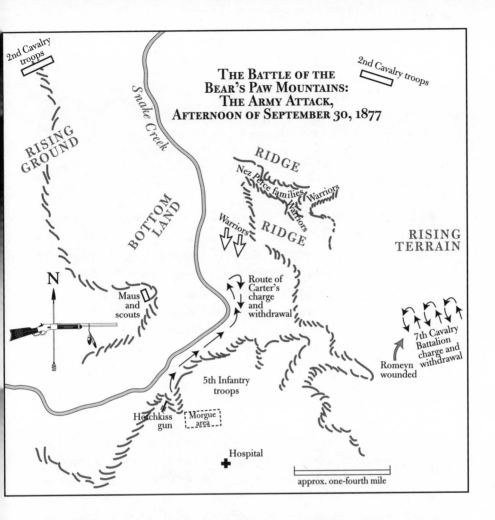

THE BATTLE OF THE
BEAR'S PAW MOUNTAINS:
THE ARMY ATTACK,
AFTERNOON OF SEPTEMBER 30, 1877

2nd Cavalry troops

2nd Cavalry troops

Snake Creek

RISING GROUND

RIDGE

Nez Perce families

Warriors

Warriors

RIDGE

Warriors

RISING TERRAIN

N

BOTTOM LAND

Maus and scouts

Route of Carter's charge and withdrawal

7th Cavalry Battalion charge and withdrawal

Romeyn wounded

5th Infantry troops

Hotchkiss gun

Morgue area

Hospital

approx. one-fourth mile

some of Tyler's Second Cavalry soldiers held the hills below the north end of the camp on either side of Snake Creek. Miles now decided that a general assault on the tribesmen from the east and southwest would dislodge them and force their destruction or capitulation. "The only thing to do," wrote Lieutenant Woodruff, adjutant of the Fifth Infantry battalion, "was to make a clean sweep by charging along the whole line and drive them from the ravines and their village out into the open plains."[55]

Shortly after 3:00 P.M., orders to attack went out to the soldiers of the Fifth and Seventh battalions. Lieutenant Romeyn, in command of his own Company G and of the Seventh Cavalry battalion pulled back on the ridge beyond the ravine to the right of the Fifth Infantry, readied his men for action.[56] As he rose to his feet to signal the infantry to start with a wave of his hat, bullets from the Nez Perce positions several hundred yards away struck him, one passing through a lung. The lieutenant walked about seventy-five yards toward the rear and collapsed.

> An enlisted man that had been cooking for me saw me soon afterward, and he and others dragged me still further to the rear and laid me along side of several other wounded men and officers. My cook gave me some water from his canteen and by and by the surgeon came and had a look at me.[57]

Romeyn's command, which had advanced with a cheer, quickly withdrew to its former position, several of the men also hit by the warriors' fire.[58] Consequently, only a unit composed of Companies I (fifteen men) and F (ten men), Fifth Infantry, besides "two or three odd men,"[59] under Lieutenant Mason Carter, moved ahead at the appointed moment. They started forward through the ravine on the left of the Fifth's blufftop position while covering marksmen stationed there opened fire. Across Snake Creek, Lieutenant Maus and the Cheyenne and Lakota scouts, probably stationed on the point of land lately occupied by Jerome, likewise raked with gunfire the ravines inhabited by the families.[60] Woodruff, who accompanied the assault group, said that "we yelled and cheered and went over the steep bluffs, across a deep ravine, and right into the village."[61]

There in the camp (which was at Joseph's sector) the approach abruptly stopped. Warriors ensconced in pits and gullies in the rising ground on the right front sent forth volleys that halted the troops and forced them back to the deep gully in their rear. Eight men were wounded (two of whom died) in the attack and withdrawal. The charge had failed, maintained Woodruff, "for the lack of support on the right and left."[62]

Carter's men remained refuged in the ravine above the village for several hours, randomly shooting at the warriors when opportunity demanded. Woodruff, meanwhile, made his way back across the ground bordering the creek to report to Captain Snyder and Miles and to give instructions to Maus. Then he returned to Carter with orders to initiate a withdrawal from the position, and at sundown the troops started back, keeping from exposing themselves "by crawling on our hands and knees along a little ravine for about 20 yards."[63] Miles later appraised Carter's attempt:

> The deadly fire of the Indians with magazine guns disabled 35 per centum of his men, and rendered it impossible for them to take the

remainder of the village; they, however, inflicted severe loss upon the enemy, and held their ground until withdrawn. The attack showed that any charge, even if successful, would be attended with severe loss on our part.[64]

At 5:30 P.M., Miles prepared a message notifying Howard, Sturgis, and Captain Brotherton of his situation:

I have this day surprised the hostile Nez Perces in their camp and have had a very sharp fight. I have several officers and men wounded—about 30. About 25 [250?] Indians are still in their camp, which is still protected.

We capture[d] the most of their herd, but I may have * * * * [difficulty?] in moving, on account of my wounded. Please move forward with caution and rapidity.[65]

Confronted with an exceedingly high percentage of loss in his assaults on the Nez Perce village, Miles determined that further such strikes would be equally unsuccessful. The fact that he had captured the people's livestock, thereby preventing their escape, decided him to prosecute them by laying siege to their position—in effect, to surround their lines with soldiers and strategically placed artillery and to pound and starve them into submission. Furthermore, Sitting Bull remained on his mind. Thus, as he wrote: "I determined to maintain the position secured, prevent the escape of the Indians, and make preparation to meet the reenforcements from the north that the Nez Perces evidently expected."[66]

By midafternoon of the thirtieth, Miles's force already held the high ground commanding the village and the primary Nez Perce refuge in the large slough running east from the northernmost camp, that of Toohoolhoolzote. It was into this broad coulee, covered by abruptly rising slopes on either side, that the women, children, and elderly had fled when the shooting erupted. Most of the warriors took advantage of the natural features of the ground in guarding this location from approach by the soldiers, and as the hours passed into the late afternoon, the people used whatever utensils were available (including some trowel bayonets taken from Gibbon's soldiers at the Big Hole) to begin to excavate more permanent entrenchments in the coulee floor. This work continued through the night, as the Nez Perces, desperate to protect themselves from the gunfire, worked to connect their shelter pits with each other—some via underground tunnels—and with the labyrinth of ravines and washes that emptied into the main draw. The loamy nature of the soil permitted the creation of cavities deep enough to accommodate whole families and their requisite supplies, moved in from the village.

The defenders further secured their works by piling saddles and other items on the edges and covering these with earth removed from the interiors of the pits. "We digged the trenches with camas hooks and butcher knives," said one woman. "With pans we threw out the dirt. We could not do much cooking. Dried meat and some other grub would be handed around."[67] At least forty-one of these shelter pits were excavated or enlarged during the night of September 30–October 1. At the same time, to further protect the people, Nee-Me-Poo warriors prepared at least fifteen rifle pits ("in the most approved manner") along the inside slope of the ridges forming the sides of the ravine. "The next morning we had dirt and rocks piled up around pits, with holes to shoot through," remembered Yellow Bull. These entrenchments not only served to further protect the people sheltered in the pits below, but furnished additional and commanding points from which to return the fire of the soldiers. Yellow Wolf claimed that, should these points be overrun by the troops, the shelter pits were to provide the last line of defense for the people.[68]

While the Nez Perces began work to fortify their position, the army worked to consolidate theirs. The Fifth Infantry still occupied the bluff south of the village, while the Second Cavalry companies maintained positions on the plateau west and northwest of the village, and on the rising ground east of Snake Creek and northeast of the camp. The severely decimated units of the Seventh Cavalry battalion held the ascending terrain east and southeast of the camp. It was from the positions held by the Fifth and Seventh battalions that the last charge on the village had begun. Late in the day, and particularly with the approach of darkness when the gunfire lessened, these positions were further advanced and secured with the establishment of rifle pits along the crests of the ridges east and southeast of the village.[69] Perhaps because of the surer accuracy promised by infantry riflemen, if not because of the exhausted condition of the cavalry, the troops of those two units switched places after nightfall, with detachments of the Seventh occupying the bluff south of the camp, as well as a ridge west of Snake Creek, and the infantrymen taking station on the high ground on the east.[70] Lieutenant Woodruff reported that the infantrymen "encamped on the

The Hotchkiss 1.65-inch breechloading mountain gun, employed by the army at the Battle of the Bear's Paw Mountains, was light enough to be carried by a mule and could be operated by only two men.

ILLUSTRATED . . . CATALOGUE OF MILITARY GOODS

ridge where we had established the Hospital, keeping strong pickets out to watch the Indians and prevent them from escaping the village."[71] And regarding Company G of the Second Cavalry, Lieutenant McClernand remembered that,

> several hours after dark, we were ordered to shift our position nearer to the other troops and astride the ravine in which the Indians were. It was very dark and we had great difficulty in getting located, especially as an officer who was to show "F" & "G" Troops their position had taken himself off to visit in another part of the command. Here the battalion [company] remained until the next night, when after dark we were shifted back to our former position.[72]

As the investment of the Nez Perces proceeded on the evening of September 30, the soldiers also improved the position of the Hotchkiss gun. Poised on the ridge west of the south bluff[73] and closely trained on the ravines harboring the people, the piece was readied to open fire at first light. The gun was a prototype, the first of its kind in the United

States, and at Bear's Paw it saw its inaugural use in the combat with the Nez Perces. The steel breech-loading weapon weighed but 116 pounds, had a caliber of 1.65 inches, and employed a charge of six ounces of black powder to propel a two-pound explosive percussion shell a distance of as much as fifteen hundred yards. It was mounted on a light pressed-steel carriage that weighed 220 pounds.[74] East of the Hotchkiss, and behind the line on the bluff top, the dead who had been retrieved were laid out in a row and covered with blankets.[75] One thousand yards west of the gun and the camp of its supporting detachment, and beyond the camp of the Seventh Cavalry, Miles placed his headquarters in a protective bend on the right side of the creek bottom.[76] Farther west lay the infantry camp—the place where the foot soldiers congregated, slept, and ate when not on the line. Somewhere in the vicinity, probably adjoining the infantry camp, the pack mules were corralled. And one thousand yards away, across Snake Creek along a tributary to the northwest, the Second Cavalry battalion established its camp. For the moment, Dr. Tilton's hospital—evidently one tent—remained on the south bluff, in the depression behind the infantry line.[77]

Late in the day, the shooting abated, the men on the line, including the Cheyenne and Lakota scouts, seemingly intent on picking off particular Nez Perce marksmen posted in ravines and rifle pits who kept up a harassing intermittent fire. "Yellowstone" Kelly and his scouts, who reached the command during the afternoon, took part in this action, and it was during the long-range dueling that Kelly's companion, Corporal John Haddo, took a bullet in the heart and died. Kelly also reported how one of the Indian scouts, Hump, "a bold and picturesque fellow," engaged a Nez Perce sharpshooter hidden in a rifle pit during an encounter that left the Nez Perce dead and the Lakota wounded.[78] Scout Louis Shambo remembered that "those Indians were the best shots I ever saw. I would put a small stone on top of my rock and they would get it every time. They were hitting the rock behind where I was lying which made me duck so hard that it made my nose bleed."[79] Sometime late in the afternoon one of Miles's packers who could speak the Nez Perce language hailed the Indians; one of them replied in English: "Come and take our hair[!]"[80]

Many soldiers wounded in the day's fighting lay stranded between the lines and could not immediately be rescued. "[These] were left lying, except those that were able to crawl in our lines & that was few," stated one man.[81] Those who were able sought treatment at the hospital where Surgeons Tilton and Gardner labored to contend with the large number of casualties. In reference to the Nez Perces, Tilton wrote, "their marksmanship was excellent, and from the very opening of the fight, [we doctors] . . . had our hands full." One who received medical treatment was Private Allen, whose arm had been shattered during the initial fighting with Captain Hale's company. He described the scene:

> [When I arrived] at the Hospital Tent, several wounded were already there, all calling for the Doctor, and begging for water, some cursing, some praying, some crying, and some laughing. Soon after we arrived, Doctor Tilton . . . came to where I was sitting . . . and remarked, "Young man, I'll wait on you now, I notice you haven't been calling for the Doctor." Until the Doctor came to me I had been sitting there taking in the entire situation. After my wound was dressed there came a soldier by the name of "Toba" [Private Emil Taube, Company K, Seventh Cavalry] who had been wounded in the head, and blood was all over his face and breast.[82]

Like Allen, Captain Godfrey sought attention for his injury received in the opening action. He related that he found Dr. Gardner, who examined the wound:

> [The doctor] promptly began to probe for any foreign substances. "Well," he said, "I see your backbone. A quarter of an inch more to the right and it would have been all up for you." I told him he was consoling but that he was not adding to my comfort by punching me with his probe. He then . . . bandaged my wounds and gave me a stiff drink of brandy and opium.[83]

And Dr. Tilton recounted an incident involving Private Jean B. Gallenne, Company M, Seventh Cavalry, Hospital Steward Second Class, who was assisting the surgeons on the battlefield:

> Some time before the [afternoon] charge was made on the village, 1st Lt. Romeyn of the Infy made an appeal to me to visit some of his men who were in urgent need of attention. They were behind a hill, but separated from the balance of the wounded by a depression which was under fire from the village. . . . I directed the Steward [Gallenne] to accompany me and we all three ran across without receiving any salute from the Indians. Upon opening the medicine case, I saw that the dressings were used up, and directed him [Gallenne] to return

to the supplies, fill the case and come back to me. He deliberately walked over. I called to him to run, but he replied, "Oh, they won't hit me." He got across safely; but in returning in the same way he was shot through the left ankle, and it was some time before he could be brought out. He crawled some distance and when the attention of the Indians was occupied in another direction, two men helped him to the Hospital. As he had the keys to the pannier and a box of dressings, I was obliged to break open one box, besides doing without his services. By making a slight detour I returned to the place where the wounded were being received, without his help.[84]

The soldiers wounded close to the Nez Perce positions who could not crawl to safety were of particular concern to the command. As the day turned to night and the firing subsided on both sides, plummeting temperatures and a wind-driven snow added greatly to their discomfort as they lay among comrades who had been killed. One man reportedly cried out to his comrades back on the line: "If some of you fellows don't take the blankets off them dead horses, I'll be damned if I won't freeze to death."[85] Some died; those who did not feared that the warriors would come and finish them off and perhaps mutilate them. Such fears proved unwarranted, for though some Nez Perce men came among them during the night, they came to take their weapons and ammunition. In one instance, a disabled sergeant readied his revolver as a warrior approached him in the darkness. The warrior spoke to him in English, telling him he would not harm him, then took the pistol and the man's cartridge belt, besides his watch and whatever money he had in his pockets.[86] Similarly, in another encounter an injured soldier begging for water lost only his ammunition belt, and the warrior left him a can filled with water.[87] The wounded in the hospital also passed a cold and dreary night. With neither wood nor troops to be spared to find some, there were few fires, only those made with buffalo chips for heating coffee. "Yellowstone" Kelly unrolled his blanket near the headquarters and noticed the soldiers sleeping nearby. Dr. Tilton distributed thirty blankets, and others were taken from the pack train, "but we felt the need of fire." Before dawn, Kelly was awakened and sent out to find the wagon train and guide it forward.[88] As Miles assessed the casualties for September 30, he found that his assault had been extremely costly. Of the three companies composing the Seventh Cavalry battalion, two officers and fourteen enlisted men had been killed, with two officers and twenty-nine men wounded (two died later); of the four companies of the battalion of the mounted Fifth Infantry, two enlisted men had been killed and four officers and twelve men wounded (three died later); and of the three companies of the Second Cavalry battalion one man was wounded. Total casualties thus numbered two officers and sixteen men killed, and four officers and forty-two men wounded. Two Indian scouts had also been wounded.[89]

Scarcely one-half mile away across the battleground, as many as six hundred men, women, and children braced against the falling sleet and snow, many laboring through the night to improve their earthen pits and all awaiting to see what would happen next. Some buried relatives from among the twenty-two killed this day, but other bodies were too close to the soldiers' lines to be retrieved. "Children crying with cold," remembered Yellow Wolf. "No fire. There could be no light. Everywhere the crying, the death wail."[90] Among those who had fought hard that day and survived were Peopeo Tholekt, Two Moon, Shot in Head, Black Eagle, and Roaring Eagle. Among the dead were Chief Toohoolhoolzote, shot in a rifle pit on a ridge north of his camp; Ollokot, killed in the initial fighting; and three men killed accidentally by the Palouse leader Husis Kute—Koyehkown, Kowwaspo, and Peopeo Ipsewahk (Lone Bird)—while they were far in advance toward the soldier position southeast of the village and thought to be enemy scouts. Lone Bird had been one who complained of the slow pace of the assemblage as it passed through the Bitterroot Valley before the Big Hole battle. Ironically, Poker Joe (Lean Elk), in charge of moving the people in the wake of that encounter until they passed Cow Island, also lay among the dead—also the victim of mistaken identity. Not far from where Toohoolhoolzote's body lay, at a place later called "Death's Point of Rocks" about three hundred yards below the northernmost camp, five more Nez Perce men lay dead; two more had been wounded there.[91] The total number of Nez Perces wounded on the first day at Bear's Paw is not known.[92]

13

Bear's Paw: Siege and Surrender

BAD WEATHER CONTINUED through the night. "The snow descends, it hails, then freezes. . . . We have no fires to relieve the cold or dry the stiffened, frozen garments of the men," wrote Lieutenant Long.[1] Daylight Monday, October 1, opened with wind and mist obscuring distant objects. Among the troops there occurred repeated announcements of mounted columns of men being sighted on the northern horizon. "They could see black horses, pinto horses, and every other kind," said Louis Shambo, reflecting the anxiety of Miles and his soldiers over the feared arrival of reinforcements for the Nez Perces.[2] Then two lines of moving objects were spotted to the south, in the rear of Miles's command. Moving slowly forward "on either flank," they appeared at first to be troops from Sturgis's command or—more threateningly—Sitting Bull's warriors coming to help the besieged Nez Perces. "Many anxious moments were spent before we determined that they were buffalo marching in single file with all the regularity and precision of soldiers," related Tilton.[3]

This incident represented a very real concern of Miles and his officers that lasted for the duration of the siege of the Nez Perces.[4] The Lakotas of Sitting Bull were keenly aware of the location of the Nez Perces, although it is unclear if they knew yet of Miles's attack. While the siege progressed, the Sioux leaders in Canada met in council preliminary to crossing the border. But they were ultimately dissuaded from lending

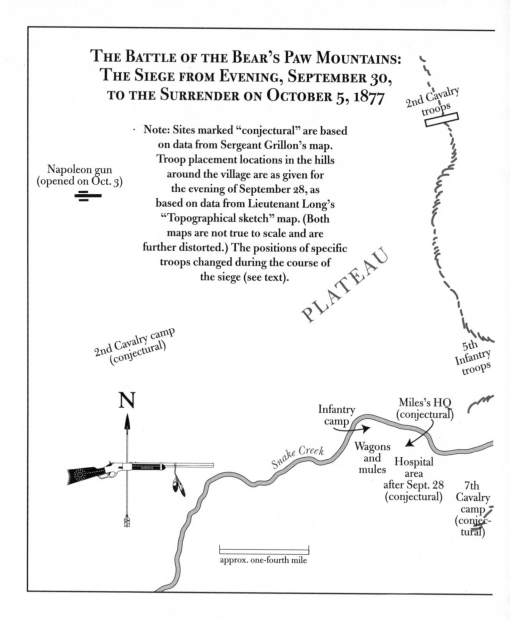

THE BATTLE OF THE BEAR'S PAW MOUNTAINS:
THE SIEGE FROM EVENING, SEPTEMBER 30,
TO THE SURRENDER ON OCTOBER 5, 1877

· Note: Sites marked "conjectural" are based
on data from Sergeant Grillon's map.
Troop placement locations in the hills
around the village are as given for
the evening of September 28, as
based on data from Lieutenant Long's
"Topographical sketch" map. (Both
maps are not true to scale and are
further distorted.) The positions of specific
troops changed during the course of
the siege (see text).

2nd Cavalry troops

Napoleon gun
(opened on Oct. 3)

PLATEAU

2nd Cavalry camp
(conjectural)

5th
Infantry
troops

N

Infantry
camp

Miles's HQ
(conjectural)

Snake Creek

Wagons
and
mules

Hospital
area
after Sept. 28
(conjectural)

7th
Cavalry
camp
(conjec-
tural)

approx. one-fourth mile

their aid by the forceful presence of Major James M. Walsh, superintendent of the North-West Mounted Police, who admonished Sitting Bull
that Canada would no longer provide them sanctuary if they moved below the line; if the warriors departed for the Bear's Paws, Walsh told
them, he would drive their women and children below the boundary.
Finally, at a subsequent council session, the chiefs concluded that any
extension of support for the Nez Perces would be suicidal for them; unknown to them, by that time (October 7) it was already too late to help.[5]

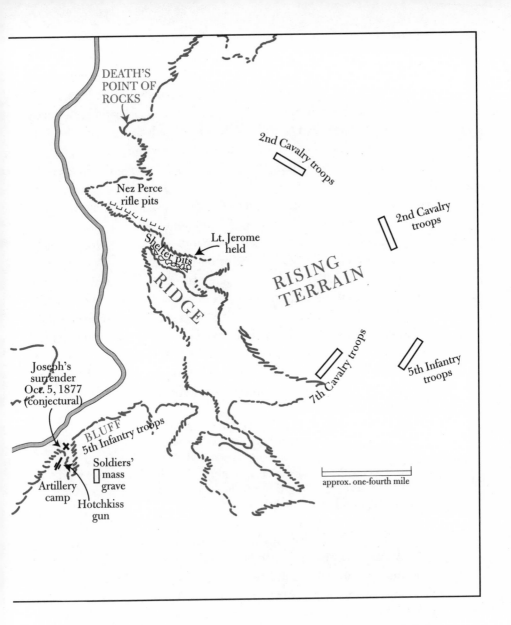

During the night of September 30, the Nez Perces improved their shelters and fortifications and seemingly prepared themselves for the worst. Equipped with the provisions taken at Cow Island, and able to live on the meat of the horses killed by the soldiers, the tribesmen could be expected to hold out indefinitely.[6] Moreover, the people retained access to the water in Snake Creek by digging two waterholes, or cisterns, in the soil below the mouth of the refuge slough and northwest of Toohoolhoolzote's camp.[7] By morning, however, not all of the Nez

Perce leaders were adamantly opposed to opening a dialogue with Miles to save lives, and Joseph was one of these.[8] During the previous day's fighting, Miles had ridden the line calling out and soliciting the tribesmen's surrender, requests that were initially met with defiance from the warriors.[9] Now at least some of them seemed more inclined to talk.

It appears that Miles's Indian scouts helped facilitate a meeting between the colonel and Joseph. After daylight, three of them, High Wolf, Young Two Moon, and Starving Elk, initiated contact in hopes of saving the women and children. As they approached the breastworks, three Nez Perces came out and shook hands with them. One, a young girl, gave Starving Elk a necklace of beads. Young Two Moon recollected that "the camp was a sad looking place. . . . Just outside of the breastworks were a few dead soldiers, but in the camp the bodies of the Nez Perces were everywhere."[10] The Cheyennes told the three that Miles would listen to them; then they rode back and reported to Miles. At the colonel's behest, Young Two Moon and three other scouts returned to the Nez Perces and convinced Joseph and several followers to come out. Young Two Moon remembered:

> As they went up on the hill, the soldiers stood in line on either side in a V with General Miles at a distance at the angle of the V. When they reached General Miles the soldiers closed in behind them. A little later a Nez Perce rode up on a cavalry horse, which his people must have captured. He came through the soldiers to where General Miles was. He could speak English and interpreted for General Miles.[11]

Although the Cheyennes factored significantly in the initiation of talks, Miles apparently pursued other avenues, too, and what happened subsequently probably reflected a mix of several efforts. Early that morning, one of the packers hailed the Nez Perces. The warrior Yellow Bull advanced under a white flag and met the man, then took his message back to Joseph.[12] "General Miles wished me to consider the situation; that he did not want to kill my people unnecessarily," remembered Joseph.[13] Joseph initially demurred, responding that he needed time to decide. Then the scout John Bruguier, perhaps with some Cheyenne scouts, went to the Nez Perce camp, and Joseph subsequently appeared and walked over to Miles's tent,[14] situated behind the lines and likely near the head of the ravine that cut between the south bluff and the hill on which the Hotchkiss gun stood.[15] Tilton described him as "a young man of fine presence. He appeared very sad. . . . He said they were short of rations and could not move without their ponies."[16] Joseph was preceded in his approach by five men, one of them an interpreter, Tom Hill, a mixed-blood Nez Perce with Delaware lineage, who Tilton said was "a man of marked presence" with "large bright black eyes and sharp cut features." "He spoke English in a very deliberate way, uttering each word slowly without emphasizing any particular one."[17]

Under the truce, the men of both sides advanced to retrieve their dead and wounded from the previous day's fighting. Some of the injured soldiers had died in the night from their wounds or from exposure. "One man was found with his throat cut," penned a Second cavalryman. "He was shot through the bowels. It's supposed that he did it with his own hands."[18] Everywhere between the lines the scene was of carnage and devastation. "The sight is frightful to see so many dead soldiers, Indians, horses & ponies lying about," observed a trooper.[19] With the gunfire suspended, burials began, the soldiers placing the bodies in a trench excavated about 150 yards back from the edge on the south bluff where part of the Seventh Cavalry attack had been repelled.[20]

At the tent, the meeting between Joseph and Miles proceeded. Joseph shook hands with the colonel, who invited him to sit inside and "talk this matter over." The meeting that followed was noncommittal on the part of Joseph. Through Tom Hill, he told Miles that in the fighting of the previous day his brother, Ollokot, among others, had been killed. He probably mentioned the loss of Toohoolhoolzote, as well as that of Looking Glass, who was shot through the head as he stood in a pit to see what he thought might be the approach of reinforcing Sioux.[21] Joseph told Miles that, although he wanted to surrender, his views did not necessarily extend to the others and that, in fact, many of the people opposed giving up. What happened next in this meeting is not altogether clear. Miles maintained that he instructed Joseph that he must surrender and bring his arms forward and place them on the ground; partial compliance yielded but a few weapons "which amounted to nothing," declared Miles. Joseph hesitated about giving up any more, explaining that his people required some guns for hunting game.[22] Eventually, at the apparent stalemate, the Nez Perce leader and his colleagues started back to their people, but Miles, despite the armistice and with no explanation then or later for his actions, intervened and took Joseph prisoner, turning him over to Lieutenant Long to guard.[23] Tom Hill described this event: "Joseph and the other four started to the camp, but Miles told me to remain. They had gone only about twenty-five yards, when Miles told me to call Joseph back. When the chief came back, the General sent me over to the camp and kept Joseph."[24] Miles's action was a clear affront to the Nez Perces as well as a direct violation of the concept of truce.[25] It is apparent that Miles promoted the suspension of arms in order to foster a dialogue with the Nez Perce leadership while gaining information about the people's condition. The truce also allowed for retrieval of the casualties between the lines. But what Miles did in arresting Joseph was to denounce his own armistice through an act of perfidy. In conventional warfare, governed by custom and well-established rules, it is doubtful that Miles would have breached such a truce. But in his quest for victory, he likely rationalized that the unconventional nature of warfare with Indians gave him license to disregard formality, despite the obvious duplicity of his actions.[26]

But what followed frustrated whatever plan Miles had devised and created consternation throughout the army command. It involved Second Lieutenant Lovell H. Jerome, Company H, Second Cavalry, a well-bred New Yorker who had graduated from West Point in 1870.[27] Apparently on Miles's direction to take advantage of the suspension of hostilities and find out the condition and circumstances of the besieged tribesmen, Jerome rode directly into the Nez Perce entrenchments.[28] According to some of those present, "he was instructed to review and report upon the Indian position and every detail of the Indian fortifications."[29] Jerome, described by Yellow Wolf as "a strong looking young man" wearing a yellow slicker,[30] was apparently in the company of some Cheyennes when he entered the camp. He was in the act of looking around when the Nez Perces received word that Joseph had been forcibly detained by Miles, whereon the warriors seized the officer to insure that no harm would come to their leader. The Cheyenne, Young Two Moon, recalled the alarm given by another scout to "try and get out of the camp and leave the Nez Perces to themselves." Some shooting, presumably from the soldier positions, erupted after the scouts had cleared the entrenchments, but apparently ceased within moments. Young Two Moon looked back and saw "three men holding the lieutenant's horse." Two more warriors were holding Jerome's arms and leading him back inside the defenses. "He did not resist."[31]

Yellow Wolf said that the Nez Perce White Bull became angry

after learning what had happened to Joseph and wanted to kill Jerome but was restrained by the others, who turned the officer over to Yellow Bull and Wottolen, who took good care of him.[32] Jerome left several accounts of his time with the Nez Perces, each of which became increasingly cloudy as time elapsed from the event. Perhaps his best account was that given in the presence of his fellow officers within two weeks of Bear's Paw:

> What I did while I was in the Indian camp was to look around for the best place for Miles to put in his shells, and to see how their rifle pits were arranged, and whether it would be possible for us to take them by assault. I had the whole thing in my mind by the next day, when I expected to leave. On that day [October 1] I received a message from Miles early in the forenoon. Miles evidently wanted to keep Joseph, but wanted me to escape. I believe now that if I had not gone into that camp under the General's order, he, being deprived of the information which I gave him afterward, would have withdrawn—holding Joseph as his prisoner—with his force to the cover of the distant woods, and there entrenched himself. The fact is he was very anxious, as all of us were, lest Sitting Bull should come to the Nez Perces' assistance. I can testify that the Nez Perces really expected that Sitting Bull would aid them, though of course I don't know how well their hope was grounded. While I was in their camp several warriors spoke of this matter.[33]

In his account, Jerome noted that soon after he had been taken hostage the Nez Perces placed him into a shelter pit with about fifteen other people. Soon he noticed shots being fired into the Nez Perce position despite the presence of the truce flag. "I was alarmed and disgusted," he said. Presently, two warriors—one of them Tom Hill—accompanied him to another pit because they feared that others might harm him. There, with two blankets to cover him, he spent an uneasy night. Throughout his presence in the camp, Jerome was treated well to the extent of being allowed to retain his pistol, although because of the occasional heavy firing, nobody slept. The lieutenant was struck by the buoyant cheerfulness of the Nez Perces despite their circumstances, one warrior commenting to him with obvious humor: "If it don't get warmer than this we'll have to go to fighting again."[34]

Miles was not at all pleased to learn of Jerome's detention in the Nez Perce camp, for it confounded his own incarceration of Joseph probably for purposes of seeking the people's final submission.[35] As frustrated as Miles became over the ill-timed venture, the officers and soldiers held decidedly mixed opinions about it. Lieutenant Woodruff wrote home that the command had little sympathy with Jerome. "We were all very much incensed at him."[36] And Captain Snyder noted in his diary that Jerome's dilemma had been brought on by "his own folly."[37] Apparently his company members, however, supported his boldness and bragged about it later, saying "that Jerome had performed as foolhardy an act as, up to that time, had occurred."[38] In any event, as evidenced by his subsequent assignments in regard to the Terry commission, Jerome was in no way penalized for the ruin of Miles's plan.[39]

Nez Perce reminiscent statements indicate that while Jerome fared well among his captors, Joseph did not. Yellow Wolf said that "Joseph was hobbled hands and feet. They took a double blanket. Soldiers rolled him in it like you roll papoose on cradle board. Chief Joseph could not use arms, could not walk about. He was put where there were mules, and not in soldier tent."[40] Yellow Wolf further said that a note from Jerome to Miles on the morning of October 2 describing his own good treatment led the soldiers to remove the hobbles from Joseph.[41] None of the military accounts—either official or personal—confirm that such extreme measures were employed. And Joseph did not mention this treatment in his account of the conflict, only that when Yellow Bull visited to check on his condition "General Miles would not let me leave the tent to see my friend alone."[42]

Because Jerome's predicament had compromised any meaningful result Miles may have entertained by holding Joseph indefinitely, plans were made to exchange the hostages on the morning of October 2. Messages passed between the camps. At the appointed time, Joseph appeared, accompanied by Miles and Lieutenant Maus, and they advanced under a white flag carried by Maus to a halfway point between the lines. There, Joseph and Jerome shook hands, then turned and went with their respective parties to their lines.[43] Jerome described the scene:

> There were three Indians along with me. I suppose that was an interesting position. With the suspicion of treachery on both sides, thirteen of our men lay in their trenches scarcely forty rods off, with the rifles held at a dead rest on Joseph and my three Indian guards. More than twenty Indians had an equally sure sight over their Winchester's and Henry's [sic] straight at General Miles and me. I have since learned

that Miles' staff officer held a cocked revolver in his bosom ready to fix Joseph if I should be harmed. The transfer passed without trouble, and I was restored to the command of my company.[44]

Jerome passed on to Miles whatever intelligence he had gained during his tenure in the camp. He had counted only about 250 people, of whom but 100 were warriors. He said that when the men entered the rifle pits they carried three guns apiece, "one a repeating rifle for close quarters."[45] The warriors, meanwhile, debated mounting an all-out charge on the troops to free themselves. Tom Hill started forward with his gun, but attracted only two followers and turned back. "I made up my mind to tell the people to quit fighting," he said.[46]

At about 4:00 P.M. on the afternoon of October 1, while Joseph and Jerome still reposed in their respective detainment areas, Quartermaster Francis M. Gibson's wagon train finally pulled up with Captain Brotherton's escort, eliciting a rousing cheer from the troops. "Yellowstone" Kelly and another scout, sent by Miles the preceding night to guide it forward, had passed the train in the darkness and had then been diverted by the discovery of some stampeded cavalry horses two miles from the army camp that Kelly later rounded up and brought in. With the train came the tents for the command and especially for the wounded. But the placement of the latter after dark drew fire from the warriors when their interiors were lighted, compelling Tilton to move the wounded via stretchers back to a more protected hospital site next to Miles's headquarters along the Snake Creek bottom. There, remembered a sergeant, "the tents where the wounded were were put down and walled up to protect them fr[om] cold."[47] Of the two ambulances that had accompanied the train, one had been abandoned on the trail, and the other was in dilapidated shape, its top missing.[48] Also arriving was the bronze twelve-pounder Napoleon gun, whose presence would soon add a new and horrifying dimension to Miles's efforts to dislodge the people.[49]

Despite the arrival of the tents and supplies, the night of October 1 seems to have been even more miserable for the soldiers than the previous night. One man was killed and another wounded during the day's action.[50] These two represented the last army casualties at Bear's Paw. Seventh Cavalry Sergeant Stanislaus Roy, who arrived with the train, recalled the scene that evening: "The Troops were all on the skirmish line and the fight was still on. . . . Coffee was made for the troops and carried on [the] skirmish line to the men, and I took charge of the Troop on the line that night."[51] "The wagon train . . . brought little fuel and it snowed that night and some of the wounded had their feet frozen."[52] Lieutenant McClernand recalled that "that night I suffered more than I ever did in my life."

> At nine o'clock it commenced raining, and this at midnight turned into snow. The men in our squadron did not have their blankets, I had not even an overcoat. Under the circumstances we did not find the bare ground especially warm, . . . and the next morning, being unable to mount my horse, I was taken to the hospital tent. Here a fire was made from pieces of wagons which had been broken up after the arrival of the train.[53]

And Tilton observed that "the men's blankets are wet and they are cold and uncomfortable."[54]

During the night, the infantry and cavalry units again shifted positions, with Snyder's battalion of the Fifth occupying a tract "in front of the village," and Tyler's Second battalion, now short one officer in Lieutenant Jerome's absence, moving inadvertently closer to the north side of the Nez Perce camp.[55] "We could distinctly hear their voices in ordinary conversation," said McClernand, who described the activity on the line that night:

> The command was dismounted, the horses led a little to the rear, and the men, after being deployed as skirmishers, were directed to lie down. Occasionally some Indians would try to escape, when the skirmishers in their front would open fire, directing their fire by the noise made, as it was too dark to see. A few of the Nez Perces succeeded in dashing through between our skirmishers, followed by a perfect volley of wildly directed shots. However, several dead Indians were found in our front next morning. One horse in my troop was killed, and my own horse stampeded and fell into the hands of the Indians. As there were only two officers present, we were obliged to pass frequently from one end of the line to the other. Each man was required to call softly to his neighbor at intervals of about five minutes. It was in this way one man was found to be dead, having been shot through the body—probably by the Indians who broke through our lines. Even this frequent calling to each other was not sufficient to prevent some of the men from falling asleep, they were so worn out with fatigue and benumbed by cold.[56]

An artistic, and not altogether accurate, view of the Bear's Paw battlefield, as represented to the American public in HARPER'S WEEKLY, *November 17, 1877.*

Along the encircling line of rifle pits, army cooks made their rounds only after darkness fell. The unsteady truce continued through the night and all day Tuesday, October 2, with but occasional shots being fired on both sides. Early that day, a crew of six soldiers and six civilian packers started with sixteen pack mules for the foothills to get firewood, returning in the afternoon with mules and horses fully loaded.[57] On the lines, the prolonged lulls provoked interesting colloquies between the soldiers and the warriors, and it was reported that at one point during the fighting, when Miles was heard to yell, "Charge them to hell!" an informed Nez Perce called back in English: "Charge, hell, you God d—n sons of b———s! You ain't fighting Sioux!"[58] Meantime, Sergeant McHugh worked to prepare his ordnance for service, with earthworks being raised to protect the gun crews. "We will see what tomorrow will bring forth," wrote Private Zimmer.[59] On the evening of October 2, the Second Cavalry troops moved "from the extreme right flank to the [extreme?] left, covering a field gun poised so as to command the place where the Indians came down in the evening to get water."[60] Similarly, Zimmer noted that "our battalion was supporting the big guns [sic] on the north [sic—west] side of their camp."[61] This position of the twelve-pounder lay approximately fifteen hundred yards directly west of the noncombatant-occupied ravine and afforded the gun a clear and direct access with its projectiles into the entire east-west alignment of that

This Civil War-era model 1857 bronze twelve-pounder Napoleon cannon weighed more than twelve hundred pounds. It was mounted on a wooden carriage and used by Miles's command to send fuse-detonated explosive shells against Nez Perce noncombatants at Bear's Paw.
COURTESY PAUL L. HEDREN

ravine. Supporting rifle pits to be manned by Second cavalrymen were raised while the cannon was emplaced.[62] In the camp, the people used the prolonged reprieve to improve their defenses. For warmth, they burned some tipi poles dragged over from the village.[63] Joseph broached the issue of surrendering, but the people remained divided. He later remarked: "We could have escaped from Bear Paw Mountain if we had left our wounded, old women, and children behind. We were unwilling to do this. We had never heard of a wounded Indian recovering while in the hands of white men."[64]

At daybreak Wednesday, the white flag still floated over the Nez Perces' line. Miles used the time to move his camp a bit more upstream "so as to be better protected from the rifle pits of the Indians."[65] He also sought to ready his twelve-pounder, decreeing that if the tribesmen did not come to terms by midmorning he would turn his artillery on them.[66] While the breech-loading Hotchkiss was a new addition to the command, Miles had earlier used the Napoleon gun against the Sioux and Northern Cheyennes at Wolf Mountains, Montana, the previous January, an engagement that resulted in the surrender of many of those tribesmen. Named for Emperor Louis Napoleon, under whom its use became popular in France, the gun with its wooden carriage and limber weighed thirty-two hundred pounds and was drawn by six mules. It delivered explosive shells with pronounced effect against targets as far off as seventeen hundred yards, and its principal benefit lay in its capability to vary its trajectory from flat to arcing like a howitzer. Although prized during the Civil War as an effective anti-personnel weapon over quarter-mile distances, the great weight and lack of easy maneuverability of the Napoleon made it a cumbersome field component on the plains frontier.[67]

Because of space limitations posed by the wagon transportation, only twenty-four shells had been carried with the train and were available for use at Bear's Paw.[68] Yet when the gun opened on the morning of the third, it quickly had a deadly physical and psychological impact among the tribesmen. "At 11 o.c. A.M.," wrote Tilton, "firing began on the village with both field pieces and small arms."[69] Lieutenant Romeyn said of the twelve-pounder, "its boom told the Indians that a new element had entered for their destruction." Describing the effect of the Napoleon's fire, Romeyn continued:

> It was almost impossible, owing to the shape of the ground, to bring it to bear on the pits now occupied by the hostiles, who . . . took refuge in the banks of the crooked "coulees" where no direct fire could be made to reach and where the shells, if burst over them, were likewise liable to injure our men on the high ground behind. A dropping or mortar fire was, however, obtained by sinking the trail of the gun in a pit dug for it and using a high elevation with a small charge of powder. This made the fire effective.[70]

The cannon fire, however, must have occurred sparingly because of the small number of rounds on hand. As the shooting went on, the sun briefly appeared, but then it clouded over and snow fell intermittently.[71] The artillery fire had an immediate impact among the people. A packer remembered that "when that big gun went off you never heard such howling from squaws, dogs and kids."[72] Other than this, there was little response. The warriors fired only a few shots in return. "They are either short of ammunition or else we are too well entrenched for them to waste ammunition upon us," wrote Captain Snyder. He believed that the tribesmen would not surrender and "we will have to starve them out. To charge them would be madness."[73] Zimmer recorded that despite "a good shelling" of their camp, the Nez Perces "are well fixed & intend to wear us out."[74] That night Miles started a courier to Fort Benton with dispatches for Terry describing his action to date, his casualties, and the Nez Perces' situation. "Joseph gave me a solemn pledge yesterday that he would surrender," he wrote, "but did not, and they are evidently waiting for other Indians. They say that the Sioux are coming to their aid. . . . They fight with more desperation than any Indians I ever met."[75] Miles also took the opportunity to send a letter to his wife with an optimistic notation: "At present we have them closely surrounded and under fire, and they may yet give up."[76] Dr. Tilton prepared an account of casualties for delivery to department headquarters and noted that in anticipation of removing the wounded to Fort Buford he was already constructing litters and travois.[77]

The musketry and artillery fire continued the morning of the fourth, "a disagreeable, raw, chilly, cloudy day," said Tilton.[78] The twelve-pounder continued its discharge, delivering a harrowing impact among the people. Yellow Wolf told how one shell burst in a shelter pit, burying a small boy, a girl about twelve years old named Atsipeeten, and four women. The girl and her grandmother both died, while the others were rescued.[79] On the army line, an enlisted man described his unit's activities at getting wood and herding the captured stock. "Some were in the rifle pits popping at the Indians whenever one made his appearance."[80] This morning, Company F, Fifth Infantry, which had been on the line continuously since the thirtieth, was relieved by Brotherton's Company K. Miles later called on his battalion commanders to account for their men, animals, and equipment, with surplus horses and supplies to be delivered to Lieutenant Gibson. Several attempts were made to open talks with the Nez Perces, but they were not so inclined.[81]

Just at dusk, riders appeared from the south. They proved to be General Howard with two aides and an escort of twenty-one men, besides several scouts, one white interpreter, and two elderly Nez Perce men.[82] After leaving Sturgis with the main force at Carroll and ascending aboard the *Benton* to Cow Island with part of his foot troops, Howard had set out on October 3 on the trail with only this small party, which included the general's son, Lieutenant Guy Howard, and Lieutenant

Charles E. S. Wood, anxiously intent on finding Miles. Scout Redington wrote of the Nez Perces, who but recently had raided the stores at Cow Island, that "for many miles up Cow Creek and Bull Creek we could trail them by the packages of finecut tobacco, beans and coffee that had trickled and dropped off their packs."[83] During the afternoon of the fourth, Howard's group met two men carrying dispatches from Sturgis to Miles and first learned of the battle then underway. (Unknown to Howard, Colonel Sturgis, meanwhile, had on October 2 received Miles's dispatch of the thirtieth announcing the battle, mobilized his troops, and crossed the Missouri on the steamers *Meade* and *Silver City*.[84] Pushing north with ten days' rations, Sturgis had covered thirty miles to the base of the Little Rocky Mountains by evening, October 4.[85]) Soon after, Howard's party crested the divide south of the battlefield and saw campfires in the growing twilight. A few bullets from the Nez Perce position whistling past their heads momentarily caused Howard to think that his party was mistakenly under attack by the pickets. Then Miles appeared, saying, "We have the Indians corralled down yonder," and with an escort conducted them forward.[86]

At a meeting that evening, Howard told Miles that he had no wish to assume command and that the colonel would be free to complete the work he had started. That view probably brought Miles certain relief, knowing that his imminent victory over the Nez Perces and whatever laurels and promotional possibilities it might entail remained secure.[87] Because the end of the siege did not appear immediately at hand, however, and because the Sitting Bull factor remained, Howard prepared dispatches directing reinforcements ahead from his command. Unaware of Sturgis's movement north, he also sent word directing Major Mason (who was with Sturgis) to supervise the transport of the supplies at Cow Island and Carroll to the mouth of Little Rocky Creek on the Missouri, and there to await Miles's wagon train, which would be bringing the wounded from the battlefield for conveyance to Fort Buford on the *Benton* along with Captain Miller's artillerymen.[88] Finally, Howard suggested using his two Nez Perces, Jokais (Lazy), known as Captain John, and Meopkowit (Baby, or Know Nothing), known as Old George,[89] both with daughters among the besieged people, to try to induce their surrender, an idea that Miles supported. Howard then prepared a status report for General McDowell in San Francisco, complimentarily concluding that Miles's "successful march . . . of three hundred miles could not be excelled in quickness of conception and promptitude of execution."[90]

Friday, October 5 arrived "a beautiful morning."[91] The bombardment of the Nez Perce camp, which had gone on at intervals all during the night, finally began to subside. Doctors Tilton and Gardner had finished performing three amputations at the hospital,[92] and Lieutenant Guy Howard at his father's direction sent a message to Sturgis telling him to bring along the howitzer, as it was "in special demand here." (In fact, Sturgis had left the gun behind because the horses were too weak to carry it.)[93] Then, at 8:00 A.M., all firing ceased.[94] The two Nez Perces who had come with Howard, Captain John and Old George, stepped forward under a white flag, descended to the Snake Creek bottom, and crossed into the Nez Perce position. Hours passed. The two returned, reported to Miles and Howard, and then went back to the Nez Perces.[95] "They were getting very tired of the siege," related Tilton. "They report that one shell killed three, and wounded others.[96] They had sent runners to the Assiniboines, who had been killed. The soldiers fired at them; citizens fired at them; and Indians fired at them. They were ready to surrender."[97]

In the space since Howard's arrival, Joseph had learned of the presence of Arthur Chapman, the interpreter who was his friend. "We could now talk understandingly," he remembered.[98] But the major face-to-face consultations involved the two Nez Perces Howard had brought with him. Reminiscent accounts of the talks in the camp between the besieged and Captain John and Old George were given by Yellow Wolf and Tom Hill, both of whom were present. Perhaps at about 9:00 A.M.,[99] Captain John and Old George, who had attached themselves to Howard's army in an effort to find and retrieve their children and who had been primed by Howard through Chapman, entered the Nez Perces lines to mixed greetings. White Bull, who had wanted to kill Lieutenant Jerome, also wanted to kill these men, but was ordered away from them. "We see your sons and relations lying dead, but we are glad to shake hands with you today," said Old George. Captain John said that Howard had sent word that the people need not be afraid. Then they told them that Howard's army was but a day behind, that a surrender would bring no executions, and that the people would be treated well and given blankets and food. Probably, too, the two Nez Perces told the leaders that the people would be sent to the Lapwai Reservation, as this was what Miles and Howard believed was expected.[100]

At Joseph's direction, the two emissaries passed back to the soldier's lines. While they were gone, the men counciled over the proposal. Some were inclined to believe that the leaders, notably Joseph, would be hanged. Others wanted assurances that they would be compensated for the property taken from them before the warfare had erupted. Yellow Wolf remembered seeing General Howard standing in the distance and calling to the Nez Perces. Then Captain John and Old George returned with a message from Miles asking to speak directly to Joseph. The leaders counciled again and decided that Joseph should go forward.[101] All realized that the individual bands could decide unilaterally and might not act together, and, moreover, that each individual was free to choose his or her own course.[102] Tom Hill said that Joseph asked him to accompany him, saying that to quit fighting "is the best thing we can do."[103] Captain John and Old George returned to the army command, this time likely carrying the reply from Joseph that has since defined Bear's Paw and the conclusion of the Nez Perce War while assuring the stature of Chief Joseph in history and in legend.[104] When the two emissaries, at Joseph's direction, passed back to the soldiers' line, Captain John, "with tears in his eyes," relayed (and possibly paraphrased)—through Chapman—Joseph's response to Howard, an oral report on the Nez Perces' stricken condition, in essence, that became known as Joseph's surrender speech.[105] As transcribed in pencil by Lieutenant Wood, Howard's adjutant, the historic message read:

> Tell General Howard I know his heart. What he told me before I have in my heart. I am tired of fighting. Our chiefs are killed. Looking Glass is dead. Tu-hul-hul-sote is dead. The old men are all dead. It is the young men who say yes or no. He who led on the young men is dead. It is cold and we have no blankets. The little children are freezing to death. My people, some of them, have run away to the hills, and have no blankets, no food; no one knows where they are— perhaps freezing to death. I want to have time to look for my children and see how many of them I can find. Maybe I shall find them among the dead. Hear me, my chiefs. I am tired; my heart is sick and sad. From where the sun now stands I will fight no more forever.[106]

Halfway between the lines, Joseph, with Tom Hill and some other Nez Perces, all apparently unidentified, met with Miles and Howard and Chapman. "I remember well the council held, in a circle on the grass, in full view of the camp," wrote Kelly.[107] At this meeting, the proceedings of which were evidently not transcribed, Joseph indicated his intention of surrendering his own band and himself, leaving to others to decide the respective fates of the other Nee-Me-Poo. He later related that "General Miles said to me in plain words, 'If you will come out and give up your arms, I will spare your lives and send you to your reservation.'"[108] White Bird did not attend, but reportedly concurred with Joseph's decision to surrender, sending word that "What Joseph does is all right; I have nothing to say."[109] Yellow Wolf, who apparently was not present at this council, mentioned some minor perturbation of Howard and said that, after the officers promised to provide food and supplies to the people, the leaders and commanders shook hands all around. Joseph said, "Now we understand these words, and will go with General Miles." At 11:00 A.M., October 5, Joseph's negotiated surrender was thus complete.[110]

At midafternoon, in formal consummation of the agreement, Joseph mounted a pony and, closely surrounded on either side by five men afoot who clung to his person and spoke softly yet intently to him, slowly rode out of the Nez Perce entrenchments. In appearance, according to Wood,

> His scalp-lock was tied with otter fur. The rest of his hair hung in a thick plait on each side of his head. He wore buckskin leggings and a gray woolen shawl, through which were the marks of four or five bullets. . . . His forehead and wrist were also scratched by bullets.[111]

His hands were crossed on the pommel of his saddle, his Winchester carbine straddling his knees, and his head hanging down. Contemporary observers said that Joseph rode up a hill. Quite logically, he passed across the creek bottom to the west side of the bluff opposite the south end of the camp, then ascended the slightly rising tableland adjoining the west side of the coulee through which Carter's assault party had come on September 30. This rise is between the south bluff and that adjacent on the west where the Hotchkiss gun stood. The site, while not far from that presently designated for the formal surrender, is furthermore shielded from known warrior positions to the northwest and would have been within the protective encirclement of the army line situated back from the edges of the bluffs.[112] Probably there, Miles and Howard stood waiting to receive him.[113] It was 2:20 P.M., according to Lieutenant Wood.[114] On his approach, Joseph sat upright, then gracefully dismounted before the senior officers, who were accompanied by Lieutenants Wood, Long, and Howard, besides the interpreter, Arthur

Heinmot Tooyalakekt, or Chief Joseph, was photographed by John H. Fouch at Tongue River Cantonment shortly after the arrival of the Nez Perce prisoners on October 23, three weeks following the surrender at Bear's Paw battlefield.

Chapman, and an unidentified enlisted orderly. Some distance away, a courier stood by his horse, bridle in hand.[115] The other warriors and headmen fell back as Joseph raised his head, walked forward, and "with an impulsive gesture" extended his Winchester carbine to General Howard.[116] The general, true to his word, stepped back and motioned the Nez Perce leader over to Miles, who received the gun.[117] It is not certain if he uttered any statement, although Howard told a newspaperman that Joseph had said, doubtless in his own language: "From where the sun stands, forever and ever, I will never fight again."[118] Wood remembered: "Those present shook hands with Joseph, whose worn and anxious face lighted with a sad smile as silently he took each offered hand. Presently turning away, he walked to the tent provided for him." Howard and Miles, riding on either side, accompanied Joseph to the rear, where Lieutenant Wood took charge of him.[119] The chief was described as "in great distress" over the whereabouts of his daughter, who had escaped at the time of the initial attack. "He was afraid she would perish from the cold, as she had on very little clothing at the time," related Tilton.[120] Then, almost randomly, probably as they concluded that capitulation was the only alternative, other groups of Nez Perces came filing out of the pits to turn in their weapons in an impromptu demonstration that lasted until dusk. Wrote a witness: "The other chiefs and their companions who had followed Joseph into the camp performed the same ceremony. . . . In reversing their weapons [they] gave a significance to the act easily appreciated by the veterans who were silent witnesses of it."[121]

During the remainder of the day, sixty-seven warriors and an unspecified number of noncombatants had turned themselves in. Besides Nez Perces, they included the Palouses of Husis Kute. Howard recalled the "forlorn procession" as "covered with dirt, their clothing was torn, and their ponies, such as they were, were thin and lame."[122] By dark, not all of the people ensconced in the earthworks had committed to surrender, and the military lines were maintained through the night.[123] Nonetheless, that evening Miles prepared a dispatch for delivery to General Terry:

> We have had our usual success. We made a very direct and rapid march across the country, and after a severe engagement, and being kept under fire for three [sic] days, the hostile camp of Nez Perces, under Chief Joseph, surrendered at two o'clock to-day.[124]

Not all of the people chose to follow Joseph's course, however. At least seventy of the tribesmen had managed to escape Miles's investment on September 30 in the opening moments of the attack. Most of them had eluded the Second Cavalry pursuit and continued north toward the British possessions. And during the course of the siege, under the cover of darkness other bodies of tribesmen, probably numbering as many as one hundred—sometimes including whole families—had managed to penetrate the military cordon and escape. Now, in the hours following Joseph's surrender, White Bird and many other people chose to attempt to escape and drive for Canada and what they hoped would be freedom and a reunion with those friends and relatives who had gotten away ear-lier.[125] At about 9:00 P.M., aided by darkness, White Bird's party, perhaps as many as fifty people, quietly made its way north along the Snake Creek bottom, somehow eluding the attention of the army pickets, and headed toward Milk River and beyond.[126] The next morning, the chief not hav-ing appeared, Howard and Miles visited the Nez Perce entrenchments to find him and there learned of his departure.[127] Howard, oblivious to the nature of Nee-Me-Poo societal dynamics, considered White Bird's escape, "after the terms of surrender had been agreed upon," a violation of the accord.[128] As Yellow Wolf later explained, "All who wanted to surrender took their guns to General Miles and gave them up. Those who did not want to surrender, kept their guns. The surrender was just for those who did not longer want to fight. Joseph spoke only for his own band, what they wanted to do."[129]

Early Saturday, Miles and Howard sent word to Sturgis and Mason to halt and await the arrival of the command "at the first good camp."[130] Miles also prepared a report describing his movements and the battle for filing with department headquarters.[131] Through the morning of Octo-ber 6, more of the people came in, and Miles's final tally—including small parties of Nez Perces who were picked up by ranging troops over the next two weeks—totaled 448.[132] The prisoners included several wounded Nez Perces who were taken to the hospital for treatment by Doctors Tilton and Gardner.[133] "A few wounded Indians came to our camp last night," wrote Tilton, "but it was too late to attend to them. More are brought this morning and the urgent cases attended to—balls extracted and broken bones put in splints."[134] Wagons were sent to the mountains to get more poles for constructing litters and travois.[135] Miles also directed that his battalion and company commanders ensure sufficient quantities of willow brush and hay for use in transporting the wounded.[136] Wrote Tilton:

> Instructions were given to make six litters and four travois, but the poles were so short (about 16 feet long) that they had to be used as travois. Unless the rear mule can see where to step, he walks off side very like a crab. Willows were put into the wagons and these covered by a liberal amount of grass, which made a very comfortable means of conveyance for many cases.[137]

Meanwhile, the hungry tribesmen consumed food issued to them, perhaps savoring the several buffalo shot the night before by the wood party. Yellow Wolf commented: "General Miles was good to the surrendered Indians with food. The little boys and girls loved him for that. They could now have hot food and fires to warm by."[138] At Miles's authority, most of the Cheyenne scouts started back to the cantonment with the ponies they had selected from the captured herd. Bruguier and the Lakota, Hump, left to overtake the scouts, but Young Two Moon soon caught up, saying that Miles instead wanted them to halt and await the command.[139]

As the intermittent procession of Nez Perces continued on the sixth, some of the officers took the occasion to explore their position, marveling at the ingenuity exhibited by the tribesmen in fashioning their semisubterranean dwellings. "These intrenchments," related one witness, "consisted mainly of a series of rifle pits dug deep into the earth, and they were arranged in some respects with a skill which would have done credit to an educated military engineer."[139] By the layout of the shelter pits in the bottoms and sides of the coulees, Miles's officers at last understood fully why their gunfire had taken little effect. Lieutenant Wood, one of the visitors, explained that "the ravines were so crooked as to prevent enfilade fire, and so protected by hills as to be safe from our sharpshooters."[140] Tilton also examined the works. "There were a series of holes in the bottom of a ravine which branched out in three directions; these holes were from 3 to 5 feet deep and from 3 to 10 feet in diameter. They gave perfect protection from small arms fire. Dead horses were utilized to increase the breastworks."[141] During the examination, some soldiers sent in "to overhaul their works" stumbled on a Nez Perce man, still armed, who had been wounded in the thigh. Private Zimmer said the man was in a tunnel between two pits and had kept supplies for several days with him. "It's likely he expected some of his escaped friends would come for him."[142] The men also uncovered caches of "saddles, robes, flour, sugar, beans, ammunition and a few arms" that allegedly belonged to those who had escaped north during the fighting. Late in the day, the people used army wagons to transport their property to a new and clean village site selected upstream and on the west side of Snake Creek, closer to the army camp.[143] "Our guard duty will be much lighter this evening," concluded Zimmer.[144]

Miles's losses at the Battle of the Bear's Paw totaled two officers and nineteen enlisted men killed, four officers and forty-six men wounded (three more enlisted men would die from their wounds), besides two Indian scouts wounded.[145] "Some of our wounded claimed to have been struck by explosive bullets, and they had ugly looking wounds," said Tilton.

> I was disposed to doubt it, until I saw some explosive balls in the village. I secured two of .50 cal. and a package of .44 cal. I have since learned that the Nez Perces raided a place, owned by a prosperous Englishman who was an amateur stock ranchman in Idaho, and secured a quantity of ammunition, explosive bullets among other things.[146]

As the surgeons prepared the wounded for removal on the following day, the bodies of the soldiers killed on September 30 and after were covered over in the trench with earth and marked with rocks gathered by their comrades.[147] The remains of Captain Hale and Lieutenant Biddle were wrapped in blankets preparatory to moving with the troops back to the Missouri River to be shipped downstream to their respective families for interment.[148]

Nez Perce losses at Bear's Paw were not precisely determined because many of the dead had been buried in unmarked graves in or next to the shelter pits and were not readily found by the troops. Tilton, however, said that seventeen of the people had been killed and forty wounded as of October 3, although his source for the information is unknown.[149] McWhorter concluded from his sources that the number of dead did not exceed twenty-five, including twenty-two killed the first day. The number of wounded estimated by Tilton as of October 3 was forty, while Miles, after the surrender, reported that between fifty and sixty had been wounded, five of whom died on the way to the cantonment.[150] In his postsurrender report, Dr. Tilton wrote regarding the wounded Nez Perces:

> It would be difficult to ascertain the number of wounded among them. Some cases not very severe they pay very little attention to. I saw a fractured radius, a humerus, a femur, a clavicle, and one of the metacarpophalangeal joint of the left thumb. This last case the patient fixed up for himself and it appears to be doing very well.[151]

Tilton also commented on the cases of Hump, the Lakota, and White Wolf, the Northern Cheyenne, both scouts who had been shot, the latter in the head. "Both [of] these men returned to the Cantonment and swam the Yellowstone River with their horses. White Wolf has had several small pieces of the skull removed by a brother warrior; he continues to ride around the post as if his wound were a trifling affair."[152]

Beyond those accorded Colonel Miles, the Battle of the Bear's Paw yielded no immediate individual honors for the soldiers who fought there. In June 1878, Miles recommended Lieutenants Baird, Carter, Romeyn, and McClernand for recognition via brevet promotions or Medals of Honor. It was not, however, until after 1890, when brevets for Indian wars service were at last authorized, that Carter and McClernand were so recognized, along with Lieutenant Woodruff and Captains Snyder, Moylan, and Godfrey.[153] And only in 1894 did Baird, Carter, Romeyn, McClernand, Godfrey, Moylan, Long, Tilton, and First Sergeant Henry Hogan, Company G, Fifth Infantry, receive coveted Medals of Honor for their services at Bear's Paw.[154] It is not known why the award of the medals was delayed for so many years, nor why only one enlisted man was deemed worthy for the honor.[155] Indeed, some of the awards, such as those for McClernand, Tilton, and Long seem to have been unwarranted based on knowledge of their roles in the action, which were no greater than those normally expected for officers in combat. And Baird, Moylan, and Godfrey were performing no distinguished acts of bravery when they were wounded. That received by Sergeant Hogan resulted from the recommendation of Henry Romeyn, who reported that Hogan had assembled the party that "carried me off the field" and "whose action probably enabled me to live."[156] Finally, Private John Gorham (John Quinn) was cited for gallant service at Bear's Paw, and—in perhaps the oddest recognition of all—Lieutenant Guy Howard was acknowledged for "accompanying the Department Commander through a hostile Indian country, with a small party, from [the] Missouri River to the battlefield at Bear [Paw] Mountain."[157]

While individual recognition was elusive in the years ahead, Miles on October 7 issued a general order applauding his men on their signal victory over the Nez Perces. He offered his congratulations "for the recent exhibition they have given of the highest degree of endurance with hardships and unyielding fortitude in battle." He noted that "it is an added source of congratulations that Gen. O. O. Howard . . . was present to witness the completion of his arduous and thankless undertaking."[158] Soon after that, General Howard assumed command, directing Miles to keep the Nez Perces within the District of the Yellowstone until next spring owing to the transportation costs required for moving them to the Pacific Coast. "Then," Howard told Miles, "unless you receive instructions from higher authority, you are hereby directed to have them sent, under proper guard, to my Department. . . . You will treat them as prisoners of war, and provide for them accordingly, until the pleasure of the President concerning them shall be made known." He told Miles he would move his own force back to their home stations, and he relinquished his command of Sturgis's men, requesting that they, too, be permitted to return to Fort Lincoln to recuperate from the severities of the campaign. "I am gratified to have been present," concluded Howard, "and to have contributed ever so little to facilitate the surrender."[159]

In reality, both Howard and Miles owed thanks to the native peoples living in the vicinity of the Bear's Paws. Even before the presence of troops in the area, word had reached the local tribes of the government's expectations regarding the war with the Nez Perces. The Gros Ventres (Atsinas) and Assiniboines had earlier sent parties to the Missouri River to watch for the Nez Perces. On October 3, a party of Gros Ventre warriors, assisted by some Assiniboines, encountered some Nez Perces on a fork of Box Elder Creek, killing five men and capturing two women. Later, they helped the army search for Bear's Paw refugees. Twenty-five Gros Ventres received a supply of tobacco as a reward for providing information about the location of some Nee-Me-Poo. Forty mounted Gros Ventres also ranged through the western Bear's Paw Mountains searching for escapees. And when several families of Nez Perces approached the Gros Ventre camps, they were turned away.[160] For their part, the Assiniboines had been formally solicited by the army leadership at Fort Benton to help contain the Nez Perces, and Miles sent word to them from the battlefield "that they could fight any that escaped and take their arms and ponies." The Assiniboines succeeded in capturing some army horses and mules near Milk River, and they claimed to have killed seven Nez Perces and captured four more.[161] On the other hand, there is evidence that Plains Cree Indians took in some Nez Perce refugees in the area of Milk River, provided them with food and blankets, and helped them in crossing into Canada.[162]

Against this backdrop and before he left Bear's Paw, Miles sent a request to Terry at Fort Benton to send supplies to meet Tyler's Second Cavalry battalion, which would start for that point to join the commission to the Sioux. On Major Ilges's direction, Second Lieutenant Hugh L. Scott left Fort Benton with a train of provisions, escorted by Company E, Seventh Cavalry, under First Lieutenant Charles C. DeRudio. Both officers had lately been in the national park at the approximate time of the Nez Perce passage. On October 10, as Scott and six of his men approached the trading post of Fort Belknap (discontinued as an Indian agency in 1876) along Milk River near the present community of Chinook, they stumbled on the remains of five Nez Perces. Assiniboines gathered at the former agency readily admitted that some of their young men had killed and scalped these people.[163] Meanwhile, as early as the fifth, Miles had sent detachments of troops (and evidently some selected Nez Perces, too[164]) to scour the countryside for tribesmen who had escaped the besieging force, either having gone with White Bird or with myriad parties that had broken away since the fighting began.

Lieutenant Maus headed one of these detachments. Near Fort Belknap, after turning over his provisions to Tyler's battalion, Scott shortly encountered Maus and his ten men ranging over the area searching for refugee Nez Perces. Two warriors who had been in the camp at Bear's Paw, Tippit and Nez Perce John, were with Maus. While DeRudio headed the wagons to a rendezvous point at Three Buttes near the Little Rockies, Scott and Maus traveled down Milk River to a village of so-called "Red River half-breeds"—Metis hunters from Pembina—where they found twelve Nez Perces (mainly women and children, but also two wounded men) who had stopped there instead of proceeding directly to the line. Maus rented two wood-wheeled Red River carts and loaded the people aboard, and he and Scott started for Three Buttes and DeRudio's wagons, passing over the battlefield on the way. "It had gotten very cold then," recalled Scott. "Maus and I had . . . one robe & two saddle blankets & slept together shivering all night. We killed buffalo & we wrapped the children in fresh green buffalo hides to keep them from freezing."[165] From Three Buttes, they proceeded with their captives to meet Miles at the Missouri River.[166] Elsewhere, on the seventh Major Ilges reported that the Gros Ventres were turning a Nez Perce woman and a child over to him.[167]

Miles started his command on the back trail to the Musselshell crossing of the Missouri at noon Sunday, exactly one week after the Battle of the Bear's Paw Mountains opened. The Seventh Cavalry and Fifth Infantry troops escorted the Nez Perce prisoners, many riding ponies from the captured herd, their truck being transported in the wagons. Tyler's Second Cavalry battalion, Dr. Gardner accompanying, prepared to head for the agency at Fort Belknap en route to Fort Benton, there to join Terry's commission as originally planned. Wrote Tilton: "The Indians clad in lively colors and strung out in a long line; the pack train, the pony herd, the mounted troops, the wagons, the wounded on travois, all combine to make an unusual and striking picture."[168] Over the course of the ten miles traveled this day, seven of the wounded soldiers rode on travois, while the two amputation cases occupied the broken ambulance. Other injured men rode on grass and willow branches in the wagons, while two more of the travois were given over to the Nez Perces for their injured. On the trail, two ambulances from Sturgis's command arrived, and next day Lieutenant Romeyn, shot through the lung, boarded one of them, and two of the wounded men the other, for the balance of the journey. On the night of the seventh, a lightning and thunder storm struck, but subsided before causing a stampede of the stock; on the eighth a torrential downpour kept the command in camp all day.[169]

On the eighth, Howard prepared a dispatch for General McDowell, specifying his role in bringing about the surrender, explaining the Nez Perces' casualties (Ollokot, Looking Glass, Toohoolhoolzote, besides "33 warriors, either in battle or as fugitives to other tribes") and telling him that "the Camas Prairie murderers [are] now all killed in action." He also recounted his directive to Miles regarding removing the prisoners to Tongue River. Howard then departed, intending to send his command homeward down the Missouri. Joining Major Mason, he reached the mouth of Little Rocky Creek on the ninth and left aboard the *Benton* for Squaw Creek next afternoon to prepare the steamers *Meade* and *Silver City* to receive Miles's wounded and cross his troops. Meanwhile, Miles continued by slow marches on his diagonal trail back to the Missouri opposite the mouth of Squaw Creek.[170] On the ninth,

Miles lifted the restriction on firing, and the men and prisoners dined on antelope steaks that evening. Over the next several days, they passed Peoples, Beaver, and Fourchette creeks, and on the afternoon of the thirteenth they arrived at the Missouri, "Joseph and some of his people riding with Miles at the head of the column."[171] That afternoon, Howard and his troops started home. The general would visit in St. Paul and Chicago en route, while the Twenty-first infantrymen and Fourth artillerymen would go by steamer to Omaha, then via rail to San Francisco, and by steamship to Portland. Leaving the reunited and resupplied Seventh Cavalry at "Camp Owen Hale" on the north side of the river as a precaution against Sitting Bull's possible resurgence, Miles and the Fifth Infantry and the Nez Perce prisoners Sunday and Monday forded the river aboard the *Silver City*. That afternoon, the most serious cases of wounded soldiers were placed aboard the *Silver City* for transport to hospitals at Forts Buford and Lincoln. On Tuesday Miles struck out cross-country for the Yellowstone and the cantonment. More than a week later, at noon on October 23, the troops and prisoners, several wounded of which had died en route, pulled up on the north bank opposite the post.[172] "As the command filed down the ravine," recorded Tilton, "flags were unfurled, the band struck up, 'Hail to the Chief,' while cannon thundered forth a salute of welcome to the troops who had so successfully ended the campaign against the Nez Perces."[173]

The significance of the Bear's Paw engagement in ending the Nez Perce War of 1877 cannot be overstated. While the large percentage of deaths among the troops created certain consternation among the army hierarchy and the public, for the Nez Perce people—both those directly involved and those "treaty" people who had remained in Idaho—the final battle contained long-range implications that affected the respective Nez Perce groups for decades, to say nothing of their relationships with the tribes that helped or supported the government pursuit and capture of the people. Most immediately, the physical and psychological impact of Bear's Paw meant that many Nez Perces lost relatives and friends among the killed. In addition, families were torn apart, if not by death, then by separation of those who made their escape and went into Canada not knowing if their loved ones had survived the encounter with Miles's troops. And the later exile and incarceration of the prisoners exacerbated the pain and confusion over family members' whereabouts. Bear's Paw was the climactic engagement of the long, grueling ordeal of the people

"Gen. Miles and Command crossing the Yellowstone with Joseph."
Miles's arrival with Nez Perce prisoners at Tongue River Cantonment on
October 23, 1877, was captured by post photographer John H. Fouch.
Courtesy Wayne T. Norman and Jeanne Norman Chiarot

affected by the government decision to take their land—and the lives of
the Nee-Me-Poo were never the same afterwards. Physically dominated,
the people's spirits nonetheless remained buoyant, and they managed
to live productive, meaningful lives despite the tragedy of 1877 as ex-
emplified at the Bear's Paw Mountains battle.

For the army, the larger moral question concerned whether the government intimidation resulting in the expulsion of the Wallowa band of
Nez Perces from their homeland with their supporting bands justified
the vigorous and costly pursuit and the resultant deaths of so many soldiers and Indians.[174] Certainly, by modern standards it did not, but to
such an institution as the post–Civil War U.S. Army, beset by budgetary

and organizational problems and an increasingly negative public perception in the wake of the Sioux conflict, the frustratingly embarrassing Nez Perce campaign only afforded more of the same. As public opinion gradually turned in favor of the Nez Perces, it conversely turned against the army and its leaders, particularly Howard.[175] And although many officers, including Howard, sympathized with the tribesmen in their plight, they were institutionally bound to prosecute the conflict, despite the consensus of white Americans in favor of the Nez Perces. Even though certain figures, such as Miles, would eventually derive personal gain from the event, in its broadest sense the war with the tribesmen, as epitomized in Bear's Paw, advantaged no one at all.

Because of its significance as the climactic engagement of the Nez Perce War—both in terms of the numbers of casualties that occurred there and its status as the place where Joseph surrendered—Bear's Paw battlefield continued to attract interest after the encounter ended. One of the earliest post-surrender visitors was Scout "Yellowstone" Kelly, who accompanied Terry's commission to the Sioux after the battle, then stopped to look over the site on his return to the Tongue River Cantonment. When he reached the field, Kelly found some Gros Ventre Indians rifling a Nez Perce cache of goods seized at Cow Island. "The battle field, forsaken of life, looked gruesome enough with its scattered bones of cavalry horses and mounds of freshly piled earth that covered the remains of soldiers and warriors who had addressed their last rollcall." The cache disclosed all sorts of items—cooking gear, pillows, flour, and sugar—"mingled in the utmost confusion."[176] It is known that in January 1878, Major Guido Ilges also visited the Bear's Paw battlefield while on business at Fort Belknap, although his reaction to the site is not known.[177] Almost thirty years later, in October 1907, Indian Inspector James McLaughlin toured the field. By then, the evidence of warfare at the Bear's Paw site was disappearing due to time and nature. As McLaughlin observed:

> The battlefield is wholly neglected. It presents no other proof of the fact that it was the scene of one of the decisive battles of the Indian wars, except the disturbed face of the ground where the rifle-pits were dug, and a yawning trench, some thirty feet long and six feet wide, where the fallen soldiers were hastily buried. . . . In a few years the roller of time will have utterly removed even these evidences of the past.[178]

By the time of McLaughlin's visit, the Bear's Paw army dead had been removed from the trench grave for reinterment at Fort Assinniboine, which had been established near Havre in 1879. In 1902, largely at the urging of then-Commanding General Miles, who had spent several days hunting prairie chickens near Fort Assinniboine (and whose aide-de-camp, then-Colonel Marion P. Maus—a battle participant—had visited the site), a detail from the post went to the battlefield where they found "a trench fifty feet in length by four feet wide surrounded by a circle of rocks several feet high," which they temporarily opened to reveal the twenty soldier dead of Bear's Paw. The remains were not exhumed, however, until August 1903, when they were brought to Havre in a wagon drawn by six mules for reburial in the post cemetery under the direction of the post quartermaster, Captain John B. McDonald, Third Cavalry.[179] Soldiers of the Twenty-fourth Infantry escorted the remains (contained in two wooden coffins) to the cemetery, served as pallbearers during the Episcopal service, and furnished the firing squad. The Third Cavalry band played appropriate airs. In 1908, the Bear's Paw army dead, along with others interred in the Fort Assinniboine cemetery, were moved to the Custer Battlefield National Cemetery south of Hardin, Montana.[180]

Meanwhile, as early as 1902, the imminent reburials of the Bear's Paw soldier dead seem to have sparked a local campaign seeking official recognition of the Bear's Paw site. In 1902, landowner Henry Winters, on whose tract the trench grave was situated, offered to deed the land back to the government so that it might be designated a "national burying ground and set aside for its historic interest." Senator Paris Gibson (D-Montana) pursued legislation for a national park designation and funding for a suitable monument to the dead; in anticipation of that, a section of battlefield land was withdrawn from entry by the General Land Office. But this effort waned, and all but 160 acres of the core site was restored to entry. It was not until after 1925—when a party headed by Major General Hugh L. Scott and Governor John E. Erickson of Montana came to the battlefield—and the later efforts of Blaine County Commissioner L. V. Bogy and others of Chinook, that Congress in 1930 passed legislation authorizing a marker on the battlefield.[181] In 1929, the Daughters of the American Revolution, aided by the Chinook Lions Club, had placed a memorial on the site dedicated to the soldiers who were killed there. And in September 1931, the congressionally sanctioned monument, consisting of an eight-ton rock with bronze plaque, was installed on the field.[182] In addition, the work of Lucullus V. McWhorter and Blaine County Surveyor C. Raymond Noyes, aided by Yellow Wolf, White Hawk, Peopeo Tholekt, and the interpreter Many Wounds—to mark localized places on the battlefield in the late 1920s and mid-1930s—helped to ensure its historical integrity while enhancing its potential for interpretation, thus making Bear's Paw one of the best preserved Indian wars battlefields in the country, commensurate with its importance in American history.[183]

Consequences

GENERAL HOWARD'S SOLDIERS steamed down the Missouri River aboard the *Benton* and reached Omaha on November 3. Next day, the four hundred officers and men boarded Union Pacific cars for the West Coast. Citizens and military personnel from the Platte department headquarters saw them off, noting that the men appeared "dirty, ragged and footsore—[and] presented a sorry appearance."[1] By estimate, the troops had marched more than seventeen hundred miles since leaving Kamiah, Idaho Territory, on July 30, and most of them, by the time they reached their home stations, had gone approximately seven thousand miles. Howard's march was termed in the media "the most remarkable on record."[2] The army, of course, tried to cast the most favorable light possible on what had really been at best a haphazard campaign and, at worst, a sloppy one. The most immediate encomiums went to Miles for the quickness of his victory, which contrasted greatly with the plodding nature of Howard's lengthy pursuit. Congratulations were extended to Miles after Bear's Paw from Generals Sherman, Sheridan, and Terry. Colonel Gibbon sent kudos from Fort Shaw, too, telling Miles that "after coming so far this way to carry off 'our' Indians you might have come a little farther & paid us a visit here." Later, Sherman issued an order thanking Howard's command "that pursued them, as well as the commands of Colonels Sturgis and Miles that headed them off and finally captured them."[3] Regimental general orders thanked officers

and men of the units involved,[4] and Secretary of War McCrary proclaimed his "grateful recognition to the zeal, energy, endurance, courage, and skill displayed by General Howard, Colonel Gibbon, and
Colonel Miles, and the officers and men under their command, in the
prosecution of this most remarkable campaign."[5]

On the evening of November 13, a gala in Howard's honor took
place in Portland with many officers on hand who served under him
during the campaign. The reception was held at Turn Halle, and Washington and Oregon militia units accompanied the general into the fes-
tooned hall to an artillery salute. After welcoming speeches and
recitations about the campaign, Howard rose to a thunderous ovation
and told the throng: "There has been one campaign continuous, and,
we claim, systematic, extending from the time the savage murderers of
Idaho forced the unequal battle of White Bird Canyon to the last scene
when Col. Miles stood at my side to receive the surrendered rifle of the
Indian Chief."[6] On December 1, 1877, Howard issued General Field
Orders No. 8, congratulating the men of the Department of the Columbia who participated in his campaign, including "officers and soldiers of the Army, volunteers, scouts, and other citizens, who rendered
in various capacities willing and valuable aid as occasion demanded."

> From the 14th of June to the 5th of October the pursuit was con-
> tinuous—not a day passed that some part of the force was not march-
> ing, crossing torrents, climbing mountains or threading their rocky
> defiles. From the Snake and Salmon Rivers in Northeastern Idaho,
> across the Continent, to within a day's march of the "British Line,"
> you pursued a foe, at first cruel, arrogant, and boastful; but after the
> successful battle of the Clearwater, intent only on escaping and elud-
> ing your attack.[7]

The tributes to and from Howard, while sincere, also helped as-
suage the bitter and sometimes unjust criticism he had received throughout most of the course of the campaign. Although Howard rationalized
his performance to the best advantage, it was perceived generally in a
negative light by the media, especially after Miles's sudden victory at
Bear's Paw. In his report of August 27, 1877, written at Henry's Lake,
Howard—already under scrutiny by the press—had enumerated the
positive results of his campaign thus far as (1) the end of citizen murders by the Nez Perces after the Battle of White Bird Canyon; (2) the

ejection of the tribesmen from the Salmon-Snake river country and the destruction of Looking Glass's village; (3) the anticipation of the movements of the Nez Perces at Cottonwood, leading to the victory at the Battle of the Clearwater; and (4) the driving of the Nez Perces out of Kamiah, their pursuit out of Idaho into the buffalo country, and "the Department of the Columbia freed from their presence."[8] Before Howard's departure from Idaho Territory, his campaign drew little negative editorial comment in the regional press, even if the New York *Herald* had mentioned the government's deliberation over replacing him with Crook as early as July 16. His perceived ambulatory progress began to draw sharp notice after the post-Clearwater failure to check the tribesmen before they headed out over the Lolo Trail. After the Fort Fizzle episode, Howard complained of the editorial criticism to Governor Potts in a letter that was widely reproduced. Later, when Sherman contemplated replacing Howard with Lieutenant Colonel Gilbert, the news found its way into print.[9] The Philadelphia *Times* called Howard a "feeble braggart" whose "career, both military and civil, has been a lamentable failure."[10] After Camas Meadows, the New York *Herald* averred that "Howard now finds himself reviled as a failure by a public which supposed that he was pursuing the Indians when, in fact, they were pursuing him."[11] (In fact, the Nez Perces themselves grew contemptuous of the general, applying to him the sobriquet, "Day After Tomorrow," because of his propensity to fall so far behind them.[12]) Howard believed that the newspaper abuse of him for a perceived lack of aggressiveness was patently unfair. He was likely correct, for it is implausible that anybody could have done more under the circumstances that existed regarding terrain and logistics, factors augmented by the extreme determination and mobility of the Nez Perces. Even McDowell failed to appreciate these realities, and his own critique of Howard's campaign to his department commander was devastating.[13] A major criticism of Howard, however, has to be leveled at his role in the councils preceding the Salmon River murders. At the least, his lack of diplomatic sensitivity at Fort Lapwai contributed to creating an atmosphere that promoted the outbreak of violence. Moreover, the presence of troops to bolster the dictums of agents of the Indian Bureau only exacerbated existing intratribal tensions and promoted the inevitability of open conflict.

Conversely, in Howard's support it must be said that he did what he could initially with the limited force at his disposal; requests for reinforcements were in process when the fight at White Bird Canyon commenced. And later, with a weary, footsore army, he kept moving forward, although the realities of the march made whatever progress he achieved nearly unbearable. Persistent criticism that he remained in camp every Sunday to conduct church services for his men was unfounded. "As to the story that he peddled out Bibles to the soldiers, . . . there was not one in the force, the General himself only having a 'Daily Food' selection of Bible texts, which he carried in his vest pocket."[14] The *Army and Navy Journal* went to Howard's defense:

> Howard followed his game untiringly through two [sic—three] departments and over twelve hundred miles of territory, and 'got in at the death,' in hunter's phrase. The fact is equally plain and equally to his credit that after he had hunted his prey successively into the grasp of Sturgis and Miles, General Howard refused to appropriate any of the glory of the final exploit to himself, leaving the command in the hands of Miles.[15]

In an attempt to defuse the censure, Howard issued a highly defensive "Supplementary Report" of his campaign, most of which was drafted by Lieutenant Wood, and which was published at the end of the *Report of the Secretary of War, 1877*, as well as in a separate edition. So averse was he to the criticism of his reputed slothful pace throughout the expedition that he closed the paper with a point-by-point rebuttal to specific charges regarding his rate of march to White Bird Canyon and to the battlefield at Clearwater, his perceived delay in starting over the Lolo trail, and his proximity to the Nez Perces at various points of the march. In support of his contention, he offered a statistical summary showing, for example, that "the march to Captain Perry's battle-field, of 80 miles, averaged 2 5/8 miles per hour, including all rests and halts." He also presented a computation of "exceptional marches" made by his total force, which included the mileage of treks of consecutive days, and a table showing that in seventy-five days his force traveled 1,321 miles from Weippe in Idaho Territory to the embarkation point on the Missouri River, making an average daily distance of 17.61 miles.[16] While the data must have contributed to clearing up the record in Howard's mind, the public perception of his tardiness in the Nez Perce War, created in large measure by the media, remained.

The combination of bad luck and bad press dogged Howard beyond the end of the campaign. While he continued to draw heated criticism, Miles, conversely, basked in the publicity for his work at Bear's Paw and emerged as the leading Indian fighter in the army, notably rivaling Crook and supplanting the dead Custer.[17] Unfortunately, the controversy that swirled between Howard and Miles in the weeks and months following the surrender at Bear's Paw only added to Howard's woes and tarnished what had earlier been touted as an air of cooperation that had brought about the final success of arms. Miles's initial messages from the battlefield following the capitulation of the Nez Perces slighted (probably purposefully) Howard's presence there. In his announcement of victory on October 5, Miles stated that "We have had our usual success," but made no mention of Howard or the role of his two Nez Perce interpreters in undertaking the negotiations leading to the surrender. And in his more lengthy report of the next day, the colonel acknowledged only that Howard "arrived on the evening of the 4th, having come forward in advance with a small escort," and only at the very end of his dispatch. He was more gracious in his congratulatory message of October 7, in which he cited the general's presence "to witness the completion of his arduous and thankless undertaking."[18] For his part, Howard seemed satisfied. "Permit me to congratulate you with all my heart," he intoned in his letter of October 7 to Miles, "and give you, your officers and men, my sincere thanks for your grand success."[19]

But in the aftermath of the event, Howard's attitude soured. He believed that Miles's initial dispatch—purportedly mentioning that Howard was present and had assisted in the surrender—had been forwarded purposefully omitting any reference to himself; in fact, the brief statement of October 5 announcing Joseph's surrender (and subsequently published both in tabloids and in *Report of the Secretary of War, 1877*) did not contain a reference to Howard. The dispatch of the following day, while alluding to his presence, was not published in its entirety, and the portion published did not include the reference to Howard. Thus, the acknowledgment did not appear in the newspapers, and editorially Miles was credited solely with the victory. Howard, deprived of any of the initial reward, came to believe that the original dispatch *had* mentioned him, but that Miles had deviously expunged the reference before his courier departed the battlefield.

Howard learned of the omission on arriving in Bismarck. He was, recalled Lieutenant Wood, at once "heart-broken and furious." On October 22, he telegraphed to Sheridan a report in which he stressed

his intentional slowing of his command to let Miles overtake the tribesmen, as well as the role of his Nez Perce interpreters in producing the
surrender. Then he and Wood journeyed to Chicago, ostensibly to discuss the arrangements he had made with Miles respecting the Nez
Perces. There Wood delivered an account of the surrender, together
with a copy of Howard's report to Sheridan—"a flattering account of
his share in the hostilities"— to the Chicago *Tribune* (published the
morning of October 25). Howard also granted a disconsolate and para-
noiac interview to the Chicago *Times* (published October 26) and then
sought an audience with a fuming Sheridan—who believed the publication of the dispatch to be a breach of military formality—to set the
record straight.[20] In a letter to the division commander, a contrite
Howard wrote:

> I wish to assume the entire responsibility for the publication of the
> dispatch sent to you from the Missouri River. I wished the publica-
> tion made with a view of placing in succinct form before the public
> the facts of the campaign as they appeared to me and I did not dream
> of there being any objection from yourself in the premises, and I am
> very sorry to have compromised you in any way.[21]

Miles initially stayed aloof from the brewing storm, but eventually
he could not resist getting involved, despite Sherman's private admonition to him to "Keep quiet."[22] In December, Howard addressed a note
to Miles: "In my presence, in your tent, you inserted the fact of my
being with you—giving, I think, the arrival, the evening before. Were
the words of this struck out before the dispatch left you or after?"[23]
More than a month later, Miles wrote back, assuring Howard that the
October 6 dispatch had gone forward in its entirety; he also noted that
the newspapers had omitted the last paragraph of his general order of
the seventh in which Howard's presence was mentioned. Miles continued: "If this garbling of official documents has been done by one officer to the prejudice of another, it has been done without my knowledge
and outside of my command, and in my opinion is a dishonorable act."
Then he took Howard to task:

> Your statements in public, your official documents and comments
> thereon, particularly your congratulatory order, have been received
> with just indignation, as the representations contained therein are
> not considered in accordance with well-known facts, or your letters

written to me at the time. I can appreciate your desire to compli-
ment your own troops, but I regret that you should have found it
necessary to claim that which you were not entitled to, as well as to
ignore the bloody engagements on this side of the mountains, for in
so doing, you do an injustice to those who were killed and wounded,
days after you, with your command, had abandoned the pursuit.[24]

For the next several months, Howard and Miles exchanged a bitter
correspondence over the affair, with Miles just as adamantly critical of
the general's slighting of his command's role in his public accounts. In
one letter to Miles in 1878, Howard claimed to be "astonished" at Miles's
allegations. Howard wrote that:

My own report has, I think, done you and your officers no injustice.
I claim nothing but simple truth, and would, as you know, rather
have honored you than myself. You fought the battle and succeeded
and if there is any language in which I can state it to the credit of
yourself, your officers and your men I was willing, and remain willing to do so.[25]

Miles responded to Howard: "You virtually gave up the pursuit." But
the dispute always came back to the initial announcement of the victory. Almost twenty years later, Howard still complained that "the telegram . . . should not have been altered so as to leave out the fact of my
being there. Who changed the telegram I do not know. Gen. Miles was
my devoted friend till then."[26]

Beyond the rift and ultimate rupture of relations between Howard
and Miles over distribution of honors, the army underwent something of
an institutional evaluation of its cavalry following its debatable performance during the four-months-long pursuit of the Nez Perces. Although
the procedural investigation took place in Howard's department and consequently could have turned into a self-serving exercise tailored to the
department commander's publicity-conscious agenda, the resulting report fairly critiqued then-current field techniques and afforded an important insight into the workings of field commands during the Nez Perce
and, presumably, other period Indian campaigns. Howard believed that
the performance of his cavalry, as manifested particularly at White Bird
Canyon, but also at Looking Glass's camp, Clearwater, Weippe, and
Camas Meadows, was below par, and at the request of General McDowell,
he solicited information from the many cavalry officers who took part in

his field operations. Among the recommendations for improvement were
(1) establishment of a cavalry school to provide more drill for both horses
and soldiers ("Our Cavalry soldiers have been obliged to work as laborers, and have not . . . been drilled enough. . . . It should be remembered
that the Cavalry soldier has a double part to perform, namely: to care for
and manage his horse, and besides to acquire even more skill with his
arms than the Infantry man. . . ."); (2) increased drill with arms, including
firing with blanks to keep the animals from bolting, and target practice
from horseback; (3) arming the troops with Springfield rifles or with
carbines with lengthened barrels; (4) improved training in skirmishing
from horseback; (5) development of improved proficiency with the saber
("in drill, if not in campaign") to increase soldiers' confidence and agil-
ity; (6) relinquishment of the revolver for combat in favor of the long
arm; (7) increased practice in swimming cavalry horses across rivers ("at
Salmon river, [some] . . . had to be towed over by boats two and four at a
time"); and (8) implementation of a system of reward and recognition for
the cavalry soldier (who has "more to do in the way of preparation and
subsequent work than the Infantry soldier"), including increased com-
pensation.[27] Beyond improved training in marksmanship, few of these
recommendations were immediately implemented, the army opting to
continue its overall sluggish and reactive performance throughout the
remaining years of the Indian wars.

Army losses in the course of the fighting through June, July, August,
September, and early October of 1877, numbered 6 officers, 101 enlisted
men, and 6 citizen employees killed (total killed: 113); plus 13 officers,
125 enlisted men, 4 citizens, and 2 Indian scouts wounded (total wounded:
144—of whom 2 later died). Aggregate casualties stood at 257.[28] Total
monetary cost of the military campaign—exclusive of private property
destroyed or otherwise lost—was $1,873,410.43[29] (approximately
$22,405,989.00 in 1990 dollars). As a direct result of the Nez Perce
campaign, a new post was erected near Milk River in northern Montana to keep watch over the activities of the Sioux and Nez Perces in
the country adjoining the Canadian border. Fort Assinniboine was also
strategically situated between the boundary and the Missouri River to
oversee the Assiniboines, Gros Ventres, Crows, and Blackfeet. But by
the time the fort was constructed in 1879, the need for it seemingly had
passed, for with the surrender of the Lakotas in 1880 and 1881, and the
dissipation of the Nez Perce threat, the potential for further large-scale

Among the people surrendering to Miles at Bear's Paw were two unidentified Nez Perce youths, photographed by John H. Fouch at the Tongue River Cantonment in late October or early November 1877.

COURTESY JAMES S. BRUST

Indian conflicts ceased to exist. Nonetheless, Fort Assinniboine operated until 1911.[30]

The post–Bear's Paw period brought manifold changes for the Nee-Me-Poo. It involved the incarceration of the people who had surrendered to Miles, as well as the troubled coexistence of White Bird's followers and other of the tribesmen who, one way or another, had managed to escape before or during the tumult of Bear's Paw, with the followers of the Hunkpapa Lakota leader, Sitting Bull, in the Cypress

Hills region of the Northwest Territories (present southern Saskatchewan). The odyssey of the Nez Perce prisoners began almost immediately following their arrival at the Tongue River Cantonment on October 23, 1877. While Miles and his command basked in the favorable publicity engendered by their victory, the prisoners raised their lodges and shelters on the south side of the Yellowstone in a grove of cottonwood trees where troops kept careful watch over them.[31] In the days after their arrival at the cantonment, Joseph and others of his people sat before the camera of photographer John H. Fouch.[32] Yet Miles's plan to keep them at the post through the winter and return them to Idaho in the spring—presurrender terms agreed upon by Miles, Howard, and Joseph at Bear's Paw—quickly dissipated with receipt of a directive from General Sheridan that the tribesmen were to be sent to Fort Abraham Lincoln, Dakota Territory. Even before the prisoners had reached Tongue River, Commanding General Sherman had effectually nullified the surrender accord, believing that as an example to other tribes the Nez Perces should be punished and never allowed to return home, and he directed their conveyance instead to the Indian Territory. Sheridan told Sherman that he agreed with him, but cited the expense of feeding the Nez Perces at Tongue River, and he recommended that the people be "shipped to Yankton" to await their future disposition.[33] When Miles learned of Sheridan's intention, he directed a letter to departmental headquarters:

> I presume the Government is not aware of the severe punishment the Nez Perces received or the number of badly wounded. I have brought them 265 miles from the battle-field; three (3) died on the road, two (2) on arrival and others cannot live. I consider it inhuman to compel them to travel farther at this season of the year.[34]

But this appeal was too late. The decision had already been made. Finally, Secretary of War McCrary directed Sheridan to remove the Nez Perces either to Yankton or Bismarck (Fort Lincoln), and the general chose Bismarck. On the evening of October 29, Miles received the order to transport the Nez Perces to Fort Lincoln, which would be but a stop en route to the Indian Territory.[35] Joseph quoted Miles as telling him: "I have endeavored to keep my word, but the chief who is over me has given the order, and I must obey it or resign."[36]

On October 29, accompanied by a detachment of troops, the Nez Perces who could stand the trip (along with seventeen Northern

Cheyenne prisoners) started down the road to Fort Buford, at the confluence of the Yellowstone and Missouri rivers.[37] Two days later, the ill, wounded, and women and children set out via fourteen mackinaws—each about thirty-two feet long by eight feet wide—to the same destination. Miles traveled in a boat until he overtook the party traveling by land. The journey was difficult, and the people agonized greatly from the cold. On November 6, Lieutenant Frank Baldwin wrote of the movement as "most inhumane, and if the public could get a hold of it, they would raise a glorious row. The General can't sleep or take any comfort thinking as he does of their suffering."[38] The people traveling by boat reached Fort Buford on November 5; those coming by wagon and horseback arrived at the post on the seventh.[39] A Fifth infantry officer remembered that "when we reached the Missouri, cakes of ice were floating in it, . . . but many of the Nez Perces took off their clothing and jumped in the water for a bath."[40] At Buford they rejoined fifteen refugees (including those taken by Lieutenants Maus and Scott at Milk River) who had been forwarded from the Seventh Cavalry camp opposite Squaw Creek on the Missouri.[41] Also, one of the men died and was buried "near the water's edge, where the Missouri and the Yellowstone, meeting, form angle."[42] Between November 8 and 10, the people left Fort Buford for Fort Lincoln, some two hundred departing aboard the boats on November 9 guarded by two companies of the First Infantry, the others on horseback escorted by troops of the Seventh Cavalry en route to their winter quarters.[43] At the Fort Berthold Indian Agency, the flotilla stopped briefly and the tribesmen took the occasion to meet some members of the Mandan tribe before starting downstream again. The mackinaws reached Bismarck on Monday evening, the nineteenth.[44]

The citizens of Bismarck turned out en masse to welcome the Nez Perce prisoners, providing a sumptuous buffet for them and the troops composing their military escort. Miles stood with Joseph while a band played the "Star Spangled Banner."[45] The tribesmen encamped across the river at Fort Abraham Lincoln, remaining there for four days. Miles's request to accompany a number of the Nez Perces to Washington, D.C., "in order that they may learn the intention of the Government and be satisfied that no wrong is intended" was turned down, and Sheridan's petition that the tribesmen be transferred to Fort Leavenworth won Sherman's speedy concurrence.[46] Joseph's response on learning of the new destination was: "When will these white chiefs tell the truth?"[47] On the nineteenth, Miles was feted at a banquet given by the city of Bismarck. Following the colonel's departure for St. Paul, the townspeople similarly honored Joseph with an expressly prepared invitation to him, as "Head Chief of Nez Perces," to dine with them at the Sheridan House. Joseph "and other chiefs" attended a reception at the Sheridan, where he "was presented to a number of the ladies of the house." At the dinner, Joseph ate salmon and reportedly said that it reminded him of his own country.[48]

On November 23, the Nez Perce prisoners loaded their lodges and equipment in freight cars and themselves into eleven rail coaches, and they started down the tracks to Fort Leavenworth, Kansas, escorted by Companies B and G, First Infantry.[49] The route lay east, through Jamestown, Dakota, and to St. Paul, Minnesota, then southwest through Marshalltown, Iowa, to Fort Leavenworth.[50] They reached the post on Monday afternoon, November 26. There the tribesmen, wrote Sherman, would be "held as prisoners of war until spring, when I trust the Indian Bureau will provide them homes on the Indian reservation near the Modocs. . . . They should never again be allowed to return to Oregon or Lapwai."[51] At Fort Leavenworth, however, Major General John Pope, commander of the Department of the Missouri, informed that he had only tents to shelter the Nez Perces and recommended that they be transferred to either Fort Riley, Fort Larned, or Fort Hays, where they might better be accommodated through the winter in barracks. Sheridan denied this application to remove the Indians, and they stayed at Fort Leavenworth in 108 army tents arranged in the Missouri River bottom about two miles above the garrison.[52] Howard's request that thirty-nine more Nez Perce prisoners being held at Forts Vancouver, Lapwai, and Missoula be sent to join their kin was summarily rejected by General Sherman, who directed that they instead "be sent to the Agency near Lapwai and then released."[53]

Army records indicate that the number of Nez Perces arriving at Fort Leavenworth consisted of 87 men, 184 women, and 147 children—a total of 418 people. The discrepancy between that figure and the number 448 given by Miles as having surrendered to his command is probably not accountable, although several of the people had died since the action at Bear's Paw. Other Nez Perces who subsequently turned themselves in to the military authorities were also sent to Fort Leavenworth.[54] Regardless of the numbers, the tribesmen remained in the center of a defunct race track on the alternating cold, humid, and hot Missouri River flats from the time of their arrival until July 1878.[55] Officials of the Bureau of Indian Affairs who visited the Nez Perces denounced the location "between a lagoon and the river, [as] the worst possible place that could have been selected." A doctor reported that "one-half could be said to be sick, and all were affected by the poisonous malaria of the camp."[56] Late that month, the Nez Perces—now numbering 410— embarked for a new home on the Quawpaw reservation in extreme northeastern Indian Territory. Three children died en route south from Fort Leavenworth, and at the new location 260 of the people became sick, many from malaria. Within months, more than 100 had died.[57]

The subsequent history of the Nez Perce prisoners in the Indian Territory was just as tragic. Joseph and his people longed to return to the mountains of their homeland. In 1879, when the tribesmen took up lands west of the Ponca tribe in the Cherokee Outlet to practice agriculture and ranching, Joseph visited Washington, D.C., to lobby to that end. He published his views, translated into polished English by an unknown person, in the popular *North American Review*, in which he stated: "I cannot understand how the Government sends out a man to fight us, as it did General Miles, and then breaks his word. Such a Government has something wrong with it."[58] Miles worked hard to remedy the obvious injustice meted to the Nez Perces, including writing arguments to President Rutherford B. Hayes and Interior Secretary Carl Schurz in favor of their removal back to their homeland. In addition, the Presbyterian Church and the Indian Rights Association labored on behalf of the people. Finally, Miles's own promotion in 1880 to command the Department of the Columbia worked in favor of bringing the tribesmen back to the Northwest. But the bureaucratic machinery moved slowly, and it was not until 1885 that legislation appropriating removal funds paved the way for the return of the Nez Perces. To protect themselves from legal indictments in Idaho as well as from physical injury by whites living there, 150 of the people—including Joseph—opted to go to the Colville Reservation in Washington Territory; the remaining 118 went to the Lapwai Reservation. On May 22, 1885, the 268 people—all who were left—boarded a train at Arkansas City to start homeward. Once on the train, "the Indians commenced howling and crying" in sorrowful manifestation of leaving more than one hundred of their dead behind in "Eeikish Pah"—"the Hot Place."[59]

For many of the Nez Perces, Bear's Paw was not the end of their quest for freedom from the U.S. Army. Those who made it out of the village at that place and into Canada found extended respite from their immediate troubles. For many, however, the experience of living in juxtaposition with the Sioux was less than appealing, and the uncertainty of the whereabouts and condition of their friends and relatives captured or killed at Bear's Paw only compounded the feelings of separation and despair they felt after their long flight. The trek into the British Possessions ended with small bands of hungry, impoverished people, some with horses and some without, straggling across the boundary to seek help and sustenance from the exiled Lakotas. Evidently, the number of tribesmen who broke away from the Bear's Paw village between September 30 and October 5 totaled as many as 233, according to the estimate of Black Eagle, one of those who made his way north.[60] The wife of Wounded Head described the ordeal of her party on escaping the Bear's Paw village on the first day of the fighting:

> We mounted horses and left. Only one blanket, I rode bareback as did the rest. Going quite a distance, we stopped. We listened to the guns back where they were fighting. I cannot tell the distance, but we were outside the battle. There we stayed till the evening drew on. The night darkness came about us, and still we do not travel further. Not only ourselves, but Chief Joseph's older wife and daughter are with us. But people are scattered everywhere, hungry, freezing. Almost naked, they had escaped from the camp when the soldiers came charging and shooting. Thus we remained overnight. We must not build a fire. No bedding, cold and chilly, we stood or sat holding our horses. We cried with misery and loneliness, as we still heard the guns of the battle. Daylight came, and we moved a little farther down from that place. . . . Nothing to eat all that day, all that night we remained there. Though no food nor fire, I grow sleepy. All of us fall asleep. After awhile we feel as if a blanket is covering us. It is snow. . . . Four suns in all we are hiding, no food, starving and cold. No moccasins, I am barefooted. . . . Then we travel toward Sitting Bull's camp. Moving that fifth day, towards evening the men killed a buffalo bull. A fire is built. Meat is cooked by roasting, and we have supper. . . . Next day we come to some Chippewa Indians. They are nice people. They give us food. I am given a pair of moccasins. Then I feel better.[61]

Some warriors and their families managed to get away during the siege, making their way through the soldier lines after dark and striking north. The warrior Many Wounds claimed to have killed two soldiers during the day after his escape and to have taken their clothing to keep warm, giving one of the uniforms to another refugee. Later, the Crees gave him other clothes. "They told me I would be killed if found wearing soldier uniform."[62] Some groups of escapees likely congregated into larger bodies before crossing into Canada. One North-West Mounted Police official reported seeing a party of "fifty men, forty women, and a large number of children, besides about three hundred horses" come in to Sitting Bull's camp.[63] Certainly one of the largest groups to get away from Bear's Paw was that headed by White Bird, whose party—perhaps numbering more than fifty people—left the night of October 5 following Joseph's surrender.[64] They were better prepared for the journey, but it was nonetheless rigorous. According to Ollokot's widow:

> We walked out, leaving many of our friends. Some were too bad wounded to travel and had to stay. . . . Night drew on as we left. We had blankets but not too heavy for the traveling. Not enough to keep us warm when camping. . . . I do not know how long, but it must have been several days we were on that journey. Two days we had nothing to eat. Then antelopes were seen, and some of them killed.[65]

In their course north, this party encountered the Catholic missionary Father J. B. M. Genin with the so-called "Red River Halfbreeds," or Metis, along Milk River. The priest treated White Bird's wounded and gave them food before sending them on their way to Canada.[66]

Because of the bad weather and the fact that the tribesmen were slowed by the presence of wounded along with many children among them, besides the fact that they were not at all certain of the route they followed, the travel into Canada took several days. After reaching the Lakota encampment, the Nez Perces had trouble conversing with them, and mostly used sign talk. There was confusion over the gesture for "water," and when the Nez Perces tried to explain "stream," meaning Snake Creek, the Sioux thought they meant the Missouri River—too far distant for a relief force to travel with hope of accomplishing much. The confusion was rectified after one arriving Nez Perce explained what was meant in the Crow language, which some Lakotas understood.[67] The knowledge of the nearby presence of Miles and his soldiers seems to have whipped up a flurry of excitement among the Sioux, and Superintendent Walsh issued stern warnings to the chiefs to rein in their warriors and by no means cross the line. Many Lakotas believed that Miles's troops were going to come over and attack them.[68] When White Bird and some other late arrivals reached their kinsmen already with the Sioux, they told of the death and destruction at Bear's Paw, of the killing of the leaders (some by accident), and of Joseph's surrender. The news resulted in much grieving among the people.[69]

White Bird approached the Lakotas with certain trepidation, for they were traditional enemies of the Nee-Me-Poo, and he did not know how his people would be received. The chief later told Duncan MacDonald that Sitting Bull personally greeted him with a group of warriors and communicated that he was sorry he had not been aware of the fighting at Bear's Paw.[70] A small party continued to the scene of the battle, however, apparently arriving after the troops and prisoners had departed. One of the group, Peopeo Tholekt, remembered that "nothing living was seen anywhere on that field. But we found some of our dead who were unburied, and buried them as best we could."[71] Then they returned into Canada. Nez Perce sources suggest that the initial response by the Sioux to their presence was empathy, for many of their own people had experienced similar tragedy in their relations with the army. As the refugees explained what had happened to them, the Sioux witnesses, including Sitting Bull, broke into sympathetic crying and wailing.[72]

In mid-October, General Terry's much-delayed entourage—escorted by a company of the Seventh Infantry as well as the three companies of Second Cavalry so recently engaged at Bear's Paw—arrived at the border hopeful of settling difficulties with the refugee Lakotas who had crossed into Canada in early 1877, during the closing stages of the Great Sioux War.[73] While Terry's mission was to convince Sitting Bull to return to the United States, it was obvious that the recent tribulation of the Nez Perces dominated the Hunkpapa leader's thinking, and if there had existed any prospect that the Tetons would return, the specter of wounded Nez Perces coming among the Sioux fresh from Bear's Paw— a vivid reminder of their own ordeal—contributed to dash it away.[74] Any promise of good faith by United States government authorities had a hollow ring to it. Terry's council with the tribesmen occurred on October 17 at Fort Walsh. He found the Sioux disposed against returning and surrendering. Finally, Sitting Bull told him: "This part of the country does not belong to your people. You belong on the other side, this side belongs to us." Terry's party went back to Fort Benton, and the general returned to St. Paul.[75] In their official report of the meeting, the commissioners concluded: "To the lawless and ill-disposed, to those who commit offenses against the property and persons of the whites, the refugee camp will be a secure asylum. . . . We have already an illustration of this danger in the fact that more than one hundred of the Nez Perces defeated at Bear's Paw Mountain [sic] are now in Sitting Bull's camp."[76]

Over the next several weeks and months, the Sioux shared their tipis with the Nez Perces, giving them food and clothing until the people could begin to provide for themselves. Eventually, the Nez Perces raised their own lodges and established an independent camp, but continued hunting buffalo with the Lakotas, occasionally going below the international line to kill the beasts. During the winter of 1877–78, both tribes eked out a marginal existence, forced as they were to share the game resources with the Gros Ventres, Assiniboines, and other tribes that hunted the region.[77] There is evidence, too, that some Nez Perces, together with some of their Lakota hosts, journeyed as far south as Cow Creek early in November to raise caches left there following the raid on the stores at Cow Island. And in December 1877, Sitting Bull together with some Nez Perces traveled from a large Lakota village on Frenchman's Creek near Milk River to the Bear's Paw battlefield "and returned with a large quantity of ammunition which had been cached by [the] Nez Perces previous to their surrender." Still other Nez Perces were reported to be among the Metis camped along Milk River.[78]

On October 22, after the excitement had subsided in Sitting Bull's encampment following the Terry council and after the Nez Perces had settled into their new environs, Superintendent Walsh met with them to formalize their presence on British soil. At that time, White Bird explained what had happened to his people to incite them to warfare against the whites in Idaho and against the U.S. Army. He told Walsh that the Nez Perces were undecided about what to do; some hoped to remain with the Sioux, while others wanted to move farther north to the Cypress Hills. White Bird movingly concluded that "the white man wanted the wealth our people possessed; he got it by the destruction of our people. . . . We have no country, no people, no home."[79] Walsh's impression of White Bird was that he seemed "a very intelligent man of fine and good judgment, less diplomatic than [Sitting] Bull but more clear in perception and quicker in decision—a greater General than

Bull."[80] It was clear, however, that the people were now totally dependent on the Lakotas for their existence and would remain so as long as they stayed in Canada. Yet rumors circulated regarding the treatment of the Nez Perces by the Sioux. Colonel Gibbon wired Sheridan that they were being "whipped and treated as slaves" and wanted to come back to the United States.[81] And in March 1878, Assistant Commissioner Acheson G. Irvine of the North-West Mounted Police heard "all the Nez Perces" were entertaining notions of returning.[82] Father Genin, meanwhile, who was trying to convince the Sioux to return south, criticized the North-West Mounted Police for coddling the people of both tribes and not sending them below the boundary line. Genin's quest to broker the delivery of the Sioux and Nez Perces to the United States was finally quelled by a missive from Major Ilges at Fort Benton, who told the priest in no uncertain terms to "hereafter abstain from meddling with any of our Indians."[83] Still, Walsh's objective remained the return of the people of both tribes to the United States.[84]

The exodus of the Nez Perces back into the United States from Canada began in the late spring of 1878. Many people thought they could quietly go back to the agency at Lapwai and there live with their Lapwai relatives. The first departees left in June, after warm weather had arrived. One party numbered seven warriors. Another consisted of four men and a woman. Another, probably the largest body of returnees, comprised at least twenty-four tribesmen led by Wottolen and including Yellow Wolf, Peopeo Tholekt, Black Eagle, and Joseph's daughter, Kapkap Ponmi. Perhaps unaware of the fate of Joseph's followers, this group journeyed south through Montana Territory, the men stealing horses and killing cattle to sustain them. They encountered both enemy tribesmen and settlers on their way.[85] At a point below Philipsburg, the warriors confronted three placer miners and, primarily for food, killed them before proceeding into Idaho. Rumors spread that these Nez Perces intended to join the Flatheads in all-out warfare, causing some settlers to congregate in makeshift defenses. Meanwhile, the party of seven men that had left Canada earlier was captured and confined in the Fort Lapwai guard house as "prisoners of war." The other small party had gone to the country of the Pend d'Oreilles.[86] On July 15, a detachment of mounted infantrymen under First Lieutenant Thomas S. Wallace operating out of Fort Missoula pursued a party of

Nez Perce refugees heading home and alleged to have committed murders in Montana. The troops caught up with them on the Middle Fork of the Clearwater River. In the skirmishing that ensued, Wallace's men supposedly killed six Nez Perces and wounded three (neither sex nor age was reported), and captured thirty-one horses and mules and killed twenty-three others.[87]

One returning Nez Perce woman named Lucy told Captain William Falck, Second Infantry, something of her party's struggle to join the Umatillas, with whom they had planned to live:

> They left Sitting Bull's camp about the 20th of June; in ten days they struck Milk River in a southwesterly direction from the camp, and in five days thereafter the Rocky Mountains. They came through the Blackfeet country and saw no whites until they reached Bitter Root Mountains; thence they came in by the Elk City trail. . . . When in the Bitter Root Valley the women were left in charge of two men, with directions to take the Elk City trail, while the men were to take the Lo Lo trail, but on the following day the women overtook the men and found the latter in possession of a large and fine band of horses and mules. They went in camp about 90 miles from Elk City, and while resting there the following day were overtaken in the afternoon by a party of thirty white men, who attacked them and fought them at long range until evening. The white men were successful in capturing all of the horses and mules, including the horses and saddles of the entire party, excepting six on which they mounted the squaws, the men marching until they reached the reservation, where they again provided themselves with mounts by stealing from Kamiah Indians. In this fight the squaw says one white man was killed and no Indians. The entire party camped near Clear Creek; when James Lawyer's first party [sent out from the agency] found them they all refused to surrender, and declared their determination to join the Snakes. During the night five squaws escaped and surrendered to Lawyer. Three women and children are still left with the party, who are probably gone to the Salmon River, there to open some caches left by their people last year, containing money, blankets, provisions, &c.[88]

By mid-August 1878, fourteen Nez Perce men, including Yellow Wolf, had been incarcerated in the post guard house at Fort Lapwai, the women and children allowed to roam free at Kamiah. Most of these people were later sent to the Indian Territory to join Joseph. Three others, Wottolen, Black Eagle, and a Bannock Indian who had traveled with the party, decided to return to Canada and live with the Sioux.[89]

While these events were unfolding, the U.S. government initiated a formal attempt to bring the Nez Perce refugees back to American soil for imprisonment with Joseph's people at Fort Leavenworth. To facilitate talks with their kinsmen in Canada, General Terry sent three of the people from Kansas—Yellow Bull, Husis Kute, and Estoweaz—with the celebrated scout and interpreter, Benjamin H. Clark, to Fort Buford and instructed Colonel Miles to undertake arrangements for their passage onto British soil.[90] "If the Nez Perces . . . come over and surrender," he told Miles, "they should be brought to Buford, there to await further orders . . . for their transfer to their own people at Leavenworth."[91] At Fort Keogh, Miles selected his aide, Lieutenant George W. Baird, who had been wounded at Bear's Paw, to lead the delegation into Canada and, "with the consent of the Canadian authorities, to return the Nez Perces [sic] Indians to their tribe, should they desire to do so."[92] Armed with an introductory letter, Baird and his party crossed the international boundary on June 15 to consult with the North-West Mounted Police and the Nez Perces. Christopher Gilson, an interpreter who could converse in the Nee-Me-Poo language, joined the party in Canada. On the twenty-second, Commissioner James F. Macleod wrote Baird acknowledging that that officer was only to take charge of the Nez Perces if they agreed to return to the United States on assurance that they would be granted "the same terms as were granted those captured at the 'Bear Paw' by General Miles."[93] For fear of inciting the Sioux by their presence, Baird, Clark, and Gilson were denied the opportunity of going to the Nez Perce camp, and only the three Nez Perces "captured at the battle of 'Bear Paw,'" along with Assistant Commissioner Irvine, arranged to speak with White Bird.[94] Eventually, however, Irvine convinced White Bird to come to Fort Walsh and talk directly to Baird, and on July 1 and 2 the delegation confronted the veteran Nee-Me-Poo leader and seven of his people in the presence of Macleod and Irvine.

At the opening of the meeting July 1, Baird lied outright to White Bird, extending to the chief the likelihood that he and his people would be allowed to return to their Idaho homeland, although he knew that the opposite was true. In his opening comments Baird said:

> If you, on this side of the line, wish to go to Joseph, you will be treated just as well and have the same protection as Joseph and his

people. Joseph and his Indians will be put on a good Reservation, and have an opportunity to live comfortably. . . . The Great Father wrote to General Miles to ask him what he thought about sending Joseph back to his old home. General Miles told him he thought they ought to go back to their old home and be protected there. If you here go back to Joseph, you will be with him, and it may be at your old home. Joseph and the Nez Perces have a great many friends among the Americans, and they tell the Great Father that they ought to go back to their old home. . . . The Americans are your friends, and want you to go back to your old home, and if you don't, you will go to some other good Reservation.

On Tuesday, the three people from Joseph spoke to the group, mainly to affirm the surrender agreement, although one of them, Husis Kute, cast a dubious prognosis on an anticipated return to Idaho while seemingly negating what Baird had told them: "Joseph thinks to-day that, because General Miles promised him he would go back to his own country, he will go, he and his people. Joseph does not want to go further south, because it is not healthy; his people die even at Leavenworth." Attempting to reconcile the remarks, Baird said:

If White Bird and the Nez Perces, who are here, will go over and join Joseph, there is a very good prospect that they will go back [to Idaho]; but if White Bird and his people stay here, there is not a good prospect that Joseph and his people will go back, and I will tell you why: The Great Father may say, "White Bird and his people are living with my enemies, the Sioux, and as long as they live with my enemies I don't want Joseph and his people to go back to their old home."

To this White Bird responded:

For my part, I want Joseph to come back to our [old] part of the country. I don't wish to stop [stay] with the Sioux. If Joseph comes back to our part of the country, to a good Reservation, I will join him. I don't like the Sioux, and don't want to stop with them. I don't care for the Sioux; I just camp there to pass the time. My heart is very good, there is not a bit of bad in it.

At that juncture, Commissioner Macleod pointed out to White Bird that "this is a very kind and generous offer on behalf of the President, and if you do not accept it now it may never occur again."

That afternoon the meeting reconvened. White Bird told the

members that he had counseled with his people and that he had decided he would not go. Lieutenant Baird and Macleod appealed to the other Nez Perces to decide for themselves if they wanted to return. Baird told them that if they returned one at a time they would be "arrested as hostile Indians." Again he held out the likelihood that they would be returned to Idaho, and now he made Joseph's future contingent on their decision: "I think you ought to go because if you go now you have a good chance to go to your old home, but if you don't, you will not have a good chance of going, or Joseph either." Macleod then asked, "Do any of you want to say anything? When White Bird spoke, he spoke for himself; now I want to hear from the others whether they will accept the kind offer of the American Government." "You know what I said," interjected White Bird. "Yes," said McLeod. "You spoke for yourself; now I want to hear the others." White Bird responded: "What I said, I said for all my people." Later that evening, White Bird delivered his final word on the matter: "We will not go."[95]

According to Duncan MacDonald, a mixed-blood of Scottish and Nez Perce ancestry who was engaged as an interpreter at the conference, White Bird had with him in Canada thirty-two lodges inhabited by as many as 120 people. Years later, MacDonald recalled that at the dramatic climax White Bird rose to his feet, pointed his finger at Baird, and told him: "I want you to understand what I am saying. You go back and bring Chief Joseph to Idaho. I will know it. I will hear of it. Do this, and I promise to surrender."[96] (This, however, is not verified in the Canadian transcript of the proceedings.) MacDonald quoted White Bird as saying that those who had expressed a willingness to return to the United States (and, in fact, had left in June) were not his followers and belonged to another band. He acknowledged, however, that some of his people "are deserting me; they do so when I am sound asleep in my bed; they run off at night, and if these men commit depredations, I am not to blame." He affirmed that if the government sent Joseph back to Idaho, "I will at once go back and make peace."[97]

It became apparent that—true to Nee-Me-Poo cultural dynamics—White Bird's hold on his own followers did not necessarily extend to those who belonged to other bands. Soon after the Baird mission, mounted police officials learned that some Nez Perces intended to move west into the country occupied by tribes of the Blackfeet Indians. There the Nez Perces would try to break away to their former homes in Idaho and Oregon. The news caused concern at Forts Walsh and Macleod, where the police hoped to prevent clashes between the two tribes. But such trouble never happened; instead, the North-West Mounted Police became concerned when Sitting Bull succeeded in making peace with his Blackfeet and Cree neighbors.[98] And of even more direct import regarding the Nez Perces and the Sioux came reports that White Bird's people had attempted to make peace with the Crows—that a party had ventured south of the line in September and had received assurances that, if the Americans attempted to take their arms and horses, the Crows would fight and then cross into Canada and join the Lakotas and Nez Perces, and that such a combined force would be sufficient to combat American troops sent over the line to punish them. With Sioux concurrence, Nez Perce representatives were sent to the Crows in December bearing peace tobacco to assert that the Nez Perces and Lakotas desired friendship with them. The plan did not find favor among the British officials, who concluded that "the Sioux and Nez Perces (by the Canadian authorities) and the Crows (by the American authorities) should be made to understand at once, that under no circumstances will the Crows be permitted to find an asylum in Canada."[99]

Nor did the Crows seem to favor a coalition with their traditional Sioux enemies, despite the diplomacy of the Nez Perces to forge such a union. They responded to the proposal by promptly raiding the Sioux pony herd and instigating an indignant war frenzy by the Lakotas. Inspector Walsh visited the Sioux camp on January 23, 1879, and found the camps of Sitting Bull and White Bird more than two miles below the forty-ninth parallel. Confronting Sitting Bull, Walsh told the Hunkpapa that the American authorities "would be called upon to put a stop to such raids into Canadian territory." He further told Sitting Bull:

> I believe that you and the Nez Perces are to blame for this raid by the Crows. If you had not tried to plant sedition in the Crow tribe, by sending messengers to induce them to leave their Reservation which the good men of the tribe would not listen to, the Crows would never have sent their young men into the White Mother's country to steal horses from the Sioux. There are perhaps a few dissatisfied men in the Crow tribe that listened to your messengers,—men that would not care if they brought destruction on their people; but the wise and good men sent your messengers off from their camp, telling them never to return. You still persisted, and sent messages, and I suppose the Crows found the only way to stop

you was to commence stealing your horses. I have been informed
that one of the messages you sent the Crows was for them to leave
their Reservation and join you in the White Mother's country, where
the buffalo were numerous, and that guns and ammunition were
sold to the Indians by all the traders.[100]

Sitting Bull confessed his role in the affair and heeded Walsh's advice.
His war ardor waned, and his and White Bird's people instead undertook a buffalo hunt below the line. Sitting Bull's and White Bird's efforts at intertribal confederation ended after that.[101]

Despite White Bird's efforts to work with Sitting Bull, it is clear that
the Nez Perces in Canada were tired of that existence and longed for
home. Others continued to trickle across the border in 1878 and 1879,
although many of these were destined to go the Indian Territory to join
Joseph. In December 1878, such a party of seventeen Nez Perces who
had returned from Canada was taken under escort via Portland, San Francisco, and Omaha to join the incarcerated people.[102] But over the next
few years, the homeward imperative was strong. Some wandered about
for years, staying on reservations of friendly tribes. The parents of
Suhmkeen (Samuel Tilden) came back into Montana, located on a ranch
near the Alberta border, and did chores for white settlers until 1880,
when they settled on the Flathead Reservation. They remained there
until 1910, when they went home to Lapwai.[103] Some returnees found
their way back to Lapwai and took residence with those Nee-Me-Poo
who had not taken part in the war of 1877. Ollokot's widow stayed with
the Spokans after she departed Canada in 1879, but eventually returned
to Lapwai. The warrior Two Moon said that, after passing a year with the
Sioux, he joined the Flatheads for two winters before joining the Lemhi
Shoshones in southern Idaho Territory. He then visited the Spokans and
finally joined Joseph's band at Nespelum, Washington, after their return
from the Indian Territory. Likewise, Red Wolf III left Canada after two
years, joining—of all people—the Blackfeet for one year. He next spent
time with the Flatheads and Umatillas before coming back to Lapwai.[104]

Meantime, the dwindling herds of buffalo that failed to sustain
them caused Sitting Bull's people to begin crossing the line and surrendering in 1880, and the Hunkpapa leader himself eventually yielded to
U.S. military authorities at Fort Buford. When the chief came into the
garrison on July 19, 1881, among his followers was a Shoshone-Bannock
man named Seeskoomkee (Steps, also called No Feet), who had gone

through the war of 1877 with the Nez Perces.[105] Instead of returning himself, White Bird moved his few remaining lodges west to Pincher Creek and near the Piegan reserve. These people built stout cabins of poplar and pine. Some of them went to work for freighters around Fort Macleod, while others sold berries to survive. A settler remarked that they "had to rustle their own living and came to us with blueberries, gooseberries, fish, and sometimes venison or mountain sheep meat, which they were glad to 'swap' for tea, sugar and flour, etc."[106]

Seemingly by the 1890s, only a few families of Nez Perces remained in Canada with White Bird. Few, if any, made any effort to join Joseph's people in Nespelum after 1885, and White Bird was apparently content to stay north of the line for good. In 1892, almost eleven years after Sitting Bull had gone over to the Americans, White Bird became involved in a quarrel with another Nez Perce, a man named Lamnisnim Husis (Shriveled Head), also known as Hasenahmahkikt, but locally called Nez Perce Sam. Sam accused White Bird of threatening supernatural powers against his son and other family members. On the evening of March 6, Sam confronted the aged chief with an axe and killed him not far from his house. North-West Mounted Police officers arrested Sam. He was tried and sentenced to be executed in the Manitoba Penitentiary in July, but through the exertions of local religious leaders, Sam's death sentence was commuted to a life term. He died in prison in October 1893. The remaining Nez Perces dispersed following White Bird's murder, some going to live on the Piegan reserve while the others eventually moved back to Lapwai or gradually died off in Canada. In 1898, Nez Perce Sam's wife, Sara, was pronounced "the only remaining Nez Perce woman" in the Canadian settlement. She died of tuberculosis in 1899, and her daughters subsequently moved down to Lapwai. After his murder, White Bird was buried near the Pincher Creek settlement. The site of his unmarked grave was obliterated after the remaining Nez Perces had either died or departed the area.[107]

In the aftermath of the Nez Perce War, the public sentiment that had long favored the Nez Perces continued. Even the military foes of the tribesmen complimented them for their sagacity, enterprise, and resourcefulness in eluding the army's frustrating pursuit for so long. Based on his only confrontation with them, Nelson A. Miles, in the tenor of the time, offered solid praise for their military prowess and accomplishments and extended hope for their future:

> I consider these Nez Perces decidedly [the] most dangerous Indian enemies that the Government has had to contend with. Nearly all understand English and many speak it; they have all the cunning of wild Indians, and many of the arts of civilized warfare. . . . From what I have seen of both, I should say that Joseph is decidedly the superior of Sitting Bull, less a savage and superior in intelligence and personal courage, and as this trouble was commenced with fraud and injustice I am satisfied these Indians can be made loyal friends of the government in six months with anything like honesty and justice on the part of the representatives of the government.[108]

In fact, the general military success of the Nez Perces over the long road from Camas Prairie to Bear's Paw was not so much the result of one individual but of the interband community of the people, coupled with the leadership of the different bands, including well-qualified military persons, operating together for the common good. While the movement of the assorted families and dunnage, along with the immense herd of stock, under the constant threat of attack was not always efficient and seems to have often lacked security-consciousness, it succeeded enough to overcome the mediocrity of the army's own performance until Bear's Paw.

The Nez Perces lost at least 96 people and perhaps as many as 145—with at least 36 of them women and children—within the three and one-half months between White Bird Canyon and Bear's Paw. Many more suffered from injuries received in the fighting or from the cumulative effects of the long march and the bad weather near the end.[109] The heartrending agonies of noncombatant women and children and the elderly, coupled with the plucky performance of the Indians in eluding Howard's pursuit and besting the troops in several encounters after White Bird Canyon, contributed to their successful enlistment of public opinion over much of the course of their struggle. Most Americans knew from reading of the Wallowa controversy that the Nez Perces had been defrauded in their own country by the government. Thus, their effort to remove themselves from the seat of the corruption and to leave their homeland became a noble ambition to many white Americans. Whereas editorial opinion in Idaho often enlarged on the problems emerging from the Fort Lapwai councils, much of the territorial press in Montana came to root for the tribesmen, especially in the wake of the Fort Fizzle embarrassment. As they passed through the Bitterroot Valley, their stock continued to soar, and journalists urged "that it is best to let them go in peace." Despite the fighting at Big Hole, where army casualties were high, and amid rising criticism of Howard's performance, the papers generally viewed the Nez Perces in a favorable light.[110] Initial reports of the tribesmen's capture of the tourist parties in the national park created horrific consternation, but later accounts by the captives themselves tended to show that they had been largely well treated.

Following Bear's Paw, the press elevated Joseph—the only surviving chief present—as something of a hero, fostering the myth of his martial leadership that dominated accounts of the warfare for decades. The nontreaty Nez Perces became a people that white Americans could relate to. Despite the horrors of the initial outbreak, the public took comfort in the knowledge that the wronged tribesmen had, presumably because of their Christian-inspired traits, showed humanity on the battleground in not killing the wounded or scalping the dead. Moreover, they represented a portion of a tribe that had a solid history of friendship toward the government and that had supposedly benefited from an awareness of Christianity and a knowledge of the English language—both of which factors doubtless made the nontreaty people more acceptable as foes than other tribes that had battled the whites. Their estrangement from a large segment of their own people made their actions difficult to comprehend and exacerbated an intratribal schism that still challenges reconciliation. But the definitive truth was that—no matter the perception within or without the tribe—in their hearts they transcended all to grasp what they believed the only course left to them. Irrefutably, they had just cause, and in the end the Nez Perces carried through with dignity and forbearance, an apotheosis of being and of the human spirit.

Epilogue: Later Lives

COLONEL NELSON A. MILES gained the most benefit from his participation in the Nez Perce War. His success at Bear's Paw boosted his stock among the leading Indian-fighting officers of the army. In 1880, Miles won the rank of brigadier general commanding the Department of the Columbia, succeeding Howard in this assignment. Five years later, he took command of the Department of the Missouri, headquartered at Fort Leavenworth. In 1886, he supplanted General Crook in the campaign against the Chiricahua Apaches, finally forcing Geronimo's surrender. When Crook died in 1890, Miles moved to Chicago to command the Division of the Missouri, and in 1895, based on seniority, he became Commanding General of the Army. Yet Miles's astounding lack of strategic vision about how the army should change as it assumed new responsibilities in the world during and following the Spanish-American War, as well as his obstinate and increasingly outspoken disposition, rendered him expendable, and he retired in 1903. Largely forgotten in the years that followed, he collapsed and died in 1925, while attending a circus with his grandchildren in Washington, D.C.[1]

Brigadier General Oliver O. Howard went on to oversee field operations during the Bannock War of 1878, in which he vastly improved his performance over that of the previous year. While he never overcame the criticism of his work in the Nez Perce War, Howard nonetheless continued his army career in departmental and divisional commands for another seventeen years, and he served as superintendent of the military academy at West Point. In 1893, Howard received a Medal of Honor for his service in the Civil War Battle of Fair Oaks, where he had lost his right arm. After retirement, he settled in Burlington, Vermont, where he wrote books and continued his activities on behalf of religious and educational causes, including helping to establish Lincoln Memorial University in Tennessee. He died in 1909. His son, Guy, who had accompanied him during the long march of 1877, was killed as a major in the Philippines in 1899.[2]

Among the army personnel who had participated in the rout at White Bird Canyon on June 17, 1877, Captain David Perry endured questions regarding his performance there and at Cottonwood and Clearwater. He was exonerated of all charges of misconduct in courts of inquiry held in 1877 and 1878, and he enjoyed a comparatively quiet remainder of his army career. He eventually became colonel of the all-black Ninth Cavalry before his retirement in 1898. Perry died ten years later and was buried in Arlington National Cemetery.[3] His two subordinates, Lieutenants William R. Parnell and Joel G. Trimble testified, respectively, for and against Perry in the courts of inquiry. Parnell stayed in the army for another ten years and was promoted to major before retiring because of a disability. Awarded the Medal of Honor in 1897 for his performance at White Bird Canyon, he retired to San Francisco, where he worked as an instructor in military science at a private school. Parnell died in 1910 after sustaining injuries in a fall from a streetcar. Trimble also retired on a disability in 1879 and died in California in 1911.[4]

Captain Stephen G. Whipple—who led the attack on Looking Glass's camp, commanded at Cottonwood, and fought in the Battle of the Clearwater—retired from the army in 1884 with twenty-one years of military service; he died in 1895.[5] Colonel Edward McConville, of the Lewiston, Idaho, volunteers who fought the tribesmen at Misery Hill, later became a major and brevet brigadier general of the First Idaho Volunteer Infantry Regiment during the Spanish-American War. Sent to the Philippines, McConville was killed on February 5, 1899, at the outset of the native insurrection.[6] Captain Marcus P. Miller, who charged the Nez Perce positions at Clearwater, continued his distinguished army career, serving with Howard in the field in 1879 and commanding various artillery regiments until 1898, when, appointed brigadier general of volunteers during the Spanish-American War, he led U.S. troops against Philippine insurgents. In 1899, at age sixty-four, Miller retired.[7] His colleague at the Clearwater, Major and Surgeon George Miller Sternberg in 1893 became Surgeon General and one of the most important doctor-scientists in U.S. Army history through his work in bacteriology.[8]

Colonel John Gibbon commanded the departments of Dakota, the Platte, and the Columbia at various times after 1877, rising to the grade of brigadier general before retiring in 1891. He later served a term as commander of the Loyal Legion, a society of veteran officers of the Civil War. At his home in Baltimore, he authored numerous articles about his army service, including those about the Battle of the Big Hole. Gibbon died at his home in February 1896, from complications of pneumonia, and was buried in Arlington National Cemetery.[9] Of the officers who pursued the Nez Perces after they attacked the army bivouac at Camas Meadows on August 20, 1877, Captain Randolph Norwood had endured the longest and most dangerous encounter. Despite his apparent hypochondria, Norwood stayed in the army until 1889, when he was discharged for disability.[10] Of the tourists who encountered the Nez Perces, Frank and Ida Carpenter both died within a decade of their captivity, while George and Emma Cowan lived long, happy lives. George became a school teacher and an attorney in Montana and eventually became a district judge. In the years after his experience with the warriors, Cowan kept on his watch chain the bullet from his forehead that had almost killed him. He lived to age eighty-five, dying in Spokane, Washington, in December 1926. His wife, Emma, who had suffered the trauma of being captured and seeing her husband shot, lived until 1938, the last survivor of the encounters with the Nez Perces in Yellowstone.[11]

Colonel Samuel G. Sturgis, who pursued the Nez Perces after they emerged from the national park, and who met their warriors at Canyon Creek, subsequently commanded Fort Meade, Dakota, until 1881, when he became governor of the Soldier's Home in Washington, D.C. He retired in 1886 at age sixty-four and died three years later in St. Paul, Minnesota.[12] Sturgis's co-battalion commander at Canyon Creek, Captain Frederick W. Benteen, was promoted to major in the Ninth Cavalry, was court-martialed for drunkenness and disorderly conduct and suspended from rank and one-half pay for one year, and retired in 1888 to his home in Atlanta, where he argumentatively pontificated about Custer and the Little Bighorn until his death ten years later.[13]

Captain Edward S. Godfrey enjoyed a lengthy career in the cavalry. His Bear's Paw wound caused him discomfort in later years and made it difficult for him to wear a belt or carry arms. Nevertheless, he continued his facility for being involved in all of the Seventh's Indian campaigns with his participation in the fighting at Wounded Knee in 1890. Godfrey served in Cuba during the Spanish-American War and rose to brigadier general before his retirement in 1907. He lived at Cookstown, New Jersey, until his death in 1932.[14] Captain Henry Romeyn, who took over command of the disabled Seventh Cavalry battalion at Bear's Paw, continued in the army but never recovered from his wound, which brought him frequent paroxysms of pain. Court-martialed in 1897 for striking a junior officer after having made slanderous remarks about the man's wife, Romeyn won a remittal of his sentence and retired. He died in 1913 while a patient at Walter Reed General Hospital.[15] Lieutenant Charles Erskine Scott Wood continued as Howard's adjutant after the general became superintendent of West Point. Wood resigned his army commission in 1884 and practiced law in Portland, Oregon, becoming a defender of radical and feminist causes. He also cultivated his interests in literature and the arts, and during the early twentieth century, he became a noted poet and satirist, authoring *Heavenly Discourse*, among other widely heralded works. Wood lived until 1944 at his estate, "The Cats," in Los Gatos, California.[16]

Lieutenant Lovell H. Jerome's promising army career ended tragically after his brave but controversial performance in going into the Nez Perce camp at Bear's Paw. Bibulous habits forced him to resign his commission in 1879 while awaiting sentence of a court-martial. In 1880, Jerome enlisted in the Eighth Cavalry, determined to "go to Texas and win my commission back or never return." Promoted corporal, he took and passed the requisite exams and was recommended for appointment, but regressed, was cited for "frequent acts of drunkenness," and was reduced to the ranks and confined. He later appeared inebriated at inspection and "committed a nuisance on the troop street." On October 30, 1881, Jerome "became so drunk as to be unable to saddle his horse." To avoid "the disgrace attending his trial and conviction," and after an appeal from his father to the secretary of war that he be separated from the service "as speedily as possible," Jerome was discharged on January

31, 1882. In later years, he worked for the U.S. Customs Service, held mining interests in Alaska, and became involved in the McKinley-Roosevelt election campaign of 1900. Jerome became the founder of Alumni Day at West Point, and until shortly before his death in 1935, he remained active in reunion activities at the academy.[17]

Most of the nontreaty Nee-Me-Poo leaders were killed at Bear's Paw. White Bird, of course, remained in Canada until his death. Some surviving warriors and headmen—those who returned from Canada and the Indian Territory—lived out their remaining lives on the Nez Perce Reservation at Lapwai or on the Colville Reservation two hundred miles away at Nespelem, Washington. Husis Kute, the Palouse leader, went to Fort Leavenworth and the Indian Territory with Joseph and served as spiritual mentor to the exiled tribesmen. In 1885, he returned to Lapwai with the Nez Perces assigned there, but later emigrated to the Colville Reservation, where he died.[18] In the years after Bear's Paw, Yellow Bull emerged as an able leader and, along with Joseph, worked tirelessly for his people in the Indian Territory and after. He settled at Colville, but six years later accepted a land allotment and removed his family to Lapwai.[19]

Decades later, many Nez Perce men and women related their experiences with the army in 1877, adding significantly to the knowledge, but also to the perspective, of that history. Among them were Wottolen, the tribal historian (who lived to age 109), Two Moon, White Hawk, and Peopeo Tholekt, all participants in the battles and skirmishes. Over the course of almost three decades, Yellow Wolf, who as a young warrior had lived through the events, gave data to historian Lucullus V. McWhorter and accompanied him several times to the sites of the actions, including Big Hole and Bear's Paw. His reminiscences comprise a vital body of information essential to understanding the course of the struggle from Camas Prairie through Bear's Paw, Canada, the Indian Territory, and after. Yellow Wolf died at the Colville Reservation in 1935.[20] The last Nez Perce survivor of the odyssey was Josiah Red Wolf, who had been but a child when the war took place. He passed away on March 23, 1971, at age ninety-nine.[21]

Joseph lived for twenty-seven years after the fighting ended. Although he had not been the leader of all the nontreaty Nez Perces in their historic trek, that perception by the army, the media, and the American public endured, and to a great extent he came to assume that mantle in the years that followed. Joseph became an anchor for his troubled people during and after their exile in the Indian Territory; he traveled to the nation's capital on their behalf. His favorable persona enhanced his positive image and aided in the final determination to move his tribesmen back to the Northwest in 1885. At Colville, however, he was not initially welcomed by resident tribes, and army troops had to help settle his followers. In 1897, Joseph journeyed again to Washington, D.C., to protest the opening to whites of a substantial portion of the Colville reserve. He visited New York City, and in company with his old nemeses, Generals Oliver O. Howard and Nelson A. Miles, he rode in the dedicatory parade for Grant's Tomb—ironically honoring the president whose policies had brought on the Wallowa crisis. In 1899, he finally got to see his beloved valley in eastern Oregon, but during the visit, white residents told him he could never live there again. Joseph never stopped trying. Four years later, he beseeched an audience in Seattle to help him return home: "I have but a few years to live and would like to die in my old home. My father is buried there, my children are buried there, and I would like to rest by their side." On September 21, 1904, Joseph died in Nespelem, where he was laid to rest.[22]

U.S. Army Casualties, Nez Perce War, 1877

I. WHITE BIRD CANYON, June 17, 1877.
(Sources: Secretary of War, *Report . . . 1877*, 131–32. Corrected as per McDermott, *Forlorn Hope*, and other materials.)

KILLED

No.	NAME	RANK	COMPANY	REGIMENT
1.	Edward R. Theller	First lieut.	G	Twenty-first Infantry
2.	Roman D. Lee	Corporal	H	First Cavalry
3.	Michael Curran	Corporal	H	First Cavalry
4.	Frank A. Marshall	Trumpeter	H	First Cavalry
5.	John Galvin	Saddler	H	First Cavalry
6.	Adalaska B. Crawford	Private	H	First Cavalry
7.	Valentine Edwards	Private	H	First Cavalry
8.	Laurence Kavanagh	Private	H	First Cavalry
9.	James E. Morrisey	Private	H	First Cavalry
10.	John J. Murphy	Private	H	First Cavalry
11.	Olaf Nielson	Private	H	First Cavalry
12.	John Shea	Private	H	First Cavalry
13.	John Simpson	Private	H	First Cavalry
14.	Andrew Werner	Private	H	First Cavalry
15.	Patrick H. Gunn	Sergeant	F	First Cavalry
16.	Thomas Ryan	Sergeant	F	First Cavalry
17.	John L. Thompson	Corporal	F	First Cavalry
18.	John Jones	Trumpeter	F	First Cavalry

19.	Charles Armstrong	Private	F	First Cavalry
20.	Joseph Blaine	Private	F	First Cavalry
21.	Frank E. Burch	Private	F	First Cavalry
22.	James C. Colbert	Private	F	First Cavalry
23.	Patrick Connolly	Private	F	First Cavalry
24.	Lawrence K. Dauch	Private	F	First Cavalry
25.	John H. Donne	Private	F	First Cavalry
26.	William L. Hurlbert	Private	F	First Cavalry
27.	James S. Lewis	Private	F	First Cavalry
28.	William Liston	Private	F	First Cavalry
29.	John M. Martin	Private	F	First Cavalry
30.	John R. Mosforth	Private	F	First Cavalry
31.	David Quinlan	Private	F	First Cavalry
32.	Peter Schullein	Private	F	First Cavalry
33.	Andrew Shaw	Private	F	First Cavalry
34.	Charles Sullivan	Private	F	First Cavalry

WOUNDED

1. Thomas McLaughlin Private   F   First Cavalry
—conical ball; right arm and forearm; flesh wound.
2. Joseph Kelly   Private   H   First Cavalry
—conical ball; left thigh; flesh wound.

II. LOOKING GLASS'S CAMP, July 1, 1877.

NO ARMY CASUALTIES

IIIa. RAINS'S ENCOUNTER, COTTONWOOD, July 3, 1877.
(Sources: Secretary of War, *Report . . . 1877*, 132; and Assistant Surgeon
William R. Hall to Medical Director, Department of the Columbia, July 6,
1877, entry 624, box 1, Office of the Adjutant General. Corrected as per
Regimental Returns . . . First Cavalry, July 1877, roll 166.)

KILLED

No.	NAME	RANK	COMPANY	REGIMENT
1.	Sevier M. Rains	Second lieut.	L	First Cavalry
2.	Charles Lampman	Sergeant	E	First Cavalry
3.	John Burk	Private	E	First Cavalry
4.	Patrick Quinn	Private	E	First Cavalry
5.	Daniel Ryan	Private	E	First Cavalry
6.	William Roche	Private	E	First Cavalry
7.	Franklin Moody	Private	L	First Cavalry

8.	Frederick Meyer	Private	L	First Cavalry
9.	George H. Dinteman	Private	L	First Cavalry
10.	Otto H. Richter	Private	L	First Cavalry
11.	David Carroll	Private	L	First Cavalry

CIVILIANS KILLED
1 William Foster
2. Charles Blewett

IIIb. COTTONWOOD SKIRMISH, July 4, 1877.

NO ARMY CASUALTIES

IIIc. VOLUNTEERS' FIGHT, COTTONWOOD, July 5, 1877.
(Source: Frank Fenn, "The Cottonwood Fight,"
Kooskia, Idaho, *Mountaineer*, April 23, 1927.)

CIVILIANS KILLED
1. Darius B. Randall
2. Benjamin Evans
3. D. H. Howser (*died of wounds*)

CIVILIANS WOUNDED
1. Charles Johnson
2. Alonzo B. Leland

IV. CLEARWATER, July 11–12, 1877.
(Sources: Secretary of War, *Report . . . 1877*, 32–33; "List of Wounded in
Gen. Howard's expedition . . . Battle of Clearwater." Corrected as per
Regimental Returns . . . First Cavalry, July 1877, roll 166; Regimental
Returns . . . Fourth Artillery, July 1877, roll 30; and Regimental Returns . . .
Twenty-first Infantry, July 1877, roll 220.)

KILLED

No.	NAME	RANK	COMPANY	REGIMENT	DATE
1.	James A. Workman	Sergeant	A	Fourth Artillery	7/12
2.	Charles Marquardt	Corporal	A	Fourth Artillery	7/12
3.	James Doyle	Corporal	I	Twenty-first Infantry	7/11
4.	Charles Clark	Private	I	Twenty-first Infantry	7/11
5.	Juan Platta	Private	E	First Cavalry	7/11
6.	Alson Compton	Private	I	Twenty-first Infantry	7/12

7.	Fred Montaudon	Private	E	Fourth Artillery	7/11
8.	William Hutchinson	Private	C	Twenty-first Infantry	7/11
9.	Maier Cohn	Private	H	First Cavalry	7/12
10.	Edward Wykoff	Private	B	Twenty-first Infantry	7/11
11.	David McNally	Private	E	Twenty-first Infantry	7/11
12.	Frederick Sandmier	Blacksmith	E	First Cavalry	7/11
13.	Charles Simonds	Private	G	Fourth Artillery	7/12

—originally carried as missing in action morning of 7/12.

WOUNDED

1. Eugene A. Bancroft   Captain   A   Fourth Artillery   7/11
   —conical ball; left shoulder and thorax; severe wound; apex of lung wounded; ball extracted from shoulder.
2. Charles A. Williams   Second lieut. C   Twenty-first Infantry 7/11
   —conical ball; right forearm and right thigh; slight wound; flesh wound.
3. Abraham Repert   Sergeant   I   Twenty-first Infantry 7/11
   —conical ball; left buttock; severe wound; ball not found.
4. Levis Shaffner   Private   I   Twenty-first Infantry 7/11
   —conical ball; right thigh, left thigh, and left leg; three flesh wounds; ball extracted.
5. Richard Hanson   Sergeant   E   First Cavalry   Unk
   —conical ball; right leg; slight wound; flesh wound.
6. William Buckow   Private   B   Twenty-first Infantry 7/11
   —right thigh; severe wound; compound fracture of lower extremity of femur; amputated through middle third.
7. Daniel McGrath   Private   H   Twenty-first Infantry 7/11
   —conical ball; left arm; severe wound; resection of three inches of humerus.
8. Henry V. Richit   First sergeant C   Twenty-first Infantry 7/11
   —round ball; left thorax; severe wound; perforating wound of thorax.
9. George Graham   Private   E   Fourth Artillery   7/11
   —round ball; back and jaw; slight wound; two flesh wounds.
10. Bernard Simpson   Sergeant   L   First Cavalry   7/12
    —conical ball; left leg; severe wound; ball not found.
11. William Garvean   Private   I   Twenty-first Infantry 7/11
    —conical ball; scalp wound; slight wound.
12. Ephraim Hess   Corporal   A   Fourth Artillery   7/11
    —conical ball; left arm; severe wound; fracture of the humerus, not comminuted; wound enlarged and explored.
13. Joseph Held   Trumpeter   H   First Cavalry   7/12
    —conical ball; left foot; slight wound; flesh wound.
14. Francis Winters   Private   B   Twenty-first Infantry 7/11
    —conical ball; left thigh; slight wound; flesh wound.

15. Gottleib Weikerle   Private   I   Twenty-first Infantry 7/11
    —conical ball; buttock; severe wound; flesh wound through both buttocks.
16. Fritz Heber   Private   M   First Cavalry   Unk
    —conical ball; right arm and right leg; severe wound; flesh wounds.
17. Peter Murphy   Corporal   I   Twenty-first Infantry 7/11
    —conical ball; right arm and thorax; flesh wounds; ball extracted.
18. William Kenkle   First sergeant I   Twenty-first Infantry 7/11
    —conical ball; thorax; flesh wound.
19. Thomas Burns   Corporal   E   Fourth Artillery   7/11
    —conical ball; left foot; flesh wound.
20. Thomas Connelly   Corporal   H   Twenty-first Infantry 7/11
    —round ball; back; slight wound; flesh wound; ball extracted.
21. Samuel Ferguson   Private   E   First Cavalry   Unk
    —round ball; left thigh; slight wound; flesh wound.
22. Frederick Schickler   Private   H   Twenty-first Infantry 7/11
    —round ball; right arm, left thigh, and right hand; three flesh wounds.
23. Peter Blumenberg   Sergeant   E   Fourth Artillery   7/11
    —conical ball; thorax; probably not a penetrating wound of thorax; ball
    extracted.
24. William Barton   Private   B   Twenty-first Infantry 7/11
    —round ball; left shoulder; flesh wound.
25. Eugene McFilmore   Corporal   E   Fourth Artillery   7/11
    —conical ball; left arm; severe wound; fracture of humerus, not
    comminuted; wound enlarged and explored.
26. Charles Carlin   Corporal   I   Twenty-first Infantry 7/13
    —conical ball; left leg; posterior of artery wounded; severe wound;
    femoral artery tied. *Died en route* from exhaustion due to loss of blood
    on the field.
27. John G. Hinneman   Musician   I   Twenty-first Infantry 7/13
    —conical ball; hip; severe wound; ball passed into the abdominal cavity;
    urine escaping from wound. *Died en route* from the field to hospital.

V. KAMIAH, July 13, 1877.
(Source: Secretary of War, *Report . . . 1877*, 133.)

WOUNDED

No.	NAME	RANK	COMPANY	REGIMENT

1. William Mulcahy   Corporal   A   Fourth Artillery
   —rifle ball; wounded by a sharpshooter; gunshot wound of the forehead
   and gouging of frontal bone.

VI. WEIPPE PRAIRIE, July 17, 1877.
(Source: McWhorter, *Hear Me*, 338; and McWhorter, *Yellow Wolf*, 106.)

INDIAN SCOUTS KILLED
1. Nez Perce scout John Levi (Sheared Wolf)

INDIAN SCOUTS WOUNDED
1. Nez Perce scout Abraham Brooks—wounded in shoulder. *Died later.*
2. Nez Perce scout James Reuben

VII. BIG HOLE, August 9–10, 1877.
(Source: Aubrey Haines, *An Elusive Victory*, 155–62.)

KILLED

No.	Name	Rank	Company	Regiment
1.	James H. Bradley	First lieut.	B	Seventh Infantry
2.	William L. English	First lieut.	I	Seventh Infantry
3.	William Logan	Captain	A	Seventh Infantry
4.	Herman Broetz	Private	I	Seventh Infantry
5.	Mathew Butterly	Private	E*	Seventh Infantry
6.	McKindra L. Drake	Private	H	Seventh Infantry
7.	Robert L. Edgeworth	First sergeant	G	Seventh Infantry
8.	Jacob Eisenhut	Corporal	D	Seventh Infantry
9.	Michael Gallagher	Musician	D	Seventh Infantry
10.	Michael Hogan	Sergeant	I	Seventh Infantry
11.	John Kleis	Artificer	K	Seventh Infantry
12.	Gottlieb Mantz	Private	G	Seventh Infantry
13.	William H. Martin	Sergeant	G	Seventh Infantry
14.	Daniel McCaffery	Corporal	I	Seventh Infantry
15.	James McGuire	Private	F	Seventh Infantry
16.	F. John O'Brien	Private	G	Seventh Infantry
17.	Dominick O'Connor	Corporal	G	Seventh Infantry
18.	Edward Page	Sergeant	L	Second Cavalry
19.	William H. Payne	Corporal	D	Seventh Infantry
20.	William D. Pomeroy	Private	F	Seventh Infantry
21.	Robert E. Sale	Corporal	G	Seventh Infantry
22.	John B. Smith	Private	A	Seventh Infantry
23.	Thomas P. Stinebaker	Musician	K	Seventh Infantry
24.	Frederick Stortz	First sergeant	K	Seventh Infantry
25.	William W. Watson	Sergeant	F	Seventh Infantry

WOUNDED

1.	Charles A. Coolidge	First lieut.	A	Seventh Infantry
2.	John Gibbon	Colonel	CO	Seventh Infantry
3.	Constant Williams	Captain	F	Seventh Infantry
4.	Charles A. Woodruff	First lieut.	K	Seventh Infantry
5.	John Abbott	Corporal	D	Seventh Infantry
6.	Charles Alberts	Private	A	Seventh Infantry
7.	George Banghart	Private	G	Seventh Infantry
8.	James Bell	Sergeant	E*	Seventh Infantry
9.	Robert Bensinger	Sergeant	G	Seventh Infantry
10.	Lorenzo D. Brown	Private	A	Seventh Infantry
11.	James Burk	Private	G	Seventh Infantry
12.	John Burns	Corporal	E*	Seventh Infantry
13.	Washington Clark	Private	I	Seventh Infantry
14.	John J. Connor	Private	G	Seventh Infantry
15.	Timothy Cronan	Musician	D	Seventh Infantry
16.	Richard N. Cunliffe	Corporal	I	Seventh Infantry
17.	Patrick C. Daly	Sergeant	D	Seventh Infantry
18.	Mathew Devine	Private	K	Seventh Infantry
19.	Joseph Devoss	Private	I	Seventh Infantry
20.	John Erickson	Musician	F	Seventh Infantry
21.	Patrick Fallon	Private	I	Seventh Infantry
22.	John W. H. Frederick	Sergeant	G	Seventh Infantry
23.	Charles B. Gould	Private	F	Second Cavalry
24.	Davis Heaton	Private	K	Seventh Infantry
25.	Edward D. Hunter	Private	F	Seventh Infantry
26.	Philo O. Hurlburt	Private	K	Seventh Infantry
27.	James Keys	Private	D	Seventh Infantry
28.	James C. Lehmer	Private	A	Seventh Infantry
29.	George Leher	Private	A	Seventh Infantry
30.	Christian Luttman	Corporal	F	Seventh Infantry
31.	George Maurer	Private	F	Seventh Infantry
32.	Charles A. Robbecke	Private	G	Seventh Infantry
33.	William Thompson	Private	I	Seventh Infantry
34.	William Wright	Sergeant	E*	Seventh Infantry

*—Attached to Company D

CIVILIANS KILLED
1. John Armstrong
2. Henry S. Bostwick
3. Lynde C. Elliot
4. Alvin Lockwood
5. Campbell Mitchell
6. David Morrow

CIVILIANS WOUNDED
1. Jacob Baker
2. Otto Leifer
3. Myron Lockwood
4. William Ryan

VIII. CAMAS MEADOWS, August 20, 1877.
(Sources: "List of Wounded in Skirmish on Camas Meadow"; and Regimental Returns . . . Second Cavalry, August 1877, roll 719.)

KILLED

No.	Name	Rank	Company	Regiment
1.	Bernard A. Brooks	Trumpeter	B	First Cavalry

—shot in heart.

WOUNDED

1. Henry M. Benson   First lieut.   L *(attached)* Seventh Infantry
—ball; hips; severe flesh wound; simple dressing.
2. Henry Wilkins   First sergeant L   Second Cavalry
—ball; head; slight wound; simple dressing.
3. Harry Garland   Corporal   L   Second Cavalry
—ball; left iliac region; severe wound; fracture crest of ilium; simple dressing.
4. Samuel A. Glass   Farrier   L   Second Cavalry
—ball; peliose; severe wound; penetrating wound; simple dressing.
Died of wounds August 24, 1877.
5. Wilfred Clark   Private   L   Second Cavalry
—ball; left shoulder; slight wound; simple dressing.
6. Harry Trevor   Private   L   Second Cavalry
—ball; lung and left scapula; severe wound; penetrated cavity; simple dressing. *Died of wounds October 4, 1877.*
7. William H. Jones   Private   L   Second Cavalry
—ball; over right patella; slight wound; simple dressing.
8. James King   Farrier   I   First Cavalry
—ball; left forearm, upper third; severe wound; simple dressing.

IX. CANYON CREEK, September 13, 1877.
(Source: "List of Wounded . . . Canon Creek." Corrected as per Regimental Returns . . . Seventh Cavalry, September, 1877, roll 72.)

KILLED

No.	Name	Rank	Company	Regiment
1.	Nathan T. Brown	Private	L	Seventh Cavalry
2.	Frank J. Gosselin	Private	M	Seventh Cavalry

WOUNDED

1. Thomas H. French   Captain   M   Seventh Cavalry
—hand; slight wound.
2. Edson F. Archer   Blacksmith L   Seventh Cavalry
—conical ball; chest; penetrating; severe wound; opiates, simple dressing. *Died of wounds September 14, 1877.*

3. Edward Deverin   Sergeant   F   Seventh Cavalry
—conical ball; left arm; flesh wound; slight wound; simple dressing.
4. George A. Campfield Private   F   Seventh Cavalry
—conical ball; left shoulder; flesh wound; severe wound; simple dressing.
5. James Lawlor   Private   G   Seventh Cavalry
—conical ball; skull; fracture of; severe wound; opiates, simple dressing.
Died of wounds September 18, 1877.
6. William Young   Private   G   Seventh Cavalry
—conical ball; both hips; flesh; severe wound; simple dressing.
7. Edward B. Cromby   Private   I   Seventh Cavalry
—conical ball; left shoulder; flesh wound; severe wound; simple dressing.
8. Levi Weigel   Private   L   Seventh Cavalry
—conical ball; right leg; fracture; splints; right shoulder; slight flesh
wound; simple dressing.
9. Albert B. Fowler   Private   L   Seventh Cavalry
—conical ball; left leg; flesh wound; slight wound; simple dressing.
10. Jacob P. Watson   Private   M   Seventh Cavalry
—conical ball; left ankle joint; severe wound; simple dressing.
11. Lewis M. Adkins   Private   M   Seventh Cavalry
—slight wound.
12. John Rivers   Farrier   I   Seventh Cavalry

X. Cow Island, September 23, 1877.
(Sources: Fort Benton *Benton Record*, October 5, 1877;
and Hardin, Diary, September 28, 1877.)

Killed

No.	Name	Rank	Company	Regiment
1.	Byron Martin	Private	B	Seventh Infantry

Civilians Wounded
1. E. W. Buckwalter—hand and side.
2. George Trautman—right shoulder.

XI. Cow Creek Canyon, September 25, 1877.
(Source: Secretary of War, *Report . . . 1877*, 557.)

Killed
1. Citizen volunteer Edmund Bradley

XII. Bear's Paw, September 30–October 5, 1877.

(Sources: Surgeon Henry R. Tilton to Medical Director, Department of
Dakota, October 3, 1877, entry 624, box 1, Office of the Adjutant General.
Corrected as per Regimental Returns . . . Seventh Cavalry, September and
October 1877, roll 72; Regimental Returns . . . Fifth Infantry, September
and October 1877, roll 58; and Regimental Returns . . . Second Cavalry,
September and October 1877, roll 719.)

Killed

No.	Name	Rank	Company	Regiment	Date
1.	Owen Hale	Captain	K	Seventh Cavalry	9/30
2.	J. Williams Biddle	Second lieut.	K	Seventh Cavalry	9/30
3.	Otto Wilde	First sergeant	K	Seventh Cavalry	9/30
4.	Max Mielke	Sergeant	K	Seventh Cavalry	9/30
5.	Henry W. Raichel	Sergeant	K	Seventh Cavalry	9/30
6.	William Whitlow	Private	K	Seventh Cavalry	9/30
7.	Francis Roth	Private	K	Seventh Cavalry	9/30
8.	Charles F. Hardick	Private	K	Seventh Cavalry	9/30
9.	Frank Knaupp	Private	K	Seventh Cavalry	9/30
10.	George W. McDermott	First sergeant	A	Seventh Cavalry	9/30
11.	John E. Cleveland	Private	A	Seventh Cavalry	9/30
12.	Lewis Kelly	Private	A	Seventh Cavalry	9/30
13.	Samuel McIntyre	Private	A	Seventh Cavalry	9/30
14.	Michael Martin	First sergeant	D	Seventh Cavalry	9/30
15.	James H. Alberts	Sergeant	D	Seventh Cavalry	9/30
16.	William I. Randall	Private	D	Seventh Cavalry	9/30
17.	David E. Dawsey	Private	D	Seventh Cavalry	9/30
18.	John Haddo	Corporal	B	Fifth Infantry	9/30
19.	Thomas Geogehgan	Private	C	Fifth Infantry	9/30
20.	Richard M. Peshall	Private	G	Fifth Infantry	9/30
21.	John Irving	Private	G	Second Cavalry	10/1

Wounded

1. Myles Moylan   Captain   A   Seventh Cavalry   9/30
—gunshot wound; right thigh (flesh); severe wound.
2. Edward S. Godfrey   Captain   D   Seventh Cavalry   9/30
—gunshot wound; left lumbar region; flesh wound; slight wound.
3. Henry Romeyn   First lieut.   A   Fifth Infantry   9/30
—gunshot wound; right chest (penetrating); severe wound.
4. George W. Baird   First lieut.   AAAG   Fifth Infantry   9/30
—gunshot fracture; left forearm and left ear; slight wound; severe wound.
5. Daniel S. Wright   Private   A   Seventh Cavalry   9/30
—gunshot wound; right thigh; severe wound.

6. Thomas D. Godman   Sergeant   A   Seventh Cavalry   9/30
    —gunshot wound; left hand and left shoulder; slight wound.

7. Thomas Denning   Private   A   Seventh Cavalry   9/30
    —gunshot wound; right popliteal region; slight wound.

8. Charles Miller   Private   A   Seventh Cavalry   9/30
    —gunshot wound; neck and right shoulder; severe wound.

9. Otto Durselen   Sergeant   A   Seventh Cavalry   9/30
    —gunshot wound; right hip and bladder. *Died of wounds.*

10. Michael Gilbert   Private   A   Seventh Cavalry   9/30
    —gunshot wound; right shoulder; severe wound.

11. George W. Savage   Private   A   Seventh Cavalry   9/30
    —gunshot wound; both thighs (flesh); severe wound.

12. Howard H. Weaver   Private   A   Seventh Cavalry   9/30
    —gunshot wound; right arm; slight wound.

13. James E. Christopher Trumpeter   A   Seventh Cavalry   9/30
    —gunshot wound; left knee; severe wound.

14. James Clark   Private   D   Seventh Cavalry   9/30
    —gunshot wound; right shoulder; severe wound.

15. Frederick W. Deetline Private   D   Seventh Cavalry   9/30
    —gunshot wound; right shoulder and left elbow; severe wound.

16. John Curran   Private   D   Seventh Cavalry   9/30
    —gunshot wound; left hand; index finger amputated.

17. Charles H. Welch   Sergeant   D   Seventh Cavalry   9/30
    —gunshot fracture; right thigh and left thigh; severe wound; flesh wound.

18. Uriah S. Lewis   Private   D   Seventh Cavalry   9/30
    —gunshot wound; right calf; slight wound.

19. John M. Jones   Private   D   Seventh Cavalry   9/30
    —gunshot wound; left shoulder and left arm; slight wound. Carried on
    some reports as James H. Johnson.

20. Thomas Herwood   Trumpeter   D   Seventh Cavalry   9/30
    —gunshot wound; left side chest; penetrating wound.

21. John Quinn   Corporal   D   Seventh Cavalry   9/30
    —gunshot wound; left shoulder; severe wound.

22. David E. Baker   Private   D   Seventh Cavalry   9/30
    —gunshot wound; right thigh; severe wound.

23. Michael Delany   Corporal   K   Seventh Cavalry   9/30
    —gunshot wound; right chest; penetrating wound; dangerous.

24. Peter Allen   Private   K   Seventh Cavalry   9/30
    —gunshot fracture; left radius; arm amputated.

25. William H. McGee   Private   K   Seventh Cavalry   9/30
    —gunshot wound; right leg.

26. John Schwerer   Private   K   Seventh Cavalry   9/30
    —gunshot wound; left leg.

27. John Meyers   Saddler   K   Seventh Cavalry   9/30
    —gunshot wound; left hand.
28. George A. Sorrell   Private   K   Seventh Cavalry   9/30
    —gunshot wound; right wrist and left hand.
29. John Shawer   Private   K   Seventh Cavalry   9/30
    —gunshot wound; left heel; slight wound.
30. John Nolan   Sergeant   K   Seventh Cavalry   9/30
    —gunshot wound; left lumbar region (hip).
31. Emil Taube   Private   K   Seventh Cavalry   9/30
    —gunshot wound; scalp; slight wound.
32. Michael Murphy   Private   K   Seventh Cavalry   9/30
    —gunshot wound; chest and abdomen; dangerous wound.
33. John Foley   Private   K   Seventh Cavalry   9/30
34. Charles L. Smith   Private   K   Seventh Cavalry   9/30
    —gunshot wound; left thigh; severe wound.
35. George A. Dowell   Private   K   Seventh Cavalry   Unk
    —right wrist and left hand; slight wound.
36. Daniel Lyons   Blacksmith   K   Seventh Cavalry   9/30
37. Jean B. D. Gallenne   Private   M   Seventh Cavalry   9/30
                         (Hosp. Stwd)
    —gunshot fracture; left ankle.
38. James Farrell   Private   F   Second Cavalry   9/30
    —gunshot wound, right elbow.
39. Patrick Martin   Private   F   Second Cavalry   9/30
40. Lewis Gensler   Private   I   Fifth Infantry   9/30
    —gunshot wound; fractured left forearm; arm amputated.
41. Joseph A. Cable   Sergeant   I   Fifth Infantry   9/30
    —gunshot fracture; left femur; flesh wound; right thigh; severe wound.
    Died of wounds October 15, 1877.
42. Patrick McCanna   Private   I   Fifth Infantry   9/30
    —gunshot wound; right hip; slight wound.
43. John Andrews   Private   I   Fifth Infantry   9/30
    —gunshot wound; left side face.
44. Nicholas B. Ward   Private   I   Fifth Infantry   9/30
    —gunshot wound; both thighs (flesh); severe wound.
45. Joseph Kohler   Private   I   Fifth Infantry   9/30
    —gunshot wound; abdomen. *Died of wounds October 1, 1877.*
46. George Krager   Sergeant   G   Fifth Infantry   9/30
    —gunshot wound; left side face and right hand; severe wound.
47. Daniel Horgan   Private   G   Fifth Infantry   9/30
    —gunshot wound; right leg; slight wound.
48. John Ferrons   Private   D   Fifth Infantry   9/30
    —gunshot wound; left leg; slight wound.

49. Fleming S. Griffith	Private	G	Fifth Infantry	9/30
50. Jesse O'Neill	Musician	G	Fifth Infantry	9/30

—gunshot fracture; left thigh.

INDIAN SCOUTS WOUNDED

1. Hump, Minneconjou Lakota   9/30
   —right shoulder; slight.
2. White Wolf, Northern Cheyenne   9/30
   —skull fractured.

Known Nez Perce Casualties, 1877

(Sources: McWhorter, *Hear Me*, 253–54, 267–71, 292, 323, 328 n. 7,
336–39, 374, 424–25, 486; McWhorter, *Yellow Wolf*, 60, 76–77, 186 n. 5,
290; MacDonald, "Nez Perces," 243–44; "Nez Perce Warriors, 1877";
Aubrey Haines, *An Elusive Victory*, 167–69; and Otis Halfmoon,
telephone communication with author, May 2, 1996.)

I. WHITE BIRD CANYON, June 17, 1877.

NONE KILLED

WOUNDED
Chellooyeen (Bow and Arrow Case)—wounded, right side waist.
Espowyes (Heavy Weapon)—shot in side of abdomen, not serious.

II. LOOKING GLASS'S CAMP, July 1, 1877.

KILLED
Nennin Chekoostin (Black Raven)—died of wounds.
Unidentified woman—drowned.
Unidentified infant—drowned.

WOUNDED
Temme Ilppilp (Red Heart)—gunshot wound in right thigh.
Tahkoopen (Shot Leg)—flesh wound in leg.
Peopeo Tholekt (Bird Alighting)—gunshot wound in right leg.

IIIa. Rains's Encounter, Cottonwood, July 3, 1877.

NONE KILLED OR WOUNDED.

IIIb. Cottonwood Skirmish, July 4, 1877.

NONE KILLED OR WOUNDED.

IIIc. Volunteers' Fight, Cottonwood, July 5, 1877.

KILLED
Weesculatat, or Mimpow Owyeen (Open Mouth)—died of wounds.

WOUNDED
Two unidentified warriors

IV. Clearwater, July 11–12, 1877.

KILLED
Wayakat (Going Across)
Yoomtis Kunin (Grizzly Bear Blanket)—died of wounds.
Heinmot Ilppilp (Red Thunder)
Lelooskin (Whittling)

WOUNDED
Howwallits (Mean Man)—injured by howitzer fire in village.
Kipkip Owyeen (Wounded Breast)—wound, serious.
Pahkatos Owyeen (Five Wounds)—wounded in right hand.
Old Yellow Wolf—head wounds.
Heinmot Hihhih (Yellow Wolf)—gunshot wound, left arm near wrist; under
    left eye.
Elaskolatat (Animal Entering a Hole)—leg wound.

V. Kamiah, July 13, 1877.

NONE KILLED OR WOUNDED.

VI. Weippe Prairie, July 17, 1877.

NONE KILLED OR WOUNDED.

VII. BIG HOLE, August 9-10, 1877.

KILLED

Wahlitits (Shore Crossing)
Wife of Wahlitits
Sarpsis Ilppilp (Red Moccasin Tops)
Wahchumyas (Rainbow)
Pahkatos (Five Wounds)
Hahtelekin
Pahka Tahtahank (Five Fogs)
Watyetmas Likleinen
Wife of Watyetmas Likleinen
Tahkinpalloo
Tewit Toitoi
Wisookaankith
Tonawihnikth (woman)
Oyema (woman)
Iptsalatat (woman)
Tosciiahpoa
Ipnasapahyutsan

Heyumtananmi
Ellisyacon
Ipnanyetama Lilpith
Tsiayah
No Heart
Patsakonmi
Wife of Watyetmasliklinin
Red-headed Woodpecker
Chemih
Black Owl
Wahkinkinno Ilppilp
Watisto Kaiikth
Otsilwah (woman)
White Hawk (woman)
Toktawetisha (woman)
Wayatanatolatpath (woman)

(In addition to these individuals, at least nine other Indian men, women, and children of undetermined identities died at the Big Hole, with total fatalities perhaps numbering between sixty and ninety killed.)

WOUNDED

Jekamkun
Wahnistas Aswettesk
White Eagle—*died later.*
Gray Eagle—*died later.*
Weweetsa (Log)
Red Heart—*died later.*
Wife of Tom Hill
Daughter of Blacktail Eagle
Takiyaya
Mother of Elliuyatsitskon
Welatolikakats (shot by citizens after leaving battlefield)

Black Tail
White Feather
Toktawetisha—*died later.*
Quiloishkish
Strong Eagle
Elliutalatkit
Hiumath
Wife of Melmelistalikaia
Wife of Ispanyes
Lakantessin
John Dog

(Certainly many more Nee-Me-Poo were wounded in the fighting at the Big Hole.)

VIII. Camas Meadows, August 20, 1877.

Killed
Unknown, but possibly six warriors killed in Norwood's encounter.

Wounded
Exact number unknown. One was Peopeo Tholekt—wounded in head.

IX. Canyon Creek, September 13, 1877.

Killed
Tookleiks (Fish Trap)—possibly killed on September 14, 1877.

Wounded
Silooyelam—left ankle.
Eeahlokoon—right leg.
Elaskolatat (Animal Entering a Hole)—left hip and thigh.

X. Cow Island, September 23, 1877.

Killed
None

Wounded
Husis Owyeen (Wounded Head)—grazed by wood splintered by bullet.

XI. Cow Creek Canyon, September 25, 1877.

Casualties unknown.

XII. Bear's Paw, September 30–October 5, 1877.

Killed

Toohoolhoolzote
Ollokot
Looking Glass
Tohtohaliken
Lakoyee
Timlihpoosman
Young Sookoups

Koyehknown
Kowwaspo
Peopeo Ipsewahk (Lone Bird)
Red Legs
Eagle Necklace, Sr.
Lying

Heyoomeekahlikt (Grizzly Bear on His Back)
Wawookya Wasaaw (Lean Elk—Poker Joe)

(At least eleven other people died during the fighting at Bear's Paw, most of them killed during the first day's combat.)

Wounded
Eagle Necklace, Jr.   Tomyahnin
Rainbow, Jr.

(Estimates of the number of wounded in the six days of fighting at Bear's Paw range between forty and sixty.)

XIII. Killed by enemy tribesmen during the course of the war.

Ahtailakin—killed by Crows.   Mulmulken
Tahwistokaitat   Sotahwa
Watyetmestahmoe Wiyun   Hemene Haihaiih—killed by Blackfeet.
Tipyahlanah Kapskaps (Strong Eagle) White Hark (Hawk?)
Pitpeelulin   Tipsus
Wamaskayah   Jouwolkonkon
Teweyannah   Wainatakacan
Weyahtanatolakawit—killed by Blackfeet.

XIV. Killed, but with place and circumstances unknown.

Imnawahna

Notes

In referencing works in the notes, short citations have been used, as have the abbreviations listed below. Complete references can be found in the bibliography.

BYU   Harold B. Lee Library, Brigham Young University
DPL   Western History Department, Denver Public Library
IU   Lilly Library, Indiana University
LBNM   Little Bighorn Battlefield National Monument
LC   Library of Congress
MHI   U.S. Army Military History Institute, Army War College
NA   National Archives
USGS   United States Geographical Survey

CHAPTER I

1. Also given as Nimipu, Nimiipu, Numepo, Nu-me-poo, and Ne-mee-poo. The spelling, "Nee-Me-Poo," is subscribed to by the member offices of the Nez Perce (Nee-Me-Poo) National Historic Trail Advisory Council, i.e., the Department of Agriculture (Forest Service), the Department of the Interior (National Park Service, Bureau of Land Management), the Nez Perce Tribe of Idaho, the Nez Perce Tribe of Washington, and the states of Oregon, Idaho, Wyoming, and Montana. See *Nez Perce . . . Trail Comprehensive Plan*, 3. For the variety of spellings, as well as other names given the people by other tribes, see Swanton, *Indian Tribes*, 400–401; and Hodge, *Handbook of American Indians*, 2:67.

2. For further details of the physical setting of the Nez Perce homeland, see the following, from which the above description was drawn: Atwood, *Physiographic Provinces*, 408–14; Fenneman, *Physiography of Western United States*, 225, 237–39, 248–49; Thomson and Ballard, *Geology and Gold . . . North Central Idaho*, 12–17; Warren Wagner, *A Geological Reconnaissance . . . Snake and Salmon Rivers*, 1–3; Alfred Anderson, *The Geology . . . Orofino, Idaho*, 5–6; and Lindgren, *Geological Reconnaissance*, 59, 61. The area traditionally occupied by the Nez Perces approximates all or parts of the following modern counties: *Idaho*—Idaho, Clearwater,

Nez Perce, Adams, Latah, and Lewis; *Oregon*—Wallowa, Baker, and Union; *Washington*—Asotin, Garfield, and Columbia.

3. This overview of Nee-Me-Poo culture is drawn from the following sources: Hodge, *Handbook of American Indians*, 2:65–67, 519–20; Swanton, *Indian Tribes*, 400–403; Spinden, *Nez Perce Indians*, passim; McBeth, *Nez Perces*, passim; Josephy, *Nez Perce Indians*, 14–30; Josephy, *Patriot Chiefs*, 315, 317; Francis Haines, *Nez Perces*, 8–16; Walker, *Conflict and Schism*, 13, 16–17; Coale, "Ethnohistorical Sources"; Allan Smith, "Traditional Culture"; McWhorter, *Yellow Wolf*, 295–300; and Otis Halfmoon, communication with author, Nez Perce National Historical Park, Spalding, Idaho, November 8, 1995, and April 23, 1996. See in particular the discussion of the term, "Nez Perce," in Thompson, *Historic Resource Study, Spalding Area*, 1–2.

In addition, for Nez Perce prehistory, see Aikens, "Far West"; Josephy, "Origins of the Nez Perce Indians," 4–13, much of which is in Josephy, *Nez Perce Indians*. For the Nez Perce language and examples of tribal folklore, see Aoki, *Nez Perce Texts*.

4. While discussions of the impact of the acquisition of horses among the Nez Perces is included in many of the titles in note 3, see in addition Ewers, "Horse Complex"; and Francis Haines, "Nez Perce Horses."

5. Francis Haines, "Nez Perce Horses," 10–11; Francis Haines, *Nez Perces*, 17–22; Josephy, *Nez Perce Indians*, 19–20, 33–34; Thomas, "Pi.Lu'.Ye.Kin," 1, 4, 6–8. The intertribal influences were reciprocal, with the Nez Perces contributing significantly to the Crows' culture, as well. Diana Miles, communication with author, Nez Perce National Historical Park, Spalding, Idaho, January 22, 1996.

6. Whalen, "Nez Perces' Relationship to Their Land," 30–32. See also Josephy, *Nez Perce Indians*, 24–25.

7. It should be noted that many so-called "Christian tenets" were already long-practiced traditions in Nez Perce society. For example, they believed in a single creator deity called Hunywat long before the coming of the missionaries and their "God." Otis Halfmoon, communication with author, Nez Perce National Historical Park, Spalding, Idaho, November 8, 1995; and Diana Miles, communication with author, Spalding, Idaho, January 22, 1996.

8. Walker, *Conflict and Schism*, 32–44. In-depth treatment of the fur traders and missionaries among the Nez Perces is in Francis Haines, *Nez Perces*, 46–56, 71–110; Josephy, *Nez Perce Indians*, 40–78, 81–103ff.; and Thompson, *Historic Resource Study, Spalding Area*, 5–66. Discussion of the religion-based schism is in Josephy, *Nez Perce Indians*, 245–48. See also Ray, "Ethnohistory of the Joseph Band."

9. For the Dreamer religion and its appearance and application among the Nez Perces, see Francis Haines, *Nez Perces*, 193–96; Josephy, *Nez Perce Indians*, 434–46; Hodge, *Handbook of American Indians*, 2:602–3; and Burns, *Jesuits and the Indian Wars*, 365. An in-depth, though dated, study is in Mooney, "Ghost-Dance Religion," 708–45.

10. Information presented here about the Nez Perce bands is derived from Josephy, *Patriot Chiefs*, 314; Lebain, Interview, Camp Manscripts, IU; Yellow Bull, Interview, BYU; Thomas, "Pi.Lu'.Ye.Kin," 7–8. For the Palouse, see Swanton, *Indian Tribes*, 433–34; Hodge, *Handbook of American Indians*, 2:195; and Trafzer and Scheureman, *Chief Joseph's Allies*.

Knowledge about the number, identification, and distribution of early Nez Perce bands is sketchy. Francis Haines stated that the entire tribe occupied as many as seventy villages (Haines, *Nez Perces*, 15), presumably, though unstated, with several of them representing single bands. From data derived from the 1855 treaty councils, McWhorter (McWhorter, *Hear Me*, 608–9) listed twenty-one locations of Nez Perce chiefs and their followers, while Josephy (Josephy, *Nez Perce Indians*, 162–63) presents similar village locations for sixteen leaders for the period 1836–47. These villages, scattered as they appeared, seem to have politically coalesced to constitute the few major distinct bands acknowledged by the time of the treaties of 1855 and 1863 and the years preceding the war of 1877.

11. Drury, "Lawyer, Head Chief," 2–7. A comprehensive treatment of Lawyer appears in Drury, *Chief Lawyer*. Many Nez Perce names are either not translatable into English, or, when translatable, are too lengthy and complexly convoluted by English for textual use. Throughout this document, the Nee-Me-Poo name will be retained unless a preferred and commonly accepted English equivalent exists. In all instances, Nez Perce names will be introduced phonetically in Nee-Me-Poo whenever that equivalent is known. Generally, long-established spelling will be followed as presented in McWhorter, *Yellow Wolf*; McWhorter, *Hear Me*; and Josephy, *Nez Perce Indians*.

12. For Old Joseph, see Josephy, *Nez Perce Indians*, 182, 189–91, 447–50, and passim; Francis Haines, *Nez Perces*, 77, 92, 115–17; Josephy, *Patriot Chiefs*, 319–20. Quote is from Commissioner of Indian Affairs, *Report . . . 1859*, 420–21, as quoted in Francis Haines, *Nez Perces*, 152.

13. For specifics, see Royce, "Indian Land Cessions," Pt. 2:806–7, pl. 16; Kappler, *Indian Affairs*, 2:702–6; and Kip, *Indian Council at Walla Walla*. A nonlegal description of the reservation is as follows: "The lands reserved by the treaty of 1855 embraced all the country enclosed by a line beginning at the source of the south fork of the Palouse, extending south-westerly to the mouth of the Tucannon, up the Tucannon to its source in the Blue Mountains, along this range in a general southerly direction to a point on Grand[e] Rond[e] River, midway between the Grand[e] Rond[e] and Wallowa Creek, along the divide between the Wallowa Creek and Powder River, crossing Snake River at the mouth of Powder River, thence in an easterly direction to Salmon River fifty miles above the mouth of the Little Salmon, thence north to the Bitter Root Mountains, and thence west to the place of beginning." Bancroft, *History of Washington, Idaho, and Montana*, 485. See also the comprehensive accounts of the 1855 treaty council in Josephy, *Nez Perce Indians*, 315–38; and Francis Haines, *Nez Perces*, 119–32. Captain Benjamin L. E. Bonneville first used the term "Lower Nez Perces" to distinguish the Wallowa people from those east of Snake River. Josephy, *Nez Perce Indians*, 108.

14. Walker, *Conflict and Schism*, 45; Thompson, *Historic Resource Study, Spalding Area*, 85; and MacDonald, "Nez Perces," 222–23. MacDonald's account, originally published serially in 1878 in the Deer Lodge *New North-West*, presented the first Nez Perce view of events surrounding their troubles in 1877 with the U.S. government. MacDonald was part Nez Perce, knew and was related to many of the principals within the tribe, and fluently spoke both Nez Perce and English. He interviewed tribesmen in Canada, notably Chief White Bird, to gain the Nez Perce perspective.

15. Stevens to Commissioner of Indian Affairs, October 22, 1856, roll 907, Letters Received by the Office of Indian Affairs, as quoted in Thompson, *Historic Resource Study, Spalding Area*, 83.

16. F. L. M., "Nez Perce War," 820–22; Bancroft, *History of Washington, Idaho, and Montana*, 490; Josephy, *Nez Perce Indians*, 387; Paul, *Mining Frontiers of the Far West*, 138, 143; Ross, *Mining History of South-Central Idaho*, 3–5; and Bolino, "Role of Mining," 116–51. Lawyer's remark is in "Grievances of the Nez Perce," 7. Quote from "Treaty of Agreement 10th April 1861," in Talkington, "History of the Nez Perce," 3; Commissioner of Indian Affairs, *Report . . . 1877*, 9–10.

17. Talkington, "History of the Nez Perce," 6–8, 10; F. L. M., "Nez Perce War," 822; Walker, *Conflict and Schism*, 46; Josephy, *Nez Perce Indians*, 388–407, 433–34. Fort Lapwai (originally Camp Lapwai), established on August 6, 1862, by troops of the First Oregon Cavalry on orders from District of Oregon commander, Brigadier General Benjamin Alvord, stood on Lapwai Creek four miles above its confluence with the Clearwater and the Lapwai Agency. Because of the ongoing Civil War, Fort Lapwai was not occupied by regular troops until 1866. Intermittently abandoned and reoccupied over the next two decades, the post finally closed in 1884. A thorough history is in Thompson, *Historic Resource Study, Fort Lapwai*.

18. More specifically, the treaty "reserved an extent of country bounded by a line beginning at a point on the north bank of the Clearwater, three miles below the mouth of Lapwai Creek, crossing to the north bank at Hatwai Creek and taking in a strip of country seven miles wide along the river, reaching to the North Fork, thence in a general southerly course to the 46th parallel, and thence west and north to the place of beginning. . . ." Bancroft, *History of Washington, Idaho, and Montana*, 489. The treaty was slightly amended in 1868 to permit tribal use of lands within the tract formerly reserved for agency and military purposes. Kappler, *Indian Affairs*, 2:1024–25. For full discussion of the treaty of 1863, see Josephy, *Nez Perce Indians*, 410–31; Francis Haines, *Nez Perces*, 159–64; and Thompson, *Historic Resource Study, Spalding Area*, 95–97. The treaty surrendered 6,932,270 acres of the Nez Perce land recognized in 1855. Josephy, *Nez Perce Indians*, 429.

19. Josephy, *Nez Perce Indians*, 429; Royce, "Indian Land Cessions," Pt. 2:826–27; Kappler, *Indian Affairs*, 2:843–48, and, as amended in 1868, 2:1024–25; Drury, "Lawyer, Head Chief," 11; Walker, *Conflict and Schism*, 46–48, 51–52; Josephy, *Nez Perce Indians*, 433, 437–38. Annuities and monies promised under the 1863 treaty were likewise delayed, partly because of the ongoing Civil War. Bancroft, *History of Washington, Idaho, and Montana*, 490–91.

20. Josephy, *Patriot Chiefs*, 321. Quote is from F. L. M., "Nez Perce War," 823.

21. Quoted in F. L. M., "Nez Perce War," 823. See also Commissioner of Indian Affairs, *Report . . . 1873*, 18; Royce, "Indian Land Cessions," Pt. 2:864–65; Bancroft, *History of Washington, Idaho, and Montana*, 494; and the discussion in Francis Haines, *Nez Perces*, 215ff. For details of the formulation of the executive order, which was considerably based on apparently confused information regarding respective Nez Perce and white use of the Wallowa area, see Josephy, *Nez Perce Indians*, 456–57.

22. Rowton, Interview; Lebain, Interview, LBNM, 138–39, 143–44.

23. Quote is from Monteith's report, September 9, 1873, in Commissioner of Indian Affairs, *Report . . . 1873*, 246. In 1874, Monteith requested troops to oversee such a rendezvous near Pierce City on the reservation. See editorial in Boise, Idaho *Statesman*, July 14, 1877.

24. For the Ott affair, see "Lawrence Ott," in *Illustrated History of North Idaho*, 513; Josephy, *Nez Perce Indians*, 512–13; Francis Haines, *Nez Perces*, 210;

and McWhorter, *Hear Me*, 122. Lawrence Ott maintained that he had killed a Umatilla Indian named Bear's Heart, and that "the Nez Perce had no grievances against me because of this affair, but they had against a man [Samuel] Benedict, who lived near the mouth of the W.B. [White Bird Creek], because of a N.P. he killed about 6 months before the war." Ott stated that a Nez Perce council had declared his killing of the Umatilla an act of self-defense. For Ott's detailed description of the encounter, see Ott, Interview.

25. Bancroft, *History of Washington, Idaho, and Montana*, 495. See Grover, *Report*, 62–64.

26. Royce, "Indian Land Cessions," Pt. 2:864–65.

27. Quote is from Board of Indian Commissioners, *Eighth Annual Report*, 50.

28. At Howard's direction, Major Wood had become expert with regard to the Nez Perce and their treaties, privately publishing his *The Treaty Status of Young Joseph and His Band of Nez Perce Indians* in Portland in January 1876. The document's conclusions appeared in the *Army and Navy Journal*, issues of July 7, 1877, and (with corrections by Wood) September 8, 1877.

29. Commissioner of Indian Affairs, *Report . . . 1877*, 10–11; Josephy, *Patriot Chiefs*, 321–22. Quotes are from F. L. M., "Nez Perce War," 822, 824. The full statement of Old Joseph respecting his views of selling the Wallowa homeland is quoted by Young Joseph in Joseph [Heinmot Tooyalakekt], "An Indian's Views," 419 (republished as "Chief Joseph's Own Story," in Brady, *Northwestern Fights and Fighters*, 44–75.)

30. McDowell, "Report," 113. Just how close this incident came to instigating warfare in September 1876 is evident in documents contained in the Forse Papers. First Lieutenant Albert G. Forse commanded the troops from Fort Walla Walla and recalled the following details: "I made a forced march of over 80 miles in 24 hours, arriving there [Wallowa Valley] before daylight Sunday morning [Joseph's deadline], and in time to prevent an outbreak. . . . I went alone with a guide 7 miles to where Joseph was with his warriors. I found them well posted on a high ridge, stripped . . . to the breech clout, and in war paint and ready to commence hostilities. I went alone for the reason . . . [that] had I taken my troop the volunteers would have followed and . . . we would have had an Indian war upon our hands. . . . I was in danger of being shot at any time . . . and was in more danger than I have ever been in [in] an engagement." Forse to Howard, April 4, 1895, in ibid. Forse not only convinced Joseph that the murderers would be indicted, but obtained a penciled statement from one of two Nez Perce witnesses and arranged for them to testify before the court at Union, Oregon. See Forse's draft report, September 11, 1876; his "Statement of Indians"; and Forse to Judge Brainard, September 15, 1876, in Forse Papers. See also Josephy's description of this and succeeding events in Josephy, *Nez Perce Indians*, 445–84.

31. Josephy, *Patriot Chiefs*, 319–20; Josephy, *Nez Perce Indians*, 486–91; and Francis Haines, *Nez Perces*, 214.

32. Commissioner of Indian Affairs, "Report . . . Nez Perce Indians," 211–12.

33. Quote from transcript of the proceedings in Board of Indian Commissioners, *Eighth Annual Report*, 58.

34. Ibid., 62–63. In their digest of the proceedings, published in Commissioner of Indian Affairs, *Report . . . 1877*, the commissioners succinctly paraphrased Joseph's view as follows: "The 'Creative Power,' when he made the earth, made no

marks, no lines of division or separation upon it, and . . . it should be allowed to remain as then made. The earth was his [Joseph's] mother. He was made of the earth and grew up on its bosom. The earth, as his mother and nurse, was sacred to his affections, too sacred to be valued by or sold for silver and gold. He could not consent to sever his affections from the land that bore him. He was content to live upon such fruits as the 'Creative Power' placed within and upon it, and unwilling to barter these and his free habits away for the new modes of life. . . ." Commissioner of Indian Affairs, *Report . . . 1877,* 212.

35. Quote from transcript in Board of Indian Commissioners, *Eighth Annual Report,* 60.

36. Quote is from ibid., 63. For full details of the murder incident, see Horner and Butterfield, "Nez Perce–Findley Affair," 40–51; and also, for its conclusion, Josephy, *Nez Perce Indians,* 483–84.

37. Board of Indian Commissioners, *Eighth Annual Report,* 58; F. L. M., "Nez Perce War," 825–26; Josephy, *Patriot Chiefs,* 322–23. An overview of Howard's involvement in the proceedings is in John Carpenter, *Sword and Olive Branch,* 246–47.

38. Monteith to Commissioner of Indian Affairs J. Q. Smith, February 9, 1877, in McDowell, "Report," 115; Howard, "Report," 590 (this report was drafted after the conclusion of the Nez Perce campaign by Second Lieutenant Charles Erskine Scott Wood, Howard's aide as of late July 1877. Howard inserted material before submitting the document to his superiors. What appears to be the original draft is in the C. E. S. Wood Collection); "Report of the General of the Army," November 7, 1877, in Secretary of War, *Report . . . 1877,* 8–9. Howard's report was also published separately, as *Supplementary Report.*

39. Howard, "Report," 587–88.

40. Ibid., 589.

41. Quoted in MacDonald, "Nez Perces," 230. Howard's responses are on pages 228–30.

42. Monteith to Howard, March 19, 1877, Howard Collection, correspondence, 1877; Howard, "Report," 592–94; Howard, *My Life and Experiences,* 250.

43. Howard, *My Life and Experiences,* 252.

44. Howard, "Report," 594. A slightly variant account is in Howard, *My Life and Experiences,* 254–55.

45. Joseph [Heinmot Tooyalakekt], "An Indian's Views," 422. For other Nez Perce views of this episode, see MacDonald, "Nez Perces," 232, and the Chuslum Moxmox (Yellow Bull) account in Curtis, *North American Indian,* 8:163–64. Howard's counterpoint to Joseph's "An Indian's Views," in which Howard frequently cited official transcripts of the proceedings to correct Joseph's comments, is in Howard, "True Story . . . Wallowa Campaign," (and republished in Brady, *Northwestern Fights and Fighters,* 76–89). In its March 29, 1879 issue, the *Army and Navy Journal* questioned the accuracy of Joseph [Heinmot Tooyalakekt], "An Indian's Views," stating that "it is a great mistake . . . not to give the name of the interpreter; for the English is not Chief Joseph's English, and the name of the interpreter (assuming that the story was told by the chief in his own tongue), and also of the writer who interpreted the interpreter, or prepared the article for publication, would furnish Army officers [and others] with the means of ascertaining the point of first consideration, how accurately the language conveys Chief Joseph's views and thoughts." Howard's aide, Wilkinson, referred to Toohoolhoolzote as

"six feet and over of badness." *Army and Navy Journal*, August 18, 1877. The opinion that Howard's treatment of Toohoolhoolzote violated established council decorum is advanced by his former aide, C. E. S. Wood, in a letter to the editor, Portland *Daily Oregonian*, June 19, 1928.

46. Howard, "Report," 594–95.

47. Joseph [Heinmot Tooyalakekt], "An Indian's Views," 422.

48. Howard, *My Life and Experiences*, 257.

49. Howard, "Report," 595.

50. Joseph [Heinmot Tooyalakekt], "An Indian's Views," 422. One Nez Perce view is that six months would be required to round up the herds and report to the agency, and that because the people had, in essence, agreed to come in, the greater period of time should have been allowed. Slickpoo and Walker, *Noon Nee-Me-Poo*, 183–84. On the other hand, a document prepared on May 12—three days before the final council meeting—by Howard's aide, First Lieutenant Melville C. Wilkinson, indicates that Joseph thought thirty days was ample and, in fact, may have suggested that amount of time: "Joseph says it may be a month before he can get all of his stock over the Snake River. The General has given this length of time." Wilkinson to Captain Stephen G. Whipple, May 12, 1877, Department of the Columbia, Letters Sent, 2, 19, National Archives, quoted in John Carpenter, "General Howard," 132.

51. Howard, "Report," 596.

52. Ibid., 596–97. For additional accounts of the Fort Lapwai council, see Howard, "True Story . . . Wallowa Campaign," 59–64 (also published in *Army and Navy Journal*, June 28, 1879); Howard, *Famous Indian Chiefs*, 189–94; Howard, *Nez Perce Joseph*, 51–53; First Lieutenant Melville C. Wilkinson letter in *Army and Navy Journal*, August 18, 1877; FitzGerald, *Army Doctor's Wife*, 246–52. See also John Carpenter, *Sword and Olive Branch*, 248–49; Francis Haines, *Nez Perces*, 238–42; Josephy, *Nez Perce Indians*, 497–508; and Thompson, *Historic Resource Study, Fort Lapwai*, 70–74. Nez Perce accounts appear in Joseph [Heinmot Tooyalakekt], "An Indian's Views," 230–33; and McWhorter, *Yellow Wolf*, 37–41. Contemporary discussions of the Nez Perce situation that are based largely on Joseph's *North American Review* ("An Indian's Views") account, and that are sympathetic to the Indians, appear in Jackson, *Century of Dishonor*, 103–35; and Dunn, *Massacres of the Mountains*, 527–66. For an editorial perspective favorable to the Nez Perces, see "Responsibility for the Idaho War," 69–70.

53. Crook, *General George Crook*, 169.

54. This sketch of Howard is composed from the following works: Cullum, *Biographical Register*, 2:369–70; George C. Rable, "Oliver Otis Howard," in Spiller, *Dictionary of American Military Biography*, 2:493–96; Utley, "Oliver Otis Howard," 55–63; Robert M. Utley, introduction to reprint edition of Howard, *My Life and Experiences*, v–xvii; Ellis, "Humanitarian Generals," 169–70; Hutton, *Soldiers West*, 119. See also Howard's works as cited above; Howard, *Autobiography*; and the full biographical treatment in John Carpenter, *Sword and Olive Branch*.

CHAPTER 2

1. "Scene of the Outbreak," inset drawing in Fletcher, "Department of Columbia Map" (this map also appears in foldout format in Secretary of War, *Report . . . 1877*); John Wilson, "Map of Clearwater River"; Portland *Daily Oregonian*,

June 18, 1877; Howard, "Nez Perces Campaign of 1877," July 11, 1878; and Thian, *Notes Illustrating the Military Geography*, 26, 56.

2. Howard, "Report," 599.

3. McCarthy, Diary, June 4, 12, and 14, 1877. Internal references suggest that this "diary" was prepared many years—possibly decades—later, probably from a diary kept on the march.

4. The letter was from Loyal P. Brown and had been mistakenly dated June 15. C. E. S. Wood, "Journal." This daily journal appears to be an official account of the campaign composed and kept by Wood at the behest of General Howard.

5. These figures are from Francis Haines, "Chief Joseph," 1. See also Josephy, *Nez Perce Indians*, 511; McWhorter, *Hear Me*, 177–86; and McDermott, *Forlorn Hope*, 81 n. 8.

6. Yellow Bull, Interview, BYU; Camp Manuscript Field Notes, 540, Camp Papers, LBNM; Lott, Interview; Lee Rhodes, "Chief Joseph's Leadership," 99–100; McWhorter, *Hear Me*, 181–83, 265; Josephy, *Nez Perce Indians*, 374 n. 527; Francis Haines, *Nez Perces*, 16, 262–63; and Mark Brown, "Joseph Legend," 56.

7. There are several scenarios regarding the challenge to Shore Crossing that precipitated the outbreak. See Josephy, *Nez Perce Indians*, 512–13. Shore Crossing reportedly did not drink alcohol. Otis Halfmoon, communication with author, Nez Perce National Historical Park, Spalding, Idaho, November 16, 1995.

8. The accounts of the Tolo Lake gathering and initial attacks on the Salmon River settlers often are imprecise and disagree on many details, and particularly the chronology of events. This reconstruction is based on information in Josephy, *Nez Perce Indians*, 511–14; McDermott, *Forlorn Hope*, 3–12; Francis Haines, *Nez Perces*, 217–19; McWhorter, *Hear Me*, 175–77, 188–96; MacDonald, "Nez Perces," 234–36; Yellow Bull account in Curtis, *North American Indian*, 8:164–65; "Story of Kawownonilpilp"; Pinkham, *Hundredth Anniversay of the Nez Perce War*; Slickpoo and Walker, *Noon Nee-Me-Poo*, 184; Trafzer and Scheureman, *Chief Joseph's Allies*, 10–12; Camp Manuscript Field Notes, 142–44, 149, 169, Camp Papers, LBNM; Riley, "Nez Perce Struggle," 41; Lebain, Interview, IU; and Elizabeth Wilson, "Outbreak of the Nez Perce War." Tolo Lake is named for Too-lah, or Aleblemot, a Nez Perce woman who aided the settlers on Slate Creek by riding to the mining community of Florence for help during the first days of the conflict. Robert Bailey, *River of No Return*, 252–53, 255. At her death, Tolo was buried in Red Rock Canyon, where the American Legion Auxiliary erected a memorial at her grave in 1939. Elsensohn, *Pioneer Days in Idaho County*, 1:281–82.

9. The treatment of Walsh and Osborn is substantiated in McCarthy, Diary, June 26, 1877.

10. Norton, "True Story," 99; Howard, "Nez Perces Campaign of 1877," July 4, 1878; Portland *Morning Oregonian*, June 19, July 4, 1877; Lewiston *Morning Tribune*, June 19, 1927; Rowton, Interview; Fenn, Interview; Francis Haines, *Nez Perces*, 219–20; Elsensohn, *Pioneer Days in Idaho County*, 1:114–17, 131, 280–82; Robert Bailey, *River of No Return*, 254–60; and Bosler, Reminiscence. See also "Statement of Mrs. W. W. Bowman." For the most comprehensive and well-documented telling of the outbreak on the Salmon, see McDermott, *Forlorn Hope*, 3–43. The controversy surrounding the demise of Mrs. Manuel and her daughter is treated at length in ibid., 157–60.

11. The attack on the Norton party was one of the most publicized episodes

of the evolving conflict. For details, see Nez Perce Campaign—1877, Wilmot Papers; "Victim of Nez Perces Tells Story of Indian Atrocities," *Winners of the West*, February 15, 1926; Adkison, *Nez Perce Indian War*, 21–25, 36–39, 43–44; Elsensohn, *Pioneer Days in Idaho County*, 1:297–300; Arnold, *Indian Wars of Idaho*, 154–61; and, especially, McDermott, *Forlorn Hope*, 27–32, 41–42. The rape of Mrs. Chamberlin is attested to in James Chamberlin claim (John's father), no. 8632, entry 700, Claim for Indian Depredations, U.S. Bureau of Indian Affairs.

12. Adkison, *Nez Perce Indian War*, 44. See Canby, "Report of Indian depredations"; Drum, "Report . . . Indian depredations." Settlers claimed to have lost 280 horses, 941 cattle, 20 sheep, and 174 hogs either killed, stolen, or lost during the initial outbreak, for a total value of $73,186.81. One of those submitting a claim for livestock was Lawrence Ott. "He is the man, who murdered an Indian near Slate Creek, about three years ago," wrote Captain William F. Drum, "and has not lived on his Ranch until quite recently. He may have lost some stock but I would recommend that this claim be suspended, until Ott can prove that he has not run off more Indian stock than would pay his claim if it were a good one. It is believed that he has been engaged in that business." Drum, "Report . . . Indian depredations."

13. This explanation of the Nez Perces' behavior is adapted from a thesis cogently expressed, with regard to the Delaware Indians, in Weslager, *Delaware Indians*, 230; and, with regard to the Northern Cheyenne Indians, in Powers, "Northern Cheyenne Trek," 10–11, 31–32 n. 29.

14. Howard, "Report," 600–601; "Report of the General of the Army," November 7, 1877, in Secretary of War, *Report . . . 1877*, 9; McCarthy, Diary, June 15, 1877; C. E. S. Wood, "Journal," June 15, 1877; Captain Melville C. Wilkinson letter in *Army and Navy Journal*, August 18, 1877; Howard, "Nez Perces Campaign of 1877," June 27, 1878; Redfield, "Reminiscences of Francis M. Redfield," 70; Thompson, "Summer of '77," 12–13; John P. Schorr to L. V. McWhorter, May 20, 1926, McWhorter Papers; John Carpenter, *Sword and Olive Branch*, 249; McDermott, *Forlorn Hope*, 49–54. One citizen wired President Rutherford B. Hayes directly, urging him to send Brigadier General George Crook to the scene of the outbreak. Crook, regarded as one of the leading Indian fighters in the army, had conducted operations against other Northwest tribes in previous years. Thomas Donaldson to Hayes, June 21, 1877, item 3565, roll 336, Nez Perce War Papers.

At the outset, Howard exhibited an abysmal ignorance of the complexities and intricacies involved in the outbreak, as well as of Nee-Me-Poo tribal band dynamics, in ascribing the outbreak to the premeditation of thirteen "thieving desperadoes of White Bird's band" who had terrorized the countryside for years. See marginal notations by Major General Irvin McDowell in "Copies of letters and telegrams."

15. For further background on Companies F and H, see McDermott, *Forlorn Hope*, 59–68. For specifics of period army clothing and equipment, see McChristian, *U.S. Army in the West*; and Steffen, *The Frontier*.

16. Biographical data on Perry, Theller, Trimble, and Parnell is variously from *Records of Living Officers of the United States Army*, 103, 160, 430; Powell, *Powell's Records*, 447–48, 457, 602; and Heitman, *Historical Register and Dictionary*, 1:771, 785, 952, 970. See also McDermott, *Forlorn Hope*, 57–68. An obituary of Theller is in Boise, Idaho *Tri-Weekly Statesman*, June 23, 1877.

17. The names of the eleven citizen volunteers were as follows: Herman A. Faxon, Frank A. Fenn, Vincent Tullis, William B. Bloomer, John W. (Jack) Rainey,

John O. Barber, George M. Shearer, William Coram, Charles L. Crooks, Theodore D. Swarts, and Arthur I. ("Ad") Chapman. Another citizen, Asa Jones, started with the troops, but was unarmed and returned to Mount Idaho. Walter M. Camp to Swarts, August 7, 1915, folder 2, box 2, Camp Papers, BYU; Swarts to Camp, January 21, 1917, folder 3, box 2, ibid.; Swarts, Interview.

18. New York *Herald*, September 10, 1877, quoted in Parnell, "Nez Perce Indian War," 373. Parnell's account was republished with several additions and modifications in Parnell, "Battle of White Bird Cañon."

19. Swarts, Interview.

20. While this account of the battle draws heavily from the military record, the following Nez Perce sources were consulted: "Story of Kawownonilpilp"; Lebain, Interview, IU; "Incidents of the Nez Perce War," in Curtis, *North American Indian*, 8:165; MacDonald, "Nez Perces," 236–37; Redfield, "Reminiscences of Francis M. Redfield," 72–73; Francis Haines, *Nez Perces*, 223–28; Francis Haines, "Chief Joseph," 2–3. McWhorter, *Hear Me*, 236, stated that the Nez Perces had surveilled Perry's advance from the time his troops left Cottonwood Ranch. See, in ibid., the accounts of Husis Owyeen (Wounded Head), 239–41; Two Moon, 244–48; Weyahwahtsitskan, 248–49; Tipyahlahnah (Roaring Eagle), 251–52 n; Chelooyeen (Bow and Arrow Case), 53–54; and Kowtoliks, 255. See also McWhorter, *Yellow Wolf*, 54–64; Josephy, *Nez Perce Indians*, 523–26; and McDermott, *Forlorn Hope*, passim, which does an excellent job of integrating Nez Perce testimony.

21. Sergeant Michael McCarthy claimed that the first soldier killed in the Battle of White Bird Canyon, as well as in the conflict generally known as the Nez Perce War, fell at this point. He was Corporal Roman D. Lee, of Company H, First Cavalry. "He was shot in body, . . . and when lifted from his horse to the ground, in confusion, wandered down towards indian [sic] camp. We found the body 3 weeks afterwards, very close to indian camp lying in a dry gulley. Some of the boys wanted to stop and bury it, [and] I gave them permission to fall out, but the comdr was in a hurry and had them recalled to the command." McCarthy, Scrapbook.

22. Swarts, Interview.

23. McCarthy, Diary, June 17, 1877.

24. Perry, "Battle of White Bird Cañon,"116.

25. Coram, Interview.

26. Perry, "Battle of White Bird Cañon," 116.

27. McCarthy, Diary, June 17, 1877.

28. Ibid.

29. Swarts, Interview. Frank A. Fenn claimed that Swarts's wound was self-inflicted. "I . . . assisted him in extinguishing the fire that had been started in his clothing by the discharge." Some of the civilians veered to the right off Parnell's route, instead going up the ridges farther east of the road until they struck a stock trail, which they followed up and over the mountain and onto the prairie, well ahead of the other civilians and the troops. Fenn to Camp, September 19, 1915, folder 2, box 2, Camp Papers, BYU.

30. Years later, Volunteer Frank Fenn reported on Theller's movement: "To Lieut. Theller I believe is due the credit for saving the greater number of those who escaped. I personally heard Captain Perry appeal to Theller to try to stop the headlong flight of the men and I was one of a party of ten or twelve who responded to Theller's call for a stand just south of the point where the road crosses

the long ridge. . . . By the time the head of the retreating soldiers reached this point the Indians were coming up the ridge in considerable numbers. . . . The party with Theller was well in hand and he directed their fire with such good effect that the Indian advance was thoroughly checked and the Indian column was turned down the hill to the east. At the bottom of this hill on that side the canyon is quite brushy and there the Indians took shelter but kept moving up the canyon in a course generally parallel with the road. After thus checking the Indians, Theller very quietly directed his men to take to the road again with the view of getting ahead of the Indians a second time and in that way cover the retreat as well as possible. He explained briefly to the men just what he wished to do and it was in the carrying out of that intention that he and the most of his party was killed about a half mile farther up the road. When Theller ordered his party to resume the movement along the road I left them. . . [and joined some other civilians going out via an old stock trail]." Fenn to Camp, September 19, 1915, folder 2, box 2, Camp Papers, BYU.

31. Parnell, "Nez Perce Indian War," 370. Parnell's singular movement drew plaudits in the press: "There is no doubt but the Indians would have pursued and massacred every one of the command were it not for the bravery and determined pluck of Lieutenant Parnell. . . . This officer, gathering a few men around him, occupied knolls here and there after gaining the high ground, and so vigorous and effective was the fire poured into the victorious Indians that they (the Indians) did not deem it prudent to come within range, but instead circled to the right and left, when Lieutenant Parnell would so change his position as to again check them. This, of course, gave the rest of the troops time to get far enough to the rear to organize and prepare for defense, which they did." New York *Herald*, September 10, 1877.

32. Frank Fenn witnessed this brief action. Years later he described the trooper as "an old, gray headed sergeant, one who had, no doubt, passed through many campaigns against hostile Indians." Fenn noted that a memorial shaft raised at the battlefield in the 1920s marked the spot where the sergeant had died. *Winners of the West*, December 30, 1925. Another White Bird Canyon veteran, John P. Schorr, identified the man as Sergeant Patrick Gunn, of Company F, First Cavalry, "gray headed and on his fourth enlistment" when killed. *Winners of the West*, March 15, 1926.

33. Coram, Interview. An Indian named Wounded Head found Mrs. Benedict and protected her before permitting her to go on her way. See "Wounded Head's Narrative," in McWhorter, *Hear Me*, 239–41.

34. Parnell, "Nez Perce Indian War," 372. Besides those quoted above, this account of the Battle of White Bird Canyon incorporates material from the following sources: Howard, "Report," 602; McCarthy, "Journal," 8–12; Kirkwood, "The Nez Perce Indian War," August 17, 1950; Wilmot, "White Bird"; Frank L. Powers to Camp, November 24, 1913, Ellison Collection; Howard, "Nez Perces Campaign of 1877," July 11, 18, 1878; Francis Haines, *Nez Perces*, 255–60; Carroll, *Papers of the Order of Indian Wars*, 217–18; Howard, *My Life and Experiences*, 283–86; and Beyer and Keydel, *Deeds of Valor*, 2:239–44. The most comprehensive treatment of the entire affair, and on which this account has significantly depended, appears in McDermott, *Forlorn Hope*. This book also contains pertinent excerpts from the transcript of Perry's Court of Inquiry of 1878–79.

35. Perry thought that Trimble had deserted him during the retreat, while Trimble questioned many of Perry's actions during the encounter. Despite courts of inquiry, the issues between the men were never settled. See McDermott, *Forlorn Hope*, 96–98, 165–76, and passim.

36. "Report of Casualties"; and "Report of the Surgeon-General," in Secretary of War, *Report . . . 1877*, 359. For names of the army killed and wounded, see Appendix A. Volunteer Swarts, who later homesteaded on the battlefield, described the army fatalities and their locations on the field: "The first man killed was a soldier whose horse ran away and carried him about half way between the 'fort' [rocky hill where most of the soldiers were stationed at the start of the battle] and the hill where we civilians were [on the left of the line]. He ran into Inds [sic] and was killed. The next killed were five soldiers in a group, just to west of present stage road [1915] about ½ mile N.E. of the 'fort.' Another body lay in the road perhaps ½ mile further on, and another on the hillside a little S.E. of where I was shot. Another body was tied in the top of a thorn tree that stands by the mail box in front of my house [1915]. (The privates had been cut from this body and stuck into the mouth.) About ½ mile further on were two more bodies and a mile or so above my house in a thorn gulch in S.W. ¼ or N.E. ¼ Sec. 25 Twp [Township] 29N lay Lieut. Theller and 7 bodies, probably having tried to make a stand (three of these bodies and one of the group of 5, above referred to, are still there, not being found when the bodies were removed). Up on the top of the hill were two more bodies. I think that all or nearly all of these bodies were of dismounted men, who either lost their horses by not cinching their saddles before retreating or who lost their horses through the excitement of their horseholders, who let them go when the stampede started. Some half dozen of the soldiers went back bareback by losing saddles. . . . My house stands at about the center of the strip of fighting ground, the principle part of which is comprised in E ½ of Sec. 36 Twp 29N Range 1 E. Boise Meridian." Swarts, Interview.

37. For details of McCarthy's remarkable escape, see McCarthy, Diary, June 17–19, 1877 (reprinted in McDermott, *Forlorn Hope*, 106–7). Twenty years later, in November, 1897, McCarthy received a Medal of Honor for his performance at White Bird Canyon. The citation, erroneous to some degree, read: "Was detailed with six men to hold a commanding position, and held it with great gallantry until the troops fell back. He then fought his way through the Indians, rejoined a portion of his command, and continued the fight in retreat. He had two horses shot under him, and was captured, but escaped and reported for duty after 3 days' hiding and wandering in the mountains." *The Medal of Honor*, 224. See also the account featuring McCarthy in Beyer and Keydel, *Deeds of Valor*, 2:240–44. Lieutenant Parnell also received a Medal of Honor in 1897 for his service at White Bird Canyon. *The Medal of Honor*, 230.

38. Nez Perce casualties are discussed in McWhorter, *Hear Me*, 253–56; and McWhorter, *Yellow Wolf*, 60. See Appendix B.

39. Howard, "Nez Perces Campaign of 1877," July 18, 1878.

40. McCarthy, "Journal," 18–19.

41. On this point, Howard's aide, First Lieutenant Charles E. S. Wood, wrote in 1918: "The volunteers fled and were never seen or heard of again. . . . Joseph has told me of this. Perry and Parnell told me of it. . . . It was a notorious fact known to every survivor and within three [nine] days I helped bury the dead and

there was not a civilian among them." Wood to C. J. Brosnan, January 7, 1918, in *The Bookmark*, a ca. 1940 publication of the University of Idaho Library, Brosnan Collection.

42. "Summary of Reports . . . Non-Effectiveness," 8, 13.

43. *U.S. Army Gallantry and Meritorious Conduct*, 75. As late as 1913, White Bird Canyon survivor Frank L. Powers, a private in H Company during the fight, described it as "the worst managed affair I was ever in." Powers to Camp, November 24, 1913, Ellison Collection.

44. Possibly the first report of the fight was that of a friendly Nez Perce that was received at Fort Lapwai at 1:00 P.M. on June 17. It read: "Last evening the troops left Idaho City [sic] and went to Chapman's Ranch and from there toward Salmon River and slept there a little. Near the river they met a small party of Indians who began an attack of the troops. The troops advanced their force and one half went to the right and the other to the left to surround the Indians. The Indians attacked the one party and drove them back, but the other came to their assistance and held the ground. Two horse of the officers were killed, but up to the time of the Indians [illeg.] having no success, but some of the soldiers horses were stampeded. Joseph is in command of the Indians and in the fight." "Statement of Indian." Other messages announcing the action came out of Mount Idaho after 9:00 A.M. June 17, but must have reached Fort Lapwai considerably later that day. See Portland *Daily Oregonian*, June 21, 1877.

45. Howard, "Nez Perces Campaign of 1877," August 22, 1878.

46. McCarthy, Diary, June 20, 21, 22, 23, 1877; C. E. S. Wood, "Journal," June 23, 1877; Howard, "Report," 602; "Report of the General of the Army," November 7, 1877, in Secretary of War, *Report . . . 1877*, 9; McDowell to General William T. Sherman, telegram, June 20, 1877, item 3505, roll 336, Nez Perce War Papers; *Army and Navy Journal*, June 30, 1877; Howard, "Nez Perces Campaign of 1877," August 1, 1878; New York *Herald*, September 10, 1877; and John Carpenter, "General Howard," 134. For Trimble's movement to Slate Creek, see Parnell, "Salmon River Expedition," 127-30. Providing rare contemporary insight into the emotions of soldiers bound for the front during an Indian campaign, Second Lieutenant Charles E. S. Wood jotted the following impressions in his notebook as Howard's troops entered the zone of the outbreak: "Nearing the field, peculiar nervous feelings of going to death, [and] shrinking from the exposure; about desire to be out of the expedition. Old soldiers [feel] the same way. Each fright more dreaded than the last. The desire to investigate immortality, thoughts on death, inability to change the morals and tenor of life and thought; each one's expectation that *he* will escape." C. E. S. Wood, "Notes on Nez Perces Expedition," June 23, 1877.

47. Harry Bailey, "An Infantry Second Lieutenant." The body was that of Sergeant Patrick Gunn. McDermott, *Forlorn Hope*, 122.

48. Howard, "Nez Perces Campaign of 1877," September 5, 1878; Kirkwood, "The Nez Perce Indian War," August 17, 1950; and Brimlow, "Nez Perce War Diary," 28. Some bodies were strewn over the back trail three or four miles from the battlefield, the men having been shot from their horses during the retreat. Howard to Assistant Adjutant General, Division of the Pacific, June 26, 1877, item 4026, roll 336, Nez Perce War Papers. For details of the deployment of troops in approaching and securing the battlefield, see C. E. S. Wood, "Journal,"

June 26, 1877. This document states that Theller and his few men were buried on June 27. Ibid., June 27, 1877. Elsewhere, Wood commented on the dead: "Horrible stench, arms and cheeks gone, bellies swollen, blackened faces, mutilations, heads gone—tragic." C. E. S. Wood, "Notes on the Nez Perce Expedition," June 27, 1877. Theller's widow issued an unusual request for the return of items of jewelry stripped from his body by the Nez Perces, in particular asking that an heirloom presentation gold watch belonging to her husband's father be forwarded to her should it and other articles "fall into the hands of white persons." Bozeman *Times*, August 30, 1877. In September, two companies of the Second Infantry traveled to White Bird Canyon to improve on the burials of June 26–27. During that expedition, two additional bodies were found that had not been previously buried. At that time, too, "Lieutenant [Robert P. P.] Wainwright [First Cavalry] partially uncovered Lieut. Theller's grave and cut from the uniform part of the blouse showing the braid and a portion of the stripe from his pants. He also left a paper in the rocks showing the position of the grave." Unidentified to Acting Assistant Adjutant General, District of the Clearwater, September 9, 1877, entry 897, box 1, part 3, 1877, U.S. Army Continental Commands. Theller's remains were exhumed in December 1877 and shipped for interment in San Francisco. First Lieutenant Joseph A. Sladen to Commanding Officer, District of the Clearwater, December 14, 1877, ibid. Sergeant Gunn was buried at Fort Lapwai by a fraternal organization, while the White Bird Canyon dead stayed buried on the battlefield until 1879, when they were removed to the post cemetery at Fort Lapwai. That post was abandoned in 1885, and in November 1890, the soldiers' remains were exhumed and reinterred at Fort Walla Walla. McDermott, *Forlorn Hope*, 129, 163; *Winners of the West*, March 15, 1926; and A. F. Parker to Brigadier General William Carey Brown (ret.), September 28, 1927, William Brown Papers.

49. Howard to Assistant Adjutant General, Department of the Columbia, June 26, 1877, item 4026, roll 336, Nez Perce War Papers.

50. Howard to Trimble, June 26, 1877, entry 897, box 1, part 3, 1877, U.S. Army Continental Commands.

51. Howard, "Nez Perces Campaign of 1877," August 22, 29, September 5, 19, 1878. The shooting between the Nez Perces and Howard's command has been termed the "Salmon River Demonstration." Jocelyn, *Mostly Alkali*, 210.

52. Lieutenant Wood wrote of this exchange: "Enemy hard to discover, but just at night came out in full [view] of the advance signal . . . post where Hdqrs were at the time. . . . Joseph burned house on opposite side of river as notice of our approach." C. E. S. Wood, "Journal," June 27, 1877.

53. C. E. S. Wood, "Notes on Nez Perces Expedition," June 27, 1877.

54. Howard, "Report," 603. Wood described this action: "10.30 [A.M.], order troops forward to take crossing of Salmon River. Capt. Whipple ordered to support Infantry advance. 1 P.M., about one hundred Indians charge down (opposite side of river) a ravine to the right of the secured crossing. Captain Wilkinson, Capt. Page [sic] & the General's orderlies fire upon them as they approach river bank, turning them back. After firing, Indians assemble on hill tops & watch until Soldiers retire to camp." C. E. S. Wood, "Journal," June 28, 1877. See also Wood's notations in C. E. S. Wood, "Notes on Nez Perces Expedition," June 28, 1877.

55. Harry Bailey, "An Infantry Second Lieutenant," 11; Alexander B. Dyer, "The Fourth Regiment of Artillery," in Rodenbough and Haskin, *Army of the United*

States, 373; Howard, "Report," 602–3; Eugene Wilson, "Nez Perce Campaign" (later published as Eugene Wilson, *Hawks and Doves*); *Army and Navy Journal*, July 7, 1877; Portland *Daily Oregonian*, July 6, 1877; Boise, Idaho *Tri-Weekly Statesman*, July 7, 1877; Adkison, *Indian Braves*, 19; and Elsensohn, *Pioneer Days in Idaho County*, 1:285, 293–94.

56. C. E. S. Wood, "Journal," June 29, 1877; and Howard, "Report," 603.

C H A P T E R   3

1. Wagner, *A Geological Reconnaissance . . . Snake and Salmon Rivers*, 1–3. Much of the area traversed by the Nez Perces and the army in 1877 is today called the Joseph Plains. Ibid., 3; Howard, "Report," 603; C. E. S. Wood, "Journal," July 1, 2, 3, 4, 5, and 6, 1877; C. E. S. Wood, "Notes on Nez Perces Expedition," July 1, 2, 3, 4, 5, 6, 1877; Eugene Wilson, "Nez Perce Campaign," 4–5; McCarthy, Diary, July 1, 2, 1877; Parnell, "Salmon River Expedition," 128–29; Portland *Daily Standard*, July 7, 9, 1877; Portland *Daily Oregonian*, July 9, 1877; "Nez Perce War Letters," 62–63; and McDowell's marginal notes on various communiqués, especially on 46, 50, 51, 56, 60, 63, in "Copies of letters and telegrams"; Wood to C. J. Brosnan, January 7, 1918, in *The Bookmark*, a ca. 1940 publication of the University of Idaho Library, Brosnan Collection; Adkison, *Indian Braves*, 19; Howard to Commanding Officer, Cottonwood, July 6, 1877, entry 896, box 1, part 3, 1877, U.S. Army Continental Commands. During Howard's activity near the Salmon, one man was accidentally wounded and another was killed, on June 30 and July 7, 1877, respectively. Regimental Returns . . . First Cavalry, June and July 1877, roll 166; Regimental Returns . . . Fourth Artillery, July 1877, roll 30; General Orders No. 8, Headquarters, Department of the Columbia, copy in Paddock, Appointment, Commission, and Personal File.

2. McCarthy, "Journal," 14.

3. Howard to James Lawyer, June 24, 1877, entry 897, box 1, part 3, 1877, U.S. Army Continental Commands.

4. Boise, Idaho *Weekly Statesman*, July 7, 10, 1877; Portland *Daily Oregonian*, July 7, 1877; Watkins to Bureau of Indian Affairs Commissioner J. Q. Smith, July 8, 1877, item 4499, roll 336, Nez Perce War Papers; Howard, "Report," 603; Howard, "Nez Perces Campaign of 1877," September 19, 1878; and Lewiston *Morning Tribune*, June 19, 1927. The newspaper dates support the contention of raids in the area of the Clearwater; inexplicably, both Dempster and Silverwood filed depredation claims for damages inflicted on July 8—well after the attack on Looking Glass's camp. Canby, "Report of Indian depredations."

5. Quoted in Howard, "Nez Perces Campaign of 1877," September 19, 1878.

6. Boise, Idaho *Weekly Statesman*, July 14, 1877. McWhorter erroneously believed that Whipple used the guns to attack Looking Glass's camp. Peopeo Tholekt, his Nez Perce informant, however, was correct in declaring "he saw no cannon or Gatling guns." McWhorter, *Hear Me*, 270. That two men per Gatling gun were left at Mount Idaho is presumed based on information of the minimal number of gunners (1) and cannoneers (1) required to operate the pieces. *Artillery Tactics*, 78–79.

7. These figures are derived from information contained in Boise, Idaho *Weekly Statesman*, July 14, 1877; and Regimental Returns . . . First Cavalry, July 1877, roll 166.

8. *Records of Living Officers of the United States Army*, 101, 104; Heitman, *Historical Register and Dictionary*, 1:429, 712, 880, 1051; and Cullum, *Biographical Register*, 3:43, 200.

9. For discussion of this controversial combat procedure, see Wooster, *The Military and United States Indian Policy*, 127, 135–43; and Greene, *Yellowstone Command*, 10–12.

10. Howard, "Report," 603. The specific time that the troops reached the village is given in a letter from Loyal P. Brown of Mount Idaho dated July 2. Portland *Daily Oregonian*, July 7, 1877. Corporal Frederick Mayer of Company L gave the time as about 5:00 A.M., which is probably the time Whipple originally wanted to attack. Mayer also gave the wrong date—July 2. Brimlow, "Nez Perce War Diary," 28.

11. The size of the camp is graphically represented in a sketch map drawn by Nez Perce participant Peopeo Tholekt in 1927. Peopeo Tholekt, "Attack on Chief Looking Glass' Village." Duncan MacDonald's contemporary account also stated that the village contained eleven tipis. MacDonald, "Nez Perces," 239. Possibly some villagers were living in Plains-type brush shelters called wickiups.

12. According to McWhorter, the term, "Kamnaha [Kamnaka]," has not been defined. McWhorter, *Hear Me*, 264 n.

13. Josephy, *Nez Perce Indians*, 111; and McWhorter, *Hear Me*, 182–83, 264.

14. This figure is based on the numbers estimated for Looking Glass's band in chapter two.

15. Whipple's report is excerpted in Howard, "Nez Perces Campaign of 1877," September 19, 1878. The Nee-Me-Poo account taken by Duncan MacDonald also indicated that Looking Glass personally tried to surrender. MacDonald, "Nez Perces," 238–39. Peopeo Tholekt insisted that at no time did Looking Glass agree to surrender and had, in fact, avoided meeting the soldiers at all. McWhorter, *Hear Me*, 270–71.

16. McWhorter, *Hear Me*, 266. Apparently, some of the officers thought that Peopeo Tholekt was Looking Glass, and one insistently poked him in the ribs with his carbine. Ibid., 266–67. The volunteers must have known the chief, however, as he had visited Mount Idaho previously and had, in fact, delivered a "speech of amity" to a gathering there the previous year. Miscellaneous notes, Camp Manuscripts, IU. Duncan McDonald's contemporary account, utilizing Nez Perce recollections, stated that a white man in Looking Glass's village initially came forward, but became intimidated and returned to the chief, whereupon they both approached the soldiers. When the shooting started, the white man ran to the soldiers while Looking Glass "returned to his camp and told his men to do the best they could." MacDonald, "Nez Perces," 238–39.

17. The individual who fired the first shot was probably a volunteer, most likely David Ousterholt or Dutch Holmes. See McWhorter, *Hear Me*, 273. One account stated that a trumpet suddenly sounded from the cavalry, causing "astonishment among Whipple's men and consternation in the camp of the Indians," that led to their evacuation before the shot was fired "by some impulsive person on the hill." Frank A. Fenn, "Disarming Looking Glass, An Episode in the Nez Perce War," Kooskia *Mountaineer*, May 11, 18, 1927. (Although Fenn was a Mount Idaho volunteer, he may not have been present in this action, judging from his lack of first person usage in describing it, when compared with his account of the

subsequent Cottonwood action, in which he took part.) However, a contemporary description of the event emanating from Mount Idaho criticized Whipple for balking at directing the attack. "The Col. [Captain] would not cross the river where the boys were, but remained in a perfectly safe position until the Indians had secured all their arms, saddled their horses, and attempted to escape. Capt. Winters and Lieut. Rains and a large majority of the soldiers were eager for the fight, but were held in check by the Col. Our boys finally became indignant and opened fire." Boise, Idaho *Weekly Statesman*, July 14, 1877. Still another report maintained that the villagers fired the first shot. Boise, Idaho *Weekly Statesman*, July 10, 1877.

18. While this account is heavily based on that of Peopeo Tholekt in McWhorter, *Hear Me*, 264–72, see, in addition, Yellow Bull, Interview, BYU; Lebain, Interview, IU; and MacDonald, "Nez Perces," 238–39. See also Francis Haines, *Nez Perces*, 263–64; and Josephy, *Nez Perce Indians*, 535–37.

19. Forse to Howard, April 4, 1895, Forse Papers.

20. *U.S. Army Gallantry and Meritorious Conduct*, 75. Rains's citation was granted posthumously, for he died in combat two days later.

21. Boise, Idaho *Weekly Statesman*, July 14, 1877.

22. *Army and Navy Journal*, July 14, 1877; and Watkins to Smith, July 8, 1877, item 4499, roll 337, Nez Perce War Papers. The Indian casualties are from Peopeo Tholekt, in McWhorter, *Hear Me*, 267–71. The wounded were Red Heart, Tahkoopen (Shot Leg), and Peopeo Tholekt. The killed were the woman and her infant who drowned, and Nennin Chekoostin (Black Raven), who died from his wounds. Ibid. See Appendix B. One newspaper wildly accounted for seventeen Indians killed. Portland *Daily Oregonian*, July 9, 1877.

23. Most army reports gave an inflated figure for the number of ponies captured— from 1,000 to 1,200—far more than the narrow confines of Clear Creek Canyon and its hillsides could sustain. In a directive of July 18, Howard noted that 622 animals—doubtless those captured at Looking Glass's camp—"were receipted for by the Mount Idaho Company." This figure more realistically reflects the number of ponies that would have been grazed at Clear Creek. Howard to George Shearer, July 18, 1877, Shearer Papers.

24. McWhorter, *Hear Me*, 270.

25. Howard to Whipple, July 3, 1877, entry 897, box 1, part 3, 1877, U.S. Army Continental Commands. See also Howard, "Report," 603.

26. Yellow Bull, Account; and Weptas Nut (No Feather), Interview. Probably the attack further tilted the Palouses toward joining with the Nez Perces, as many had relatives in Looking Glass's village. Trafzer and Scheureman, *Chief Joseph's Allies*, 18. When Looking Glass and his people joined the main Nez Perce camp, he reportedly addressed the council, saying among other things, "Two days ago my camp was attacked by the soldiers. I tried to surrender in every way I could. . . . Now, my people, as long as I live I will never make peace with the treacherous Americans. . . . The officer may say it was a mistake. It is a lie. He is a dog, and I have been treated worse than a dog by him. He lies if he says he did not know it was my camp. I am ready for war." MacDonald, "Nez Perces," 241.

27. Howard to Whipple, July 3, 1877, entry 897, box 1, part 3, 1877, U.S. Army Continental Commands. In his article, Howard, "Nez Perce Campaign of 1877," September 19, 1878, Howard gave the following as his order to Whipple: "Proceed without delay to Cottonwood (Norton's) and form junction with Captain

Perry—the object being to gain the earliest information of the movements of the enemy, should he, as is thought probably, re-cross the Salmon." Information that Howard knew as early as July 1 that the Nez Perces were recrossing the Salmon is in Boise, Idaho *Weekly Statesman*, July 14, 1877.

28. Howard, "Report," 603.

29. Elsensohn, *Pioneer Days in Idaho County*, 1:297; and McDermott, *Forlorn Hope*, 27 n. 3. The site was favored "because of its good water and being protected from winds and storms." John L. Rooke to L. V. McWhorter, February 9, 1934, folder 151B, McWhorter Papers. A pen and ink sketch of Cottonwood made by First Lieutenant Robert H. Fletcher shows the main buildings and the Lewiston–Mount Idaho road in 1877. "Cottonwood House," inset drawing in Fletcher, "Department of the Columbia Map." Several late-nineteenth century views of Cottonwood are in the Idaho State Historical Society, Boise. See, in particular, numbers 75–228.16/A (ca. 1889); 75–228.16/C (ca. 1898); and 78–203.32(E99.N5), titled "Pack train encamped at Cottonwood during 1877 war." The Norton house burned in 1908. A hotel was later erected on its site. Rooke to McWhorter, February 2, 1934, folder 151B, McWhorter Papers.

30. Fenn to Colonel William Carey Brown (ret.), May 11, 1927, folder 19, box 8, William Brown Papers; and Canby, "Report of Indian depredations."

31. Wilmot, "The Raines [sic] Massacre."

32. Regarding Blewett, Whipple wrote on July 6: "The fate of Charles Blewett is not positively known. . . . [Foster reported] that he saw Blewett dismounted at a little distance, probably from his horse having stumbled. Foster thought the Indians had not seen the young man and that he would be able to evade them, but as the mountains was [sic] then full of Indians, my hope of his safety is but faint. I had taken Blewett into my own mess, and we had all become much attached to him." Portland *Daily Oregonian*, July 18, 1877. Company E, First Cavalry, while scouting the region on August 22, discovered Blewett's body and brought it to Norton's Ranch for burial. Report of McConville to Governor Mason Brayman, August, 1877, in "Nez Perce War Letters," 72. Oddly, a spurious Blewett cropped up in 1931 to claim participation in the Battle of White Bird Canyon. He claimed he had been struck on the head in that action, rendering him unconscious and then amnesiac for the next fourteen years. *Winners of the West*, December 30, 1931.

33. Boise, Idaho *Tri-Weekly Statesman*, July 14, 1877.

34. Quoted in Howard, "Nez Perces Campaign of 1877," September 19, 1878.

35. Besides Rains and Foster, the advance guard included Company E Sergeant Charles Lampman and privates John Burk, Patrick Quinn, William Roche, and Daniel Ryan; and Company L privates David Carroll, George H. Dinteman, Frederick Meyer, Franklin Moody, and Otto H. Richter. Regimental Returns . . . First Cavalry, July 1877, roll 166. Sergeant Lampman was a field correspondent for the Walla Walla *Watchman*. Portland *Daily Oregonian*, July 18, 1877.

36. Josephy described both the senior Rains's involvement on the Northwest frontier, as well as his son's demise at the hands of the Nez Perces. Josephy, *Nez Perce Indians*, 305, 315, 346, 347, 357, 537–38.

37. Rains, Appointment, Commission, and Personal File. Rains had also applied for an appointment in the Fourth Cavalry, which its commander, Colonel Ranald S. Mackenzie, endorsed, noting that "Sandy Rodgers [Second Lieutenant

Alexander Rodgers] who serves in my Regiment from the last class says young Rains is a very excellent young man." Mackenzie to General William T. Sherman, June 8, 1876, ibid. See also Cullum, *Biographical Register*, 3:259.

38. See Fenn to Brown, May 11, 1927, folder 19, box 8, William Brown Papers. The army losses as officially registered appear in Appendix A.

39. Frank A. Fenn, who examined the site of the Rains fight a few days later, speculated that "the body of Indians that had been drawn up in the saddle, when the near approach of Whipple was discovered, hastily abandoned their position on the run, joined their companions on the mountain slopes around the cove where they could more effectively unite in the fight against Rains. That the Indians did not leave the saddle until Whipple was close upon them is evidenced by the fact that members of the command distinctly saw a lot of the hostiles fleeing from the saddle just as the command reached its brink." Fenn to Brown, May 11, 1927, folder 19, box 8, William Brown Papers. Whipple had but fifty-six effectives after every fourth man fell back to hold the horses. Brimlow, "Nez Perce War Diary," 29.

40. Boise, Idaho *Tri-Weekly Statesman*, July 14, 1877.

41. "Proceedings [of] Court of Inquiry"; Brimlow, "Nez Perce War Diary," 29; and Boise, Idaho *Tri-Weekly Statesman*, July 14, 1877. A volunteer on the scene within a few days of the Rains fight maintained that the lieutenant's "life was needlessly sacrificed," likely an index of the general tenor of thought at the time. Fenn to Brown, May 11, 1927, folder 19, box 8, William Brown Papers. Despite the contention in the *Statesman* that Whipple's men did not fire at the warriors, Corporal Frederick Mayer of Company L, who participated, reported that the soldiers returned the fire "whenever we got a shot." Mayer to Brown, undated, ca. 1927, Brimlow File.

42. Whipple's testimony in "Proceedings [of] Court of Inquiry"; Boise, Idaho *Tri-Weekly Statesman*, July 14, 1877; Boise, Idaho *Weekly Statesman*, July 17, 1877; Howard, "Nez Perces Campaign of 1877," September 19, 1878; and Portland *Daily Oregonian*, July 10, 1877. The *Oregonian* piece has been published without identification in Johansen, "The Nez Perce War," 167–70.

43. "Proceedings [of] Court of Inquiry"; and Brimlow, "Nez Perce War Diary," 29. Besides the sources cited, this account of the Rains fight has been compiled from information in Kirkwood, "The Nez Perce Indian War," August 17, 1950, which contains the reminiscence of T. J. ("Eph") Bunker, a volunteer; Grangeville *Idaho County Free Press*, August 31, 1950; *Army and Navy Journal*, July 14, 1877; Elsensohn, *Pioneer Days in Idaho County*, 1:300–302; and Francis Haines, "Chief Joseph," 4.

44. Two Moon's account in McWhorter, *Hear Me*, 283.

45. Ibid., 284–85; and McWhorter, *Yellow Wolf*, 71–74.

46. "Story of Kawownonilpilp."

47. MacDonald, "Nez Perces," 28.

48. McWhorter, *Yellow Wolf*, 77–78; and Lewiston *Tribune*, undated (ca. 1957) news item, clippings file, Idaho State Historical Society, Boise.

49. Harry Bailey, "An Infantry Second Lieutenant," 23. The ring was sent to Rains's sister. Ibid. See also Bailey to McWhorter, item 182, McWhorter Papers. In his memory, Rains's West Point classmates presented his mother with a framed crayon portrait of the lieutenant. *Army and Navy Journal*, December 1, 1877. Following White Bird Canyon, Rains was the officer in charge of burying Lieutenant

Theller and marking the grave so that it would be easily found. With Rains's own death, Theller's widow feared that the site would now be lost. FitzGerald, *Army Doctor's Wife*, 274.

50. T. J. Bunker account in Kirkwood, "The Nez Perce Indian War," August 31, 1950.

51. Hall to Medical Director, Department of the Columbia, July 6, 1877, entry 624, box 1, Office of the Adjutant General; "Report of the Surgeon-General," in Secretary of War, *Report . . . 1878*, 427–28; and Wilmot, "The Raines [sic] Massacre."

52. Brimlow, "Nez Perce War Diary," 30; and Thompson, "Thirteen U.S. Soldiers," 47. In October 1877, a party passing the scene of Rains's encounter described it thusly: "We came on 2 little mounds of fresh earth, close by the wayside. They were the graves of the scouts. Farther on were 3 others, the graves of some of Rains' men. I rode off to a cluster of low rocks which cropped out on the prairie a short distance from the trail. Behind these 7 men had made their last stand, only to be shot down. The rocks were literally covered with marks of bullets. Farther on, in a little depression of the prairie, Lieutenant Rains' body was found." The author of this article noted that some burials occurred back of the Norton house, and this is probably where Rains was buried. Brooke, "Land of the Nez Perces," 355–56. The Rains family requested that the lieutenant's remains lie "undisturbed" where he was initially buried. *Army and Navy Journal*, September 22, 1877. Sergeant Michael McCarthy described the services at Fort Lapwai on June 10, 1878: "All the troops were turned out. It was a sort of double funeral, each having (that is, the officer and the 10 men) its own funeral party &c. The 6 senior noncoms were pall bearers for Lt. Rains, and I was one of the 6. His coffin was draped with the flag and covered, even piled high, with wreaths, crosses &c of flowers, prepared by the officers' ladies of the Post. It was a graceful tribute to his worth and bravery, for Lt. Rains was a gallant gentleman. But behind came a big square pine box containing the bones of the 10 men, on which no flag was draped or flowers placed. They, too, were brave men. Every man of the 10 had volunteered for the duty. When the coffins were laid by the graves nearly side by side for the closing ceremonies, the contrast was great, and to me painful." McCarthy, "Reminiscence"; and Thompson, *Historic Resource Study, Fort Lapwai*, 89. A monument stands in the Fort Walla Walla post cemetery over the common grave of the ten men, its inscription reading: "IN MEMORY OF ENLISTED MEN. 1ST U.S. CAVALRY. KILLED IN ACTION AT COTTONWOOD CAÑON IDAHO. JULY 3rd 1877." The names of the enlisted men are imprinted below the inscription. Lieutenant Rains's grave is located among a row of headstones several yards south of the monument.

53. *U.S. Army Gallantry and Meritorious Conduct*, 75.

54. Elsensohn, *Pioneer Days of Idaho County*, 1:303.

55. "Proceedings [of] Court of Inquiry."

56. Mayer to Brown, undated, ca. 1927, Brimlow File. Volunteer Luther P. Wilmot reported that this earthwork was called "Fort Perry." Wilmot, "The Cottonwood Fight."

57. Mount Idaho volunteer George M. Shearer, who with three others had arrived that afternoon from Mount Idaho, claimed that Perry put him in charge of the fortifications. As he remembered, "Strange that a civilian should be placed in

such an important position, to the exclusion of experienced army officers, and particularly so, when so many of them were unoccupied or seemed to be idle in the gulch below where there was no danger." Shearer to Major Edwin C. Mason, July 28, 1877, Shearer Papers. Another observer commented that Captain Perry "remained at the house" during the fight. Boise, Idaho *Tri-Weekly Statesman*, July 14, 1877.

58. "Proceedings [of] Court of Inquiry." See also Whipple's testimony in ibid.

59. Mayer to Brown, undated, ca. 1927, Brimlow File.

60. Boise, Idaho *Tri-Weekly Statesman*, July 14, 1877.

61. Ibid.

62. Howard, "Nez Perces Campaign of 1877," September 19, 1878.

63. For the action of July fourth, see—besides the sources cited above—John P. Schorr to McWhorter, May 20, 1926, McWhorter Papers; Schorr to McWhorter, February 5, 1935, item 179, ibid.; and *Army and Navy Journal*, July 14, 1877.

64. "Story of Kawownonilpilp."

65. MacDonald, "Nez Perces," 242; Regimental Returns . . . First Cavalry, July 1877, roll 166.

66. "Proceedings [of] Court of Inquiry."

67. The seventeen volunteers were as follows: Captain Randall, First Lieutenant James C. Cearley, Second Lieutenant Luther P. Wilmot, Orderly Sergeant Frank A. Fenn, and Privates Henry C. Johnson, Charles Johnson, Cassius M. Day, D. H. Howser, Benjamin F. Evans, Al B. Leland, A. D. Bartley, George Riggins, Frank D. Vansise, Charles W. Case, James Buchanan, William B. Beamer, and F. J. Bunker. Henry Johnson, "Some Reminiscences," 4.

68. For background on Randall, see Chedsey and Frei, *Idaho County Voices*, 210–11, 257.

69. McWhorter, *Yellow Wolf*, 76–77; McWhorter, *Hear Me*, 292; and "Story of Kawownonilpilp." Yellow Bull stated that White Bird led the warriors in the fight with the seventeen white men. Yellow Bull, Account. Duncan MacDonald reported that the Nez Perces had one man killed and two wounded on July 5. MacDonald, "Nez Perces," 243.

70. Whipple's testimony in "Proceedings [of] Court of Inquiry." Whipple is also quoted by Howard in Howard, "Nez Perces Campaign of 1877," September 19, 1878. However, Perry maintained that "I at once rushed my front line down the hill and sent a mounted detachment to their rescue, which drove the Indians off and brought the party in." Perry, "Affair at Cottonwood," 125.

71. Shearer to Mason, July 26, 1877, Shearer Papers.

72. Reportedly, Perry placed Simpson under arrest for insubordination, but reinstated him at the Clearwater battle, where Simpson was wounded. Frank A. Fenn, "The Cottonwood Fight," Kooskia *Mountaineer*, April 20, 27, 1927; and Fenn to A. F. Parker, March 9, 1927, folder 2, box 12, William Brown Papers. One newspaper wrote that Perry "seemed to be very backward about coming forward" and suggested that his timidity resulted from the "big scare" he had received at White Bird Canyon. Boise, Idaho *Weekly Statesman*, July 17, 1877. Much of the negative newspaper coverage was ascribed to Orin Morrill, of Lewiston, "who was at Cottonwood at the time, but who altho' armed remained ensconced in the little fortification there instead of going with the soldiers to the aid of his imperiled fellow citizens." McDowell to Adjutant General, telegram, July 18, 1877, item

4109, roll 336, Nez Perce War Papers (also published in *Army and Navy Journal*, July 28, 1877). Because of continued criticism of his behavior at Cottonwood, Perry requested yet another court of inquiry to investigate his performance. The court concluded that (1) the volunteers could not be recognized as white men until the engagement commenced; (2) Perry took ten minutes to order the relief party out, but that the delay was not excessive; (3) that "no additional injury resulted from this delay, as all the casualties occurred at the first volley; and (4) that "there is not a word of testimony which reflects upon the personal courage of Captain Perry, and the opinion of the Court exonerates him from the charge of having made any improper delay . . . nearly surrounded, as he evidently was, by hostile Indians, then undoubtedly outnumbering his troops." General Orders No. 23, Headquarters, Department of the Columbia, November 30, 1877, item 7782, roll 339, Nez Perce War Papers. A court examining Perry's overall performance at White Bird Canyon, Cottonwood, and Clearwater convened in late 1878. Regarding Cottonwood, it concluded that Perry's "conduct there appears to have been in accordance with good judgment and prudence, particularly as the enemy was flushed with success, and a part of his [Perry's] command at least, had but recently suffered from a severe disaster." "Proceedings [of] Court of Inquiry."

73. "Proceedings [of] Court of Inquiry."

74. The other wounded volunteers were Charles Johnson and Al B. Leland. Frank A. Fenn, "The Cottonwood Fight," Kooskia *Mountaineer*, April 23, 1927. Civilian and Nez Perce casualties are listed in Appendices A and B, respectively. In addition to those cited, this account of the volunteers' fight and relief has been compiled from the following sources: Mayer to Brown, undated, ca. 1927, Brimlow File; Wilmot, "The Cottonwood Fight"; Henry Johnson, "Some Reminiscences"; Portland *Daily Oregonian*, July 16, 1877; T. J. Bunker account in Kirkwood, "The Nez Perce Indian War,"August 24, 31, 1950; New York *Herald*, September 10, 1877; Francis Haines, "Skirmish at Cottonwood," 2–7; and Elsensohn, *Pioneer Days in Idaho County*, 1:303–10.

75. C. E. S. Wood, "Journal," July 8, 1877; Eugene Wilson, "Nez Perce Campaign," 6–7; Hunter, *Reminiscences of an Old Timer*, 337–39; Howard, "Report," 604; McCarthy, Diary, July 8, 9, 1877; McCarthy, "Journal," 15; Trimble, "Battle of the Clearwater," 139; and Howard, "Nez Perces Campaign of 1877," September 19, 1878.

CHAPTER 4

1. For specifics, see Canby, "Report of Indian depredations."

2. McWhorter, *Hear Me*, 295; McWhorter, *Yellow Wolf*, 78; Lewiston *Teller*, undated clipping ca. July 1927, clippings file, Idaho State Historical Society, Boise; Josephy, *Nez Perce Indians*, 543–44; and Francis Haines, "Chief Joseph," 4.

3. The reorganization of the Dayton, Lewiston, Grangeville, and Mount Idaho volunteers into a single "regimental" organization resulted in the following command hierarchy: Colonel Edward McConville, Lieutenant Colonel George Hunter, Major George Shearer, and Adjutant (Captain) Benjamin F. Morris. McConvillle to Governor Mason Brayman, August, 1877, in "Nez Perce War Letters," 65. The reorganization also aggravated a feud between volunteers Eugene T. Wilson and George Hunter, in which the former shot and wounded the latter, necessitating Wilson's arrest and Hunter's recuperation at the hotel hospital at Mount Idaho

while the events at Fort Misery transpired. For details, see Wilmot, "Misery Hill"; and Hunter, *Reminiscences of an Old Timer*, 339–40.

4. McConville to Brayman, August, 1877, in "Nez Perce War Letters," 65–66.

5. Wilmot, "Misery Hill."

6. The volunteers, particularly the Mount Idahoans, lacked faith in Howard's ability to find the Indians and bring them to battle. "They fear that the murdering redskins will get away or run to Howard for a compromise and protection." Boise, Idaho *Tri-Weekly Statesman*, July 21, 1877.

7. Wilmot wrote that "everything was going fine until . . . John Atkinson while monkeying with a 50 cal. Springfield rifle let it go off accidentally. Never did I hear . . . a rifle make such a report. . . . Our camp was thrown into quite a commotion." Wilmot, "Misery Hill."

8. Ibid.

9. Account of Misery Hill by T. J. Bunker in Kirkwood, "The Nez Perce Indian War," August 4, 1950.

10. Just how "strong" the fire of the Nez Perces was in the middle of the night is questionable, it being doubtful that the warriors would expend much of their ammunition wastefully. Moreover, other accounts of Misery Hill say little about actual shooting during the nighttime encounter. That of T. J. Bunker stated, in fact, that McConville directed him to check out a rifle pit of one of the volunteers after prolonged and frequent shooting from that source. Bunker approached the volunteer. "I said, 'Sam, what are you shooting at?' He replied: 'I don't know. It is so dark I can't see, but I thought it a good idea to keep the ark a-moving.' I suggested that it might be a good plan to save his ammunition for a greater need." Account of Misery Hill in Kirkwood, "The Nez Perce Indian War," August 4, 1950.

11. Bunker stated that "they hailed us, saying: 'We are going to breakfast allee same Hotel de France (a popular hotel in Lewiston). Come over and eat with us.' Not to be outdone . . . , we returned the invitation, when they replied, 'You ain't got anything to eat, you —,' swearing at us in English. . . . Somehow they had stumbled onto the truth, for we did not have much." Bunker also described the warriors' threatening movement: "Just after sunrise, they appeared strung out on the crest of the [opposite] hill, sending out horsemen right and left, maneuvering in true Indian style, waving red blankets, and, as we supposed, trying to draw our fire. . . . After favoring us with a display of their force with no apparent object, they silently withdrew without firing a gun." Ibid.

12. This message is contained in U.S. House, *Nez Perce and Bannock Wars*, 4.

13. Boise, Idaho *Tri-Weekly Statesman*, July 21, 1877.

14. Apparently Wilmot here engaged in a lively altercation with Captain Perry and other officers over the Cottonwood affair that resulted in Howard's threatening him with arrest before he left the army camp. Wilmot, "Misery Hill." See also McCarthy, Diary, July 10, 1877; and Wood, "Journal," July 11, 1877.

15. McConville to Brayman, August 1877, in "Nez Perce War Letters," 66–68. For additional coverage of Misery Hill, see Howard, "Report," 604; Eugene Wilson, "Nez Perce Campaign"; Adkison, *Nez Perce Indian War*, 33–35, which presents a variant account (probably revised by Adkison) of Luther P. Wilmot. One volunteer allowed that, at Mount Idaho at least, "our bloodless expedition proved a full-fledged, fizzling joke." Frank Allen in McWhorter, *Hear Me*, 297 n. 6.

16. McWhorter, *Yellow Wolf,* 79–80, 83–84; McWhorter, *Hear Me,* 295–97. The site of Misery Hill is approximately six miles south of Kamiah and can be reached by traveling via Highway 162 generally south and west to the Fort Misery Road. The privately owned site encompasses about forty acres and is unmarked. Some of McConville's rock defenses remain atop the hill. Lillian Pethtel, communication with author, Kamiah, Idaho, February 17, 1995. See Thain White, "Relics from Fort Misery." This paper describes approximately ten rock "barricades" on the north, south, and east sides of the top of Misery Hill, besides the discovery there of expended cartridge cases and other items (12–13).

17. Howard, "Report," 604; Howard, "Nez Perces Campaign of 1877," September 19, 1878. The Looking Glass village site was also near a ford of the Middle Clearwater, and Howard may have believed that Joseph and the Nez Perces would attempt a crossing there. Boise, Idaho *Weekly Statesman,* July 14, 1877. Sergeant McCarthy noted that "We had crossed the Clearwater so as to head them off." McCarthy, "Journal," 21.

18. Wall's place had been virtually destroyed. The following August he filed a claim for $3,445 to cover the loss of four houses burned and furniture, agricultural implements, clothing, chickens, and "12 large hogs" destroyed. But the claim also included twenty-five fruit trees, two acres of cabbage, two acres of potatoes and onions, fifteen acres of wheat, and ten acres of timothy destroyed by Howard's soldiers on July 9, 10, 1877. Canby, "Report of Indian depredations."

19. C. E. S. Wood, "Journal," July 9, 10, 1877; Howard, "Nez Perces Campaign of 1877," September 26, 1878; and McCarthy, Diary, July 10, 1877.

20. Besides Silverwood and Chapman, other scouts known to be with the command were Daniel Gallagher, George Bingham, John Bingham, and Benjamin Penny (who had earlier been with McConville's command). Boise, Idaho *Tri-Weekly Statesman,* July 19, 1877.

21. The infantry and artillery soldiers were uniformed and outfitted similarly to the cavalrymen (see chapter two). The dismounted men wore shoes and carried slung canteens and haversacks or valises. The infantrymen wore bayonets (possibly trowel-shaped for digging entrenchments) for use with the Springfield rifles they carried. The foot soldiers carried no pistols. Each man's overcoat, blanket, and rubber blanket were rolled lengthwise and worn looped across his shoulder. For specifics, see McChristian, *U.S. Army in the West,* passim.

22. The order of march is from Trimble, "Battle of the Clearwater," 140–41; and Captain Marcus P. Miller to Assistant Adjutant General, Department of the Columbia, July 18, 1877, in Leary, Appointment, Commission, and Personal File. Miller's subsequent references to his battalion of the Fourth Artillery in the Clearwater action invariably omitted Captain Charles B. Throckmorton's Company M. That Company M was present there was no doubt; perhaps the unit did not occupy a front line position in the fighting but was used to guard the pack train.

23. Boise, Idaho *Tri-Weekly Statesman,* July 19, 1877.

24. Lieutenant Wood noted in his journal that Howard ordered "forward two Gatling guns & supports them by all the troops except Capt. Trimble's Co. of Cavalry." Wood made no mention of a howitzer at this location. C. E. S. Wood, "Journal," July 11, 1877. The 12-pounder mountain howitzer was "a small, light, bronze piece about 3 feet long, weighing 220 pounds, capable of being easily removed from its carriage, and transported upon the back of a mule. The shell weighs,

when strapped and charged, 9.35 pounds, and the maximum range of the piece is about 1000 yards." Wilhelm, *Military Dictionary and Gazetteer*, 229–30.

25. The movement of the guns came on the advice of Ad Chapman, who told Howard that "'the ravine the Indians are ascending can be reached from there [pointing to the bluff beyond Stites Canyon]. It is a mile back by the way to go.' Gen'l Howard orders the Howitzer to go with all speed thither, and supports it by Winters['] Co. with gatling [sic] guns." C. E. S. Wood, "Journal," July 11, 1877.

26. Miller to Assistant Adjutant General, Department of the Columbia, July 18, 1877, in Leary, Appointment, Commission, and Personal File.

27. C. E. S. Wood, "Chief Joseph, the Nez Perce," 137.

28. Sergeant McCarthy remembered details of the initial deployment of his company: "When the rear of the column became engaged we [Company H] were halted on the Bluff overlooking the Clearwater, about a mile or so below the camp. With my glass we could see the Indians moving up the river or riding around their herds. We heard the firing back towards our rear but supposed it was only the howitzers shelling the retreating Indians. The column had strung out as usual with big gaps here and there, and only the sound of the big guns reached us. Our captain [Trimble], after a leisurely survey of the scene on the river below, took it into his head that a little drill would be a useful way to kill time, so we practised dismounting to fight on foot, mounting, etc. I became nervous and called the attention of the Captain to the firing, now growing heavier way back in [the] rear. The hills were rolling and concealed movements of [the] rest of [the] command. We mounted and awaited orders. A courier made signals to come back, and moving back we found Capt. Rodney's company and the packtrain in a sort of uncertain state." McCarthy, "Journal," 21.

29. Harry Bailey, "An Infantry Second Lieutenant," 14.

30. Accounts of Yellow Wolf in McWhorter, *Yellow Wolf*, 85–88; Ollokot's wife (Springtime) and Peopeo Tholekt in McWhorter, *Hear Me*, 298–99, 302–3. Ollokot's presence is indicated in ibid., 318. There is no mention of Looking Glass's involvement in the battle, although Joseph evidently took part. Ibid., 319–20.

31. Years later a Nez Perce named Johnson Boyd identified himself as one of those who attacked the pack train. Lewiston *Tribune*, undated ca. 1957 news item, clippings file, Idaho State Historical Society, Boise. See also McWhorter, *Yellow Wolf*, 94. One of the packers killed was Louis Pecha, who resided on Salmon River and who had been employed by the army since June. Canby, "Report of Indian depredations."

32. The Nez Perce Roaring Eagle recalled that "we pushed those soldiers back on the pack-saddle fort . . . but we could not stand before the soldiers' big guns. We were forced back from that part of the field." McWhorter, *Hear Me*, 303–4.

33. Second Lieutenant Edward S. Farrow wrote that the guns were moved "to a second bluff in that direction, beyond a deep and rocky transverse ravine [the identical ravine as cited by Howard, above], almost at right angles to the cañon." Farrow, "Assembling of the Soldiers," 156. Likewise, First Lieutenant Albert G. Forse recalled that "the howitzers [sic] were brought into requisition and shelling began, but at each explosion the Indians would shout in derision. Captain Winters was finally sent with his troop, supported by a company of infantry, to a projecting bluff higher up the river from which it was thought the howitzers would be effective." Forse, "Chief Joseph as a Commander," 3. This

second position for the artillery pieces, on the bluff immediately south of the present Stites Canyon, was recommended by Chapman, who told Howard that "the ravine the Indians are ascending can be reached from there." Account in Portland *Daily Oregonian*, July 27, 1877. See also Correspondent Thomas A. Sutherland's account in Portland *Daily Standard*, July 23, 1877, and his account in Sutherland, *Howard's Campaign*, 12.

34. Report of Captain Stephen P. Jocelyn, September 2, 1877, quoted in Jocelyn, *Mostly Alkali*, 237.

35. McCarthy, "Journal," 24.

36. Ibid.

37. For Miles's record, see Heitman, *Historical Register and Dictionary*, 1:708. Lieutenant Harry L. Bailey stated that Miles "was so nervous in this campaign that he was very wearing on all under him." Bailey to L. V. McWhorter, March 6, 1931, folder 182, McWhorter Papers.

38. Williams was first shot in the thigh. As he attempted to stem the bleeding by applying a tourniquet, he received the second wound. Jocelyn, *Mostly Alkali*, 235. Bancroft described his experience thus: "I was shot about 3 o'clock in the afternoon; lay on the field all that day and night and part of the next day. . . . Two of my best men, Sergeant [James A.] Workman and Corporal [Charles] Marguarandt [Marquardt], were killed by my side. While I was being carried to the rear by one of my men, . . . he had one ear shot clean away, and I did not know it till after he had laid me down." Portland *Daily Standard*, September 6, 1877.

39. Miller to Assistant Adjutant General, Department of the Columbia, July 18, 1877, in Leary, Appointment, Commission, and Personal File.

40. Boise, Idaho *Tri-Weekly Statesman*, July 19, 1877.

41. In 1890, the Army awarded LeMay a Certificate of Merit for his performance. *U.S. Army Gallantry and Meritorious Conduct*, 76.

42. Miller to Assistant Adjutant General, Department of the Columbia, July 18, 1877, in Leary, Appointment, Commission, and Personal File.

43. New York *Herald*, September 10, 1877.

44. Yellow Bull account in Curtis, *North American Indian*, 8:165–66. It is uncertain exactly when this incident occurred.

45. Miller to Assistant Adjutant General, Department of the Columbia, July 18, 1877, in Leary, Appointment, Commission, and Personal File. An 1858 West Point graduate, Miller had spent his entire career in the Fourth Artillery. In the Civil War, he fought at Richmond, Antietam, Fredericksburg, and Chancellorsville, later served with Major General Philip H. Sheridan in the Shenandoah Valley, and fought with General Ulysses S. Grant at Petersburg during the closing operations. Miller's most notable prior western service had occurred during the Modoc Indian campaign, when he led a battalion of artillery and infantry in rescuing the survivors of the peace commission after the murder of Major General Edward R. S. Canby. Miller, Appointment, Commission, and Personal File; Powell, *Powell's Records*, 402; Cullum, *Biographical Register*, 2:702–3; Heitman, *Historical Register and Dictionary*, 1:711.

46. New York *Herald*, September 10, 1877.

47. Harry Bailey, "An Infantry Second Lieutenant," 14; Bailey to McWhorter, March 5, 1933, folder 182, McWhorter Papers. One of the casualties of this action was Private Francis Winters of Company B, Twenty-first Infantry. Wrote

Lieutenant Bailey: "He was wounded severely in the hip. . . . He was near me and had his hat shot off three times, and his cartridge belt cut entirely off by a bullet, the leather being cut as by a knife, as I saw it at the moment it occurred. . . . He kept saying that some of our own men had shot him." Bailey to his father, September 14, 1877, quoted in Jocelyn, *Mostly Alkali*, 232 n. 8. See also the letter from Bailey describing this incident in Farrow, "Assembling of the Soldiers," 162–63. At the left of Miller's advanced position stood a large, lone pine tree, behind which at least one Nez Perce sharpshooter was posted. John P. Schorr to McWhorter, ca. January 1934, folder 179, McWhorter Papers. Evidently, this man was shot and fell back near the stone barricades. Bailey mentioned later seeing a dead warrior there with a shell hole in his head possibly inflicted by the howitzer, and Peopeo Tholekt identified the man as Lelooskin (Whittling). Bailey to McWhorter, March 6, 1931, folder 182, McWhorter Papers; McWhorter, *Hear Me*, 312. After this happened, some of Miller's men took up position at the tree. A reporter noted: "There were two boys behind a big pine tree, and I made the third. The Indians would rise out of the grass, take a rapid look, drop down and then fire as fast as they could. The bark of our tree was cut to pieces. The Indians were not more than twenty yards from us. One of the boys, quite a lad, just gloried in the fun. He put his hat on his rifle and held it out. As we expected, our Indians rose up and fired." Boise, Idaho *Tri-Weekly Statesman*, July 19, 1877. It is apparently this tree that is pictured in Lieutenant Fletcher's sketch, "Battle of Clearwater," inset drawing in Fletcher, "Department of Columbia Map."

   48. Harry Bailey, "An Infantry Second Lieutenant," 15.
   49. Howard, "Report," 605.
   50. McWhorter, *Yellow Wolf*, 88.
   51. Ibid., 89–91; McWhorter, *Hear Me*, 305, 312–13.
   52. McWhorter, *Hear Me*, 309–10.
   53. Trimble, "Battle of the Clearwater," 143.
   54. On this tendency of the Indians, see the report of Captain George H. Burton in "Summary of Reports . . . Non-Effectiveness."
   55. McCarthy, Diary, July 11, 1877. See also McCarthy, "Journal," 22.
   56. Comment by Captain Whipple in "Proceedings [of] Court of Inquiry."
   57. McCarthy, Diary, July 11, 1877.
   58. Trimble, "Battle of the Clearwater," 144–45.
   59. Howard's report states that "during the night stone barricades and rifle-pits were constructed by ourselves and the enemy." Howard, "Report," 605.
   60. Harry Bailey, "An Infantry Second Lieutenant," 16.
   61. Boise, Idaho *Tri-Weekly Statesman*, July 19, 1877.
   62. McCarthy wrote that "some of the Infantry armed with trowel bayonets finding themselves where there was [sic] no stones dug little rifle pits. Where there was most danger the breastworks were larger and contained sometimes 2, 3, and I believe even 4 men. On our side of the semicircle, the least exposed [side], the men occupied each alternate breastwork during the night." McCarthy, Diary, July 11, 1877.
   63. This reference to warriors firing from treetops appears in several accounts. The Nez Perce Many Wounds told McWhorter that his informants always denied that sharpshooters fired from the tops, but allowed that "soldiers might have thought shots came from among the branches of the trees." Grizzly

Bear Blanket "was on a point or knoll back of [a] tree from where he could see whole group of soldiers. To them it must have looked like he was up the tree." McWhorter, *Hear Me*, 306.

64. First Lieutenant Melville C. Wilkinson letter, July 17, 1877, in *Army and Navy Journal*, August 18, 1877.

65. McWhorter, *Yellow Wolf*, 92; McWhorter, *Hear Me*, 312–13; Pouliot and White, "Clearwater Battlefield," 6.

66. First Lieutenant Melville C. Wilkinson letter, July 17, 1877, in *Army and Navy Journal*, August 18, 1877.

67. Lieutenant Bailey was appointed to prepare the line troops to attack in support of Miller's charge. He recalled that none of the other officers wanted to help arrange the soldiers, and that he and First Lieutenant Charles F. Humphrey had to do it alone. "When approaching the trench of Capt. [First Lieutenant] [James A.] Haugh[e]y and [Second] Lieut. [Francis E.] Eltonhead, they yelled at me to 'lie down,' as I was drawing fire. . . . They had stuck to their trench all thru, and certainly looked very sweaty and dirty." Harry Bailey, "An Infantry Second Lieutenant," 18. Bailey had trouble with the enlisted men, too. "I had . . . difficulty in making the men KEEP the skirmish line after I had arranged them, for they would run back and jump into the holes." Bailey to McWhorter, January 12, 1931, folder 182, McWhorter Papers.

68. Lewiston *Teller*, July 21, 1877.

69. Miller to Assistant Adjutant General, Department of the Columbia, July 18, 1877, in Leary, Appointment, Commission, and Personal File.

70. Howard, "Report," 605.

71. Farrow to James T. Gray, July 16, 1877, Gray, Correspondence.

72. McCarthy, Diary, July 12, 1877.

73. Ibid. See also McCarthy, "Journal," 24–25.

74. McWhorter, *Yellow Wolf*, 96 n. 2; and McWhorter, *Hear Me*, 314–15. One of the men, Teeweeyownah (Over the Point), went to the smoking lodge and found many warriors, who had been riding back and forth from the village, "sitting around smoking." He scolded them repeatedly for their dereliction, then untied and released their horses. This angered the warriors. Over the Point then returned to the ravine and notified the others about what was happening, and the leaders decided that without the warriors' support it would be better to protect the camp. They left and were followed by those from the smoking lodge. McWhorter, *Hear Me*, 315–16 n. 35. Haines stated that the disagreement actually began during the fighting on July 11 and carried over to the twelfth. Francis Haines, *Nez Perces*, 237; Francis Haines, "Chief Joseph," 5.

75. McWhorter, *Yellow Wolf*, 100–101.

76. Ibid., 96–98, 100–101.

77. Quoted in McWhorter, *Hear Me*, 314–15.

78. Quoted in ibid., 317.

79. McWhorter, *Yellow Wolf*, 97; and McWhorter, *Hear Me*, 320. Another Nez Perce account stated that Looking Glass was responsible for directing the camp to move. MacDonald, "Nez Perces," 244.

80. Parnell, "Salmon River Expedition," 132. Captain Perry once more came under criticism for not pressing the pursuit of the fleeing Nez Perces beyond the river, the argument being that this was the first and most logical opportunity since

the battle started to make efficient use of the cavalry. Together with his actions at White Bird and Cottonwood, it became a lively topic of conversation in the command, as well as an element for investigation in Perry's subsequent court of inquiry. The court exonerated him from blame at Clearwater, specifying that Perry "appears to have done all required of him, and all that, under the circumstances, could have been reasonably expected of him,—the Commanding General being present." "Proceedings [of] Court of Inquiry."

81. Wilkinson to McConville, July 12, 1877, entry 897, box 1, part 3, 1877, U.S. Army Continental Commands.

82. C. E. S. Wood, "Journal," July 11, 1877.

83. The caches were hollows in the ground so well covered with sod that their presence was nearly imperceptible and would likely not have been discovered but for the citizen guides who were familiar with the practice. Harry Bailey, "An Infantry Second Lieutenant," 18. In another description, Bailey wrote that the caches "were holes in the ground or rocks about three or four feet wide and about six feet deep, and cunningly covered with earth and ashes and trampled over with horses. The manner of finding them was by punching ramrods or stakes into the ground until the feel of buffalo hides a few feet below the surface gave the evidence." Quoted in Mrs. Harry B. Longworth to McWhorter, January 12, 1943, folder 182, McWhorter Papers.

84. On the other hand, a message from Howard noted that there were "arms captured in the battle of the 11th & 12th," along with "several hundred rounds of metallic ammunition . . . found in the hostile camp." This and other factors led army officers to conclude that the Nez Perces armed themselves with Henrys, Winchesters, Springfield carbines and rifles, "and apparently some long range target rifles—name unknown." Howard to Assistant Adjutant General, Division of the Pacific, July 28, 1877, entry 897, box 1, part 3, 1877, U.S. Army Continental Commands.

85. Lieutenant Bailey retrieved several items from the South Fork village. In 1927 he donated a fringed buckskin shirt, a powder horn, a beaded sheath, and six bronze bells to the Allen County Historical and Archeological Society at Lima, Ohio. Longworth to McWhorter, January 12, 1943, folder 182, McWhorter Papers. Some of these items were returned to the Nez Perces in 1999.

In addition to the materials previously cited, this account of the Clearwater engagement is reconstructed from an amalgam of data drawn from the following materials: McDowell to Adjutant General, telegram (Howard's initial report), July 14, 1877, item 3973, roll 336, Nez Perce War Papers; Surgeon (Major) Charles T. Alexander to Medical Director, Department of the Columbia, July 14, 1877, entry 624, box 1, Office of the Adjutant General; C. E. S. Wood, "Notes on Nez Perces Expedition," July 11, 12, 1877; pen and ink sketch titled, "Battle of Clearwater," inset drawing in Fletcher, "Department of Columbia Map"; Brimlow, "Nez Perce War Diary," 30; Albert G. Forse to Howard, April 4, 1895, Forse Papers; Harry L. Bailey to McWhorter, December 9, 1932, folder 182, McWhorter Papers; Bailey to McWhorter (including sketch map), January 29, 1934, item 88, McWhorter Papers; C. E. S. Wood to C. J. Brosnan, January 7, 1918, in *The Bookmark*, a ca. 1940 publication of the University of Idaho Library, p. 236, Brosnan Collection; Portland *Daily Oregonian*, July 16, 1877; Boise, Idaho *Tri-Weekly Statesman*, July 17, 1877; Portland *Daily Standard*, July 14, 1877; Howard, "Nez Perces Campaign of 1877," September 26, 1878, and October 3, 1878; Howard, *My Life and Experiences*, 288–89; R. P. Page Wainwright, "The First Regiment of Cavalry," in Rodenbough and Haskin, *Army of the United States*, 169; Alexander B. Dyer, "The Fourth Regiment of Artillery," in ibid., 373–74; Fred H. E. Ebstein, "Twenty-first Regiment of Infantry," in ibid., 677; Sternberg, *George Miller Sternberg*, 60–61; Charles Rhodes, "Chief Joseph," 219–20; Francis Haines, *Nez Perces*, 235–38; and Josephy, *Nez Perce Indians*, 546–52. Contemporary artistic renditions of events associated with the Clearwater engagement, based upon "sketches by an officer of General Howard's staff," appear in the New York *Daily Graphic*, August 3, 1877.

Nee-Me-Poo accounts of the Clearwater action are few and, except for those noted above (mostly in McWhorter's books or materials), are generally vague as to specifics and locale. McWhorter's *Yellow Wolf* and *Hear Me* contain much more conversationally derived and descriptive anecdotal material; the essence alone is presented here. Nonetheless, for other Nez Perce accounts not previously cited, see "Story of Kawownonilpilp"; Weptas Nut (No Feather), Interview; and Joseph [Heinmot Tooyalakekt], "An Indian's Views," 426. Two possible pictographic renderings of incidents at the Clearwater battle appear in a sketchbook in the Special Collections of the University of Oregon Library, Eugene. See Stern, Schmitt, and Halfmoon, "A Cayuse–Nez Perce Sketchbook," 360–62.

86. "List of Wounded in Gen. Howard's expedition . . . Battle of Clear Water"; Captain Evan Miles to Adjutant General, November 24, 1877, entry 624, box 1 (two sheets), Office of the Adjutant General; "Report of the Killed, Wounded and Missing"; "Classified Return . . . Battle of Clearwater." A complete list of army casualties is in Appendix A. Regarding the missing man, he was Private Charles E. Simonds, Battery G, Fourth Artillery, who was reported missing effective July 12. Yellow Wolf mentioned seeing a dead soldier on the previous day and presumed he had deserted. McWhorter, *Yellow Wolf*, 85. And about twenty years after the battle, settlers in the area found the remains of a soldier "back of one of the hills near Stites," along with four canteens, some army buttons, and silver coins. Nez Perce Indians Wars 2, 153, Camp Manuscript Field Notes, Camp Papers, LBNM.

87. C. E. S. Wood, "Chief Joseph, the Nez Perce," 137.

88. McCarthy, Diary, July 12, 1877. Captain Jocelyn alluded to a diagram that located the grave "just in rear of the hospital, within the limits of the camp held by the troops during the engagement." Jocelyn, *Mostly Alkali*, 237. Presumably, but not certainly, the dead were eventually removed to Fort Lapwai, and later to the post cemetery at Fort Walla Walla, where a small granite marker is all that recognizes the thirteen killed at Clearwater. Thompson, "Thirteen U.S. Soldiers," 47, 63.

89. Two men died en route. One was buried along the road and the other at Grangeville. Sternberg to Colonel E. I. Baily, Medical Director, Department of the Columbia, July 15, 1877, entry 624, box 1, Office of the Adjutant General (also published in "Report of the Surgeon-General," in Secretary of War, *Report . . . 1878*, 428.) See also a variant form of this letter in Sternberg to the Surgeon General, July 15, 1877, in ibid.

90. Sternberg to the Surgeon General, July 22, 1877, entry 624, box 1, Office of the Adjutant General; Sternberg, *George Miller Sternberg*, 62-63; and Kober, *Reminiscences of George Martin Kober*, 358, 359. For a contemporary discussion of the matter of moving the wounded by mule litter during the Indian wars, see Otis, *Transport of Sick and Wounded*.

91. Howard, "Report," 606. Howard reported that "about 300 warriors, aided by their women," (ibid.) faced his command at the Clearwater, a figure that—based on approximations of the strength of the various bands—is unreasonable. It is more likely that the Nez Perce warriors at the Clearwater numbered fewer than 150—about half of Howard's strength.

92. McWhorter, *Yellow Wolf*, 98–100; McWhorter, *Hear Me*, 323; and Joseph [Heinmot Tooyalakekt], "An Indian's Views," 426. Duncan MacDonald's informants told him that the Nez Perces lost four killed and four wounded, all on the first day of the battle. MacDonald, "Nez Perces," 244. See listing in Appendix B.

93. "Report of the General of the Army," November 7, 1877, in Secretary of War, *Report . . . 1877*, 10; Sutherland, *Howard's Campaign*, 13; John Carpenter, *Sword and Olive Branch*, 251; and Francis Haines, "Chief Joseph," 5.

94. Wood to Hayes, telegram, July 14, 1877, entry 107, box 2, part 3, 1877, U.S. Army Continental Commands; Corbett to McCrary, July 14, 1877, ibid: and Dolph to Hayes, July 14, 1877, ibid. McDowell informed Wood that he "as Division Commander reserves to himself alone the privilege of communicating direct with the President." Lieutenant Colonel John C. Kelton to Wood, July 21, 1877, ibid. The New York *World*, July 14, 1877, reported that "Howard's inefficiency" had caused the administration to consider replacing him with Crook and that "it is entirely possible Howard may be superseded to-morrow." See also John Carpenter, "General Howard," 134–35.

95. Grostein and Binnard to Howard, July 26, 1877, entry 107, box 2, part 3, 1877, U.S. Army Continental Commands.

96. General Field Orders No. 2, Headquarters, Department of the Columbia (In the Field), July 16, 1877, entry 897, box 1, part 3, 1877, U.S. Army Continental Commands.

97. Beyer and Keydel, *Deeds of Valor*, 2:244; *The Medal of Honor*, 230; *U.S. Army Gallantry and Meritorious Conduct*, 75–77, 87.

CHAPTER 5

1. McCarthy, Diary, July 13, 1877. The Nez Perces crossed the river adjacent to the geologic and cultural feature Heart of the Monster, which figures prominently in Nee-Me-Poo origin folklore and history and is an interpretive unit of Nez Perce National Historical Park. In 1877, a wire ferry that forded passengers across the river had been disabled prior to Howard's arrival. Lillian Pethtel, communication with author, Kamiah, Idaho, February 28, 1995.

2. McCarthy, Diary, July 13, 1877; Trimble's testimony in "Proceedings [of] Court of Inquiry"; and McCarthy, "Journal," 16. The order of the troops as they descended the bluffs to Kamiah was as follows: "Captain Jackson's Co. in advanced [sic], Miles' command, gatling [sic] guns, howitzers, then Miller's artillery command, Cavalry, pack train, Trimble as rear guard." C. E. S. Wood, "Journal," July 13, 1877.

3. Whipple's testimony in "Proceedings [of] Court of Inquiry."

4. "Summary of Reports . . . Non-Effectiveness," 2.

5. Brimlow, "Nez Perce War Diary," 30.

6. Sutherland, *Howard's Campaign*, 15.

7. Trimble's testimony in "Proceedings [of] Court of Inquiry." Trimble also wrote that the cavalry approached the river "rather incautiously and receiving several volleys retired in some haste, if not confusion." Trimble, "Battle of the

Clearwater," 149. Oddly, although many senior officers considered sabres out-
moded for cavalry combat by 1877, Howard endorsed their use: "The effect of a
charge in a body was seen when our Cavalry came down the steep hills upon the
retreating Indians at Kamiah. Sabres would have added to the terror-inspiring
movement." "Summary of Reports . . . Non-Effectiveness," 3.

8. One man was apparently wounded superficially and thus not formally reported in the medical log (a common procedure in Indian combat), although the
casualty is mentioned in the official reports. See, for example, Howard to Adjutant
General, Division of the Pacific, July 15, 1877, items 6718 and 6724, roll 338, Nez
Perce War Papers. The severely wounded man was Corporal William Mulcahy,
Company A, Fourth Artillery, who was evidently on duty with the cavalry and was
shot in the head. McDowell, "Report," 133.

9. Brooks to sister, July 21, 1877, in Bennett, "History and Legend of . . .
Brooks," 39.

10. Harry L. Bailey to C. W. Risley, July 26, 1877, folder 182, McWhorter
Papers. McWhorter's sources indicated that no Nez Perces were injured in this
brief action. McWhorter, *Hear Me*, 328 n. 7; McWhorter, *Yellow Wolf*, 103. See
also Yellow Bull account in Curtis, *North American Indian*, 8:166.

11. Howard's encampment was where the Kamiah airport is today. Probably
his soldiers raised earthworks at appropriate points about the bivouac. See
McWhorter, *Hear Me*, 330. For the events at Kamiah, see also Josephy, *Nez Perce
Indians*, 553.

12. Howard to McDowell, July 15, 1877, entry 897, box 1, part 3, 1877, U.S.
Army Continental Commands; Portland *Daily Oregonian*, July 19, 1877; and *Army
and Navy Journal*, July 28, 1877.

13. Contained in entry 897, box 1, part 3, 1877, U.S. Army Continental
Commands. The intended recipient of this message is not known. Sutherland,
Howard's Campaign, 17, published one that was practically identical, stating that it
was "Howard's answer to Joseph" regarding his proposed surrender. However, too
many internal nuances suggest otherwise, and that the word "may" was intended
in the conditional, rather than the permissive, sense. Perhaps it was an informal
note for his adjutant at Portland or for General McDowell. Regardless, Major
Mason, as in Howard's formal missive, was more definite, stating that "Joseph
promises to come in tomorrow morning with all his people and surrender immediately." Mason to wife, July 15, 1877, quoted in Mark Brown, "Joseph Myth," 7.
Yellow Wolf identified the Nez Perce messenger as Zya Timenna (No Heart).
McWhorter, *Hear Me*, 329.

14. John Carpenter, "General Howard" 135. On the sixteenth, Lieutenant
Farrow wrote a friend: "We are expecting Joseph to come and surrender to day—
he says he can't fight any more, and that he is whipped and wants to give up. We
demand an unconditional surrender. If he surrenders Looking Glass and White
Bird will claim our attention." Edward S. Farrow to James T. Gray, July 16, 1877,
Gray, Correspondence.

15. The group, eventually imprisoned at Fort Vancouver, Washington Territory, included the following people: "Old" Chief Red Heart, Nenetsukusten (son
of Red Heart), Tmenah Ilppilp (son of Red Heart), "Old Man" Halfmoon, Tsalahe,
Nosm, John Reuben, Little Bear, Alex Hayes, Teponoth, Hahatsi Hekelantsa, "Old"
Chief Jacob, Ayokkasie, Pile of Clouds, Walweyes, James Hines, Quul Quul Tami,

Jim Powers, Pacuslawatakth, George Raymond, Kaiyewich, Tsacope, Hemakio Autway, Petolwetalooth, Hamolitshamolits, Petolackyoth, Wetahweenonmi, Talwenommi, Ilsoopop, and an unnamed son of Little Bear. List compiled by Black Eagle in May 1930, and provided to the author by Otis Halfmoon, Nez Perce National Historical Park, Spalding, Idaho, December 12, 1995. The events of July 15 are described in McCarthy, Diary, July 16, 1877; Trimble's testimony in "Proceedings [of] Court of Inquiry"; Howard, "Report," 606; McConville to Governor Mason Brayman, August, 1877, in "Nez Perce War Letters," 68; Howard, "Nez Perces Campaign of 1877," October 3, 1878; Wilmot, "Battle of the Clearwater"; McDowell to Adjutant General, July 19, 1877, item 4110, roll 336, Nez Perce War Papers; Sutherland, *Howard's Campaign,* 16; *Frank Leslie's Illustrated Newspaper,* August 4, 1877; Forse, "Chief Joseph as a Commander," 5–6; Josephy, *Nez Perce Indians,* 554–55; and Francis Haines, *Nez Perces,* 275–76. There is a story, perhaps apocryphal, that the messenger kept Howard occupied while the Indians packed toward the Lolo trail. He then "fired a shot from his rifle in Howard's direction, slapped that portion of his anatomy which his leggins did not reach, and rode off." Eugene Wilson, "Nez Perce Campaign," 10–11. See also McWhorter, *Hear Me,* 329. Red Heart had apparently been in Looking Glass's village when it was attacked on July 1, but had decided against subsequently joining in the fighting against the soldiers. McWhorter, *Hear Me,* 332. See also McWhorter, *Yellow Wolf,* 104–5, 310–12; and Francis Haines, *Nez Perces,* 239–40.

16. Captain Babbitt wrote that the Nez Perces "are said to be divided in opinion and quarreling among themselves. Small parties are constantly breaking away from the main band and surrendering." Quoted in Boise, Idaho *Tri-Weekly Statesman,* July 21, 1877.

17. McCarthy, Diary, July 16, 1877. See also Brimlow, "Nez Perce War Diary," 31. Because the ferry was out of commission, the troops crossed ten at a time in the single boat available. Redfield, "Reminiscences of Francis M. Redfield," 75. The order of crossing was infantry, artillery, and cavalry, with Jackson's company fording last. Howard to Perry, July 15, 1877, entry 897, box 1, part 3, 1877, U.S. Army Continental Commands.

18. Eugene Wilson, "Nez Perce Campaign," 13.

19. Ibid., 14.

20. McConville to Governor Mason Brayman, August 1877, in "Nez Perce War Letters," 69.

21. During a halt soon after this incident, Lieutenant Parnell and others discovered sawdust on the ground. Parnell maintained that "many of the trees had been sawed off . . . leaving the trees still standing on their stumps." The object, theorized Parnell, was "to let us pass until our rearguard had advanced beyond that point, whereupon some fifty or sixty warriors . . . were to drop the trees across the trail and block our retreat while they would attack us." Parnell, "Salmon River Expedition," 134–35. McWhorter's Nez Perce informants denied using this improbable tactic, and McWhorter dismissed it as sensationalism. McWhorter, *Hear Me,* 341–42.

22. Eugene Wilson, "Nez Perce Campaign," 16–17; McCarthy, Diary, July 17, 1877; Trimble's testimony in "Proceedings [of] Court of Inquiry"; McCarthy, "Journal," 16–17; Brimlow, "Nez Perce War Diary," 31; Monteith to Commissioner of Indian Affairs John Q. Smith, July 31, 1877, item 6877, roll 337, Nez

Perce War Papers; Howard, "Report," 606; McConville to Brayman, August, 1877, in "Nez Perce War Letters," 68–69; Portland *Daily Standard*, July 21, 1877; Portland *Daily Standard*, August 4, 1877; Sutherland, *Howard's Campaign*, 18; Howard, "Nez Perces Campaign of 1877," October 3, 1878; Trimble, "Battle of the Clearwater," 149–50; Josephy, *Nez Perce Indians*, 558–59. Trimble, as well as other officers, believed that "the Cavalry retreated rather quickly" in this affair. "Proceedings [of] Court of Inquiry." Scout Abraham Brooks eventually died at Lapwai from his wounds. McWhorter, *Hear Me*, 338–39. See the accounts of Seekumses Kunnin (Horse Blanket) and Two Moon in McWhorter, *Hear Me*, 338, 340; and that of Yellow Wolf in McWhorter, *Yellow Wolf*, 106. Yet another Nez Perce account of their confrontation with the army scouts—this one containing much verbal reprimand directed against them—is in MacDonald, "Nez Perces," 245–46. The volunteers' simmering dislike of the regulars is pervasive in nearly all documents generated by the volunteers in the Idaho portion of the conflict. For example, George Hunter described the Lolo reconnaissance as follows: "The Indian scouts, through their tactics, drew the attention of the hostiles, so as to let McConville and his men out of the snap, and seeing that the whole force of the regulars had taken to flight, he found it necessary to follow them rather than suffer his handful of men to be cut off." Portland *Daily Oregonian*, July 21, 1877.

23. McCarthy, Diary, July 15, 16, 17, 18, 1877.

24. Portland *Daily Oregonian*, July 17, 1877; Howard to George Shearer, July 18, 1877, Shearer Papers; and Memorandum Order, August 28, 1877, Headquarters, North Idaho Volunteers, ibid. For details of the subsequent work of the volunteers, see Boise, Idaho *Weekly Statesman*, August 11, 1877.

25. McCarthy, Diary, July 20, 1877.

26. McDowell to Adjutant General, July 19, 1877, item 4110, roll 336, Nez Perce War Papers; Howard, "Report," 607; McCarthy, Diary, July 20, 1877; McCarthy, "Journal," 26; MacDonald, "Nez Perces," 245; and Monteith to Smith, July 31, 1877, item 6877, roll 337, Nez Perce War Papers. Wrote Monteith in ibid.: "The treaty Indians have lost a great deal by the hostiles, and the troops have destroyed fences, crops, &c., belonging to the Kamiah Indians, which will leave many in want. Col. Watkins [Indian Inspector] will probably . . . recommend an appropriation to reimburse them. They should receive the same consideration as settlers who have lost by the hostiles." See also Josephy, *Nez Perce Indians*, 560; and Francis Haines, *Nez Perces*, 278.

27. Croasdaile filed a claim for damage incurred not only by the Nez Perces but by the army. Wrote Major Canby in August 1877: "His house at Sheep Ranch ½ mile from residence is occupied by Colonel John Green as Headquarters, & his barn, corral, & fields, occupied by troops and horses. . . . The Indians entered the [dwelling] house first and destroyed most of the furniture &c and were followed by the soldiers & volunteers, who completed the destruction." Canby, "Report of Indian depredations." Of significance were some explosive bullets taken from the homestead of Croasdaile, a retired British officer. Some of the cartridges saw later use by Nez Perce warriors at the battles of the Big Hole and Bear's Paw Mountains (see discussion in chapter 13).

28. Howard, "Report," 607–8; General Field Orders No. 3, Headquarters Department of the Columbia (in the field), July 23, 1877, entry 107, box 2, part 3, 1877, U.S. Army Continental Commands; "Department of the Columbia, Roster

of Troops"; *Army and Navy Journal*, August 4, 1877; Portland *Daily Oregonian*, July 27, 1877; William M. Wright, "The Second Regiment of Infantry," in Rodenbough and Haskins, *Army of the United States*, 430.

29. Howard, "Report," 608; C. E. S. Wood, "Journal," July 28, 29, and 30, 1877; McDowell to Adjutant General, July 6, 1877, item 3792, roll 336, Nez Perce War Papers; Howard to Colonel Alfred Sully, July 24, 1877, entry 897, box 1, part 3, 1877, U.S. Army Continental Commands; Jocelyn, *Mostly Alkali*, 239–41; Sutherland, *Howard's Campaign*, 18–19; Boise, Idaho *Tri-Weekly Statesman*, July 21, 1877; Portland *Daily Oregonian*, July 27, 1877; FitzGerald, *Army Doctor's Wife*, 283, 284; R. P. Page Wainwright, "The First Regiment of Cavalry," in Rodenbough and Haskin, *Army of the United States*, 169; Alexander B. Dyer, "The Fourth Regiment of Artillery," in ibid., 374. For background on the Bannocks, see Madsen, *Bannock of Idaho*. The Coehorn was a small, bronze 24-pounder Model 1841 siege and garrison mortar mounted on a small wooden bed. It had a maximum range of 1,200 yards. The piece, including its bed, weighed about 296 pounds and was easily transportable. Ripley, *Artillery and Ammunition*, 58–59. This gun was not used in the Clearwater battle and presumably arrived with the fresh Fourth Artillery companies from San Francisco.

30. Lindgren, *Geological Reconnaissance*, 33, 34; Dingler and Breckenridge, "Glacial Reconnaissance," 645, 646; and Space, *Lolo Trail*, 1–4, 43–45 (much of this work is encompassed in Space's larger study, Space, *Clearwater Story*). McWhorter gave the name of the fur trapper as Joseph Lolo, or Lulu, killed by a bear in 1852. For details, see McWhorter, *Hear Me*, 343 n. 1.

31. The Weippe council and its aftermath is in McWhorter, *Hear Me*, 334–36, 340; McWhorter, *Yellow Wolf*, 104–5; MacDonald, "Nez Perces," 245; Yellow Bull account in Curtis, *North American Indian*, 8:166; Yellow Bull, Account; Francis Haines, "Chief Joseph," 5–6; and Otis Halfmoon, communication with author, Nez Perce National Historical Park, Spalding, Idaho, December 12, 1995. See also Josephy, *Nez Perce Indians*, 555–57; and Francis Haines, *Nez Perces*, 274–75.

32. The Nee-Me-Poo Albert Moore commented on the traditional use of the site: "We always camped below the Lolo Hot Springs. We camped coming through there on our way home to the Bitterroot. . . . We would make a tipi and stay two or three nights. When we moved on, we piled up these poles to have there when we returned." Thomas, "Pi.Lu'.Ye.Kin," 2.

33. MacDonald, "Nez Perces," 247.

34. Thian, *Notes Illustrating the Military Geography*, 24, 58.

35. Frazer, *Forts of the West*, 83.

36. Rawn to Acting Assistant Adjutant General, District of Montana, July 16, 1877, Fort Missoula Letterbook. Background on Rawn is in Heitman, *Historical Register and Dictionary*, 1:817. Fortification of the Missoula post is discussed in Charles N. Loynes, "Battle of the 'Big Hole,'" *Winners of the West*, March 1925 (this account also appears in *Winners of the West*, April and May, 1924, under the title, "With the Seventh Infantry in Montana"). For the Flathead factor, see Fahey, *Flathead Indians*, 189–90.

37. Space, *Lolo Trail*, 46.

38. The news that reached the Bitterroot Valley about the appearance of the Nez Perces was augmented by the report of their presence at Lolo Hot Springs brought by two youths, William Silverthorn and Peter Matt, of Stevensville, who

encountered the tribesmen while on a holiday at the springs. The Nez Perces detained them, but the two managed to escape and reached Stevensville to alert the residents. Henry Buck, "Nez Perce Indian Campaign," 15. The Salt Lake *Daily Tribune*, July 26, 1877, reported that Silverthorn (no mention of Matt) had been en route to Lewiston when captured by the Nez Perces, who held him for eight days. Silverthorn escaped during the night of July 22 and reached Woodbridge's pickets.

39. Captain Charles C. Rawn report, September 30, 1877, in Terry, "Report," 500–501. There was some opinion that the Nez Perces might circumvent Rawn's command, taking one of several trails and ravines out of Lolo Canyon either to reach the Jocko (Kutenai) Reservation to the north or to head east directly through Missoula and up the Big Blackfoot River. Ferdinand Kennett letter, July 25, 1877, copy in vertical files, Indians—Wars—1877, Parmly Billings Library, Billings, Mont.

40. Corporal Charles Loynes account in McWhorter, *Hear Me*, 347.

41. Rawn to First Lieutenant Levi F. Burnett, July 25, 1877, Fort Missoula Letterbook; and Portland *Daily Oregonian*, July 27, 1877

42. Henry Buck, "Nez Perce Indian Campaign," 18; Mark Brown, "Joseph Legend," 51. Rawn stated that he arranged the second meeting "for the purpose of gaining time for General Howard's forces to get up and for General Gibbon to arrive from Fort Shaw." Captain Charles C. Rawn report, September 30, 1877, in Terry, "Report," 501. It is clear that Looking Glass was in charge of these events from the Nez Perce side, and that Joseph's role was at this point subordinate. See MacDonald, "Nez Perces," 248. Henry Buck identified the principals with Rawn as volunteers William Baker, Amos Buck, and Cole B. Sanders. Henry Buck, "Nez Perce Indian Campaign," 18.

43. Helena *Daily Independent—Extra*, July 29, 1877; and Barsness and Dickinson, "Minutemen of Montana," 4–5.

44. Henry Buck, "Nez Perce Indian Campaign," 19; and Volunteer Alfred Cave account in Boise, Idaho *Weekly Statesman*, September 6, 1877.

45. "Narrative of John Buckhouse."

46. Wilson Harlan, "Fiasco at 'Fort Fizzle,'" 65 (Harlan's reminiscence also appears in Gilbert Harlan, "Diary of Wilson Barber Harlan"). Information about Delaware Jim, who had reportedly scouted for John C. Frémont in the 1840s and had worked in the area during the 1850s and 1860s as a hunter, guide, and interpreter, is in Weisel, *Men and Trade*, 117–18.

47. Captain Charles C. Rawn report, September 30, 1877, in Terry, "Report," 501. According to the Nez Perces, Rawn told Looking Glass that "any further communication he had to make must be made under a flag of truce at the fortified camp." MacDonald, "Nez Perces," 250. Governor Potts's political interests are outlined in Olson, "The Nez Perce," 165, 192–95. See also Josephy, *Nez Perce Indians*, 568–69.

48. Rawn to Burnett, July 27, 1877, Fort Missoula Letterbook. Rawn's report of September 30, 1877, apparently confuses the dates of the various meetings with the Nez Perces. Nez Perce sources maintained that only one meeting was held with Rawn. See the accounts of Two Moon and Wottolen in McWhorter, *Hear Me*, 352–54, and that of Yellow Wolf in McWhorter, *Yellow Wolf*, 106–7.

49. Charles N. Loynes, "Battle of the 'Big Hole,'" *Winners of the West*, March 1925. While the full extent and configuration of the works is unknown, one axis

that is today marked ran east and west with a probable "L" to the north at the west end, all occupying the higher alluvial fan bench north of Lolo Creek. Kermit M. Edmonds, telephone communication with author, January 25, 1996.

50. "Narrative of John Buckhouse."

51. Wilson Harlan, "Fiasco at 'Fort Fizzle,'" 65.

52. Henry Buck, "Nez Perce Indian Campaign," 19; and Fahey, *Flathead Indians*, 194.

53. Captain Charles C. Rawn report, September 30, 1877, in Terry, "Report," 501; and Rawn to Adjutant General, Department of the Columbia, August 1, 1877, Fort Missoula Letterbook. One feasible interpretation of Rawn's meeting on July 27 is that the Nez Perces agreed not to cause harm if allowed to pass through the Bitterroot without hindrance, and that Governor Potts and Rawn fashioned a "treaty" or secret nonaggression pact with them to that effect. See Francis Haines, *Nez Perces*, 247. For a thorough airing of the circumstantial evidence favoring this explanation, see Olson, "The Nez Perce," 165, 192–94. In support of this view, it should be noted that Joseph later told of having "made a treaty with these soldiers" just before the Fort Fizzle episode. Joseph [Heinmot Tooyalakekt], "An Indian's Views," 426. And Howard reported that: "It seems that the Indians really negotiated their way by promising the citizens that they would do them no harm if permitted to pass by unmolested. Captain Rawn thought it wiser under the circumstances to let them go than attempt a fight, which he feared would be disastrous." Howard, "Report," 609. Yet another contemporary reference stated: "As usual the volunteers weakened, particularly when the Indians, upon being interviewed, agreed to pass through the valley doing no harm if they were themselves unmolested." Captain Stephen P. Jocelyn letter, August 9, 1877, in Jocelyn, *Mostly Alkali*, 243.

54. McWhorter identified the three as Tom Hill, Thunder Eyes (George Amos), and an elderly man named Honan, or Kannah. The three had gone to see the soldiers over the objections of the Nez Perce leadership. The army jailed them at the Missoula post for the remainder of the war. McWhorter, *Hear Me*, 348 n. 14, 349 n. 15. (However, Hill was present at Bear's Paw in September.) Corporal Loynes remembered that there were four people in the party. "They were conducted to the rear, their feet and hands tied, and a guard placed over them." Charles N. Loynes, "Battle of the 'Big Hole,'" *Winners of the West*, March 1925. For a Nez Perce explanation of the events attendant on the arrival of Hill and the others, see MacDonald, "Nez Perces," 247.

55. Boise, Idaho *Tri-Weekly Statesman*, August 21, 1877, quoting the Deer Lodge *New North-West*. This reporter perhaps overextolled the Nez Perces' maneuver as "the boldest, most fearless, audacious and confident tactical movement we have known. It surpassed McClellan's flank movement from the Chickahomany [sic] to James River, or Grant's from the Rapidan to Richmond." The side movement led out of Lolo Canyon to Sleeman Creek and rejoined Lolo Creek about two and one-half miles west of its junction with the Bitterroot River. Space, *Lolo Trail*, 46.

56. Wilson Harlan, "Fiasco at 'Fort Fizzle,'" 66. Harlan believed that Rawn was incapacitated by drink during the incident of the Nez Perces' passing by his command. For an account that suggests that Rawn's pickets were purposely withdrawn to facilitate the Indians' movement (thereby endorsing the "secret agreement" scenario), see that of former Missoula volunteer John L. Humble in McWhorter, *Hear Me*, 351 n. 21.

57. Charles N. Loynes account in McWhorter, *Hear Me*, 352; Charles N. Loynes, "Battle of the 'Big Hole,'" *Winners of the West*, March 1925; Wilson Harlan, "Fiasco at 'Fort Fizzle,'"66. Quote is from Henry Buck, "Nez Perce Indian Campaign," 22. At least one volunteer ascribed the Nez Perces' reluctance to attack Rawn to the presence of the Flatheads with the command. Amos Buck, "Battle of the Big Hole," 119–20. See also Josephy, *Nez Perce Indians*, 567–72; and Francis Haines, *Nez Perces*, 284.

58. Captain Charles C. Rawn report, September 30, 1877, in Terry, "Report," 501. Aggressive logging and skidding operations, along with a fire in 1934, destroyed surface evidence of Fort Fizzle in Lolo Canyon. Barsness and Dickinson, "Minutemen of Montana," 7 n. 8. Today U.S. Highway 12 and a U.S. Forest Service picnic and recreation area cover the southern periphery of the site.

59. A Bitterroot volunteer described the aftermath somewhat more anticlimactically, perhaps indicative of the rather loose state of affairs among the Nez Perces, having left Idaho behind: "A squad of our men had been ordered down the creek [by Rawn], and had got mixed up with the Indians, and finally had a talk with them, and after this others, of our men, met or overtook them and talked with them, when they avowed their intentions to pass through the valley peaceably, if possible. About sundown a number of the valley men met Looking Glass and he agreed to molest no one, and go on through the valley as fast as possible if he was not molested." Alfred Cave account in Boise, Idaho *Weekly Statesman*, September 6, 1877.

60. Deer Lodge *New North-West*, quoted in Boise, Idaho *Tri-Weekly Statesman*, August 21, 1877.

61. Boise, Idaho *Weekly Statesman*, September 6, 1877.

62. Helena *Daily Herald*, July 30, 1877.

63. Alfred Cave account in Boise, Idaho *Weekly Statesman*, September 6, 1877.

64. Portland *Daily Standard*, September 6, 1877.

65. MacDonald, "Nez Perces," 251.

66. For the accusations against Rawn, as well as notice of the dissension appearing among the different Montana communities regarding what was or was not done at Fort Fizzle, see Olson, "The Nez Perce," 164–70. Thorough coverage of the Fort Fizzle affair, together with a discussion of events in Montana preceding the episode, is in Aubrey Haines, *An Elusive Victory*, 7–30.

67. The delay incensed General McDowell, who later critiqued his department commander: "Whilst Howard delayed to organize this combined movement of his two columns and a reserve, the indians [sic] all get beyond Missoula! The day this order was issued—July 23—Gov. Potts reports the indians seeking to pass through Montana. July [illeg.] they are reported on the Lolo trail thirty miles from Missoula!—and July 28th reported as having turned Rawn's position and gone to the Buffalo country!!! And Howard's march was to commence July 30th." Marginal notations by McDowell in "Copies of letters and telegrams."

68. New York *Herald*, September 1, 1877.

69. Howard, "Report," 608.

70. FitzGerald, *Army Doctor's Wife*, 291.

71. Boise, Idaho *Weekly Statesman*, August 18, 21, 1877; "Summary of Reports . . . Non-Effectiveness," 6; Mason to Sanford, August 2, 1877, entry 897, box 1, part 3, 1877, U.S. Army Continental Commands; Howard to Commanding Officer, Missoula, August 3, 1877, ibid.; and Boise, Idaho *Weekly Statesman*, August 11, 1877.

72. Boise, Idaho *Weekly Statesman*, August 18, 1877.

73. On August 1, Lieutenant Wood observed that dispatches received indicated that the Nez Perces were "said to be blocked at the mouth of the trail in Montana." C. E. S. Wood, "Journal," August 1, 1877. On August 2 or 3, Captain Jocelyn wrote: "Two Co's at Missoula were holding them in check. If we can strike them from this side they are in a close place. I do not however expect it. They doubtless know of our movements and will get away. . . . " Jocelyn, *Mostly Alkali*, 241.

74. C. E. S. Wood, "Chief Joseph, the Nez Perce," 138.

75. FitzGerald, *Army Doctor's Wife*, 296. The modern locations of Howard's bivouacs along the Lolo trail are believed to be as follows: July 30, Weippe Prairie; July 31, Musselshell Meadows; August 1, Soldier Meadows; August 2, Weitas Meadows; August 3, Bald Mountain; August 4, Camp Howard; August 5, where Lolo trail crosses Crooked Fork; August 6, Lolo Hot Springs; and August 7, present site of Lolo, Montana. Space, *Lolo Trail*, 46–47.

76. John Carpenter, *Sword and Olive Branch*, 255; and Jocelyn, *Mostly Alkali*, 243.

77. Howard, "Report," 609; and Monteith to Smith, July 31, 1877, item 6877, roll 337, Nez Perce War Papers.

78. Howard to Gibbon, August 6, 1877, entry 897, box 1, part 3, 1877, U.S. Army Continental Commands. See also C. E. S. Wood, "Journal," August 4, 1877. In later years, cannonballs thought to be for use with Howard's guns were found at Bald Mountain and Camp Howard. Also, legend has it that one of Howard's howitzers was abandoned on the trail, a most unlikely occurrence. See Space, *Lolo Trail*, 47–48.

79. Howard to First Lieutenant Joseph A. Sladen, August 5, 1877, entry 897, box 1, part 3, 1877, U.S. Army Continental Commands.

80. Howard to Gibbon, August 6, 1877 entry 897, box 1, part 3, 1877, U.S. Army Continental Commands.

81. Howard, "Report," 609.

82. Howard to Wheaton, August 7 [9], 1877, entry 897, box 1, part 3, 1877, U.S. Army Continental Commands; and Wheaton to Howard, August 18, 1877, in Howard, "Report," 652–53. After leaving Lewiston on July 30, Wheaton's force camped atop the Lewiston grade, then followed a route that took them to the site of present Moscow, Idaho, then on to Palouse City, the site of present Farmington, then followed Hangman's Creek to the Mullan Road, and arrived at Spokane Falls, Washington Territory, on August 10, 1877. Burgunder, "Nez Perce War." Wheaton had, in effect, traveled in an opposite direction from Howard. When he learned that the Nez Perces had turned south up the Bitterroot, he wrote the general that "this column . . . can hardly hope to cooperate very directly with the pursuing troops, who are separated from us by a range of great mountains, and moving in a different direction." Wheaton to Howard, August 10, 1877, in Howard, "Report," 652.

CHAPTER 6

1. McWhorter's informants identified the men as two Nez Perces and a Yakima—Ugly Grizzly Bear Boy, Tepsus (Horn Hide Dresser), and Owhi (the Yakima). McWhorter, *Hear Me*, 357.

2. Another preferred route was up the Big Blackfoot, then through Deer Lodge Valley and down Madison River to the Yellowstone country. Unidentified newspaper (Billings *Gazette?*), November 16, 1928, clipping, entry "Nez Perce—Blackfeet," scrapbooks, Parmly Billings Library, Billings, Mont.

3. Yellow Bull identified this individual as Pile of Clouds. He was not Eapalekthiloom, the Nez Perce war leader of the same name who died in 1859. McWhorter, *Hear Me*, 553–57. The name could have been erroneously interpreted.

4. Yellow Bull mentioned the indecision among the Nee-Me-Poo after the Lolo trail experience over where to go, with some advocating going back into Idaho or heading east "to seek asylum among the Crows." Yellow Bull, Interview, BYU; and "Yellow Bull's Story." One of the people's traditional routes from Idaho to the buffalo plains lay through Nez Perce Pass, then through Big Hole Basin and streams east to the Yellowstone. For mention of Nez Perce Pass, see note by Theodore Swarts, unclassified envelope 122, 564, Camp Manuscript Field Notes, Camp Papers, LBNM.

5. No Feather recalled in 1915 that "when we started we did not know where we were going, nor did we at the time of the battle of Big Hole. At that time we had not thought of going to Canada. Tuhul Hutsut [Toohoolhoolzote] wanted to go over to the Crow Reservation." Weptas Nut (No Feather), Interview. However, McWhorter stated that Toohoolhoolzote aligned with White Bird on the matter. McWhorter, *Hear Me*, 357. See also Walter M. Camp to Brigadier General Hugh L. Scott, January 11, 1914, folder 1, box 2, Camp Papers, BYU.

6. The essence of this critical meeting of the Nee-Me-Poo leadership is here fused from the several Nez Perce sources that treat it. See, in particular, MacDonald, "Nez Perces," 252–53, 255 (which clearly mentions the British Possessions as an objective); Yellow Bull account in Curtis, *North American Indian*, 8:166; and McWhorter, *Hear Me*, 357–58 (which does not at this point entertain the possibility of Canada being an objective). See also the discussion in Francis Haines, *Nez Perces*, 248–49.

7. Fahey, *Flathead Indians*, 196; Francis Haines, *Nez Perces*, 249; and Dunlay, *Wolves*, 120. Nez Perce sources state that Looking Glass tried to visit Charlo, whereupon the Flathead refused to shake his hand, saying, "Why should I shake hands with men whose hands are bloody?" Looking Glass replied, "Your hands are as bloody as ours." MacDonald, "Nez Perces," 256.

8. In one well-documented example of Crow–Nez Perce mutual assistance, the Nez Perces of Looking Glass helped turn back an attack by Sioux at the mouth of Pryor Creek in 1874. Linderman, *American*, 260; and Marquis, *Memoirs of a White Crow Indian*, 88–97.

9. Francis Haines, *Nez Perces*, 250–51; Bradley, *The Handsome People*, 97–99; Marquis, *Memoirs of a White Crow Indian*, 97–98; and William White, *Custer, Cavalry, and Crows*, 134. For the Crows, see Hoxie, *Parading through History*.

10. Athearn, *William Tecumseh Sherman*, 317; and Dunlay, *Wolves*, 120. As an example of the continuing Nez Perce presence in Montana, on April 5, 1877, an army detachment from Fort Benton on the upper Missouri River escorted twenty-five lodges of Nez Perces, returning from a hunt on Milk River, past the settlements near Fort Shaw. Terry, "Report," 554. And a party of Nez Perces and Umatillas was encountered near the community of Yellowstone, Montana Territory, on April 14. Bozeman *Times*, April 19, 1877.

11. Lindgren, *Geological Reconnaissance*, 28. For the history of Fort Owen, see Weisel, *Men and Trade*, 135–36, 139–40; and Henry Buck, "Nez Perce Indian Campaign," 8–11. "The old historic fort was made of adobe or sun-dried bricks and covered an area 250 feet north and south by 125 feet east and west; the walls were

15 feet high and two feet thick. On the south end were two square bastions built and raised to two stories high, one on each corner. Long narrow perpendicular port holes were constructed on either side to serve as look-outs and for rifle shooting in case of attack. Prior to the Nez Perce War there had been four of these bastions, one on each of the four corners of the inclosure, but by 1877 only the two at the south end were standing." See Henry Buck, "Nez Perce Indian Campaign," 9–10, for further specifics of Fort Owen.

12. Although only Stevensville and Corvallis existed in 1877, the course of the Nez Perces through the Bitterroot took them through or near what are today the towns of Lolo, Florence, Stevensville, Corvallis, Hamilton, Como, Darby, Conner, and Sula. Dusenberry, "Chief Joseph's Flight," 47.

13. Henry Buck, "Nez Perce Indian Campaign," 11–12, 14; and Myers, "Settlers and the Nez Perce," 22. Another account indicated that the citizens of Skalkaho "built a stockade of logs, and then built a house inside large enough to accommodate the women and children." Catlin, "The Battle of the Big Hole."

14. Harlan to Potts (?), July 10, 1877, in Paul Phillips, "Battle of the Big Hole," 66.

15. The most extensive reminiscent account of the meeting between the Bitterroot volunteers and Looking Glass is in Wilson Harlan, "Fiasco at 'Fort Fizzle,'" 67–68. In essence, at their request, the chief came to speak with them, and at first upbraided them for having earlier borne arms against his people, but concluded that the men could go through to their homes. Wrote Wilson Harlan: "He and his warriors then rode back to camp, we following slowly in single file. The Indians were lined up on both sides of the road with guns in their hands. . . . As we passed the last Redskin, each of us urged his horse to a lope and stopped for nothing until we had reached the fort." See also the remarkably similar Nez Perce recollections in MacDonald, "Nez Perces," 252.

16. Henry Buck, "Nez Perce Indian Campaign," 23–24.

17. Boise, Idaho *Tri-Weekly Statesman*, August 21, 1877.

18. Henry Buck, "Nez Perce Indian Campaign," 26.

19. Fahey, *Flathead Indians*, 196.

20. Henry Buck, "Nez Perce Indian Campaign," 27.

21. Ibid., 28.

22. Boise, Idaho *Statesman*, September 6, 1877.

23. Gibbon, "Report of Colonel Gibbon," 68.

24. Henry Buck, "Nez Perce Indian Campaign," 30–31, 32–33, 36–37. Buck misidentified the chief as White Bird. See ibid., 28, 29, 32. For coverage of the Stevensville visitation, see also Wilson Harlan, "Fiasco at 'Fort Fizzle,'" 68–69; MacDonald, "Nez Perces," 256–57; Washington McCormick to Potts, August 3, 1877, in Paul Phillips, "Battle of the Big Hole," 75; Gibbon, "Pursuit of Joseph," 325–26; Francis Haines, *Nez Perces*, 252; and Fahey, *Flathead Indians*, 196–97.

25. Duncan MacDonald believed that this band was headed by a man named Perish Bull Head and that Poker Joe was a warrior in the group. McWhorter, *Hear Me*, 360 n. 6.

26. Rawn to Gibbon, August 1, 1877; Rawn to Captain C. P. Higgins, August 1, 1877; Rawn to Potts, August 1, 1877; Rawn to Adjutant General, Department of the Columbia, August 1, 1877; Rawn to Gibbon, August 2, 1877 (quoted); all in Fort Missoula Letterbook.

27. Sherman to Secretary of War George W. McCrary, August 3, 1877, in Sheridan and Sherman, *Report*, 32.

28. Helena *Daily Herald*, July 30, 1877; Helena *Daily Herald—Extra*, July 31, 1877; Deer Lodge *New North-West—Extra*, August 3, 1877; Barsness and Dickinson, "Minutemen of Montana," 5; Athearn, *William Tecumseh Sherman*, 316–17; Athearn, "Frontier Critics," 26–27; and Olson, "The Nez Perce," 170–71.

29. Sherman to McCrary, August 3, 1877, in Sheridan and Sherman, *Report*, 32.

30. This enormous eighteenth-century ponderosa pine still stands east of U.S. Highway 93 a few miles south of Darby, Montana. For its background, see McWhorter, *Hear Me*, 364.

31. MacDonald, "Nez Perces," 257–58; McWhorter, *Hear Me*, 361; Yellow Bull, Account; miscellaneous notes, Camp Manuscripts, IU; Sutherland, *Howard's Campaign*, 29; Francis Haines, *Nez Perces*, 252, 254; and Fahey, *Flathead Indians*, 197–98.

32. Yellow Bull, Account.

33. Gibbon, "Report of Colonel Gibbon," 68; Rawn to Gibbon, August 2, 1877, Fort Missoula Letterbook; and Henry Buck, "Nez Perce Indian Campaign," 38. Gibbon had anticipated possibly meeting the Nez Perces if they attempted to come through Cadotte Pass, writing Governor Potts that "I might be unable to do more than check them" and encouraging the governor to provide armed militia to assist Rawn, who would necessarily follow the tribesmen up the Blackfoot. Gibbon to Potts, July 27, 1877, in Paul Phillips, "Battle of the Big Hole," 73.

34. Gibbon to Potts, August 2, 1877, in Paul Phillips, "Battle of the Big Hole," 73–74. Initially, Gibbon hoped to catch the Nez Perces before they left the Bitterroot Valley and by hard marching overtake them in two days. McCormick to Potts, August 3, 1877, in Paul Phillips, "Battle of the Big Hole," 75.

35. Heitman, *Historical Register and Dictionary*, 1:452; and Dennis S. Lavery, "John Gibbon," in Spiller, *Dictionary of American Military Biography*, 1:380–83. For a selection of Gibbon's writings, see Gibbon, *Adventures*, which includes Gibbon's reminiscence of the Battle of the Big Hole (203–18).

36. Gibbon, "Report of Colonel Gibbon," 69; and Gibbon, "Pursuit of Joseph," 328.

37. Gibbon, "Report of Colonel Gibbon," 69; Gibbon, "Pursuit of Joseph," 329–30; Terry, "Report," 501; *Army and Navy Journal*, August 11, 1877, citing dispatches from the Department of the Columbia; Henry Buck, "Nez Perce Indian Campaign," 38–39; Catlin, "The Battle of the Big Hole," 2; Gibbon, "Pursuit of Joseph," 327–28; and Charles N. Loynes, "Battle of the 'Big Hole,'" *Winners of the West*, March 1925.

38. Gibbon, "Report of Colonel Gibbon," 69.

39. Hardin, Diary, August 8, 1877; and Charles Woodruff, "Battle of the Big Hole," 105, 107. Corporal Loynes recalled that "in places the trail was so steep that the mules were detached from the army wagons, and with ropes were drawn up the steep sides." Charles N. Loynes, "Battle of the 'Big Hole,'" *Winners of the West*, March 1925.

40. Gibbon, "Pursuit of Joseph," 332.

41. Charles Woodruff, "Battle of the Big Hole," 106.

42. Gibbon, "Report of Colonel Gibbon," 69; Gibbon, "Pursuit of Joseph," 331–32; and Charles Woodruff, "Battle of the Big Hole," 106–7.

43. Heitman, *Historical Register and Dictionary*, 1:238; Deer Lodge *New North-West*, August 17, 1877; Bozeman *Times*, March 15, April 5, 1877; and *Army and Navy Journal*, September 1, 1877.

44. Gibbon, "Pursuit of Joseph," 334.

45. Gibbon, "Report of Colonel Gibbon," 69.

46. Ibid.

47. Gibbon, "Pursuit of Joseph," 335–36; Charles N. Loynes, "Battle of the 'Big Hole,'" *Winners of the West*, March 1925; Charles Woodruff, "Battle of the Big Hole," 107; and Henry Buck, "Nez Perce Indian Campaign," 42–43.

48. Gibbon, "Report of Colonel Gibbon," 70.

49. Horace B. Mulkey letter in *National Tribune*, August 29, 1929.

50. Charles N. Loynes, "Battle of the 'Big Hole,'" *Winners of the West*, March 1925.

51. Charles Woodruff, "Battle of the Big Hole," 109.

52. Ibid.

53. The loss of Bradley elicited mourning throughout the region, where he was well known, and he was commemorated in a poem entitled, "Bradley the Brave." Norris, *The Calumet*, 90–91.

54. Account based on information of William H. Edwards in the Deer Lodge *New North-West*, August 17, 1877.

55. Horace B. Mulkey letter in *National Tribune*, August 29, 1929.

56. Charles Woodruff, Letter.

57. "Battle Briefs Gleaned from Enlisted Men of the Seventh Infantry," Helena *Daily Herald*, August 23, 1877. "Officers [had] issued orders against killing non-combattant [sic] squaws or children and the order was respected, but . . . in numerous instances both were found fighting with pistol, gun and knife. Many were doubtless killed in the charge of the tepees." Deer Lodge *New North-West*, August 24, 1877.

58. Charles N. Loynes, "Battle of the 'Big Hole,'" *Winners of the West*, March 1925.

59. Gibbon, "Pursuit of Joseph," 336–37.

60. Otis Halfmoon, telephone communication with author, January 25, 1996.

61. McWhorter, *Yellow Wolf*, 115.

62. "Wounded Head's Narrative," in McWhorter, *Hear Me*, 372.

63. "Young White Bird's Story," in ibid., 376.

64. McWhorter, *Yellow Wolf*, 118.

65. "Story of Kawownonilpilp."

66. Gibbon, "Report of Colonel Gibbon," 70.

67. Charles Woodruff, Letter. A published version appears in Stewart, "Letters from the Big Hole," 55–56.

68. Gibbon, "Battle of the Big Hole," 4. Gibbon testified that the warriors at this point "got off on the hills and in the brush, and while we had to be up and at work, of course they laid low, and at almost every shot of their rifles one of our men fell, and this, too, when our men were at a distance from the enemy, such as rendered it utterly impossible for them to compete with the Indians [armed with Winchesters, or "hunting rifles"] in their accuracy of fire." U.S. House, *Report of a Sub-Committee . . . Relating to the Reorganization of the Army*, 264.

69. MacDonald, "Nez Perces," 260–61.

70. "Peopeo Tholekt's Story," in McWhorter, *Hear Me*, 392.

71. Charles Woodruff, Letter.

72. Woodruff, "Battle of the Big Hole," 111.

73. Gibbon, "Report of Colonel Gibbon," 70–71; Howard, "Report," 609; and Hunt, "Sergeant Sutherland's Ride," 39–46.

74. Gibbon, "Report of Colonel Gibbon," 71; "Report of the Surgeon-General," in Secretary of War, *Report . . . 1877*, 428; Gibbon, "Pursuit of Joseph," 342; Hardin, Diary, August 10, 1877; and Horace B. Mulkey letter in *National Tribune*, August 29, 1929. A complete list of army casualties is in Appendix A. This overview of the Battle of the Big Hole is drawn from the several primary accounts from which quoted material presented above is cited, in addition to the following: reports of Captain Richard Comba and Colonel John Gibbon, in Terry, "Report," 561–63; *Record of Engagements*, 70–71; Helena *Daily Independent*, August 12, 1877; Deer Lodge *New North-West*, August 24, 1877; *Army and Navy Journal*, August 18, 25, September 22, 1877; New York *Herald*, September 10, 1877; Sherrill, "Battle of the Big Hole"; Shields, "Battle of the Big Hole"; and excerpts from Coon, "Outbreak of Chief Joseph," also in Rickey, *Forty Miles a Day*, 293–94. These sources and many more are the basis of the principal published authority on the battle, on which this description has liberally depended, Aubrey Haines, *An Elusive Victory*. In addition, a thorough analysis of the troops' deployment and progressive movements, as well as Nez Perce movements throughout the battle, based on archeological discoveries and on knowledge of contemporary tactical dispositions and group and individual behavioral patterns, is in Douglas D. Scott, *A Sharp Little Affair*. This volume also contains discussions about army and Nez Perce material culture, including clothing, weapons, and equipment, based on investigations conducted at Big Hole National Battlefield in 1990.

Next to the Battle of the Little Bighorn, that of the Big Hole is doubtless the best-chronicled in terms of Indian participant accounts of all the trans-Mississippi Indian-white battles, thanks largely to the efforts of Lucullus V. McWhorter early in the twentieth century. Besides those quoted above, this account has benefitted from the following: "Two Moons's Narrative," in McWhorter, *Hear Me*, 384–88; the accounts of Eloosykasit (Standing on a Point), Penahwenonmi (Helping Another), Owyeen (Wounded), Wetatonmi—Ollokot's wife, Young White Bird (a fuller account than in *Hear Me*), Red Elk, Eelahweemah (About Asleep), Pahit Palikt, Kowtoliks, Black Eagle, and Samuel Tilden, in McWhorter, *Yellow Wolf*, 134–46; Yellow Bull account in Curtis, *North American Indian*, 8:167; unclassified envelope 127, 563, Camp Manuscript Field Notes, Camp Papers, LBNM; Yellow Bull, Interview, BYU; Joseph [Heinmot Tooyalakekt], "An Indian's Views," 426–27; and Alcorn and Alcorn, "Old Nez Perce Recalls," 66–67. More reminiscent Indian sources are integrated in the thorough Aubrey Haines, *An Elusive Victory*, and for modern accounts weighted heavily toward the Nez Perce perspective, though utilizing other sources, too, see Garcia, *Tough Trip Through Paradise*, 286–92; Trafzer and Scheureman, *Chief Joseph's Allies*, 19–20; Francis Haines, "Chief Joseph," 6; Francis Haines, *Nez Perces*, 255–56; and, especially, Josephy, *Nez Perce Indians*, 580–88. Nez Perce historical pictographic sources possibly related to Big Hole are discussed in Stern, Schmitt, and Halfmoon, "A Cayuse–Nez Perce Sketchbook," 361–62.

75. Although the Nez Perces had learned of Howard's imminent arrival, it was not for that reason that they refrained from further combat with the command. In 1889 Joseph told Gibbon that his warriors watched the troops in the

aftermath of the fighting on the tenth and that both Joseph and Looking Glass agreed to leave the soldiers alone. "I said let us give up this thing; it is not a fair fight; I do not like this kind of fighting; in the morning, if they catch up with us, we will fight to the death. Looking Glass said, 'Very well; let us go.'" Letter from Gibbon to the editor of the Portland *Oregonian*, as reprinted in *Army and Navy Register*, December 14, 1889.

76. Gibbon, "Report of Colonel Gibbon," 71; Howard, "Report," 609–10; "Report of the Surgeon-General," in Secretary of War, *Report . . . 1877*, 428; Jocelyn, *Mostly Alkali*, 242–43; C. E. S. Wood, "Journal," August 11, 12, 1988; FitzGerald, *Army Doctor's Wife*, 302–5; Davison, "A Century Ago," 8–10; and John Carpenter, "General Howard," 136–37.

77. *Army and Navy Journal*, August 18, 1877.

78. *U.S. Army Gallantry and Meritorious Conduct*. Medal winners were First Sergeant William D. Edwards, Sergeant Patrick Rogan, Private Lorenzo D. Brown, Musician John McLennon, and Sergeant Milden H. Wilson, all of the Seventh Infantry; and Private Wilfred Clark, Second Cavalry, whose award was partly for Big Hole and partly for his participation in the fight at Camas Meadows, Idaho Territory. *The Medal of Honor*, 230–31. The Montana Volunteers won belated validation for their part in the Nez Perce War in 1881, when the federal government authorized payment to them of one dollar per day and entitled those wounded or disabled, and the heirs of those killed while assisting the regular troops, to applicable pension benefits. The volunteers were also reimbursed for horses and guns lost during their service. *Statutes . . . 1879 . . . 1881*, 641.

CHAPTER 7

1. Gibbon,"Report of Colonel Gibbon," 71; Howard, "Report," 610; Henry Buck, "Nez Perce Indian Campaign," 51; and Charles N. Loynes, "Battle of the 'Big Hole,'" *Winners of the West*, March 1925. In September a party from Deer Lodge under Lieutenant Van Orsdale returned to the battlefield and reburied the army dead, fourteen of whom had been disinterred in the interim and the officers' remains scalped. Van Orsdale counted the remains of eighty Indians "visible or partially so" in the makeshift graves. Van Orsdale to Adjutant, Post at Missoula, September 29, 1877, in Terry, "Report," 549–50.

2. Howard, "Report," 610; and Regimental Returns . . . Fourth Artillery, August 1877, roll 30.

3. Mason to wife, August 13, 1877, in Davison, "A Century Ago," 9–10. In 1877 the Department of the Platte included "so much of the Territory of Idaho as lies east of a line formed by the extension of the western boundary of Utah to the northeastern boundary of Idaho, embracing Fort Hall [near present Pocatello]." Thian, *Notes Illustrating the Military Geography*, 89. On August 14, Howard notified McDowell that he was entering the Department of the Platte that day; three days later, McDowell relayed that information to Sheridan at Chicago. Nez Perce War, 1877, Division of the Missouri, Special File, roll 5.

4. Howard, "Report," 610; and Howard to Adjutant General, Military Division of the Pacific, August 14, 1877, quoted in John Carpenter, *Sword and Olive Branch*, 255. In a letter of August 14, Surgeon FitzGerald informed his wife that indications were that the Indians "were moving rapidly toward headwaters of the Yellowstone River via a place on the maps designated Pleasant Valley. General

Howard said . . . he would pursue them as far as that point. Then if he did not succeed in overtaking them, he would notify General McDowell and terminate the campaign." FitzGerald, *Army Doctor's Wife*, 304-5.

5. Howard to Miller, August 13, 1877, entry 897, box 1, part 3, 1877, U.S. Army Continental Commands; and Portland *Daily Standard*, August 28, 1877.

6. Despite published references to the contrary in secondary literature about the 1877 war, there is no documentation in the Nez Perce sources to support the contention that the people altered by any great degree their intended route to the Yellowstone country following the Big Hole encounter. See, for example, Mark Brown, "Joseph Myth," 9.

7. For a participant account of the citizens' reaction to the Nez Perces' presence in the area, see Barrett, "A Near Encounter." (Also published in Dillon *Examiner*, July 25, 1962.) Comprehensive trail studies of the route of the Nez Perces after leaving the Bitterroot Valley through the Battle of the Big Hole and until they reached the Lemhi Valley of southeast Idaho Territory are in Hagelin, *Nez Perce . . . Trail*; and Gard, *Nez Perce . . . Trail*.

8. This brief account of the activity on Horse Prairie is based on information contained in Helena *Daily Herald*, August 13, 15, 1877; Deer Lodge *New North-West*, August 24, 1877; Cruikshank, "Chasing Hostile Indians"; Alva Noyes, "Story of Andrews [sic] Myers"; Redington, "Scouting in Montana," 57; Vaughn, *Then and Now*, 220-21; McWhorter, *Yellow Wolf*, 162 n. 2; and McWhorter, *Hear Me*, 407-8. The view that the strikes were motivated by the fury of the people in the wake of the Big Hole is consistent with Nez Perce revelations given Duncan MacDonald and presented in MacDonald, "Nez Perces," 265.

9. Dusenberry, "Chief Joseph's Flight," 48; Roeser, "Territory of Idaho."

10. Quoted in McWhorter, *Hear Me*, 406.

11. Ibid., 406-7. This probable marching order is based on information in Thomas, "Pi.Lu'.Ye.Kin," 7, quoting Curtis, *North American Indian*, 8:46; Coale, "Ethnohistorical Sources," pt. 1, 250; "Yellow Bull's Story"; and unclassified envelope 91, 541, Camp Manuscript Field Notes, Camp Papers, LBNM. A settler at Junction, Idaho Territory, described the marching order of the procession as: women "and families leading, next quite a number of drags or litters, carrying the wounded, then . . . 1,500 or more ponies, ending with about 300 warriors." Clough, "Recollections."

12. Rifle pits discovered in 1965 numbered about thirty in an area covering three acres. Missoula *Missoulian*, December 28, 1965. For the Junction settlers' preparations and response to the Nez Perces' presence, see Clough, "Recollections."

13. Fred Phillips claim, no. 1782, April 13, 1878, entry 700, Claim for Indian Depredations, U.S. Bureau of Indian Affairs. The freight train belonged to Fred Phillips, who was not present during the incident.

14. Deer Lodge *New North-West*, August 31, 1877; Clough, "Recollections"; J. D. Wood, Reminiscence; Cruikshank, "Chasing Hostile Indians"; Cruikshank, "Birch Creek"; clipping of newspaper article by Alexander Cruikshank, vertical files, Parmly Billings Library, Billings, Mont.; and Shoup, "Birch Creek Massacre" (originally published in the Salmon City, Idaho, *Recorder-Herald*, August 22, 1940). The incident, as told through Albert Lyon, appears in DeCost Smith, *Indian Experiences*, 258-69; and M. I. McCreight, "An Incident in Chief Joseph's War," unidentified periodical, clipping ca. 1952, Yellowstone National Park Research Library, Mam-

moth, Wyo. Accounts from the Nez Perce perspective, which cite the influence of whiskey on the warriors' actions, are in Curtis, *North American Indian*, 8:167; McWhorter, *Yellow Wolf*, 164–65, 164 n. 4; McWhorter, *Hear Me*, 409–10; and MacDonald, "Nez Perces," 265–66. "While under the influence of the whiskey captured from the train, one of the bravest and best warriors in the Nez Perce band was killed and another narrowly escaped death at the hands of their comrades." MacDonald, "Nez Perces," 266. McWhorter's informants identified the dead warrior as Stripes Turned Down, who had helped capture the howitzer at the Big Hole. McWhorter, *Hear Me*, 410. In later years, the site attracted passersby who placed rocks on a cairn at the place the train was attacked. By the 1940s, the cairn had become indistinguishable. DeCost Smith, *Indian Experiences*, 269. The grave of one of the unidentified victims is one mile from the site. The four other dead were removed in January 1878 for reburial in Salmon City, where a monument was erected to their memory. Clough, "Recollections"; and Falkner, Letter. For the route from Utah, see Madsen and Madsen, "Diamond-R Rolls Out."

15. Granville Stuart in Nez Perce Indian Wars 1, 160, Camp Manuscript Field Notes, Camp Papers, LBNM; Bozeman *Times*, August 23, 1877; Dusenberry, "Chief Joseph's Flight," 43; and Chicago *Tribune*, August 24, 1877. Sutherland wrote that the Nez Perces passed through "cutting and carefully coiling the telegraph wire before leaving." Portland *Daily Standard*, September 6, 1877. For discussion of the construction and maintenance of the telegraph line between Salt Lake City and Virginia City and Helena, see Madsen and Madsen, *North to Montana!*, 108–9.

16. Quoted in Davison, "A Century Ago," 10. See also Sutherland, *Howard's Campaign*, 32.

17. Sutherland, *Howard's Campaign*, 32. Howard responded to Shoup, telling him, "The more you can do to draw them towards you the better till I get upon the old Mormon Road. I expect to reach a point near the mouth of the [Medicine Lodge Creek?] canyon tomorrow night. If I get word that the Indians have gone up the Mormon Road, that is, eastward, I shall make a wider detour to the left as quick as possible to try & intercept them." Howard to Shoup, August 15, 1877, entry 897, box 1, part 3, 1877, U.S. Army Continental Commands. See also C. E. S. Wood, "Journal," August 15, 16, 1877.

18. Howard asked the volunteers to cooperate with his plan, but they insisted on following their own course, which the general feared would "result as a diversion in favor of the enemy." Howard, "Report," 610. Howard's instructions to the volunteers are in Wood to Captain William A. Clark, Montana Volunteers, August 16, 1877, entry 897, box 1, part 3, 1877, U.S. Army Continental Commands. But see also the lengthy explanation for this dispute in C. E. S. Wood, "Journal," August 16, 1877. Bozeman *Times*, August 23, 1877, reported that the volunteers became miffed and returned home when Howard directed them to "march in the rear, or retire altogether." Sutherland wrote of this episode: "Sixty volunteers, under Messrs. Stuart and Clark, from Deer Lodge, joined us, but apparently not wishing to fight the Indians if they had to chase them for it, they returned home after traveling about five miles in the direction of the hostiles." Sutherland, *Howard's Campaign*, 32.

19. Howard to Miller, August 16, 1877, entry 897, box 1, part 3, 1877, U.S. Army Continental Commands.

20. Henry Buck, "Nez Perce Indian Campaign," 55.

21. Howard's orders to Bacon were as follows: "You will proceed with your command to the vicinity of Henry Lake and Reynolds [sic—Raynolds] Pass. The object of the expedition is to ascertain whether the hostile Indians are passing into the buffalo country by the above-mentioned route. Should you find the Indians you will take a defensible position and while observing their movements do all you can with your force to harass them. Exercise at the same time prudence and caution. You will send a courier back to these headquarters with information as soon as you discover the Indians and form an opinion of their intended movement. Should you not at the expiration of 48 hours discover any trace of the hostiles, you will return to this camp by easy marches, sending a courier in advance." Quoted in Davison, "A Century Ago," 11–12.

22. Howard, "Report," 610–11; C. E. S. Wood, "Journal," August 17, 1877; Sutherland, *Howard's Campaign*, 32; Lew L. Callaway to L. V. McWhorter, May 1, 1931, folder 158, McWhorter Papers; and Helena *Daily Independent*, June 13, 1896.

23. Davis, "Incident," 561. (This article, retitled, "The Battle of Camas Meadows," is reprinted in Brady, *Northwestern Fights and Fighters*, 191–97.)

24. Major James S. Brisbin to Assistant Adjutant General, Department of Dakota, October 26, 1877, in Secretary of War, *Report . . . 1877*, 553; Regimental Returns . . . Second Cavalry, August 1877, roll 166; Mason to wife, August 19, 1877, in Davison, "A Century Ago," 10; Chicago *Tribune*, August 24, 1877; Sutherland, *Howard's Campaign*, 33; C. E. S. Wood, "Journal," August 18, 1877; and Howard to Mason containing sketch map of the Nez Perces' route crossing stage route possibly headed to a southeastwardly leading trail along the Teton River, with scout's notation: "I think from the cors [sic] the Indians are taking they are trying to go to Wind River." Howard to Mason, August 18, 1877, entry 897, box 1, part 3, 1877, U.S. Army Continental Commands.

25. General Land Office Survey Plat. Geological data is from Embree, McBroome, and Doherty, "Preliminary Stratigraphic Framework," 333–34.

26. Howard, "Report," 611. A man in the ranks stated that the troops pitched camp "on a knoll of lava rocks." New York *Herald*, September 10, 1877. Howard remembered that the meadow had been cut and that "large stacks of meadow hay" lay scattered across the ground. Howard, *Nez Perce Joseph*, 221. Wood stated that the camp was "double picketed." C. E. S. Wood, "Journal," August 19, 1877.

27. Howard, *Nez Perce Joseph*, 224–25.

28. The following citizens were present at Camas Meadows: James E. Callaway (captain), G. W. Peck, George Thexton, Henry Sermon, J. Harkness, C. Chadduck, J. S. McCormick, J. B. Allebaugh, Hugh Kelly, J. Bucklin, Henry Fishback, Thomas Garvey, L. C. Smith, R. O. Hickman, Frank Lelleher, Dr. E. T. Yager, J. Bogin [Rogin?], Thomas T. Baker, Henry Browne, Henry O'Donnell, D. W. Sumner, Walter Wynne, W. H. Patrick, Sargent Hall, A. Shellbarger, J. W. Barley, Frank Daddow, W. W. Stevens, George Odell, J. M. Kyle, W. M. Alward, James Mitchell, J. F. Hart, Thomas Baker, A. Talbott, C. B. Houser, Thomas J. Farrell, Simeon R. Buford, William Morris, and Samuel Word. "Special correspondent" Thomas T. Baker account in Virginia City *Madisonian*, August 25, 1877. The identity of Baker is confirmed in Helena *Daily Independent*, June 13, 1896.

29. Virginia City *Madisonian*, August 25, 1877. Sergeant Davis wrote years later that "at night guards were posted, and a picket post was established some five

hundred yards upstream, near the creek and on a rocky knoll, and two at other points." Davis, "Incident," 562.

30. Howard, "Report," 611; and Sutherland, *Howard's Campaign*, 34. However, Sutherland stated that "all the cavalry horses and wagon mules were tied up on the rocky mound where we were encamped." Ibid., 35. See also the sketch map by Edmonds, "Howard's Camp."

31. Davis, "Incident," 562.

32. Powell, *Powell's Records*, 13, 57, 112, 155, 308, 520. In addition, for Sanford, see Hagemann, *Fighting Rebels and Redskins*; however, this is largely a Civil War memoir.

33. The complainant continued: "He has leave of absence on Sick account, but judging from the number of women that he states he is 'Intimate' with—He cannot be very sick. . . . The people here think it an outrage." S. B. Underwood to Secretary of War, January 21, 1876, in Norwood, Appointment, Commission, and Personal File. Norwood eventually retired from the army in 1889 on disability; he died May 24, 1901. Powell, *Powell's Records*, 439; Norwood, Appointment, Commission, and Personal File; and Greene, *Yellowstone Command*, 206–11.

34. At least two accounts mention the rainy weather and the moon; however, Howard described the night as "starlight, but no moon." Howard, *Nez Perce Joseph*, 225.

35. Accounts vary as to the time of the Nez Perces' attack, with most specifying either 3:00 A.M. or 4:00 A.M. or sometime in between. See, for examples, Boise, Idaho *Tri-Weekly Statesman*, September 18, 1877; and New York *Herald*, September 10, 1877. Wood stated that the command was "awakened at 4 A.M. by reveille of musketry." C. E. S. Wood, "Journal," August 20, 1877.

36. Ibid., September 10, 1877.

37. Norwood to Gibbon, August 24, 1877, item 6154, roll 338, Nez Perce War Papers.

38. Virginia City *Madisonian*, August 25, 1877. "We discovered that a band of screaming Indians were behind our entire mule train, 110 in number, and our loose horses." New York *Herald*, September 10, 1877.

39. Frank T. Conway reminiscence in Helena *Daily Independent*, June 13, 1896. Howard was critical of the volunteers' response. "One takes another's gun, some get the wrong belts, others drop their percussion caps; their horses get into a regular stampede, and rush in the darkness toward the herd of mules, and all the animals scamper off together, while the citizens plunge into the water above their knees, and cross to the regular troops at a double-quick." Howard, *Nez Perce Joseph*, 226.

40. Frank T. Conway, a twelve-year-old helper with a freight train from Corrine that had attached itself to the command until the Nez Perce threat passed, recalled the following incident during the attack: "A well known [Virginia City] stockman, it is said, for some reason best known to himself, climbed into the forks of a big cottonwood tree and was halloing for some one to do something, when a famous criminal lawyer, who had made a dive through the creek, and was wet up to his neck, took shelter beneath the same tree, and called through his chattering teeth: 'For God's sake, dry up, Tom, it is a general attack.'" The remark inspired the following doggerel, entitled, "Our Volunteers": "Lay low boys, it is a general attack/Down in the creek or you'll get shot in the back,/I pledge you my word I wish I hadn't come,/And I'll bet you ten to one we'll have to foot it home./Oh, I

am one of the volunteers, who marched right home on the tramp, the tramp,/ When Joseph set the boys afoot, At the battle of Callaway's camp." Helena *Daily Independent*, June 13, 1896.

41. Davis, "Incident," 562. Another account stated that "everybody sprung out of their blankets, cartridge belt and rifle in hand." Boise, Idaho *Tri-Weekly Statesman*, September 18, 1877.

42. Virginia City *Madisonian*, August 25, 1877.

43. Sutherland, *Howard's Campaign*, 34. See also Sutherland's account in Portland *Daily Standard*, September 6, 1877.

44. Davis, "Incident," 562.

45. Howard, "Report," 611. Citizen John Davis received a slight wound in the head, and Dr. E. T. Yager was hit in the knee by a spent bullet. Helena *Daily Herald*, August 30, 1877. (This account also appears in *Army and Navy Journal*, October 6, 1877.) A rough drawing of the area of the Camas Meadows attack, however, suggests that the warriors headed northwest, toward the Centennial Range, a seemingly implausible direction considering the subsequent chase by the cavalry companies. See "Fight at Camas Meadows," inset drawing in Fletcher, "Department of Columbia Map." For a sketch showing the layout of the army camp at the outset of the Nez Perces' attack, see the New York *Daily Graphic*, September 8, 1877.

46. See MacDonald, "Nez Perces," 266–67; and McWhorter, *Hear Me*, 417.

47. Yellow Bull stated that Looking Glass had counseled against attacking the soldiers, but was overruled. Yellow Bull, Interview, LBNM, 165.

48. McWhorter, *Hear Me*, 421 n. 45; Yellow Bull account in Curtis, *North American Indian*, 8:167; and MacDonald, "Nez Perces," 267.

49. See "Story of Kawownonilpilp."

50. To which the verbal response among the Nez Perces was something like "Ise tanin kenek kun nawas kunya tim onina padkuta?"—"Who in hell fire that gun?" McWhorter, *Hear Me*, 167 n. 5; see also account of Wottolen in McWhorter, *Hear Me*, 419.

51. See the following Nez Perce sources, upon which this synopsis of their testimony is based: MacDonald, "Nez Perces," 266–68; McWhorter, *Yellow Wolf*, 165–68; and McWhorter, *Hear Me*, 414–23, which includes the accounts of Peopeo Tholekt and Wottolen. Yellow Wolf succinctly stated that "Joseph was not along." McWhorter, *Yellow Wolf*, 166; and Alcorn and Alcorn, "Old Nez Perce Recalls," 69. For synthesized accounts drawing heavily on Nez Perce testimony, see Francis Haines, "Chief Joseph," 6–7; Francis Haines, *Nez Perces*, 260–61; and Josephy, *Nez Perce Indians*, 595–96. In his own account, Joseph [Heinmot Tooyalakekt], "An Indian's Views," 427, Joseph barely acknowledged the action. In an alternative explanation for the fight at Camas Meadows, Yellow Bull explained that: "We decided to attack the soldiers in their camp at night as they had done to us at Big Hole. We tried to do this but blundered in some way . . . and the noise of the firing stampeded the pack mules. Having failed to jump the camp of the soldiers, we took the stampeded mules, which was the only advantage gained, and they fell to us more by accident than by design, or as a stroke of good luck." Yellow Bull, Interview, LBNM, 165.

52. Davis, "Incident," 562.

53. Ibid.

54. Davis claimed that the recovered animals had been "dropped" by the tribesmen. Ibid. Another account stated that Norwood "ordered a citizen and a soldier to get ahead of and drive back about 40 or 50 animals that had been cut off from the herd." Account by "Participant" in Helena *Daily Herald*, August 30, 1877. Yet another account declared that it was Captain Carr's company that retook the mounts. New York *Herald*, September 10, 1877.

55. See New York *Herald*, September 10, 1877. Howard indicated years later that he "was surprised and somewhat vexed" at the retirement of the cavalry. Howard to then-Major James Jackson, October 3, 1895, copy provided by Eileen Bennett, Kilgore, Idaho.

56. The twenty-one-year-old Brooks had enlisted in October 1875, at age nineteen, having received his parents' permission. A contemporary account reported that Brooks was killed while delivering a message. "He was a very promising youth, and his loss was mourned by all who knew him." Boise, Idaho *Tri-Weekly Statesman*, September 18, 1877. A literary account of the death of Brooks appears in Redington, "Bugler Brooks." This article is reprinted, with additions, in Redington, "Story of Bugler Brooks." (Technically, Brooks was a trumpeter of the Second Cavalry; the bugle was the instrument of the infantry.) The latter piece states that Charles Gibbons purportedly shot the warrior who had killed Brooks. Redington, "Story of Bugler Brooks," 200 n. Five days earlier, Brooks had written his last letter home from a drugstore in Bannack City, where he had gone with officers from Howard's command to purchase horses. "Good by [sic] for the present. You will hear from me soon again," he penned his sister, who, through some bureaucratic oversight, learned nothing of Brooks's death from the War Department until the following summer. Bennett, "History and Legend of . . . Brooks," 41–42.

57. Howard, "Report," 611–12; and Helena *Daily Herald*, August 30, 1877.

58. Davis, "Incident," 562.

59. Notation by Norwood accompanying clipping in Virginia City *Madisonian*, August 25, 1877, item 5816, roll 338, Nez Perce War Papers.

60. Norwood to Gibbon, August 24, 1877, item 6154, roll 338, Nez Perce War Papers.

61. Davis, "Incident," 563.

62. There is disagreement among the accounts over the distance of the withdrawal to where Norwood made his stand. Whereas the captain stated that he withdrew twelve hundred yards, the account of "Participant" made the distance "about 1,000 yards." Helena *Daily Herald*, August 30, 1877. Sergeant Davis, writing more than twenty-five years after the events, thought that the distance was "more than five hundred yards." Davis, "Incident," 563. Yet another source stated that Norwood withdrew "half a mile," which would have been some five hundred yards farther than the figure given by the captain. Virginia City *Madisonian*, August 25, 1877. Because Norwood's and "Participant's" statements are immediate to the event, the distance of one thousand to twelve hundred yards is probably close to correct.

63. Norwood to Gibbon, August 24, 1877, item 6154, roll 338, Nez Perce War Papers. (Norwood's report was also published in Secretary of War, *Report . . . 1877*, 572–73). A source told the Virginia City *Madisonian*, August 25, 1877, that Norwood's fight lasted a rather specific "two hours and forty-five minutes," while Sergeant Davis thought that it took "two hours." Davis, "Incident," 563. Four hours is likely the *total* time of Norwood's engagement, from the inception of the

fighting through Norwood's withdrawal and fight at the "frying pan." Helena *Daily Herald*, August 30, 1877.

64. Davis, "Incident," 563.

65. Boise, Idaho *Tri-Weekly Statesman*, September 18, 1877. The other casualties were: First Sergeant Henry Wilkins, scalp wound; Farrier William Jones, right knee, slightly; and Private Wilfred Clark, left shoulder, slightly. Field Return, Battalion Second Cavalry, August 1877, Regimental Returns . . . Second Cavalry, roll 166. One man of Company I, Farrier James King, was also wounded. "List of Wounded in Skirmish on Camas Meadow." Another listing of casualties stated that "during the same action many slight flesh wounds [were] received by men of Companies 'B' & 'I' 1st Cavalry." Sanford to Assistant Adjutant General, Department of the Columbia, December 6, 1877, box 1, entry 624, Office of the Adjutant General. See also Davis, "Incident," 563. A complete account of army casualties at Camas Meadows is in appendix A. Scout Willie L. Curry, who was with Norwood, was the son of the governor of Oregon. Boise, Idaho *Tri-Weekly Statesman*, September 20, 1877.

66. "Story of Kawownonilpilp"; and Deer Lodge *New North-West*, September 14, 1877.

67. McWhorter ascribed this call to Trumpeter Brooks, who was with Company B, First Cavalry. McWhorter, *Hear Me*, 425 n. 54. But it almost precisely conforms to the account of Sergeant Davis, "Incident," 563, who was with Norwood's Company L. Moreover, the movement described by Peopeo Tholekt aligns with that known to have occurred during Norwood's withdrawal from his advanced skirmish position.

68. McWhorter, *Hear Me*, 424–25. See also McWhorter, *Yellow Wolf*, 168–69. MacDonald's informants told him that Looking Glass tried to trap Norwood's company by positioning two lines on either side, but Norwood failed to advance between the lines and instead "retreated to a point of timber." MacDonald, "Nez Perces," 268.

69. Howard, *Nez Perce Joseph*, 227.

70. Penciled, undated note, "Headquarters, Department of Columbia," part 3, 1877, box 2, entry 107, U.S. Army Continental Commands.

71. Ibid.

72. Howard, "Report," 612. The exchange between Howard and Sanford is in Howard, *Nez Perce Joseph*, 228.

73. Norwood to Gibbon, August 24, 1877, roll 338, item 6154, Nez Perce War Papers.

74. Helena *Daily Independent*, June 13, 1896.

75. This is a liberal estimate based on knowledge of the approximate start of the Nez Perce raid, say 3:30 A.M., to probably 4:15 A.M., when the troops went in chase of the pack animals and horses, to perhaps 5:30 A.M. when they fell into line facing the warriors, to about 9:30 A.M., when the warriors retired before Norwood's final position, to 11:30 A.M. or even mid-afternoon, when the troops likely arrived back in camp with the dead and wounded. However, Howard's aide, Lieutenant Wood, wrote eleven years later that the fighting ended at 2:00 P.M. C. E. S. Wood, "Chief Joseph, the Nez Perce," 140.

76. Virginia City *Madisonian*, August 25, 1877. Davis wrote: "I could never understand how those two companies of the 1st Cavalry could have missed the

Indians [sic—they did not] and gotten entirely out of touch with us, when we started together and we were fighting within half an hour and kept it up for nearly three hours." Davis, "Incident," 564.

77. New York *Herald*, September 10, 1877.

78. C. E. S. Wood, "Journal," August 20, 1877.

79. Howard, *Nez Perce Joseph*, 229.

80. Howard, "Report," 612; and Henry Buck, "Nez Perce Indian Campaign," 60–61. Other sources, besides those cited above, that have contributed to this record of the Camas Meadows fight are: McDowell to Adjutant General, Washington, D.C. (containing Howard's initial report of the event), August 22, 1877, roll 337, item 5282, Nez Perce War Papers; Portland *Daily Standard*, September 6, 1877; FitzGerald, *Army Doctor's Wife*, 307; Lew L. Callaway account in Great Falls *Rocky Mountain Husbandman*, September 4, 1941; C. E. S. Wood, "Indian Epic is Re-Told"; Charles Rhodes, "Chief Joseph," 224; and Baily, "Nez Perces in Yellowstone," 5–7.

81. Medal of Honor, Special File; *The Medal of Honor*, 229–31; copies of Jackson Medal of Honor documents provided by Eileen Bennett, Kilgore, Idaho; Beyer and Keydel, *Deeds of Valor*, 2:248; and *U.S. Army Gallantry and Meritorious Conduct*, 80–81.

82. Glass's grave, complete with U.S. Quartermaster Department–provided marker, overlooks Pleasant Valley west of Interstate 15. It can be reached via the exit at the community of Humphreys, then south on an old two-lane highway for nearly three miles, then under the interstate and north on a gravel road for about one mile to the solitary grave above the valley.

83. Henry Buck, "Nez Perce Indian Campaign," 63.

84. Howard, "Report," 612; Chicago *Tribune*, August 24, 1877; and *Army and Navy Journal*, September 1, 1877.

85. New York *Herald*, September 10, 1877.

86. Howard to Bainbridge, August 21, 1877, entry 897, box 1, part 3, 1877, U.S. Army Continental Commands. The Bannocks proved to be effective scouts for the army, despite the stated desire of their leader, Buffalo Horn, to kill the Nez Perce herders with the command, a request that Howard quickly refused. Howard, *Nez Perce Joseph*, 175. Howard also expected to receive forty Lemhi Shoshones under Chief Tendoy who he wanted also to go after the stolen animals. "If Ten-Doy comes up," he wrote Bainbridge, "he can join you as I believe his people and yours are friendly." Howard, *Nez Perce Joseph*, 175. See also Howard to Shoup, August 20, 1877, entry 897, box 1, part 3, 1877, U.S. Army Continental Commands.

87. Years later, Howard complained that "Lieutenant Bacon let him [Joseph] go by and pass through the narrow gateway [Targhee Pass] without firing a shot." Howard, *My Life and Experiences*, 293. Yet it is obvious in his orders that Bacon was to scout Raynolds Pass, not Targhee. Davison, "A Century Ago," 12.

88. For extracts of medical reports testifying to the poor condition of the men, see Howard, "Report," 617.

89. Ibid., 612; Sutherland, *Howard's Campaign*, 36–37; Chicago *Tribune*, August 24, 1877; and Henry Buck, "Nez Perce Indian Campaign," 64–70.

90. Howard, "Report," 613.

91. Mason to wife, August 24, 1877, quoted in Davison, "A Century Ago," 12.

92. Captain Robert Pollock to wife, August 25, 1877, in Pollock, *Grandfather, Chief Joseph and Psychodynamics*, 83.

93. New York *Herald*, September 10, 1877.

94. Howard to Assistant Adjutant General, Military Division of the Pacific, August 24, 1877, quoted in John Carpenter, *Sword and Olive Branch*, 257.

95. "Report of the General of the Army," November 7, 1877, in Secretary of War, *Report . . . 1877*, 12–13.

96. Ibid., 13.

97. Ibid. See the in-depth discussion of the Howard-McDowell-Sherman telegraphic round robin in John Carpenter, *Sword and Olive Branch*, 254–57.

CHAPTER 8

1. Sheridan to Terry, telegrams, August 13, 1877, and Terry to Howard, August 14, 1877, folder: Nez Perce War, box 3, Sladen Family Papers.

2. Miles to Doane, August 3, 1877, Baird Papers.

3. Doane's army career, including his work with the Crow scouts, is detailed in Bonney and Bonney, *Battle Drums and Geysers*, 71–87.

4. Terry, "Report," 506–7.

5. First Lieutenant George W. Baird to Doane, August 12, 1877, Baird Papers.

6. Colonel Samuel D. Sturgis report, December 5, 1877, in Secretary of War, *Report . . . 1877*, 507–8. See also *Army and Navy Journal*, April 30, 1878.

7. Howard to Sturgis, August 25, 1877, entry 897, box 1, part 3, 1877, U.S. Army Continental Commands.

8. Colonel Samuel D. Sturgis report, December 5, 1877, in Secretary of War, *Report . . . 1877*, 508; and Bonney and Bonney, *Battle Drums and Geysers*, 76–77.

9. Howard, "Report," 616.

10. Howard's orders to Cushing are in ibid.

11. Sherman to Sheridan, August 29, 1877, roll 5, Nez Perce War, 1877, Division of the Missouri, Special File.

12. Terry, "Report," 506.

13. Sherman to Howard, August 29, 1877, roll 5, Nez Perce War, 1877, Division of the Missouri, Special File.

14. Sherman to Sheridan, August 31, 1877, item 5542, roll 338, Nez Perce War Papers.

15. Howard, "Report," 617–18.

16. U.S. Senate, *Letter from the Secretary of the Interior . . . 1872*, 1–2; "Report on the Yellowstone National Park," 841; and Chittenden, *Yellowstone National Park*, 175–76. For the background and history of Yellowstone National Park, see Aubrey Haines, *Yellowstone Story*; Bartlett, *Yellowstone*; Aubrey Haines, *Yellowstone National Park*; and Beal, *Story of Man in Yellowstone*.

17. August 3, 1877, letter, in Sheridan and Sherman, *Report*, 33. The statement about native beliefs was untrue. Indians were *not* afraid of the park's hot springs, but thanks to Sherman's statement and others like it (from Euro-Americans who did not know the truth), Yellowstone National Park has been plagued by that misconception ever since. Historian Lee H. Whittlesey, letter to author, May 1995. Confirming this view, at least one aged Nez Perce recalled that his people had used the hot springs for cooking food during their passage in 1877. Kearns, "Nez Perce Chief," 41.

18. Sherman to McCrary, August 19, 1877, in Sheridan and Sherman, *Report*, 35.

19. Sherman to McCrary, August 29, 1877, ibid., 37.

20. Ibid.

21. Gibbon, "Wonders of the Yellowstone"; and Gibbon, "Rambles in the Rocky Mountains," 312–36, 455–75 (reprinted in Gibbon, *Adventures*).

22. Gibbon to Howard, August 26, 1877, entry 395, 141–42, part 3, Letterbook, January 1870–April 1879, U.S. Army Continental Commands.

23. The sole substantive Nez Perce account that is known to date is that of Yellow Wolf, given to L. V. McWhorter early in the twentieth century. Yellow Wolf, however, as will be seen, was part of a group of warriors that splintered off from the main column and traveled north, so that his recollections are limited in explaining the extent of movement of the principal assemblage. See McWhorter, *Yellow Wolf*, 170–80; and Guie and McWhorter, *Adventures in Geyser Land*. The primary first-person non-Indian account that posits the locations of the Nez Perces through much of their passage through the park is that of Fisher, in charge of the Bannock scouts, as contained in Fisher, "Journal of S. G. Fisher." A typescript of Fisher's original journal, which contains slight differences in wording and phrasing from the published version, is Fisher, Journal, Idaho State Historical Society. A reminiscent account of some value is in Woodward, "Service of J. W. Redington" which contains not only Redington's recollections of his days in Yellowstone working with Fisher, but verbatim excerpts from period tabloids covering his experiences.

For a sampling of recent thinking regarding the route of the Nez Perces through Yellowstone based partly on the above materials but with widely divergent results, see Goodenough, "Lost on Cold Creek"; and Lang, "Where Did the Nez Perces Go?".

24. Fisher, "Journal of S. G. Fisher," 270–71.

25. For details of the course of the Bannock Trail and its many divisions, see Replogle, *Yellowstone's Bannock Indian Trails*, 22–30. See also Aubrey Haines, *Yellowstone Story*, 1:27–29; and Aubrey Haines, "Bannock Indian Trails."

26. John Shively gave his age as sixty-two in March 1887, when he filed for losses incurred from his experience with the Nez Perces ten years earlier. By all accounts, he must have appeared older than his age. Frank D. Carpenter, one of the Radersburg tourists, called him "the most wretched looking specimen of humanity I had ever seen." Guie and McWhorter, *Adventures in Geyser Land*, 68. See John Shively claim, no. 4049, entry 700, Claim for Indian Depredations, U.S. Bureau of Indian Affairs. Shively's accounts appear in the Bozeman *Times*, September 13, 1877; Deer Lodge *New North-West*, September 14, 1877; and Helena *Daily Independent*, September 12, 1877. See also Shively's narrative in Stanley, *Rambles in Wonderland*, 175–79.

27. See the concerned accounts, as follows: Fisher, "Journal of S. G. Fisher," 270; McWhorter, *Hear Me*, 435; McWhorter, *Yellow Wolf*, 170–71; "Yellow Wolf's Story," in Guie and McWhorter, *Adventures in Geyser Land*, 275; and "Shively, Guide for the Nez Perces," in ibid., 281.

28. See Norris, *The Calumet*, 250, for a close-to-contemporary description of this site.

29. Fisher, "Journal of S. G. Fisher," 272–73; Bozeman *Times*, September 30, 1877; and McWhorter, *Hear Me*, 436–37.

30. Hayden, "Yellowstone National Park"; and "Sketch of the Yellowstone Lake and . . . Upper Yellowstone River." Pelican Creek was named in 1864. Whittlesey, *Yellowstone Place Names*, 119.

31. Deer Lodge *New North-West*, September 14, 1877; and Bozeman *Times*, September 13, 1877. On being informed that they were on the Yellowstone, Shively recalled, "there was more rejoicing among them than among the children of Israel when they first viewed the Promised Land." Bozeman *Times*, September 13, 1877.

32. Fisher, "Journal of S. G. Fisher," 274.

33. Boise, Idaho *Tri-Weekly Statesman*, September 20, 1877. An abbreviated version of the dispatch is in Howard to Commanding Officer, Fort Ellis, September 2, 1877, entry 897, box 1, part 3, 1877, U.S. Army Continental Commands. Private Irwin had been discharged on July 17 on surgeon's certificate of disability. Regimental Returns . . . Second Cavalry, August 1877, roll 166.

34. Portland *Daily Standard*, September 30, 1877.

35. Fisher, "Journal of S. G. Fisher," 274.

36. Ibid., 275.

37. Lake District Ranger John Lounsbury, telephone communication with author, April 25, 1995.

38. It should be noted that Scout John W. Redington said that he reached Fisher on the morning of September 4 by traveling "up Pelican creek" on the third and passing through an "awful stretch of down timber." In an article published in 1933, fifty-six years after the events, Redington recalled that on the morning of September 4, Fisher "took me up to the top of a ridge, from which we could look across a deep canyon and see the Nez Perce camp on the next ridge." Redington, "Scouting in Montana," 58. In a statement made in 1934, Redington said that he and Fisher "surveyed the camp in the next valley." Woodward, "Service of J. W. Redington," 5.

39. Fisher, "Journal of S. G. Fisher," 275.

40. See Goodenough, "Lost on Cold Creek," 26, 28.

41. Fisher, "Journal of S. G. Fisher," 275.

42. Shively carefully prepared a brush shelter, then stole away in the night, heading northwest for Baronett's bridge. He was guided by Soda Butte and the North Star. He reached Bozeman on September 5. Deer Lodge *New North-West*, September 14, 1877.

43. Quoted in Kearns, "Nez Perce Retreat," 36.

44. Fisher, "Journal of S. G. Fisher," 276.

45. Fisher's manuscript journal is slightly different, but just as imprecise, stating that the scouts encountered "the enemy's trail" at "a point where it [East Fork] formed a junction with another Stream [Cache Creek?] betwixt the Stream we followed down [Miller Creek?] and Soda Butte Creek. They [the Nez Perces] then turned South of East following up this middle stream." Quoted, without bracketed inserts, in Lang, "Where Did the Nez Perces Go?," 27. Discussion of the likelihood that the Nez Perces had separated into two or more groups (perhaps by bands) is in Lang, "Where Did the Nez Perces Go?," 28.

46. This course would have put the Nez Perces on what was essentially the last leg of the main Bannock Trail leading out of the park to Clark's Fork River. See Replogle, *Yellowstone's Bannock Indian Trails*, 30.

47. The cattle belonged to James C. Beatty, who grazed the animals in the area of the East Fork of the Yellowstone in exchange for providing milk to the

park superintendent. Goodenough, "Lost on Cold Creek," 29; and Bozeman *Times*, September 2, 1877.

48. Fisher, "Journal of S. G. Fisher," 276.

49. Bozeman *Times*, September 13, 1877; and Deer Lodge *New North-West*, September 14, 1877.

50. Historian Aubrey L. Haines staked the site of the camp in 1962 as based on the substantiation of Jack Ellis Haynes, who had been present in 1902 when the Cowans identified the site for Park Engineer Hiram M. Chittenden. Aubrey L. Haines, letter to author, August 23, 1995. Haines marked the site on the copy of Hague, *Atlas*, Geology Sheet XX, in the Yellowstone National Park Research Library, Mammoth, Wyo.

51. Guie and McWhorter, *Adventures in Geyser Land*, 97.

52. Cowan and Arnold said that they were encouraged to start for home by "one of the Indians who told them that they need apprehend no danger, as they were friends to the white man, and he would himself escort the party safely by all of the band, and they could then proceed without molestation toward home. They were, however, soon surrounded by about seventy-five or one hundred warriors who told them that it would not be safe to travel that road as there were some bad Indians behind who would probably meet them . . . [and] that their only safe plan would be to turn back and go with them; that they would protect them from the bad Indians." Bozeman *Times*, September 27, 1877. Yellow Wolf, who was one of the warriors who initially approached the tourists, said that he tried to explain that the Indians were "double-minded," or of mixed temperament, toward the whites, and that Cowan's party had insisted upon seeing Chief Joseph. McWhorter, *Yellow Wolf*, 174 n. 4.

53. Cowan, "Reminiscences," 168. Yellow Wolf indicated that the "other Indians"— the rearguard of the train supposedly composed of hotheads—took over at this point. "They did not listen to anybody. Mad, those warriors took the white people from us." McWhorter, *Yellow Wolf*, 175. Yellow Bull said that "they were young men from Lapwai, who had joined us after the fighting began." Yellow Bull account in Curtis, *North American Indian*, 8:167.

54. Carpenter met Looking Glass and described him thus: "Looking Glass is a man of medium height, and is apparently forty-five years of age, his hair being streaked with grey. He has a wide, flat face, almost square, with a small mouth running from ear to ear. His ears were decorated with rings of purest brass, and down the side of his face hung a braid of hair, adorned at the end with brass wire wound around it. The ornament worn by him, that was most conspicuous, was a tin lookinglass, which he wore about his neck and suspended in front. . . . He wore nothing on his head and had two or three feathers plaited in his back hair." Guie and McWhorter, *Adventures in Geyser Land*, 103.

55. When Carpenter met this individual he thought he was White Bird. Ibid., 104.

56. Boise, Idaho *Tri-Weekly Statesman*, September 18, 1877.

57. Bozeman *Times*, September 27, 1877.

58. Boise, Idaho *Tri-Weekly Statesman*, September 18, 1877.

59. Bozeman *Times*, September 27, 1877. The Nez Perces said later that the man who shot Cowan was Umtillilpcown. Duncan MacDonald, "The Captives Attacked," excerpt from 1879 series in the Deer Lodge *New North-West*, in Guie and McWhorter, *Adventures in Geyser Land*, 216.

60. Cowan, "Reminiscences," 171.

61. The man who confronted Frank Carpenter was Red Scout. Duncan MacDonald, "The Captives Attacked," excerpt from 1879 series in the Deer Lodge *New North-West*, in Guie and McWhorter, *Adventures in Geyser Land*, 216.

62. Ten years later, Arnold filed a claim for loss of property valued at $305. Andrew J. Arnold claim, no. 4185, November 1887, entry 700, Claim for Indian Depredations, U.S. Bureau of Indian Affairs.

63. George F. Cowan, born in Ohio in 1842, had served in the Civil War in the Wisconsin volunteer infantry. Great Falls *Tribune*, December 26, 1926.

64. Yellow Wolf, who was with the main caravan when the trouble erupted on the back trail, remembered that "it was the bad boys killing some of the white men." McWhorter, *Yellow Wolf*, 176.

65. Cowan, "Reminiscences," 172.

66. Ibid., 173.

67. Guie and McWhorter, *Adventures in Geyser Land*, 129. Philetus W. Norris wrote in 1883: "In the open pines of the summit, just east of the lake, is the remains of Chief Joseph's corral in 1877." Norris, *The Calumet*, 260.

68. Guie and McWhorter, *Adventures in Geyser Land*, 135.

69. McWhorter, *Yellow Wolf*, 177. In Joseph [Heinmot Tooyalakekt], "An Indian's Views," 427, Joseph is quoted as saying of the three captives, "They were treated kindly. The women were not insulted." Frank Carpenter, however, through the veiled language of the time strongly hinted that Emma Cowan and Ida Carpenter had been abused during their captivity. See Guie and McWhorter, *Adventures in Geyser Land*, 133, 155.

70. One of those who accompanied the Cowan-Carpenter group from the park was the inimitable John B. ("Texas Jack") Omohundro, erstwhile army scout, showman, and colleague of William F. ("Buffalo Bill") Cody, who had been guiding some Englishmen (the Earl of Dunraven and Dr. George Kingsley) around "Wonderland," but had headed to Mammoth on learning of the presence of the Nez Perces. Omohundro gave the papers a ridiculous yarn about Frank Carpenter being tied to a tree "to be burned, when he was recognized by Joseph, his father having formerly been a trader among the Nez Perces, and by order of that chieftain was, with the two ladies, released." Cheyenne *Daily Leader*, September 12, 1877.

71. This account of the Radersburg party's encounter with the Nez Perces is compiled from the following materials: Bozeman *Times*, September 27, 1877; Boise, Idaho *Tri-Weekly Statesman*, September 15, 18, 1877; Helena *Daily Herald*, August 27, 1877; New York *Herald*, September 18, 1877; Cowan, "Reminiscences," 178–85; Albert Oldham account in *Forest & Stream* undated clipping, scrapbook 4208, 124, Yellowstone National Park Research Library, Mammoth, Wyo.; Frank Carpenter's account in Guie and McWhorter, *Adventures in Geyser Land*, 91–186; Oldham's account in ibid., 201–5; George F. Cowan's account in ibid., 206–16; A. J. Arnold's account in ibid., 217–31; McWhorter, *Yellow Wolf*, 173–77; Topping, *Chronicles of the Yellowstone*, 213–15; Chittenden, *Yellowstone National Park*, 152–62; Walgamott, *Reminiscences*, 44–47; and Aubrey Haines, *Yellowstone Story*, 1:222–27. In 1888, both Cowan and Oldham filed depredations claims against the Nez Perces for their losses. Cowan claimed $3,910 for the theft of his horses and property and damages to himself, while Oldham claimed $2,011 for "property stolen

&c., personal injuries." George Cowan claim, no. 4186, entry 700, and Albert Oldham claim, no. 4187, entry 700, Claim for Indian Depredations, U.S. Bureau of Indian Affairs. The Cowans revisited the park in 1882 and 1901 and, during the latter tour, helped identify places significant to the routes of the Nez Perces and Howard's army in 1877. Topping, *Chronicles of the Yellowstone*, 215; and Chittenden, *Yellowstone National Park*, 162 n.

72. Ben Stone's account in Bozeman *Avant Courier*, September 6, 1877.

73. Weikert, "Journal of the Tour," 159. Hiram M. Chittenden, an early park engineer and historian, examined the site of the Helena group's camp and commented as follows: "The camp site on Otter Creek was well chosen for defense, but its natural advantages were absolutely ignored by the party. It was a triangular knoll between the forks of the stream, and some twenty feet above them. It commanded every approach, and with the slightest vigilance and intelligent preparation, could have been made impregnable to the . . . Indians who attacked it. But while the camp was properly pitched in a little depression back of the crest, the men themselves all staid back where the view around them was entirely cut off. They kept no guard, and were, therefore, in a worse position than if actually out in the open plain below. The Indians approached under cover of the hill, climbed its sides, and burst over its crest directly into camp before any one suspected their presence." Chittenden, *Yellowstone National Park*, 165. For a fairly contemporary description of this site, see Norris, *The Calumet*, 265.

74. Before dawn on August 26, Emma Cowan, Frank Carpenter, and Ida Carpenter, released the previous day by the Nez Perces, passed by the Helena party's camp and could hear somebody chopping wood. Fearful of being captured again by the Nez Perces, they kept moving north toward Tower Fall. Cowan, "Reminiscences," 171.

75. Irwin later came under criticism for what he apparently told the Nez Perces about tourists in the park. Because he was still in uniform (he said he had brought it from the Black Hills), Irwin told the tribesmen that he belonged to one of the excursion parties. "His sole motive in his talk and movements were to preserve his own life, which is a natural impulse." Bozeman *Times*, September 20, 1877.

76. McWhorter, *Yellow Wolf*, 177.

77. Stone's account in Bozeman *Avant Courier*, September 6, 1877.

78. John Stewart's account in Bozeman *Avant Courier*, September 27, 1877.

79. In 1887, Leslie N. Wilkie and Leander Duncan claimed $675.75 for items taken by the Nez Perces, including horses, pack saddles, a cooking outfit, an ax, various wearing apparel, and fishing tackle. "List of articles stolen from Leslie N. Wilkie and Leander Duncan." Andrew Weikert also filed a claim for "property stolen or destroyed and injuries." Andrew Weikert claim, August 1877, no. 4189, entry 700, Claim for Indian Depredations, U.S. Bureau of Indian Affairs.

80. One contemporary secondary account stated that this incident occurred "on the plateau between Blacktail [Deer] creek and Gardiner [sic] river," an area now designated Blacktail Deer Plateau. Topping, *Chronicles of the Yellowstone*, 217.

81. Weikert, "Journal of the Tour," 171.

82. This account of the Helena party is drawn from the following sources: Weikert, "Journal of the Tour," 153–74; Stone's accounts in Bozeman *Avant Courier*, September 6, 13, 1877; Frederic J. Pfister's account in Bozeman *Times*, August 30, 1877; John Stewart's account in Bozeman *Avant Courier*, September 27, 1877; Cowan,

"Reminiscences," 178; Chittenden, *Yellowstone National Park*, 163–66; and Aubrey Haines, *Yellowstone Story*, 1:220–31.

83. It is not known if this was the same body of warriors that struck the Helena tourists or an altogether different group. According to Yellow Wolf, he was with the party that later struck Mammoth and Henderson's Ranch. While it is possible that this group had nothing to do with the earlier raid, available Nez Perce sources unfortunately provide little that might clarify the matter. Historian William L. Lang concluded that the bodies of warriors that hit Henderson's Ranch and the Helena party were different and that the men involved in the former incident made their way up the Yellowstone and forded the river at Tower Fall before passing up the East Fork (Lamar) to rejoin the main Nez Perce assemblage. Lang, "Where Did the Nez Perces Go?," 17, 24.

84. Gibbon to Assistant Adjutant General, Department of Dakota, October 18, 1877, in Secretary of War, *Report . . . 1877*, 522.

85. Private William H. White claimed to have been riding in advance with some of Doane's scouts when they came on the ongoing action at Henderson's. White rode back to the column and told the officers what was happening, but they did nothing. "No direct relief went from any of the soldiers to the white men being attacked. But the ordinary course of movement of the entire body brought them nearer to the scene. By this undesigned means the Indians were frightened away." William White, *Custer, Cavalry, and Crows*, 136–37.

86. Yellow Wolf was with the group that killed Dietrich: "I shot at him, but I missed. At the same time he makes for his gun, but the next Indian by me, shot him before he could reach his gun. Then we go into the house and we take everything we could, especially in clothes." McWhorter, *Hear Me*, 439. However, in McWhorter, *Yellow Wolf*, 177, Yellow Wolf stated that Naked-footed Bull only winged Dietrich and identified Yettahtapnat Alwum (Shooting Thunder) as the man who killed him by shooting him in the stomach. Yellow Wolf also cited a skirmish with the soldiers near the hotel at about dusk, but other sources do not bear this out. See McWhorter, *Yellow Wolf*, 178–79. For background on Dietrich, see Whittlesey, *Death in Yellowstone*, 134–35.

87. Hugh Scott, *Some Memories of a Soldier*, 62.

88. In later years, Hugh Scott believed that his presence at Mammoth Hot Springs in the wake of the attack on Henderson's ranch convinced the Nez Perce leadership not to head out of the park by that route. In 1913, the then General Scott wrote that Joseph had told him after the surrender that "my [Scott's] rapid advance with 10 men at Mammoth hot springs & chase of his advance guard or rather scouts . . . made him think I had a strong force behind me and he turned off at the Mud Geysers, crossed the Yellowstone there below the lake, went up Pelican Creek & East Fork, then down Clarks Fork, crossing the Yellowstone about 100 miles nearer Gen. Miles at Fort Keogh [sic—Tongue River Cantonment]. . . . Had the 7th Cav messenger had 100 miles more to take Miles the news he would have gotten across the [British] line [or to the buffalo grounds if that was still an objective]. Miles would never have caught him." Scott to Walter M. Camp, September 22, 1913, folder 23, box 1, Camp Papers, BYU. See also Hugh Scott, *Some Memories of a Soldier*, 65. In fact, the date (August 31) conforms with the main camp's likely presence along the upper East Fork, rather than the ford near Mud Volcano. The Nez Perces also told Scott "that before such change of plan [in their

route] they had not intended going to Canada; before that they had intended going only as far as the buffalo country." Scott to Camp, January 11, 1914, folder 1, box 2, Camp Papers, BYU.

89. Ben Stone's account in Bozeman *Avant Courier*, September 13, 1877; Bozeman *Times*, September 6, 1877; Weikert, "Journal of the Tour," 174; Hugh Scott, *Some Memories of a Soldier*, 61–63; Topping, *Chronicles of the Yellowstone*, 217–18; McWhorter, *Hear Me*, 438–41 (which has confused the sequence of events); Aubrey Haines, *Yellowstone Story*, 1:232–33; Aubrey Haines, "Burning of Henderson's Ranch"; and Mark Brown, "Yellowstone Tourists and the Nez Perce." A purported account by Ben Stone of unknown derivation and suspected veracity, complete with affected Negro dialect (Stone was black), is provided by Frank Carpenter in Guie and McWhorter, *Adventures in Geyser Land*, 194–95. Kenck and Dietrich were the first Euro-Americans known to be killed by Indians in the area constituting the national park since 1839, when Piegan tribesmen killed five fur trappers near present Indian Pond. Whittlesey, *Death in Yellowstone*, 131–32.

90. Scott claimed that Doane had initially directed Lieutenant Charles C. DeRudio to lead the scout, but that "DeRudio flatly refused to go." Camp Manuscript Field Notes, 181, Camp Papers, BYU.

91. Hugh Scott, *Some Memories of a Soldier*, 63. A more detailed description of Scott's scouting technique is in Camp Manuscript Field Notes, 181, Camp Papers, BYU.

92. One reference to this incident stated that it occurred near the head of Little Blacktail Deer Creek and that Leonard and Groff had fought off the attackers from a point of rocks by the trail. Topping, *Chronicles of the Yellowstone*, 219.

93. For Doane's background, see Heitman, *Historical Register and Dictionary*, 1:375. While noted for his regional explorations (he authored *Journals of Yellowstone Exploration of 1870* and *Snake River Explorations of 1876–77*) as well as for his work with the Crow scouts, Doane received heavy criticism from the Crow agent, George W. Frost, and Major James S. Brisbin, Second Cavalry. The former complained that Doane had exceeded his authority and that the Crows harbored "a very bitter feeling against him," while Brisbin said that Doane "consorted with squaws and he and his men greatly demoralized the Crow camp." Frost to Brisbin, October 10, 1877, with Brisbin's endorsement, October 21, 1877, entry 107, box 3, part 3, "Letters and Telegrams Received by District of the Yellowstone Headquarters, September 1877–April 1878," U.S. Army Continental Commands.

94. Quoted in Bonney and Bonney, *Battle Drums and Geysers*, 83.

95. Quoted in ibid., 83–84.

96. Hugh Scott, *Some Memories of a Soldier*, 68.

97. Phinney, *Jirah Isham Allen*, 99.

98. Gilbert to Assistant Adjutant General, Department of Dakota, October 2, 1877, in Secretary of War, *Report . . . 1877*, 561; Hugh Scott, *Some Memories of a Soldier*, 67–69; Camp Manuscript Field Notes, 183, Camp Papers, BYU; Bozeman *Times*, September 6, 1877; Phinney, *Jirah Isham Allen*, 97–100; Grinnell, *Hunting at High Altitudes*, 60, 62; Topping, *Chronicles of the Yellowstone*, 218–19; Bonney and Bonney, *Battle Drums and Geysers*, 84–86; and "Charles Champion Gilbert," in Warner, *Generals in Blue*, 173–74. In an incident of Gilbert's march, Scout Jirah Isham Allen was directed to help several dismounted Seventh Cavalry troopers in fording streams on the way to camp. He found that their sabres so hampered them

when afoot that he ordered the men stick them in the ground and leave them, an action for which he was chastised for disarming the soldiers. Jirah Isham Allen, Letter.

99. Howard, "Report," 618.

100. Howard to Commanding Officer, Fort Ellis, August 29, 1877, in ibid.

101. General Field Order No. 6, in ibid., 619.

102. Mason to wife, August 29, in Davison, "A Century Ago," 13.

103. Henry Buck, "Nez Perce Indian Campaign," 72–73. In his report, Howard stated that Oldham was found on August 28, while Buck, writing many years after the events, stated that Oldham was found on the thirtieth. The date of August 29 was given by Mason in a letter written on that day.

104. Howard, "Report," 620.

105. Henry Buck, "Nez Perce Indian Campaign," 76. In 1923, Henry Buck relocated Howard's camp on Nez Perce Creek, about one mile above its mouth. "I pointed out . . . the ground occupied by our wagon train, next, the infantry camp, and above that the cavalry." Henry Buck, "Nez Perce Indian Campaign," Appendix B, 7.

106. In 1923, Henry Buck visited the 1877 trail below Mary Mountain, reporting that "in places the old road was quite visible showing the remains of corduroy laid across swampy places. In one instance the wreckage of a bridge over a small stream was still in evidence." Henry Buck, "Nez Perce Indian Campaign," Appendix B, 8.

107. Henry Buck revisited this site in 1923, noting that at that date a signboard nailed to a tree specified the spot as the place where the Nez Perces deliberated regarding the fate of the Cowan party. Buck stated that "this spot was also the place where the command made camp on the night of August 31st." Ibid.

108. William F. Spurgin (1838–1907) served from Indiana during the Civil War and afterwards saw duty with the Freedmen's Bureau, which Howard headed. He rose to the rank of brigadier general in 1902, in which year he retired. Heitman, *Historical Register and Dictionary*, 1:913. The skilled laborers comprised fifty-two frontiersmen organized as a company of engineers. Armed as infantry, they brought their own horses and received three dollars per day plus rations. Chittenden, *Yellowstone National Park*, 170.

109. Henry Buck, "Nez Perce Indian Campaign," 83.

110. The approximate route of Howard's road is in Hayden, "Yellowstone National Park."

111. New York *Herald*, September 18, 1877.

112. Henry Buck in 1923 stated that in 1877 "on account of so much sulphur present we christened this 'Sulphur Mountain,' but this is several miles west of what is now called 'Sulphur Mountain.'" Henry Buck, "Nez Perce Indian Campaign," Appendix B, 10. Buck was probably talking about present Highland Hot Springs. Historian Lee H. Whittlesey, telephone communication with author, May 1995.

113. Henry Buck,"Nez Perce Indian Campaign," 87–88. In 1921, Henry Buck traveled his 1877 route through Yellowstone National Park. He and his son climbed the ridge where the "beaver slide" enabled the wagons to descend. Wrote Buck: "We counted ten trees rope burned that will ever give evidence as long as the trees may stand of the spot where we took our slide down five hundred feet." Henry Buck,"Nez Perce Indian Campaign," Appendix A, 5. Unfortunately, the fires of 1988 in Yellowstone evidently destroyed the rope-burned trees that re-

mained from the "beaver slide." Lake District Ranger John Lounsbury, communication with author, Yellowstone National Park, June 5, 1994.

114. Henry Buck, "Nez Perce Indian Campaign," 89.

115. Ibid. Evidence of the cutting of timber for Spurgin's road is still present
in the area of Cascade Creek. Historian Aubrey L. Haines, letter to author, August
23, 1995.

116. Pollock to wife, September 2, 1877, in Pollock, *Grandfather, Chief Joseph and Psychodynamics*, 97. Scout John W. Redington recalled years later: "We
had a rather hungry time in Yellowstone Park, but found plenty of wormy trout to
fill up on. Tobacco was all out, but chewers found something just as good by cutting out the pockets where they had carried tobacco and chewing the rags."
Redington, Letter.

117. Howard, "Report," 620.

118. Henry Buck, "Nez Perce Indian Campaign," 88.

119. First Lieutenant Robert H. Fletcher to Second Lieutenant Charles A.
Worden, September 4, 1877, entry 897, box 1, part 3, 1877, U.S. Army Continental Commands. The white scout Thomas H. Leforge said that he met with Looking Glass and assured him that he would try and dissuade the Crows from helping
to intercept the Nez Perces on their way through the reservation. Marquis, *Memoirs of a White Crow Indian*, 128. See also Francis Haines, *Nez Perces*, 263.

120. Henry Buck, "Nez Perce Indian Campaign," 90–98. Spurgin was cited
"for conspicuous and arduous service in advance of the column which pursued the
hostile Nez Perce Indians, from Kamiah, Idaho, to the Yellowstone River, commanding the pioneer party." *U.S. Army Gallantry and Meritorious Conduct*, 78. In
August 1962, historian Aubrey L. Haines and Wayne Replogle traced 1,237 feet
of Captain Spurgin's road from Hayden Valley to the Yellowstone Canyon. For a
description of the road's appearance at that time, see Aubrey Haines, "Retracement
of Spurgin's road"; and letter, Haines to author, August 24, 1995. Vestiges of
Spurgin's road are still evident along the north side of Dunraven Pass and on the
flat where Carnelian Creek joins with Tower Creek. Lake District Ranger John
Lounsbury, letter to author, June 4, 1995; Historian Aubrey L. Haines, letter to
author, August 23, 1995.

Spurgin reached Fort Ellis on September 15. After a few days, he refitted his
wagons and started down the Yellowstone to meet Howard. He reached a point
120 miles below Fort Ellis when orders directed his return to that post. At Fort
Ellis, Spurgin discharged his engineers and journeyed back to Lewiston, Idaho,
via stagecoach, train, and steamer. He wrote his parents in Indiana; "I lost 27
pounds this summer. My clothes are all too large." Letter in Greencastle *Banner*,
December 6, 1877.

121. Deer Lodge *New North-West*, September 14, 1877; and Lang, "Where
Did the Nez Perces Go in Yellowstone?," 24.

122. Howard to Cushing, September 8, 1877, in Howard, "Report," 620.

123. Boise, Idaho *Tri-Weekly Statesman*, September 29, 1877.

124. Information about Howard's course through the park is from Howard,
"Report," 620–22; New York *Herald*, October 1, 1877; Connolly, Diary, August
30–September 6, 1877; Sutherland, *Howard's Campaign*, 38–39; Jocelyn, *Mostly
Alkali*, 255; Chittenden, *Yellowstone National Park*, 170–73; Howard, *My Life and
Experiences*, 293–94; and Davison, "A Century Ago," 13–15.

CHAPTER 9

1. Sherman to Sheridan, August 26, 1877, roll 5, Nez Perce War, 1877, Division of the Missouri, Special File.

2. Five of these companies had but recently returned from Omaha and Chicago, where they were posted during the railroad riots in July. Price, *Across the Continent*, 167–68. For a history of Camp Brown, see McDermott, *Dangerous Duty*, 105–11.

3. Crook, "Report," 90; Cheyenne *Daily Leader*, August 31, 1877; and Hart to Sheridan, telegram, September 5, 1877, roll 5, Nez Perce War, 1877, Division of the Missouri, Special File. As of August 30, Sheridan wanted Crook to send out some Shoshone scouts and "invite unconditional surrender of Joseph's band." In preparation for confronting the Nez Perces, however, Sheridan directed that 250 Sioux scouts under White Horse be sent to accompany Major Hart's battalion. Sheridan to Sherman, telegram, August 30, 1877, item 5542, roll 338, Nez Perce War Papers; and Cheyenne *Daily Leader*, November 2, 1877. Only 150 actually departed Red Cloud Agency on August 30 for Hart's command. Apparently, the scouts were recalled on Crook's advice. Lieutenant Colonel Robert Williams, Assistant Adjutant General, Department of the Platte, to Sheridan, telegram, August 30, 1877, roll 282, Letters Received, Adjutant General's Office, June 1877–October 1877, Sioux War Papers. For Crook's involvement in the Nez Perce campaign vis-à-vis the unfolding events at Camp Robinson, Nebraska, surrounding Crazy Horse's death, see Buecker, *Fort Robinson*, 110–13.

4. Sheridan sent word to Hart to "make for Stinking Water." With the help of the Sioux scouts, Sheridan wrote, "you will be able to kill or capture the hostile band of Nez-Perces . . . ," and "if you should get on their trail do not give it up till you overtake them." Enclosed in Sheridan to Williams, Assistant Adjutant General, Department of the Platte, August 30, 1877, roll 282, Letters Received, AGO, June 1877–October 1877, Sioux War Papers. Major Hart's battalion consisted of Companies B (Captain Robert H. Montgomery), H (Captain John M. Hamilton), I (Captain Sanford C. Kellogg), and L (First Lieutenant Charles H. Rockwell), along with twenty-five scouts headed by the noted frontiersman Frank Grouard. Second Lieutenant Edwin P. Andrus was adjutant. Wheeler, *Buffalo Days*, 202–3. On September 4, Sheridan had received a suggestion from Gibbon "that Hart be pushed up Stinking Water as far as he can go. Would it not be well to put Merritt up into the park on [Captain William A.] Jones [1873] trail [east of Yellowstone Lake] to pick up any straggling hostiles[?] . . . It is not impossible finding themselves headed off by Sturgis that they may turn back & make their way south by the trail East of the lake & so reach Snake river again." Gibbon to Sheridan, telegram, September 4, 1877, roll 5, Nez Perce War, 1877, Division of the Missouri, Special File.

5. Crook to Sheridan, September 10, 1877, roll 5, Nez Perce War, 1877, Division of the Missouri, Special File.

6. Ibid.; Assistant Adjutant General (Robert Williams) to Sheridan, August 27, 1877, roll 5, Nez Perce War, 1877, Division of the Missouri, Special File; Sheridan to Adjutant General (E. D. Townsend), August 28, 1877, item 5398, roll 337, Nez Perce War Papers; Cheyenne *Daily Leader*, September 13, 1877; Chicago *Tribune*, September 12, 1877; and King, *Indian Campaigns*, 86. Merritt's command consisted of Companies C (Captain Emil Adams), D (Captain Samuel S. Sumner), E (Captain George F. Price), F (Captain J. Scott Payne), K (Captain

Albert E. Woodson), and M (Second Lieutenant Charles H. Watts), Fifth Cavalry; and Company K (Captain Gerald Russell), Third Cavalry. Merritt's adjutant was Charles King, his regimental quartermaster First Lieutenant William P. Hall, and his medical officer Assistant Surgeon Charles Smart. Second Lieutenant Hoel S. Bishop commanded the Shoshone scouts. *Army and Navy Journal*, September 23, 1877.

7. Crook, "Report," 89–90; *Army and Navy Journal*, September 23, 1877; New York *Herald*, September 23, 1877; "Record of Medical History of Fort Washakie," 55, 56, 59; King, *Indian Campaigns*, 86–88; Price, *Across the Continent*, 168; Wheeler, *Buffalo Days*, 202–4, 206; DeBarthe, *Life and Adventures of Frank Grouard*, 188–89 (in which Grouard confused Hart's command, with which he served, with Merritt's); Daly, "U.S. vs. Joseph," 44; and Hedren, "Eben Swift's Army Service," 148–49.

8. First Lieutenant George W. Baird to Sturgis, August 11, 1877, Baird Papers.

9. Miles to Sturgis, August 12, 1877, ibid.

10. With Sturgis, the questions seemed not to do with his bravery but with his judgment. For his background, see Cullum, *Biographical Register*, 2:278–80; Warner, *Generals in Blue*, 486–87; Boatner, *Civil War Dictionary*, 816–17; and Hammer, *Biographies of the Seventh Cavalry*, 5.

11. Colonel Samuel D. Sturgis report, December 5, 1877, in Secretary of War, *Report . . . 1877*, 507; Regimental Returns . . . Seventh Cavalry, August 1877, roll 72; and Mills, *Harvest of Barren Regrets*, 298. General Terry's original plan was to send out the battalion of Second Cavalry that was under Miles's command, but as that unit was scouting for Sioux in the Little Missouri country to the east, Miles—anticipating the need for troops to head off the Nez Perces—had already dispatched Sturgis's Seventh cavalrymen by the time Terry's directive arrived. Miles to Assistant Adjutant General, Department of Dakota, August 19, 1877, roll 5, Nez Perce War, 1877, Division of the Missouri, Special File.

12. For details of the rations problem, see Goldin, *Bit of the Nez Perce Campaign*, 4–8.

13. Baird to Sturgis, August 16, 1877; and Miles to Sturgis, August 19, 1877, Baird Papers.

14. Hare, "Report of Lieut. L. R. Hare," 1677 (reprinted as *After the Battle*).

15. Fuller left the Tongue River Cantonment on the night of August 11. Years later he stated that "I was ordered to make all practicable speed, and if practicable, reach Ft. Ellis in five days, there to deliver my dispatches to the commanding officer to be forwarded to General Sherman, who was then in the national park, and whom [Brevet] General Miles desired to have advised that the Indians might pass through the Park, as they afterwards did, after which I was to get into communication with the Governor of Montana and General Gibbon, then colonel of the Seventh Infantry. . . . In the meantime, any information [that] might be received was to be communicated to [Brevet] General Sturgis." Fuller's account in Goldin, Biography, chap. 14, 289–97.

16. Colonel Samuel D. Sturgis report, December 5, 1877, in Secretary of War, *Report . . . 1877*, 508.

17. Miles to Sturgis, August 26, 1877, ibid.

18. Miles to Sturgis, August 27, 1877, ibid.

19. Beyond the sources cited above, the early movements of Sturgis's command are described variously in Goldin to L. V. McWhorter, August 30, 1929, and September 10, 1929, folder 177, McWhorter Papers; Hare, "Report of Lieut.

L. R. Hare," 1676–78; Goldin, Biography, 288–89, 297–301; Goldin, "Seventh Cavalry at Cañon Creek," 204–6; Benteen to wife, August 11, 1877, in Carroll, *Camp Talk*, 84–85; Sturgis to Potts, August 23, 1877, reprinted in Paul Phillips, "Battle of the Big Hole," 79; and Bonney and Bonney, *Battle Drums and Geysers*, 76–77.

20. Colonel Samuel D. Sturgis report, December 5, 1877, in Secretary of War, *Report . . . 1877*, 509.

21. On this date, Captain Benteen wrote: "To-day we labored under the impression for a while that we found the Nez Perces, caused by six of our indian [sic] scouts . . . firing into a herd of elk. M Co. went out to ascertain the cause of the firing—and commenced shooting elk themselves. 'Boots and Saddles' were sounded—and we awaited developments. Soon the six indians came in." Benteen to wife, September 5, 1877, in Carroll, *Camp Talk*, 90–91. For descriptions of the fishing, see Goldin, *Bit of the Nez Perce Campaign*, 8; and Benteen, "Trouting on Clark's Fork," 234–35.

22. Sturgis's September 6, 1877, notice "To the Miners and others at the Smelting Works" was also published in the Bozeman *Times*, September 13, 1877.

23. Yellow Wolf and Otskai shot these men while scouting for the main body of the Nez Perces. Yellow Wolf also claimed they attacked the party transporting the wounded man to the agency. For particulars, see McWhorter, *Yellow Wolf*, 182–84.

24. Colonel Samuel D. Sturgis report, December 5, 1877, in Secretary of War, *Report . . . 1877*, 510.

25. In his often confused accounts of Sturgis's movements, Goldin stated that on this or another night pickets fired on a horseman in the darkness and next morning found unshod pony tracks in the vicinity. See, for example, Goldin, "Seventh Cavalry at Cañon Creek," 210–11; and Goldin to McWhorter, September 27, 1933, folder 177, McWhorter Papers.

26. Hare, "Report of Lieut. L. R. Hare," 1678. Details of the march to the Stinking Water, from a former enlisted man's perspective, are in Goldin, *Bit of the Nez Perce Campaign*, 10–11; Goldin, Biography, 301–9; and Goldin, "Seventh Cavalry at Cañon Creek," 206–12.

27. It was Sturgis's trail in this area that Merritt found one week later.

28. On the eleventh, Hare commented, "on coming down the mountain-side it was found that the Indians had gone down Clark's Fork the same day that we had started for the Stinkingwater." Hare, "Report of Lieut. L. R. Hare," 1679. This assessment of Sturgis's maneuver to the Stinking Water is based upon data contained in the above-cited works, as well as in Regimental Returns . . . Seventh Cavalry, September 1877, roll 72; Goldin to McWhorter, March 20, 1939, August 30, 1929, and December 4, 1934, folders 159 and 177, McWhorter Papers; and Roy Johnson, *Jacob Horner*, 17–18. A route at some variance with the above is given in Mills, *Harvest of Barren Regrets*, 299–303.

29. Howard to Sturgis, September 8, 1877, entry 897, box 1, part 3, 1877, U.S. Army Continental Commands.

30. Fisher, "Journal of S. G. Fisher," 277.

31. This assessment of the Nez Perces' course in reaching Clark's Fork is based on communication with Stuart Conner, Michael Bryant, and Kenneth J. Feyhl, of Billings, Mont., who jointly over many years have worked to determine that route as precisely as possible. Of great benefit to this study has been Stuart Conner, letters to author, January 18, 1996, February 2, 1996, February 9, 1996,

and April 11, 1996; Kenneth J. Feyhl, letter to author, February 8, 1996; and Michael Bryant, Stuart Conner, and Kenneth J. Feyhl, various telephone communications with author, February 1996.

32. Mason to wife, September 11, 1877, in Davison, "A Century Ago," 15.

33. It is unclear exactly how many prospectors were killed, or whether they had been killed in one spot or several. Fisher accounted for three bodies found on Clark's Fork ("they were Danes or Norwegians from the Black Hills") and mentioned finding the German whose two colleagues had been killed on Crandall Creek. Fisher, "Journal of S. G. Fisher," 277. Redington, in "Scouting in Montana," 59, stated only that the scouts had found where the Nez Perces "had cleaned out a prospector's camp." He gave no number. Sutherland, writing in the Portland *Daily Standard*, October 5, 1877, said that eight men had been killed, four of them Scandinavians named Olsen, Kannard, Anderson, and Nelson.

34. Mason to wife, September 11, 1877, in Davison, "A Century Ago," 15.

35. Howard to Sturgis, September 10, 1877, entry 897, box 1, part 3, 1877, U.S. Army Continental Commands.

36. Colonel Samuel D. Sturgis report, December 5, 1877, in Secretary of War, *Report . . . 1877*, 510.

37. New York *Herald*, October 1, 1877. "What hurt us worse than all else," remembered Private Goldin years later, "was the discovery that the Indian trail entered the valley hardly more than a mile or two above the camp from which we had so recently started on that night march [September 8]. Had we remained where we were the Indians would almost have walked into our arms." Goldin, Biography, 310.

38. See Howard to Sturgis, September 11, 1877, in Howard, "Report," 622. Sturgis originally desired to send one of his battalions under Major Merrill or Captain Benteen rapidly ahead to find the Indians, but was deterred by his officers from thus splitting his command. Benteen to Goldin, November 17, 1891, in Carroll, *Benteen-Goldin Letters*, 203.

39. Howard, "Report," 623. See also Colonel Samuel D. Sturgis report, December 5, 1877, in Secretary of War, *Report . . . 1877*, 510.

40. Goldin, Biography, 311.

41. Goldin, *Bit of the Nez Perce Campaign*, 13.

42. The movements of Howard and Sturgis on Clark's Fork are documented in the sources quoted above, as well as in Hare, "Report of Lieut. L. R. Hare," 1679; Fisher, "Journal of S. G. Fisher," 277–78; Connolly, Diary, September 8, 9, 10, 11, 12, 1877; Goldin to McWhorter, February 27, 1929, folder 159, McWhorter Papers; Goldin to Earl A. Brininstool, January 13, 1929, Brininstool Collection; Redington, "Scouting in Montana," 58–59; Sutherland, *Howard's Campaign*, 40–41; William White, *Custer, Cavalry, and Crows*, 140–41; Pickard, Interview; Andrew Garcia account in Billings *Gazette*, August 14, 1932; Goldin, "Seventh Cavalry at Cañon Creek," 213–15; and John Carpenter, "General Howard," 140.

43. Weptas Nut (No Feather), Interview; and Yellow Bull's account in Curtis, *North American Indian*, 8:168. See also Francis Haines, *Nez Perces*, 265–66; and Josephy, *Nez Perce Indians*, 606–8. On their way down Clark's Fork, the tribesmen passed through or near the sites of the modern communities of Belfry, Bridger, Fromberg, Edgar, and Silesia, approximating the route of part of U.S. Highway 310 into Laurel. Dusenberry, "Chief Joseph's Flight," 49.

44. Harold Hagan, communication with author, Billings, Mont., May 24, 1995.

45. Redington, "Scouting in Montana," 61.

46. McWhorter's informants identified the six members of the Nez Perce party as Kalotas, Yellow Wolf, Sr., Iskiloom, Wattes Kunnin (Earth Blanket), John Mulkamkan, and Owhi. McWhorter, *Hear Me*, 457–58 n. 26. In another list, a seventh man's name was given as Tomsusliwi (complete name is illegible, but is probably Tumsuslehit [Rosebush]). List of Nez Perce informants to L. V. McWhorter.

47. The warriors who traveled as far as thirty miles to reach the area of present Huntley probably did not rejoin the main group until late that day, after the fight with Sturgis was over. Accounts of the Yellowstone Valley raiding by the Nez Perces on September 13, 1877, are often confusing and unclear, seemingly sometimes combining two or more events into one. This account is based on information in Bozeman *Times*, September 20, 1877; Portland *Daily Standard*, October 5, 1877; Fort Benton *Record*, September 21, 1877; Carroll, *Benteen-Goldin Letters*, 201–2; Topping, *Chronicles of the Yellowstone*, 221–22; Cascade *Courier*, February 28, 1930; Billings *Gazette*, June 30, 1927; Forrest Young account in "Forrest Young," Billings *Gazette*, undated clipping (ca. 1945), Indians—Wars—1877, vertical files, Parmly Billings Library, Billings, Mont.; Ed Forrest account in Billings *Gazette*, September 14, 1941; "Joe Cochran, 'First Resident of Billings,'" unidentified newspaper (Billings *Gazette*?), clipping apparently dated 1934, Montana scrapbook 3, Parmly Billings Library, Billings Mont.; Billings *Gazette*, July 6, 1958; Redington, "Scouting in Montana," 59, 60; and Redington, "The Stolen Stage Coach." See also Joseph M. V. Cochran claim, no. 2391, entry 700, and Bela B. Brockway claim, no. 3202, entry 700, Claim for Indian Depredations, U.S. Bureau of Indian Affairs. In 1882, the Indian agent on the Oakland Reservation, Indian Territory, presented Cochran's claim to Joseph and other Nez Perces. A warrior named Multitude said that he had taken part in the raid and acknowledged having taken some items, but that most had been abandoned soon afterwards. Joseph told the agent: "When the war broke out between my people and the whites, the property of either that fell into the other's hands was considered to belong to the captors; it was the fortune of war. . . . If we had money we might consider this claim and perhaps pay it; but we have nothing now to pay with. All our property fell into the hands of the whites." "Proceedings of a Council." Cochran never received payment. Billings *Gazette*, June 30, 1927, April 18, 1991. In an apparent tongue-in-cheek story related to his experiences on the campaign, J. W. Redington described the claim of a settler against the government for, among other things, a seven hundred dollar piano. Captain Fisher purportedly remarked: "Everything the scouts had was always in plain sight on their horses, and a piano would make a sightly package. There was no piano in the hostile camp at the wind-up; none dropped along the trail. There must be a mistake. It may have been a jewsharp that was stolen." Redington, "Who Stole the Piano?," 292–93.

48. Theodore Goldin identified this scout as Pawnee Tom. Goldin, Biography, 311. John W. Redington stated in 1930 that Sturgis's scouts saw a Nez Perce scout "on the northern bluffs" who disappeared as the command started on the trail. Redington, "The Stolen Stage Coach."

49. Fisher, "Journal of S. G. Fisher," 278. Goldin recalled hearing gunfire from downstream. Goldin, Biography, 311.

50. Redington, who watched the Nez Perces' procession up Canyon Creek, stated that the captured stage coach with its horses was following behind, driven by a warrior, and that "when these hostiles saw us they quickly unhitched the stage horses, mounted their cayuses, and dashed into skirmish line flanking their outfit. . . . The old stage was abandoned in the sagebrush." Redington, "The Stolen Stage Coach." See also Redington, "Scouting in Montana," 60; and Jocelyn, *Mostly Alkali*, 257. The firm of Gilman and Saulsbury, of Bozeman, operated the Bozeman–Miles City stage line, and the coach belonged to them. The vehicle was not a Concord coach, but a "jerky"—"a springless wagon with a covered body and two boots, fore and aft." The coach eventually went back into service on the line. "Wiley King, Tells of Stage-Coaching," unidentified newspaper (Billings *Gazette?*), undated clipping, Montana scrapbook 3, Parmly Billings Library, Billings, Mont.

51. Both Merrill and Benteen were officers of wide experience. Both had seen extensive Civil War service and had received numerous brevets for their respective performances in that conflict. Merrill (1834–1896) had joined the Seventh Cavalry in 1868 and had accompanied the regiment during its tenures in the West and South, but was on duty in the East when the Little Bighorn disaster occurred in June 1876. Cullum, *Biographical Register*, 2:624–25; and Hammer, *Biographies of the Seventh Cavalry*, 7. Benteen (1834–1898) was a forty-three-year-old Virginian who had joined the Seventh in 1866 and took part in much of its Indian campaigning and Reconstruction activities thereafter. As one of Custer's two principal subordinates at the Little Bighorn, Benteen found himself entangled in controversy for the rest of his military career. A brave officer, Benteen was also a chronic complainer who was ever ready to criticize those he considered his inferiors, which included just about everybody. Mills, *Harvest of Barren Regrets*; Heitman, *Historical Register and Dictionary*, 1:212; and Carroll and Price, *Roll Call on the Little Big Horn*, 117.

52. Fisher, "Journal of S. G. Fisher," 278.

53. Major Lewis Merrill report, September 18, 1877, in Secretary of War, *Report . . .1877*, 570. General Howard, reporting later on the character of the soldiers' arms during the war with the Nez Perces, noted that "quite a number" of the Seventh Cavalry carried Springfield rifles rather than carbines, an exchange that Howard approved because "there is greater distance between the sights, and . . . the larger charge gives relatively greater velocity to the ball." He further believed that the cavalrymen "all felt increase of confidence from this fact." "Summary of Reports . . . Non-Effectiveness," 3. See also McChristian, *Army of Marksmen*, 37–38. The Seventh Cavalrymen at Canyon Creek did not carry the regulation M1858 cavalry sabres, according to Theodore Goldin. They had been turned in at the Tongue River Cantonment before the troops started for the field. "They were a useless appendage in an Indian campaign. . . . We [previously] used them as toasting forks, rattle snake killers and . . . tent poles for our dog [shelter] tents." Goldin to McWhorter, July 12, 1932, folder 32, McWhorter Papers.

54. Major Lewis Merrill report, September 18, 1877, in Secretary of War, *Report . . . 1877*, 570.

55. Fisher, "Journal of S. G. Fisher," 278.

56. Benteen maintained that it was he who suggested this initiative to Sturgis. Carroll, *Benteen-Goldin Letters*, 203. Private Jacob Horner also confirmed that Benteen approached Sturgis and got permission for his movement. Roy Johnson, *Jacob Horner*, 20.

57. Colonel Samuel D. Sturgis report, December 5, 1877, in Secretary of War, *Report . . . 1877*, 511.

58. Ibid.

59. The withdrawal of Benteen's command, not mentioned in the official reports, is referenced in Fisher, "Journal of S. G. Fisher," 279. One of Howard's scouts who witnessed the engagement confirmed what apparently was this maneuver. The soldiers "would charge to the creek bank where the Nez Perces lay concealed, and who held their fire until the soldiers came close by, when the Indians would discharge a murderous volley, resulting in a confused stampede wherein were horses running in every direction; some with empty saddles, some unmanageable and running away with soldiers and men being wounded and others shot to pieces." Cruikshank, "Chasing Hostile Indians," 13.

60. Colonel Samuel D. Sturgis report, December 5, 1877, in Secretary of War, *Report . . . 1877*, 511. Wrote Goldin many years later: "So far as I ever knew, Benteen did not capture any part of the pony herd which, with the retreating village was well out in the valley out of long range fire from our [Benteen's] column. Seeing that we could not reach the village, Benteen deployed in some scrub timber and had a long range fight with the Indians on the side of the bluffs and at the entrance to the canyon affecting but little." Goldin to McWhorter, August 13, 1933, folder 159, McWhorter Papers. A soldier named Pickard claimed that "we got several hundred of their horses. Our Indian scouts captured these." Pickard, Interview. And Sutherland wrote for the Portland *Daily Standard*, October 5, 1877, that about one hundred ponies "were run off by the Crow Indians."

61. Fisher, "Journal of S. G. Fisher," 279.

62. Major Lewis Merrill report, September 18, 1877, in Secretary of War, *Report . . . 1877*, 570.

63. Fisher, "Journal of S. G. Fisher," 279. In most of his various writings, Goldin erroneously identified the officer in charge of the howitzers as Howard's son, Second Lieutenant Guy Howard, of the Twelfth Infantry, who had been in the army for less than one year (and who was probably not present at Canyon Creek but with his father coming down Clark's Fork). See, for example, Goldin, *Bit of the Nez Perce Campaign*, 15, wherein Goldin stated that Lieutenant Howard fired the howitzers while they were still strapped to the pack mules in an incident so ridiculous that it could never have happened as described.

64. This despite claims to the contrary by Goldin and others. See, for example, Goldin, "Seventh Cavalry at Cañon Creek," 217; Goldin, Biography, 313; and an account of teamster Andrew Garcia in Billings *Gazette*, August 14, 1932. A former trooper told McWhorter that Sturgis directed a howitzer round be fired into the Nez Perces' pony herd to start the fighting. William C. Slaper to McWhorter, April 22, 1929, folder 159, McWhorter Papers. A newspaper correspondent suggested that the howitzer was to have played a major role in securing a victory at Canyon Creek. "An attempt was made to hem the hostiles in by taking possession of the rear end of the cañon with a howitzer, but, as the heights were all so steep, it was found impossible to drag the gun up, and the plan had to be abandoned and the Indians escaped." New York *Herald*, October 1, 1877. Wrote Sturgis: "In spite of energetic efforts on the part of Lieutenant Otis, that officer was unable to render his little gun available, as his animals were totally worn out." Colonel Samuel D. Sturgis report, December 5, 1877, in Secretary of War, *Report . . . 1877*, 511.

65. Goldin, *Bit of the Nez Perce Campaign*, 15–16.

66. Goldin, Biography, 313–14. In a letter to McWhorter, Goldin provided more data about this movement. "I have no recollection that any communication came from Sturgis to Benteen [in fact, it did], but the latter finding he was making no headway [in the valley] figured that by moving to the left and passing around the end of this high bluff he might be able to force the Indian position. The squadron was mounted, G Troop under Lieut. Wallace on the right and the squadron at a gallop struck back along this high bluff. All went well for a short time, but the Indians were evidently closely watching our movement as ere we had gone half the distance along the face of this bluff, we were assailed by a heavy fire from the top. Lieut. Wallace charged on through, while H [M?] and I think it was B [Bendire's K, First Cavalry?] Troops hesitated for a few moments then, apparently without orders, the men charged the bluff. Only a few shots were fired and when we reached the top not an Indian was to be seen. We moved cautiously across the level plateau on top of the bluff until we reached the farther side, when we discovered the Indian[s] beyond rifle shot among the ravines. There was no use in pursuing them [as] they had every advantage." Goldin to McWhorter, February 3, 1933, folder 35, McWhorter Papers.

67. Fisher, "Journal of S. G. Fisher," 279–80.

68. Ibid., 280. Times for the start and end of the action were given by the wounded to Assistant Surgeon Holmes O. Paulding at the Tongue River Cantonment. Paulding to Medical Director, Department of Dakota, September 22, 1877, entry 624, box 1, Office of the Adjutant General; and also Return for Company G, September 1877, roll 72, Regimental Returns . . . Seventh Cavalry. In addition, this reconstruction of the Canyon Creek action is drawn from the following sources: Colonel Samuel D. Sturgis report, December 5, 1877, Major Lewis Merrill report, September 18, 1877, Benteen to Adjutant, Seventh Cavalry, September 18, 1877, and October 8, 1877, all in Secretary of War, *Report . . . 1877*, 511–12, 569–71, 572, respectively; Regimental Returns . . . Seventh Cavalry, September 1877, roll 72; pen and ink sketch titled, "Fight at Cañon Creek, Sturgis," inset drawing in Fletcher, "Department of Columbia Map"; Fisher, "Plan of the [Canyon Creek] Battle Ground," (this manuscript map was prepared to accompany publication of Fisher's journal but was deleted before the volume went to press); *Record of Engagements*, 72; sketch map of Canyon Creek by John W. Redington, in Redington to McWhorter, April 1930, folder 159, McWhorter Papers; sketch map by I. D. O'Donnell, 1944, ibid.; Pickard, Interview; Lynch, Interview; Sutherland (who arrived later with Howard), *Howard's Campaign*, 41; Forrest Young account in "Forrest Young," Billings *Gazette*, undated clipping (ca. 1945), Indians—Wars—1877, vertical files, Parmly Billings Library, Billings, Mont. (see also Forrest Young account in Stanford *Judith Basin County Press*, February 13, 1930); Andrew Garcia account in Laurel *Outlook*, June 23, 1937 (reprinted in Laurel *Outlook*, August 5, 1954, and August 2, 1989); and particularly valuable research conclusions based upon on-site archeological finds contributed by Michael Blohm of Laurel, Mont. See Douglas D. Scott, "Historical Archaeological Overview . . . Canyon Creek,"4–6. See also Taylor, "Canyon Creek Battlefield," which is especially useful in its on-ground placement of activities during the battle and post-battle phases according to section/township designation.

The numerous materials associated with enlisted man Theodore W. Goldin appear to be of dubious merit and have been used cautiously. While Goldin did much writing late in his life, his memory appears to have been faulty on numerous matters relating to Canyon Creek, particularly as it related to command objectives and other affairs in which he as a private soldier had no special knowledge. He was, moreover, prone to exaggeration and apparent creation of yarns to add color to his accounts. His materials, however, are useful for events in which he personally participated. The sources in question are: Goldin, Biography, 311–14; Goldin, *Bit of the Nez Perce Campaign*, 13–17; Goldin, "Seventh Cavalry at Cañon Creek," 215–20 (which Goldin accused Brady, *Northwestern Fights and Fighters*, of rewriting for his book); letters to McWhorter, February 27, 1929, March 20, 1929, March 14, 1932, July 12, 1932, August 1, 1932, February 3, 1933, August 13, 1933, and December 4, 1934, all in folders 159 and 177, McWhorter Papers; and Goldin to Brininstool, January 13, 1929, Brininstool Collection. Goldin was a participant in the Little Bighorn battle, too, and his recollections of that affair are likewise suspect in several areas. For a sketch of his life and service, see Hammer, *Biographies of the Seventh Cavalry*, 143–44.

69. Quoted in Sheridan to Adjutant General, September 17, 1877, item 5828, roll 338, Nez Perce War Papers.

70. Paulding to Medical Director, Department of Dakota, September 22, 1877, entry 624, box 1, Office of the Adjutant General; "List of Wounded . . . Cañon Creek"; and New York *Herald*, September 23, 1877. In addition, Lieutenants Gresham and Nicholson appear to have suffered very slight wounds of unspecified nature. Cheyenne *Daily Leader*, September 23, 1877; Sheridan to Adjutant General, September 26, 1877, item 6002, roll 338, Nez Perce War Papers; addendum to Major Lewis Merrill report, September 18, 1877, in Secretary of War, *Report . . . 1877*, 571; and Benteen to Adjutant, Seventh Cavalry, September 18, 1877, and October 8, 1877, in Secretary of War, *Report . . . 1877*, 571–72. A capsule biography of Brown (as well as several of the Canyon Creek wounded) is in Hammer, *Biographies of the Seventh Cavalry*, 210 and passim. See Appendix A for a complete list of the Canyon Creek army casualties.

71. Cruikshank, "Chasing Hostile Indians," 15. It must be stated that while Cruikshank's procedural description of the burials is likely correct, he was altogether wrong in his recollection of the number of casualties. Two of the Canyon Creek burials were exposed in December 1915 by workmen on the Cove Orchard Project. The remains, found about two hundred yards from Horse Cache Butte, were removed for reburial in Custer Battlefield National Cemetery, where they lie today. Billings *Gazette*, December 6, 1960 (citing issue of December 6, 1915). See also Glendolin Wagner, *Old Neutriment*, 223–26 n. 18.

72. Fisher, "Journal of S. G. Fisher," 280–81.

73. Major Lewis Merrill report, September 18, 1877, in Secretary of War, *Report . . . 1877*, 571.

74. San Francisco *Chronicle*, August 15, 1927.

75. Redington, "Scouting in Montana," 60.

76. Ibid.

77. Quoted in Roy Johnson, *Jacob Horner*, 19. See also Burdick and Hart, *Jacob Horner*, 21–22.

78. Quoted in Roy Johnson, *Jacob Horner*, 19.

79. Ibid., 19–20.

80. Lynch, Interview. Benteen acknowledged that he had carried a fishing

pole in at least part of the action at Canyon Creek. See Benteen to Goldin, November 17, 1891, in Carroll, *Benteen-Goldin Letters*, 204. For examples of criticism directed toward Sturgis ("Sturgis should have given the word to charge in on that sagebrush flat and wind up the war."), see Redington to Colonel William Carey Brown, October 28, 1926, folder 8, box 12, William Brown Papers; Redington, "Scouting in Montana," 60; and Goldin to McWhorter, various letters as cited above, and his sundry accounts. And the scout Alexander Cruikshank said that "everyone felt that the General had blundered as he surely had a sufficient force to have corralled the entire Indian outfit." Cruikshank, "Chasing Hostile Indians," 14. The characteristically blunt Benteen wrote Goldin (whose views may have been thus colored): "From the fact of having struck the reds at Canyon Creek, what was left of Sturgis's reputation was saved. . . . Sturgis was never very warm with me after the Canyon Creek affair. Why? Because he knew that I thought he was a coward." Carroll, *Benteen-Goldin Letters*, 204. Strong censure was directed at Sturgis by Ami Frank Mulford in a generally worthless (yet frequently cited) account: "Sturgis posted himself on a bluff, with a body guard, fully a mile from the reds, and viewed proceedings through his field glass. A bullet from a long-range gun in the hands of an Indian . . . struck the ground a short distance in front of the General, who lowered his glass, remarking that it was getting dangerous up there, and got out of danger." Mulford, *Fighting Indians!*, 115. This is hearsay, if Mulford was where he was supposed to be during the combat. Furthermore, the commanding officer's position in the rear supervising the engagement would have been entirely appropriate. For Horner's complimentary remarks, see Burdick and Hart, *Jacob Horner*, 22. It must be noted that even had Sturgis managed to block the mouth of the canyon, there existed two other routes allowing egress to the plains just five miles east of Canyon Creek. Harold Hagan, communication with author, Billings, Mont., May 24, 1995.

81. Goldin to McWhorter, February 27, 1929, folder 159, Goldin to McWhorter, August 1, 1932, folder 177, and Goldin to McWhorter, September 10, 1929, folder 159, McWhorter Papers.

82. Slaper to McWhorter, April 22, 1929, folder 129, McWhorter Papers.

83. FitzGerald to wife, September 16, 1877, in FitzGerald, *Army Doctor's Wife*, 312.

84. McWhorter and Many Wounds, "Colonel Sturgis Fight"; and McWhorter, *Hear Me*, 461.

85. McWhorter, *Yellow Wolf*, 185.

86. Ibid., 186.

87. Colonel Samuel D. Sturgis report, December 5, 1877, in Secretary of War, *Report . . . 1877*, 512; and McWhorter, "Fight with Sturgis." However, in McWhorter, *Yellow Wolf*, 194, Yellow Wolf indicated that the Crows killed this man along with another named Wetyetmas Hapima (Surrounded Goose) the next day. Yellow Wolf stated that the only casualties were the three wounded men. McWhorter, *Yellow Wolf*, 186 n. 5. William Connolly recorded that he "saw 4 dedd [sic] Indians" on the battlefield. Connolly, "Diary," September 13, 1877. The reporter Thomas Sutherland (*Howard's Campaign*, 41) stated that six Nez Perce bodies were found on the field, a figure uncorroborated by other accounts.

88. McWhorter, *Hear Me*, 462. According to McWhorter, Teeto Hoonnod was "noted for his courage and strategic ability." In his defense, he was joined for

a time by Swan Necklace, but evidently maintained his position alone until the families and horses passed inside the canyon walls. McWhorter, *Yellow Wolf*, 185 n. 3; and McWhorter, *Hear Me*, 462.

89. McWhorter, *Yellow Wolf*, 186–87. Theodore Goldin confirmed the presence of this barricade, writing that in the chase the next day, September 14, "we found the trail blocked by logs and boulders, evidently placed there by the fleeing Indians, and as we struggled through these obstacles or sought to remove them, we realized how completely we would have been exposed to ambush and annihilation." Goldin, Biography, 315.

90. McWhorter, *Yellow Wolf*, 187. In 1935 the aged warrior White Hawk told McWhorter that the Nee-Me-Poo camped a very far distance up the creek bottom. "Far across an open valley hemmed in by sloping hills, he designated where the trail entered a dark woods. Their camp that night, he said, was a considerable distance beyond, and he could not recall whether it was pitched by a stream or a spring." McWhorter and Many Wounds, "Colonel Sturgis Fight." See also McWhorter to Major Thomas A. Reiner, December 18, 1935, folder 159, McWhorter Papers. The modern route of the Burlington Northern Railroad along Canyon Creek probably closely—if not directly—parallels the Nez Perces' historical route for its entire distance through the canyon.

Nez Perce accounts of Canyon Creek testify to the loud reports of one of their guns during the fighting. On being questioned years later by L. V. McWhorter, the aged warrior Many Wounds recounted that a rifle capable of making such a noise had been for many years among the Nee-Me-Poo. McWhorter later learned that a large-caliber weapon, possibly a long-range Sharps buffalo gun weighing as much as fifteen pounds, had been captured on the Salmon by the young man, Shore Crossing (subsequently killed at the Big Hole). He further learned from Peopeo Tholekt that Poker Joe possessed such an arm at Canyon Creek and, after exhausting his ammunition for it, disposed of it by burying it among the rocks at the Nez Perce camp that night. McWhorter, *Hear Me*, 462–63 n. 37; McWhorter, "Poker Joe's Big Rifle"; and McWhorter to Reiner, December 18, 1935, folder 159, McWhorter Papers. Regarding Canyon Creek, correspondent Frank J. Parker noted that "that Indian with the loud reporting rifle was again heard, as he always is, and did his share of the killing." Boise, Idaho *Tri-Weekly Statesman*, October 2, 1877. See also Redington, "Scouting in Montana," 65.

91. Yellow Bull, Interview, BYU. For other brief accounts of Canyon Creek based largely on Nee-Me-Poo perspectives, see Garcia, *Tough Trip Through Paradise*, 292–93; Francis Haines, "Chief Joseph," 7; and Josephy, *Nez Perce Indians*, 608–10.

92. "Yellow Bull's Story." See also Yellow Bull, Interview, BYU; unclassified envelope 91, 541, Camp Manuscript Field Notes, Camp Papers, BYU; and Camp Manuscript Field Notes, Nez Perce Indian Wars 1, 138, Camp Papers, LBNM. Also, the supply of ammunition—mostly taken from the soldiers at White Bird Canyon, Big Hole, and other engagements—was clearly dwindling by this time. McWhorter, "Fight with Sturgis."

93. For other Nez Perce mention of Canyon Creek, see Joseph [Heinmot Tooyalakekt], "An Indian's Views," 427; "Story of Kawownonilpilp"; and Yellow Bull account in Curtis, *North American Indian*, 8:168, wherein it is stated that during the night following the fighting fifty Nez Perce men captured twenty-seven horses (their own?) from the soldiers.

94. Paulding to Medical Director, Department of Dakota, September 22, 1877, entry 624, box 1, Office of the Adjutant General; Major George Gibson to Assistant Adjutant General Department of Dakota, October 1, 1877, in Terry, "Report," 547; Burdick and Hart, *Jacob Horner*, 21; Coughlan, *Varnum*, 23; McWhorter, "Unpublished Incidents"; and Upton, *Fort Custer*, 40. A biographical sketch of Lawler is in Hammer, *Biographies of the Seventh Cavalry*, 146.

95. *U.S. Army Gallantry and Meritorious Conduct*, 82–84. All of the enlisted men had been recommended by Merrill and Benteen in their respective reports of September 1877.

CHAPTER 10

1. Dusenberry, "Chief Joseph's Flight," 50; and unclassified envelope 134, 656–57, Camp Manuscript Field Notes, Camp Papers, LBNM.

2. Agent George W. Frost of the Crow Agency explained the augmentation of the number of Crows with Sturgis. During the descent of Clark's Fork, the scouts had picked up a number of mounts abandoned by the Nez Perces and took them to the agency, causing frenzied excitement there and prompting many more covetous warriors to set forth in hopes of securing more Nez Perce ponies. Bozeman *Times*, September 20, 1877. Private Goldin remembered that the Crows had arrived during the night. "[They] came dashing into camp, shouting and singing, and from that time on until early dawn sleep was an impossibility." Goldin, *Bit of the Nez Perce Campaign*, 17.

3. Colonel Samuel D. Sturgis report, December 5, 1877, in Secretary of War, *Report . . . 1877*, 512.

4. Nez Perce casualties in the skirmish with the Crows and Bannocks are difficult to determine. According to McWhorter, Yellow Wolf claimed that the Crows killed but one warrior, Teeweeyownah, and two old men, Fish Trap and Surrounded Goose—all of whom were also listed as having been killed at Canyon Creek. Yellow Wolf reported that he received a slight thigh wound in the fighting with the Crows. For the discrepancy regarding Nez Perce casualties, see McWhorter, *Yellow Wolf*, 188, 192, 193–94; McWhorter, *Hear Me*, 467; and McWhorter, "Fight with Sturgis."

5. McWhorter, *Yellow Wolf*, 187, 194. For the Nez Perces' reaction to seeing the Crows and Bannocks descending on them, see *Yellow Wolf*, 187–88.

6. See Walter M. Camp to Brigadier General Hugh L. Scott, September 22, 1913 (on which letter Scott responded), folder 23, box 1, Camp Papers, BYU. Yellow Wolf denied that the Crows took any large number of the Nez Perces' horses. McWhorter, *Yellow Wolf*, 188. Yellow Wolf's personal role in the attempt by the Crows and Bannocks to corral the non-combatants is in McWhorter, *Yellow Wolf*, 190–93.

7. Goldin, Biography, 316. However, in a letter, Goldin stated that he did not see the action but was told of it later by a mixed-blood Crow. For further reference to the Crow–Nez Perce action, see Goldin to L. V. McWhorter, August 1, 1932, folder 177, McWhorter Papers. See also Goldin to McWhorter, February 27, 1929, Goldin to McWhorter, March 20, 1929, Goldin to McWhorter, September 10, 1929, Goldin to McWhorter, August 13, 1933, Goldin to McWhorter, December 4, 1934, ibid.; and Goldin, *Bit of the Nez Perce Campaign*, 17–18. On returning to their agency, the Crows reported that Sturgis had sent them home because the troops were not going to fight the Nez Perces any more.

Captain Daniel W. Benham to Sheridan, September 22, 1877, quoted in Cheyenne *Daily Leader*, September 23, 1877. Crow accounts of what is probably this
encounter are in Dixon, *Vanishing Race*, 148–49 (account of Goes Ahead); and
Medicine Crow, *From the Heart of Crow Country*, 47–48 (account of Medicine Crow).

8. Colonel Samuel D. Sturgis report, December 5, 1877, in Secretary of
War, *Report . . . 1877*, 512.

9. Brigadier General Edward S. Godfrey, who was at the Battle of the Bear's
Paw as a captain in the Seventh Cavalry, recalled that the disease that afflicted
Sturgis's horses also was found among the horses of the surrendered Nez Perces.
If their flesh was injured "in any way it would fester up badly." Godfrey, Interview.

10. Colonel Samuel D. Sturgis report, December 5, 1877, in Secretary of
War, *Report . . . 1877*, 512.

11. Quoted in Howard, "Report," 627.

12. Sturgis's order is from New York *Herald*, September 29, 1877. The critical comment is from Mulford, *Fighting Indians!*, 116.

13. Redington, "Scouting in Montana," 61. Information about Sturgis's movement to the Musselshell is in Fisher, "Journal of S. G. Fisher," 281; Hare, "Report of
Lieut. L. R. Hare," 1679; Assistant Surgeon Holmes O. Paulding to Medical Director, Department of Dakota, September 22, 1877, entry 624, box 1, Office of the Adjutant General; Regimental Returns . . . Seventh Cavalry, September 1877, roll 72;
Mulford, *Fighting Indians!*, 116; Boise, Idaho *Tri-Weekly Statesman*, October 2, 1877;
Cheyenne *Daily Leader*, September 23, 1877; *Record of Engagements*, 72; Ernest A.
Garlington, "The Seventh Regiment of Cavalry," in Rodenbough and Haskin, *Army
of the United States*, 261; and Goldin, "Seventh Cavalry at Cañon Creek," 220–21.

14. Howard, "Report," 627–28; Connolly, Diary, September 16–22, 1877;
Mason to wife, September 15, 18, 1877, in Davison, "A Century Ago," 16; Jocelyn,
Mostly Alkali, 256–57; Portland *Daily Standard*, September 23, 1877; and Forrest
Young account in "Forrest Young," Billings *Gazette*, undated clipping (ca. 1945),
Indians—Wars—1877, vertical files, Parmly Billings Library, Billings, Mont.

15. See Howard, "Report," 628; and Colonel Samuel D. Sturgis report, December 5, 1877, in Secretary of War, *Report . . . 1877*, 512. On September 20,
Howard sent a message to Miles describing his current movements and noted:
"We have stopped forced marching to get enough life into our fagged animals to
make another vigorous push, intending to move forward, via Judith Gap, tomorrow. We shall not hasten the pursuit over much in order to give you time to get
into position." Howard to Miles, September 20, 1877, entry 107, box 3, part 3,
1877, U.S. Army Continental Commands.

16. Letter of September 23, 1877, quoted in Jocelyn, *Mostly Alkali*, 257.

17. Redington, "Scouting in Montana," 62. Agent Frost referenced the presence of the River Crows in front of the troops in a dispatch to Captain Benham at
Fort Ellis on September 14. Bozeman *Times*, September 20, 1877. "Dumb Bull" is
perhaps "The Dumb" (or "Deaf Bull"?) who was among the River Crow headmen
who assented to the agreement of 1873 redefining their reservation. See Commissioner of Indian Affairs, *Report . . . 1873*, 122.

18. The First cavalrymen arrived at Fort Ellis on October 3, left that post on
the thirteenth, passed through Virginia City on the nineteenth, passing down the
stage road to reach the railroad near Corrine, Utah Territory, on November 3. Company B arrived at Fort Klamath, Oregon, on November 19, 1877. Connolly, Diary,

dates specified. Correspondent Frank J. Parker, among those departing with Sanford's troops, wrote: "We all left the main command with regret. So far as I can see no one had any fault to find, except a few chronic growlers. . . . In almost every instance I have found that the growlers belong to that class whose chief merit consists in always being among the first at the 'grub pile' and whose terrific onslaughts on the bean pot more than offsets their tardy assistance, begrudgingly given when work or service of any kind was required of them. In fact, they are invincible in peace and decidedly invisible in war." Boise, Idaho *Tri-Weekly Statesman*, October 16, 1877. The companies were assigned as follows: B (Jackson), Fort Klamath, Oregon; C (Wagner), Camp McDermitt, Nevada; I (Carr), Camp Halleck, California; K (Bendire), Camp Harney, Oregon. Orders No. 2, Headquarters, First Cavalry Battalion, Fort Ellis, Montana, October 4, 1877, entry E-633, U.S. Regular Army Mobile Units; "Orders . . . Major Sanford's Battalion," vol. 1.

19. Mason to wife, October 2, 1877, in Davison, "A Century Ago," 18. This description of the movements of Howard and Sturgis to the Missouri is based on data cited above and in Howard, "Report," 628–29; Colonel Samuel D. Sturgis report, December 5, 1877, in Secretary of War, *Report . . . 1877*, 512; Hare, "Report of Lieut. L. R. Hare," 1679–80; Regimental Returns . . . Seventh Cavalry, September 1877, roll 72; Boise, Idaho *Tri-Weekly Statesman*, October 9, 1877; and New York *Herald*, October 4, 1877.

20. See Stevens, "Missouri River 1877." The location of the depot above the mouth of Cow Creek has been verified through documentary and photographic research and through on-site investigation. See LeRoy Anderson, "Nez Perce Trail," 1.

21. The Nez Perces probably approached the Missouri through Woodhawk Canyon. See LeRoy Anderson, "Nez Perce Trail," passim.

22. The other soldiers present were Sergeant Briggs, Corporal Cookly, and Privates Clark, Denver, Ford, Krefer, Malvihill, Reap, Rice, Watson, and Williams. The other civilians were George Trautman, E. W. Buckwalter, and Hugh Huggins. Fort Benton *Record*, October 5, 1877; and Clendenin to Second Lieutenant Hobart K. Bailey, September 24, 1877, entry 107, box 3, part 3, Letters and Telegrams Received by District of the Yellowstone Headquarters, September 1877–April 1878, U.S. Army Continental Commands.

23. Reed's Fort was owned by Alonzo S. Reed. Miller and Cohen, *Military and Trading Posts of Montana*, 73; Fort Benton *Record*, September 21, 1877; and Redington, "Scouting in Montana," 62.

24. This route of crossing the river, explicitly stated by George Clendenin in his letter of the following day ("The Nez Perces . . . crossed above, below & directly opposite the landing at 2 P.M.") Clendenin to Bailey, September 24, 1877 (entry 107, box 3, part 3, Letters and Telegrams Received by District of the Yellowstone Headquarters, September 1877–April 1878, U.S. Army Continental Commands), conforms well with the immediate topography of the area as well as the known location of the Cow Island ford. Anderson, "Nez Perce Trail," 1.

25. Molchert, Letter. Michael Foley's own account of the proceedings, originally rendered early in the twentieth century, appeared in Great Falls *Rocky Mountain Husbandman*, January 8, 1942. It is substantially different from Molchert's, notably in recounting Foley's role in the discussion that preceded the assault and Molchert's virtual non-participation in it. In his account, Foley described a lengthy conversation between himself and leaders Joseph and Looking Glass that resulted in

his permitting the people to take whatever provisions they wanted. "I went with them down to the freight pile and the squaws took several sacks of sugar, some hams, hardtack and a lot of other truck. They carried it about a half mile up the river, to a little benchland, where the whole lousy outfit had a feast and pow-wow." Regarding the defenders in the ensuing fight, Foley maintained that "I took command of that little party." In 1888, Foley filed a claim for lost personal possessions amounting to $598 in the destruction at Cow Island. Michael Foley claim, no. 4466, entry 700, Claims for Indian Depredations, U.S. Bureau of Indian Affairs.

26. Molchert, Letter. The number of charges by the warriors against the Cow Island entrenchments varies according to accounts. Major Guido Ilges wrote on September 24 that the warriors charged seven times. Ilges to Gibbon, in New York *Herald*, September 29, 1877.

27. Buckwalter received wounds in the hand and side, while Trautman was shot in the right shoulder. Fort Benton *Record*, October 5, 1877. However, Molchert accounted for the death of a private who was riding a horse down from Dauphin Rapids with which to tow a boat laden with provisions back up to the project. Wrote Molchert: "Before this fighting commenced we heard a shot and I told the boys, I bet that is Private Pearce . . . , and sure enough we [later] found his body and buried [him] right there at Cow Island." Molchert, Letter. This individual, in fact, was probably the same man mentioned in Second Lieutenant Edward E. Hardin's diary entry for September 28: "Found Pvt. Byron Martin Co. B 7th Infantry and buried him near the road on the right-hand side about 300 yds from the Bull creek crossing and about 20 yds from the road." Hardin, Diary.

28. Quoted in Fort Benton *Record*, October 5, 1877.

29. Fort Benton *Record*, October 5, 1877. Clendenin reported that the Nez Perces "took & destroyed 200 sks Sugar, a large pile of tobacco, 150 sacks Bacon, & everything I had (except the clothes I wore), books, papers, trunks—a thorough clean-up." Clendenin to Bailey, September 24, 1877, entry 107, box 3, part 3, Letters and Telegrams Received by District of the Yellowstone Headquarters, September 1877–April 1878, U.S. Army Continental Commands.

30. In addition to the above-cited sources, this description of the Cow Island affair is compiled based on data in Terry, "Report," 516–17; Ilges to Gibbon, September 24, 1877, in New York *Herald*, September 29, 1877; Sheridan to Adjutant General, September 28, 1877 (enclosing Terry to Sheridan, September 27, 1877), item 6048, roll 338, Nez Perce War Papers; *Record of Engagements*, 73; James, "Sergeant Molchert's Perils," 63–65; and Mueller, "Prelude to Surrender." Primary Nez Perce sources are in McWhorter, *Yellow Wolf*, 198–99; and McWhorter, *Hear Me*, 469–72. See Yellow Bull account in Curtis, *North American Indian*, 8:168; and Josephy, *Nez Perce Indians*, 612–14.

31. Years later, Molchert remembered that he had been complimented by Ilges for his defense of Cow Island. "The Major looked over the whole thing and then sent for me and said to me, 'Sergt., you have done very well to save yourself and men, it was impossible for you to save the freight.'" Molchert, Letter.

32. Fort Benton *Record*, October 5, 1877.

33. For Ilges's background, see Heitman, *Historical Register and Dictionary*, 1:562; and Henry, *Military Record of Civilian Appointments*, 347–48.

34. Ilges to Assistant Adjutant General, Department of Dakota, October 21, 1877, contained in Terry, "Report," 557.

35. Ibid.

36. It is unclear why Ilges waited until September 27 to send couriers to Miles respecting the location of the Nez Perces. In a letter to the editor of the *Army and Navy Register*, September 1, 1883, Ilges stated that he sent the two volunteers to Miles on the night of the twenty-fifth, paying them three hundred dollars to make the journey down the Missouri. But the dispatch was, in fact, dated the twenty-seventh. Entry 107, box 3, part 3, 1877, U.S. Army Continental Commands. A piece in the Helena *Weekly Independent*, October 11, 1877, stated that Ilges's couriers left for Miles's command on the morning of September 28.

37. See Stevens, "Missouri River 1877," which indicates a "Blockhouse" on the bank approximately four hundred feet above the area designated as "Landings."

38. In addition to the sources cited above, this account of Ilges's fight in Cow Creek Canyon and the burning of the wagon train is based on material drawn from the following: Ilges to Assistant Adjutant General, Department of Dakota, October 21, 1877, contained in Terry, "Report," 557; Ilges to Assistant Adjutant General, Department of Dakota, May 18, 1878 (enclosing Jonathan J. Donnelly to Ilges, May 10, 1878), roll 401, Nez Perce War Claims; Clendenin to Bailey, September 24, 1877, entry 107, box 3, part 3, Letters and Telegrams Received by District of the Yellowstone Headquarters, September 1877–April 1878, U.S. Army Continental Commands; Hardin, Diary, September 21–28, 1877; Terry, "Report," 516–17; *Army and Navy Journal*, October 6, 1877; Fort Benton *Record*, September 28, October 5, 1877; *Record of Engagements*, 73; Samples, Letter, describing the battle of Cow Creek Canyon; Michael Foley's account of Cow Island in Great Falls *Rocky Mountain Husbandman*, January 8, 1942; Al H. Wilkins account, unidentified newspaper, ca. 1927 clipping, Indians—Wars—1877, vertical files, Parmly Billings Library, Billings, Mont.; Chappell, "Early Life"; and McWhorter, *Yellow Wolf*, 202. Ever after, Ilges believed that his command was ignored in the parceling out of praise following the Nez Perce campaign. "Although these services rendered by my command have for some unaccountable reason never been publicly recognized, either officially or otherwise, I hold in my possession a private note from General Miles of subsequent date, in which he acknowledges the receipt of my information and service rendered, of which he made good use." *Army and Navy Register*, September 1, 1883. The howitzer that accompanied Ilges for part of his movement is in the Museum of the Upper Missouri at Fort Benton.

39. Fort Benton *Record*, October 5, 1877.

40. The dispute between Looking Glass and Poker Joe was recounted by Many Wounds in McWhorter, *Hear Me*, 473–74, but see also McWhorter, *Yellow Wolf*, 203, for McWhorter's commentary. The route north from Cow Island is authoritatively estimated in LeRoy Anderson, "Nez Perce Trail," 3. That the tribesmen were perfectly aware that they were not yet in Canada is specified in McWhorter, *Hear Me*, 473 and 473 n. 19; and McWhorter, *Yellow Wolf*, 202.

CHAPTER 11

1. Gibbon, "Report of the Commanding General," 66. See also DeMontravel, "Miles," 269–70.

2. For the military operations against the Lakotas and Northern Cheyennes out of the Tongue River Cantonment, see Greene, *Yellowstone Command*.

3. Miles to Howard, February 1, 1877, correspondence (1877), Howard Collection.

4. The district consisted of "the Posts on the Tongue and Big Horn Rivers and Fort Peck; [and] such portion of the garrison of Fort Buford, D.T., as may, under authority received from Dept. Hdqrs, be called into the field. . . . The Hdqrs of the District will, until further orders, be at Cantonment on Tongue River, or with the Commanding Officer in the field." General Orders No. 1, Headquarters, District of the Yellowstone, Cantonment at Tongue River, M.T., September 4, 1877, entry 903, part 3, General Orders and Circulars, Sept. 1877–June 1881, District of the Yellowstone, U.S. Army Continental Commands. During the Indian campaigns of the post–Civil War period, Miles was in demand because of his proactive leadership and direct involvement, impressing not only his superior officers but also the enlisted men of his command. "General Miles [is] the Best Indian Fighter there is on the Prairie today since Custer Fell," wrote Private Oliver P. Howe, Company H, Second Cavalry, soon after the Nez Perce campaign. Howe to Samuel J. Howe, October 11, 1877, Howe Letters. Miles later became commanding general of the army before his retirement in 1903. For background on his career, see Wooster, *Nelson A. Miles*; Pohanka, *Nelson A. Miles*; DeMontravel, "Miles"; and Virginia Johnson, *Unregimented General*. Autobiographies are in Miles, *Personal Recollections*; and Miles, *Serving the Republic*.

5. Miles, *Personal Recollections*, 260–61; Regimental Returns . . . Fifth Infantry, September 1877, roll 58; and Kelly, *"Yellowstone Kelly,"* 186.

6. Miles to Sturgis, August 19, 1877, Baird Papers.

7. Major George Gibson to Assistant Adjutant General, Department of Dakota, October 1, 1877, in Terry, "Report," 546–47; and Zimmer, *Frontier Soldier*, 114. Originally, Company B, Seventh Cavalry, under Captain Thomas B. McDougall, was ordered to join the commission, but McDougall took sick ("drunk," according to Edward S. Godfrey's account) and Hale's unit started instead. Edward S. Godfrey, account of the Bear's Paw Campaign, October 31, 1877, Godfrey Papers, LC.

8. Miles later recalled receiving the dispatch: "During the afternoon of September 17th I observed a dark object appear over the high bluff to the west and move down the trail to the bank of the Yellowstone. He was soon ferried across, and, riding up, dismounted and saluted. Without waiting for him to report, I asked him if they had had a fight. He replied, 'No, but we have had a good chance.'" Miles, *Serving the Republic*, 172.

9. Terry, "Report," 514; and Colonel Samuel D. Sturgis report, December 5, 1877, in Secretary of War, *Report . . . 1877*, 73. The message was accompanied by a report from Sturgis accounting for his failure to stop the Nez Perces and blaming it on "the absence of a single guide, who had ever been in the country in which we were operating, taken in connection with our ignorance of it, and its exceeding rough and broken character, and my inability to learn anything of Howard's position, [all of which] enabled them to elude me at the very moment I felt sure of success. This is extremely mortifying to me." Sturgis to Miles, September 13, 1877, in Colonel Samuel D. Sturgis report, December 5, 1877, in Secretary of War, *Report*, 1877, 73-74. It must be stated that Terry's message was not an order directing Miles to action, but a request for assistance, since technically Howard was from another military department to which Miles was not subjected. Accord-

ing to military protocol, however, should the two meet in the field, Howard, by virtue of his rank, could assume command of a combined force; until then, Miles subscribed directly to the orders of Generals Terry and Sheridan, and Commanding General Sherman. For this discussion, see William H. C. Bowen to the editor, *The Spectator*, September 21, 1929, folder—correspondence of William Bowen, 1908–1931, box—William Bowen personal papers, Bowen Papers.

10. Miles to Terry, September 17, 1877, in Colonel Samuel D. Sturgis report, December 5, 1877, in Secretary of War, *Report . . . 1877*, 73. Miles sent Howard an almost identical message, explaining his plan for "intersecting the Nez Perces" before they could reach Sitting Bull's camp. Miles to Howard, September 17, 1877, copy in folder: Nez Perce War, box 3, Sladen Family Papers. The troops remaining on the Yellowstone included the First Infantry companies at Bighorn Post, and Companies A, C, D, E, Fifth Infantry, and Company C, Seventh Cavalry, which garrisoned the Tongue River Cantonment. Regimental Returns . . . Fifth Infantry, September 1877, roll 58; and Regimental Returns . . . Seventh Cavalry, September 1877, roll 72. Miles's adjutant, First Lieutenant George W. Baird, described Miles's proposed route of march as being "along the hypothenuse of a triangle, to intercept a rapidly marching force which was following the perpendicular and had had five days the start." Baird, "General Miles's Indian Campaigns," 363.

11. Miles to Howard, September 17, 1877, copy in folder: Nez Perce War, box 3, Sladen Family Papers.

12. An enlisted man remembered: "On September 17, just after midnight, there was loud knocking at the door of D Company, Fifth Infantry. We heard the headquarters orderly tell the first sergeant to turn out the company for a 30 days scout in light marching order. Fort Keogh [sic] was soon in a buzz of preparation for an Indian campaign. By daylight the next morning the command . . . was moving out." *Winners of the West*, October 30, 1936.

13. Snyder, "Diary," September 17, 1877.

14. Alice Baldwin, *Memoirs . . . Baldwin*, 191.

15. Miles, *Personal Recollections*, 262.

16. Fragmentary note dated October 3, 1877, in Edward S. Godfrey's hand, item 16, container 1, Godfrey Papers, LC; Gibson to Assistant Adjutant General, Department of Dakota, October 1, 1877, in Terry, "Report," 547; Miles, "Report," 527; Circular, September 17, 1877, entry 903, part 3, General Orders and Circulars, September 1877–June 1881, District of the Yellowstone, U.S. Army Continental Commands; and *Army and Navy Journal*, December 8, 1877. Most previous estimates of the size of Miles's command on the Nez Perce campaign have been far too low. This approximate figure is reconstructed based on examination of several sources, notably the following: Regimental Returns . . . Seventh Cavalry, August and September, 1877, roll 72; Regimental Returns . . . Second Cavalry, August and September, 1877, roll 19; Regimental Returns . . . Fifth Infantry, August and September, 1877, roll 58; Surgeon Henry R. Tilton to Surgeon General, October 26, 1877, entry 624, box 1, Office of the Adjutant General; and Godfrey, Interview.

17. Basic information about these officers is in Heitman, *Historical Register and Dictionary* as follows: Hale (1:487), Biddle (1:217), Moylan (1:733), Godfrey (1:461), Eckerson (1:396), Tyler (1:977), McClernand (1:657), Jerome (1:573),

Bennett (1:211), Woodruff (1:1058), Snyder (1:907), Romeyn (1:844), Carter (1:287), Baird (1:183), Long (1:640), Maus (1:698), Tilton (1:836), and Gardner (1:445). In addition, for Hale and Biddle, see *Army and Navy Journal*, October 13, 1877; and for Godfrey, whose extensive and action-filled frontier career commanded special interest, see Carroll and Price, *Roll Call on the Little Big Horn*, 61–63; and Chandler, *Of Garry Owen in Glory*, 360–62. Godfrey's article about the Little Bighorn is an oft-reprinted classic (Godfrey, "Custer's Last Battle").

18. First Lieutenant Frank D. Baldwin to Tyler, September 18, 1877, entry 107, box 3, part 3, 1877, U.S. Army Continental Commands. See also Tyler to Baldwin, September 19, 1877, ibid., which contains details of Tyler's and Hale's marches. Hale had been notified of the change on September 17 and had been directed to return his company to the cantonment. News of the Nez Perce situation, however, changed that directive, and instead of turning back, Hale awaited the arrival of Tyler's battalion. Biddle, Diary, September 17, 18, 1877.

19. Long, "Journal of the Marches," 1697.

20. Miles, *Personal Recollections*, 263. Lieutenant Henry Romeyn, writing long after the fact, maintained that these scouts had located "flankers" of the Nez Perce column. If so, the sightings went unacknowledged in the official reports. See Romeyn, "Capture of Chief Joseph," 285.

21. Zimmer, *Frontier Soldier*, 117. Miles's directive prohibiting shooting is in Circular, September 21, 1877, entry 903, part 3, General Orders and Circulars, September 1877–June 1881, District of the Yellowstone, U.S. Army Continental Commands.

22. Tilton, "After the Nez Perces," 403. A condensation of this piece appears in *Army and Navy Journal*, February 9, 1878.

23. Howard to Miles, September 20, 1877, folder: Nez Perce War, box 3, Sladen Family Papers. Biddle's own account of the stopping of the *Fontenelle* is in Biddle to Mother, n.d. [September 24, 1877], box 2, Biddle Collection. Biddle's mother wrote on the top of this letter, "The last letter my darling ever wrote."

24. Johnson was a highly regarded scout who had served Miles valuably during the Sioux campaigns, and his death was keenly felt. He mistook the swift-running Missouri for the Musselshell and tried to swim his horse across. See Miles, *Personal Recollections*, 263; Tilton to Surgeon General, October 26, 1877, entry 624, box 1, Office of the Adjutant General; and, particularly, Barker, "Campaign and Capture," (December 1922): 7, 30.

25. Long, "Journal of the Marches," 1698. In his books, Miles, *Personal Recollections* (263) and Miles, *Serving the Republic* (173), Miles fondly boasted that his men marched fifty-two miles within twenty-four hours to reach the Missouri on September 23. In fact, in two days' marching on the twenty-second and twenty-third, the men made 57.45 miles—35.83 miles the first day and 21.57 miles the second—according to Long, "Journal of the Marches," 1697–98. This description of Miles's march to the Missouri is drawn from material in Long, "Journal of the Marches," 1696–98; Miles, "Report," 527; Snyder, "Diary," September 18–23, 1877; Tilton to Surgeon General, October 26, 1877, entry 624, box 1, Office of the Adjutant General; Zimmer, *Frontier Soldier*, 117–18; Romeyn, "Capture of Chief Joseph," 284–85; *Army and Navy Journal*, February 9, 1878; Baird, "Capture of Chief Joseph," 209–11; Baird, "General Miles's Indian Campaigns," 363; Miles, *Personal Recollections*, 261–64; and Miles, *Serving the Republic*, 173–74.

26. Biddle to Mother, n.d. [September 24, 1877], box 2, Biddle Collection.

27. Baldwin to Tyler, September 24, 1877, entry 107, box 3, part 3, 1877, U.S. Army Continental Commands. See also Miles, *Personal Recollections*, 264.

28. Miles to Terry, September 24, 1877, Department of Dakota, Letters Sent, item 4043, entry 1167, U.S. Army Continental Commands.

29. Snyder, "Diary," September 24, 1877; Zimmer, *Frontier Soldier*, 118; Tilton to Surgeon General, October 26, 1877, entry 624, box 1, Office of the Adjutant General; Godfrey, Interview; and Circular, September 24, 1877, entry 903, part 3, General Orders and Circulars, September 1877–June 1881, District of the Yellowstone, U.S. Army Continental Commands.

30. Long, "Journal of the Marches," 1698.

31. Tilton to Surgeon General, October 26, 1877, entry 624, box 1, Office of the Adjutant General; Kelly, *"Yellowstone Kelly,"* 186; and Kelly, "Capture of Nez Perces."

32. Bailey to Baldwin, 9:15 A.M., September 25, 1877, entry 107, box 3, part 3, 1877, U.S. Army Continental Commands.

33. Clendenin to Bailey, September 24, 1877, ibid. See also Barker, "Campaign and Capture," (December 1922): 30.

34. Miles, "Report," 528. See also Miles, "Report of Col. Nelson A. Miles," October 6, 1877, in Secretary of War, *Report . . . 1877*, 74.

35. The fuses on the projectiles were shortened to insure their bursting high in the air. Baldwin, Interview. See Miles, *Personal Recollections*, 265; Miles, *Serving the Republic*, 174–75; and Steinbach, *Long March*, 129–30. Godfrey stated that the Napoleon gun was used to signal the craft. Godfrey, Interview.

36. Long, "Journal of the Marches," 1698; Miles, "Report," 527; Snyder, "Diary," September 25, 1877; Zimmer, *Frontier Soldier*, 118; Tilton to Surgeon General, October 26, 1877, entry 624, box 1, Office of the Adjutant General; Godfrey, Interview; and Kelly, "Capture of Nez Perces." Private Luther Barker remembered that the crossing necessitated unloading the supplies from the wagons and carrying them aboard the steamer. Then "the wagons had to be taken apart and carried a piece at a time on board the steamer." Barker, "Campaign and Capture," (January 1923): 7. For background on Kelly (1849–1928), Miles's most trusted civilian scout during his campaigns on the northern plains, see his autobiography, Kelly, *"Yellowstone Kelly"*; and Keenan, "Yellowstone Kelly."

37. Miles to Mary Miles, September 26, 1877, quoted in Virginia Johnson, *Unregimented General*, 197.

38. Long, "Journal of the Marches," 1699.

39. Ibid.

40. Ibid.

41. Tilton to Surgeon General, October 26, 1877, entry 624, box 1, Office of the Adjutant General.

42. Tilton, "After the Nez Perces," 403.

43. Snyder stated that this camp was on "Dry Fork of Milk River," but it might, in fact, have been on an affluent of the South Fork of Beaver Creek, an often dry tributary of Milk River. Snyder, "Diary," September 27, 1877. For activities of September 26 and 27, see appropriate entries in Snyder, "Diary"; Zimmer, *Frontier Soldier*, 120; Long, "Journal of the Marches," 1699; Tilton to Surgeon General, October 26, 1877, entry 624, box 1, Office of the Adjutant General;

Howe to Howe, November 11, 1877, Howe Letters; and Romeyn, "Capture of Chief Joseph," 285–86.

44. There is some evidence that a few of the Cheyenne scouts contacted the Nez Perces during this period, probably as the families moved north toward Snake Creek from Cow Creek Canyon. The Cheyennes reportedly lied, telling the Nez Perces they were not scouts, whereupon the tribesmen took them into their village and gave them food. By the time the Cheyennes returned to Miles with intelligence of the Nez Perces, the colonel already knew of the location of the village. See Stands In Timber and Liberty, *Cheyenne Memories*, 227; and Brown and Felton, *Frontier Years*, 107, 244 (citing Rufus Wallowing to the authors, April 1951).

45. Miles, *Personal Recollections*, 266.

46. Long, "Journal of the Marches," 1699.

47. Long described the route on September 28 thus: "Our trail still clings closely to the northern side of the Little Rockies, and at 4.10 P.M. we cross People's Creek; it has a gravelly bed, running spring-water, but no wood in sight. Passing over several small branches of this creek which wind among the foot-hills of the mountains at 6 P.M., after a march of 28.36 miles, we finally encamp on one of them near the gap or pass of the Little Rockies that tower above us. The pass is the only one through these mountains, and not a little difficulty is experienced in following its intricate windings." Ibid., 1699–700.

48. Ilges to Miles, September 27, 1877, entry 107, box 3, part 3, 1877, U.S. Army Continental Commands; Helena *Weekly Independent*, October 11, 1877; and Ilges's letter in *Army and Navy Register*, September 1, 1883.

49. Long, "Journal of the Marches," 1700.

50. Godfrey, Interview.

51. Kelly, *"Yellowstone Kelly,"* 188.

52. Miles, *Personal Recollections*, 267. The message from Howard to Miles, September 26, 1877, and Miles's response, September 29, 1877, are in folder: Nez Perce War, box 3, Sladen Family Papers. Miles might also have received two other dispatches at this time. (Private Ami Frank Mulford, Seventh Cavalry, claimed to have ridden from Sturgis to Miles before the Bear's Paw engagement opened. See Mulford, *Fighting Indians!*, 117). One, sent via Fort Ellis from Terry at Fort Shaw, offered plausible vindication for his future movements, stating: "I revoke any order forbidding movement to the North prior to the return of the Commission. I leave the whole subject to your discretion and best judgement." Terry to Miles, September 26, 1877, entry 107, box 3, part 3, 1877, U.S. Army Continental Commands. The other, a penciled personal note from Howard at the Musselshell, referenced Miles's dispatch of September 17 and bemoaned his continued criticism by the press. Howard to Miles, September 20, 1877, Miles Family Papers, LC. Beyond the material quoted above, this description of the events of September 28 and 29 is based on accounts in Miles, *Personal Recollections*, 266–67; Miles, "Report," 528; Miles, "Report of Col. Nelson A. Miles," October 6, 1877, in Secretary of War, *Report . . . 1877*, 74; Long, "Journal of the Marches," 1699–700; Snyder, "Diary," September 28, 29, 1877; Howe to Howe, November 11, 1877, Howe Letters; Zimmer, *Frontier Soldier*, 121; Tilton to Surgeon General, October 26, 1877, entry 624, box 1, Office of the Adjutant General; Godfrey, Interview; Gaybower, Interview; Baird, "General Miles's Indian Campaigns," 363; Kelly, *"Yellowstone Kelly,"* 188–90; and Romeyn, "Capture of Chief Joseph," 286.

53. William F. Schmalsle is mentioned in Bailey to Baldwin, September 25, 1877, entry 107, box 3, part 3, 1877, U.S. Army Continental Commands. In a 1914 letter, the retired Marion Maus wrote that "I had 32 Cheyennes besides the whites, Trippe [sic], Smalze [sic] and Yellowstone Kelly." Maus to Walter M. Camp, February 2, 1914, folder 1, box 2, Camp Papers, BYU. Maus's engagement with the Indians on September 29 is described in "Memoranda of Active Service . . . Maus." It is referenced in a letter, Miles to Adjutant General, March 26, 1894, Medal of Honor, Special File. In another letter, Maus wrote: "We had a fight with the Indians on the 29th wounding or killing two and capturing a herd of horses. This about 25 miles from the scene of fight & surrender at Bear Paw." Maus to Camp, February 2, 1914, folder 1, box 2, Camp Papers, BYU. "Yellowstone" Kelly described what was probably this encounter, but mistakenly had it occurring on the thirtieth. Kelly, *"Yellowstone Kelly,"* 191–92. See also Kelly, "Capture of Nez Perces."

54. "Map of Milk River Indian Country." See Josephy, *Nez Perce Indians,* 33–35, for general commentary on tribal interrelationships, but for a comprehensive discussion, see McGinnis, *Counting Coup and Cutting Horses,* passim.

55. Weed and Pirsson, "The Bearpaw Mountains," 283–87. On the origin of the range's name, the article states: "The name of the mountain group is itself derived from the Indian designation for Black Butte near Fort Assinniboine [1896], called by them the Bear's Paw. The mountains of course became known as the Mountains of the Bear's Paw." Weed and Pirsson, "The Bearpaw Mountains," 284. According to legend, however, the origin of the mountains, and hence their name, "Bear's Paw," came from area Indians (which tribe or tribes is not stated). Centennial Mountain, in the extreme part of the range, in shape resembles a dead or prostrate bear. The legend states that, because of the presence of many bears, the tribesmen never hunted there. One winter, however, a brave Indian hunter ventured to camp on Big Sandy Creek, killed a deer, and was leaving the mountains with the deer when the Master Bear appeared and held the warrior to the ground with his paw. The Indian, who needed the game for his starving people, appealed to a supreme deity, who ordered the bear to release him. When the bear refused, the deity let loose bolts of lightning that severed the animal's paw, freeing the Indian, and killing all the bears in the mountains. Appropriately, at the point of severance of the bear's paw near Centennial Mountain exists a geological fault that adds credence to the legend, while adjacent Box Elder Butte represents the paw. This account, attributed by geologist William Pecora to Montana state senator William Cowan, is in Pecora, Letter. See also Chinook *Opinion,* August 25, 1955. Through the years, the nomenclature has included Bear's Paw, Bearpaw (USGS, 1987), Bears Paw (USGS, 1987), and Bear Paw, in reference to this range; historically, however, the term, "Bear's Paw" predominated over all others, and for that reason it has been retained in the present narrative. The Nez Perces called them the Wolf's Paw Mountains. Yellow Bull, Interview, LBNM; and Camp to Romeyn, March 27, 1918, Ellison Collection. The U.S. Geological Survey has designated the range the Bearpaw Mountains, and the National Park Service, as of October 1994, determined that the name of the unit of Nez Perce National Historical Park would be Bear Paw Battlefield.

56. Yellow Bull, Interview, BYU.

57. This account is from "Yellow Bull's Story." See also McWhorter, *Hear Me,* 478; McWhorter, *Yellow Wolf,* 204; and the recollections of Suhmkeen (later

known as Samuel Tilden), in Alcorn and Alcorn, "Old Nez Perce Recalls," 70. The Nez Perce James Stewart told Camp that the people had a somewhat different reason for stopping: "[They] knew they had a big start on Howard and the women and children wanted to rest. Some of the warriors were for going on and all intended to do so the next day [September 30]. They knew they were near the Canadian border. Dissensions and jealousies had also arisen and some of those who had taken a leading part all along in conducting affairs became disgusted and the morale of the whole band had fallen into a rather bad way. These men knew the trails through the mountains and through the buffalo country." Unclassified envelope 91, Camp Manuscript Field Notes, Camp Papers, BYU. Most Nez Perce accounts are specific in stating that the people realized that they had not already crossed into Canada. Joseph claimed such in Joseph [Heinmot Tooyalakekt], "An Indian's Views," 429, soon after the warfare ended. Indian Superintendent James McLaughlin stated that he conversed with Joseph in 1900 about the 1877 war and that Joseph told him: "I had made a mistake by not crossing into the country of the Red Coats, also in not keeping the country scouted in my rear." McLaughlin, *My Friend the Indian*, 363 (see also 361).

58. This description of the location of the Nee-Me-Poo encampment is based upon information derived from James Magera, various communications with author, Havre, Mont., 1994 and 1995; author's field notes, June 9, 1994; New York *Herald*, October 11, 1877; C. Raymond Noyes, plat, "Battle of the Bear's Paw," NA; Romeyn, "Capture of Chief Joseph," 287; Alva Noyes, *In the Land of the Chinook*, 71–73; Francis Haines, "Chief Joseph," 7; Francis Haines, *Nez Perces*, 273; and Josephy, *Nez Perce Indians*, 615–16. The camping sites of the different bands were identified by two aged warriors, Many Wounds and White Hawk, who had fought at Bear's Paw and who accompanied Lucullus V. McWhorter to the field in 1928 and 1935. Within specific camp circles, they identified the following individuals (presumably with families) as among the occupants: [Joseph's camp] Poker Joe, Young Buffalo Bull, Many Coyotes, Lone Bird, Red Spy, Kowtolikts, Black Trail, Lahpeealoot (Geese Three Times Alighting on Water), Joseph, Eagle Necklace Sr., John Dog, Howithowit, Ollokot, Red Wolf, and Koosouyeen (Going Alone); [Looking Glass's camp] Husis Kute, Kolkolhkequtolekt, Looking Glass, Sahpunmas (Vomiting), Toonahon, Peopeo Tholekt, White Bull, and No Hunt (Looking Glass's brother); [White Bird's camp] White Bird, Weyahsimlikt, Yellow Bull, Koolkool Snehee (Red Owl), Yellow Grizzly Bear, Wayatanatoo Latpah (Sun Tied), Peopeo Yahnaptah, Koolkool Stahlihken, Two Moons, Blacktail Eagle, and Shot in Head; and [Toohoolhoolzote's camp] Toohoolhoolzote, White Eagle, Struck by Lightning, Rainbow Sr., Five Times, Wenottahkahcikoon, No Fingers, Wottolen (Hair Combed Over Eyes), Ipnoutoosahkown, Shot in Breast, Tom Hill, Buffalo Horn, Eagle Necklace Sr. (also listed as being in Joseph's camp), Charging Hawk, and Nicyotscoohume. McWhorter, "Stake Tabulation, Chief Joseph's Camp" (this appears to be the first draft); and McWhorter, "Stake Tabulation of the Bear's Paw Mountain Battlefield." Both of these lists place the Palouse leader Husis Kute in Looking Glass's camp. Information on tabulation is correlated on C. Raymond Noyes, plat, "Battle of the Bear's Paw," NA. See also McWhorter, *Yellow Wolf*, 323–38 (index); and McWhorter, *Hear Me*, 633–40 (index), for confirmation of individuals' names.

59. Maus's party seemingly did not return to the column until the battle at Snake Creek was well underway. See Kelly, *"Yellowstone Kelly,"* 192.

60. Shambo, "Reminiscences." Shambo's account is reprinted in Alva Noyes, *In the Land of the Chinook*, 73–77.

61. The Northern Cheyenne scouts with Miles included the following: Brave Wolf, Old Wolf, Magpie Eagle, Crazy Mule, Young Two Moon (John Two Moon), High Wolf, Starving Elk, Tall White Elk (or Tall White Antelope?), White Wolf, Little Sun, Spotted Blackbird (later known as Medicine Top), Little Yellow Man, Stands Different, Timber, Sa-huts, Yellow Weasel, Little Old Man, Medicine Flying, Ridge Bear, White Bear, White Bird, Big Head, War Bonnet, Bear Rope, Elk Shows His Horns, and Hail. Lakota scouts present included Hump, Roman Nosed Sioux, Iron Shield (or Iron Shirt?), and No Scalplock. A number of the listed Cheyennes were, in fact, not scouts but volunteers who hoped to acquire Nez Perce horses by participating in the venture. Two of the Cheyennes, White Bear and White Bird, apparently scouted so far away from the command that they did not participate in the action at Bear's Paw. This information has been compiled from Young Two Moon, Account. A slightly variant version is "Capture of the Nez Perces, Young Two Moon's Account." In a second-generation statement, John Stands-in-Timber contended in 1954 that Young Two Moon and High Wolf had discovered the Nez Perce village on September 29. Dusenberry, "Northern Cheyenne," 27.

62. Tilton, "After the Nez Perces," 403.

63. Romeyn, "Capture of Chief Joseph," 286. For the formation of the column, see also Moylan to Ernest Garlington, August 16, 1878, copy in Godfrey Papers, LC. (This document is reprinted in Chandler, *Of Garry Owen in Glory*, 74–76.)

64. Long to Miles, August 16, 1890, Long Papers; and Godfrey, Interview.

65. Description based on an interview with Charles K. Bucknam and G. H. Snow, New York *Herald*, October 11, 1877. (This account is abbreviated in *Frank Leslie's Illustrated Newspaper*, October 27, 1877.) Bucknam was one of the Fort Benton volunteers dispatched by Ilges to Miles after the Cow Island/Cow Creek Canyon affairs. *Army and Navy Register*, September 1, 1883.

66. Godfrey, Interview. Former Private Fremont Kipp, Company D, Seventh Cavalry, told Walter M. Camp: "When we got within 5 or 6 miles of the camp that morning we got within 1000 yds of a Nez Perce outpost of 3 Inds [sic] who were sitting by a fire. When they saw us they rode off bare back, leaving their saddles. We were coming from the S.E. & had not struck the main trail yet. They evidently thought we were going direct to the village & so instead of trying to mislead us struck out for the village themselves & our scouts followed them." Kipp, Interview.

67. Undated fragmentary note penciled in Godfrey's hand, part of which is in container 1, folios 14–15, Godfrey Papers, LC, while a continuation page is in the Godfrey Papers, MHI. A contemporary account by Lieutenant Jerome of the Second Cavalry partly dispelled Hale's purported statement: "The story about Hale's saying, 'My God! am I going to be killed so early in the morning?' is probably a fiction. What did occur was this. When the command halted . . . , Hale, who was spoiling for a fight, but who was evidently nervous and troubled, took out a charm given to him by a lady, which he wore around his neck and said:—'Jerome, if I should get killed this morning I want you to see that this gets back'—mentioning the lady's name. I bantered him a moment about it. Then he took it in his hand and threw it with a gesture against his heart, laughed in his peculiar manner and exclaimed:—'There, nothing is going to harm me now.'" New York *Herald*, October 30, 1877. Still another story of Hale's portent had him saying, on the eve of his departure from the cantonment:

"Pray for me, for I am never coming back!" Alice Baldwin, *Memoirs of . . . Baldwin*, 192. See also Carriker and Carriker, *An Army Wife*, 106–7.

68. Titus, "Last Stand," 148. This article, while containing inaccurate and undocumented information, is to some degree useful because Titus was able to have then-Colonel Edward S. Godfrey, a participant, review and correct the manuscript. Godfrey evidently concurred with the statement regarding the viewing of the herd from the ridge "between Peoples Creek and Snake Creek." Nelson Titus to Godfrey, June 11, 1905, Godfrey Papers, LC.

69. Romeyn, "Capture of Chief Joseph," 286; Miles, *Personal Recollections*, 267. It is doubtful that Miles or any of his command, save perhaps the white scouts, ever knew the full extent of the pre-action involving the Northern Cheyennes at the Nez Perce camp; only their own accounts, given to selected whites years later, described the introductory skirmishing in any detail.

70. This description of the advance has been reconstructed from the sources quoted or cited in explanatory footnotes, besides the following: Miles, "Report," 528; Miles, "Report of Col. Nelson A. Miles," October 6, 1877, in Secretary of War, *Report . . . 1877*, 74; Long, "Journal of the Marches," 1700; Zimmer, *Frontier Soldier*, 121–22; Snyder, "Diary," September 30, 1877; Howe to Howe, November 11, 1877, Howe Letters; Moylan to Garlington, August 16, 1878, copy in Godfrey Papers, LC; and Baird, "General Miles's Indian Campaigns," 363.

71. For details of the Lame Deer fight, see Greene, *Yellowstone Command*, 205–13. For descriptions and assessments of the army's tactical recourses during the so-called Indian wars of the 1870s, see ibid., 10–12; and Wooster, *The Military and United States Indian Policy*, 135–42. For an overview of the procedures and pitfalls of the system, including the surprise tactic, during this period, see Cook, "Art of Fighting Indians."

72. This estimate of the village population is derived from knowledge of the estimates given by Shively and Irwin in the national park, as well as the surrender figures given by McWhorter's Nez Perce sources in McWhorter, *Hear Me*, 499; and estimates by Black Eagle regarding the number of people who escaped to Canada, presented in McWhorter, *Hear Me*, 499. Also considered was the tabulation of surrendered Nez Perces given in "Report of Indians . . . District of the Yellowstone."

73. Pre-battle activities in the Nez Perce camp are described in McWhorter, *Yellow Wolf*, 205; McWhorter, *Hear Me*, 478–81; Joseph [Heinmot Tooyalakekt], "An Indian's Views," 428; and Garcia, *Tough Trip through Paradise*, 293.

74. McWhorter, *Yellow Wolf*, 205. Ten-year-old Suhmkeen recalled that the man "yelled, then he fired his rifle in the air, at the same time he waved a blanket giving us the signal . . . 'Soldiers coming—soldiers coming.'" Alcorn and Alcorn, "Old Nez Perce Recalls," 71.

75. McWhorter, *Yellow Wolf*, 205. For the alarm in the camp, see McWhorter, *Yellow Wolf*, 205; McWhorter, *Hear Me*, 479, 481; Yellow Bull, Interview, LBNM; MacDonald, "Nez Perces," 269; and Francis Haines, *Nez Perces*, 274–75.

CHAPTER 12

1. This is approximate, all the major Nez Perce and army sources—most stated long after the fact—specifying only a range between approximately 7:30 A.M. and 10:00 A.M. for the time of attack, but with the majority coalescing around

8:30 A.M. to 9:15 A.M.. Private Abram Brant wrote home that the village was first sighted four miles ahead at 9:00 A.M. Brant, Letter.

2. Edward J. McClernand, *With the Indian*, 104.

3. In describing the advance, Miles wrote that "a more light-hearted, resolute body of men never moved over any field. An occasional laugh, a happy witticism, and radiant smiles were heard and seen along the lines, and one officer complacently rode into action humming the air 'What Shall the Harvest be?'—the melody of the song timed to the footfalls of his galloping steed." Miles, *Personal Recollections*, 268.

4. For technical descriptions of the permutations of period cavalry, such as the force engaged at Bear's Paw, see *Cavalry Tactics*.

5. Lieutenant Henry Romeyn stated that, in the initial charge, the mounted Fifth infantrymen followed "about 800 or 900 yards behind" the Seventh Cavalry. Romeyn, Interview.

6. The evident mistake by Tyler in leading his battalion to the left rather than straight toward the camp was significantly ignored in Miles's battle reports, probably because it contributed importantly to the ultimate outcome of the fighting at Bear's Paw through the capture of most of the pony herd. (Tyler, most likely, would have gone after the herd after carrying his charge through the village, as was customary in such assaults.) In his annual report, in fact, Miles termed Tyler's movement "a slight detour, to attack in the rear and cut off and secure the herd." Miles, "Report," 528. And Adjutant Baird later maintained that he carried the order from Miles to Tyler, directing the latter to "sweep around to the left and cut off the camp from the herd"—this, apparently, after Tyler's diversion left was well underway. Baird, "General Miles's Indian Campaigns," 363. This description (using much of the same verbiage) was echoed in Miles, *Personal Recollections*, 268. Of course, despite the first day's action, the ultimate military result of Bear's Paw was success with potential enhancement for Miles's reputation and career. Probably because of this, the error was ignored; that it occurred, however, is documented in Godfrey, Interview; and undated fragmentary note penciled in Godfrey's hand, part of which is in container 1, folios 14–15, Godfrey Papers, LC, while a continuation page is in the Godfrey Papers, MHI. Yet another fragmentary note by Godfrey stated the following: "Capt. Taylor [sic] with his 3 troops of the 2 Cavy was designated to make the attack, & the 3 troops of the 7" were to act as support. In his advance, however, Taylor had mistaken the direction & diverged so far to the left that the 7th were ordered to make the attack & Taylor was ordered to cut off the Pony herds." Godfrey, "Gen. Godfrey's Story." In an account that appeared in the Boston *Sunday Post*, however, Godfrey modified his position somewhat, stating that "Captain Tyler of the 2nd Cavalry immediately made for the herd [implying no mistake had been made]. Then the 7th Cavalry was ordered to make the attack." In a slightly variant account, enlisted man Frederick Gaybower recollected that "Miles ordered one co. of 2nd Cav. to take the herd, and by mistake all 3 cos. of 2nd Cav went after the horses." Gaybower, Interview. Another enlisted man of the Seventh told Camp virtually the same thing. James Clark, Interview.

7. This according to an interview with Charles K. Bucknam and G. H. Snow, New York *Herald*, October 11, 1877.

8. Miles, *Personal Recollections*, 268.

9. Moylan stated that, after cresting the divide leading toward Snake Creek, the battalion deployed into line formation, as opposed to columns of fours. Moylan

to Ernest Garlington, August 16, 1878, copy in Godfrey Papers, LC. It is clear from Godfrey's account, however, that the charge was made by the three companies in column rather than in line, which would have been illogical given the topographical constraints encountered in the approach as well as at the site where the fighting erupted.

10. Godfrey remembered that "as the terrain appeared to give access to the village on Moylan's side, I started toward him. He had found the bluffs too abrupt along his assigned front, and had started toward my part of the line, so we bumped together." Boston *Sunday Post*, August 23, 1931.

11. Kipp, Interview.

12. McAlpine, "Memoirs."

13. Moylan to Garlington, August 16, 1878, copy in Godfrey Papers, LC.

14. Godfrey, Interview.

15. Ibid.; Godfrey to Adjutant General, February 24, 1882, Godfrey Papers, LC. See also Moylan to Garlington, August 16, 1878, copy in Godfrey Papers, LC; and Mulford, *Fighting Indians!*, 122.

16. Moylan placed the distance at "200 or 300 yards to the rear" of the former position. Moylan to Garlington, August 16, 1878, copy in Godfrey Papers, LC. See also the discussion of the cavalry assault and repulse on the bluff and the advent of the Fifth Infantry in Walter M. Camp to Romeyn, March 27, 1912, and Romeyn's reply of June 13, 1912, on verso, item 19, Camp Papers, DPL.

17. The casualty figure is from Garlington, "Seventh Regiment," but see also Moylan to Garlington, August 16, 1878, copy in Godfrey Papers, LC. Godfrey later stated that "the Indians were so close that they shot too high." Garlington, "Seventh Regiment." An enlisted man, perhaps referring to the same topography at the site, remembered that "men and horses went down pretty fast before the battalion [companies A and D] could fall back over the ridge out of sight." *Winners of the West*, October 30, 1936. One man killed on the line was Private David E. Dawsey. His "bunkie," Private Abram B. Brant, described to Dawsey's brother how he died: "David and myself were together, the fighting was then very hot. Your Brother was shot while on the line, through the left Brest [sic]. He called to me at once and I crawled up to him and drew him in a hollow out of range of the firing. He says Abe old boy, if this thing kills me, write to my Mother with my love and tell her I hope[d] to see her this winter. I was then obliged to leave him and go back in the line, and after dark, when I went to him, he was dead." Brant, Letter.

18. Statement in Peter Allen, "Military Expedition . . . Bear Paw Mountains." Allen's recollection is important in establishing the relative chronology of the deaths of Biddle and Hale. After he and an injured comrade walked back to the field hospital, "having to cross a washout or dry creek bed on the way," Allen, who had witnessed Biddle's death, noted that while with the surgeons "a wounded man came in and said that Capt. Hale, capt. of my Co. (K) had been killed." Peter Allen, Interview.

19. Godfrey, Interview.

20. Kipp recalled: "Just as we crossed the big coulee a Nez Perce Ind[ian] stood in the coulee & kept firing into us until we got within 15 feet of him when he was killed and we swept on past him." Kipp, Interview. The wounding of Baird is described in Miles to Adjutant General, March 27, 1877, Medal of Honor, Special File.

21. In his account, Godfrey said that he "had just 'jumped' a corporal, whom I saw 'ducking' and I thought trying to stop in a ravine," when he was shot. In fact, he probably had encountered Corporal John Quinn, who under his real name of John

Gorham, related his experience fifty-four years later: "The command . . . formed in skirmish line moving forward. At this time it was my misfortune to have met with an accident caused by my carbine getting between my legs while on the run, causing me to fall heavily to the ground; the breechlock of the carbine coming against my groin, causing a painful injury which rendered me helpless for a time. In the meantime, . . . Godfrey, having overcome his loss of mount, was hastening to join the troops, which was [sic] just ahead. Seeing me prone on the ground, he stopped, and while in the act of talking to me he was shot through the side of his waist. . . . As soon as I was able I joined the troop." Quinn was himself later wounded as he tried to rescue the mortally wounded Trooper Dawsey. John Gorham letter, August 19, 1931, in Boston *Herald*, undated clipping (ca. August 22, 1931), Godfrey Papers, LC.

22. Private Kipp of Company D told Walter Camp that Hale, in response to Eckerson's observation that their position was good, said: "We will charge them again, that's what we'll do." They were his last words. Kipp, Interview. George Baird recorded that a staff officer carried a message from Miles to Hale, who was lying on the ground seeking cover with his men. "[He] began the familiar formula—'The General's compliments and he directs'—when observing that no response was given he looked more intently and saw that he was saluting the dead." Baird, "General Miles's Indian Campaigns," 363–64. Lieutenant Long identified the staff officer as himself in Long to Miles, August 16, 1890, Long Papers, and in Beyer and Keydel, *Deeds of Valor*, 2:252, while Miles confirmed his action in connecting the companies following Hale's death. Long, "Brief of services." The Charles K. Bucknam and G. H. Snow account in New York *Herald*, October 11, 1877, stated that Hale had also received an earlier wound while leading a charge. Eckerson's feat in going for the ammunition is recounted in *Army and Navy Journal*, April 27, 1878. A perhaps anecdotal story had Eckerson witnessing the deaths and wounding of his colleague officers and rushing up to Miles, saying, "I am the only damned man of the Seventh Cavalry who wears shoulder straps, alive." Titus, "Last Stand," 149.

23. Portland *Daily Standard*, November 4, 1877. Walter Camp, citing James Stewart's recollections, wrote: "The Nez Perce had orders to pick off the bugler first and the officers next. This was a standing order in the fighting all along. . . . By picking off the buglers, the officers could not give commands at critical times, and by getting the officers out of the way they would demoralize the men." Unclassified envelope 91, 537, Camp Manuscript Field Notes, Camp Papers, LBNM.

24. Peter Allen, Interview.

25. Tilton, "After the Nez Perces," 403.

26. Romeyn, "Capture of Chief Joseph," 288.

27. Tilton, "After the Nez Perces," 403.

28. Long to Miles, August 16, 1890, Long Papers.

29. Baird, "Capture of Chief Joseph," 212–13.

30. Miles, *Personal Recollections*, 272.

31. The movement of Romeyn's Company G, Fifth Infantry, across the ravine to aid the Seventh troopers is precisely mentioned in Second Lieutenant (and Fifth Infantry battalion adjutant) Thomas M. Woodruff, Letter; published as Thomas M. Woodruff, "'We have Joseph," 32.

32. This account of the opening attack at Bear's Paw comprises a fusion of information drawn from the materials already cited in documenting quotes and explanatory references above, as well as the following: Miles, "Report," 528; Long to Miles,

August 16, 1890, Long Papers; Surgeon Henry R. Tilton to Surgeon General, October 26, 1877, entry 624, box 1, Office of the Adjutant General; Zimmer, *Frontier Soldier*, 122–23; New York *Herald*, October 11, 1877; *Army and Navy Journal*, December 8, 1877; Romeyn, Interview; Henry P. Jones to Camp, January 26, 1912, folder 2, box 1, Camp Papers, BYU; James Clark, Interview; "Summary of Reports . . . Non-Effectiveness"; *Harper's Weekly*, November 17, 1877; *Record of Engagements*, 73–74; Garlington, "Seventh Regiment," 261–62; Miles, *Serving the Republic*, 176–77; and Nelson A. Miles, "Chief Joseph's Surrender," New York *Tribune*, August 4, 1907. See also the following historical maps: sketch map accompanying Allen, "Military Expedition . . . Bear Paw Mountains"; Grillon, "Battle of Snake Creek"; and "Topographical Sketch . . . 'Bear's Paw Mts.'" This last map was probably drawn by Lieutenant Long. See Long to Baird, March 14, 1890, Baird Papers.

33. Black Eagle's account in McWhorter, *Hear Me*, 479–80.

34. Joseph [Heinmot Tooyalakekt], "An Indian's Views," 428.

35. Shot in Head's account in McWhorter, *Hear Me*, 482–83.

36. McWhorter, *Yellow Wolf*, 206.

37. Ibid., 207. McWhorter's interpretation of Yellow Wolf's narration at this point is unclear. See McWhorter, *Yellow Wolf*, 208 n. 5. It is possible that the account described Carter's attack on the village later that afternoon. Francis Haines, in *Nez Perces*, 313, stated that White Bird and 120 men met the Seventh's attack at the crest of the bluff, but provided no documentation. MacDonald's sources said only that "White Bird ordered his warriors to prepare for a defense." MacDonald, "Nez Perces," 269. Josephy, *Nez Perce Indians*, 618–19, made no statement regarding White Bird or the identity of others who repelled the assault. Unfortunately, beyond the possibility of Yellow Wolf, the names of the defenders who turned back the cavalrymen on the bluff seem to be unknown. McWhorter's on-site informants, Many Wounds and White Hawk, however, named several individuals who fought in the vicinity of the east and northeast edges of the bluff: Wottolen, Young Soo-koups (killed there), Akh-tai-la-ken, Lone Bird, Shooting Thunder, and Red Spy. McWhorter, "Stake Tabulation of the Bear's Paw Mountain Battle Field"; and C. Raymond Noyes, plat, "Battle of the Bear's Paw," NA.

38. Yellow Bull, Interview, LBNM.

39. Scout Kelly believed that "the Sioux and Cheyennes were so eager for horses that they precipitated the fight before General Miles was ready." Kelly, "Capture of Nez Perces."

40. One Nee-Me-Poo, Grizzly Bear Lying Down, conversed in sign with the Cheyenne scout leader. He inquired why the Cheyennes were helping the soldiers, saying: "You have a red skin, red blood. You must be crazy! You are fighting your friends. We are Indians. We are humans." The Cheyenne said he would not shoot, but, according to Yellow Wolf, he lied to them. McWhorter, *Yellow Wolf*, 207. "The way I look at it," Yellow Wolf told McWhorter, "we did not make war with any of those tribes [Crows, Bannocks, Sioux, Northern Cheyennes]. Our war was with the whites. Started by General Howard at our Lapwai council." McWhorter, *Yellow Wolf*, 208.

41. Nee-Me-Poo sources indicate that the Cheyennes killed a woman. Shot in Head stated: "A strange Indian chief wearing a great-tailed war bonnet was pursuing a woman on a cream-colored horse, riding as fast as she could whip her horse. I heard her begging for her life." McWhorter, *Hear Me*, 482. See also

Ealahweemah's account in McWhorter, *Hear Me*, 484. Yellow Wolf said that the Cheyenne killed the woman with his revolver. McWhorter, *Yellow Wolf*, 207.

42. The action of the scouts is documented in Young Two Moon, Account, and is essentially the same in "Capture of the Nez Perces, Young Two Moon's Account." See also Stands In Timber and Liberty, *Cheyenne Memories*, 228. Dr. Tilton reported of the Nez Perces that "the first intimation they had of our presence, was the firing upon the village by the Cheyenne Indians." Surgeon Henry R. Tilton to Surgeon General, October 26, 1877, entry 624, box 1, Office of the Adjutant General. The figure of possibly seventy Nez Perces leaving the village is given in Edward J. McClernand, *With the Indian*, 105.

43. Godfrey remembered that the captured ponies "were diseased, and that if their flesh was wounded in any way it would fester up badly." Godfrey, Interview.

44. Peopeo Tholekt dueled with a Cheyenne scout on the tableland about six thousand feet northeast of the battlefield, finally wounding the Cheyenne. See his account, and Peopeo Tholekt's pictographic rendering (citing Cheetham, "Peopeo Tholekt's Artistry"), both in Thain White, "Relics from the Bear's Paw Battlefield." The site of this encounter is defined on C. Raymond Noyes, plat, "Battle of the Bear's Paw," NA.

45. "Capture of the Nez Perces, Young Two Moon's Account."

46. Edward G. McClernand, Letter.

47. Ibid. The Cheyenne, Young Two Moon, offered his view of this episode: "Looking back, the officer in command of the troops saw that he had left a man who could not mount his horse and he wheeled his troops and charged back to save this man. Here the soldiers and the Nez Perces got pretty close together. When this troop of cavalry got down into a gulch, the Nez Perces formed a line on both sides and so surrounded the troops and the three scouts who were with them. There was hot fighting here down in this gulch for two and a half hours. Then the Nez Perces left them." "Capture of the Nez Perces, Young Two Moon's Account."

48. Ealahweemah's account in McWhorter, *Hear Me*, 483–84.

49. Arthur, Interview, 560. Young Suhmkeen (later Samuel Tilden) also managed to escape, despite being shot at by one of the Cheyenne scouts. Alcorn and Alcorn, "Old Nez Perce Recalls," 71.

50. Miles stated that the captured stock totaled seven hundred horses, ponies, and mules (Miles, "Report of Col. Nelson A. Miles," October 6, 1877, in Secretary of War, *Report . . . 1877*, 74), but raised that figure to eight hundred in Miles, *Personal Recollections*, 273. Not all of the animals were confiscated; some ran off and were later reported in the vicinity of the Fort Belknap Indian Agency about fifteen miles north. Fort Benton *Record*, October 12, 1877.

51. Edward G. McClernand, Letter.

52. Besides the sources indicated above, this account of the capture of the herd is based on material in Edward J. McClernand, *With the Indian*, 105–6; Romeyn, "Capture of Chief Joseph," 287; Bruce, "Comments"; and Baird, "General Miles's Indian Campaigns," 364.

53. This action is referenced in an interview with Jerome in the New York *Herald*, October 30, 1877, and the anonymous participant account in *Army and Navy Journal*, December 8, 1877. And Private William Zimmer, of Company F, noted that "H Co. went to the assistance of the 7th & infantry, while our co. were engaged

in gathering up the loose ponies that were scattered about the prairie. After this was done . . . the rest of us went in the skirmish line." Zimmer, *Frontier Soldier*, 122.

54. Jerome, "Inquiries."

55. Thomas M. Woodruff, Letter. Miles reported that, based upon the Nez Perces' fixed positions in the ravines, "it soon became apparent they could only be forced by a charge or by siege." Miles, "Report," 528. Henry Romeyn believed the attack was planned as part of a siege operation in order "to get possession of the course of the creek to cut the Indians off from water." Romeyn, "Capture of Chief Joseph," 288. See also Baird, "Capture of Chief Joseph," 212. In Miles, *Personal Recollections* (272), Miles denied that he attempted this multidirectional assault: "I did not . . . order a general assault, as I knew it must result in the loss of many valuable lives and possibly might end in a massacre."

56. Woodruff claimed that Romeyn never received the directive because the orderly carrying it was shot. Thomas M. Woodruff, Letter. Godfrey recollected that "Genl Miles had ordered a charge by the whole battalion [meaning the Seventh Cavalry as well as the Fifth Infantry troops] but the line failed to advance very far, except the few men . . . [of Carter's party who went] down the creek bottom. Genl Miles was not satisfied and sent word to the companies that when he gave the command charge, the whole battalion should charge. . . . I suggested to the General that perhaps, owing to the noise of the firing, etc., they could not hear his command and that the trumpeter sounding the charge could be better heard. I don't think the General liked the 'suggestion' but he acted on it and had the charge sounded in addition to his word of command." Godfrey, Interview.

57. New York *Tribune*, undated clipping in Romeyn, Appointment, Commission, and Personal File. See also Romeyn, "Capture of Chief Joseph," 288–29. That the wounding of Romeyn is one of the most documented injuries on record during the Indian wars period was largely due to Romeyn himself. On October 8, he wrote an acquaintance: "I was shot through the right lung, the ball striking about two inches below the nipple, breaking a rib where it entered and again where it came out (about two inches from the spine)." Romeyn to H. A. Colvin, October 8, 1877, in unidentified newspaper clipping, in Romeyn, Appointment, Commission, and Personal File. See other accounts of Romeyn's injury in *Army and Navy Journal*, March 9, 1878; and Beyer and Keydel, *Deeds of Valor*, 2:252. Woodruff observed that Romeyn's wounding came about because he "unnecessarily exposed himself. . . . His horse received two severe wounds [that killed the animal], his field glass case was shot away and another shot cut his sword belt at the left side, striking the handle of his knife, which with his belt and pistol fell to the ground." Thomas M. Woodruff, Letter. First Sergeant Henry Hogan carried Romeyn off the field in the midst of heavy fire by the warriors. *The Medal of Honor*, 227.

58. A Seventh Cavalry anecdote related to Lieutenant Eckerson possibly referenced this action: An acquaintance in "the states" had sent Eckerson a fine pipe with a long stem of amber. At Bear's Paw, as the lieutenant halted with his unit behind a ledge, a bullet shattered his pipe bowl "into dozens of pieces, filling his face with ashes, burning tobacco and fragments of the pipe, leaving him with only part of the stem clenched between his teeth. The look that came over his face was so comical [that] the men simply had to laugh." Goldin, Biography, 331.

59. Thomas M. Woodruff, Letter. The "odd men" may have numbered more than "two or three" and probably included members of Jerome's Company H,

Second Cavalry (see below). Godfrey stated that the attacking force included some of the Cheyenne scouts. Godfrey, Interview.

60. Woodruff stated that "I had sent word previously to have some troops sent over the creek to the left so as to enfilade the ravines that the Indians held, and Lt. Maus with ten men was sent there." Thomas M. Woodruff, Letter. Maus recounted that "I was sent, with scouts, on the opposite side of their camp to drive the indians [sic] out of a ravine where they were sheltered and were keeping up a damaging fire on parts of our command. This we did as we had, from our position, a fire enfilading their position. I was out nine (9) hours on this line." "Memoranda of Active Service. . . Maus."

61. Thomas M. Woodruff, Letter.

62. Private Oliver P. Howe described what was apparently this action in which he participated: "H compy 2" [was] facing Right into the Village. We were ordered to dismount and charge it on foot and we got a galing [sic] fire for we had to Charge over a little Knoll and down into a Ravine and as soon as we Reached the top of the Knoll we got it from all quarters but only wounding two men [mortally?] on our side." Oliver P. Howe to Samuel J. Howe, November 11, 1877, Howe Letters. Godfrey stated that Carter's troops "found their way blocked by the Nez Perces who were working their way toward the positions held by the Company on the bluffs," and that the encounter was "hand to hand." Godfrey, Interview. Woodruff, who was there, made no such assertion regarding the nature of the combat. Thomas M. Woodruff, Letter.

63. Thomas M. Woodruff, Letter.

64. Miles, "Report," 528. Nez Perce participants made few references to the infantry assault. One of them was by Joseph, whose camp was directly involved. He observed: "Ten or twelve soldiers charged into our camp and got possession of two lodges, killing three Nez Perces and losing three of their men, who fell inside our lines. I called my men to drive them back. We fought at close range, not more than twenty steps apart, and drove the soldiers back upon their main line, leaving their dead in our hands. We secured their arms and ammunition." Joseph [Heinmot Tooyalakekt], "An Indian's Views," 428. Yellow Wolf might well have been referencing this action instead of that involving the Seventh Cavalry at the start of the battle. McWhorter, *Yellow Wolf*, 207–8.

65. Miles to Howard, Sturgis, and Brotherton, September 30, 1877, folder: Nez Perce War, box 3, Sladen Family Papers. The asterisks and bracketed word are in the copy. Unaccountably, Miles did not inform of the large proportion of men killed in his command. And his low estimate of the number of Nez Perces still before him is equally confusing.

66. Miles, "Report," 528.

67. Unnamed woman in McWhorter, *Hear Me*, 485.

68. McWhorter, *Yellow Wolf*, 211; McWhorter, *Hear Me*, 485–86; Yellow Bull, Interview, LBNM; and Fort Benton *Record*, October 12, 1877. Delineation of the shelter and rifle pits is in McWhorter, "Stake Tabulation of the Bear's Paw Mountain Battle Field"; and C. Raymond Noyes, plat, "Battle of the Bear's Paw," NA. The complimentary quote is from Long, "Journal of the Marches," 1701. Years later, former sergeant Stanislaus Roy, Company A, Seventh Cavalry, described a feature he remembered among the Nez Perce fortifications: "The Indian lookout . . . was a round hole dug in the earth about 4 feet in diameter and about 2 ½ ft. deep,

and above the earth was a stone wall walled up round like a well for 4 ft. high. This wall protruded above the ground and the lookout enabled two men to stand up and be protected in it. It was on the edge of the Hill [sic] in plain view of Indian Intrenchments and how an Indian got into it or got out of it I don't know, but it was talked about at the time and [that?] there was an undermine [underground?] outlet. Now I have come to the conclusion that if you found a pile of bolders [sic] and rocks that that must be the place and that the rocks has fell in [and] covered up the hole." Roy to Camp, August 13, 1911, folder 19, box 1, Camp Papers, BYU.

69. The construction of rifle pits is documented in Long, "Journal of the Marches," 1701; Grillon, "Battle of Snake Creek"; Fort Benton *Record*, November 16, 1877; McAlpine, "Memoirs"; and New York *Herald*, October 15, 1877 (which stated that the pits, "from night to night, when concealment was possible among the barren gulches and ravines, were dug nearer and nearer to the lines of the Indians"). Private Zimmer noted that "after dark our skirmish line was brought around so as to completely hem them in to prevent their escape." Zimmer, *Frontier Soldier*, 122. It is likely that some of the rock cairns located in recent years on the battlefield relate to positions occupied by members of the Fifth Infantry and Seventh Cavalry during the night of September 30, and by other units as they changed places over the course of the siege. Because of the cover afforded by darkness, it is possible that the line of cairns located approximately 630 yards from the Nez Perce position represents rifle pits established by the Seventh cavalrymen or Fifth infantrymen that night. Another line of cairns located on higher ground about fifteen hundred yards east-southeast of the Nez Perce position (still within carbine range) might represent either an earlier-held position of the troops following the warriors' repulse of Hale's men, or a strategic post continuously occupied by infantry or cavalry to provide constant oversight of the field. The latter position conforms well with a line designated as held by a company of Fifth Infantry, apparently late on September 30. See "Topographical Sketch . . . 'Bear's Paw Mts.'" The cairns are delineated and discussed in LeRoy Anderson, "Bear Paw Battlefield." See also Douglas D. Scott, "Historic Archaeological Overview . . . Bear Paw," which encloses this and other documents related to the historical archeology of the site (see, in particular, fig. 2), including the highly significant reports of Thain White and Gordon L. Pouliot (see bibliography for complete listing); Rennie and Brumley, "Prehistoric Archaelogical Overview . . . Bear's Paw," 5; and Jellum, *Fire in the Wind*, 277–79. The map, Grillon, "Battle of Snake Creek," which is distorted in scale, posits four army rifle pits generally in the areas discussed above. One more appears to be at the northeast side of the south bluff and conforms with that shown on C. Raymond Noyes, plat, "Battle of the Bear's Paw," NA. Grillon, "Battle of Snake Creek," further indicates three more pits constructed on the west side of Snake Creek at points flanking the village.

70. "Topographical Sketch . . . 'Bear's Paw Mts.'" Grillon, "Battle of Snake Creek," shows the Seventh Cavalry camp located some distance in the rear of the artillery position on the south bluff. That the troop positions were changed periodically throughout the siege is evident in "Memoranda of Active Service . . . Maus," wherein Maus stated: "I was employed by the general in assisting him in changing and locating the line surrounding the hostiles from day to day."

71. Thomas M. Woodruff, Letter.

72. Edward G. McClernand, Letter.

73. "Topographical Sketch . . . 'Bear's Paw Mts.'"; and Grillon, "Battle of Snake Creek."

74. The gun, invented by Benjamin B. Hotchkiss, answered an 1876 request by Miles for "a rifled gun, probably a breech-loader, that can travel with cavalry, and has an effective shell range beyond that of rifled small-arms." "Report of the Chief of Ordnance," in Secretary of War, *Report . . . 1878*, xiii. The gun was manufactured at the Hotchkiss Armory, Paris, France. Aubrey L. Haines to Jack Williams, January 18, 1962, copy in research files, Big Hole National Monument, Wisdom, Mont. See also Miles's testimony in U.S. House, *Report of a Sub-Committee . . . Relating to the Reorganization of the Army*, 241.

75. This according to Scout Kelly. Kelly, *"Yellowstone Kelly,"* 193.

76. This location for Miles's headquarters varies from that established by McWhorter on the basis of information gathered in 1935 from Charles Smith, who had been a teamster with the troops. Smith claimed that Miles's headquarters were back up the draw between the south bluff and the neighboring point where the Hotchkiss gun stood. McWhorter to Smith, November 8 and 9, 1935, folder 61 and folder 3, McWhorter Papers. Indeed, Smith's designated point may, in fact, have served as the colonel's front line command post.

77. These positions are correlatively postulated on the basis of information delineated on the map, Grillon, "Battle of Snake Creek." It is likely that Tilton's "field hospital" was back from the edge of the bluff behind the infantry position during the opening hours of the fighting. See Kipp, Interview. The pack mules bearing ammunition were hurried forward by Lieutenant Long when the village was discovered. Once in the vicinity of the ongoing action, they required proximity to the command as well as protection, which Long provided. Long to Miles, August 16, 1890, Long Papers. Their probable location is based on Grillon's designation of the area where the wagon train was placed after its arrival. One account stated that Miles parked the train eight hundred yards "to the rear," a placement that roughly conforms with that shown on Grillon, "Battle of Snake Creek."

78. For details of this incident, see Kelly, *"Yellowstone Kelly,"* 193–95; and Kelly, "Capture of Nez Perces." The incident involved the Cheyenne scouts' rescue of one of their own, White Wolf, who had been wounded in the head by the sharpshooter. Hump had purposefully drawn fire while Starving Elk and Young Two Moon reached the injured scout and dragged him off. "Capture of the Nez Perces, Young Two Moon's Account." After this incident, White Wolf got a new name—Shot in the Head. Marquis, *Warrior Who Fought Custer*, 326.

79. Shambo's account in Alva Noyes, *In the Land of the Chinook*, 76.

80. Tilton to Surgeon General, October 26, 1877, entry 624, box 1, Office of the Adjutant General.

81. Zimmer, *Frontier Soldier*, 123.

82. Peter Allen, "Military Expedition . . . Bear Paw Mountains." Allen's arm was amputated above the elbow on October 5.

83. Godfrey, Interview.

84. Tilton to Surgeon General, October 26, 1877, entry 624, box 1, Office of the Adjutant General. Steward Gallenne's leg was amputated on October 14.

85. New York *Herald*, October 11, 1877.

86. Ibid.

87. Portland *Daily Standard*, November 4, 1877. Tilton wrote: "The Indians came up to some of our wounded, and when they offered resistance, called out to them, 'don't shoot, we won't hurt you, we only want your [cartridge] belts,' and they were as good as their word." Tilton also commented: "They not only did not disturb the wounded beyond taking their equipments, but in at least two instances gave them water to drink." Tilton to Surgeon General, October 26, 1877, entry 624, box 1, Office of the Adjutant General. Dr. Tilton later requested that the words, "not only," and "but in two instances gave them water to drink" be excised from his report because "I am convinced upon further inquiry that the statement is not correct." Tilton to Surgeon General, December 17, 1877, entry 624, box 1, Office of the Adjutant General.

88. Tilton to Surgeon General, December 17, 1877, entry 624, box 1, Office of the Adjutant General; Romeyn, "Capture of Chief Joseph," 289; Kelly, *"Yellowstone Kelly,"* 196; and Tilton to Surgeon General, October 26, 1877, entry 624, box 1, Office of the Adjutant General.

89. "List of Wounded in the Yellowstone Command . . . Bears Paw"; Regimental Returns . . . Seventh Cavalry, September 1877, roll 72; Regimental Returns . . . Fifth Infantry, September and October 1877, roll 58; Regimental Returns . . . Second Cavalry, September 1877, roll 719; and Tilton to Medical Director, Department of Dakota, October 3, 1877, entry 624, box 1, Office of the Adjutant General.

90. McWhorter, *Yellow Wolf*, 211.

91. The dead at "Death's Point of Rocks," allegedly killed by the Cheyenne scouts, were Tohtohaliken (mortally wounded and died), Lakoyee, Timlihpoosman, Eagle Necklace, Sr., and Heyoomeekahlikt (Grizzly Bear Lying on His Back). The wounded were Eagle Necklace, Jr., and Tomyahnin. Philip Williams to McWhorter, July 19, 1936, folder 93, McWhorter Papers; McWhorter, "Stake Tabulation of the Bear's Paw Mountain Battle Field"; and C. Raymond Noyes, plat, "Battle of the Bear's Paw," NA.

92. Information on the extent and identity of Nez Perce casualties on September 30 is from McWhorter, *Hear Me*, 363–64, 482, 486; and McWhorter, *Yellow Wolf*, 209. Joseph accounted for eighteen men and three women in Joseph [Heinmot Tooyalakekt], "An Indian's Views," 428, and Kawownonilpilp stated that five people were killed. "Story of Kawownonilpilp." See also Josephy, *Nez Perce Indians*, 621. Wottolen told McWhorter that a noncombatant elderly man kept track of day-to-day incidents throughout the engagement and announced them to the group. "All knew him and reported to him who had been wounded or killed in battle, who was missing or had disappeared. The names of all were known throughout the band." McWhorter, *Hear Me*, 486 n. 23.

C H A P T E R   1 3

1. Long, "Journal of the Marches," 1700.

2. Shambo's account in Alva Noyes, *In the Land of the Chinook*, 76.

3. Tilton to Surgeon General, October 26, 1877, entry 624, box 1, Office of the Adjutant General. Shambo said, "I told them it was buffalo. You see it had snowed that night and the snow had blown into the hair of the buffalo and made them look white and spotted." Shambo's account in Alva Noyes, *In the Land of the Chinook*, 76. Shambo stated that Miles sent him to reconnoiter and that he shot one of the animals, and that the rest of the herd "charged right down through" the

army and Indian positions. Havre *Plaindealer*, August 22, 1903. See also *Army and Navy Journal*, December 8, 1877; Baird, "General Miles's Indian Campaigns," 364; Miles, *Personal Recollections*, 274–75; and Miles, *Serving the Republic*, 178.

4. Just what action Miles would have taken if confronted with several hundred Lakota warriors in addition to the Nez Perces is uncertain. In Miles, *Personal Recollections* (275), he stated only that "I concluded that we could use our artillery and quite a large portion of our troops against any additional enemy and still hold the fruits of the victory already gained."

5. For details of the Sioux factor, see Cheyenne *Daily Leader*, October 6, 1877, as cited in DeMontravel, "Miles," 4–5; John Turner, *North-West Mounted Police*, 2:340–41; Manzione, "*I Am Looking to the North for My Life*," 82–98; and, especially, Utley, *Lance and the Shield*, 193, 371–72 n. 14.

6. Romeyn, "Capture of Chief Joseph," 289.

7. Ibid.; McWhorter, "Stake Tabulation of the Bear's Paw Mountain Battle Field"; and C. Raymond Noyes, plat, "Battle of the Bear's Paw," NA. Regarding the cisterns, see Mrs. M. E. Plassman, "Disputed Points Relating to Events Incident to the Battle of the Bear Paws," Eureka *Journal*, April 28, 1926.

8. The willingness of some Nez Perces to negotiate on October 1 and again on the fifth suggests not only the traditional independence of the Nee-Me-Poo band units, but perhaps also the continuation of the factiousness that had plagued the people since Canyon Creek.

9. Baird, "Capture of Chief Joseph," 212–13.

10. "Capture of the Nez Perces, Young Two Moon's Account." The Nez Perce No Feather said that "no Cheyenne or Sioux scouts visited our camp at Bear's Paw at any time nor did they talk with us." Weptas Nut (No Feather), Interview.

11. "Capture of the Nez Perces, Young Two Moon's Account." In another Cheyenne version, Miles got angry at the scouts for going among the Nez Perces, whereupon High Wolf grabbed the colonel by the collar and said: "You told us to try to get these people to come in and not be harmed. They are Indians like us. Why don't you talk to them?" It is not clear from this account whether this incident preceded the negotiations of October 1 or those of October 5 leading to the surrender. Stands In Timber and Liberty, *Cheyenne Memories*, 228.

12. Yellow Bull (who described the meeting as having occurred on October 2) maintained that the soldiers raised the white flag. McWhorter, *Yellow Wolf*, 214. This is very likely correct given the fact that Miles initiated the communication. Charles K. Bucknam and G. H. Snow, who were present, stated that "during the temporary truce a white flag floated over the Nez Perces' stronghold. The flag stayed during the whole of the second day, and was visible on the morning of the third. It consisted of a whole sheet of stolen bunting." New York *Herald*, October 11, 1877.

13. Joseph [Heinmot Tooyalakekt], "An Indian's Views," 428.

14. Tilton to Surgeon General, October 26, 1877, entry 624, box 1, Office of the Adjutant General; and Joseph [Heinmot Tooyalakekt], "An Indian's Views," 428.

15. Author's field notes, August 27, 1995.

16. Tilton to Surgeon General, October 26, 1877, entry 624, box 1, Office of the Adjutant General. Elsewhere, Tilton said of Joseph: "He is a man of splendid physique, dignified bearing and handsome features. His usual expression was serious, but occasionally a smile would light up his face, which impressed us very favorably." Tilton, "After the Nez Perces," 403.

17. Tilton said that this man was the "one whose portrait was given in Harpers Weekly as Joseph." Tilton to Surgeon General, October 26, 1877, entry 624, box 1, Office of the Adjutant General. Tom Hill stated that he had a precouncil meeting with Miles, who interrogated him about the Nez Perce leadership—who was present in the camp and which leaders had been killed. After receiving a hearty meal, Tom Hill and Miles went half way to the Nez Perce position, and Hill called over for Joseph to come forth and he did. Hill's account is in U.S. Senate, *Memorial of the Nez Perce*, 31–34. A similar account by Tom Hill is in Curtis, *North American Indian*, 8:171–72, in which he identified the other four men as Hiyatommon (Shouter), Wepteshwahaiuht, Kalowit, and Pahwema (171), although in Hill's account to the Senate, he stated that Joseph came over with but two other men (32). See also Walter M. Camp to Scott, September 22, 1913, folder 23, box 1, Camp Papers, BYU. A Nez Perce account largely derived from White Bird stated that "General Miles, like many others, supposed Joseph to be the leader of the hostiles and wanted his surrender in place of the real leader—Looking Glass. This suited the Indians exactly and they allowed Joseph to go to the camp of the soldiers." MacDonald, "Nez Perces," 270.

18. Zimmer, *Frontier Soldier*, 123.

19. Ibid.

20. Ibid. Captain Snyder noted: "No shots fired today, the time being consumed in negotiations looking to surrender of the Indians." Snyder, "Diary," October 1, 1877. It is not certain if the burials occurred immediately or later. Sergeant Stanislaus Roy, who arrived with the wagon train late on the first, remembered that "to my sad surprise there layed [sic] my two friends Sgt. McDermott and Dreslew and 18 others dead layed in line on a little noled [knoll] covered over with their own blankets. Capt Hale and Biddle [a] little to the right, also Dead." Roy to Camp, December 18, 1909, folder 11, box 1, Camp Papers, BYU.

21. See Tilton to Surgeon General, October 26, 1877, entry 624, box 1, Office of the Adjutant General; and Miles, *Personal Recollections*, 274. Most non-Indian accounts mentioned that Looking Glass had been killed by the time of the Joseph-Miles meeting October 1, and Yellow Wolf's account seems to concur. Yellow Wolf confusedly stated that Looking Glass was killed on the "third sun of battle," preceding the first meeting with Miles, which was actually on the second day of the fighting. See McWhorter, *Yellow Wolf*, 213–14. Other Nez Perce sources indicate that he was killed on the day of the surrender. See McWhorter, *Hear Me*, 495; and MacDonald, "Nez Perces," 271. Yet the tight chronology of the existing cease-fire, Joseph's message (in which the death of Looking Glass is mentioned), and the capitulation—all on the morning of October 5 (see below)—does not favor the latter view. McWhorter, on the basis of an opinion of former teamster Charles A. Smith, stated that Scout Milan Tripp fired the shot that struck Looking Glass in the left forehead. Another view is that he was killed by a shell from the twelve-pounder. McWhorter, *Yellow Wolf*, 214 n. 2. McWhorter's informants pointed out the spot where Looking Glass died at the lower end of the ridge occupied by Hale's battalion of cavalry. C. Raymond Noyes, plat, "Battle of the Bear's Paw," NA. The spot was marked by a shaft in 1928.

22. Miles, *Personal Recollections*, 274. Yellow Wolf concurred that "some guns were given up." McWhorter, *Yellow Wolf*, 215. See also U.S. Senate, *Memorial of the Nez Perce*, 32. Another account stated that Joseph "proposed to close the en-

gagement by surrendering the arms he had taken from the dead soldiers." Charles K. Bucknam and G. H. Snow account in New York *Herald*, October 11, 1877.

23. Long to Miles, August 16, 1890, Long Papers.

24. Hill recollection in Curtis, *North American Indian*, 8:171.

25. McWhorter, *Hear Me*, 488. "During a truce, it is dishonorable to . . . resort to any act which would confer advantage." Wilhelm, *Military Dictionary and Gazetteer*, 602.

26. For the formalities and historically recognized rules pertaining to armistices, see *Rules for Land Warfare*, 88–96.

27. Jerome was the son of prominent financier and businessman Lawrence R. Jerome of New York City, friend to powerful politicians and newspaper publishers during the Gilded Age. He was also the nephew of Leonard W. Jerome, the so-called "King of Wall Street," whose daughter, Jennie, became the mother of Winston Churchill. His younger brother was William Travers Jerome, who became district attorney of New York City. For more background, see Davies, *Ten Days on the Plains*, 135–39; *Winners of the West*, February 28, 1935; and Stearns, "Volunteer Hostage," 87–89.

28. The matter of whether Jerome acted on his own volition or in response to a request from Miles remains a matter of some controversy. In his report, Miles stated that Jerome was directed "to ascertain what was being done in the Indian village." Miles, "Report," 528. However, Miles later stated that "I directed Lieutenant Jerome to ascertain what the Indians were doing in the village, supposing that he would go to the edge of the bluff and look down into the camp. Misunderstanding my instructions, he went down into the ravine, he was seized and held until he was exchanged for Chief Joseph." Miles, *Personal Recollections*, 274. However, Lieutenant Long wrote Miles in 1890: "When you thought it might be advisable for some officer to enter the camp then under the protection of flag of truce, I volunteered to go . . . [but] . . . you thought best for Jerome to perform this work." Long to Miles, August 16, 1890, Long Papers.

29. Charles K. Bucknam and G. H. Snow account in New York *Herald*, October 11, 1877.

30. McWhorter, *Yellow Wolf*, 215.

31. "Capture of the Nez Perces, Young Two Moon's Account."

32. McWhorter, *Yellow Wolf*, 215–16.

33. Jerome's account in New York *Herald*, October 30, 1877. In Jerome, "Jerome's Own Story," Jerome gave an account (first published in the Otsego *Journal*, July 17, 1930, and later in *Winners of the West*, April 30, 1935) that is often cited in describing the event. It originated in an interview conducted by Robert Bruce at Jerome's New York City apartment in 1930. In it he claimed to have initiated contact with Joseph leading to the meeting with Miles and even accompanied the leader back to his camp to explain the proposed surrender. After Joseph returned to Miles with "20 or 30 guns he had collected," the two enjoyed coffee while Jerome returned to the camp on Miles's order "to see that they don't cache any of their guns." Jerome, "Jerome's Own Story," 337–38. There is indeed some basis for believing that Jerome entered the camp twice, the first time volunteering to assist in the retrieval of some arms and the second in response to Miles's request for information. Years later, seeking a Medal of Honor, he wrote Miles: "The first time I went into the Indian camp I volunteered, or asked permission. The second

time when I was detained and held prisoner I went in by your order." Jerome to Miles, April 1, 1898, in Jerome, Appointment, Commission, and Personal File. An article in the Fort Benton *Record*, October 12, 1877, stated that Jerome had entered the camp twice. And Lieutenant McClernand, writing of the event that involved his fellow officer of the Second Cavalry, observed the following: "Jerome was sent into the village to see if Chief Looking Glass was killed, as reported, and perhaps to observe generally. He went and returned all right, but not satisfied with having accomplished all he was instructed to do, he let his curiosity lead him back again." Edward J. McClernand, *With the Indian*, 106.

34. Jerome account in New York *Herald*, October 30, 1877. In his 1930 memoir, Jerome stated that "my food was brought from our camp by an orderly." It is extremely doubtful that this happened and is probably an elaboration by the aged Jerome. Jerome, "Jerome's Own Story," 338.

35. See, for example, Edward J. McClernand, *With the Indian*, 107. Lieutenant Wood, Howard's aide, who was not yet present, declared that Miles "was furious. He swore at Lt. Jerome, saying that now he would be compelled to return Joseph to his camp." Wood to Harry S. Howard, February 20, 1942, folder 34, McWhorter Papers.

36. Thomas M. Woodruff, Letter.

37. Snyder, "Diary," October 1, 1877.

38. Memorandum containing Brigadier General John F. Weston recollection, September 22, 1900, in Jerome, Appointment, Commission, and Personal File.

39. *Army and Navy Journal*, November 24, 1877. That Jerome was in no way reprimanded suggests that Miles may have apprehended certain political fallout from among the powerful Jerome family's associates and supporters.

40. McWhorter, *Yellow Wolf*, 217. See also McWhorter, *Hear Me*, 489–90.

41. McWhorter, *Yellow Wolf*, 217. McWhorter cited an account of Wottolen that said that Joseph's hands were cuffed behind him and his feet drawn up behind him and tied to the cuffs. McWhorter, *Yellow Wolf*, 217 n. 6. Tom Hill likewise said that Joseph, on his return, told the people that he had been tied up and hobbled. U.S. Senate, *Memorial of the Nez Perce*.

42. Joseph [Heinmot Tooyalakekt], "An Indian's Views," 429. The former Lieutenant Wood, on learning of Yellow Wolf's statements, responded that "the account that General Miles hobbled Joseph and held him corralled with the mules . . . is absolutely rot without any slightest foundation whatever." Wood to Harry S. Howard, folder 34, McWhorter Papers, February 20, 1942. And Miles himself denied that Joseph was handcuffed, though he allowed that he had been guarded closely. See Curtis, *North American Indian*, 8:172 n. 1. Private Barker recalled that Joseph was kept in a tent with a bed and darkened lantern. "An infantryman sat on a camp stool with fixed bayonet," while two cavalrymen stood guard outside. Barker, "Campaign and Capture," (January 1923): 30.

43. McWhorter, *Yellow Wolf*, 218; "Memoranda of Active Service . . . Maus"; Maus to Adjutant General, August 29, 1890, box 2, Halstead-Maus Family Papers; Havre *Plaindealer*, August 23, 1902; and Maus to Camp, February 20, 1914, folder 1, box 2, Camp Papers, BYU. Young Two Moon maintained that the Cheyenne scouts completed the exchange at Miles's direction. "Capture of the Nez Perces, Young Two Moon's Account."

44. Jerome's account in New York *Herald*, October 30, 1877. The fact that Joseph had been dealing with Miles led to a story that, to protect himself against warriors prone to picking off officers and senior noncommissioned officers, Miles promptly shaved off his mustache to change his appearance (see Kipp, Interview). Jerome termed the imputation "rot." Jerome, "Inquiries." Denied a brevet promotion for his service under Miles at the Lame Deer Fight and at Bear's Paw (legally, because of his circumstances, Jerome was then neither an active duty officer nor on the retired list), Jerome in 1898 began a campaign to receive a Medal of Honor. Miles, again perhaps politically conscious, recommended the medal, but ultimately Jerome's direct application to President Theodore Roosevelt (who detested Miles) was denied. "The medal . . . can not be awarded to you for participation in the [May 1877] charge on Lame Deer's camp, because there is nothing to show that you distinguished yourself . . . , and the medal cannot be awarded to you on account of your visit to Chief Joseph's camp, because the official record shows that you made that visit while Chief Joseph was in Colonel Miles' camp, thus giving reasonable assurance that you would not be harmed." Jerome, Appointment, Commission, and Personal File.

45. Tilton to Surgeon General, October 26, 1877, entry 624, box 1, Office of the Adjutant General. See also Zimmer, *Frontier Soldier*, 127.

46. The plan to break out is mentioned in McWhorter, *Yellow Wolf*, 218–19. Hill's recollection is in Curtis, *North American Indian*, 8:172.

47. Roy to Camp, August 13, 1911, folder 19, box 1, Camp Papers, BYU. See also Tilton to Medical Director, Department of Dakota, October 3, 1877, entry 624, box 1, Office of the Adjutant General.

48. Tilton to Surgeon General, October 26, 1877, entry 624, box 1, Office of the Adjutant General.

49. For the arrival of the train, see Kelly, *"Yellowstone Kelly,"* 196–97; Tilton to Surgeon General, October 26, 1877, entry 624, box 1, Office of the Adjutant General; and Romeyn, "Capture of Chief Joseph," 289–90. Particulars of the advance of the wagon train by a member of its escort are in Barker, "Campaign and Capture," (January 1923): 7.

50. The dead man was Private John Irving, Company G, Second Cavalry; the wounded man was Private Charles Smith, Company K, Seventh Cavalry. Tilton to Medical Director, Department of Dakota, October 3, 1877, entry 624, box 1, Office of the Adjutant General.

51. Roy to Camp, December 18, 1909, folder 11, box 1, Camp Papers, BYU.

52. Roy to Camp, August 13, 1911, folder 19, box 1, Camp Papers, BYU.

53. Edward J. McClernand, *With the Indian*, 107. Captain Snyder described the night as "one of the most disagreeable I ever spent." Snyder, "Diary," October 2, 1877.

54. Tilton to Surgeon General, October 26, 1877, entry 624, box 1, Office of the Adjutant General.

55. Snyder, "Diary," October 1, 1877; Edward G. McClernand, Letter.

56. Barker, "Campaign and Capture," (February 1923): 7; and Edward G. McClernand, Letter. The dead man was Trooper Irving, as cited in note 50 above.

57. Roy to Camp, December 18, 1909, folder 11, box 1, Camp Papers, BYU.

58. Charles K. Bucknam and G. H. Snow account in New York *Herald*, October 11, 1877. The account is not clear as to which day this incident happened. In

what was perhaps a typical overstatement by an enlisted man, Private John McAlpine recalled of his time on the line that "I never saw an officer for the whole five days of the battle. They stayed in the rear with the grub and hot coffee." McAlpine, "Memoirs."

59. Zimmer, *Frontier Soldier*, 127.

60. Edward G. McClernand, Letter. Private Zimmer, of Company H, Second Cavalry, wrote: "Our battalion got relieved off of the skirmish line this evening." Zimmer, *Frontier Soldier*, 126. It is not clear whether the Napoleon gun fired a round at the Nez Perces' position at dusk on the second. In Edward J. McClernand, *With the Indian*, 107, McClernand stated that it did, but on "the evening of the 6th day," somehow confusing his chronology. In Edward G. McClernand, Letter, McClernand said only that the gun was pointed to command the place where the Nez Perces obtained water.

61. Zimmer, *Frontier Soldier*, 127.

62. Author's field notes, August 27, 1995.

63. Long, "Journal of the Marches," 1701; and Kipp, Interview.

64. Joseph [Heinmot Tooyalakekt], "An Indian's Views," 429. A Nee-Me-Poo account of Peyanahalkpowwit noted that the council of leaders believed that, since Miles ignorantly recognized Joseph as chief of all the people, he should continue talking as a means of delaying. But if he indeed wanted to surrender, he was talking only for himself. Pinkham, *Hundredth Anniversary of the Nez Perce War*.

65. Tilton to Surgeon General, October 26, 1877, entry 624, box 1, Office of the Adjutant General.

66. It is clear that a deadline had been established. Woodruff stated that "the Indians had raised a flag of truce on the morning of the 1st and had kept it up, but we sent word to them that if they did not surrender by 10:30 (the 3rd) we should open fire on them, and we did, for they were not inclined to accept our terms." Thomas M. Woodruff, Letter. Snyder remarked that "the Indians not coming to terms, [we] opened fire upon them about noon." Snyder, "Diary," October 3, 1877.

67. Ripley, *Artillery and Ammunition*, 26–29; and Aubrey L. Haines to Jack Williams, January 18, 1962, copy in the research files, Big Hole National Monument, Wisdom, Mont. For use of the twelve-pounder at Wolf Mountains, see Greene, *Yellowstone Command*, 166–76. Inexplicably, there is little mention in any of the accounts of the activity, much less the performance, of the Hotchkiss gun at Bear's Paw, beyond the fact that it was present throughout the encounter stationed on the point adjacent to the south bluff. However, fragments of its projectiles have been found on the battlefield, bearing witness to its use during the siege.

68. *Army and Navy Journal*, December 8, 1877; Baird, "Capture of Chief Joseph," 213; and Baird, "General Miles's Indian Campaigns," 364.

69. Tilton to Surgeon General, October 26, 1877, entry 624, box 1, Office of the Adjutant General. One report stated that the flag of truce above the Nez Perce position "was cut down by a single shot from the French breechloader." Fort Benton *Record*, October 12, 1877. Young Two Moon said that "General Miles told the Nez Perces that unless they surrendered this afternoon the soldiers would fire at them. The sign would be by bugle calls. After a time the troops did fire on the Nez Perces and the firing did not cease until sundown." "Capture of the Nez Perces, Young Two Moon's Account." However, the relative chronology of both of the above references to the events of the siege is unclear.

70. Romeyn, "Capture of Chief Joseph," 290. Romeyn's chronology for the

opening of the twelve-pounder is in error; he said October 2, but he meant the third, which is specified in the other accounts. Furthermore, Romeyn indicated that the gun was repositioned on the morning of October 4 (he meant the fifth), which was probably not correct, as there is no further evidence that the twelve-pounder was relocated after it opened fire directly on the noncombatant-occupied coulee on October 3. Romeyn's chronology is off one day beginning with his entry for October 2 on page 290.

71. Tilton to Surgeon General, October 26, 1877, entry 624, box 1, Office of the Adjutant General.

72. Butte *Miner*, May 26, 1925.

73. Snyder, "Diary," October 3, 1877.

74. Zimmer, *Frontier Soldier*, 127.

75. Copy in New York *Herald*, October 8, 1877; and *Army and Navy Journal*, October 13, 1877.

76. Miles to Mary Miles, October 3, 1877, quoted in Virginia Johnson, *Unregimented General*, 203. The courier who took the dispatches to Fort Benton was Charles Bucknam, who had earlier joined the command from Major Ilges. Helena *Weekly Independent*, October 11, 1877.

77. Tilton to Medical Director, Department of Dakota, October 3, 1877, entry 624, box 1, Office of the Adjutant General.

78. Tilton to Surgeon General, October 26, 1877, entry 624, box 1, Office of the Adjutant General.

79. McWhorter, *Yellow Wolf*, 220; and McWhorter, *Hear Me*, 495.

80. Zimmer, *Frontier Soldier*, 127.

81. Barker, "Campaign and Capture," (January 1923): 30; and Circular, Headquarters, District of the Yellowstone, October 4, 1877, entry 903, part 3, General Orders and Circulars, Sept. 1877–June 1881, District of the Yellowstone, U.S. Army Continental Commands.

82. Miles, "Report," 528–29; Howard to Sheridan, October 19, 1877, in Secretary of War, *Report . . . 1877*, 76; Tilton to Surgeon General, October 26, 1877, entry 624, box 1, Office of the Adjutant General; Snyder, "Diary," October 4, 1877; and Portland *Daily Standard*, November 4, 1877.

83. Redington, "Scouting in Montana," 63. Redington reported finding the body of "a colored courier," dead about two hours with his dispatches torn up and scattered about along with a box of cigars.

84. Benteen to wife, October 2, 1877, in Carroll, *Camp Talk*, 92, 94. Sturgis forwarded a congratulatory message to Miles. "I will begin crossing the troops at once to march toward you as rapidly as our jaded animals will permit." He also sent orders to the troops at Cow Island to move out immediately. Sturgis's cavalry crossed at Carroll, while the infantry and artillery troops and their wagons ascended to Little Rocky Creek, there to move over a shorter distance and rejoin Sturgis near the Little Rocky Mountains. Sturgis to Miles, October 2, 1877, entry 107, box 3, part 3, 1877, U.S. Army Continental Commands. See also Sturgis to Miles, October 4, 1877, ibid.

85. Sturgis to Miles, October 4, 1877, entry 107, box 3, part 3, 1877, U.S. Army Continental Commands

86. Howard, "Report," 629–30; Mason to wife, October 2 and 3, 1877, in Davison, "A Century Ago," 18; Hardin, Diary, October 2, 1877; Howard, *My Life and*

Experiences, 298–99; and John Carpenter, *Sword and Olive Branch*, 259–60. Howard had not received any of Miles's dispatches and, according to Wood, was worried that Miles might have been wiped out. C. E. S. Wood, "Indian Epic is Re-Told."

87. Lieutenant Wood, who was present at this meeting in Howard's tent, said years later that Howard told Miles: "'I have not come to rob you of any credit. I know you are after a star, and I shall stand back and let you receive the surrender, which I am sure will take place tomorrow.' When Miles left the tent, I told General Howard I thought he made a mistake. . . . He laid his one hand on my shoulder and said: 'Wood, Miles was my aide-de-camp in the Civil War. . . . I got him his first command. I trust him as I would trust you.'" C. E. S. Wood, "Indian Epic is Re-Told." See also John Carpenter, "General Howard," 112. Miles told his wife that Howard "did not assume command or give any directions. He had really nothing to do but witness the completion of the work. I was very glad to have him come up as he has been so badly abused that I am willing to give him any help or share any credit with him." Miles to Mary Miles, October 14, 1877, quoted in Virginia Johnson, *Unregimented General*, 207. On the other hand, interpreter Arthur ("Ad") Chapman said that he was also present and that Howard proposed assuming command, reportedly saying: "'When two commands join the ranking officer takes command of both.' Miles replied: 'Where is your command,' and Howard said, 'I have my staff here.' Miles said, 'Your staff is not your command.'" Chapman, Interview, 138. This story was relayed to Walter Camp by "Ad" Chapman's brother Winfield in 1913, six years after "Ad" Chapman's death.

88. Wood to Mason, October 4, 1877, entry 897, box 1, part 3, 1877, U.S. Army Continental Commands; and Mason to wife, October 6, 1877, in Davison, "A Century Ago," 18.

89. McWhorter, *Hear Me*, 493; and McWhorter, *Yellow Wolf*, 222 n. 3.

90. Quoted in Portland *Daily Oregonian*, October 19, 1877. See also John Carpenter, "General Howard," 142. The meeting is discussed in Howard, "Report," 630; and Howard, *My Life and Experiences*, 299. Lieutenant Wood remembered that the two Nez Perces were brought along "as witnesses to the proximity of his [Howard's] entire force and as possible negotiators." Wood, draft of letter account to Edward D. Lyman, January 17, 1939, C. E. S. Wood Collection. (This letter is reprinted in Erskine Wood, *Charles Erskine Scott Wood*, 16–20.)

91. Tilton to Surgeon General, October 26, 1877, entry 624, box 1, Office of the Adjutant General. Zimmer said: "It froze very hard last night, but the sun came out bright & warm this morning." Zimmer, *Frontier Soldier*, 128.

92. Tilton to Surgeon General, October 26, 1877, entry 624, box 1, Office of the Adjutant General.

93. Guy Howard to Sturgis, October 5, 1877, Letters Sent, Department of the Columbia, U.S. Army Continental Commands, quoted in John Carpenter, "General Howard," 142; and Sturgis to Miles, October 2, 1877, entry 107, box 3, part 3, 1877, U.S. Army Continental Commands.

94. Snyder, "Diary," October 5, 1877. Zimmer, *Frontier Soldier*, 128, carried this notation: "Last night our men crawled up on the Indian works, within 50 yards, & dug pits under the shelter of the darkness & a heavy fire from our men. As soon as it was dawn our boys began to pour lead into their pits and by ten A.M. they squealed. White rags could be seen in all directions in their camp."

95. Snyder, "Diary," October 5, 1877; U.S. Senate, *Memorial of the Nez Perce*;

and Tilton to Surgeon General, October 26, 1877, entry 624, box 1, Office of the Adjutant General. Howard stated that "we did not have very long to wait" for the two Nez Perces to return. Howard, *My Life and Experiences*, 299.

96. Probably in reference to the shelling of the preceding day.

97. Tilton to Surgeon General, October 26, 1877, entry 624, box 1, Office of the Adjutant General.

98. Joseph [Heinmot Tooyalakekt], "An Indian's Views," 429.

99. This time is speculative, based on documentation of the approximate time of succeeding events. Sutherland, who probably heard of the proceedings from Lieutenant Wood, gave the time that Captain John and Old George went over as "about 11 o'clock," in Portland *Daily Standard*, November 4, 1877.

100. McWhorter, *Yellow Wolf*, 222–23; McWhorter, *Hear Me*, 493–94; Hill recollection in Curtis, *North American Indian*, 8:172; and U.S. Senate, *Memorial of the Nez Perce*. McWhorter stated that some Nez Perces believed they would be returned to the Wallowa and Imnaha valleys, but most realized that Lapwai was meant. McWhorter, *Hear Me*, 494. On this point, Wood maintained that while in strictest terms the imminent surrender was considered "unconditional," in actuality, based on McDowell's telegram to Adjutant General, September 1, 1877, respecting the return of the people to the Department of the Columbia, and that expectation being common knowledge among the command, the scouts probably relayed it on to Joseph and other Nez Perces in the camp. Wood to L. V. McWhorter, March 17, 1929, folder 25, McWhorter Papers. Miles was more definite, however, stating (probably after consultation with Howard) that "I acted on what I supposed was the original design of the government to place these Indians on their own reservation, and so informed them. . . . [I told them] that they would be taken to Tongue River [Cantonment] and retained for a time, and sent across the mountains as soon as the weather permitted in the spring." Miles, "Report," 529. Wood also said that the Nez Perces were told they would not be tried or executed for past transgressions. C. E. S. Wood, "Pursuit and Capture," 328.

101. McWhorter, *Yellow Wolf*, 224.

102. McWhorter, *Hear Me*, 494.

103. Hill recollection in Curtis, *North American Indian*, 8:172.

104. The roles of Captain John and Old George in concluding the surrender cannot be overstated. In 1939, Howard's former aide, Lieutenant Wood, recollected their work in considerable detail: "Myself . . . , Lieutenant Guy Howard, the General's son, . . . Arthur Chapman, as interpreter, Old George and Capt. John as messengers, also Lieutenant Oscar Long, Col. Miles' Adjutant, and a Cavalryman, dismounted and standing at his horse's head a little apart, were out on a bare knoll, or rolling hill, one slope of which led down to the creek and valley. . . . Nobody was allowed to come on the outpost knoll where we stood. Presently, General Howard and Col. Miles came to where we were, walking slowly and talking as they came. When the[y] arrived where we were, and after we had made the formal salutes, which the two senior officers acknowledged, they went to one side, somewhat away from us and began talking. They then called Chapman and gave him instructions what to say to Old George and Capt. John and these two messengers started down the slope to Joseph's camp. They remained a long time, at least an hour, and we were walking around to keep warm and to break the monotony. Presently the two old Indians came up the slope and Chapman walked over and

484 Notes to page 309

stood by Gen. Howard and Col. Miles who had also been walking about talking. What message the Indians brought no one ever knew but Gen. Howard, Col. Miles, Arthur Chapman, Old George and Capt. John. After a fairly short consultation, the two old Indian messengers were sent back. . . . I wish to emphasize that the negotiations between Joseph's camp and General Howard with Col. Miles on the hilltop were carried on entirely by Old George and Capt. John, always as a couple, going back and forth, bringing messages to Howard and Miles which no one heard but Howard, Miles and Chapman, the interpreter, and taking replies which also no one heard but these three. So the day progressed." Wood, draft of letter account to Lyman, January 17, 1939, C. E. S. Wood Collection.

105. Howard indicated in his report that "Joseph sent the following reply," which constituted his "speech." Howard, "Report," 630. Captain John was identified by Lieutenant Wood as the speaker in *Harper's Weekly*, November 17, 1877. Major Mason (not present, but a confidante to Howard) later reported that Joseph's statement was given to Captain John in response to Howard's offer of "good terms." Omaha *Herald*, March 15, 1883. For succinct background studies on Wood (1852–1944), see "Men and Women"; and, especially, Bingham, *Charles Erskine Scott Wood*. Regarding the "speech," Wood later claimed that "no one was interested to take it. Oscar Long, Miles['s] adjutant, was there to take it down but did not. No one was told to take it down. I was not told. The speeches of Indians were not considered important. I took it for my own benefit as a literary item." Park City *Park Record*, March 16, 1944.

106. This is the version of the statement "taken verbatim on the spot" by Wood and subsequently published in *Harper's Weekly*, November 17, 1877, and in Howard, "Supplementary Report," 630. The earliest *published* version of the statement appeared in the Bismarck *Tri-Weekly Tribune*, October 26, 1877, with slight variations from that published in Howard's report. Notably, the *Tribune* version spelled the chief's name "Ta-hool-hool-shoot," and it contained the following differences: "he who leads the young men," "may be freezing to death," and "I want time to look for my children." (Four other and slightly different renderings by Wood of the address are in, respectively, C. E. S. Wood, "Chief Joseph, the Nez-Perce," 141, (1884); Wood to Moorfield Storey, May 27, 1895, published in *Oregon Inn-Side News*, 1 (November-December, 1947), 5–6, copy in the C. E. S. Wood Collection; C. E. S. Wood, "Pursuit and Capture," 330, (ca. 1935); and Wood to C. J. Brosnan, January 7, 1918, p. 236, in *The Bookmark*, a ca. 1940 publication of the University of Idaho Library, Brosnan Collection. In 1939, after considerable reflection, Wood revised the last line of Joseph's "speech" to: "Joseph will fight no more forever." Wood, draft of letter account to Lyman, January 17, 1939, C. E. S. Wood Collection. The original penciled note was turned over to the War Department and subsequently lost, according to Wood in C. E. S. Wood, "Pursuit and Capture," 331. His wife insinuated that Miles had there destroyed it. Sara Bard Field to McWhorter, July 2, 1935, folder 35, McWhorter Papers. For analysis and discussion of the four variations of the speech purported to have originated with Wood, see Aoki, *Nez Perce Texts*, 120–23 (a fifth with minor punctuation differences is in C. E. S. Wood, "Famous Indians," 439); and Aoki, "Chief Joseph's Words." Aoki concluded that the "speech" was indeed a message that was likely embellished upon by Wood, who had literary interests (and became a leading writer during the early twentieth century) and, as such, does not exemplify

American Indian oratory. Aoki also believed that the reminiscence of Yellow Wolf regarding the discussion preceding the surrender signified that the Nez Perces believed they were agreeing to only a cease-fire. Aoki, "Chief Joseph's Words," 20–21. Given the condition of the people, this was unlikely; besides, technically, a truce was already in place. For various Nee-Me-Poo language translations from English, see Aoki, *Nez Perce Texts*, 123–25; John Thomas to Camp, April 15, 1912, item 27, Ellison Collection; Camp Manuscript Field Notes, Nez Perce Indian Wars 1, 141, Camp Papers, LBNM; and notes by Starr J. Maxwell and Samuel Morris of Lapwai, January 20, 1913, ibid., 147. See also Mark Brown, "Joseph Myth," 14–17.

107. Kelly, "Capture of Nez Perces."

108. Joseph [Heinmot Tooyalakekt], "An Indian's Views," 429. Joseph added: "General Miles had promised that we might return to our own country with what stock we had left. I thought we could start again."

109. Howard, "Report," 630.

110. McWhorter, *Yellow Wolf*, 224–26; McWhorter, *Hear Me*, 496; and Hill recollection in Curtis, *North American Indian*, 8:172. This time is given in Thomas M. Woodruff, Letter. Miles wrote his wife that Chief Joseph surrendered "this morning." Miles to Mary Miles, October 5, 1877, quoted in Virginia Johnson, *Unregimented General*, 206. However, in his somewhat unreliable Miles, *Personal Recollections*, 275, Miles stated that Joseph surrendered at 10:00 A.M., but described the formal surrender, which occurred later, as depicted below. Afterwards, there was talk that Joseph had asked for and received help from a force of soldiers in searching for his lost daughter. Cheyenne *Daily Leader*, December 6, 1877. She, in fact, had escaped before the initial battle on the thirtieth and had reached Canada.

111. C. E. S. Wood, "Chief Joseph, the Nez-Perce," 142. In later years, Wood variously remembered that Joseph's hair was braided on either side of his face and tied with fur, that he wore a woolen shirt—either gray or army blue, he thought—a blanket, probably gray with a black stripe, and buckskin moccasins and fringed leggings. Wood to McWhorter, January 31, 1936, quoted in McWhorter, *Hear Me*, 498; Wood, draft of letter account to Lyman, January 17, 1939, C. E. S. Wood Collection; and Park City *Park Record*, March 16, 1944. In *Harper's Weekly*, November 17, 1877, Wood reported that Joseph's clothes bore so many bullet holes that "Colonel Miles begged his shirt as a curiosity."

112. Author's field notes, August 27, 1995.

113. Wood, in *Harper's Weekly*, November 17, 1877, stated that the party came "up the hill," a reference repeated in C. E. S. Wood, "Chief Joseph, the Nez-Perce," 141. In 1895, Wood repeated his view that "Joseph came up to the crest of the hill, upon which stood Gen. Howard, Gen. Miles, an interpreter [Chapman] and myself." Wood to Storey, May 27, 1895, published in *Oregon Inn-Side News*, 1 (November–December, 1947), 5–6, copy in the C. E. S. Wood Collection. In C. E. S. Wood, "Pursuit and Capture," ca. 1935, Wood said that the Nez Perces "came from the ravine below, up to the knoll on which we were standing" (329). See also the repeated references to the site in Wood, draft of letter account to Lyman, January 17, 1939, C. E. S. Wood Collection. And in a letter written decades after the event to Howard's son, Wood said that Joseph's party "approached us on the little hill." Wood to Howard, February 20, 1942, folder 34, McWhorter Papers. This site is at variance with that advanced by McWhorter in the 1930s, based upon the statements of Charles A. Smith, who had been a teamster with

Miles in 1877. "He came out to the field, and I had him point out the location of the formality of surender [sic], as he remembered." McWhorter to Joseph G. Masters, October 27, 1936, Masters Papers. McWhorter wrote to Wood about this new information, and Wood responded that he thought the site was "on higher ground." Nonetheless, McWhorter wrote Smith that "I had a talk with my Noyes, and he agreed that the location decided on by you should be marked on the map and promised me that he would so make it, as designated by you." McWhorter to Smith, November 8, 1935, folder 61, McWhorter Papers. (See also C. Raymond Noyes, plat, "Battle of the Bear's Paw," NA.) The next day, McWhorter wrote Smith that "I now have absolute proof that you are correct in the location of Col. Miles [sic] Headquarters being located up that 'draw' or canyon, at the mouth of which you pointed out where the surrender took place." McWhorter to Smith, November 9, 1935, folder 3, McWhorter Papers. McWhorter did not state the nature of his "absolute proof." Yet this site seems illogical from a military stand-point; besides being at variance with accounts that specifically mention Joseph riding up a hill, the fact that it was located on relatively open terrain—where Miles and Howard would be vulnerable to Nez Perce sharpshooters beyond the enclosed perimeter of the army line—would seem to negate it as the surrender site. The correspondent for the New York *Herald* (October 15, 1877) noted that "Joseph entered the lines established by General Miles." This postulated surren-der site may also qualify as the place where Joseph approached during the cease-fire of October 1 (see Young Two Moon, Account).

114. Wood to Mason, October 6, 1877, entry 897, box 1, part 3, 1877, U.S. Army Continental Commands. The Charles K. Bucknam and G. H. Snow ac-count in New York *Herald*, October 11, 1877, stated that "at half past two in the afternoon . . . Joseph came into General Miles' camp and shook hands and pro-posed a surrender, which was instantly granted."

115. C. E. S. Wood, "Pursuit and Capture," 329.

116. See also Wood to Storey, May 27, 1895, published in *Oregon Inn-Side News*, 1 (November-December, 1947), 5–6, copy in the C. E. S. Wood Collection. The gun that Chief Joseph delivered to Miles was a brass-receivered Model 1866 Winchester .44 rimfire lever-action carbine. Its serial number of 102 596 indicates an 1872 manufacturing date. The gun was donated in 1957 to the Museum of the Upper Missouri, in Fort Benton, where it reposes today. Statement of William T. Morrison; accession agreement; and exhibit text, all provided to author by John G. Lepley, February 8, 1996. For a purported Joseph surrender weapon, see Charles Phillips, "Chief Joseph's Gun."

117. The account in Portland *Daily Standard*, October 13, 1877, supposedly by Sutherland (apparently using information provided by Lieutenant Wood when both were subsequently on the Missouri River), and Lieutenant Guy Howard's account of the Joseph-Howard-Miles incident in the New York *Herald*, October 22, 1877, are in agreement as to its essentials as described above. See also Wood-ward, "Service of J. W. Redington" (ca. 1934); C. E. S. Wood, "Pursuit and Cap-ture," 329; and Wood, draft of letter account to Lyman, January 17, 1939, C. E. S. Wood Collection, all of which concur. An account published earlier in the New York *Herald*, October 15, 1877, is the apparent source for the scenario in which Joseph spurned Howard, passing by him "in surly silence" and approaching Miles to say, "I want to surrender to you." This version of the event—practically verba-

tim in some particulars—was pirated by Mulford in Mulford, *Fighting Indians!*, 123–24, thus further compromising this book's value. While there may have been certain substance to this view of the event, there is no indication in the accounts of the primary participants—Joseph, Miles, and Howard—that such animosity existed between Joseph and Howard—in fact, every indication is that only an hour or so earlier Joseph had responded favorably in referring to Howard. Chicago *Inter-Ocean*, October 26, 1877, editorialized: "All that clap-trap about Chief Joseph of the Nez Perces contemptuously declining to surrender to General Howard . . . is exploded [by] a dispatch to the New York *Herald* and other reports by officers present at the surrender." See also *Army and Navy Journal*, November 3, 1877. Nonetheless, the story of Joseph's repudiation of Howard at the surrender persisted. In the 1920s, two civilian employees of the army in 1877, Jack Conley and James Boyd, maintained that it happened. Conley said that "Chief Joseph reached out his gun and General Howard reached out to take it, but Chief Joseph pulled it back and handed it to General Miles. . . . We all threw our hats in the air and cheered." Butte *Miner*, May 26, 1925. James Boyd said of Joseph: "He had a Winchester rifle and presented arms, then handed the gun to Howard with the muzzle pointed towards the general. Howard reached out his only hand to take it and Joseph quickly withdrew it, reversed the gun and handed it stock forward to General Miles. This is just how it happened and we talked it over afterwards as to just what Joseph meant." Boyd, Interview. Samuel Tilden said it was commonly believed among the Nez Perces in Canada that "Joseph refused to give his gun to Howard but deliberately walked over and gave it to Miles," a view with which the Reverend Stephen Reuben, another Nez Perce, agreed. C. T. Stranahan to McWhorter, August 31, 1941, folder 44, McWhorter Papers. In an interview the year before his death, Joseph said in broken English of the event: "I give gun Miles. He say: 'Give gun General Howard.' I say: 'No, I give you my gun; Howard no catch me.'" Washington, D.C., *Evening Star*, December 12, 1903. McWhorter believed that the leaders had discussed in council who to surrender to and favored Miles because they thought that Howard would have the leaders hanged. McWhorter, *Hear Me*, 497 n. 10. But another prevailing view among the Nez Perces was that Howard would be more likely to take them back home than Miles would. McWhorter to Many Wounds, February 11, 1930, containing Many Wounds's responses to questions, folder 160, McWhorter Papers. See McWhorter, *Hear Me*, 497 n. 10, for yet further (and questionable) scenarios regarding the Joseph-Howard-Miles surrender incident.

118. Chicago *Times*, October 26, 1877. And in Joseph [Heinmot Tooyalakekt], "An Indian's Views," (429) Joseph stated that he said: "From where the sun now stands I will fight no more." In his 1903 interview, he stated: "I point to sun; I say: 'I fight white man no more.'" Washington, D.C., *Evening Star*, December 12, 1903. Baird wrote in Baird, "General Miles's Indian Campaigns" (364), and Miles wrote in Miles, *Personal Recollections* (275) that Joseph said: "From where the sun now stands, I fight no more against the white man." Thus, it is possible that Joseph uttered an abbreviated form of his earlier remarks. See Aoki, *Nez Perce Texts*, 121–22. More likely, these accounts may be among the earliest attempts to link the longer message to the formal surrender proceedings, contributing to the misconception about the delivery of the "speech" that is present today. By 1895, it seems, Wood himself had come to believe that Joseph made the speech in dramatic

gesture when he turned his weapon over to Miles. "Standing back, he folded his blanket again across his chest, leaving one arm free, somewhat in the manner of a Roman senator with his toga . . . [and began to speak.]" Wood to Storey, May 27, 1895, published in *Oregon Inn-Side News*, 1 (November-December, 1947), 5–6, copy in the C. E. S. Wood Collection. And in 1936 Wood wrote that Joseph "stepped back, adjusted his blanket to leave his right arm free, and began his speech." Wood to McWhorter, January 31, 1936, quoted in McWhorter, *Hear Me*, 497–98. (See also C. E. S. Wood, "Pursuit and Capture," 330.) And as he wrote Howard's son: "Joseph swung himself down from his horse and offered his rifle to your father, and your father signed to him to give it to Miles, which Joseph did. Joseph stepped back a little and began his surrender speech, which was translated by Chapman and I took it on my paper pad." Wood to Howard, February 20, 1942, folder 34, McWhorter Papers. Scout Redington claimed to have watched the surrender. "I have always thought writers took poetic license in translating Joseph's speech. . . . I heard Joseph say something and the interpreter blah blah blah something back. That was all. I don't know what was said." Quoted in Woodward, "Service of J. W. Redington."

119. C. E. S. Wood, "Chief Joseph, the Nez Perce," 142; and Wood to Brosnan, January 7, 1918, C. E. S. Wood Collection. Wood remembered that Howard turned to him "and said, 'Mr. Wood, take charge of Chief Joseph as a prisoner of war. See that he is made comfortable and in no way is molested or troubled.' Chapman translated this to Joseph. I approached him, smiling pleasantly, a guard was designated for us and we walked together to Miles' camp where a large tent had been prepared for Joseph. I entered the tent with him and remained some time, with Chapman to interpret, trying to make Joseph feel at home, conversing with him about the outbreak of this unhappy war." Wood, draft of letter account to Lyman, January 17, 1939, C. E. S. Wood Collection.

120. Tilton to Surgeon General, October 26, 1877, entry 624, box 1, Office of the Adjutant General. One report stated that Joseph, as a condition of his submission, insisted that Miles send out a force to try and find his daughter, which was agreed to. See comment of Second Lieutenant Ernest A. Garlington, Seventh Cavalry, cited in Cheyenne *Daily Leader*, December 6, 1877.

121. New York *Herald*, October 15, 1877.

122. Howard, *My Life and Experiences*, 299.

123. New York *Herald*, October 15, 1877. In addition, contemporary accounts of the surrender proceedings on which this description is based are in *Harper's Weekly*, November 17, 1877, which contains Wood's account (that in the Portland *Daily Standard*, October 13, 1877, purportedly by Sutherland, is in fact Wood's); Snyder, "Diary," October 5, 6, 1877; New York *Herald*, October 22, 1877; and Sutherland, *Howard's Campaign*, 44 (again, using information presumably acquired from Wood). Memoir accounts include Miles, *Personal Recollections*, 275; Miles, *Serving the Republic*, 178–79; Nelson A. Miles, "Chief Joseph's Surrender," New York *Tribune*, August 4, 1907, 6; and Howard, *My Life and Experiences*, 299–300; Howard, *Nez Perce Joseph*, 265–67; and Howard, *Famous Indian Chiefs*, 197–98. For the Palouses, see Trafzer and Scheuerman, *Chief Joseph's Allies*, 23.

124. Miles, "Report," 515.

125. These figures are based on the estimate of Black Eagle, himself an escapee, who told McWhorter that 233 people—140 men and boys and 93 women

and girls—had managed to leave the Bear's Paw village either at the outset of the fighting, breaking away in small parties during succeeding nights, or with White Bird at the end. McWhorter, *Hear Me*, 499. The numbers tally well with known Nez Perce surrender and death figures in accounting for the size of the Nez Perce village.

126. White Bird's escape from Bear's Paw on the night of October 5 is documented in Zimmer, *Frontier Soldier*, 128; Snyder, "Diary," October 6, 1877; and Howard, "Report," 631, wherein the general stated that the chief, his 2 wives, and "about 14 warriors, crept out between the pickets and fled to British Columbia [sic]." Both the date and the number of people who left with White Bird is at issue. In one instance, Yellow Bull said that White Bird's escapees numbered 103 and left the night of September 30. Yellow Bull, Interview, LBNM. Later, however, he stated that White Bird and 50 people escaped on the night of October 2. Yellow Bull, Interview, BYU, 719. Yet Edward Lebain also said the Indians left on the night of the thirtieth. Lebain "has talked with many of the old warriors about this & they all have said it was the night of the first day." Lebain, Interview, IU. White Bird's wife, Hiyom Tiyatkehct, told Camp that during the escape "they crept out quietly. Soldiers saw them but did not fire." See Yellow Bull, Interview, BYU, 719. No Feather also went with White Bird. He said that "more than 40 people" accompanied the chief. "We slipped out at night quietly and were not fired upon by soldiers." Weptas Nut (No Feather), Interview. Duncan MacDonald's sources (who included White Bird) said that there were 103 warriors, 60 women, and 8 children. MacDonald, "Nez Perces," 271.

127. New York *Herald*, October 15, 1877. This account related that when a Nez Perce man volunteered to go find White Bird if Miles would provide him with a mule, the colonel "turned to General Howard, saying:—'I haven't got any use for White Bird. I've got all his traps [property?], and don't think he is worth a mule.'"

128. Howard, "True Story . . . Wallowa Campaign," 63.

129. McWhorter, *Yellow Wolf*, 225–26.

130. Wood to Mason, October 6, 1877, entry 897, box 1, part 3, 1877, U.S. Army Continental Commands. Sturgis received the notice on October 7. Mills, *Harvest of Barren Regrets*, 308; and Davison, "A Century Ago," 19. Mason had joined Sturgis on October 5. On the sixth, they had marched eighteen miles and, on the seventh, had gone ten miles when news of the surrender reached them. "Mem. of Marches." On October 8, Sturgis's camp was located "at the upper end of [Little?] Peoples Creek close to the [Little Rocky] mountains." Sturgis to Miles, October 8, 1877, entry 107, box 3, part 3, 1877, U.S. Army Continental Commands.

131. Miles to Assistant Adjutant General, Department of Dakota, October 6, 1877, in Terry, "Report," 515–16.

132. "Report of Indians . . . District of the Yellowstone." This figure aligns approximately with the Nez Perces' estimate of 87 men, 184 women, and 147 children—total 418—given in McWhorter, *Hear Me*, 499 and 499 n. 14. The number 418 is the same as that given by Baird, "General Miles's Indian Campaigns," 364. Howard reported that about 100 warriors and 300 women and children surrendered. Howard, "Report," 631. Dr. Tilton reported that "the total number of Nez Perces who surrendered was 405, a large number of them squaws and children." Tilton to Surgeon General, October 26, 1877, entry 624, box 1, Office of the Adjutant General. Finally, Miles told a Chicago newsman that 424 Nez Perces

had surrendered to him—perhaps the true figure of those who came over to him at Bear's Paw. Leavenworth *Daily Times*, November 29, 1877.

133. New York *Herald*, October 15, 1877.

134. Tilton to Surgeon General, October 26, 1877, entry 624, box 1, Office of the Adjutant General.

135. Long, "Journal of the Marches," 1701.

136. Circular, Headquarters, District of the Yellowstone, October 6, 1877, entry 903, part 3, U.S. Army Continental Commands.

137. Tilton to Surgeon General, October 26, 1877, entry 624, box 1, Office of the Adjutant General.

138. McWhorter, *Yellow Wolf*, 225.

139. "Capture of the Nez Perces, Young Two Moon's Account." The scouts, in fact, may have left on the fifth. Some of them evidently joined in the search for Bear's Paw refugees in the Milk River country over the next week or two. See Zimmer, *Frontier Soldier*, 130.

140. *Harper's Weekly*, November 17, 1877.

141. Tilton to Surgeon General, October 26, 1877, entry 624, box 1, Office of the Adjutant General.

142. Zimmer, *Frontier Soldier*, 128; and Tilton to Surgeon General, October 26, 1877, entry 624, box 1, Office of the Adjutant General.

143. Tilton to Surgeon General, October 26, 1877, entry 624, box 1, Office of the Adjutant General; and Grillon, "Battle of Snake Creek."

144. Zimmer, *Frontier Soldier*, 128.

145. Tilton to Medical Director, Department of Dakota, October 3, 1877, entry 624, box 1, Office of the Adjutant General; "List of Wounded in the Yellowstone Command . . . Bears Paw Mountains"; and Miles, "Report of Col. Nelson A. Miles," October 6, 1877, in Secretary of War, *Report . . . 1877*, 74–75. A complete list of army casualties is in Appendix A.

146. Tilton to Surgeon General, October 26, 1877, entry 624, box 1, Office of the Adjutant General. Tilton noted two cases among the wounded that seemed to have been caused by explosive bullets. "List of Wounded in the Yellowstone Command . . . Bears Paw." An illustration of an explosive bullet found in the Nez Perce camp, along with an accounting by Tilton of wounds rendered by these missiles, is in Otis and Huntington, *Surgical History*, 702 n. 1. Miles said of the Nez Perce warriors he fought at Bear's Paw: "They are the best marksmen I have ever met, and understand the use of improved sights and the measurement of distances; they were principally armed with Sharp's, Springfield, and Henry rifles, and used explosive bullets." Quoted in Captain Otho E. Michaelis to Adjutant General, January 22, 1879, in "Reports on Indian Arms," appendix 5, p. 323, in "Report of the Chief of Ordnance," in Secretary of War, *Report . . . 1879*. Explosive bullets had seen limited use during the Civil War. Each had a tiny fuse that detonated after discharge from the piece, so that a bullet would either explode in the flesh after striking a person or in the air before impact, becoming then a lethal knifelike missile. Hardy, "Explosive Bullets," 43. Evidently, the Nez Perces had confiscated a supply of these bullets from the ranch of Henry Croasdaile on Cottonwood Creek near Mount Idaho (see chapter five). There were reports that some of these bullets had been used by the warriors at the Big Hole. See Aubrey Haines, *An Elusive Victory*, 88.

147. Romeyn, "Capture of Chief Joseph," 291. Lieutenant Wood remarked that when he arrived with Howard on the night of October 4 "the dead soldiers were lying side by side in a long row on the prairie. . . . I have never forgotten that cordwood line of dead bodies." C. E. S. Wood, "History by One"; and Havre *Plaindealer*, August 16, 1902.

148. Zimmer, *Frontier Soldier*, 129; Havre *Plaindealer*, August 29, 1903; Theodore Goldin to McWhorter, June 20, 1930, McWhorter Papers; and Goldin, Biography, 331.

149. Tilton to Medical Director, Department of Dakota, October 3, 1877, entry 624, box 1, Office of the Adjutant General.

150. McWhorter, *Hear Me*, 486; Tilton to Medical Director, Department of Dakota, October 3, 1877, entry 624, box 1, Office of the Adjutant General; and Leavenworth *Daily Times*, November 29, 1877. Known Nez Perce casualties are listed in Appendix B.

151. Tilton to Surgeon General, October 26, 1877, entry 624, box 1, Office of the Adjutant General.

152. Ibid.

153. For brevet appointments for Bear's Paw, see Heitman, *Historical Register and Dictionary*, 1:183, 287, 461, 657, 733, 844, 907, 1058.

154. Miles to Adjutant General, June 7, 1878, folder: campaigns against Sioux and Nez Perce, box T-2: 5th Infantry to Aug. 1887, Miles Papers, MHI.

155. Captain Godfrey in 1882 recommended that Trumpeter Herwood, who had helped save him after he had been thrown from his horse in the initial charge, be awarded a Certificate of Merit. Herwood, who was himself wounded, was discharged on a surgeon's certificate of disability and apparently never received the recommended award. Godfrey to Adjutant General, February 24, 1882, Godfrey Papers, LC.

156. Romeyn to Adjutant General, May 23, 1894, Medal of Honor, Special File. Hogan also received the medal for his performance at Cedar Creek, Montana, October 21, 1876, in the Great Sioux War. For citations of the recipients, see *The Medal of Honor*, 227, 231. For applications on behalf of Carter, Romeyn, and Baird, see Miles to Adjutant General, March 26 and 27, 1894, Medal of Honor, Special File. See also Beyer and Keydel, *Deeds of Valor*, 2:249–53. Miles also applied for a medal for Lieutenant Marion P. Maus for Bear's Paw, but Maus received a Medal of Honor in 1894 for his work in the Geronimo Campaign of 1886. Miles to Adjutant General, March 26, 1894, Medal of Honor, Special File; and Heitman, *Historical Register and Dictionary*, 1:698.

157. *U.S. Army Gallantry and Meritorious Conduct*, 94.

158. General Orders No. 3, Headquarters, District of the Yellowstone, October 7, 1877, entry 903, part 3, U.S. Army Continental Commands. Also published in *Army and Navy Journal*, December 8, 1877; Howard, "Report," 632; and Mulford, *Fighting Indians!*, 129–30.

159. Howard to Miles, October 7, 1877, folder: Nez Perce War, box 3, Sladen Family Papers. Also published in Howard, "Report" 631–32. See also C. E. S. Wood, "History by One."

160. Fort Benton *Record*, October 5, 12, 1877; Terry to Miles, October 5, 1877, entry 107, box 3, part 3, 1877, U.S. Army Continental Commands; *Army and Navy Journal*, November 24, 1877; and Bell, "Life of 'Ne-cot-ta'," 391–94.

161. Moccasin, Affidavit; Speak Thunder, Affidavit; and Miles to Mary Miles,

October 14, 1877, quoted in Virginia Johnson, *Unregimented General*, 207. For the treatment of one Nez Perce woman captive of the Assiniboines, see Garcia, *Tough Trip Through Paradise*, 294–96; and Billings *Gazette*, August 14, 1932.

162. Alcorn and Alcorn, "Old Nez Perce Recalls," 71.

163. Yellow Bull identified the five Nez Perce scouts as Tipyilana Kapskaps (Strong Eagle), Pitpiluhin (Calf of the Leg), Tipsas (Hide Scraper), Pitomyanon Haihchaihc (White Hawk), and Wamushkaiya. Yellow Bull, Interview, BYU, 715. MacDonald stated that the Assiniboines and Gros Ventres killed seven warriors and identified one as Umtililpcown, one of those who had initiated the Salmon River murders in Idaho. MacDonald, "Nez Perces," 272. An account by Mrs. James Dorrity, who as a child was at Fort Belknap, seemingly described the same incident, but defined the group of Nez Perces as composed of two women and three men and ascribed the killings to the Gros Ventres. "Mrs. James Dorrity's Story," in Alva Noyes, *In the Land of the Chinook*, 81. Similarly, General Terry reported that on October 3 the Gros Ventres—on Box Elder Creek—"killed five men and took two women prisoners" who told the Gros Ventres of the existence of the main village in the Bear's Paws. Terry to Sturgis, October 5, 1877, entry 107, box 3, part 3, 1877, U.S. Army Continental Commands.

164. Tom Hill said that he and others "were ordered to go out in the prairie and out among the other tribes of Indians to look for Nez Perce Indians. . . . I obeyed the order and I left for good." U.S. Senate, *Memorial of the Nez Perce*. Supporting this contention, an enlisted man noted that some of the Nez Perces "want to hear from their people in the hills first before they surrender, so a few were let go to hold council with them, but leaving their arms." Zimmer, *Frontier Soldier*, 128.

165. Scott to Camp, September 2, 1913, folder 23, box 1, Camp Papers, BYU.

166. Miles to Terry, October 5, 1877, in Terry, "Report," 515; Zimmer, *Frontier Soldier*, 131; "Memoranda of Active Service . . . Maus"; penciled receipts, "Half Breed Camp, Milk River M.T. Oct. 13 77," and "Camp on Peoples Cr. Oct 14th 1877," entry 107, box 3, part 3, 1877, U.S. Army Continental Commands; Scott to Camp, January 18, 1914, folder 1, box 2, Camp Papers, BYU; Maus to Camp, February 2 [?], 1914, ibid.; Hugh Scott, *Some Memories of a Soldier*, 75–79; and unclassified envelope 110, 639, Camp Manuscript Field Notes, Camp Papers, LBNM. On crossing the battlefield, Scott viewed Looking Glass's unburied body still in the pit where he died.

167. Ilges to Miles, October 7, 1877, entry 107, box 3, part 3, 1877, U.S. Army Continental Commands. Ilges had led his citizen force on a reconnaissance along the western slopes of the Bear's Paws to Milk River at Terry's direction, intending to "pick up any small outlying parties of Nez Perces." Terry to Miles, n.d., entry 107, box 3, part 3, 1877, U.S. Army Continental Commands.

168. Tilton, "After the Nez Perces," 403.

169. Zimmer, *Frontier Soldier*, 129–30; Snyder, "Diary," October 7, 8, 1877; Tilton to Surgeon General, October 26, 1877, entry 624, box 1, Office of the Adjutant General; Tilton, "After the Nez Perces," 403; Romeyn, "Capture of Chief Joseph," 291; Edward J. McClernand, "The Second Regiment of Cavalry, 1866–91," in Rodenbough and Haskin, *Army of the United States*, 189; and Fort Benton *Record*, October 12, 1877.

170. Howard, "Report," 632–33; Mason to wife, October 6 and 11, 1877, in Davison, "A Century Ago," 18–19; and Miles to Howard, October 10, 1877, and

Howard to Miles, October 11, 1877, folder: Nez Perce War, box 3, Sladen Family Papers.

171. Mason to wife, October 13, 1877, in Davison, "A Century Ago," 19.

172. Miles to Howard, October 12, 1877, folder: Nez Perce War, box 3, Sladen Family Papers; Colonel Orlando H. Moore to Assistant Adjutant General, Department of Dakota, October 1, 1877, in Secretary of War, *Report . . . 1877*, 559; Regimental Returns . . . Seventh Cavalry, October 1877, roll 72; Tilton to Surgeon General, October 26, 1877, entry 624, box 1, Office of the Adjutant General; Romeyn, "Capture of Chief Joseph," 291; Mason to wife, October 13, 1877, in Davison, "A Century Ago," 19; Redington, "Scouting in Montana," 68; Snyder, "Diary," October 9–23, 1877; Tilton, "After the Nez Perces," 404; and Long, "Journal of the Marches," 1701.

173. Tilton, "After the Nez Perces," 404. Miles recalled that "as we were ferried over the band played, 'Hail to the Chief,' when suddenly they stopped and played a bar of that then familiar air, 'Not for Joe, oh no, no, not for Joseph!' etc., and then resumed the former air." Miles, *Serving the Republic*, 180–81. See also Miles, *Personal Recollections*, 278–79. This popular song, written by Arthur Lloyd, had been published in 1868 by C. H. Ditson and Company, New York City. The Cheyenne and Lakota scouts had arrived at the cantonment several days before the soldiers and prisoners and had created considerable anxiety among the families present there. Miles, *Personal Recollections*, 278. For the "welcome home" activities of the cantonment garrison, see Miles, *Personal Recollections*, 278–79; and Alice Baldwin, *Memoirs of . . . Baldwin*, 193–94 (reprinted in Carriker and Carriker, *An Army Wife*, 108–9).

174. Along these lines, the Chicago *Inter-Ocean*, October 19, 1877, allowed that "the captured Nez Perces Indians [sic] are a white elephant on the hands of the War Department, and it would have been a measure of economy, and saved much trouble if Chief Joseph had escaped General Miles and followed Sitting Bull into Canada."

175. See Olson, "The Nez Perce," 186, 189. For examples of pro–Nez Perces editorial coverage, see *Army and Navy Journal*, October 13, 1877; New York *Times*, October 15, 1877; *The Nation*, October 18, 1877; Bismarck *Tri-Weekly Tribune*, November 23, 1877; and especially, New York *Daily Graphic*, October 15, 1877, which called for "some tribute of respect . . . be paid these Nez Perce chiefs. If it is possible, in the enlargement of our regular army which must take place this winter, every one of these copper-colored leaders ought be made a second lieutenant."

176. Kelly, *"Yellowstone Kelly,"* 205.

177. Hardin, Diary, January 17, 1878.

178. McLaughlin, *My Friend the Indian*, 370.

179. Havre *Plaindealer*, June 21, August 16, 1902, April 18, 1903, August 29, 1903. Members of the contracted exhumation detail from Havre included Fred Atkins, Wesley Lay, George Aldars, Paul Worthall, Bob Mills, Walt Shamrick, Bill Eklarse, Fred Gierall, John McCarthy, and messrs. Purcy, Harvey, and Stone (first names unknown). Photograph and information provided by James Magera, Havre. Local tradition stated that the mass grave was attended through the years by range-riding cowboys, with whom it became a custom "to make frequent pilgrimages to the trench" and add "more rocks to the growing heap atop the grave." Great Falls *Tribune*, December 20, 1925.

180. "Ft. Assinniboine, Mont. Reburial"; and "Record of Funeral."

181. Havre *Plaindealer*, August 23, 30, October 11, 1902, February 26, 1921, July 23, 1925; Havre *Hill County Democrat*, September 8, 1925; Great Falls *Tribune*, December 20, 1925; U.S. House, *Marking the Site*, 1–2; and U.S. Senate, *Marking the Site*, 1–2. For General Scott's speech on July 19, 1925, on the Bear's Paw battlefield, see Laut, *Blazed Trail*, 134, 144–48. For details of the land transactions concerning the battlefield, 1901–15, see Jellum, *Fire in the Wind*, 276–77.

182. Great Falls *Tribune*, September 18, 1960.

183. Edward Fredlund to McWhorter, December 5, 1932, folder 5, and McWhorter to County Surveyor, July 7, 1935, folder 28, both in McWhorter Papers. The markers were set in concrete in 1964. Great Falls *Tribune*, September 28, 1964; and Billings *Gazette*, December 19, 1965.

Chapter 14

1. Cheyenne *Daily Leader*, November 6, 1877.

2. New York *Herald*, October 23, 1877.

3. Chicago *Tribune*, October 12, 1877; Gibbon to Miles, October 21, 1877, Miles Family Papers, LC; and *Army and Navy Journal*, December 1, 1877.

4. See, for example, General Orders No. 10, Headquarters, Second Cavalry, November 9, 1877, entry 107, box 3, part 3, 1877, U.S. Army Continental Commands.

5. Secretary of War, *Report . . . 1877*, xv.

6. *Army and Navy Journal*, December 15, 1877; and Boise, Idaho *Tri-Weekly Statesman*, November 20, 1877.

7. Entry 897, box 1, part 3, 1877, U.S. Army Continental Commands. See also Howard, "Report," 634–35; and *Army and Navy Journal*, December 29, 1877.

8. Howard to Adjutant General, Military Division of the Pacific, August 27, 1877, in Secretary of War, *Report . . . 1877*, 124–25.

9. Olson, "The Nez Perce," 182–86. Howard's letter to Potts appears, for example, in the Portland *Daily Oregonian*, September 4, 1877. For media fallout from the Sherman-Howard-Gilbert dispatch, see *Army and Navy Journal*, September 29, 1877.

10. Quoted in the Portland *Daily Oregonian*, September 7, 1877. The *Oregonian*, which supported Howard, deflected the criticism to his superior, McDowell, who himself had criticized Howard and who the paper cast as a "mere martinet" and as "a parlor general." Portland *Daily Oregonian*, September 7, 1877.

11. New York *Herald*, September 15, 1877.

12. Unclassified envelope 91, 537, Camp Manuscript Field Notes, Camp Papers, BYU. See also the Nez Perce opinion of Howard in the Cheyenne *Daily Leader*, November 3, 1877.

13. See the marginal notations by McDowell in "Copies of letters and telegrams."

14. Chicago *Inter-Ocean*, October 17, 1877. See, too, the evaluation of Howard's performance in John Carpenter, "General Howard," 144–45; and John Carpenter, *Sword and Olive Branch*, 264–65. Howard's apologia appeared in Howard, "True Story . . . Wallowa Campaign."

15. *Army and Navy Journal*, November 3, 1877.

16. Howard, "Report," 635–38.

17. DeMontravel, "Miles," 264–65.

18. Miles, "Report," 515; Miles, "Report of Col. Nelson A. Miles," October 6, 1877, in Secretary of War, *Report . . . 1877*, 75 (also in Miles, "Report," 515-16); and *Army and Navy Journal*, December 8, 1877.

19. Howard, "Report," 632.

20. C. E. S. Wood, "History by One"; Howard to Sheridan, October 19, 1877, in Howard, "Report," 633-34 (also in *Army and Navy Journal*, November 3, 1877); and Sheridan to Sherman, with enclosures, October 25, 1877, item 7113, roll 339, Nez Perce War Papers. See also the pro-Howard editorial probably generated by Wood in Chicago *Inter-Ocean*, October 17, 1877 (also in *Army and Navy Journal*, November 3, 1877); and Sara Bard Field (Mrs. C. E. S. Wood) to L. V. McWhorter, June 25, 1925, , folder 36, McWhorter Papers. The "flattering" quote is in the Boise, Idaho *Tri-Weekly Statesman*, November 1, 1877. Compounding the flap, General Terry called into question the propriety of Howard's having given Miles any orders on October 7 respecting the prisoners, terming the action a violation of the Articles of War, since Howard had had no command with him at the time. "His true position," wrote Terry, "was that of a spectator on the field." Furthermore, Terry questioned Howard's assumption and maintenance of command of Sturgis and his troops after the Nez Perces' surrender when their primary object for being in the area remained Sitting Bull's Sioux. General Sherman concurred in Terry's complaint, writing that "General Howard was clearly wrong in giving orders to Col. Miles concerning the future disposition of the Nez Perce prisoners—and still more so in his . . . giving instructions to Col. Sturgis." Terry to Sheridan, with endorsements, December 14, 1877, item 8076, roll 339, Nez Perce War Papers.

21. Howard to Sheridan, October 25, 1877, part 3, 1877, entry 897, box 1, U.S. Army Continental Commands.

22. Sherman to Miles, November 13, 1877, quoted in Wooster, *Nelson A. Miles*, 108.

23. Howard to Miles, December 26, 1877, folder: Nez Perce War, box 3, Sladen Family Papers.

24. Miles to Howard, January 31, 1878, ibid.

25. Howard to Miles, March 29, 1878, quoted in John Carpenter, *Sword and Olive Branch*, 263.

26. Howard to Wood, June 5, 1897, quoted in Wooster, *Nelson A. Miles*, 107. The dispute between Howard and Miles extended to their aides. In 1883, then-Lieutenant Colonel Edwin C. Mason erroneously asserted, in a lengthy piece in the Omaha *Herald* (March 15, 1883), that had Miles not been notified by couriers sent by Howard from Clark's Fork "he would have never been heard of in connection with the Nez Perces campaign." Miles's former aide, Major George W. Baird, wrote a blistering rejoinder: "In a word, the force of General Howard contributed nothing to the result of the campaign after the Indians left the Yellowstone three weeks before the time of . . . the surrender. The status of General Howard at the time of the surrender could not possibly have been that of a commander; he had no command." *Army and Navy Register*, July 19, 1883.

27. "Summary of Reports . . . Non-Effectiveness," 1-4. See also Lieutenant Colonel John C. Kelton to McDowell, March 13, 1878, in reference to the above summary, in *Army and Navy Journal*, May 4, 1878.

28. "Report of Casualties." Unaccountably, the Nez Perce scouts killed and wounded at Weippe Prairie on July 17, 1877, were excluded from this tally.

496 NOTES TO PAGES 332-335

29. U.S. Congress, Senate, 45th Cong., 2d sess., 1877, S. Doc. 14, p. 40, cited in McWhorter, *Hear Me*, 501.

30. Fort Benton *Record*, October 26, 1877; and Frazer, *Forts of the West*, 79.

31. Long, "Journal of the Marches," 1701; and Miles, *Personal Recollections*, 279.

32. Fouch took at least two historic photos of Joseph at the cantonment, as well as photos of the return of Miles's command with the Nez Perce prisoners on October 23. See Brust, "Into the Face of History," 107–10; James S. Brust, "The Find of a Lifetime," San Francisco *Chronicle*, February 28, 1993, *This World* section, 8–9; and Brust, "John H. Fouch," 8–9; and James S. Brust, letter to author, September 4, 1999.

33. Congratulatory telegrams are given in the Chicago *Tribune*, October 12, 1877. For the directive removing the Nez Perces, see Sherman to Sheridan, October 10, 1877, cited in Athearn, *William Tecumseh Sherman*, 320–21; and Sheridan to Adjutant General, October 10, 1877, item 6267, roll 338, Nez Perce War Papers. The Bureau of Indian Affairs notified the War Department that it harbored "grave objections" to removing the Nez Perces to Yankton or the Indian Territory and thought "they could be subsisted without difficulty at the Nez Perce Ag'cy." Adjutant General to Sheridan, October 18, 1877, roll 5, Nez Perce War, 1877, Division of the Missouri, Special File. In fact, Sheridan expressed certain support for returning the Nez Perces to Idaho, but feared that winter weather and the "reduced condition of the [captured] stock" prevented that course. Sheridan to McCrary, October 17, 1877, quoted in Chapman, "Nez Perces," 105. Besides the penalty factor, it was believed that, because of the murders and outrages in Idaho, "there would be no peace nor safety for Joseph and his Indians on their old reservation, or in its vicinity, as the friends and relatives of the victims would wage an unrelenting war upon the offenders." Commissioner of Indian Affairs, *Report . . . 1877*, 13. For Charles Erskine Scott Wood's view of how the removal of the Nez Perces "broke the real spirit of the surrender," see Wood to McWhorter, March 17, 1929, folder 25, McWhorter Papers.

34. Miles to Assistant Adjutant General, Department of Dakota, October 27, 1877, entry 107, box 3, part 3, 1877, U.S. Army Continental Commands.

35. Snyder, "Diary," October 29, 1877; Chicago *Inter-Ocean*, October 19, 1877; and Chicago *Tribune*, October 25, 1877. On October 24, Sherman wrote McDowell: "My efforts will be to send the Nez Perces where they will never disturb the people of Oregon or Idaho again." Quoted in Chapman, "Nez Perces," 105. Secretary of the Interior Carl Schurz and Commissioner of Indian Affairs Ezra A. Hayt concurred. Chapman, "Nez Perces," 105. See also Hutton, *Phil Sheridan and His Army*, 332–33.

36. Joseph [Heinmot Tooyalakekt], "An Indian's Views," 430.

37. Snyder, "Diary," October 31, 1877.

38. Baldwin to wife, November 6, 1877, quoted in Steinbach, *Long March*, 132.

39. For the river trip, which was not without mishap (one boat capsized and some of the Nez Perces apparently drowned), see Bond, *Flatboating*, 4–12.

40. Reed, "Recollections," 50–51.

41. Frederick Benteen to Assistant Adjutant General, District of the Yellowstone, October 24 and 27, 1877, entry 107, box 3, part 3, 1877, U.S. Army Continental Commands. Two of the Nez Perce warriors, Fine Hat and Bugle, had been sent

previously under military escort to Fort Lincoln. According to Miles, "these Indians committed many murders previous to the Nez Perces war, and . . . they are in a great measure responsible for the war. The Nez Perces say that they are very bad men, and outlaws." Miles to Assistant Adjutant General, Department of Dakota, October 25, 1877, item 7041, roll 339, Nez Perce War Papers. Sheridan wanted to send these men to Florida, but on Sherman's recommendation sent them instead to the military prison at Fort Leavenworth. Sheridan to Adjutant General, November 8, 1877, items 6911 and 7265, roll 339, Nez Perce War Papers.

42. "Nez Perce Funeral," 260; and Reed, "Recollections," 51.

43. Fort Buford Post Returns, November, 1877, transcribed in vol. 5, Fort Buford Records; and Regimental Returns . . . Seventh Cavalry, November 1877, roll 72.

44. Bismarck *Tri-Weekly Tribune*, November 21, 1877; Miles, *Personal Recollections*, 279–80; and Bond, *Flatboating*, 12–21.

45. Bond, *Flatboating*, 22; and Reed, "Recollections," 54–55.

46. Sheridan to Adjutant General, with Sherman's endorsement, November 15, 1877, November 14, 1877, item 7053, roll 339, Nez Perce War Papers.

47. Quoted in Chicago *Inter-Ocean*, November 23, 1877. A reporter noted that the Nez Perces "often cried and wept like children over their ill fate. Joseph cheered them, but not without tears rolling down his own cheeks." Cheyenne *Daily Leader*, November 25, 1877.

48. Francis Haines, *Nez Perce Indians*, 290–91. The other attendees were Yellow Bull, Yellow Wolf, and the Palouse, Husis Kute. *Army and Navy Journal*, December 1, 1877. For an account of other activities during the Nez Perces' stay in Bismarck, see Bismarck *Tri-Weekly Tribune*, November 21, 23, 1877.

49. Bismarck *Weekly Tribune*, November 23, 1877.

50. Full details of the trip to Fort Leavenworth are in Reed, "Recollections," 55–64.

51. "Report of the General of the Army," November 7, 1877, in Secretary of War, *Report . . . 1877*.

52. Pope to Sheridan, telegram, November 15, 1877, roll 5, Nez Perce War, 1877, Division of the Missouri, Special File; Pope to Sheridan, November 25, 1877, ibid.; and Leavenworth *Daily Times*, November 27, 1877. For details of the arrival of the Indians, see Leavenworth *Daily Times*, November 27, 1877.

53. Howard to Adjutant General, Military Division of the Pacific, November 27, 1877, item 7685, roll 339, Nez Perce War Papers; and Howard to Adjutant General, Military Division of the Pacific, with Sherman's endorsement, December 14, 1877, ibid. In declining Howard's request, Sherman wrote: "There is no reason why they should be carried at great cost to Fort Leavenworth and afterwards to the Indian Territory. They have already subjected the U.S. to enough cost and trouble."

54. Confusing things even more, Sheridan had wired Pope on November 24 that he would receive 431 Indians—79 men, 178 women, and 174 children. Pope to Assistant Adjutant General, Military Division of the Missouri, December 4, 1877, roll 5, Nez Perce War, 1877, Division of the Missouri, Special File; and Commissioner of Indian Affairs, *Report . . . 1878*, xxxiii.

55. Elvid Hunt, *History of Fort Leavenworth*, 154.

56. Quoted in Commissioner of Indian Affairs, *Report . . . 1878*, xxxiii.

57. Ibid.; and Morris and McReynolds, *Historical Atlas of Oklahoma*, map 23. In 1878, Congress appropriated twenty thousand dollars for removing the Nez Perces from Fort Leavenworth to the Indian Territory. *Statutes . . . 1877 to . . . 1879*, 74.

58. Joseph [Heinmot Tooyalakekt], "An Indian's Views," 431. For the Nez Perce tract in the Indian Territory, see Morris and McReynolds, *Historical Atlas of Oklahoma*, maps 14, 20.

59. DeMontravel, "Miles," 251–53; and Chapman, "Nez Perces," 112, 115–16, 120–21. For details of the bureaucratic machinations governing the removal of the Nez Perce prisoners to Fort Leavenworth, the Indian Territory, and the Northwest, see Chapman, "Nez Perces," 102–21. See also Stanley Clark, "Nez Perces in Exile," 213–32; and Slickpoo and Walker, *Noon Nee-Me-Poo*, 195–200. Thirty-three widows and orphans were allowed to return to Idaho in 1883. Dozier, "Nez Perce Homecoming," 23. Details of the physical removal of the people from the Indian Territory to Idaho and Washington are in Ruby, "Return of the Nez Perce." For the personal experiences of one Nez Perce tribesman (Josiah Red Wolf), see Alcorn and Alcorn, "Aged Nez Perce," 65–66. For more overviews of the removal, see Josephy, *Nez Perce Indians*, 637–42; and Francis Haines, *Nez Perces*, 330–37.

60. Black Eagle's estimate included 140 men and boys and 93 women and girls. McWhorter, *Hear Me*, 499.

61. Quoted in McWhorter, *Hear Me*, 508–9. Yellow Wolf claimed that after the surrender Joseph asked him to go find his wife and daughter. Yellow Wolf went out alone and somehow overtook this group the next day, although they supposedly had left on September 30. Despite the chronological problems in Yellow Wolf's account of his journey to Canada, it is compelling and otherwise accurate in its particulars. See McWhorter, *Yellow Wolf*, 229–33.

62. McWhorter, *Hear Me*, 510.

63. Fort Benton *Record*, November 15, 1877.

64. See chapter 13, note 126. A courier who reached Terry's commission en route to Canada on October 12 told of encountering White Bird with twenty-four men and about thirty women and children (totaling about fifty-four people). New York *Herald*, October 17, 1877.

65. Quoted in McWhorter, *Hear Me*, 510–11.

66. Genin letter, December 13, 1877, in Slaughter, "Leaves from Northwestern History," cited in McWhorter, *Hear Me*, 511 n. 4. John Howard, one of Miles's scouts, reported on October 20 that he had met White Bird "and 14 warriors & about 7 women at the Half Breed Camp about 5 miles from the line en route to the Teton camp. They were at first willing to surrender but 'White Bird' dissuaded them and in spite of all the inducements I offered I could not get the Halfbreeds to help me attack them." Howard to Miles, October 20, 1877, entry 107, box 3, part 3, 1877, U.S. Army Continental Commands.

67. Shot-in-Head, Mrs., Account.

68. John Turner, *North-West Mounted Police*, 1:340–42.

69. Alcorn and Alcorn, "Old Nez Perce Recalls," 71–72.

70. MacDonald, "Nez Perces," 272–73. McWhorter's informants told him that Sitting Bull reportedly organized a body to go to the aid of the besieged Nez Perces at Bear's Paw, but on meeting White Bird's party and learning of Joseph's surrender, it was deemed too late to help and the main relief force turned back

with the refugees to Sitting Bull's camp. McWhorter, *Hear Me*, 513. See also John Turner, *North-West Mounted Police*, 1:340–41.

71. Quoted in McWhorter, *Hear Me*, 513.

72. McWhorter, *Hear Me*, 514. The Oglala Black Elk recounted his meeting with a party of Nez Perce refugees from Bear's Paw. "When we got back to camp, everyone put their arms around the shoulders of the [Nez Perce] people and began to wail. I cried all day there." Black Elk, *Sixth Grandfather*, 207.

73. The rapprochement had been suggested by the British authorities in Canada. Members of the commission besides Terry were Diplomat Albert Gallatin Lawrence; Captain Henry C. Corbin, secretary; and Captain Edward W. Smith, Eighteenth Infantry, aide. Accompanying the commissioners were Jerome B. Stillson, correspondent for the New York *Herald*; Charles S. Diehl, correspondent for the Chicago *Times*; and John J. Healey, who reported for the Fort Benton *Record*. John Turner, *North-West Mounted Police*, 1:362; and Utley, *Lance and the Shield*, 194–97, 372–73. For Diehl's reminiscence, see Diehl, *Staff Correspondent*, 117–19, 124–31.

74. Commissioner James F. Macleod wrote: "The fact that about 100 Nez Perces men, women and children, wounded and bleeding, who had escaped from the United States troops, had come into their [Sioux] camp the day before they had left, appeared to have a great effect upon them; and they were evidently afraid that the American soldiers would not be prevented from crossing the line to attack them." Macleod to Minister of the Interior David Mills, October 27, 1877, in "Papers . . . Nez Perce Indians," 3.

75. See New York *Herald*, October 22, 1877. For digests of the council proceedings, see John Turner, *North-West Mounted Police*, 1:365–72; Utley, *Lance and the Shield*, 194–97; Hoopes, *Road to the Little Big Horn*, 233–35; and Manzione, *"I Am Looking to the North for My Life,"* 101–3. A transcript is in *Report of the Commission . . . to Meet the Sioux Indian Chief, Sitting Bull*, 6–10.

76. *Report of the Commission . . . to Meet the Sioux Indian Chief, Sitting Bull*, 12.

77. McWhorter, *Hear Me*, 515–16.

78. Scout John Howard to Miles, November 3, 1877, entry 107, box 3, part 3, 1877, U.S. Army Continental Commands; Howard to Miles, January 10, 1878, ibid.; and Lieutenant Colonel Daniel Huston to Miles, January 9, 1878, ibid. Father Genin also reported the Sioux and Nez Perce in the Bear's Paw Mountains. Bozeman *Times*, December 27, 1877. Another report of Sitting Bull's camping on the battlefield appeared in Fort Benton *Record*, November 10, reprinted, December 14, 1877. See also "Chief Joseph's People Join Sitting Bull," in Vestal, *New Sources of Indian History*, 243–44.

79. Quoted in John Turner, *North-West Mounted Police*, 1:374.

80. Quoted in MacEwan, *Sitting Bull*, 122.

81. Sheridan to Adjutant General, December 27, 1877, item 7974, roll 339, Nez Perce War Papers. The Nez Perce Captain George, who went into Canada purportedly to find Joseph's daughter, returned late in 1877 to report that the Nee-Me-Poo wanted to return to the United States and surrender and that they planned to slip across the line in small parties. *Army and Navy Journal*, January 5, 1878.

82. Irvine to Ilges, March 29, 1878, in "Papers . . . Nez Perce Indians," 19. For Irvine's explanation of how this perception came about, see Irvine to Frederick White, November 10, 1878, ibid., 18–19.

83. Quoted in John Turner, *North-West Mounted Police*, 1:374.

84. Ibid., 390, 391.

85. A detailed account, from the Nez Perce perspective, of this party's odyssey in returning to Idaho is in McWhorter, *Yellow Wolf*, 238–82.

86. Fahey, *Flathead Indians*, 201; McWhorter, *Hear Me*, 517–18; Captain William Falck, Second Infantry, to Assistant Adjutant General, Department of the Columbia, August 1, 1878, in McDowell, "Report," 180; and Thompson, *Historic Resource Study, Fort Lapwai*, 86. For details of the skirmish with the miners on Rock Creek, see Jones, "Rock Creek Massacre." The Nez Perce account of the incident is in McWhorter, *Yellow Wolf*, 254–55.

87. Details of this fight are in Gibbon, "Report of the Commanding General," 68; *Record of Engagements*, 78; and J. H. McRae, "The Third Regiment of Infantry," in Rodenbough and Haskin, *Army of the United States*, 449. For Yellow Wolf's account, in which it is claimed that no Indians were killed or wounded in the clash with Wallace's soldiers, see McWhorter, *Yellow Wolf*, 260–70 (the excerpt from Gibbon's report, "Report of the Commanding General," cited above, is reproduced in ibid., 270 n. 6).

88. Falck to Assistant Adjutant General, Department of the Columbia, August 1, 1878, in McDowell, "Report," 180–81.

89. Thompson, *Historic Resource Study, Fort Lapwai*, 86; McWhorter, *Yellow Wolf*, 283–84, 287; and McWhorter, *Hear Me*, 520.

90. "The party of Indians who left Camp Joseph Monday afternoon for Sitting Bull's camp were Yellow Bull, the brother-in-law of White Bird; Kansas Rutt [Husis Kute], a preacher, well known in Gen. Howard's report; and Espow Yous [sic], a brave noted for his truthfulness. Ben. Clark, who also accompanied them, is an old Cheyenne scout, and will go with them as far as Bismarck, where he is to join a party of 300 Cheyennes [en route to the Indian Territory (Clark's orders changed and he went on with the three Nez Perces)]. . . . The Nez Perces chiefs after leaving Bismarck will be accompanied by a guide and go via Fort Benton to Fort Walsh, where they will meet White Bird and consult with him, reporting the state in which they left Chief Joseph and his warriors, together with the women and children." *Army and Navy Journal*, May 11, 1878.

91. Assistant Adjutant General, Department of Dakota, to Miles, May 7, 1878, in "Papers . . . Nez Perce Indians," 7. Ben Clark was a favorite of General Sheridan, having served the army in the West in various capacities since the "Mormon" War of the 1850s. Sheridan trusted him implicitly, and although he could not speak the Nee-Me-Poo tongue, he was recognized as a master of Indian sign language. Hutton, *Phil Sheridan and His Army*, 300–301. Clark intimated that he was there because Joseph wanted him to bring his daughter back to him. She, of course, had returned to Idaho. "Ben Clark," 19, folder 3, box 2, Camp Manuscript Field Notes, Walter M. Camp Papers, BYU.

92. Miles to Baird, May 24, 1878, "Papers . . . Nez Perce Indians," 7–8.

93. Macleod to Baird, June 22 [?], 1878, ibid., 8. The implication here is that the tribesmen were told that they would be returned to Idaho if they surrendered.

94. Baird to Macleod, June 21, 1878, ibid., 6. Macleod wrote that the Nez Perces had told Irvine that Gilson, who was known among them, "was not wanted back again." Macleod to Baird, June 22 (?), 1878, ibid., 8.

95. The foregoing exchange has been excerpted from the transcript of the

proceedings in ibid., 9–16. For digests of the council, see John Turner, *North-West Mounted Police*, 1:395–98; *Winners of the West*, April 1940; and Manzione, "*I Am Looking to the North for My Life*," 119–24.

96. MacDonald to McWhorter, quoted in McWhorter, *Hear Me*, 522. One Nez Perce refugee, a child of one of the three from Fort Leavenworth, returned with the party to the United States. Baird to Assistant Adjutant General, Military Division of the Missouri, July 11, 1878, in McWhorter, *Hear Me*, 522–23; and "Ben Clark," 19, folder 3, box 2, Camp Manuscript Field Notes, Walter M. Camp Papers, BYU.

97. Deer Lodge *New North-West*, August 9, 1878, quoted in McWhorter, *Hear Me*, 523–24. MacDonald composed the following portrait of White Bird during his visit: "In person the White Bird, a name which implies the Pelican, . . . is upon a close view a handsome man, of about five feet nine in his moccasins, square shouldered, long-waisted and of clear, sinewy limbs. His hair when in prime of life was of a dark chestnut, rather than black; his face of a longer than rounder form, his cranium advancing, his nostril and chin expressive; his eye strong and observant; his cast of face perpendicular." MacDonald, "Nez Perce Campaign." It is not certain that MacDonald was in Canada at the time of the meeting; his account might have been hearsay derived later from Nez Perces who were there. George Kush, communication with author, Lethbridge, Alberta, August 4, 1996.

98. Irvine wrote that: "White Bird, the Nez Perce chief, can have but very few lodges with him, as during the past month I have visited many Blood and Piegan camps, and have seen several Nez Perce lodges among them." Irvine to White, November 10, 1878, in "Papers . . . Sioux Indians," 126; John Turner, *North-West Mounted Police*, 1:399; and Utley, *Lance and the Shield*, 202.

99. Walsh to Irvine, December 30, 1878, in "Papers . . . Sioux Indians," 128.

100. Walsh to Irvine, January 25, 1879, ibid., 129.

101. Ibid., 129–31; and Utley, *Lance and the Shield*, 204–6.

102. *Army and Navy Journal*, December 7, 1878.

103. Alcorn and Alcorn, "Old Nez Perce Recalls," 72.

104. McWhorter, *Hear Me*, 517 and 517 n. 22.

105. Jean Louis Lagere to Walter M. Camp, March 26, 1912, folder 21, box 1, Camp Papers, BYU.

106. Quoted in Dempsey, "An Indian's Death in Exile," 25.

107. Weptas Nut (No Feather), Interview; and Maxwell and Morris, Interview. Details of the death of White Bird and the trial and imprisonment of his assassin are comprehensively treated in Dempsey, "An Indian's Death in Exile," 26–29. See also McWhorter, *Hear Me*, 524.

108. Miles to Terry, October 17, 1877, folder: Nez Perce Campaign 1877, box T-2: 5th Infantry to Aug. 1881, Miles Papers, MHI.

109. McWhorter, *Hear Me*, 501.

110. Olson, "The Nez Perce," 186–89.

EPILOGUE

1. For Miles's later career, see Wooster, *Nelson A. Miles*, chaps. 8–15.

2. Warner, *Generals in Blue*, 238–39; and Heitman, *Historical Register and Dictionary*, 1:546.

3. McDermott, *Forlorn Hope*, 164; and Heitman, *Historical Register and Dictionary*, 1:785.

4. McDermott, *Forlorn Hope*, 140–43, 163–64; and unidentified San Francisco newspaper, August 2, 1910 clipping, copy provided by Brad Dahlquist.

5. Heitman, *Historical Register and Dictionary*, 1:1025.

6. Faust, *Campaigning in the Philippines*, photo opposite 193.

7. Miller, Appointment, Commission, and Personal File.

8. Mary E. Condon, "George Miller Sternberg," in Spiller, *Dictionary of American Military Biography*, 3:1047–50; Sternberg, *George Miller Sternberg*, passim; and Heitman, *Historical Register and Dictionary*, 1:921. See also Gibson, *Soldier in White*.

9. Warner, *Generals in Blue*, 172.

10. Powell, *Powell's Records*, 431; and Norwood, Appointment, Commission, and Personal File.

11. Guie and McWhorter, *Adventures in Geyser Land*, 7; Great Falls *Tribune*, December 26, 1926; and McWhorter, *Yellow Wolf*, 174 n. 5.

12. Warner, *Generals in Blue*, 487.

13. Hammer, *Biographies of the Seventh Cavalry*, 155.

14. Godfrey, Appointment, Commission, and Personal File; and Hammer, *Biographies of the Seventh Cavalry*, 188.

15. Romeyn, Appointment, Commission, and Personal File.

16. Heitman, *Historical Register and Dictionary*, 1:1054; and Bingham, *Charles Erskine Scott Wood*, 7–10.

17. Jerome, Appointment, Commission, and Personal File; and Barry Johnson, "Solved."

18. Trafzer and Scheureman, *Chief Joseph's Allies*, 24–26.

19. McWhorter, *Hear Me*, 546.

20. Ibid., 379, 604; and McWhorter, *Yellow Wolf*, 13–18.

21. Alcorn and Alcorn, "Aged Nez Perce," 54; and McDermott, *Forlorn Hope*, 162.

22. Gidley, *Kopet*, 35–39.

Bibliography

Adkison, Norman B. *Indian Braves and Battles with More Nez Perce Lore.* Grangeville, Idaho: Idaho County Free Press, 1967.

———. *Nez Perce Indian War and Original Stories.* Grangeville, Idaho: Idaho County Free Press, 1966.

After the Battle: Sturgis—Seventh Cavalry, Miles—Fifth Infantry. Bryan, Tex.: privately printed, 1978.

Aikens, C. Melvin. "The Far West." In *Ancient Native Americans*, edited by Jesse D. Jennings, 164–73. San Francisco: W. H. Freeman and Company, 1978.

Alcorn, Rowena L., and Gordon D. Alcorn. "Aged Nez Perce Recalls the 1877 Tragedy." *Montana The Magazine of Western History* 15 (October 1965): 54–67.

———. "Old Nez Perce Recalls Tragic Retreat of 1877." *Montana The Magazine of Western History* 13 (winter 1963): 66–74.

Allen, Jirah Isham. Letter, to C. O. Marcyes, October 10, 1927. TS copy. Yellowstone National Park Archives, Mammoth, Wyo.

Allen, Peter. Interview by Walter M. Camp. October 17, 1913. Packet FF 12. Walter M. Camp Papers. Western History Department. Denver Public Library, Denver, Colo.

———. "Military Expedition and Campaign and Battle of Bear Paw Mountains M.T., Sept. 30th, 1877." July 11, 1913. Packet FF 12. Walter M. Camp Papers. Western History Department. Denver Public Library, Denver, Colo.

Anderson, Alfred L. *The Geology and Mineral Resources of the Region about Orofino, Idaho.* Idaho Bureau of Mines and Geology. Moscow: University of Idaho, 1930.

Anderson, LeRoy. "Bear Paw Battlefield: Research and Field Notes, 1992–1993." TS. Copy provided by LeRoy Anderson in the collection of the author, Arvada, Colo.

———. "Nez Perce Trail—Blaine County, Cow Island Freighter Trail." June 15, 1992. TS. Vertical Files. Montana Historical Society Library, Helena.

Aoki, Haruo. "Chief Joseph's Words." *Idaho Yesterdays* 33 (fall 1989): 16–21.
———. *Nez Perce Texts.* Berkeley: University of California Press, 1979.
Arnold, R. Ross. *Indian Wars of Idaho.* Caldwell, Idaho: Caxton Printers, Ltd., 1932.
Arthur, Mark. Interview by Walter M. Camp. n.d. Unclassified Envelope 127. Camp Manuscript Field Notes. Walter M. Camp Papers. Little Bighorn Battlefield National Monument, Crow Agency, Mont.
Artillery Tactics, United States Army, Assimilated to the Tactics of Infantry and Cavalry. New York: D. Appleton and Company, 1874.
Athearn, Robert G. "Frontier Critics of the Western Army." *Montana The Magazine of Western History* 5 (spring 1955): 16–28.
———. *William Tecumseh Sherman and the Settlement of the West.* Norman: University of Oklahoma Press, 1956.
Atwood, Wallace W. *The Physiographic Provinces of North America.* Boston: Ginn and Company, 1940.
Bailey, Harry Lee. "An Infantry Second Lieutenant in the Nez Perce War of 1877." MS. Lucullus V. McWhorter Papers. Manuscripts, Archives and Special Collections. Holland Library, Washington State University, Pullman.
Bailey, Robert G. *River of No Return (The Great Salmon River of Idaho).* Rev. ed. Lewiston, Idaho: R. G. Bailey Printing Company, 1983.
Baily, Joe. "Nez Perces in Yellowstone." *Pacific Northwesterner* 21 (winter 1967): 1–12.
Baird, George W. "The Capture of Chief Joseph and the Nez-Perces." *International Review* 7 (August 1879): 209–15.
———. "General Miles's Indian Campaigns." *Century* 42 (July 1891): 351–70.
———. Papers. Microfilm. Kansas State Historical Society, Topeka.
Baldwin, Alice Blackwood. *Memoirs of the Late Frank D. Baldwin, Major General, U.S.A.* Los Angeles: Wetzel Publishing Company, Inc., 1929.
Baldwin, Frank D. Interview by Walter M. Camp. June 16, 1919. Interview Notes. MS 57. Box 2. Walter M. Camp Papers. Microfilm. Archives and Manuscripts Division. Harold B. Lee Library, Brigham Young University, Provo, Utah.
Bancroft, Hubert Howe. *History of Washington, Idaho, and Montana, 1845–1889.* San Francisco: History Company, Publishers, 1890.
Barker, Luther. "The Campaign and Capture of Chief Joseph." Parts 1–3. *Oregon Veteran* 5 (December 1922): 7, 30; 6 (January 1923): 7, 30; 6 (February 1923): 7, 30–31.
Barrett, Tom. "A Near Encounter with the Nez Perce Indians." n.d. TS. Research Files. Big Hole National Battlefield, Wisdom, Mont.
Barsness, John, and William Dickinson. "Minutemen of Montana." *Montana The Magazine of Western History* 20 (spring 1960): 2–9.
Bartlett, Richard A. *Yellowstone: A Wilderness Besieged.* Tucson: University of Arizona Press, 1985.

Bauer, C. Max. "The Ben Stone Incident of 1877." *Nature Notes* 19 (March–April 1942): 21–23.

Beal, Merrill D. *"I Will Fight No More Forever": Chief Joseph and the Nez Perce War*. Seattle: University of Washington Press, 1963.

———. *The Story of Man in Yellowstone*. Rev. ed. Mammoth, Wyo.: Yellowstone Library and Museum Association, 1960.

Bearss, Edwin C. "National Register of Historic Places Inventory–Nomination Form, Bear Paw Battlefield." National Park Service. 1988. National Register of Historic Places, Washington, D.C.

Bell, John T. "The Life of 'Ne-cot-ta' the Last of the Great Warrior Chiefs." MS. Collection of James Magera, Havre, Mont.

Bennett, Eileen, ed. "The History and Legend of Bugler Bernard A. Brooks in the Saga of the Nez Perce War in Clark County." *Snake River Echoes: A Quarterly of Idaho History* 13, no. 2 (1984): 31–39.

Benteen, Frederick W. "Trouting on Clark's Fork." *Recreation* 3 (July–December 1895): 234–35.

Beyer, W. F., and O. F. Keydel, eds. *Deeds of Valor*. 2 vols. Detroit: Perrien-Keydel Company, 1907.

Biddle, Henry J. Collection. Biddle Family Papers. Special Collections. Knight Library. University of Oregon, Eugene.

Biddle, Jonathan W. Diary. Box 2. Henry J. Biddle Collection. Biddle Family Papers. Special Collections. Knight Library, University of Oregon, Eugene.

Bingham, Edwin R. *Charles Erskine Scott Wood*. Western Writer Series, no. 94. Boise, Idaho: Boise State University, 1990.

Black Elk. *The Sixth Grandfather: Black Elk's Teachings Given to John G. Neihardt*. Edited by Raymond J. Demallie. Lincoln: University of Nebraska Press, 1984.

Board of Indian Commissioners. *Eighth Annual Report of the Board of Indian Commissioners for the Year 1876*. Washington, D.C.: Government Printing Office, 1877.

Boatner, Mark M., III. *The Civil War Dictionary*. New York: David McKay Company, Inc., 1959.

Bolino, August C. "The Role of Mining in the Economic Development of Idaho Territory." *Oregon Historical Quarterly* 59 (June 1958): 116–51.

Bond, Fred G. *Flatboating on the Yellowstone, 1877*. New York: New York Public Library, 1925.

Bonney, Orrin H., and Lorraine Bonney. *Battle Drums and Geysers: The Life and Journals of Lt. Gustavus Cheyney Doane, Soldier and Explorer of the Yellowstone and Snake River Regions*. Chicago: Swallow Press, Inc., 1970.

Bosler, E. R. Reminiscence. SC 183. Montana Historical Society Archives, Helena.

Bowen, William H. C. Papers. Manuscripts Division. U.S. Army Military History Institute, Army War College, Carlisle, Pa.

Boyd, James. Interview by David Heilger. Wolf Point, Mont., May 28, 1925. Collection of James Magera, Havre, Mont.

Bradley, Charles Crane, Jr. *The Handsome People: A History of the Crow Indians and the Whites*. Billings, Mont.: Council for Indian Education, 1991.

Brady, Cyrus Townsend. *Northwestern Fights and Fighters*. Garden City, N.Y.: Doubleday, Page and Company, 1907.

Brant, Abram. Letter, to Charles H. Dawsey, January 10, 1878. Folder 285. National Archives Non-Accessioned Materials. Little Bighorn Battlefield National Monument, Crow Agency, Mont.

Breckenridge, Roy M., et al. *Preliminary Review of the Geology of the Tolo Lake Fossil Site, Idaho County, Idaho*. Idaho Geological Survey. Moscow: University of Idaho, 1994.

Brimlow, George F. File. Manuscripts Division. Idaho State Historical Society, Boise.

———, ed. "Nez Perce War Diary of Private Frederick Mayer, Troop L, 1st United States Cavalry." In *Idaho State Historical Society Seventeenth Biennial Report, 1939–1940*, 27–31. Boise: State Historical Society of Idaho, 1940.

Brininstool, E. A. Collection. Archives and Manuscripts Division. Harold B. Lee Library, Brigham Young University, Provo, Utah.

Brooke, John R. "A Ride through the Land of the Nez Perces." *Recreation* 15 (November 1901): 354–56.

Brosnan, C. J. Collection. Special Collections. University of Idaho Library, Moscow.

Brown, Mark H. *The Flight of the Nez Perce*. New York: G. P. Putnam's Sons, 1967.

———. "The Joseph Legend." *Westerners' Brand Book* (Chicago) 25 (September 1968): 49–51, 55–56.

———. "The Joseph Myth." *Montana The Magazine of Western History* 22 (winter 1971): 2–17.

———. "Yellowstone Tourists and the Nez Perce." *Montana The Magazine of Western History* 16 (July 1966), 30–43.

Brown, Mark H., and W. R. Felton. *The Frontier Years: L. A. Huffman, Photographer of the Plains*. New York: Henry Holt and Company, 1965.

Brown, William Carey. Papers. Western History Collection. Norlin Library, University of Colorado, Boulder.

Bruce, Robert. "Comments of Lovell H. Jerome, December 13, 1932." TS. Folder 36. Lucullus V. McWhorter Papers. Manuscripts, Archives and Special Collections. Holland Library, Washington State University, Pullman.

Brust, James S. "Into the Face of History." *American Heritage* 43 (November 1992): 104–11.

———. "John H. Fouch: First Post Photographer at Fort Keogh." *Montana The Magazine of Western History* 44 (spring 1994): 2–17.

Buck, Amos. "Review of the Battle of the Big Hole." In vol. 7. of *Contributions to the Historical Society of Montana*, 117–30. Helena, Mont.: Historical and Miscellaneous Library, 1910.

Buck, Henry. "The Story of the Nez Perce Indian Campaign during the Summer of 1877." 1922. TS. SC 492. Montana Historical Society Archives, Helena.

Buecker, Thomas R. *Fort Robinson and the American West, 1874–1899*. Lincoln: Nebraska State Historical Society, 1999.

Burdick, Usher L., and Eugene D. Hart. *Jacob Horner and the Indian Campaigns of 1876 and 1877 (The Sioux and the Nez Perce)*. Baltimore: Wirth Brothers, 1942.

Burgunder, Benjamin. "Nez Perce War." n.d. MS. Cheney Cowles Museum, Spokane, Wash.

Burns, Robert Ignatius. *The Jesuits and the Indian Wars of the Northwest*. New Haven, Conn.: Yale University Press, 1966.

Camp, Walter M. Manuscripts. Lilly Library, Indiana University, Bloomington.

———. Papers. Little Bighorn Battlefield National Monument, Crow Agency, Mont.

———. Papers. Microfilm. Archives and Manuscripts Division. Harold B. Lee Library, Brigham Young University, Provo, Utah.

———. Papers. Western History Department. Denver Public Library, Denver, Colo.

Canby, Major James P. "Report of Indian depredations in Idaho Territory." August 27, 1877. Entry 700. Evidence Concerning Depredations Claims, 1835–96. Records of the United States Bureau of Indian Affairs. RG 75. National Archives, Washington, D.C.

"Capture of the Nez Perces, Young Two Moon's Account." Folder 59. Walter M. Camp Papers. Little Bighorn Battlefield National Monument, Crow Agency, Mont.

Carpenter, Havilah. "An Account of His Army Service by Vilah Carpenter." ca. 1937. MS. Copy provided by James H. Gordon, Post Falls, Idaho, in the collection of the author, Arvada, Colo.

Carpenter, John A. "General Howard and the Nez Perce War of 1877." *Pacific Northwest Quarterly* 49 (October 1958): 129–45.

———. *Sword and Olive Branch: Oliver Otis Howard*. Pittsburgh: University of Pittsburgh Press, 1964.

Carriker, Robert C., and Eleanor R. Carriker, eds. *An Army Wife on the Frontier: The Memoirs of Alice Blackwood Baldwin*. Salt Lake City, Utah: Tanner Trust Fund, 1975.

Carroll, John M., comp. and ed. *Camp Talk: The Very Private Letters of Frederick W. Benteen of the Seventh U.S. Cavalry to His Wife, 1871 to 1878*. Mattituck, N.Y.: J. M. Carroll and Company, 1983.

———, ed. *The Benteen-Goldin Letters on Custer and His Last Battle*. New York: Liveright, 1974.

———, ed. *The Papers of the Order of Indian Wars*. Fort Collins, Colo.: Old Army Press, 1975.

———, and Byron Price, comps. *Roll Call on the Little Big Horn, 28 June 1876*. Fort Collins, Colo.: Old Army Press, 1974.

Catlin, John B. "The Battle of the Big Hole." John B. Catlin Reminiscences. SC 520. Montana Historical Society Archives, Helena.

———. Reminiscences. SC 520. Montana Historical Society Archives, Helena.

Cavalry Tactics, United States Army, Assimilated to the Tactics of Infantry and Artillery. New York: D. Appleton and Company, 1876.

Chandler, Melbourne C., comp. *Of Garry Owen in Glory: The History of the Seventh United States Cavalry Regiment.* Annandale, Va.: Turnpike Press, Inc., 1960.

Chapman, Berlin B. "Nez Perces in the Indian Territory." *Oregon Historical Quarterly* 50 (June 1949): 98–121.

Chapman, Winfield S. Interview by Walter M. Camp. January 25, 1913. Transcribed. Nez Perce Indian Wars 1. Camp Manuscript Field Notes. Walter M. Camp Papers. Little Bighorn Battlefield National Monument, Crow Agency, Mont.

Chappell, Edith M. "Early Life of David Chambers Cummings." n.d. MS. Item 628. Federal Writers Project Collection. Wyoming State Archives and Historical Department, Cheyenne.

Chedsey, Zona, and Carolyn Frei, eds. *Idaho County Voices: A People's History from the Pioneers to the Present.* Grangeville, Idaho: Idaho County Centennial Commission, 1990.

Cheetham, R. N. "Peo-peo Tholekt's Artistry in Historical Research." In *The Record*, vol. 24., 62–65. Pullman: Washington State University, 1963.

Chittenden, Hiram M. *The Yellowstone National Park: Historical and Descriptive.* Cincinnati, Ohio: Robert Clarke Company, 1903.

Clark, J. Stanley. "The Nez Perces in Exile." *Pacific Northwest Quarterly* 26 (July 1945): 213–32.

Clark, James. Interview by Walter M. Camp. October 13, 1912. Item 10. Walter M. Camp Papers. Robert S. Ellison Collection. Western History Department. Denver Public Library, Denver, Colo.

"Classified Return of Wounds and Injuries Received in Action on the 11th & 12th days of July 1877 at Battle of Clearwater." Entry 624. Box 1. Records of the Office of the Adjutant General. RG 94. National Archives, Washington, D.C.

Clough, J. P. "Recollections of the Nez Perce Indian War of 1877, and Their Entrance into Lemhi Valley." March 1935. TS. Manuscripts Division. Idaho State Historical Society, Boise.

Coale, George L. "Ethnohistorical Sources for the Nez Perce Indians." Parts 1 and 2. *Ethnohistory*, 3 (summer, 1956): 246–55; 3 (fall 1956): 346–60.

Commissioner of Indian Affairs. "Report of Civil and Military Commission to Nez Perce Indians Washington Territory and the Northwest." December 1, 1876. In *Report of the Commissioner of Indian Affairs, 1877.* Washington, D.C.: Government Printing Office, 1877.

Commissioner of Indian Affairs. *Report of the Commissioner of Indian Affairs, 1859*. Washington, D.C.: Government Printing Office, 1859.

Commissioner of Indian Affairs. *Report of the Commissioner of Indian Affairs, 1873*. Washington, D.C.: Government Printing Office, 1874.

Commissioner of Indian Affairs. *Report of the Commissioner of Indian Affairs, 1877*. Washington, D.C.: Government Printing Office, 1877.

Commissioner of Indian Affairs. *Report of the Commissioner of Indian Affairs, 1878*. Washington, D.C.: Government Printing Office, 1878.

Companions of the Military Order of the Loyal Legion of the United States. New York: L. R. Hamersly Company, 1901.

Connolly, William. Diary. TS. Folder: Nez Perce War—1877. Vertical Files. Montana Historical Society Library, Helena.

Cook, James H. "The Art of Fighting Indians." *American Mercury* 23 (June 1931): 170–79.

Coon, Homer. "The Outbreak of Chief Joseph." MS. William R. Coe Collection. Yale University Library, New Haven, Connecticut.

"Copies of letters and telegrams from Generals McDowell and Howard in regard to Nez Perce Campaign." Items 6718 and 6724. Roll 338. Nez Perce War Papers. National Archives Microfilm Publication M666. Records of the Office of the Adjutant General. RG 94. National Archives, Washington, D.C.

Coram, William. Interview by Walter M. Camp, February 12, 1915. Item 6. Walter M. Camp Papers. Robert S. Ellison Collection. Western History Department. Denver Public Library, Denver, Colo.

Coughlan, T. M. *Varnum—Last of Custer's Lieutenants*. Edited by John M. Carroll. Bryan, Tex.: privately printed, 1980.

Cowan, Emma. "Reminiscences of Pioneer Life." In vol. 4. of *Contributions to the Historical Society of Montana*, 156–87. Helena, Mont.: Historical Society of Montana, 1903.

Crook, George. *General George Crook: His Autobiography*. Edited by Martin F. Schmitt. Norman: University of Oklahoma Press, 1946.

———. "Report of Brig. Gen. Geo. Crook." September 23, 1878. In *Report of the Secretary of War, 1878*. Washington: Government Printing Office, 1878.

Cruikshank, Alexander. "The Birch Creek Massacre." n.d. TS. SC 584. Montana Historical Society Archives, Helena.

———. "Chasing Hostile Indians. The Historical Narrative." n.d. TS. Manuscripts Division. Idaho State Historical Society, Boise.

Cullum, George W. *Biographical Register of the Officers and Graduates of the U.S. Military Academy, at West Point, N.Y., from Its Establishment, March 16, 1802, to the Army Reorganization of 1866–67*. 10 vols. New York: Van Nostrand, 1868.

Curtis, Edward S. *The North American Indian*. 20 vols. 1911. Reprint, New York: Johnson Reprint Corporation, 1976.

Daly, Henry W. "U.S. vs. Joseph." *American Legion Monthly* 8 (April 1930): 16–17, 42–46.

Davies, Henry E. *Ten Days on the Plains*. Edited by Paul A. Hutton. Dallas: DeGolyer Library, Southern Methodist University, 1985.

Davis, H. J. "The Battle of Camas Meadows." In *Northwestern Fights and Fighters*, by Cyrus Townsend Brady, 191–97. New York: Doubleday, Page and Company, 1907.

———. "An Incident of the Nez Perce Campaign." *Journal of the Military Service Institution of the United States* 36 (May–June 1905): 560–64.

Davison, Stanley R. "A Century Ago: The Tortuous Pursuit." *Montana The Magazine of Western History* 27 (October 1977): 3–19.

DeBarthe, Joe. *Life and Adventures of Frank Grouard*. Edited by Edgar I. Stewart. Norman: University of Oklahoma Press, 1958.

DeMontravel, Peter D. "The Career of Lieutenant General Nelson A. Miles from the Civil War through the Indian Wars." Ph.D. diss., St. John's University, 1982.

Dempsey, Hugh A. "An Indian's Death in Exile. Tragedy of White Bird." *Beaver* 73 (February–March 1993): 23–29.

"Department of the Columbia, Roster of Troops in the Field, Operating Against Hostile Indians, Commanded by Brigadier-General O.O. Howard, U.S. Army." Entry 107. Box 2. Part 3, Department of the Columbia Nez Perce Indian Campaign, 1877. Records of the United States Army Continental Commands. RG 393. National Archives, Washington, D.C.

Diehl, Charles S. *The Staff Correspondent*. San Antonio, Tex.: Clegg Company, 1931.

Dingler, Craig M., and Roy M. Breckenridge. "Glacial Reconnaissance of the Selway-Bitterroot Wilderness Area, Idaho." In *Cenozoic Geology of Idaho*, Idaho Department of Lands, Bureau of Mines, and Geology Bulletin 26, edited by Bill Bonnichsen and Roy M. Breckenridge, 645–60. Moscow, Idaho, 1982.

Dixon, Joseph K. *The Vanishing Race: The Last Great Indian Council*. Garden City, N.Y.: Doubleday, Page and Company, 1913.

Dozier, Jack. "1885: A Nez Perce Homecoming." *Idaho Yesterdays* 7 (fall 1963): 22–25.

Drum, W. F. "Report of Captain W. F. Drum, 2d Infantry, on Indian depredations." March 24, 1878. Entry 700. Evidence Concerning Depredations Claims, 1835–96. Records of the United States Bureau of Indian Affairs. RG 75. National Archives, Washington, D.C.

Drury, Clifford M. *Chief Lawyer of the Nez Perce Indians, 1796–1876*. Glendale, Calif.: Arthur H. Clark Company, 1979.

———. "Lawyer, Head Chief of the Nez Perce, 1848–1875." *Idaho Yesterdays* 22 (winter 1979): 2–12.

Dunlay, Thomas W. *Wolves for the Blue Soldiers: Indian Scouts and Auxiliaries with the United States Army, 1860–90*. Lincoln: University of Nebraska Press, 1982.

Dunn, J. P. *Massacres of the Mountains: A History of the Indian Wars of the Far West, 1815–1875.* New York: Harper and Brothers, 1886.

Dusenberry, Verne. "Chief Joseph's Flight through Montana: 1877." *Montana The Magazine of Western History* 2 (October 1952): 43–51.

———. "The Northern Cheyenne: All They Have Asked Is to Live in Montana." *Montana The Magazine of Western History* 5 (winter 1955): 23–40.

Edmonds, Kermit M. "Site of Captain Randolph Norwood's Defensive Position. The Camas Meadows Skirmish, Idaho, August 20, 1877," with "Description of Fortifications, Norwood's Position, Camas Meadows, Idaho." 1977. Research Files. Big Hole National Battlefield, Wisdom, Mont.

———. "Site of Howard's Camp and Nez Perce Attack and Theft of Pack Mules. The Camas Meadows Skirmish, Idaho, August 20, 1877." August 1972. Research Files. Big Hole National Battlefield, Wisdom, Mont.

Ege, Robert J. *After the Little Bighorn: Battle of Snake Creek, Montana Territory, September 30 to October 5, 1877.* Greeley, Colo.: Werner Publications, 1982.

Ellis, Richard N. "The Humanitarian Generals." *Western Historical Quarterly* 3 (April 1972): 169–78.

Ellison. Robert S. Collection. Western History Department. Denver Public Library, Denver, Colo.

Elsensohn, Sister M. Alfreda. *Pioneer Days in Idaho County.* 2 vols. 1947. Reprint, Cottonwood, Idaho: Idaho Corporation of Benedictine Sisters, 1978.

Embree, Glenn F., Lisa A. McBroome, and David J. Doherty. "Preliminary Strategic Framework of the Pliocene and Miocene Rhyolite, Eastern Snake River Plain, Idaho." In *Cenozoic Geology of Idaho,* Idaho Department of Lands, Bureau of Mines, and Geology Bulletin 26, edited by Bill Bonnichsen and Roy M. Breckenridge, 333–50. Moscow, Idaho, 1982.

Ewers, John C. "The Horse Complex in Plains Indian History." In *The North American Indians: A Sourcebook,* compiled by Roger C. Owen, James J. F. Deetz, and Anthony D. Fisher, 494–503. London: Macmillan Company, 1967.

Fahey, John. *The Flathead Indians.* Norman: University of Oklahoma Press, 1974.

Falkner, W. H. Letter, to Mrs. S. A. Groves, January 24, 1878. Transcribed copy. Manuscripts, Archives and Special Collections. Holland Library, Washington State University, Pullman.

Farrow, Edward S. "The Assembling of the Soldiers and the Battle of Clearwater." In *Northwestern Fights and Fighters,* by Cyrus Townsend Brady, 151–63. New York: Doubleday, Page and Company, 1907.

Faust, Karl Irving. *Campaigning in the Philippines.* San Francisco: Hicks-Judd Company Publishers, 1899.

Fee, Chester Anders. *Chief Joseph: The Biography of a Great Indian.* New York: Wilson-Erickson, Inc., 1936.

Fenn, F. A. Interview by Walter M. Camp. February 18, 1912. Camp Manuscript Field Notes. Walter M. Camp Papers. Little Bighorn Battlefield National Monument, Crow Agency, Mont.

Fenneman, Nevin M. *Physiography of Western United States*. New York: McGraw-Hill Book Company, 1931.

Feyhl, Kenneth J. "Chief Joseph Inscription." *Archaeology in Montana* 28 (fall 1987): 61–63.

Fisher, S. G. Journal. TS. Manuscripts Division. Idaho State Historical Society, Boise.

———. "Journal of S. G. Fisher, Chief of Scouts to General O. O. Howard during the Campaign Against the Nez Perce Indians, 1877." In vol. 2. of *Contributions to the Historical Society of Montana*, 269–82. 1896. Reprint, Boston: J. S. Canner and Company, Inc., 1966.

———. "Plan of the [Canyon Creek] Battle Ground." ca. 1896. In S. G. Fisher Diary. SC 692. Montana Historical Society Archives, Helena.

FitzGerald, Emily. *An Army Doctor's Wife on the Frontier: Letters from Alaska and the Far West, 1874–1878*. Edited by Abe Laufe. Pittsburgh: University of Pittsburgh Press, 1962.

F. L. M. "The Nez Perce War." *Galaxy* 24 (December 1877): 817–26.

Fletcher, Robert H. "Department of Columbia Map of the Nez Perce Campaign, Brig. Gen. O. O. Howard, U.S.A., Commanding." Department of the Columbia, Map 10. Records of United States Army Continental Commands. RG 393. Cartographic Archives Division. National Archives, Washington, D.C. (Printed in *Report of the Secretary of War, 1877*.)

Forse, Albert G. "Chief Joseph as a Commander." In *The Unpublished Papers of the Order of Indian Wars, Book No. 3*. New Brunswick, N.J.: privately printed, 1977.

———. Papers. Collection N-6, Order of Indian Wars. Manuscript Division. U.S. Army Military History Institute, Army War College, Carlisle, Pa.

"Ft. Assinniboine, Mont. Reburial at Custer Battlefield National Cemetery." Holland and Sons Mortuary, Havre, Mont. Collection of James Magera, Havre, Mont.

Fort Buford Records. Fort Union Trading Post National Historic Site, Williston, N.D.

Fort Missoula Letterbook. July 1, 1877–December 25, 1877. Special Collections. Mansfield Library, University of Montana, Missoula.

Frazer, Robert W. *Forts of the West: Military Forts and Presidios and Posts Commonly Called Forts West of the Mississippi River to 1898*. Norman: University of Oklahoma Press, 1965.

Garcia, Andrew. *Tough Trip through Paradise, 1878–1879*. Edited by Bennett H. Stein. Boston: Houghton Mifflin Company, 1967.

Gard, Dan. *The Nez Perce National Historic Trail. Beaverhead and Salmon-Challis National Forests. Skinner Meadows to Leadore, Idaho*. Beaverhead National Forest, Salmon-Challis National Forest, Nez Perce National Historic Trail, 1994.

Garlington, Ernest A. "Seventh Regiment of United States Cavalry." Draft. Edward S. Godfrey Papers. Manuscript Division. Library of Congress, Washington, D.C.

Gaybower, Frederick. Interview by Walter M. Camp. October 23, 1919. Item 111. Walter M. Camp Papers. Robert S. Ellison Collection. Western History Department. Denver Public Library, Denver, Colo.

General Land Office Survey Plat. Township 12 North, Range 39 East (1892). Public Room. State Office of the Bureau of Land Management, Boise, Idaho.

Gibbon, John. *Adventures on the Western Frontier*. Edited by Alan and Maureen Gaff. Bloomington: Indiana University Press, 1994.

———. "The Pursuit of Joseph." *American Catholic Quarterly Review* 4 (April 1879): 317–44.

———. "Rambles in the Rocky Mountains." *American Catholic Quarterly Review* 1 (April 1876): 312–36; 1 (July 1876): 455–75.

———. "Report of Colonel Gibbon." September 2, 1877. In *Report of the Secretary of War, 1877*. Washington, D.C.: Government Printing Office, 1877.

———. "Report of the Commanding General of the Department of Dakota, General Gibbon commanding." October 4, 1878. In *Report of the Secretary of War, 1878*. Washington, D.C.: Government Printing Office, 1878.

———. "The Wonders of the Yellowstone." *Journal of the American Geographical Society of New York* 5 (May 1873): 112–37.

Gibson, John M. *Soldier in White: The Life of General George Miller Sternberg*. Durham, N.C.: Duke University Press, 1958.

Gidley, M. *Kopet: A Documentary Narrative of Chief Joseph's Last Years*. Chicago: Contemporary Books, Inc., 1981.

Godfrey, Edward S. Appointment, Commission, and Personal File of. Records of the Office of the Adjutant General. RG 94. National Archives, Washington, D.C.

———. "Custer's Last Battle by One of His Troop Commanders." *Century* 43 (January 1892): 358–87.

———. "Gen. Godfrey's Story." Edward S. Godfrey Papers. Manuscript Division. Library of Congress, Washington, D.C.

———. Interview by Walter Camp. March 3, 1917. Interview Notes. MS 57. Box 3. Walter M. Camp Papers. Microfilm. Archives and Manuscripts Division. Harold B. Lee Library, Brigham Young University, Provo, Utah.

———. Papers. Manuscript Division. Library of Congress, Washington, D.C.

———. Papers. Manuscripts Division. U.S. Army Military History Institute, Army War College, Carlisle, Pa.

Goldin, Theodore W. Biography. MS. E. A. Brininstool Collection. Archives and Manuscripts Division. Harold B. Lee Library, Brigham Young University, Provo, Utah.

———. *A Bit of the Nez Perce Campaign*. Bryan, Tex.: privately printed, n.d.

———. "The Seventh Cavalry at Cañon Creek." In *Northwestern Fights and Fighters*, by Cyrus Townsend Brady, 203–22. New York: Doubleday, Page and Company, 1907.

Goodenough, Daniel, Jr. "Lost on Cold Creek." *Montana The Magazine of Western History* 24 (autumn 1974): 16–29.

Gray, Captain James T. Correspondence. SC 1217. Montana Historical Society Archives, Helena.

Greene, Jerome A. *Yellowstone Command: Colonel Nelson A. Miles and the Great Sioux War, 1876–1877.* Lincoln: University of Nebraska Press, 1991.

"Grievances of the Nez Perce." *Idaho Yesterdays* 4 (fall 1960): 6–7.

Grillon, Charles. "Battle of Snake Creek between U.S. Troops and Indians, Sept. 30 to Oct. 4, 1877." Map. Merrill G. Burlingame Special Collections. Montana State University Libraries, Bozeman.

Grinnell, George Bird. Papers. Braun Research Library, Southwest Museum, Los Angeles, Calif.

————, ed. *Hunting at High Altitudes: The Book of the Boone and Crockett Club.* New York: Harper and Brothers, 1913.

Grover, La Fayette. *Report of Governor Grover to General Schofield on the Modoc War, and Reports of Maj. Gen. John V. Miller and General John E. Ross, to the Governor. Also Letter of the Governor to the Secretary of the Interior on the Wallowa Valley Indian Question.* Salem, Ore.: Martin V. Brown, 1874.

Guie, Heister Dean, and Lucullus V. McWhorter, comps. *Adventures in Geyser Land.* Caldwell, Idaho: Caxton Printers, Ltd., 1935.

Hagelin, Christopher. *The Nez Perce National Historic Trail. Beaverhead National Forest. Gibbons Pass to Skinner Meadows.* Beaverhead National Forest, Nez Perce National Historic Trail, 1993.

Hagemann, E. R., ed. *Fighting Rebels and Redskins: Experiences in Army Life of Colonel George B. Sanford, 1861–1892.* Norman: University of Oklahoma Press, 1969.

Hague, Arnold. *Atlas to Accompany Monograph XXXII on the Geology of the Yellowstone National Park.* Washington, D.C.: Government Printing Office, 1904.

Haines, Aubrey L. "The Bannock Indian Trails of Yellowstone National Park." *Archaeology of Montana* 4 (March 1962): 1–8.

————. "The Burning of Henderson's Ranch." *Yellowstone Interpreter* 2 (September–October 1964): 52–54.

————. "Data on Cannon Which May Have Been Used in the Battle of Bear Paw Mountain." January 18, 1962. Research Files. Big Hole National Battlefield, Wisdom, Mont.

————. *An Elusive Victory: The Battle of the Big Hole.* West Glacier, Mont.: Glacier Natural History Association, 1991.

————. "Retracement of Spurgin's road (site 82)." Memorandum by Aubrey L. Haines to Files. August 21, 1962. Copy in collection of the author, Arvada, Colo.

————. *Yellowstone National Park: Its Exploration and Establishment.* Washington, D.C.: Government Printing Office, 1974.

————. *The Yellowstone Story: A History of Our First National Park*. 2 vols. Mammoth, Wyo.: Yellowstone Library and Museum Association, 1977.

Haines, Francis. "Chief Joseph and the Nez Perce Warriors." *Pacific Northwest Quarterly* 45 (January 1954): 1–7.

————. "Nez Perce Horses: How They Changed the Indian Way of Life." *Idaho Yesterdays* 4 (spring 1960): 8–11.

————. *The Nez Perces: Tribesmen of the Columbia Plateau*. Norman: University of Oklahoma Press, 1955.

————, ed. "The Skirmish at Cottonwood." *Idaho Yesterdays* 2 (spring 1958): 2–7.

Halstead-Maus Family Papers. Manuscripts Division. U.S. Army Military History Institute, Army War College, Carlisle, Pa.

Hammer, Kenneth. *Biographies of the Seventh Cavalry, June 25th 1876*. Fort Collins, Colo.: Old Army Press, 1972.

Hampton, Bruce. "Battle of the Big Hole." Parts 1 and 2. *Montana The Magazine of Western History* 44 (winter 1994): 2–13; 44 (spring 1994): 18–29.

————. *Children of Grace: The Nez Perce War of 1877*. New York: Henry Holt and Company, 1994.

Hardin, Second Lieutenant Edward [Edwin—sic] E. Diary. Collection of Don G. Rickey, Evergreen, Colo. Original. SC 1006. Montana Historical Society Archives, Helena.

Hardy, Robert R. "Explosive Bullets." *Civil War Times Illustrated* 5 (October 1966): 43–45.

Hare, Luther, R. "Report of Lieut. L. R. Hare, Acting Engineer Officer, of March of the Seventh Cavalry during Summer and Fall of 1877." January 24, 1878. In "Report of the Chief of Engineers, 1878." Part 3. In *Report of the Secretary of War, 1878*. Washington, D.C.: Government Printing Office, 1878.

Harlan, Gilbert Drake, ed. "The Diary of Wilson Barber Harlan—Part III (Conclusion)—Farming in the Bitterroot and the Fiasco at 'Fort Fizzle.'" *Journal of the West* 3 (October 1964): 501–16.

Harlan, Wilson B. "The Fiasco at 'Fort Fizzle' on the Lolo Trail." In *In the Land of the Chinook or the Story of Blaine County*, by Alva J. Noyes. Helena, Mont.: State Publishing Company, 1917.

Hayden, F. V. "Yellowstone National Park." 1878. Item 294. U.S. Geological and Geographical Survey of the Territories. Department of the Interior. Records of the Bureau of Indian Affairs. RG 75. Cartographic Archives Division. National Archives, Washington, D.C.

Hedren, Paul L., ed. "Eben Swift's Army Service on the Plains, 1876–1879." *Annals of Wyoming* 50 (spring 1978): 141–55.

Heitman, Francis B. *Historical Register and Dictionary of the United States Army, from Its Organization, September 29, 1789, to March 2, 1903*. 2 vols. 1903. Reprint, Urbana: University of Illinois Press, 1965.

Henry, Guy V. *Military Record of Civilian Appointments in the United States Army*. New York: Carleton, Publisher, 1869.

Hodge, Frederick Webb. *Handbook of American Indians North of Mexico.* 2 vols. Washington, D.C.: Government Printing Office, 1910.

Hoopes, Alban W. *The Road to the Little Big Horn—and Beyond.* New York: Vantage Press, 1975.

Horner, J. H., and G. Butterfield. "The Nez Perce–Findley Affair." *Oregon Historical Quarterly* 40 (March 1939): 40–51.

Howard, Oliver Otis. *Autobiography.* 2 vols. New York: Baker and Taylor Company, 1907.

———. Collection. SC 1247. Montana Historical Society Archives, Helena.

———. *Famous Indian Chiefs I Have Known.* 1908. Reprint, Lincoln: University of Nebraska Press, 1989.

———. *My Life and Experiences among Our Hostile Indians.* 1907. Reprint, New York: Da Capo Press, 1972.

———. *Nez Perce Joseph: An Account of His Ancestors, His Lands, His Confederates, His Enemies, His Murders, His War, His Pursuit and Capture.* Boston: Lee and Shepard, 1881.

———. "Nez Perces Campaign of 1877." *Advance.* Serial. January–October 1878.

———. "Report of Brigadier-General O. O. Howard." September 1, 1877. In *Report of the Secretary of War, 1877.* Washington, D.C.: Government Printing Office, 1877.

———. "Supplementary Report: Non-Treaty Nez Perce Campaign." December 26, 1877. In *Report of the Secretary of War, 1877,* 585–660. Washington, D.C.: Government Printing Office, 1877.

———. "The True Story of the Wallowa Campaign." *North American Review* 128 (July 1879): 53–64.

Howe, Oliver P. Letters. Merrill G. Burlingame Special Collections. Montana State University Libraries, Bozeman.

Hoxie, Frederick E. *Parading through History: The Making of the Crow Nation in America, 1805–1935.* Cambridge: Cambridge University Press, 1995.

Hunt, Elvid. *History of Fort Leavenworth, 1827–1917.* Fort Leavenworth, Kans.: General Service Schools Press, 1926.

Hunt, Fred A. "The Battle of Big Hole, Montana." *Pacific Monthly* 18 (December 1907): 700–707.

Hunt, Garrett B. "Sergeant Sutherland's Ride: An Incident of the Nez Perce War." *Mississippi Valley Historical Review* 14 (June 1927): 39–46.

Hunter, George. *Reminiscences of an Old Timer.* San Francisco: H. S. Crocker and Company, 1887.

Hutton, Paul A. *Phil Sheridan and His Army.* Lincoln: University of Nebraska Press, 1985.

———., ed. *Soldiers West: Biographies from the Military Frontier.* Lincoln: University of Nebraska Press, 1987.

Illustrated and Descriptive Catalogue of Military Goods for Sale by Francis Bannerman Sons. New York: Francis Bannerman Sons, 1938.

An Illustrated History of North Idaho. Spokane, Wash.: Western Historical Publishing Company, 1903.

Jackson, Helen Hunt. *A Century of Dishonor: The Early Crusade for Indian Reform*. New York: Harper and Brothers, 1881.

James, Jon G. "Sergeant Molchert's Perils: Soldiering in Montana, 1870–1880." *Montana The Magazine of Western History* 34 (spring 1984): 60–65.

Jellum, Karen, ed. *Fire in the Wind: An Account of the 1991 Blaine County Fire*. Chinook, Mont.: Milk River Genealogical Society, 1994.

Jerome, Lovell H. Appointment, Commission, and Personal File of. Records of the Office of the Adjutant General. RG 94. National Archives, Washington, D.C.

———. "Inquiries Regarding Bear's Paw Fight." Undated TS questionnaire with handwritten answers. Item 123. Walter M. Camp Papers. Robert S. Ellison Collection. Western History Department. Denver Public Library, Denver, Colo.

———. "Jerome's Own Story." In *Chief Joseph: The Biography of a Great Indian*, by Chester Anders Fee, 337–40. New York: Wilson-Erickson, Inc., 1936.

Jocelyn, Stephen Perry. *Mostly Alkali: A Biography*. Caldwell, Idaho: Caxton Printers, Ltd., 1953.

Johansen, Dorothy O., ed. "The Nez Perce War: The Battles at Cottonwood Creek, 1877." *Pacific Northwest Quarterly* 27 (April 1936): 167–70.

Johnson, Barry C. "Solved: The 'Mystery' of Lt. Lovell Jerome." *Montana The Magazine of Western History* 19 (autumn 1969): 90–91.

Johnson, Elsie P. *Laurel's Story, A Montana Heritage*. Laurel, Mont.: privately printed, 1979.

Johnson, Henry C. Manuscripts. Special Collections. University of Idaho Library, Moscow.

———. "Some Reminiscences of the Nez Perce Indian War." n.d. TS. Henry C. Johnson Manuscripts. Special Collections. University of Idaho Library, Moscow.

Johnson, Roy P. *Jacob Horner of the Seventh Cavalry*. Bismarck: State Historical Society of North Dakota. Reprinted from *North Dakota History* 16 no. 2 (April 1949).

Johnson, Virginia W. *The Unregimented General: A Biography of Nelson A. Miles*. Boston: Houghton Mifflin Company, 1962.

Jones, J. H. "The Rock Creek Massacre." ca. 1904. TS. J. H. Jones Reminiscences. SC 914. Montana Historical Society Archives, Helena.

Joseph [Heinmot Tooyalakekt]. "An Indian's Views of Indian Affairs." *North American Review* 128 (April 1879): 412–33.

Josephy, Alvin M., Jr. *The Nez Perce Indians and the Opening of the Northwest*. New Haven, Conn.: Yale University Press, 1965.

———. "Origins of the Nez Perce Indians." *Idaho Yesterdays* 6 (spring 1962): 2–13.

———. *The Patriot Chiefs: A Chronicle of American Indian Resistance*. New York: Viking Press, 1969.

Kappler, Charles J., comp. and ed. *Indian Affairs. Laws and Treaties.* 2 vols. Washington, D.C.: Government Printing Office, 1904.

Kearns, William E. "A Nez Perce Chief Re-Visits Yellowstone." *Yellowstone Nature Notes* 12 (July–August 1935): 41.

———. "The Nez Perce Retreat through Yellowstone Park." *Yellowstone Nature Notes* 12 (July–August 1935): 35–41.

Keenan, Jerry. "Yellowstone Kelly: From New York to Paradise." *Montana The Magazine of Western History* 40 (summer 1990): 15–27.

Kelly, Luther S. "Capture of Nez Perces." 1909. MS. Item 441. George B. Grinnell Papers. Braun Research Library, Southwest Museum, Los Angeles.

———. *"Yellowstone Kelly": The Memoirs of Luther S. Kelly.* Edited by Milo Milton Quaife. New Haven, Conn.: Yale University Press, 1926.

King, Charles. *Indian Campaigns: Sketches of Cavalry Service in Arizona and on the Northern Plains.* Edited by Harry H. Anderson. Fort Collins, Colo.: Old Army Press, 1984.

Kip, Lawrence. *The Indian Council at Walla Walla, May and June, 1855.* Sources of the History of Oregon, vol. 1, pt. 2. Eugene, Ore.: Star Job Office, 1897.

Kipp, Fremont. Interview by Walter M. Camp. n.d. (ca. 1921–24). Item 108. Walter M. Camp Papers. Robert S. Ellison Collection. Western History Department. Denver Public Library, Denver, Colo.

Kirkwood, Charlotte M. "The Nez Perce Indian War Under Chiefs Joseph and Whitebird." *Idaho County Free Press.* Serial. August 4–31, 1950.

Kober, George Martin. *Reminiscences of George Martin Kober, M.D., LL.D..* Washington, D.C.: Kober Foundation of Georgetown University, 1930.

Lang, William L. "Where Did the Nez Perces Go in Yellowstone in 1877?" *Montana The Magazine of Western History* 40 (winter 1990): 14–29.

Laut, Agnes C. *The Blazed Trail of the Old Frontier.* New York: Robert M. McBride and Company, 1926.

Lavender, David. *Let Me Be Free: The Nez Perce Tragedy.* New York: Harper Collins, 1992.

Leary, Peter, Jr. Appointment, Commission, and Personal File of. Records of the Office of the Adjutant General. RG 94. National Archives, Washington, D.C.

Lebain, Edward. Interview by Walter M. Camp. Joseph, Oregon, January 30, 1913. Walter M. Camp Manuscripts. Lilly Library, Indiana University, Bloomington.

———. Interview by Walter M. Camp. Joseph, Oregon, January 30, 1913. Camp Manuscript Field Notes. Walter M. Camp Papers. Little Bighorn Battlefield National Monument, Crow Agency, Mont.

Leeson, Michael A. *History of Montana, 1739–1885.* Chicago: Werner, Beers and Company, 1885.

Letters Received by the Office of Indian Affairs, 1824–1881. National Archives Microfilm Publication M234. National Archives, Washington, D.C.

Linderman, Frank B. *American: The Life Story of a Great Indian.* New York: World Book Company, 1930.

Lindgren, Waldemar. *A Geological Reconnaissance across the Bitterroot Range and Clearwater Mountains in Montana and Idaho*. Washington, D.C.: Government Printing Office, 1904.

"List of articles stolen from Leslie N. Wilkie and Leander Duncan by the Nez-Perce Indians in the Yellowstone National Park in the month of August 1877." In Leslie N. Wilkie and Leander Duncan Claim, August 1877, No. 4190. Entry 700. Claim for Indian Depredations. Records of the United States Bureau of Indian Affairs. RG 75. National Archives, Washington, D.C.

List of Nez Perce informants to L. V. McWhorter. Research Files. Big Hole National Battlefield Park, Wisdom, Mont.

"List of Wounded in Gen. Howard's expedition against hostile Nez Perce Indians at the Battle of Clear Water on the 11" & 12" day of July, 1877." Entry 624. Box 1 (two sheets). Records of the Office of the Adjutant General. RG 94. National Archives, Washington, D.C.

"List of Wounded in Skirmish on Camas Meadow, M.T." Entry 624. Box 1. Records of the Office of the Adjutant General. RG 94. National Archives, Washington, D.C.

"List of Wounded in the Battalion of the 7th U.S. Cavalry (Cos. F, G, H, I, L, M) of Depart. of Dakota, at the Battle of Cañon Creek, M.T. on the Thirteenth day of September, 1877." Entry 624. Box 1. Records of the Office of the Adjutant General. RG 94. National Archives, Washington, D.C.

"List of Wounded in the Yellowstone Command, Army of Dept. of Dakota, at the Battle of Bears Paw Mountains on the 30th day of Sept. 1877." Entry 624. Box 1. Records of the Office of the Adjutant General. RG 94. National Archives, Washington, D.C.

Long, Oscar F. "Brief of services of 1st Lieut. Oscar F. Long, 5th U.S. Infantry." In Appointment, Commission, and Personal File of Oscar F. Long. Records of the Office of the Adjutant General. RG 94. National Archives, Washington, D.C.

———. "Journal of the Marches Made by the Forces under the Command of Colonel Nelson A. Miles, Fifth Infantry, in 1876 and 1877. By Lieut. O. F. Long." In *Report of the Secretary of War, 1878*. Washington, D.C.: Government Printing Office, 1877.

———. Papers. Bancroft Library, University of California, Berkeley.

Lott, Sam. Interview by L. V. McWhorter. n.d. Research Files. Big Hole National Monument, Wisdom, Mont.

Lynch, Dennis. Interview by Walter M. Camp. October 1908 and February 8, 1909. Box 2. Walter M. Camp Papers. Microfilm. Archives and Manuscripts Division. Harold B. Lee Library, Brigham Young University, Provo, Utah.

MacDonald, Duncan. "Nez Perce Campaign." Duncan MacDonald Papers. SC 429. Montana Historical Society Archives, Helena.

———. "The Nez Perces: The History of Their Troubles and the Campaign of 1877." In *In Pursuit of the Nez Perces: The Nez Perce War of 1877*, compiled by Linwood Laughy, 215–73. Wrangell, Alaska: Mountain Meadow Press, 1993.

MacEwan, Grant. *Sitting Bull: The Years in Canada*. Edmonton, Alberta: Hurtig Publishers, 1973.

Madsen, Brigham D. *The Bannock of Idaho*. Caldwell, Idaho: Caxton Printers, Ltd., 1958.

Madsen, Brigham D., and Betty M. Madsen. *North to Montana! Jehus, Bullwhackers, and Mule Skinners on the Montana Trail*. Salt Lake City: University of Utah Press, 1980.

———. "The Diamond-R Rolls Out." *Montana The Magazine of Western History* 21 (April 1971): 2–17.

Manzione, Joseph. *"I Am Looking to the North for My Life": Sitting Bull, 1876–1881*. Salt Lake City: University of Utah Press, 1991.

"Map of Milk River Indian Country Showing Location of Indian Tribes." October 7, 1871. Cartographic Archives Division. National Archives, Washington, D.C.

"Map of the Route of the Yellowstone Expedition Escort Commanded by Lieut. G. C. Doane U.S.A." September 1870. Cartographic Archives Division. National Archives, Washington, D.C.

Marquis, Thomas B. *Memoirs of a White Crow Indian*. New York: Century Company, 1928.

———. *A Warrior Who Fought Custer*. Minneapolis: Midwest Company, 1931.

Masters, Joseph G. Papers. MS 1225. Microfilm. Kansas State Historical Society, Topeka.

Maxwell, Starr J., and Samuel Morris. Interview by Walter M. Camp. January 29, 1913. Walter M. Camp Manuscripts. Lilly Library. Indiana University, Bloomington.

McAlpine, John. "Memoirs of a Frontier Soldier." 1938. MS. Collection of George Kush, Monarch, Alberta.

McBeth, Kate C. *The Nez Perces since Lewis and Clark*. New York: Fleming H. Revell Company, 1908.

McCarthy, Michael. Diary. Michael McCarthy Papers. Manuscript Division. Library of Congress, Washington, D.C.

———. "Journal of M. McCarthy." TS copy. Michael McCarthy Papers. Manuscript Division. Library of Congress, Washington, D.C.

———. Papers. Manuscript Division. Library of Congress, Washington, D.C.

———. "A Reminiscence." Item I-150. Michael McCarthy Papers. Manuscript Division. Library of Congress, Washington, D.C.

———. Scrapbook. Michael McCarthy Papers. Manuscript Division. Library of Congress, Washington, D.C.

McChristian, Douglas C. *An Army of Marksmen: The Development of United States Army Marksmanship in the Nineteenth Century*. Fort Collins, Colo.: Old Army Press, 1981.

———. *The U.S. Army in the West, 1870–1880: Uniforms, Weapons, and Equipment*. Norman: University of Oklahoma Press, 1995.

McClernand, Edward G. Letter, to Henry Romeyn, December 11, 1889. Collection of Brian C. Pohanka, Alexandria, Va.

McClernand, Edward J. *With the Indian and the Buffalo in Montana, 1870–1878*. Glendale, Calif.: Arthur H. Clark Company, 1969.

McDermott, John D. Collection. Rapid City, S. Dak.

———. *Dangerous Duty: A History of Frontier Forts in Fremont County, Wyoming*. Lander, Wyo.: Fremont County Historic Preservation Commission, 1993.

———. *Forlorn Hope: The Battle of White Bird Canyon and the Beginning of the Nez Perce War*. Boise: Idaho State Historical Society, 1978.

McDowell, Irvin. "Report of Major-General Irwin [sic] McDowell." October 17, 1877. In *Report of the Secretary of War, 1877*. Washington, D.C.: Government Printing Office, 1877.

McGinnis, Anthony. *Counting Coup and Cutting Horses: Intertribal Warfare on the Northern Plains, 1738–1889*. Evergreen, Colo.: Cordillera Press, Inc., 1990.

McLaughlin, James. *My Friend the Indian*. Boston: Houghton Mifflin Company, 1926.

McWhorter, Lucullus V. "Fight with Sturgis—Indian Killed." n.d. TS. Folder 159. Lucullus V. McWhorter Papers. Manuscripts, Archives and Special Collections. Holland Library, Washington State University, Pullman.

———. *Hear Me, My Chiefs! Nez Perce History and Legend*. Edited by Ruth Bordin. Caldwell, Idaho: Caxton Printers, Ltd., 1952.

———. Papers. Manuscripts, Archives and Special Collections. Holland Library, Washington State University, Pullman.

———. "Poker Joe's Big Rifle" n.d. TS. Folder 189. Lucullus V. McWhorter Papers. Manuscripts, Archives and Special Collections. Holland Library, Washington State University, Pullman.

———. "Stake Tabulation, Chief Joseph's Camp." Draft. Folder 162. Lucullus V. McWhorter Papers. Manuscripts, Archives and Special Collections. Holland Library, Washington State University, Pullman.

———. "Stake Tabulation of the Bear's Paw Mountain Battle Field, Blaine County, Montana." Folder 162. Lucullus V. McWhorter Papers. Manuscripts, Archives and Special Collections. Holland Library, Washington State University, Pullman.

———. "Unpublished Incidents in 'Calamity Jane's' Life." n.d. TS. Folder 196. Lucullus V. McWhorter Papers. Manuscripts, Archives and Special Collections. Holland Library, Washington State University, Pullman.

———. *Yellow Wolf: His Own Story*. Caldwell, Idaho: The Caxton Printers, Ltd., 1940.

McWhorter, Lucullus V., and Many Wounds, "The Colonel Sturgis Fight. Name of the Scene of this Engagement." 1936. TS. Folder 189. Lucullus V. McWhorter Papers. Manuscripts, Archives and Special Collections. Holland Library, Washington State University, Pullman.

The Medal of Honor of the United States Army. Washington, D.C.: Government Printing Office, 1948.

Medal of Honor, Special File. Records of the Office of the Adjutant General. RG 94. National Archives, Washington, D.C.

Medicine Crow, Joseph. *From the Heart of Crow Country: The Crow Indians' Own Stories*. New York: Orion Books, 1992.

"Mem. of Marches of Co. 'E' 21st Infantry from Carrol [sic] M.T. to place where Gen'l Sturgis left column with 7th Cavalry, to proceed to place of surrender of Nez Perce Joseph." Folder: Nez Perce Campaign 1877, Official Reports and Letters, Clippings. Box T-2: 5th Infantry to Aug. 1881. Nelson A. Miles Papers. Manuscripts Division. U.S. Army Military History Institute, Army War College, Carlisle, Pa.

"Memoranda of Active Service of Lieut. Marion P. Maus, 1st Inf'y, 1887 and 1886." Folder: Nez Perces Campaign 1877, Official Reports and Letters, Clippings. Box T-2: 5th Infantry to Aug. 1881. Nelson A. Miles Papers. Manuscripts Division. U.S. Army Military History Institute, Army War College, Carlisle, Pa.

"Men and Women: C. E. S. Wood." *Pacific Monthly* 14 (January 1903): 50–52.

Miles, Nelson A. Family Papers. Manuscript Division. Library of Congress, Washington, D.C.

———. Papers. Manuscripts Division. U.S. Army Military History Institute, Army War College, Carlisle, Pa.

———. *Personal Recollections and Observations of General Nelson A. Miles*. Chicago: Werner Company, 1896.

———. "Report of Colonel Nelson A. Miles." December 27, 1877. In *Report of the Secretary of War, 1877*. Washington, D.C.: Government Printing Office, 1877.

———. *Serving the Republic: Memoirs of the Civil and Military Life of Nelson A. Miles, Lieutenant-General, United States Army*. New York: Harper and Brothers, 1911.

Miller, Don, and Stan Cohen. *Military and Trading Posts of Montana*. Missoula, Mont.: Pictorial Histories Publishing Company, 1978.

Miller, Marcus, P. Appointment, Commission, and Personal File of. Records of the Office of the Adjutant General. RG 94. National Archives, Washington, D.C.

Mills, Charles K. *Harvest of Barren Regrets: The Army Career of Frederick William Benteen, 1834–1898*. Glendale, Calif.: Arthur H. Clark Company, 1985.

Moccasin. Affidavit. August 18, 1931. TS. SC 489. Montana Historical Society Archives, Helena.

Mo[e]lchert, William. Letter, to David Hilger, November 13, 1927. SC 491. Montana Historical Society Archives, Helena.

Mooney, James. "The Ghost-Dance Religion." In *Fourteenth Annual Report of the Bureau of Ethnology, 1892–93*, 640–1136. Washington, D.C.: Government Printing Office, 1896.

Morris, John W., and Edwin C. McReynolds. *Historical Atlas of Oklahoma*. Norman: University of Oklahoma Press, 1965.

Mueller, Oscar O. "Prelude to Surrender: The Nez Perce at Cow Island." *Montana The Magazine of Western History* 14 (April 1964): 50–53.

Mulford, Ami Frank. *Fighting Indians! In the Seventh United States Cavalry, Custer's Favorite Regiment*. Rev. ed. Corning, N.Y.: Paul Lindsley Mulford, 1925.

Myers, Rex C. "The Settlers and the Nez Perce." *Montana The Magazine of Western History* 27 (October 1977): 20–29.

"Narrative of John Buckhouse." Folder 211B. Lucullus V. McWhorter Papers. Manuscripts, Archives and Special Collections. Holland Library, Washington State University, Pullman.

"A Nez Perce Funeral." *Lippincott's Magazine of Popular Literature and Science* 22 (August 1878): 258–61.

The Nez Perce (Nee-Me-Poo) National Historic Trail Comprehensive Plan. Missoula, Mont.: U.S. Forest Service, 1991.

Nez Perce War Claims. National Archives Microfilm Publication M666. National Archives, Washington, D.C.

Nez Perce War, 1877. Division of the Missouri, Special File. National Archives Microfilm Publication M1495. National Archives, Washington, D.C.

"Nez Perce War Letters to Governor Mason Brayman." In *Fifteenth Biennial Report of the Board of Trustees of the State Historical Society of Idaho for the Years 1935–1936*, 37–128. Boise: State Historical Society of Idaho, 1936.

Nez Perce War Papers. National Archives Microfilm Publication M666. National Archives, Washington, D.C.

"Nez Perce Warriors, 1877. Recognized Members of the 'Lower Nez Perces,' Headquarters, White Bird, Idaho. Compiled by Many Wounds and Black Eagle, Sons of Wot-to-len." Lucullus V. McWhorter Papers. Manuscripts, Archives and Special Collections. Holland Library, Washington State University, Pullman.

Norris, Philetus W. *The Calumet of the Coteau, and Other Poetical Legends of the Border*. Philadelphia: J. B. Lippincott and Company, 1884.

Norton, H. B. "The True Story of the Nez Perce War." *Recreation* 20 (February 1904): 99–100.

Norwood, Randolph. Appointment, Commission, and Personal File of. Records of the Office of the Adjutant General. RG 94. National Archives, Washington, D.C.

Noyes, Alva J. *In the Land of the Chinook or the Story of Blaine County*. Helena, Mont.: State Publishing Company, 1917.

———. "Story of Andrews [sic] Myers." ca. 1915. TS. SC 559. Montana Historical Society Archives, Helena.

Noyes, C. Raymond. "Battle of the Bear's Paw between General Miles and Chief Joseph, Sept. 30 to Oct. 5–1877." Plat. January 10, 1936. Cartographic Archives Division. National Archives, Washington, D.C. Copy in Park Files. Bear Paw Unit, Nez Perce National Historical Park, Chinook, Mont.

———. "Battle of the Bear's Paw State Park," Plat. July 12–13, 1965. Park Files. Bear Paw Unit, Nez Perce National Historical Park, Chinook, Mont.

Office of the Adjutant General, Records of the. RG 94. National Archives, Washington, D.C.

Office of the Chief of Engineers, Records of the. RG 77. National Archives, Washington, D.C.

Office of the Judge Advocate General, Records of the. RG 153. National Archives, Washington, D.C.

Officers of the Army and Navy (Regular and Volunteer) Who Served in the Civil War. Philadelphia: L. R. Hamersly and Company, 1894.

Olson, Rolf Y. H. "The Nez Perce, the Montana Press and the War of 1877." Master's thesis, Montana State University–Bozeman, 1964. Copy in the library of Big Hole National Battlefield, Wisdom, Mont.

Order of Indian Wars Collection. Manuscripts Division. U.S. Army Military History Institute, Army War College, Carlisle, Pa.

"Orders, Letters and Endorsements Concerning Major Sanford's Battalion, Nez Perce War." 2 vols. Entry E-633. Records of the United States Regular Army Mobile Units. RG 391. National Archives, Washington, D.C.

Otis, George A. A Report of the Surgeon General on the Transport of Sick and Wounded by Pack Animals. Surgeon General's Office Circular No. 8. Washington, D.C.: Government Printing Office, 1877.

Otis, George A., and David L. Huntington. Surgical History. Vol. 2., pt. 3. of The Medical and Surgical History of the War of the Rebellion. Washington, D.C.: Government Printing Office, 1883.

Ott, Larry (Lawrence). Interview by Walter M. Camp. February 11, 1915. Item 6. Walter M. Camp Papers. Robert S. Ellison Collection. Western History Department. Denver Public Library, Denver, Colo.

Paddock, George H. Appointment, Commission, and Personal File of. Records of the Office of the Adjutant General. RG 94. National Archives, Washington, D.C.

"Papers Relating to the Nez Perce Indians of the United States, Who Have Taken Refuge in Canadian Territory." Governor General's Office. Public Archives of Canada, Ottawa, Ontario.

"Papers Relating to the Sioux Indians of the United States, Who Have Taken Refuge in Canadian Territory." Governor General's Office. Public Archives of Canada, Ottawa, Ontario.

Parnell, William R. "The Battle of White Bird Cañon." In Northwestern Fights and Fighters, by Cyrus Townsend Brady, 90–111. New York: Doubleday, Page and Company, 1907.

———. "The Nez Perce Indian War—1877. Battle of White-Bird Canyon." United Service, n.s., 2 (October 1889): 364–74.

———. "The Salmon River Expedition." In Northwestern Fights and Fighters, by Cyrus Townsend Brady, 127–36. New York: Doubleday, Page and Company, 1907.

Paul, Rodman Wilson. *Mining Frontiers of the Far West, 1848–1880*. New York: Holt, Rinehart and Winston, 1963.

Pecora, William. Letter, to Al Lucke, April 3, 1960. Collection of James Magera, Havre, Mont.

Peopeo Tholekt. "Attack on Chief Looking Glass' Village near (now) Kooskia, Idaho." Sketch map. 1927. Folder 151A. Lucullus V. McWhorter Papers. Manuscripts, Archives and Special Collections. Holland Library, Washington State University, Pullman.

Perry, David. "The Affair at Cottonwood." In *Northwestern Fights and Fighters*, by Cyrus Townsend Brady, 123–26. New York: Doubleday, Page and Company, 1907.

———. "The Battle of White Bird Cañon." In *Northwestern Fights and Fighters*, by Cyrus Townsend Brady, 112–18. New York: Doubleday, Page and Company, 1907.

Phillips, Charles. "Chief Joseph's Gun." *Yellowstone Nature Notes* 2 (September 18, 1925): 1–2.

Phillips, Paul C., ed. "The Battle of the Big Hole." *Frontier* 10 (November 1929): 63–80.

Phinney, Mary Allen. *Jirah Isham Allen, Montana Pioneer*. Rutland, Vt.: Tuttle Publishing Company, Inc., 1929.

Pickard, E. H. Interview by Walter M. Camp. January 26, 1913. Transcribed. Unclassified Envelope 129. Camp Manuscript Field Notes. Walter M. Camp Papers. Little Bighorn Battlefield National Monument, Crow Agency, Mont.

Pickett, William D. "The Yellowstone Park in Early Days." Parts 1 and 2. *Forest and Stream* 70 (February 1, 1908): 168–70; 70 (February 8, 1908): 208–10.

Pinkham, Ron. *Hundredth Anniversary of the Nez Perce War of 1877*. Lapwai, Idaho: Nez Perce Printing, 1977.

Plassman, Martha Edgerton. Papers. MC 78. Montana Historical Society Archives, Helena.

Pohanka, Brian C., ed. *Nelson A. Miles: A Documentary Biography of His Military Career, 1861–1903*. Glendale, Calif.: Arthur H. Clark Company, 1985.

Pollock, Robert W. *Grandfather, Chief Joseph and Psychodynamics*. Baker, Ore.: privately published, 1964.

Pouliot, Gordon L. "Addition One to Seven, Bear Paw Battleground, April 1962 to May 1969." 1969. MS. Park Files. Bear Paw Unit, Nez Perce National Historical Park, Chinook, Mont.

Pouliot, Gordon L., and Thain White. "The Clearwater Battlefield, the Nez Perce War–1877. A Preliminary Survey." September 29, 1960. MS. Research Files. Nez Perce National Historical Park, Spalding, Idaho.

———. "The Possible Site of the Rains Scouting Party Tragedy, Nez Perce War–1877." September 29, 1960. MS. Research Files. Nez Perce National Historical Park, Spalding, Idaho.

Powell, William H. *Powell's Records of Living Officers of the United States Army.* Philadelphia: L. R. Hamersly and Company, 1890.

Powers, Ramon. "The Northern Cheyenne Trek through Western Kansas in 1878: Frontiersmen, Indians, and Cultural Conflict." *Trail Guide* 17 (September, December, 1972): 1–35.

Price, George F., comp. *Across the Continent with the Fifth Cavalry.* New York: D. Van Nostrand, Publisher, 1883.

"Proceedings of a Council held on the Oakland Reservation on the 28" day of December 1882." In Joseph M. V. Cochran Claim, No. 2391, and Bela B. Brockway Claim, No. 3202. Entry 700. Claim for Indian Depredations. Records of the United States Bureau of Indian Affairs. RG 75. National Archives, Washington, D.C.

"Proceedings [of] Court of Inquiry in Case of Capt. D. Perry." Records of the Office of the Judge Advocate General. RG 153. Proceeding No. QQ 1738. National Archives, Washington, D.C.

Rains, Sevier M. Appointment, Commission, and Personal File of. Records of the Office of the Adjutant General. RG 94. National Archives, Washington, D.C.

Ray, Verne. "Ethnohistory of the Joseph Band of Nez Perce Indians." In *Nez Perce Indians.* New York: Garland Publishing Company, 1974.

Record of Engagements with Hostile Indians within the Military Division of the Missouri, from 1868 to 1882. 1882. Reprint, Bellevue, Nebr.: Old Army Press, 1969.

"Record of Funeral." October 11, 1908. Holland and Sons Mortuary, Havre, Mont. Collection of James Magera, Havre, Mont.

"Record of Medical History of Fort Washakie." April 4, 1873–June 30, 1887. TS. Collection of the author, Arvada, Colo.

Records of Living Officers of the United States Army. Philadelphia: L. R. Hamersly and Company, 1883.

Redfield, Francis M. "Reminiscences of Francis M. Redfield, Chief Joseph's War." *Pacific Northwest Quarterly* 27 (1936): 66–77.

Redington, John W. "Bugler Brooks." *Sunset Magazine* 15 (May 1905): 92–93.

———. Letter, to "Col. White," December 31, 1934. File 171.1 (1934–35). Box H-1. Yellowstone National Park Archives, Mammoth, Wyo.

———. Papers. Archives and Manuscripts Division. University of Washington Libraries, Seattle.

———. "Scouting in Montana in the 1870's." *Frontier* 13 (November 1933): 55–68.

———. "The Stolen Stage Coach." 1930. MS. Folder 159. Lucullus V. McWhorter Papers. Manuscripts, Archives and Special Collections. Holland Library, Washington State University, Pullman.

———. "Story of Bugler Brooks." In *Northwestern Fights and Fighters,* by Cyrus Townsend Brady, 198–202. New York: Doubleday, Page and Company, 1907.

————. "Who Stole the Piano?" *Sunset Magazine* 14 (January 1905): 292–93.

Reed, Hugh T. "Recollections of Colonel Hugh T. Reed, USMA 1873." 1934. MS. U.S. Military Academy Library, West Point, New York.

Regimental Returns of the Fifth Infantry, September and October, 1877. National Archives Microfilm Publication M665. National Archives, Washington, D.C.

Regimental Returns of the First Cavalry, June, July, August, and September, 1877. National Archives Microfilm Publication M744. National Archives, Washington, D.C.

Regimental Returns of the Fourth Artillery, June, July, August, September, and October, 1877. National Archives Microfilm Publication M727. National Archives, Washington, D.C.

Regimental Returns of the Fourth Cavalry, June, July, August, September, and October, 1877. National Archives Microfilm Publication M727. National Archives, Washington, D.C.

Regimental Returns of the Second Cavalry, August, September, and October, 1877. National Archives Microfilm Publication M744. National Archives, Washington, D.C.

Regimental Returns of the Seventh Cavalry, August, September, October, and November, 1877. National Archives Microfilm Publication M744. National Archives, Washington, D.C.

Regimental Returns of the Twenty-first Infantry, June, July, August, September, and October, 1877. National Archives Microfilm Publication M665. National Archives, Washington, D.C.

Rennie, Patrick J. "Prehistoric Archaeological Overview and Assessment of the Canyon Creek Battlefield Area: Yellowstone County, Montana." July 1994. MS. National Park Service Midwest Archeological Center, Lincoln, Nebr.

Rennie, Patrick J., and John H. Brumley. "Prehistoric Archaeological Overview and Assessment of the Bear's Paw Battlefield State Park, Blaine County, Montana." June 1994. MS. National Park Service Midwest Archeological Center, Lincoln, Nebr.

Replogle, Wayne F. *Yellowstone's Bannock Indian Trails*. Mammoth, Wyo.: Yellowstone Library and Museum Association, 1956.

"Report of Casualties in the Campaign against Nez Perce Indians, from June to October 1877." MS. Folder: Nez Perce Campaign 1877, Official Reports and Letters, Clippings. Box T-2: 5th Infantry to Aug. 1881. Nelson A. Miles Family Papers. Manuscript Division. Library of Congress, Washington, D.C.

"Report of Indians, that surrendered or were captured through the exertions of the troops of the District of the Yellowstone." December 15, 1881. Folder: Fifth Infantry, Ft. Keogh, M.T. Box T-2: 5th Infantry to Aug. 1881. Nelson A. Miles Papers. Manuscripts Division. U.S. Army Military History Institute, Army War College, Carlisle, Pa.

"Report of the Chief of Ordnance." October 10, 1878. In *Report of the Secretary of War, 1878*. Washington: Government Printing Office, 1878.

"Report of the Chief of Ordnance." October 20, 1879. In *Report of the Secretary of War, 1879*. Washington: Government Printing Office, 1879.

Report of the Commission Appointed by Direction of the President of the United States, under Instructions of the Honorables the Secretary of War and the Secretary of the Interior, to Meet the Sioux Indian Chief, Sitting Bull, with a View to Avert Hostile Incursions into the Territory of the United States from the Dominion of Canada. Washington, D.C.: Government Printing Office, 1877.

"Report of the General of the Army." November 7, 1877. In *Report of the Secretary of War, 1877*. Washington, D.C.: Government Printing Office, 1877.

"Report of the Killed, Wounded and Missing of the 4th Artillery Battalion commanded by Capt. M. P. Miller." Entry 624. Box 1 (two sheets). Records of the Office of the Adjutant General. RG 94. National Archives, Washington, D.C.

"Report of the Surgeon-General." October 1, 1877. In *Report of the Secretary of War, 1877*. Washington, D.C.: Government Printing Office, 1877.

"Report of the Surgeon-General." October 1, 1878. In *Report of the Secretary of War, 1878*. Washington, D.C.: Government Printing Office, 1878.

"Report on the Yellowstone National Park." October 20, 1877. In *Report of the Secretary of the Interior, 1877*. Washington: Government Printing Office, 1877.

"Responsibility for the Idaho War." *Nation*, August 2, 1877, 69–70.

Rhodes, Charles D. "Chief Joseph and the Nez Perces Campaign of 1877." In *The Papers of the Order of Indian Wars*, edited by John M. Carroll, 215–32. Fort Collins, Colo.: Old Army Press, 1975.

Rhodes, Lee. "Chief Joseph's Leadership within the Nontreaty Nez Perce Indians, 1871–1885." Ph.D. diss., United States International University, 1981.

Rickey, Don, Jr. *Forty Miles a Day on Beans and Hay: The Enlisted Soldier Fighting the Indian Wars*. Norman: University of Oklahoma Press, 1963.

Riley, Robert James. "The Nez Perce Struggle for Self Government: A History of Nez Perce Governing Bodies, 1842–1960." Master's thesis, University of Idaho, 1961.

Ripley, Warren. *Artillery and Ammunition of the Civil War*. New York: Promontory Press, 1970.

Rodenbough, Theophilus F., and William L. Haskin, eds. *The Army of the United States: Historical Sketches of Staff and Line with Portraits of Generals-in-Chief*. New York: Maynard, Merrill, and Company, 1896.

Roeser, C., comp. "Territory of Idaho, [1876]." General Land Office. Cartographic Archives Division. National Archives, Washington, D.C.

Romeyn, Henry. Appointment, Commission, and Personal File of. Records of the Office of the Adjutant General. RG 94. National Archives, Washington, D.C.

———. "The Capture of Chief Joseph and the Nez Perce Indians." In vol. 2. of *Contributions to the Historical Society of Montana*, 283–91. 1896. Reprint, Boston: J. S. Canner and Company, Inc., 1966.

———. Interview by Walter M. Camp. October 14, 1912. Transcribed. Folder 115. Camp Manuscript Field Notes. Walter M. Camp Papers. Microfilm. Archives and Manuscripts Division. Harold B. Lee Library, Brigham Young University, Provo, Utah.

Ross, Clyde P. *Mining History of South-Central Idaho*. Moscow: Idaho Bureau of Mines and Geology, 1963.

Rowton, J. G. Interview by Walter M. Camp. n.d., Kooskia, Idaho. Walter M. Camp Papers. Little Bighorn Battlefield National Monument, Crow Agency, Mont.

Royce, Charles C., comp. "Indian Land Cessions in the United States." In *Eighteenth Annual Report of the Bureau of American Ethnology, 1896–97*, Pt. 2:527–997. Washington, D.C.: Government Printing Office, 1899.

Ruby, Robert H. "Return of the Nez Perce." *Idaho Yesterdays* 12 (spring 1968): 12–15.

Rules for Land Warfare. Washington, D.C.: Government Printing Office, 1914.

Samples, John. Letter, to David Hilger, November 25, 1927. SC 715. Montana Historical Society Archives, Helena.

Schullery, Paul, and Lee H. Whittlesey. "Documentary Record of Wolves and Related Wildlife Species in the Yellowstone National Park Area Prior to 1882." In Vol. 4 of *Wolves in Yellowstone?*. Mammoth, Wyo.: Yellowstone Research Division, 1992.

Scott, Douglas D. "Archaeological Overview and Assessment of the Potential Nez Perce War Sites in Yellowstone National Park." November 1994. MS. National Park Service Midwest Archeological Center, Lincoln, Nebr.

———. "Historic Archaeological Overview and Assessment of the Bear Paw Battlefield, Blaine County, Montana." November 1994. MS. National Park Service Midwest Archeological Center, Lincoln, Nebr.

———. "Historical Archaeological Overview and Assessment of the Canyon Creek Battlefield Area: Yellowstone County, Montana." November 1994. MS. National Park Service Midwest Archeological Center, Lincoln, Nebr.

———. *A Sharp Little Affair: The Archeology of the Big Hole Battlefield*. Reprint, Lincoln, Nebr.: J & L Reprint Company, 1994.

Scott, Hugh Lenox. *Some Memories of a Soldier*. New York: Century Company, 1928.

Secretary of the Interior. *Report of the Secretary of the Interior, 1877*. Washington, D.C.: Government Printing Office, 1877.

Secretary of War. *Report of the Secretary of War, 1877*. Washington, D.C.: Government Printing Office, 1877.

Secretary of War. *Report of the Secretary of War, 1878*. Washington, D.C.: Government Printing Office, 1878.

Secretary of War. *Report of the Secretary of War, 1879*. Washington, D.C.: Government Printing Office, 1879.

Secretary of War. *Report of the Secretary of War, 1880*. Washington, D.C.: Government Printing Office, 1880.

Secretary of War. *Report of the Secretary of War, 1902*. Washington, D.C.: Government Printing Office, 1902.

Shambo, Louis. "Louis Shambow [sic] Reminiscences (Dec. 17, 1916)." Transcribed by A. J. Noyes. SC 729. Montana Historical Society Archives, Helena.

Shearer, George M. Papers. Special Collections. University of Idaho Library, Moscow.

Sheridan, P. H., and W. T. Sherman. *Report of Inspection Made in the Summer of 1877 by Generals P. H. Sheridan and W. T. Sherman of Country North of the Union Pacific Railroad*. Washington, D.C.: Government Printing Office, 1878.

Sherrill, Thomas C. "The Battle of the Big Hole as I Saw It." n.d. MS. SC 739. Montana Historical Society Archives, Helena.

Shields, G. O. "The Battle of the Big Hole." In *Northwestern Fights and Fighters*, by Cyrus Townsend Brady, 164–90. New York: Doubleday, Page and Company, 1907.

Shot-in-Head, Mrs. Account. Folder 38. Lucullus V. McWhorter Papers. Manuscripts, Archives and Special Collections. Holland Library, Washington State University, Pullman.

Shoup, George. "Birch Creek Massacre." *Snake River Echoes: A Quarterly of Idaho History* 13, no. 2 (1984): 40–41.

Sioux War Papers. National Archives Microfilm Publication M666. National Archives, Washington, D.C.

"Sketch of the Yellowstone Lake and the Valley of the Upper Yellowstone River. Route of Capt's. J. W. Barlow and D. P. Heap, Corps of Engineers, in their Reconnaissance of that Region during the Summer of 1871." In *Report of Inspection Made in the Summer of 1877 by Generals P. H. Sheridan and W. T. Sherman of Country North of the Union Pacific Railroad*, by P. H. Sheridan and W. T. Sherman. Washington, D.C.: Government Printing Office, 1878.

Sladen, Joseph. Family Papers. Manuscripts Division. U.S. Army Military History Institute, Army War College, Carlisle, Pa.

Slaughter, Linda W. "Leaves from Northwestern History." *Collections of the State Historical Society of North Dakota* 1 (1906): 274–76.

Slickpoo, Allen P., and Deward E. Walker, Jr. *Noon Nee-Me-Poo (We, the Nez Perces): Culture and History of the Nez Perces*. n.p: Nez Perce Tribe of Idaho, 1973.

Smith, Allan H. "The Traditional Culture of the Nez Perce, 1700–1835." 1985. MS. Center of Northwest Anthropology, Washington State University, Pullman.

Smith, DeCost. *Indian Experiences*. Caldwell, Idaho: Caxton Printers, Ltd., 1943.

Snyder, Simon. "Diary of Simon Snyder, Captain, Co. F, 5th U.S. Infantry, for 1877." Snyder-Ronayne Collection. Little Bighorn Battlefield National Monument, Crow Agency, Mont.

Space, Ralph S. *The Clearwater Story: A History of the Clearwater National Forest*. n.p.: U.S. Forest Service, n.d.

————. *The Lolo Trail: A History of Events Connected with the Lolo Trail*. Lewiston, Idaho: privately printed, 1988.

Speak Thunder. Affidavit. August 18, 1931. SC 767. Montana Historical Society Archives, Helena.

Spiller, Roger J. et al., eds. *Dictionary of American Military Biography*. 3 vols. Westport, Conn.: Greenwood Press, 1984.

Spinden, Herbert J. *The Nez Perce Indians*. Vol. 2, pt. 3 of *Memoirs of the American Anthropological Association*. Lancaster, Pa.: New Era Print Company, 1908.

Stands In Timber, John, and Margot Liberty. *Cheyenne Memories*. New Haven, Conn.: Yale University Press, 1967.

Stanley, Edwin J. *Rambles in Wonderland: or, Up the Yellowstone, and among the Geysers and Other Curiosities of the National Park*. New York: D. Appleton and Company, 1878.

"Statement of Indian that troops have left Idaho City [&] that Joseph is in comd &c." Entry 107. Box 2. Part 3, Department of the Columbia Nez Perce Indian Campaign, 1877. Records of the United States Army Continental Commands. RG 393. National Archives, Washington, D.C.

"Statement of Mrs. W. W. Bowman Regarding the Killing of her Mother, Mrs. John Manuel, June 14, 1877, by Nez Perce Indians. Interview with W. M. Camp, Feb. 12, 1915." Box 2. Walter M. Camp Papers. Microfilm. Archives and Manuscripts Division. Harold B. Lee Library, Brigham Young University, Provo, Utah.

The Statutes at Large of the United States of America, from October, 1877, to March, 1879. Vol. 20. Washington, D.C.: Government Printing Office, 1879.

The Statutes at Large of the United States of America, from April, 1879, to March, 1881. Vol. 21. Washington, D.C.: Government Printing Office, 1881.

Stearns, Harold G. "The Volunteer Hostage." *Montana The Magazine of Western History* 18 (October 1968): 87–89.

Steffen, Randy. *The Frontier, the Mexican War, the Civil War, the Indian Wars, 1851–1880*. Vol 2. of *The Horse Soldier, 1776–1943: The United States Cavalryman: His Uniforms, Arms, Accoutrements, and Equipments*. 4 vols. Norman: University of Oklahoma Press, 1978.

Steinbach, Robert H. *A Long March: The Lives of Frank and Alice Baldwin*. Austin: University of Texas Press, 1989.

Stern, Theodore, Martin F. Schmitt, and Alphonse Halfmoon. "A Cayuse–Nez Perce Sketchbook." *Oregon Historical Quarterly* 81 (winter 1980): 341–76.

Sternberg, Martha L. *George Miller Sternberg: A Biography*. Chicago: American Medical Association, 1920.

Stevens, H. E. "Missouri River 1877. Cow Island, Surveyed and Drawn under the Direction of Lieut. Edward Maguire Corps of Engineers U.S.A." Civil Works Map File, Q318. Records of the Office of the Chief of Engineers. RG 77. Cartographic Archives Division. National Archives, Washington, D.C.

Stewart, Edgar I., ed. "Letters from the Big Hole." *Montana The Magazine of Western History* 2 (October 1952): 53–56.

"The Story of Kawownonilpilp." Folder 100. Lucullus V. McWhorter Papers. Manuscripts, Archives and Special Collections. Holland Library, Washington State University, Pullman.

"Summary of Reports Relative to the Non-Effectiveness of Cavalry Employed on the Nez Perce Campaign, [January 18, 1878]." Folder, Nez Perce War. Box 3. Joseph Sladen Family Papers. Manuscripts Division. U.S. Army Military History Institute, Army War College, Carlisle, Pa.

Supplementary Report (Non-Treaty Nez Perce Campaign) of Brigadier-General O. O. Howard, Brevet Major-General U.S. Army, Commanding Department of the Columbia. Portland: Assistant Adjutant General's Office, Department of the Columbia, 1878.

Sutherland, Thomas A. *Howard's Campaign against the Nez Perce Indians, 1877*. Fairfield, Wash.: Ye Galleon Press, 1980.

Swanton, John R. *The Indian Tribes of North America*. Bureau of American Ethnology. Bulletin 145. Washington, D.C.: Smithsonian Institution Press, 1952.

Swarts, Theodore D. Interview by Walter M. Camp, February 10, 1915. In "Account of the battle of White Bird Canyon." Item 6. Walter M. Camp Papers. Robert S. Ellison Collection. Western History Department. Denver Public Library, Denver, Colo.

Talkington, H. L. "History of the Nez Perce Reservation and the City of Lewiston, Idaho." 1938. MS. Manuscripts Division. Idaho State Historical Society Library, Boise.

Taylor, John F. "Cultural Resource Inventory Record for Canyon Creek Battlefield." 1991. Draft. Bureau of Land Management, Billings, Mont.

Terry, Brigadier-General Alfred H. "Report of Brigadier-General Terry." November 12, 1877. In *Report of the Secretary of War, 1877*. Washington, D.C.: Government Printing Office, 1877.

Thian, Raphael P., comp. *Notes Illustrating the Military Geography of the United States, 1813–1880*. 1881. Reprint, Austin: University of Texas Press, 1979.

Thomas, Anthony E. "Pi.Lu'.Ye.Kin: The Life History of a Nez Perce Indian." In *Anthropological Studies*, 1–8. Washington, D.C.: American Anthropological Association, 1970.

Thompson, Erwin N. *Historic Resource Study, Fort Lapwai, Nez Perce National Historical Park, Idaho*. Denver: National Park Service, 1973.

———. *Historic Resource Study, Spalding Area, Nez Perce National Historical Park, Idaho.* Denver: National Park Service, 1972.

———. "The Summer of '77 at Fort Lapwai." *Idaho Yesterdays* 21 (summer 1977): 11–15.

———. "Thirteen U.S. Soldiers." *Frontier Times* 36 (spring 1962): 47, 63.

Thomson, Francis A., and Samuel M. Ballard. *Geology and Gold Resources of North Central Idaho.* Idaho Bureau of Mines and Geology. Bulletin No. 7. Moscow: University of Idaho, 1924.

Tilton, Henry Remsen. "After the Nez Perces." *Forest and Stream and Rod and Gun* 9 (December 27, 1877): 403–4.

Titus, Nelson C. "The Last Stand of the Nez Perces." *Washington Historical Quarterly* 6 (July 1915): 145–53.

"Topographical Sketch of the Battlefield of 'Bear's Paw Mts.,' Sept. 30, 1877." Nelson A. Miles Papers. Manuscripts Division. U.S. Army Military History Institute, Army War College, Carlisle, Pa.

Topping, E. S. *Chronicles of the Yellowstone.* 1883. Reprint, Minneapolis: Ross and Haines, Inc., 1968.

Trafzer, Clifford E., and Richard D. Scheureman. *Chief Joseph's Allies: The Palouse Indians and the Nez Perce War of 1877.* Sacramento, Calif.: Sierra Oaks Publishing Company, 1987.

Trimble, Joel G. "The Battle of the Clearwater." In *Northwestern Fights and Fighters,* by Cyrus Townsend Brady, 137– 50. New York: Doubleday, Page and Company, 1907.

Turner, C. Frank. *Across the Medicine Line.* Toronto: McClelland and Stewart Limited, 1973.

Turner, John Peter. *The North-West Mounted Police.* 2 vols. Ottawa: Edmond Cloutier, 1950.

United States Army Continental Commands, Records of the. RG 393. National Archives, Washington, D.C.

U.S. Army Gallantry and Meritorious Conduct, 1866–1891. Alexandria, Va.: Planchet Press, 1986.

United States Bureau of Indian Affairs, Records of the. RG 75. National Archives, Washington, D.C.

United States Geographical Survey Quadrangle Maps, 7.5 Minute Series.

United States House of Representatives. *Marking the Site of the Battle between Nez Perce Indians under Command of Chief Joseph and the Command of Nelson A. Miles.* 71st Cong., 2d sess., 1930. H. Rept. 116.

———. *Nez Perce and Bannock Wars.* 48th Cong., 1st sess., 1884, H. Rept. 386 to accompany Bill 1304.

———. *Report of a Sub-Committee of the Committee on Military Affairs Relating to the Reorganization of the Army.* 45th Cong., 2d sess., 1877. H. Misc. Rept. 56.

United States Regular Army Mobile Units, Records of the. RG 391. National Archives, Washington, D.C.

United States Senate. *Letter from the Secretary of the Interior, Accompanying A Report of the Superintendent of the Yellowstone National Park for the Year 1872.* 42d Cong., 3d sess., 1873. S. Doc. 35.

———. *Marking the Site of the Battle between Nez Perce Indians under Command of Chief Joseph and the Command of Gen. Nelson A. Miles.* 71st Cong., 2d sess., 1930. S. Rept. 190.

———. *Memorial of the Nez Perce Indians Residing in the State of Idaho to the Congress of the United States.* 62d Cong., 1st sess., 1911. S. Doc. 97.

Upton, Richard. *Fort Custer on the Big Horn, 1877–1898.* Glendale, Calif.: Arthur H. Clark Company, 1973.

Utley, Robert M. *The Lance and the Shield: The Life and Times of Sitting Bull.* New York: Henry Holt and Company, 1993.

———. "Oliver Otis Howard." *New Mexico Historical Review* 62 (January 1987): 55–63.

Vaughn, Robert. *Then and Now, or Thirty-Six Years in the Rockies.* Minneapolis: Tribune Publishing Company, 1900.

Vestal, Stanley, comp. *New Sources of Indian History, 1850–1891.* Norman: University of Oklahoma Press, 1934.

Wagner, Glendolin Damon. *Old Neutriment.* Boston: Ruth Hill, 1934.

Wagner, Warren R. *A Geological Reconnaissance between the Snake and Salmon Rivers North of Riggins, Idaho.* Idaho Bureau of Mines and Geology. Pamphlet No. 74. Moscow: University of Idaho, 1945.

Walgamott, C. S. *Reminiscences of Early Days: A Series of Historical Sketches and Happenings in the Early Days of Snake River Valley.* n.p: privately published, 1926.

Walker, Deward E., Jr. *Conflict and Schism in Nez Perce Acculturation: A Study of Religion and Politics.* Pullman: Washington State University Press, 1968; Moscow: University of Idaho Press, 1985.

Warner, Ezra J. *Generals in Blue: Lives of the Union Commanders.* Baton Rouge: Louisiana State University Press, 1964.

Weed, Walter Harvey, and Louis V. Pirsson. "The Bearpaw Mountains, Montana." Parts 1–2. *American Journal of Science,* 4th series, vol. 1 (1896): 283–301, 351–62; vol. 2: 136–48, 188–89.

Weikert, Andrew J. "Journal of the Tour through the Yellowstone National Park." In vol. 3. of *Contributions to the Historical Society of Montana,* 153–74. Helena, Mont.: State Publishing Company, 1900.

Weisel, George F., ed. *Men and Trade on the Northwest Frontier as Shown by the Fort Owen Ledger.* Missoula: Montana State University Press, 1965.

Weptas Nut (No Feather). Interview by Walter M. Camp. February 15, 1915. Camp Interview Notes. MS. 57. Box 2. Walter M. Camp Papers. Microfilm. Archives and Manuscripts Division. Harold B. Lee Library, Brigham Young University, Provo, Utah.

Weslager, C. A. *The Delaware Indians: A History.* New Brunswick, N.J.: Rutgers University Press, 1972.

Whalen, Sue. "The Nez Perces' Relationship to Their Land." *Indian Historian* 4 (fall 1971): 30–33.

Wheeler, Homer W. *Buffalo Days.* Indianapolis: Bobbs-Merrill Company, 1923.

White, Thain. "Artifacts from the Bear's Paw Battlefield, Sept. 30–Oct. 5, 1877." April 21, 1961. MS. History Group Files. Blaine County Museum, Chinook, Mont.

————. "Identification of O. W. Judge Artifacts from the Bear's Paw Battlefield." n.d. MS. History Group Files. Blaine County Museum, Chinook, Mont.

————. "Relics from Fort Misery." October 1966. MS. Department of Archives and Manuscripts. Holland Library, Washington State University, Pullman.

————. "Relics from the Bear's Paw Battlefield. Book Two." ca. 1960. MS. History Group Files. Blaine County Museum, Chinook, Mont.

————. "Supplement Number One—Artifacts—Bear's Paw Battle Ground." ca. 1961. MS. History Group Files. Blaine County Museum, Chinook, Mont.

White, William. *Custer, Cavalry, and Crows: The Story of William White as Told to Thomas Marquis.* Fort Collins, Colo.: Old Army Press, 1975.

Whittlesey, Lee H. *Death in Yellowstone: Accidents and Foolhardiness in the First National Park.* Boulder, Colo.: Roberts Rinehart Publishers, 1995.

————. "Touring in Old Yellowstone: Interpretation and Visitor Education in the National Park during Stagecoach Days, 1872–1920." 1994. MS. Yellowstone National Park Research Library, Mammoth, Wyo.

————. *Yellowstone Place Names.* Helena: Montana Historical Society Press, 1988.

Wilfong, Cheryl. *Following the Nez Perce Trail: A Guide to the Nee-Me-Poo National Historic Trail.* Corvallis: Oregon State University Press, 1990.

Wilhelm, Thomas. *A Military Dictionary and Gazetteer.* Philadelphia: L. R. Hamersly and Company, 1881.

Williams, Lewis D. "Mode of [Nez Perce] Indian Warfare." October 20, 1896. MS. National Anthropological Archives, Smithsonian Institution, Washington, D.C.

Wilmot, Luther P. "Battle of the Clearwater." ca. 1922. MS. Luther M. Wilmot Papers. Special Collections. University of Idaho Library, Moscow.

————. "The Cottonwood Fight." MS. Luther P. Wilmot Papers. Special Collections. University of Idaho Library, Moscow.

————. "Misery Hill." Luther P. Wilmot Papers. Special Collections. University of Idaho Library, Moscow.

————. Papers. Special Collections. University of Idaho Library, Moscow.

————. "The Raines [sic] Massacre." Luther P. Wilmot Papers. Special Collections. University of Idaho Library, Moscow.

————. "White Bird." Luther P. Wilmot Papers. Special Collections. University of Idaho Library, Moscow.

Wilson, Elizabeth P. "Outbreak of the Nez Perce War of 1877." In *Nez Perce Texts,* by Haruo Aoki, 116–20. Berkeley: University of California Press, 1979.

Wilson, Eugene Tallmadge. *Hawks and Doves in the Nez Perce War of 1877: Personal Recollections of Eugene Tallmadge Wilson.* Review and interpretation by Eugene Edward Wilson. Helena: Montana Historical Society, 1966.

———. "The Nez Perce Campaign: A Paper Read before the Tacoma Research Society." 1924. MS. Lucullus V. McWhorter Papers. Manuscripts, Archives and Special Collections. Holland Library, Washington State University, Pullman.

Wilson, John. "Map of Clearwater River from Mount Idaho to Lewiston, 1878." Civil Works Map File (Headquarters), W283. Records of the Office of the Chief of Engineers. RG 77. Cartographic Archives Division. National Archives, Washington, D.C.

Wood, Charles Erskine Scott. "Chief Joseph, the Nez Perce." *Century* 28 (May 1884): 135–42.

———. Collection. Department of Manuscripts. The Huntington Library, San Marino, California.

———. "Famous Indians. Portraits of Some Indian Chiefs." *Century* 46 (July 1893): 436–45.

———. "History by One Who Aided in Making It: To Whom Belongs the Credit for the Capture of Chief Joseph? Here Are the Facts." *Spectator*, July 11, 1925, 7.

———. "Indian Epic is Re-Told," *Spectator*, September 14, 1929, 23.

———. "Journal of Expedition against Hostile Nez Perce Indians, from Lewiston, I.T., to Henry's Lake, I.T." Charles Erskine Scott Wood Collection. Department of Manuscripts. The Huntington Library, San Marino, California.

———. "Notes on Nez Perces Expedition 1877. White-Bird Cañon and Battle of Clearwater, Etc." Charles Erskine Scott Wood Collection. The Huntington Library, San Marino, California.

———. "The Pursuit and Capture of Chief Joseph." In *Chief Joseph: The Biography of a Great Indian*, by Chester Anders Fee, 319–36. New York: Wilson-Erickson, Inc., 1936.

Wood, Erskine. *Life of Charles Erskine Scott Wood.* Vancouver, Wash.: Rose Wind Press, 1991.

Wood, Henry C. *The Treaty Status of Young Joseph and His Band of Nez Perce Indians.* Portland, Ore.: privately published, 1876.

Wood, J. D. Reminiscence. 1902. TS. SC 987. Montana Historical Society Archives, Helena.

Woodruff, Charles A. "Battle of the Big Hole." In vol. 7. of *Contributions to the Historical Society of Montana*, 97–134. Helena, Mont.: Historical and Miscellaneous Library, 1910.

———. Letter, to Louise, August 11, 1877. Collection of Don G. Rickey, Evergreen, Colo.

Woodruff, Thomas M. Letter, to Mother, October 15, 1877. SC 18. Montana Historical Society Archives, Helena.

———. "'We have Joseph and all his people': A Soldier Writes Home about the Final Battle." *Montana The Magazine of Western History* 27 (October 1977): 30–33.

Woodward, Arthur. "A Brief Account of the Service of J. W. Redington in the Nez Perce Campaign of 1877." ca. 1934. TS. Nez Perce National Historical Park, Spalding, Idaho.

Wooster, Robert. *The Military and United States Indian Policy, 1865–1903.* New Haven, Conn.: Yale University Press, 1988.

———. *Nelson A. Miles and the Twilight of the Frontier Army.* Lincoln: University of Nebraska Press, 1993.

Yellow Bull. Account. ca. 1912. Camp Interview Notes. Walter M. Camp Manuscripts. Lilly Library, Indiana University, Bloomington.

———. Interview by Walter M. Camp. February 13, 1915. MS 57. Folder 115. Box 2. Camp Manuscript Field Notes. Walter M. Camp Papers. Microfilm. Archives and Manuscripts Division. Harold B. Lee Library, Brigham Young University, Provo, Utah.

———. Interview by Walter M. Camp. February 17, 1912. Transcript 166. Walter M. Camp Papers. Little Bighorn Battlefield National Monument, Crow Agency, Mont.

"Yellow Bull's Story." Folder 59. Walter M. Camp Papers. Little Bighorn Battlefield National Monument, Crow Agency, Mont.

Young Two Moon. Account. Given to George Bird Grinnell. ca. 1908. MS 5. Field Notebook 348. George B. Grinnell Papers. Braun Research Library, Southwest Museum, Los Angeles.

Zimmer, William F. *Frontier Soldier: An Enlisted Man's Journal of the Sioux and Nez Perce Campaigns, 1877.* Edited by Jerome A. Greene. Helena: Montana Historical Society Press, 1998.

Newspapers

Army and Navy Journal, 1877, 1878, 1879.

Army and Navy Register, 1883, 1889.

Bozeman, Mont., *Avant Courier* , 1877.

Bozeman, Mont., *Times*, 1877.

Billings, Mont., *Gazette*, 1927, 1932, 1960, 1965.

Bismarck, N.D., *Tri-Weekly Tribune*; Bismarck, N.D., *Weekly Tribune*, 1877.

Boise, Idaho *Statesman*; Boise, Idaho *Weekly Statesman*; Boise, Idaho *Tri-Weekly Statesman*, 1877.

Boston *Herald*, 1931.

Boston *Sunday Post*, August 23, 1931.

Butte, Mont., *Miner*, 1925.

Carlisle, Pa., *Valley Sentinel*, 1877.

Cascade, Mont., *Courier*, 1930.

Cheyenne, Wyo., *Daily Leader*, 1877.

Chicago *Inter-Ocean*, 1877.

Chicago *Tribune*, 1877.

Chinook, Mont., *Opinion*, 1955, 1977.

Deer Lodge, Mont., *New North-West*, 1878.

Denver *Times*, 1902.

Dillon, Mont., *Examiner*, 1962.

Eureka, Mont., *Journal*, 1926.

Fort Benton, Mont., *Record*, 1877.

Frank Leslie's Illustrated Newspaper, 1877.

Grangeville, Idaho, *Idaho County Free Press*, 1950.

Great Falls, Mont., *Rocky Mountain Husbandman*, 1941, 1942.

Great Falls, Mont., *Tribune*, 1925, 1926, 1934, 1936, 1952, 1958, 1964.

Greencastle, Ind., *Banner*, 1877.

Harper's Weekly, 1877.

Havre, Mont., *Hill County Democrat*, 1925.

Havre, Mont., *Plaindealer*,1902, 1903, 1921, 1925.

Helena, Mont., *Daily Herald*, 1877.

Helena, Mont., *Daily Independent* , 1877.

Kooskia, Idaho, *Mountaineer*, 1927.

Laurel, Mont., *Outlook*, 1947, 1954, 1958, 1989.

Leavenworth, Kans., *Daily Times*, 1877.

Lewiston, Idaho, *Morning Tribune* and Lewiston, Idaho, *Tribune*, 1927, 1957.

Lewiston, Idaho, *Teller*, 1877, 1927.

Missoula, Mont., *Missoulian*, 1965.

National Tribune, 1929.

New York *Daily Graphic*, 1877.

New York *Herald*, 1877.

New York *Tribune*, 1877, 1907.

New York *World*, 1877.

Omaha *Herald*, 1883.

Otsego, N.Y., *Journal*, 1930.

Park City, Utah, *Park Record*, 1944.

Portland *Daily Oregonian*; Portland *Morning Oregonian*, 1877, 1928.

Portland, Oreg., *Daily Standard*, 1877.

Salmon City, Idaho, *Recorder-Herald*, 1940.

Salt Lake City, Utah, *Salt Lake Daily Tribune*, 1877.

San Francisco *Chronicle*, 1927.

Stanford, Mont., *Judith Basin County Press*, 1930.

Virginia City, Mont., *Madisonian*, 1877.

Washington, D.C., *Evening Star*, 1903.

Winners of the West, 1924, 1925, 1926, 1931, 1935, 1936, 1940.

Index